American Themes

ESSAYS IN HISTORIOGRAPHY

American Themes

ESSAYS IN HISTORIOGRAPHY

EDITED BY FRANK OTTO GATELL
AND ALLEN WEINSTEIN

New York
OXFORD UNIVERSITY PRESS
London   Toronto   1968

Introduction

This volume is designed for the student who wishes to explore the
literature of American history. From the dozens of excellent recent
essays on important themes in our national experience, the editors
have selected twenty-two that span the major periods in United
States history and examine many of its more controversial aspects.
Although both the professional scholar and the novice may find
limited use for such a collection—the one understanding too much
and the other too little about the past—most students will find it
a valuable introduction to the major writings and concerns of
American historians. The publication of monographs and articles
has expanded steadily in every field, especially in the past few
decades, making the task of historical synthesis increasingly difficult. "Keeping up with" and making sense of the vast amount of
new writing in any one field have become formidable undertakings.
The essays reprinted here serve the dual function of reviewing the
relevant literature in each area and of suggesting an interpretative
framework to assist students in its use.

The editors have included a number of works that have not

previously been reprinted, but novelty alone has not been the criterion of selection. The essays have been chosen because each represents the best available discussion of the literature in its special field. The student will discover the regularity with which perspectives of the past have been changed. Properly understood, these shifting views should not encourage a static and unyielding fatalism toward the possibility of learning from history. They suggest, instead, the student's need to recognize that not only does history change, but historians' views of the same events also vary. In reading these essays, certain questions may recur in attempting to understand a scholar's response to the past. Why did a particular viewpoint arise at a certain time? What were its premises and how did acceptance of a perspective reflect the social and intellectual background of historians holding it? Finally, what in addition to the passage of time contributed to the decline of one set of historical opinions and the overlapping growth of another? Any thoughtful historiographic discussion which attempts to answer these questions must provide more than a bibliographic survey. In studying the beliefs and values of several generations of historians, each essay thus becomes an exploration of American intellectual history itself. In varying ways, this holds true for all the writings in this volume.

The essays appear in roughly chronological order, ranging from the Colonial period to the problem of our entry into World War II. There has not been sufficient time for the accumulation of a body of literature reflecting the opinions of succeeding groups of historians on such vital questions as the origins of the Cold War, the nature of post-World War II affluence, and America's role as a world power. The concluding essays, however, offer two assessments of the present state of American historical writing. Most of the historiographic discussions are followed by a listing of major recent works that have appeared on the topic since original publication. The student can refer to these newer writings in order to gauge the present state and future course of interpretative history on the subject. The editors have also compiled the bibliography of American historiography, given at the back of the book, and offer it not as definitive but as a comprehensive guide to further reading. Like the collection of essays, its aim is not to exhaust the subject— and the student—but to introduce for additional investigation a series of still-challenging American themes.

University of California at Los Angeles   FRANK OTTO GATELL
Smith College   ALLEN WEINSTEIN
May 1968

Contents

American Themes

ESSAYS IN HISTORIOGRAPHY

I

The American Continental Colonies in the Empire

ROBERT L. MIDDLEKAUFF

Seventeenth-century Englishmen were prone to think of the founding of colonies virtually as an act in nature. Colonies were plantations; their settlement, planting, in the sense of placing seeds in the ground. English literature brims with such figures. Thus John Smith described the "first planting" of Virginia and Richard Hakluyt wrote A *Discourse of Western Planting*. Later in the colonial period men on both sides of the Atlantic commonly referred to England as the "mother" and the colonies as her "children"; and they sometimes speculated about what the "growth" of these children would yield in the future. Other terms were also used, of course, but descriptions that implied that the relationship of England and her colonies was organic were most frequently employed.

These pleasant metaphors were discarded in 1776 when Thomas Paine showed in *Common Sense* that behind the smile of the "tender mother" lurked a "devouring monster." But the old natural figures have had a persistent way of cropping up in accounts of the colonies and the Revolution. They have because they appear to be extraordinarily apt. Historians of early America face the problem of explaining enormous changes, not the least of which is how thirteen small English

From *The Historiography of the British Empire-Commonwealth; Trends, Interpretations and Resources*, Robin W. Winks, ed. (Durham: Duke University Press, 1966), pp. 23-45. Reprinted with permission.

settlements transformed themselves into an independent nation. Saying that the colonies "grew" and "matured" has proved to be a convenient answer.

Words, we all know, convey thought and the choice of words implies a way of thinking. But words may also control thought. Likening historical change in the American colonies to developments in nature has sometimes resulted in such control.

The most recent historians to offer a general interpretation of the American colonial past, the Imperial school, expressed their views in a vocabulary deeply indebted to metaphors from nature. The great men of this group, Charles McLean Andrews and George Louis Beer, found the use of these figures especially congenial because they were convinced that society follows the laws of evolution. Society, they insisted, was evolving, slowly producing higher and better institutions and ideas. The study of the past revealed this development; indeed history moved linearly. The Imperial historians customarily charted its direction with such terms as "progress" and "advance." Signs of this movement were especially clear in the American colonial past, where simple, crude beginnings had gradually produced a nation. To be sure, at many points in the accounts of the Imperial historians, their treatment implies no belief that the growth described was morphological. They clearly label much growth in inorganic terms, industrial and economic for example. But the over-all conception rests on a conviction of organic change, a growth as in nature, unresponsive to human control. Thus Andrews wrote of the American Revolution: "[Englishmen] could hardly have been expected to appreciate the fact that the colonies in cutting loose from their mother country were but obeying a law of general evolution of human society toward higher and broader forms of government and social relations."[1]

Andrews and Beer probably were not aware of the control the organic metaphor exercised over their interpretations. But both recognized, as others did not, that earlier historians had failed to think about the colonies in a meaningful context. Some neglected everything except the colonies themselves. Others, like George Bancroft, considered colonial history prefatory to the history of American democracy.[2] Bancroft's approach appeared particularly cramping because it distorted the importance of the Imperial connection to colonial development. The idea that the colonial past was simply a preface to a glorious national story obscured the fascination of the early period.

The Imperial historians insisted that the colonies must be placed within a different context. Andrews argued that the years of the English connection constituted a period which must be studied by itself, free from "all preconceptions based on later events."[3] The colonies were a part of the Empire, and they must be studied in the context of British expansion. Seeing the colonies in context also involved, according to Andrews, studying them not from within but from "without"—indeed from the vantage point of London. This angle of vision conferred a great advantage: "It brings the mother country into the forefront of the picture as the central figure, the authoritative and guiding force, the influence of which did more than anything else to shape the course of colonial achievement."[4]

Andrews' distinguished student, Lawrence Henry Gipson, is less indebted to the idea that colonial development followed organic lines. Although he agrees that the colonies must be seen within the Imperial setting, he does not believe that London offers the best vantage point. By the middle of the eighteenth century, he says, the mother country influenced the Empire less than local forces. Therefore the historian must "beat the bounds," examining from within every British colony throughout the world.[5]

George Louis Beer, on the other hand, approached British expansion largely through investigation of the old colonial system. The colonies interested him only in so far as they were affected by the system, and his work concentrated on the aspects of colonial life most affected by the system. What he may not have emphasized sufficiently was that the way colonies responded to Imperial forces depended in large part upon local conditions.

Like the conception of growth, the Imperial historians' idea of studying the colonies in the context of British expansion has been enormously influential. It has yielded excellent studies of the conditions in England favorable to colonization, of the first settlements, and of the old colonial system itself. Still, the idea has proved to be of limited value; it has not really offered a way of understanding the character of colonial culture itself. Nor has the idea of growth produced satisfactory explanations of social change. In fact it may have inhibited understanding more often than it aided it.

The Imperial historians invigorated interest in the conditions that impelled Englishmen to leave their country for America, but they did not have to stimulate interest in the first men to sail westward, the great explorers, for it had rarely drooped. Indeed the fascination of these men obscured the conditions of England's entrance in maritime enterprise and colonization. Drake and his great contemporaries are romantic figures, and most of the writing about them until fairly recently has been romance. Modern scholars have provided more substantial stuff, retelling the story of English expansion not simply in terms of heroes but as the expression of an emergent commercial capitalism and a new science. The English scholar James A. Williamson was responsible for much of the modern telling. His *Maritime Enterprise, 1485-1558* (Oxford, 1913), though now superseded on many details by later studies, blazed the way to the early history of English commerce and discovery. In his book Williamson attempted to refurbish the claims of Sebastian Cabot to exploration in the Northwest, a subject he pursued further in *The Voyages of the Cabots and the English Discovery of North America* (London, 1929). Although Williamson explained the activities of the Cabots better than anyone else has since, much evidence is still lacking about Sebastian Cabot's voyage of 1509. Williamson's *Sir John Hawkins: The Time and the Man* (Oxford, 1927) and *The Age of Drake* (4th ed., London, 1960) are still the standard books in their fields. About the time Williamson began issuing his work, William R. Scott's *The Constitution and Finance of English, Scottish and Irish Joint-Stock Companies to 1720* (3 vols.; Cambridge, 1910-12) appeared. Scott's work, like Williamson's, has been superseded on some points, but its rich coverage of the trading companies makes it still the most useful general work.

Sir Humphrey Gilbert and Sir Walter Raleigh have been the subject of romance almost as often as Drake and the English seadogs. The best work on their explorations and colonization ventures has been done recently. In his Introduction to *The Voyages and Colonising Enterprises of Sir Humphrey Gilbert* (2 vols.; London, 1940), David B. Quinn showed that unlike much English effort, Gilbert's was not in search of a Northwest Passage, but was undertaken to establish a base for piratical expeditions against Spain. Quinn also related Gilbert's experience in Ireland to his overseas adventures. In his edition of *The Roanoke Voyages, 1584-1590* (2 vols.; London, 1955), Quinn suggested that more documents on the voyages may yet turn up. But it is difficult to imagine anyone improving on his brilliant account of Raleigh's ventures in *Raleigh and the British Empire* (rev. ed., New York, 1962).

Exploration and commercial expansion provide only a partial background for the understanding of England's first colonizing efforts. As George B. Parks pointed out in *Richard Hakluyt and the English Voyages* (New York, 1928), someone had to revise old geographical conceptions and drew together the knowledge of the new world for English merchants and statesmen. The Hakluyts, of course, did just that and much more besides. Their activities are described and carefully assessed in Parks' study. Two studies of the development of English geography should also be consulted: Eva G. R. Taylor, *Tudor Geography, 1485-1583* (London, 1930) and *Late Tudor and Early Stuart Geography, 1583-1650* (London, 1934).[6] An excellent recent review is John Horace Parry's *The Age of Reconnaissance* (London, 1963).

Much of the best work on the explorations was done by English historians; American historians have followed it with intensive study of the settlements. Much of their study was given to the conditions making the founding of the colonies possible. Beer, for example, is responsible for showing the link between the belief that England was overpopulated and the encouragement of emigration. His insight has been challenged recently in an essay by Mildred Campbell, which though careful and thorough does not shake Beer's thesis.[7] Other studies of emigration to the colonies abound. At least two add much to our knowledge of the founding of the colonies: Marcus L. Hansen's *The Atlantic Migration, 1607-1860* (Cambridge, Mass., 1940), which discusses admirably the effects of a variety of colonial policies upon the flow of colonists, and Abbot E. Smith's *Colonists in Bondage: White Servitude and Convict Labor in America, 1607-1776* (Chapel Hill, 1947), which demonstrates the commercial character of the trade in servants.

Although these studies are illuminating, they all fail to match Charles McLean Andrews' *The Colonial Period of American History* in either conception or coverage. Andrews saw English expansion largely as the expression of a growing commercial capitalism. But though he argued his case persuasively and buttressed it with rich detail, he did not really sense that the seventeenth-century mind conceived of colonies in religious as well as commercial terms. Even in the founding of Virginia, Perry Miller tells us in "Religion and Society in the Early Literature of Virginia," a chapter in *Errand into the Wilderness* (Cambridge, Mass., 1956), religion "was the really energizing propulsion." Miller's essay is extravagantly phrased, but the point it insists upon—that seventeenth-century Englishmen did not make nice modern distinctions between religion, politics, and commerce—is a valid one. Andrews' massive work convinces one of the commercial motive in English promoters, but he does not persuade one of its simple purity. Miller's studies of Puritanism, *Orthodoxy in Massachusetts, 1630-1650* (Cambridge, Mass., 1933) and *The New England Mind: The Seventeenth Century* (Cambridge, Mass., 1954), have almost completely reshaped historians' conceptions of the impulses of the founding of

New England. Still, Andrews' meticulous reconstruction of the companies' charters, indeed of much of the English commercial side, remains useful. And so, for that matter, is most of his work on other seventeenth-century beginnings. In the last generation other scholars have amplified and modified to some extent portions of his work. On Virginia, Wesley Frank Craven's *The Dissolution of the Virgina Company* (New York, 1932) tells the story of the company's collapse convincingly. Craven's superb *The Southern Colonies in the Seventeenth Century, 1607-1689* (Baton Rouge, 1949) leans on Andrews' account for the beginnings of Carolina and Maryland.

Andrews' work on the beginnings of the middle colonies has also stood up well; even John E. Pomfret's admirable studies, *The Province of West New Jersey, 1609-1702* (Princeton, 1956) and *The Province of East New Jersey, 1609-1702: The Rebellious Proprietary* (Princeton, 1962), do not seriously alter his conclusions about the Jerseys, though they offer much more information. Andrews' account of the founding of Pennsylvania is excellent, but it should be supplemented by several essays in Frederick B. Tolles' *Quakers and the Atlantic Culture* (New York, 1960), and by Catherine O. Peare's *William Penn: A Biography* (Philadelphia, 1957).[8]

In his accounts of the settlements, Andrews devoted more attention to the English conditions surrounding the founding than to the first years of the colonists' desperate struggle to carve out a foothold for themselves. This focus followed from his belief that the colonies represented an expression of British expansion; the source of that expansion, Britain, seemed as important as its shape in the colonies. Like others of the Imperial school, Andrews insisted that even after settlement the colonies continued to feel the force of the British connection; indeed, their membership in the Empire was the key fact of their history.

Obviously, how the Imperial historians describe the Empire is an important matter. Andrews found that England, the center of the Empire, always placed its own interests ahead of those of the colonies. Although he and Gipson agreed that the colonies prospered within the Empire, they did not explain the colonial prosperity in the same terms. Andrews implied that the colonies were lucky: Imperial policy, which was drawn in response to mercantilist imperatives, did not by design favor their interests. Fortunately for the colonies the old colonial system, in establishing some lines of trade and prohibiting several others, encouraged activity that the colonies would have engaged in had restrictions not existed. Even when the idea of the self-sufficient Empire began dominating Imperial thinking, Andrews said, the interests of England remained paramount. Gipson, whose work covers the period in which the idea of the self-sufficient Empire was accepted, insisted that by the middle of the eighteenth century English policy-makers recognized an Imperial interest which transcended any narrow concern for the home country. British officials always consulted the colonies on questions of policy and attempted to devise plans that benefited as much of the Empire as possible.[9]

Besides disagreeing in their assessments of the purposes of Imperial policy, Andrews and Gipson also evaluated British leadership differently. Andrews described it as frequently "badly informed" about the colonies; Gipson found it intelligently concerned about colonial interests, eager and successful in discovering what the colonies really wanted. In his careful analysis of administrative agencies, Andrews suggested that their performance was uneven: the Customs Service, for example, never worked well, but the Vice-Admiralty Courts did. Although he performed no similar examination, Gipson concluded that most of the agencies that governed the Empire functioned justly and efficiently. He rated the service of the Board of Trade much higher than Andrews did.[10]

Nor did Andrews and Gipson agree on Parliament's rôle in colonial life. Andrews simply dismissed the suggestion that Parliament interfered with the "internal life or government of the colonies" before 1763 as having no basis in fact. Parliament confined itself to regulating commerce and navigation. Gipson, on the other hand, professed surprise that the colonies before 1750 did not protest against the series of parliamentary laws that "amounted in effect to a code held binding on all." Parliament, he insisted, had interfered with far more than trade and commerce long before the Revolutionary crisis: it had actually entered the internal life of the colonies. Beer, whose concern was narrower than Andrews' and Gipson's, provided an analysis substantially in agreement with Andrews.[11]

These differences should not obscure the fact that the Imperial historians have contributed much to the description of the functioning of Imperial agencies and to the analysis of English commercial policy. In a series of graceful books, Beer gave Imperial policy its first systematic analysis. His first study, *The Commercial Policy of England toward the American Colonies* (New York, 1893), revealed an interest in the medieval origins of policy, an interest he sustained throughout his work but never completely developed. His formal treatment of the beginnings of policy, *The Origins of the British Colonial System, 1578-*

1660, places most of the origins of policy in the seventeenth century. England's economic needs, the financial requirements of the government, and mercantilist theory were the determinants of England's colonial policy. The regulation of the tobacco trade in particular forced the formulation of much policy, and English statesmen tended to generalize from the experience of tobacco regulation. In *The Old Colonial System, 1660-1754* and *British Colonial Policy, 1754-1765* Beer described a fully developed British policy which sought to create a self-sufficient Empire. He emphasized that if self-sufficiency was an ideal, in functioning the system deliberately aimed to protect British interests, and that the economic interest of the colonies always remained "subordinate to that of the mother country. . . ."[12]

Although they are probably richer in the details of the making of policy, Andrews' studies of policy did not significantly alter Beer's conclusions. But Andrews did much that Beer did not: he traced the creation of the administrative apparatus, the commissions, committees, councils, and boards, by which policy was both made and superintended. The faltering beginnings of Imperial administrative agencies appear in *British Committees* (Baltimore, 1908). Andrews expressed his mature ideas in the clear-eyed essay *The Colonial Period of American History: England's Commercial and Colonial Policy* (New Haven, 1938).

Many narrower studies of policy and administration support Andrews' and Beer's view of the intentions and the functioning of the Empire rather than Gipson's. Ralph P. Bieber's *The Lords of Trade and Plantations, 1675-1696* (Allentown, Pa., 1919) suggests that administrative agencies "often failed to grasp the colonial point of view." Lawrence A. Harper's *The English Navigation Laws* (New York, 1939) asserts that the old colonial system was not "designed for the good of the empire as a whole." Similarly Oliver M. Dickerson's *American Colonial Government* (Cleveland, 1912) and Mark Thomson's *The Secretaries of State, 1681-1782* (Oxford, 1932) buttress Andrews and Beer.[13]

If all these books aid in assessing the old colonial system each has more specialized uses. Bieber's book, for example, describes the ordinary workings of the Lords of Trade carefully; Harper's account is unrivaled in its analysis of the origins and functioning of the English Navigation Acts.

The metaphor of "growth" has been especially prominent in the Imperial historians' studies of the colonial economy. In this case the metaphor has not impaired understanding but perhaps has increased it. For the components of economic growth are susceptible of description in terms other than those borrowed from nature: in short, economic growth can be analyzed empirically.

Preoccupied by the position the colonies held within the Empire, the Imperial historian attempted to assess the effects of the Acts of Navigation and Trade upon the economic life of the colonies. Gipson, in the latest statement of the Imperial historians' view, suggested that the system of restrictions imposed by Parliament was made less burdensome by the advantages that the Imperial connection conferred. To be sure the colonies paid certain duties, they could manufacture hats and woolens only on a limited scale, they could ship "enumerated" products only to Imperial ports, and they could import manufactures only through Britain. But, he points out, they received drawbacks—or rebates—of many of the duties collected; the restrictions on manufactures were either irrelevant to the facts of colonial production or, as in the case of iron, were ignored; the enumerated goods enjoyed a virtual monopoly of the English market, for foreign competition was prohibited; and the colonies were not much affected by the requirement that they import their manufactures from Britain. All in all, says Gipson, "the opportunities for legitimate financial gain opened up by the trade and navigation system seemed to have more than offset the hindrances posed by legal barriers against engaging in certain activities, industrial as well as commercial."[14]

Gipson conceded that several of these conclusions have been disputed, but he does not believe that the general position of the Imperial historians has been shaken: the colonies benefited economically from their connection to the Empire. This contention, it should be observed, rests upon the discoveries that the colonies prospered during the period before the Revolution and that Americans rarely complained before 1764 about parliamentary measures regulating their business activities.

No doubt the Imperial historians are right in insisting that the Americans were prosperous and uncomplaining, but are they justified in assuming that these facts "prove" the beneficial effects of parliamentary regulation? Probably they are, but at least one historian has argued that the costs of the Imperial connection came high to the colonials. Lawrence A. Harper, in "The Effect of the Navigation Acts," suggested that in the late eighteenth century the chief losses were absorbed by planters of tobacco and rice.[15] He calculated the cost of enumeration of tobacco as two and one-fourth cents per pound; in 1773, he says, the total loss must have been between two and three million dollars. Rice planters lost an estimated three shillings a hundred-weight, which must have totaled about $185,000 at the least in 1773. The additional charges exacted by the requirement that all manufactures must come through England ran from a half million to three million dollars. The precision of Harper's calculations may be questioned, especially when they depend upon comparisons of commercial activities before and after the American Revolution, yet the evidence he presents of the fact that Americans took some losses seems irrefutable. In his *English Navigation Acts*, Harper showed that the acts wrenched colonial commerce out of its most profitable channel, trade with the Dutch, and compelled exchanges with England. The Dutch appealed to colonials on a number of scores: Dutch credit was cheaper, their manufactures were one-third less, and their freight rates were lower. The commercial habits of the colonials, it seems, were formed by regulation, and at the beginning of regulation the colonies did complain. Later colonial silence at the requirements of the Navigation Acts may in part have been the result of the old custom of acquiescence.

What especially impressed the Imperial historians about the colonial economy was its growth towards a maturity which almost equaled that of Britain. Tracing the story of the actual working of the colonial economy has been the task of a number of historians less affected by the general conceptional framework than by a number of technical problems. Their answers to many of these problems serve to confirm the Imperial historians' insight into the importance of the Empire to early American life. But it is also clear that colonial economic activity was more complicated than anyone has suspected.

An old study, William B. Weeden's *Economic and Social History of New England, 1620-1789* (2 vols.; Boston, 1891), attempted in a rough way to sketch the interconnections between New England's economy and society. Its diffuseness and limited conception of the sources for the study of economic history decreases its value. Yet Weeden succeeded in at least touching many of the problems later historians have found interesting.

Recently historians have begun to study the economy through the men who made it work, especially the merchants and their families. Seventeenth-century merchants have been treated thoughtfully by Samuel Eliot Morison, Bernard Bailyn, and Viola Barnes.[16] Morison's short biographies of John Hull in *Builders of the Bay Colony* and "William Pynchon," in *Massachusetts Historical Society Proceedings*, LXIV (Boston, 1932), 67-107, show how important it is to give a rounded picture of merchant life. The Hull of Morison's sketch earned a fortune in trade with England and the West Indies. Yet he held medieval economic ideals: he despised "oppression" and usury and welcomed regulation of business by the state. Hull was a Puritan and his social attitudes were those of his society. The transformation of the social type which Hull represented can be followed in Bailyn's *The New England Merchants in the Seventeenth Century* (Cambridge, Mass., 1955). Bailyn exposed the alienation from the old Puritans of a new business community in New England, a community tied together by family as well as interest and oriented toward England, the center of its overseas trade. Bailyn probably claimed a cohesion for this group which it did not possess; at any rate, as he admits, the merchants split badly over the Dominion of New England. But Bailyn's suggestion that the family was an important mechanism in seventeenth-century commercial life seems irrefutable. Friends and relatives in England served as factors for New England merchants or as agents who opened up fresh contacts. Whether kinship continued to be an important commercial institution in the more complex relationships of the eighteenth century remains an open question, though Bailyn seems to assume that it did. There is considerable evidence to support his view. Samuel Rosenblatt's "The Significance of Credit in the Tobacco Consignment Trade: A Study of John Norton and Sons, 1768-1775," *William and Mary Quarterly*, 3rd ser., XIX (July, 1962), 383-99, and Jacob Price's "Who Was John Norton? A Note on the Historical Character of Some Eighteenth-Century London Firms," *ibid.*, pp. 400-407, suggest that family connections served as a means of securing credit and indeed in the organization of the tobacco trade. There is further corroboration in Price's "The Rise of Glasgow in the Chesapeake Tobacco Trade, 1707-1775," *ibid.*, XI (April, 1954), 179-99, an article which goes a long way toward explaining how Scottish factors, resident in Virginia, were able to capture much of the tobacco trade from the consignment houses after 1720.

As important as kinship was in establishing commercial relationships abroad, it was not everything. From several studies of colonial houses one might infer that kinship was important chiefly in connecting colonials to English merchants. In the sizable trade outside these lines, with the Dutch, Spanish, French, and Portuguese ports, family played no important part. Byron Fairchild's *Pepperells*, William T. Baxter's *Hancocks*, James Blaine Hedge's *Browns*, and Philip L. White's *Beekmans* all established close relationships with houses in England and elsewhere, but family played little part in the non-English connections.[17]

The histories of these merchants are rich in their details of commercial activity. Ships, cargoes, voyages, exchanges, and the merchants themselves take on a concreteness that can be achieved in written history only through the accumulation of examples. Moreover, the history of each family is a story of change. Thus Hedges' book tells of the simple beginnings of James and Obadiah Brown, who in the 1720's began trading with the West Indies with only a small amount of capital and a single ship. By the end of the colonial period, the sons of James had sent ships as far away as Africa and had branched out into the manufacture of candles and iron. Manufacturing in fact had taken on a greater scale in their enterprises than commerce. Now, in this change the Browns were not typical (though they seem to have been in many other ways) but the variety of their activities was repeated many times throughout colonial ports. Diversified economic activity was a necessity: the merchant could not specialize and still secure the necessary currency and commodities to pay for imports from England. The lack of specie and the small scale of his markets made specialization impossible.

The problems of currency and markets deserve further study. Several careful beginnings have been made on currency, the best being Curtis P. Nettels' *The Money Supply of the American Colonies before 1720* (Madison, 1934), which explains the mechanisms of exchange and the attempts by Americans to collect enough specie to make payments to Europe. All the studies of merchants already cited discuss this problem: White's *Beekmans* is especially fascinating for it shows that when a merchant had a product like flaxseed for export to a large market he experienced little difficulty. Baxter and Fairchild's studies both point up how important government contracts were to merchants—how coveted they were, and how remunerative.

But a flow of trade itself kept the exchange with England open as Richard Pares' *Yankees and Creoles: The Trade between North America and the West Indies before the American Revolution* (Cambridge, Mass., 1956) shows. In search of a way to pay English merchants for imports, the northern colonies sent ships into the West Indies and picked up the sugar (in exchange for foodstuffs, fish, and horses) which English markets demanded. Pares' book tells the story of this roundabout exchange better than it has ever been told before. But it does not sketch the history of the changes in the North America–West Indies trade, changes which occurred but which have never been exploited in the detail necessary.

Pares' study lacks the statistical base which strengthens any history of commerce. Most of the histories of merchants are similarly short on statistics. We need to know in greater precision the lines of trade, the number of ships entering colonial ports over the years, their cargoes and the value of those cargoes, the ownership of the ships, the prices obtained and so on. Recently several such accounts have appeared: Bernard Bailyn's *Massachusetts Shipping, 1697-1714: A Statistical Study* (Cambridge, Mass., 1959), based on Massachusetts shipping registers; Anne Bezanson, *et al.*, *Prices in Colonial Pennsylvania* (Philadelphia, 1935), a detailed history of prices; and Murray G. Lawson's "The Routes of Boston's Trade, 1752-1765," *Colonial Society of Massachusetts Publications*, XXXVIII (1959), 81-120. Many more studies of this sort are needed for a rounded view of colonial economic activity and its relation to the Empire.

As in the investigation of economic activity, the assumptions of the Imperial historians have also provided a rough framework within which colonial politics have been studied. Andrews and Gipson frequently comment on the growth of colonial governments and their "maturity" by the time of the Revolution. Their view merges neatly with a view of colonial political history which insists that sometime in the seventeenth century popular, local, and representative government began challenging Imperial authority. The alignments in this contest are usually assumed to have included rich merchants, grand planters, and royal officials, all led by the royal governor on one side, and opposing this elite the underprivileged, the westerners, the poor debtors, the disfranchised, the lesser merchants and planters, all men on their way up. Their successful grasping of power by 1776 represents the triumph of democracy. More often the struggle is described in terms of institutions; in fact it is seen as being practically synonomous with the "growth" of the lower house of the legislature. This story has been told in Leonard W. Labaree's admirable *Royal Government in America* (New Haven, 1930). Labaree, however, does much more than recount the fight between governor and assembly; his book is a study of almost all aspects of royal government in the colonies. Mary P. Clarke's *Parliamentary Privilege in the American Colonies* (New Haven, 1943) gives depth to a part of the familiar story by showing that by claiming "parliamentary privilege," a set of rights which Parliament exercised, colonial assemblies sought to defend their encroachments on the governor's power by invoking a great tradition.

Recently Jack P. Greene, in "The Role of the Lower Houses of Assembly in Eighteenth-Century Politics," *Journal of Southern History*

(Baton Rouge), XXVII (November, 1960), 451-74, has reviewed the whole problem, summarizing his own findings about the southern colonies and those of other scholars about the northern colonies. Greene's article, as well as his book, *The Quest for Power: The Lower Houses of Assembly in the Southern Royal Colonies, 1689-1776* (Chapel Hill, 1963), is curiously dated in its focus upon the activity of the colonial assembly. But in "Foundations of Political Power in the Virginia House of Burgesses, 1720-1776," *William and Mary Quarterly*, 3rd ser., XVI (October, 1959), 485-506, he has examined a single house with a technique which has found increasing favor in the last fifteen years. His study identifies powerful burgesses within the house by analyzing the composition of committees. After showing that a few men dominated the actions of the house, Greene provides information about these men: their educations, occupations, residences within the colony, and length of service.

Studies which make use of similar techniques are altering almost our entire conception of colonial politics. Though the Imperial connection is still considered to be important, it no longer dominates historians' thinking. Indeed their emphasis is upon the local, and upon the anonymous individual, rather than upon the Empire and its royal officials. Perhaps the key book in getting the revision of the older views started was Robert E. Brown's *Middle-Class Democracy and the Revolution in Massachusetts, 1691-1780* (Ithaca, 1955). In this study Brown contends that colonial politics were democratic, and by showing that the franchise was widely held in Massachusetts, offers much, though not compelling, evidence for his thesis. Since his book was published, Brown has found considerable support from Chilton Williamson's *American Suffrage, from Property to Democracy, 1760-1860* (Princeton, 1960), which surveys the right to vote in all thirteen colonies.[18] Brown's latest book, *Virginia, 1705-1786: Democracy or Aristocracy?* (East Lansing, 1964), written with B. Katherine Brown, extends his investigations to Virginia. The book is frankly tendentious—it seeks to demonstrate the democratic character of society and politics in Virginia. The widespread property-holding, the high degree of social mobility, the absence of class, religious, or sectional conflict, the broad franchise, and the equal representation all conspired in favor of majority—that is middle-class—desires, according to the Browns. But the investigation the Browns conducted determined their conclusions, for their inquiry does not permit an adequate assessment of the power of Virginia's gentry; and they reject the results of such an inquiry made by Charles S. Sydnor in *Gentlemen Freeholders: Political Practices in Washington's Virginia* (Chapel Hill, 1952).

A feeling for the way eighteenth-century Virginia politics actually worked is missing in the Browns' study, especially a feeling for the political style of men of family and wealth. Part of the Browns' failure arises from the focus of their interests in the objective political world—the franchise, for example, representation, and the extent of property holding. The subtle manner, so deftly described by Sydnor, in which men of social status got their way in Virginia's politics almost totally escapes the Browns. And so does the complex interplay between the gentry and their constituencies, an interplay marked by a fluidity of power but not of responsibility. Yet the Browns' work is important: it provides significant information, and it forces us to discard many of the old categories in our study of colonial politics.

Much more work needs to be done. We still lack knowledge about many of the purposes and techniques of political life in the colonies. In part our ignorance can be traced to the fact that colonial politics were local, and we have few intensive studies on a small scale. We have also assumed gratuitously that colonial politics resembled modern politics. One notable exception is the late Charles S. Grant's *Democracy in the Connecticut Frontier Town of Kent* (New York, 1961), which examines economic, political, and social opportunity from 1738 to 1800 in a western community. Grant's book provides support of a kind to Brown's thesis by showing that the opportunities for getting wealth were open in Kent. But though the vote was easily obtained, office holding remained a monopoly of the few, a fact Grant does not explain.

Class conflict as described by Roy H. Akagi, *The Town Proprietors of the New England Colonies* (Philadelphia, 1924), did not exist in Kent; proprietors were residents and debtors occupied a variety of places up and down the economic scale. Though it deals with a specific episode, the land bank controversy in Massachusetts, George A. Billias, *The Massachusetts Land Bankers of 1740* (Orono, Maine, 1959), reinforces Grant's finding that class conflict was slight in colonial society. Billias rejects completely the old view of the bank issue in Massachusetts as involving debtors against merchants by showing that merchants led the fight for the bank.

Historians who have stressed the importance of class strife in colonial politics have always found a great gulf (and frequently hostility) between leaders and their constituencies. Two recent studies, Bernard Bailyn, "Politics and Social Structure in Virginia,"[19] and Charles Sydnor, *Gentlemen Freeholders*, mentioned above, reveal that in Virginia, though social status was an important ingredient in political success, the gulf may have been exaggerated. (In New England, where class lines were less distinct than in the southern colonies, the gulf between leaders and constituencies hardly existed outside the cities and large towns.) Bailyn's essay is much more than an analysis of the recruitment of Virginia's leadership. It is an imaginative suggestion about the components of Virginia's politics and the way they should be studied. Sydnor's witty and learned book describes a political situation in which the highly cohesive gentry truly represent the best interests of their electors. The findings of these books, along with Brown's, Grant's, and Billias', suggest a reinterpretation of colonial politics is now underway. Such books reinforce the impression that colonial politics were not primarily Imperial, but local. One suspects that the importance of the royal government and the colonial assembly has been exaggerated. Colonials appear to have been far more interested in concrete and immediate issues than in the struggle for legislative autonomy. Most political issues were settled without any reference to Imperial agencies. In any case, the smallest agencies of colonial government—parishes, counties, and towns—deserve much more attention than they have received.

For the Imperial historians political growth yielded maturity and then ripeness. This American "growth" differed radically from English development. Andrews insisted that the colonies "were far more advanced, politically, socially, and morally, than the mother country"; Beer and Gipson did not suggest that American institutions were superior to English, but they found them different enough so as to make the American Revolution virtually inevitable.[20]

The existence of the differences raises again the question of the character of the Empire. Indeed one might ask whether by the middle of the eighteenth century the Empire was an entity. Whose allegiance did it enlist? Gipson, who has studied the Empire just before the American Revolution more thoroughly than anyone else, has been so sorely puzzled by these questions that he has given contradictory answers. Colonials, he has written, perceived that their interest lay with the Empire's; in fact the cement of empire was "moral force." But Gipson has also agreed with Beer that fear of the French held America within the Empire before 1763. He says that after the cession of Canada at the end of the French and Indian War the colonies were ripe for rebellion. Economically the colonies had flourished under Imperial protection and regulation. They were free and happy and secure in the

Empire. And little wonder! Presiding over this magnificent creation were ministers animated not by the crude considerations of mercantilism but by the ideal of a self-sufficient Empire. These ministers never failed to consult the colonials when decisions which affected them came up; these ministers did not represent the interests of the mother country but of the larger Empire. They are for Gipson the personification of selflessness and wisdom. But the Americans were still restless in the eighteenth century. Not fully aware of the extent of their own strength, and maturity, they remained contented until 1763, when the French were removed from their borders. Then able at last to see themselves in their full strength and liberated from an old fear, they were psychologically prepared for a break. When the British reasonably asked them for contributions for Imperial defense they were seized by "irrational" fear, balked, making absurd distinctions between external and internal taxes and, ignoring the fact that they had long submitted to a virtual code of legislation by Parliament, they suddenly discovered that Parliament lacked the right to legislate for them. And finally after further friction they declared themselves independent.[21]

There are serious flaws in Gipson's account. He misunderstands the character of American politics. Political power, he says, ignoring the revisionist work on the suffrage, was controlled by an elite. Certainly American politics were not democratic in any modern sense, but governing groups were limited by the need to consult their constituencies. Repeating the old charge that opportunism governed American political theory, Gipson describes American protests against Imperial reorganization as shifts of expediency. He characterizes American concern about the possible extension of taxation at the time of the Stamp Act as "irrational fear," even though the stamp tax was the second statute passed in two years to collect revenue.[22]

Although Gipson probably has convinced many historians that his analysis of important Revolutionary questions is correct, he and the other Imperial historians have failed to persuade the present generation of American historians that the Revolution was inevitable. The Revolutionary collision, recent accounts suggest, might have been avoided had British policy taken a different tack after 1763. Few Americans sought independence until fighting began in 1775. Americans acted only to defend themselves; and in the process they discovered what they believed about the British constitution and they fashioned a set of beliefs about the rights of man.

Two books, Edmund S. and Helen M. Morgan's *The Stamp Act Crisis, Prologue to Revolution* (Chapel Hill, 1953; rev. ed., New York,

1963), and Oliver M. Dickerson's *The Navigation Acts and the American Revolution* (Philadelphia, 1951), have shaped recent views of the Revolution. The Morgans' study has altered our views of colonial constitutional thinking. Older books, most notably Carl Lotus Becker's brilliant *The Declaration of Independence: A Study in the History of Political Ideas* (New York, 1922) and Randolph G. Adams' *Political Ideas of the American Revolution: Britannic-American Contributions to the Problem of Imperial Organization, 1765-1775* (Durham, N.C., 1922; New York, 1958), described a series of shifts in the colonial position which involved a distinction between internal and external taxes. The Morgans show that the colonials did not make this distinction; rather, they agreed in 1765 upon the constitutional principle "no taxation without representation" and never abandoned it. Colonials, the Morgans argue, were prepared to fight for their rights as early as 1765. Their political position was not based upon "abstract principles," as many historians have interpreted the Morgans; it expressed the colonists' understanding of the inseparability of liberty and property. Taxation without representation would destroy property and liberty. Had the British government accorded this position the respect that the colonies expected, no Revolution would have occurred in 1776.

But in the years following the Stamp Act the British government demonstrated an insensitivity to colonial rights and interests. The character and effects of British action is nowhere more clearly revealed than in Dickerson's study of the Navigation Acts. While agreeing with the Imperial historians that the old colonial system neither hampered the colonial economy nor provoked colonial resentment, Dickerson shows that after 1767 the creation of an American Board of Customs commissioners led to "customs racketeering," as Dickerson terms the practices of customs officials, which brought grief to merchants, ship owners, and small traders. Dickerson has also shown in "Use Made of the Revenue from the Tax on Tea," *New England Quarterly* (Boston), XXI (June, 1958), 232-43, that the feeding of the tea tax into patronage inserted a new force into American politics and alienated important commercial groups.

Dickerson's book provides an explanation of merchant leadership in the resistance to British measures after 1763. But for the story of the merchants' tangled efforts to oppose the British and at the same time repress the swelling lower-class participation in politics, one must consult Arthur M. Schlesinger's admirable *The Colonial Merchants and the American Revolution* (New York, 1918). Although many recent works demonstrate that group conflict was not as great as Schlesinger thought, his book remains one of the three or four most important books on the Revolution. Support for Schlesinger's views may be found in Carl Lotus Becker's *The History of Political Parties in the Province of New York, 1760-1776* (Madison, 1909).

One particular source of concern to merchants and to many others as well were the Vice-Admiralty Courts. Carl Ubbelohde's *The Vice-Admiralty Courts and the American Revolution* (Chapel Hill, 1960) describes their working and shows that their operating without juries was a persistent threat to liberty in colonial minds. David S. Lovejoy's "Rights Imply Equality: The Case Against Admiralty Jurisdiction in America, 1764-1776," *William and Mary Quarterly*, 3rd ser., XVI (October, 1959), 459-84, explains the American concern with clarity and force.

The intellectual and social background of the American Revolution is now being studied intensively. A pioneer volume which still merits great respect was Moses Coit Tyler's *The Literary History of the American Revolution* (2 vols.; New York, 1897). Three narrower studies have recently appeared. Caroline Robbins' *Eighteenth-Century Commonwealthman* (Cambridge, Mass., 1959) helps explain how radical seventeenth-century political thinking was perpetuated and made available to the American revolutionaries.[23] Robert Brown's study of the franchise in Massachusetts (cited above) suggests that the claims of the Americans that they sought only to defend liberties already obtained had a basis in fact. And Carl Bridenbaugh's studies of cities, *Cities in the Wilderness: The First Century of Urban Life in America, 1625-1742* (New York, 1938), and *Cities in Revolt: Urban Life in America, 1743-1776* (New York, 1955), help clarify the social setting of American protests.

The latest study of Revolutionary ideas is Bernard Bailyn's "General Introduction: The Transforming Radicalism of the American Revolution," in *Pamphlets of the American Revolution, 1750-1776* (Cambridge, Mass., 1965), pp. 1-202. In it Bailyn gives old familiar materials a fresh analysis; his application of Caroline Robbins' discoveries in her *Eighteenth-Century Commonwealthman* is especially rewarding. Perhaps the most original portion of Bailyn's study is the discussion of the American fear of conspiracy in which he shows how this fear becomes embedded in Revolutionary politics and in Revolutionary ideas.

These books, and those by the Morgans, Dickerson, and numerous studies of the coming of the Revolution in the individual states suggest that an intensive study of the American response to Imperial reorganization offers the most revealing approach for an understanding of the coming of the Revolution.[24] The focus in short should be on America, not the Empire. The Americans made the Revolution; they must be understood if the Revolution is to be comprehended. Administrative historians who study the origins of colonial policies and the workings of Imperial agencies provide useful information, but they delude themselves when they claim that they explain colonial history, or the American Revolution.

At present no general interpretation of colonial American history commands wide approval. Although the insights of the Imperial school still deserve respect, their general view seems less important than it once did. Colonial historians continue to ask the big questions about early American history, but they seem dedicated to working out their answers on a piecemeal basis. And they perhaps respect fact even more than their predecessors did.

A respect for fact and for the small-scale study are all to the good, but one must also admire the Imperial historians for their willingness to work on the broad scale. They wanted to see things whole; their histories, for all their defects, are impressive for what they attempted. We need today more such attempts, but they should focus more on the colonies themselves and less on the Empire. In particular we need fresh theories of social change; the old metaphors taken from nature are tired. We need theories—not a single theory that pretends to account for change in all the colonies. The local character of American colonial history clearly demands varieties in explanations. If in such explanations the ties to the Empire appear relatively less important than local conditions, we should not entirely forget the great idea of the Imperial historians. It should serve not as a controlling idea but as an inspiration for further attempts to reconstruct the American colonial past.

NOTES

1. Andrews, *The Colonial Background of the American Revolution* (New Haven, 1924; Yale Paperbound, 1961), p. 208. Andrews' greatest work was *The Colonial Period of American History: The Settlements* (3 vols.; New Haven, 1934-37) and *England's Commercial and Colonial Policy* (New Haven, 1938). Beer's chief works were *British Colonial Policy, 1754-1765* (New York, 1907); *The Origins of the British Colonial System, 1578-1660* (New York, 1908); and *The Old Colonial System, 1660-1754* (2 vols.; New York, 1912). These books are mentioned and discussed throughout this essay. Beer's books have recently been reissued by Peter Smith (Gloucester, Mass.).

2. Bancroft, *History of the United States* (10 vols.; New York, 1834-74).
3. *Colonial Period of American History*, p. xi.
4. *Ibid*.
5. Gipson, *The British Empire before the American Revolution* (10 vols.; Caldwell, Idaho, and New York, 1936-61). Two more volumes are anticipated.
6. Two important books which I have not been able to discuss in the text should at least be noted: Arthur P. Newton, *The European Nations in the West Indies, 1493-1688* (London, 1933), and Alfred L. Rowse, *Sir Richard Grenville of the Revenge, An Elizabethan Hero* (London, 1937). See also David B. Quinn, "Sir Thomas Smith (1513-1577) and the Beginnings of English Colonial Theory," *Proceedings of the American Philosophical Society* (Philadelphia), LXXXIX (1945), 543-60.
7. Mildred Campbell, " 'Of People Either Too Few or Too Many,' The Conflict of Opinion on Population and Its Relation to Emigration," in William Aiken and Basil Duke Henning, eds., *Conflict in Stuart England: Essays in Honor of Wallace Notestein* (New York, 1960), pp. 169-201.
8. There are many other studies of the settlements. See especially Samuel Eliot Morison, *Builders of the Bay Colony* (Boston, 1930); Wesley Frank Craven, *An Introduction to the History of Bermuda* (Williamsburg, 1938); Philip A. Bruce, *Economic History of Virginia in the Seventeenth Century* (2 vols.; New York, 1895), and *Institutional History of Virginia in the Seventeenth Century* (2 vols.; New York, 1910); and Frederick B. Tolles, *Meeting House and Countinghouse: The Quaker Merchants of Colonial Philadelphia, 1682-1763* (Chapel Hill, 1948); Herbert L. Osgood, *The American Colonies in the Seventeenth Century* (3 vols.; New York, 1904-07); Verner W. Crane, *The Southern Frontier, 1670-1732* (Durham, N.C., 1928; Ann Arbor, 1956); and Philip L. Barbour, *The Three Worlds of Captain John Smith* (Boston, 1964).
9. Andrews, *Colonial Period*, IV, 7, and *passim*; Gipson, *British Empire* (rev. ed.), I, 13, and *passim*.
10. Andrews, *Colonial Period*, IV, 221; Gipson, *British Empire*, IX, 3-21, and *passim*.
11. Andrews, *Colonial Period*, IV, 166; and Gipson, *British Empire* (rev. ed.) III, 274.
12. Beer, *British Colonial Policy*, p. 200. See also the introductory essay by Julius Goebel, Jr., in Joseph H. Smith, *Appeals to the Privy Council from the American Plantations* (New York, 1950). Goebel makes an impressive case for the medieval origins of Imperial policy and Imperial institutions.
13. The complete title of Andrews' book cited in the previous paragraph is *British Committees, Commissions, and Councils of Trade and Plantations, 1622-1675*; of Harper's, *The English Navigation Laws: A Seventeenth-Century Experiment in Social Engineering*; of Dickerson's, *American Colonial Government, 1696-1765: A Study of the British Board of Trade in Its Relation to the American Colonies, Political, Industrial, Administrative*. The quotation from Bieber is on p. 37, from Harper, p. 59. See also Louise P. Kellogg, "The American Colonial Charter: A Study of English Administration in Relation Thereto, Chiefly after 1688," *Annual Report of the American Historical Association for 1903* (Washington, 1904), I,

185-341; and Philip S. Haffenden, "The Crown and the Colonial Charters, 1675-1688," *William and Mary Quarterly* (Williamsburg), 3rd. ser., XV (July, 1958), 297-311 and (Oct., 1958), 452-66.

14. Gipson, *British Empire*, III, 292.

15. Harper, "The Effect of the Navigation Acts on the Thirteen Colonies," Richard B. Morris, ed., *Era of the American Revolution* (New York, 1939), pp. 3-39. An excellent study of the failure of Imperial policy on the manufacture of colonial iron is Arthur C. Bining, *British Regulation of the Colonial Iron Industry* (Philadelphia, 1933).

16. Viola F. Barnes, "Richard Wharton," *Publications of the Colonial Society of Massachusetts*, XXVI (Boston, 1925), 238-70. For an exhaustive listing of studies bearing on colonial economic history see Lawrence A. Harper, "Recent Contributions to American Economic History: American History to 1789," *Journal of Economic History*, XIX (March, 1959), 1-24.

17. Fairchild, *Messrs. William Pepperell* (Ithaca, 1954); Baxter, *The House of Hancock: Business in Boston, 1724-1775* (Cambridge, Mass., 1945); Hedges, *The Browns of Providence Plantations, Colonial Years* (Cambridge, Mass., 1952); and White, *The Beekmans of New York in Politics and Commerce, 1647-1877* (New York, 1956).

18. See also Richard P. McCormick, *The History of Voting in New Jersey: A Study of the Development of Election Machinery, 1664-1911* (New Brunswick, N.J., 1953); and Lucille Griffith, *Virginia House of Burgesses, 1750-1774* (Northport, Ala., 1963).

19. Bailyn's essay is in James M. Smith, ed., *Seventeenth-Century America: Essays in Colonial History* (Chapel Hill, 1959), pp. 90-115.

20. Andrews, *Colonial Background of the American Revolution*, p. 218.

21. Gipson, *British Empire, passim*, and especially X; see also his *The Coming of the Revolution, 1763-1775* (New York, 1954).

22. *British Empire*, X, 365.

23. *The Eighteenth-Century Commonwealth, Studies in the Transmission, Development and Circumstance of English Liberal Thought from the Restoration of Charles II until the War with the Thirteen Colonies.*

24. Among the best studies of the states are John R. Alden, *The South in the Revolution, 1763-1789* (Baton Rouge, 1957); Charles Albro Barker, *The Background of the Revolution in Maryland* (New Haven, 1940); Robert J. Taylor, *Western Massachusetts in the Revolution* (Providence, 1954); David S. Lovejoy, *Rhode Island Politics and the American Revolution, 1760-1776* (Providence, 1958); Theodore Thayer, *Pennsylvania Politics and the Growth of Democracy, 1740-1776* (Harrisburg, Pa., 1953); William W. Abbot, *The Royal Governors of Georgia, 1754-1775* (Chapel Hill, 1959); Kenneth Coleman, *The American Revolution in Georgia, 1763-1789* (Athens, Ga., 1958); and the volumes of Becker and Brown, previously mentioned. John C. Miller's superb biography, *Sam Adams, Pioneer in Propaganda* (Boston, 1936), adds much to our knowledge of the Revolution in Massachusetts, and his *Origins of the American Revolution* (Boston, 1943) is an able general account. Readers should also consult two recent books: Carl Bridenbaugh, *Mitre and Sceptre: Transatlantic Faiths, Ideas, Personalities, and Politics, 1689-1775* (New York, 1962) for an argument, sometimes overdrawn, about the part colonial fears of an

Anglican bishopric in America played in the coming of the Revolution; and Bernhard Knollenberg, *Origin of the American Revolution, 1759-1766* (New York, 1960), which treats the same problem briefly and well, shifting the beginnings of the Revolution to the decade of the 1750's.

RECENT STUDIES

Howard Mumford Jones, *O Strange New World: American Culture, the Formative Years* (New York: Viking Press, 1964).

Darrett B. Rutman, *Winthrop's Boston: Portrait of a Puritan Town, 1630-1649* (Chapel Hill: University of North Carolina Press, 1965).

II

Changing Interpretations of Early American Politics

JACK P. GREENE

In many respects, the extraordinary ferment in the study of early American politics over the past two decades seems to have produced at least as much confusion as understanding. Subjecting various portions of the early American political fabric to a thorough and rigorous scrutiny, a variety of scholars have demonstrated that long accepted interpretations and categories simply do not fit their particular objects of study. Unfortunately, the negative thrust of their work, though enormously valuable, has not been matched by an equally vigorous attempt at reconstruction. We now have a rather clear idea of what the nature of early American politics was not, but we are still not very sure about what exactly it was. Moreover, the bewildering mass of data produced by the new studies seems, on the surface, to defy any effort at rational classification and refinement, any attempt to make explicit and conscious the network of unrecognized, inarticulated, and, in many cases, seemingly contradictory assumptions that lie behind their conclusions. The immediate impression is that the politics of every colony was completely idiosyncratic, that there were as many species of political life as there were political environments. Yet one can discern in the

From *The Reinterpretation of Early History: Essays in Honor of John Edwin Pomfret*, Ray Allen Billington (ed.), San Marino: Henry E. Huntington Library, 1966, pp. 151-84. Reprinted with abridged annotation by permission of the Huntington Library and the author.

26

literature as a whole a slow and tentative groping toward some common, if still largely implicit, conclusions. To sort out, identify, and classify those conclusions and to put them in the perspective of the historiography of early American politics is the purpose of this essay.

[1]

The nineteenth-century approach was predominantly whig. That is, it rested upon the standard whig assumptions about the nature of man and the historical process: that man is animated largely by the desire for freedom, that self-government is, therefore, necessarily the central concern of political life, and that history itself, at least in the western European world, is the story of man's inexorable progress toward liberty and democracy. Colonial politics was, then, simply another chapter in the age-old struggle of liberty against tyranny in which liberty-loving colonials from their first landing at Jamestown in 1607 until the successful conclusion of the War for Independence in 1783 had steadily opposed the arbitrary and tyrannical attempts of the English government to interfere in their affairs, to restrict that freedom and self-government to which all men naturally aspired and for which the American environment was itself peculiarly well suited. Writers like George Bancroft, the most prolific and most admired nineteenth-century historian of early America, whose massive *History of the United States* traced the narrative of American development through the adoption of the Constitution and was the standard account of early American political development for over half a century, fitted all political happenings into this mold. The various colonial rebellions, the many manifestations of opposition to the navigation acts, the friction between assemblies and royal and proprietary governors, the resistance to Parliamentary taxation after 1763, the War for Independence itself—all were part of the colonists' relentless striving for self-government and freedom from British control.[1]

Long before Herbert Butterfield wrote his devastating exposé of this approach in 1931[2] early American historians had sensed its many inadequacies. Fiercely partisan to those men and groups who seemed to be aligned on the side of liberty, it was, because it insisted upon reading the past in terms of the present, shot through with anachronisms. Worst of all, it was starkly simplistic. Rarely more than a narrative of consecutive, if often otherwise unrelated, public events, it ignored political divisions within the colonies, made no effort to identify, much less to explain, the intricate and complex interplay of forces that normally determine political events, and failed completely to fit politics into its broad social context, to look at it, in the words of one recent critic, "in conjunction with other elements of social activity."[3]

[II]

The whig interpretation of early American politics first came under serious attack during the closing years of the nineteenth century when a number of scholarly studies appeared stressing the importance of internal divisions within the colonies in shaping early American political life;[4] but an alternative framework of interpretation, one which attempted to relate politics to social and economic life, emerged only gradually during the first three decades of the twentieth century. The basic structure of the new interpretation was first worked out in detail in two studies of politics in the middle colonies in the years immediately preceding the Declaration of Independence: C. H. Lincoln, *The Revolutionary Movement in Pennsylvania* (1901), and Carl Becker, *History of Political Parties in the Province of New York, 1760-1776* (1909). Lincoln and Becker found that politics in both Pennsylvania and New York was conditioned by deep-seated internal conflicts between rival social groups. In Pennsylvania there were "two opposing forces, one radical," composed of Scotch-Irish Presbyterians and Germans in the west and non-Quaker lower and middle-class Philadelphians in the east, and the other "conservative," consisting of the Quaker mercantile oligarchy in the east. In New York it was the radical unprivileged and unfranchised common freeholders, tenants, mechanics, and artisans against a tightly-knit land-owning and commercial aristocracy. Unleashed by the contest with Britain between 1763 and 1776, this "latent opposition of motives and interests between the privileged and unprivileged," the struggle of the radicals to push their way into the political arena and to achieve a wider area of economic and social freedom—the fight over "who should rule at home" and the radical demands for the "democratization of . . . politics and society"—and not the debate over Parliamentary authority in the colonies was the central issue in the politics of both colonies in the years immediately preceding the War for Independence.[5]

The striking similarity between developments in Pennsylvania and those in New York strongly suggested that what was true for those colonies was also true for the others, that the debate with Britain had everywhere been accompanied by an internal struggle for democracy between groups representing mutually antagonistic sectional and class interests, and that such a struggle was the distinguishing feature of early American politics. Over the next three decades, a number of scholars pushed this suggestion back into the colonial period and ahead into the years after 1776 and it became the central theme of two powerful and vividly written general interpretations of the early American past: Charles and Mary Beard, *The Rise of American Civilization*,[6] and Vernon Louis Parrington, *Main Currents in American Thought: The Colonial Mind*.[7]

By 1940 the study of early American politics had undergone a profound and seemingly permanent transformation. Applied generally to many areas of early American political life, the suggestions of Lincoln and Becker had been converted into dogma. New categories had replaced the old ones completely. Not American patriots and British tyrants, but radicals and conservatives, lower classes and upper classes, democrats and aristocrats, debtors and creditors, westerners and easterners, tenants and landlords, laborers and capitalists had become the principal actors upon the political stage. Politics was no longer an autonomous and disembodied sphere of activity but a reflection of economic and social cleavages within the colonies, and the essence of political activity was economic and social conflict between "natural" rivals: the little men—the yeomen farmers, agricultural tenants, artisans, and town laborers—against aristocratic merchants, landowners and professional men, with the former contending for human rights and democracy—the demand for greater popular participation in politics and a general equality of social and economic condition—and the latter for property rights and the maintenance of special privileges in all areas of early American life for the upper classes. If the categories had changed, however, and if the contours of political life seemed to have been thoroughly altered, the ultimate end of the political process, the standard against which every particular event and development was to be judged, remained essentially the same as it had been in the whig version. For the new historians, as for their nineteenth-century predecessors, the essential meaning of early American politics was to be found in the slow and at times halting advancement toward freedom and democracy that reached its culmination in the halcyon days of Andrew Jackson and the political triumph of the common man. The past continued to be read in terms of the present.

Although there were endless local variations, the broad outlines of early American political development according to the new interpretation seemed reasonably clear. After some early contests between the privileged and unprivileged that culminated in a series of rebellions

at the end of the seventeenth century and resulted in some temporary victories for the unprivileged, the privileged, composed of relatively small groups of wealthy men connected by kinship and interest,
gained control of the political life of every colony. Although they were
everywhere a small minority of the population, they managed to maintain their hold on government by restricting the suffrage to property
holders, refusing to extend equitable representation to egalitarian frontier areas, dominating the elective lower houses of assembly, and securing a monopoly on all appointive offices from seats on the royal and
proprietary councils down to the lowest administrative posts in towns
and counties.[8] Between 1765 and 1776 radical leaders, devoted to the
achievement of social democracy if also at times to their own advancement, "seized on British acts as heaven-sent opportunities to attack the
local aristocracy . . . under the guise of a patriotic defense of American liberties" and united the unprivileged "in what became as much
a war against the colonial aristocracy as a war for independence."[9] The
chief significance of the American Revolution was, in fact, not that it
brought the colonies their independence but that it provided the opportunity for the unprivileged to score the first great victory for American democracy by driving some of the privileged to become loyalists
and compelling others to give the forces of democracy a larger share in
the direction of public affairs. Enabled by the pressures of 1774-1776 to
wrest the lion's share of political power from the conservatives, the radicals over the next decade pushed through the Declaration of Independence, the embodiment of their ideals, and inaugurated a program of
democratic reform that succeeded in the various states according to the
strength and determination of the radicals but was checked, if only
temporarily, in 1787-1788 by the Constitution and the conservative
resurgence it represented.

This version of early American political development—frequently
designated as progressive because it was obviously shaped by the rhetoric and assumptions of Progressive politics—was so widely accepted
and so integral a part of American historical consciousness that it
seemed, even as late as 1950, eternally viable. In a real sense, however,
the progressive interpretation of early American politics was the victim
of its own success. Its very symmetry and neatness, its apparent comprehensiveness, and its seemingly easy adaptability to almost every situation combined to render it as lifeless and abstract, as little descriptive
of the complex and continually changing realities of colonial society
and politics, as the old whig interpretation. Although some scholars
continued to produce works set within the progressive mold, in the

years since World War II study after study investigating a wide range
of phenomena has shown that it is inapplicable to many political situations in early America, that it cannot be superimposed upon existing
evidence without serious distortion. The resulting erosion, gradual,
piecemeal, and still incomplete though it is, now seems to have left
the progressive interpretation as little more than a series of cliches, of
continuing importance only for what they reveal about the intellectual
fashions of the first half of the twentieth century.

[III]

The most direct assault upon the progressive interpretation of early
American politics has come from Robert E. Brown. In *Middle-Class
Democracy and the Revolution in Massachusetts, 1691-1780* (1955)
he presented a massively documented case for the propositions that
Massachusetts throughout the eighteenth century was a "middle-class
society in which property was easily acquired and in which a large
portion of the people were property-owning farmers," that 95 per cent
of the adult males were qualified to vote, that there was virtually no
inequality of representation, that the farmers—not the merchant aristocracy—had by virtue of their superior numbers "complete control of
the legislature," and that there was no "sharp internal class conflict."
Far from being an aristocracy, Massachusetts, Brown concluded, was a
middle-class democracy, and the Revolution, instead of being "an internal class conflict designed to achieve political, economic, and social
democracy," was in fact a movement "to preserve a social order rather
than to change it," to protect the democratic practices which the British government was trying "to curtail . . . as a necessary step toward
the recovery of British authority and the prevention of colonial independence."[10]

What "was true in Massachusetts," Brown suggested in a general
projection of his findings, was probably also "true in the other colonies,"[11] and he immediately set to work to substantiate this suggestion
with a similar investigation of Virginia. Undertaken in collaboration
with his wife, B. Katherine Brown, this study was published in 1964
under the title *Virginia 1705-1786: Democracy or Aristocracy?* Based
upon an even greater amount of research and more systematic analysis, it demonstrated, at least, that what was true for Massachusetts was
almost true for Virginia. The percentage of adult white males who
could meet the property requirement for voting was only 85 per cent
instead of 95 per cent, but the electorate was still wide, economic

opportunity and social mobility were great, class antagonism was slight, representation was fairly equitable throughout the colony, and the only instance of internal social conflict before or during the Revolution occurred after 1740 between a growing group of dissenters and the Anglican establishment over the privileged position of the Anglican church. These findings led the authors to conclude that Virginia society, like Massachusetts society, was "fundamentally middle-class" with a political system that was "a middle class, representative democracy" and that the Revolution in Virginia, as in Massachusetts, was not an internal social upheaval but a conservative protest movement against the attacks of the British government upon Virginia democracy.[12]

A torrent of criticism followed the publication of both of these volumes. Several critics objected that the Browns' definition of democracy as any system in which social and economic opportunity was open to all and a majority of free adult males could vote was both anachronistic and inaccurate. It was anachronistic because it was derived from twentieth-century rather than eighteenth-century conceptions of democracy and inaccurate because almost all public offices—whether appointive or elective—were held by men from upper-class groups. In the most elaborate critique of the Massachusetts volume, John Cary showed that Brown's sampling techniques were faulty, that his statistics were unreliable, and that, at least for certain selected towns, the percentage of qualified voters, though still quite high, was twenty to thirty per cent lower than Brown had originally indicated.[13]

When the smoke cleared, however, two points became clear. The first was that the Browns had not departed very far from the progressive historians they had set out to criticize. So preoccupied were they with demonstrating the factual and interpretive mistakes of the progressive account that they permitted that account to dictate the questions they asked of their materials. Borrowing wholesale their assumptions, categories, and terminology from the earlier interpretation, the Browns, like the progressive historians, were completely committed to a democratic point of view which assumed, among other things, that in any given political situation it is the people in general and what they want that are of primary importance; that the middle and lower classes have strong political interests and aspirations; and that the struggle for democracy—even though it was a struggle to preserve rather than to obtain democracy—was the central issue in early American politics. As the title of the Virginia book indicated, the Browns assumed, as had their progressive progenitors, that colonial society had to be either aristocratic or democratic, that it had to fit into one or the other of two rigid, abstract, largely self-contained, and mutually exclusive political categories. By insisting upon working entirely within two such broad and abstract polar classifications, the Browns did great violence to the diverse tendencies in early American political life and precluded the possibility of developing new and more meaningful categories for describing those tendencies.

The second point that can be made about the Browns' work is more positive. However unscientific their sampling techniques and however inexact their statistics, they established beyond serious doubt two basic facts about the society of Massachusetts and Virginia that necessitate serious modifications in the progressive conception of early American politics. First, by showing that the economic structure was highly fluid, property widely distributed, and lower-class economic and social discontent minimal they made it clear that neither colony was so rigidly stratified as to produce the kind of social conflicts which progressive historians thought were the stuff of colonial politics. Secondly, by showing that the franchise was considerably wider than had previously been supposed, they demonstrated that the predominance of the upper classes in politics did not depend upon a restricted franchise, that they had to have the support of men from all classes to gain elective office. That both of these conclusions are equally applicable to the rest of the colonies is indicated by the findings of a number of recent independent studies. Investigations of voting requirements and voter eligibility in Plymouth, Connecticut, Rhode Island, Virginia, New York, New Jersey, and Pennsylvania have revealed that the franchise in those colonies was also very wide and that the vast majority of free adult males could expect to acquire enough property during their lifetimes to meet the suffrage requirements. Similarly, Jackson Turner Main in a general examination of *The Social Structure of Revolutionary America* has argued that American society in the late eighteenth century was everywhere relatively free from poverty and had, especially by European standards, a high rate of vertical mobility, great social and economic opportunity, and a remarkably supple class structure. This combination of economic abundance and social fluidity, Main has concluded, tended "to minimize those conflicts which might have grown out of the class structure and the concentration of wealth" that was occurring in older settled areas.[14]

[IV]

Even before the Browns mounted their vigorous assault, a number of other scholars had been busy turning out a series of detailed studies of the political life of individual colonies that had been quietly effecting a major revolution in the interpretation of early American politics. This movement, which is still in progress, was inspired in part by the early works of Lincoln and Becker and in part by the prosopographical studies of eighteenth-century British politics by Sir Lewis Namier and his followers. Like Lincoln and Becker, the authors of these studies have been primarily interested in penetrating behind the formal institutional arrangements, ostensible issues, and dominant rhetoric of political life to the hard, concrete, and underlying realities. In marked contrast to the progressives, however, they have in general found broad economic and social divisions within the colonies to have been less important in determining the nature and form of political activity than the conflicting interests and ambitions of rival groups within the upper strata of society. In imitation of Namier, they have tried to sort out and describe the networks of interest, kinship, religious affiliation, and regional ties that presumably formed the basis for the major political groupings and to show how those networks related to the social and economic structure of the colonies in which they existed. In the process, they have shown how inadequate the old polar categories employed by the progressive historians actually were, how profoundly those categories obscured and distorted the complex and variegated nature of early American politics.

The first of these studies, John Bartlett Brebner's *The Neutral Yankees of Nova Scotia*, appeared as early as 1937. An exhaustive survey of the development of Nova Scotia from 1749, the year the British government inaugurated its program to turn what had previously been no more than a military garrison presiding over an unassimilated French population into a full-fledged British colony, until the conclusion of the War for Independence, this volume showed that the political life of the colony quickly came under the dominance of a powerful "little commercial group" centered in Halifax and headed by Joshua Mauger, the "economic overlord" of the colony who presided over the colony's fortunes from a London base. By virtue of Mauger's influence among imperial officials at Whitehall, members of this group by the 1760s filled most of the public offices in the colony, including the lieutenant governorship and a healthy majority of seats on the royal Council. With such extensive political power they were able to secure a virtual monopoly over both the distilling industry—the chief pillar in Nova Scotia's rudimentary economy—and the colony's London trade and to reap handsome profits from the sale of lands granted to themselves and from manipulating both the public and private debts of the colony. Because of its economic stranglehold over Halifax and because the bulk of the population, widely scattered over the rest of the province and preoccupied with eking out an existence in a new and not always hospitable environment, was politically inarticulate, disorganized, and acquiescent, this "office-holding clique" usually managed even to get its friends elected to a majority of the seats in the lower house of assembly. On the rare occasions when men from outside the clique were able to obtain a majority in the house, they only infrequently acted in concert against the merchant-official oligarchy, and when they did the members of the oligarchy in the Council could always block their efforts. Thus, except for an occasional and usually ineffective challenge from a royal governor or a newly arrived merchant who resented its monopolization of power, office, and economic opportunity, the oligarchy was free to govern Nova Scotia as its interests demanded. Its tight political control, Brebner concluded, was one of the main factors in Nova Scotia's failure to join the other colonies in the American Revolution.[15]

Brebner's work on Nova Scotia, by the author's own admission a "marginal" and relatively new colony, did not in itself demand a reexamination of the progressive conception of early American politics, but two other volumes on Maryland politics published in the 1940s indicated that that conception clearly did not apply uniformly even to all of the older colonies. After a close look at Maryland society and politics through the middle decades of the eighteenth century, Charles Albro Barker found in *The Background of the Revolution in Maryland* that political divisions in that colony contained no elements of "western populism, or evangelical democracy," or " 'class struggle.' " The conflict was not between classes, not between "plebian and patrician," but "within the upper class"—a classic struggle between "country" and "court" in which the "local squirearchy," which dominated "every phase of the growing life of the province" and expressed itself politically through the elective House of Delegates, was aligned against the absentee proprietor and his representatives who monopolized the seats on the proprietary Council and all major public offices.[16] Although individuals sometimes changed sides as the proprietor sought to lure influential members of the gentry into the proprietary camp by appointment to lucrative offices,[17] the issues which divided these two groups —the special privileges, powers, and revenues of the proprietors—remained constant, subtly shaping every political battle in pre-revolutionary Maryland. The "country party" took the lead in the protest against British policy between 1763 and 1776, and, although the increasing incidence of "election pledges, instructions to delegates, mass meetings, committees and associations" during those years tended to give "increasing force, from outside legislative doors, to the politics of protest," it resulted, Barker argued, not in the diminution but the enlargement of the influence of the gentry by bringing its members into "closer connection with the people" and giving "practical . . . meaning to the phrases about popular rights" employed in the revolutionary debate.[18] That the same group—"a relatively small class of planters, lawyers, and merchants"—continued to dominate Maryland politics after 1776 without serious challenge from below was the argument of Philip A. Crowl in *Maryland During and After the Revolution: A Political and Economic Study*, published in 1942 just two years after Barker's volume. Crowl found plenty of political conflict in Maryland, but it was neither class nor sectional in nature. Rather, it took the form of a series of struggles over opposing interests, ideas, and personalities between ad hoc coalitions of rival groups of leading men.[19]

In the years after World War II investigations of segments of the political history of Connecticut, New Jersey, and Rhode Island revealed both their distinctive features and how far the politics of each colony-state departed from the progressive model. In *Connecticut's Years of Controversy, 1750-1776*, published in 1949, Oscar Zeichner showed that the tradition of political tranquility that had earned for Connecticut its reputation as the "land of steady habits" had been shattered by the Great Awakening, which by fragmenting the colony into a variety of religious groups—Separates and New Lights on one hand and Old Lights, Arminians, and Anglicans on the other—paved the way for a succession of "long and bitterly fought factional and party conflicts." Because the eastern half of Connecticut was the main center of New Light strength while the western half was the primary stronghold of the Old Lights and Anglicans, these conflicts were to some extent sectional. But they also came to represent rival economic interests as eastern merchants and lawyers who formed the core of the Susquehannah Company, a speculative enterprise intent upon securing the support of the Connecticut government for its land schemes in Pennsylvania's Wyoming Valley, came into conflict with western leaders who opposed their project. Because the previously dominant western, Old Light, anti-Susquehannah Company group was too moderate in its resistance to the Stamp Act, the eastern, New Light, Susquehannah Company faction was able to gain the ascendancy in 1766 as the imperial question became an important issue in local politics. The New Light faction retained power until 1776, and the Old Light group gradually disintegrated as first the Old Lights and then the Arminians came to support the New Light opposition to British policy leaving only the Anglicans, many of whom subsequently became loyalists, in opposition. As in Maryland, these conflicts were not along class lines. The leaders of both groups were drawn from Connecticut's "ruling aristocracy of magistrates and ministers."[20]

Similarly, Richard P. McCormick in *Experiment in Independence: New Jersey in the Critical Period, 1781-1789*, published in 1950, found that " 'men of interest' " with powerful family connections played the preponderant role in New Jersey politics. On the state-wide level they were loosely organized into two broad sectional factions, the East Jersey and the West Jersey. But this split did not represent the "sectionalism of tidewater against backcountry, of plantation owners against yeomen, of a metropolis against the hinterlands, of a trading region against an agricultural region, or of an over-represented minority against an under-represented majority." Rather it was a sectionalism that was peculiar to New Jersey, one that followed a familiar historical and cultural cleavage that dated from the earliest settlement of the colony and had been intensified during the War for Independence as East Jersey leaders took the lead in prosecuting the war while West Jersey leaders, many of whom were Quakers, adopted "a negative or neutral attitude."[21]

David S. Lovejoy showed in *Rhode Island Politics and the American Revolution, 1760-1776* (1958), that in the decades just before the American Revolution, Rhode Island politics also revolved around sectional and factional disputes. Like the disputes in Connecticut and New Jersey, these were not the result of "the attempt of one class of people to tear down another and broaden the basis of government" but of a "struggle between equals, between people who already enjoyed the right to vote and who fought to control the government for their own ends." In contrast to the New Jersey factions, those in Rhode Island were sharply defined and well organized around two rival leaders— Samuel Ward from Newport and Stephen Hopkins from Providence —and reflected an overt and explicit contest between Newport and Providence for economic and political supremacy within the colony. That personality was of critical importance in the Ward-Hopkins controversy was indicated by the virtual dissolution of the Ward faction after Hopkins' alliance with the Wantons of Newport resulted in a humiliating defeat for Ward in the election of 1770 and his retirement from politics.[22]

Other studies have shown similarly unique political patterns in still other colonies. Between 1741 and 1767 New Hampshire politics closely resembled those of Nova Scotia. A remarkably close-knit oligarchy—

centered around Governor Benning Wentworth, bound together by close family, social, and economic ties, and well connected in official circles in London—occupied most of the important appointive offices and dominated the mast and naval stores industries, the disposition of public lands, and the overseas trade—the most lucrative segments of the New Hampshire economy; and by an effective use of the patronage and other varieties of political influence even managed to control the elected lower house. The failure of an early challenge from a rival group of leading men in the 1740s and early 1750s resulted in the disappearance of faction and the total and unchallenged political ascendancy of the Wentworth family, which governed with the support of the "vast majority of provincial inhabitants."[23] In Georgia, which, like Nova Scotia, was comparatively new and underdeveloped throughout the colonial period, there were no significant internal sectional or class conflicts prior to the Revolution, and only on the question of opposition to British policy after 1763 was there any clear political division as Governor James Wright and a small coterie of Crown officers lined up in support of British authority against the vast bulk of the colony's leading men, some of whom occupied seats on the royal Council but most of whom expressed themselves through the elected Commons House of Assembly.[24] A mild form of sectionalism appeared in the 1780s as leaders from the rapidly expanding upcountry began to compete for political prominence with traditional lowcountry leaders, but this split neither resulted in the development of coherent and permanent factions nor determined voting behavior on the major public issues.[25] Politics in Delaware after the Declaration of Independence continued to manifest a long-standing sectional rivalry between the leaders of the two dominant agricultural southern counties and the dynamic Scotch-Irish minority representing the commercial interests of New Castle in the north.[26]

Factional disputes over proprietary powers, religion, and economic interests characterized the politics of both Carolinas during the proprietary period. Under the Crown, however, the old factional disputes subsided in South Carolina after a chaotic battle over paper currency, which in general pitted the Charles Town mercantile community against the planters, had ended in the early 1730s with the stabilization of the colony's paper money system. Thereafter there were no significant political divisions.[27] Even the regulator movement of the late 1760s, a recent writer has found in sharp contrast to the old interpretation, did not reveal or produce any deep-seated class or sectional antagonism because the regulators—a combination of small planters and leading men in the backcountry—were primarily concerned with the establishment of law enforcement agencies adequate to deal with the lawless conditions that prevailed in the backcountry and, once effective courts had been secured, laid aside other subsidiary grievances against the eastern government.[28] The foundations for these grievances—a discriminatory tax system and insufficient representation for the backcountry in the legislature—were presumably to a large extent remedied by the new constitution in 1776. By contrast, North Carolina during the royal period continued to be torn by factional strife over the disposition of lands, payment of quit rents, and the unequal representation of the rapidly expanding southern section of the colony in the legislature. After a dramatic attempt by leaders of the southern counties to change the representation system had been squelched by London authorities in the early 1750s, the north-south quarrel gradually subsided, but in the late 1760s and early 1770s the colony was again plagued by sectional antagonisms as western regulators rose in protest against corrupt local administration by "eastern" appointees intent on enriching themselves at the expense of the western inhabitants. This protest, which was eventually put down with force, apparently produced a deep sectional rift that continued to affect North Carolina politics even after the conditions that produced it had disappeared.

That the progressive model is also inapplicable to the politics of the two oldest colonies, Massachusetts and Virginia, can be inferred from a spate of specialized investigations of each. In Massachusetts after the Restoration, the old Puritan leadership, which had previously been able to maintain its political predominance despite occasional challenges from a variety of discontented groups in the colony,[29] began to crack under pressures from both without and within. The external pressures, described by Michael Garibaldi Hall in *Edward Randolph and the American Colonies 1676-1703*,[30] derived from the attempts of the Crown to assert its authority over the colony, and the internal pressures, discussed by Bernard Bailyn in *The New England Merchants in the Seventeenth Century*,[31] largely from a rising group of interrelated merchants, who, though in many cases Puritans themselves, were discontented with orthodox Puritan leadership. Together with other dissatisfied groups the merchants at first cooperated with the Crown in the hope of breaking the power of the Puritans and formed the bulk of the provisional Council which in 1685 and 1686 governed Massachusetts during the interim period between the recall of the charter and the arrival of royal governor Edmund Andros. But this group, too, "multifarious" to constitute a party, as Richard S. Dunn has emphasized in an excellent study of the changing political orientation of New England at the end of the seventeenth century and the beginning of the eighteenth century,[32] made common cause with the old Puritan leadership against Andros as soon as it became clear that it could not control the Dominion government. Under the new government established under the Charter of 1691 the Council, Bailyn has argued, became the "political voice of the merchants" who, over the next forty years, used their connections in Great Britain and cooperated with the country party, which represented the lesser property owners in the House of Representatives, to make and break a succession of governors in an attempt to secure their "permanent interests."[33]

This process can be seen in John A. Schutz's account of the intrigues and maneuvers that preceded the removal of Jonathan Belcher and the appointment of William Shirley as governor of Massachusetts in 1741.[34] Though heated political controversies—which, as George Athan Billias has recently shown in connection with the land bank struggle,[35] were usually between rival groups of leading men representing opposing economic interests—occasionally arose thereafter, Shirley's appointment ushered in a period of political stability that lasted until his removal from the governorship in 1756 and was based upon his deft manipulation of the House of Representatives and a clever distribution of patronage that enabled him to draw many of the colony's leading men into his political orbit and to build a powerful political machine around "a solid core of supporters and a shifting number of auxiliaries."[36] By the 1760s resentment against the engrossment of power and office by this "oligarchy" had become widespread among the wealthy and ambitious who were not a part of it, and, when the oligarchy was cautious in opposing British measures after 1763, its opponents seized the opportunity to discredit it and to strip it of some of its power by excluding its members from the royal Council. This internal political battle, which was sharpened by the revolutionary controversy and ended in 1775 with the outbreak of war and the dissolution of the oligarchy, was played out against a backdrop of western agrarian distrust of the commercial East, which though temporarily submerged during the war, openly manifested itself again in the disturbances of the 1780s.[37] Although westerners seem to have taken the revolutionary ideal of popular sovereignty more seriously than easterners, they revealed, just like Massachusetts citizens in the eastern portion of the colony, a pronounced tendency to trust political affairs at every level of government to leading men except in times of extreme economic distress such as those which accompanied Shays' Rebellion.[38]

Virginia politics, like those of Massachusetts, proceeded through several distinct phases. The chaotic factionalism and chronic disarray of the colony's first few decades gave way under the careful efforts of Governor Sir William Berkeley to a more stable political environment after the Restoration. Berkeley, as Bernard Bailyn has shown, gathered around him many of the most successful among a new wave of immigrants who began coming to Virginia in the 1640s. Bound to Berkeley by "ties of kinship and patronage," this group, called the Green Spring faction after Berkeley's plantation, formed "an inner circle of privilege" with a virtual monopoly over the important public offices and the seats on the governor's Council; easy access to the public lands which constituted the chief form of wealth in the colony; and sufficient political influence to dominate the proceedings of the elective House of Burgesses. Bacon's Rebellion, which, as Wilcomb E. Washburn has emphasized, began over a disagreement on Indian policy and had few of the populist-democratic overtones traditionally associated with it,[39] became an occasion for the venting of pent-up resentment among county leaders outside the official group. No sooner was the rebellion over and Berkeley removed from the scene, however, than this bitter rivalry between court and country and the incipient factionalism it represented began to subside as the leading men in both groups united against a series of royal governors who, unlike Berkeley, were not intimately connected through kinship, patronage, or economic interest with the emergent planter group. For thirty-five years after the rebellion the leading planter families—a "league of local oligarchs"—becoming increasingly self-conscious and expressing themselves largely through the Council, drove one governor after another out of office.[40] Not until the end of the second decade of the eighteenth century, when Lieutenant Governor Alexander Spotswood gave up the fight and allied himself with the local leaders, was this pattern broken and the political infighting it had produced stopped. For the most part, Spotswood's successors followed the same course, and Virginia politics through the middle decades of the eighteenth century acquired a degree of stability that was rare in colonial America.[41] Personal rivalries among leading politicians never hardened into factions, and the local oligarchy, dominating the Council, the House of Burgesses, and the county courts, governed, as Charles S. Sydnor has demonstrated, with rare skill and responsibility to the general satisfaction of the entire Virginia political community.[42] Even the apparent challenge by Patrick Henry and the heated political discussions that followed the disclosure in 1766 that a long-time speaker of the House of Burgesses and colony treasurer had loaned large sums of public money to his friends among the gentry did not produce any permanent or significant divisions within the Virginia polity.[43] Not until the war and confederation periods did a serious split, apparently based upon both opposing sectional and economic interests and personal political rivalries, appear.

A number of recent studies suggests that even in Pennsylvania and New York, the prototypes for the progressive model, politics do not fit that model well. Until the mid-1770s Pennsylvania politics seems to have resembled the Maryland pattern more closely. From the first decades of the colony's history there was a more or less continuous struggle between court and country over the distribution of power between the proprietor and the Assembly. During the first quarter of the eighteenth century both the country party and the court party were Quaker, but the country party, led by lawyer David Lloyd and operating primarily through the Assembly, drew its strength mostly from the country, while the court party, "dominated by city merchants under the leadership of the Proprietor's secretary, James Logan," and in complete control of the Council, was most powerful in Philadelphia, the seat of the proprietor's government.[44] Fanned by personal rivalries and ambitions, this bitter party strife temporarily subsided after 1725 as unparalleled commercial prosperity, the tactful administration of Governor Patrick Gordon, and the disappearance of old political issues ushered in an era of good feeling and resulted in the virtual extinction of the old parties.

Political peace proved to be short-lived, however, and with the end of Gordon's administration in 1736 the old wrangling began anew, this time between a united "Quaker party"—composed of remnants from both of the older factions and supported by many non-Quakers— and the "Proprietary party"—consisting of a growing body of Anglicans, proprietary officeholders, and some Presbyterian and German back settlers—over "the authority of the Proprietors and the best means of achieving a *modus vivendi* with the Indians."[45] These two parties continued to be the principal rivals in Pennsylvania politics up through the middle 1770s, although after the exclusion crisis of 1756—after many Quakers had withdrawn from the Assembly rather than betray their pacifist principles in what, as Ralph Ketcham has recently emphasized, was a move to preserve not to relinquish Quaker political power—many of the leaders of the Quaker party were no longer Quakers.[46] Although the annual election battles between these two parties were occasionally extremely hard fought, especially from 1764 through 1766 as the proprietary party managed to exploit western discontent over the Paxton affair and resentment over the Quaker Party's moderate response to the Stamp Act to secure its only clear victories, and although both parties appealed broadly to the electorate, the conflict, as William S. Hanna has underlined, was largely a mere "jousting at the top among the gentlemen rulers and their factions" with no basic social issues at stake.[47] For reasons not entirely clear, this contest subsided after 1766, and over the next decade the internal politics of Pennsylvania were remarkably smooth. Only in 1776, when the traditional leaders were slow in deciding for independence, did a rival group of radical "independents," composed primarily of men not previously prominent politically, arise to seize control of Pennsylvania government. But this new group, David Hawke has argued in a recent assault upon the earlier interpretation of Lincoln, was not the mouthpiece of the unprivileged West, which, indeed, does not appear to have been the source of any mass discontent, or even of the urban masses of Philadelphia but rather the political arm of a relatively small group of middle-class ideologues intent upon gaining independence and reconstructing the government of Pennsylvania so that the people would have a greater share in it. The trouble was that when they "gave the people democracy" in the constitution of 1776, "the people spurned the gift," still preferring "the elite to run their affairs."[48] Although the nature of the political struggles of the fifteen years after 1776 remains to be re-examined, Hawke's conclusions suggest that they may have been largely between rival political groups with opposing conceptions of the way the polity ought to be organized and may not, therefore, have represented any fundamental divisions within society.[49]

A still different variety of factionalism characterized the politics of New York. Leisler's Rebellion, which was in part a protest against the monopolization of office and economic resources by a small group surrounding the royal governor, and its ruthless suppression inaugurated a thirty-year-long feud between Leislerians and Anti-Leislerians in which the objective was not just political control of the New York government with the economic advantages such control represented but, as Lawrence H. Leder has stressed, the complete extinction of the opposition party. Although Robert Livingston and others helped arrange a political truce during the administration of Governor Robert Hunter between 1710 and 1719 which eventually resulted in the disappearance of the old parties,[50] new factions appeared in the 1720s and remained as a constant part of the political scene. For the most part loose and temporary alliances, these factions were based upon family rivalries, conflicting economic interests, ethnic and national differences, religious tensions, sectional antagonisms, personal ambition, and political alliances with the royal governors. The principals shifted sides with astonishing ease as their interests or inclinations decreed until the 1750s, when factions solidified "around the Livingston and DeLancey families, and it was their political rivalry which underlined the history of New York until the Revolution" and shaped New York's response to British measures between 1763 and 1776.[51] The debate between the Livingston and De Lancey parties, like the debates between the amorphous factions that preceded them, usually centered upon bona fide issues, and the parties vied with each other for support from a wide electorate; but at bottom this contest was primarily an "intra-class wrangle" between rival upper-class groups and never a struggle between aristocracy and democracy as Becker had insisted. Far from being democratic upheavals, the small farmer and tenant uprisings that culminated in the "Great Rebellion of 1766," Milton M. Klein has argued, were essentially non-political in character and concerned largely with such basic economic questions as "land titles, rents, security of tenure, and . . . personal obligations to the manor lord."[52] Even the radical Sons of Liberty, who played so conspicuous a part in New York politics between 1768 and 1776, Roger Champagne has demonstrated, were largely under the control of the Livingston party and, although they held ideas with more radical implications than party leaders, had no democratic program of their own and were so loosely bound together as to be unable to play a significant role in the Livingston party's shaping of the new independent state government in 1776.

Although the picture is far from complete, it can be safely inferred from this survey that every colony-state displayed a unique combination of characteristics that produced its own peculiar configuration of politics and that the old progressive conception is either totally inapplicable or seriously distorted at every point for which there has been a detailed study. But the more important question is whether these seemingly disparate, contradictory, perpetually changing, and highly volatile political systems had enough in common to make it possible to construct an alternative framework of interpretation. Although there has been no systematic attempt to deal with this question, certain preliminary conclusions can be drawn on the basis of the findings of the specialized studies published thus far.

Politics everywhere was primarily elitist in nature. Public office—both appointive and elective—and political leadership were securely in the hands of upper-class groups, and, although there were occasional manifestations of social and economic discontent among the lower classes, that discontent never resulted in widespread demands for basic changes in the customary patterns of upper-class leadership. Political divisions were not along class lines. Rather, they revolved around the ambitions of rival factions, each faction drawing support from all segments of a broad electorate. The chaotic and explosive nature of these divisions in many places—the ease with which groups formed, dissolved, and re-formed, leaders appeared "first on one side and then on another," and issues precipitated "formations without apparent relationship to previous or succeeding groupings"[53]—has led Bernard Bailyn to conclude that colonial politics was "a constant broil of petty factions struggling almost formlessly, with little discipline or control, for the benefits of public authority." According to this characterization, the object of these "shifting, transitory, competitive groupings"—the primary and impelling force behind colonial politics—was "the search for wealth, power, and prestige" by the individuals who composed them.[54] "Uncommitted to any broad principle or program," these factions were "preoccupied with immediate concern," "local questions and selfish interests." Ideas, theories, principles thus become "mere rhetoric," weapons in the factional armory employed to rationalize the conduct of the protagonists and to distract the unwary among the electorate or the unaligned politicians from the "real" objectives in dispute.[55]

That "chaotic factionalism" is an appropriate rubric for large segments of early American politics, that the competition for wealth, power, and prestige was involved to some extent in almost every factional contest, and that ideas were always closely related to the interests of the people who used them seems beyond dispute, but this formulation, recently applied by Forrest MacDonald to the period between 1776 and 1789,[56] is not free from objection. For one thing, it assumes, like the progressive conception, an "extraordinary rationality in the political behavior of men," the ability of politicians to see not only "their interests clearly" but also "precisely how to go about securing them."[57] Secondly, it rests upon a blanket assumption—which is clearly not universally valid—that ideas are always subordinate to some concrete and tangible factors in politics. Thirdly, it does not accurately describe all portions of early American political life. Some factional divisions were extraordinarily stable, and some political environments were free from factionalism altogether. Finally, unless it falls back upon the old progressive formula of repression, manipulation, propaganda, and control, which posits a degree of efficiency and sophistication not easily associated with colonial and revolutionary America, it does not by itself explain why the electorate tolerated such a patently irresponsible brand of politics. To remedy these objections it is necessary to turn to recent writings on the "political culture" of the colonies.

[v]

As here used the term *political culture* applies to that intellectual and institutional inheritance which inevitably conditions, however slightly in many instances, all—even the most revolutionary and impulsive— political behavior. For early America the most visible elements of that culture—the formal concepts of political thought and the external forms of institutional development—have received a considerable amount of attention from historians during the past seventy-five years. What has been until recently almost completely ignored and what, it now appears, is vastly more important, is that elusive and shadowy cluster of assumptions, traditions, conventions, values, modes of expression, and habits of thought and belief that underlay those visible elements. Although the inquiry into this area has not yet proceeded very far, work already published has yielded some extremely important results.

The findings of one group of independent studies help to resolve a problem that to the progressive historians and the Browns was an incomprehensible paradox: why (in the words of J. R. Pole) "the great mass of the common people might actually have given their consent to concepts of government" that by "systematically" excluding them "from the more responsible positions of political power" restricted "their own participation in ways completely at variance with the principles of modern democracy."[58] What these studies have found through an intensive examination and "imaginative reconstruction of the values and assumptions" of early American political thought is that colonial *and* revolutionary society was essentially what Walter Bagehot called "a deferential society" that operated within an integrated structure of ideas that was fundamentally elitist in nature. That structure of ideas assumed, among other things, that government should be entrusted to men of merit; that merit was very often, though by no means always, associated with wealth and social position; that men of merit were obliged to use their talents for the benefit of the public; and that deference to them was the implicit duty of the rest of society. All society was therefore divided among the rulers and the ruled, and the rulers, including the representatives of the people, were not the tools of the people but their political superiors. "The mass of the people," Richard Buel, Jr., has argued in the most thorough exposition of these ideas, thus "elected representatives not to order them around like lackeys to do the people's bidding, but to reap benefit from the distinguished abilities of the few upon which the safety of society might in large measure depend" and to utilize the "political expertise of the realm in the people's behalf."[59]

Another group of studies has suggested that more than the simple pursuit of wealth, power, and prestige may have been involved in the factional struggles of colonial politics. Works by Perry Miller, Edmund S. Morgan, George Lee Haskins, and others on the Puritans[60] and Frederick B. Tolles on the Quakers[61] have indicated how important the special religious, social, and political ideas of each were in shaping the political behavior of the leaders of early Massachusetts Bay and Pennsylvania. Of vastly more general influence appears to have been the group of ideas analyzed by Z. S. Fink and Caroline Robbins[62] and called by J. G. A. Pocock the "Country ideology." This ideology, which appeared with minor variations and modifications in all parts of the British political world during the seventeenth and eighteenth centuries, shared certain dominant assumptions about human nature and the function and process of government: that men were imperfect creatures, perpetually self-deluded, enslaved by their passions, vanities, and interests, confined in their vision and understanding, and incapable of exercising power over one another without abusing it; that government and constitutions existed to restrain the vicious tendencies of man by checking them against one another; that to fulfill that function each of the elements in the polity had to be balanced against each of the others in such a way as to prevent any of them from gaining ascendancy over the rest; and that history was the record of a continual struggle between liberty and power, purity and corruption. A mixed constitution was the device by which this delicate balance was to be achieved, but the tendency of men in power, especially men connected with the administration (the court), to seek to increase it by corrupting Parliament —the voice of the men of independent property (the country)—was so great that the country members in Parliament had to keep a wary eye on the court to see that it did not succeed in throwing the constitution out of balance or overturning it altogether and establishing an unrestrained executive tyranny that would make free with the liberties and property of the citizenry. It was essential, therefore, both that every seeming abuse of ministerial power be immediately detected and rooted out of the polity and that every representative of the country be constantly on guard lest he somehow be seduced into the conspiracy of power and thereby betray his country and lose his own personal independence, which was regarded as the basis of "all human excellence."[63]

This fetish of independence led to the condemnation of *parties*, which perforce were the instruments of *partial* men, and to the idealization of the virtuous patriot, the man of preeminent virtue whose behavior was determined not by self-interest, not by the narrow interests of some group or region with which he was associated, but by nothing less than the welfare of the entire country.

The state of knowledge is still too imperfect for historians to be able to assess with any certainty the importance of the country ideology in giving shape and coherence to the configuration of early American politics. That all of its components including its several stock personae—the court villain, dependent court lackey, independent country patriot—as well as its conventions of behavior, its rhetoric, and its patterns and categories of thought were transferred in toto to the colonies is clear enough from the frequent application of the terms *court* and *country* to colonial politics, the oft expressed dread of arbitrary power and aversion to parties, the extent to which they infused the thought and informed the behavior of individuals, the conscious cultivation of them by colonial leaders through the middle decades of the eighteenth century, and the more or less continuous efforts of the lower houses of assembly to check the prerogative and undermine executive authority—attempts which persisted both because and in spite of the factional disputes and internal divisions in colonial politics and resulted in a roughly uniform pattern of constitutional development in all of the colonies. But it is not enough to know that the country ideology was an integral part of early American politics. We need to know as well the precise nature of its role and its relationship to other elements of political life. That role and that relationship will, of course, be different for every situation, and any generalization will therefore have to await a series of detailed investigations similar to the one conducted by Bernard Bailyn for the pre-revolutionary debate. But Bailyn's study suggests what those answers may be. He finds that ideas expressed by Americans in the debate, many of which were descended directly and in a fairly undiluted form from the country ideology, had a dual role. They were first of all *explanatory* both in the sense that they enabled the principals to explain to themselves and the world what they were about and to see themselves in some kind of cosmic, or at least historical, perspective, and in the sense that they revealed "not merely positions taken but the reasons why positions were taken." Only through these ideas, only through the beliefs, attitudes, assumptions, motivations, and professed goals that "lay behind the manifest events of the time," he insists, can the "contemporary meaning" of the Revolution be understood. However much those ideas may have distorted underlying realities, they were always thought by the participants to be true and were, therefore, as Gordon S. Wood has phrased it, "psychologically true." Because these ideas—these inherited values and habits of thought—also exerted a powerful influence upon the way Americans perceived reality, shaping into predictable and familiar patterns their interpretations of and response to imperial actions, they were also in an important and fundamental sense *determinative*.[64] Ideas, then, in all of their several forms, operate to impede men's perception of reality at the same time that they give it shape and meaning, and in some situations they may even become as real as the more tangible elements of political life and exercise greater causative power than the manifest events or the underlying interests or ambitions they were first called into the political arena to serve.

[VI]

Despite the impressive accomplishments of the past three decades, our knowledge is still too fragmentary and the character of the subject too complex to permit any firm or easy generalizations about the nature of early American politics. Out of the overwhelming tangle of interests, ideas, and ambitions that seem, at least on the surface, to make colonial politics incomprehensible, however, emerge certain basic regularities that make it possible to establish at least a rough typology of political forms into which, after the elimination of certain individual variants, most pre-1776 colonial political activity can be fitted. On the basis of present knowledge, this typology would seem to require at least four distinct, if also overlapping, and not necessarily sequential classifications.

For the first, which is probably also the most common, we can use Bailyn's term, *chaotic factionalism*. It involved a ruthless competition for dominance, power, and economic advantage among rival groups of leading men, groups which were largely ad hoc and impermanent, formed as temporary alliances on specific occasions, then dissolving as quickly as they appeared only to have the individuals who had composed them regroup in different combinations in response to later events. This form seems to have been typical of Virginia prior to 1660, Massachusetts from 1684 to 1741, New York from 1720 to 1755, Pennsylvania from 1680 to 1720, Maryland before 1689, South Carolina and New Hampshire prior to 1730, and North Carolina until 1745. To some extent, it was present in every classification, but it was the dominant characteristic only in the first.

The second type may be called *stable factionalism*. It was distinguished by the emergence of two semi-permanent opposing interest groups with relatively stable memberships and representing explicit regional—perhaps a more precise and appropriate term than sectional—economic, religious, or kinship rivalries (occasionally in combination) and, in some cases, standing for rather well-defined sets of principles and beliefs. This type appears to have predominated in Massachusetts from 1760 to 1776, Rhode Island and Connecticut after 1750, New Hampshire in the 1730s and 1740s, New York from 1690 to 1720 and again from 1755 to 1776, in New Jersey, Maryland, and perhaps Delaware through most of the eighteenth century, in Pennsylvania from 1735 to 1776, in North Carolina in the 1740s and 1750s, and in South Carolina from 1720 to 1740.

The third classification may perhaps best be described as *domination by a single, unified group*. In this type of politics all of the avenues to political power and most of the primary sources of wealth were monopolized by a dominant elite bound together by common economic interests, religious beliefs, patronage and kinship ties, or some combination of these factors. In this system faction was submerged by some form of repression, manipulation, or corruption—in the "country" sense of the term—of potential leaders of opposition elements. Massachusetts Bay prior to 1684 and again from 1741 to 1760, New York before Leisler's Rebellion, Virginia between 1660 and 1720, and New Hampshire and Nova Scotia after 1750 are examples of this type.

The fourth and rarest form was almost wholly *faction free with a maximum dispersal of political opportunity within the dominant group* composed of the elite and potential members of the elite. This type, which appears to have existed over a long period only in Virginia after 1720 and South Carolina after 1740, depended upon a homogeneity of economic interests among all regions and all social groups, a high degree of social integration, and a community of political leaders so large as to make it impossible for any single group to monopolize political power. It was, in a real sense, the epitome of the country ideal of a government composed of independent men and, at least in Virginia, was in part the result of the conscious cultivation of that ideal by the leaders of the polity.

Whatever its defects, however much it stands in need of refinement, clarification, modification, and elaboration, this typology may by providing a general frame of reference at least make it easier to discuss early American politics. Hopefully, it may also be a first step toward the development of new, less abstract categories which will more accurately reflect the political life they seek to describe. Perhaps even, it will serve as a foundation for achieving some understanding of the relationship between these early political forms and the more sophisticated party structure that emerged in the United States after 1790.

NOTES

1. (10 vols., Boston, 1834-74), *passim.*
2. *The Whig Interpretation of History* (London, 1931).
3. Bernard Bailyn, "A Whig Interpretation," *Yale Review,* new ser., L (March 1961), 438-441.
4. See, e.g., Brooks Adams, *The Emancipation of Massachusetts: The Dream and The Reality* (Boston, 1887).
5. Lincoln, *Revolutionary Movement,* 3-4, 7, 14, 39, 53-54, 77, 96-98, 150, 189-190; Becker, *History of Political Parties,* 5-24, 27-28, 51-52, 275-276.
6. (New York, 1927).
7. (New York, 1927).
8. For a capsule statement of this view see Merrill Jensen, "Democracy and the American Revolution," *Huntington Library Quarterly,* XX (1957), 321-341.
9. Merrill Jensen, *Articles of Confederation; An Interpretation* . . . (Madison, 1940), 11.
10. pp. 401-408.
11. "Reinterpretation of the Revolution and Constitution," *Social Education,* XXI (1957), 103.
12. (East Lansing, 1964), *passim.*
13. "Statistical Method and the Brown Thesis on Colonial Democracy," *William and Mary Quarterly,* 3d ser., XX (1963), 251-264. See also the rebuttal by Brown in *Ibid.,* 265-276.
14. (Princeton, 1965), esp. 270-287. The quotation is from p. 163.
15. (New York, 1937), 149-157, 207-242, 291-353.
16. The extensive patronage of the Maryland proprietor is analyzed in detail by Donnell MacClure Owings, *His Lordship's Patronage: Offices of Profit in Colonial Maryland* (Baltimore, 1953).
17. See Aubrey C. Land, *The Dulanys of Maryland: A Biographical Study of Daniel Dulany, the Elder (1685-1753) and Daniel Dulany, the Younger (1722-1797)* (Baltimore, 1955).
18. Barker, *Background* (New Haven, 1940), esp. 24, 182-183, 372-377.
19. (Baltimore, 1942), esp. 11-15. See also Crowl's "Anti-Federalism in Maryland, 1787-1788," *William and Mary Quarterly,* 3d ser., IV (1947), 446-469.
20. (Chapel Hill, 1949), 3-43, 219-235; Robert Sklar, "The Great Awakening and Colonial Politics: Connecticut's Revolution in the Minds of Men," *Connecticut Historical Society Bulletin,* XXVIII (1963), 81-95.
21. (New Brunswick, 1950), 69-102.

22. (Providence, 1958), 1-30, 193-194.
23. Jere R. Daniell, "Politics in New Hampshire under Governor Benning Wentworth, 1741-1767," *Ibid.*, XXIII (1966), 76-105.
24. W. W. Abbot, *The Royal Governors of Georgia 1754-1775* (Chapel Hill, 1959). For somewhat different conclusions see Kenneth Coleman, *The American Revolution in Georgia, 1763-1789* (Athens, 1958).
25. W. W. Abbot, "The Structure of Politics in Georgia: 1782-1789," *William and Mary Quarterly*, 3d ser., XIV (1957), 47-65.
26. John A. Munroe, *Federalist Delaware, 1775-1815* (New Brunswick, 1954).
27. These generalizations are drawn largely from M. Eugene Sirmans, *Colonial South Carolina: A Political History, 1663-1763* (Chapel Hill, 1966).
28. Richard Maxwell Brown, *The South Carolina Regulators: The Story of the First American Vigilante Movement* (Cambridge, 1963).
29. George Lee Haskins, *Law and Authority in Early Massachusetts: A Study in Tradition and Design* (New York, 1960), and Edmund S. Morgan, *The Puritan Dilemma: The Story of John Winthrop* (Boston, 1958).
30. (Chapel Hill, 1960), esp. 21-128.
31. (Cambridge, 1955).
32. *Puritans and Yankees: The Winthrop Dynasty of New England 1630-1717* (Princeton, 1962), 212-257.
33. *Ibid.*, Bailyn, *New England Merchants*, 143-197.
34. "Succession Politics in Massachusetts, 1730-1741," *William and Mary Quarterly*, 3d ser., XV (1958), 508-520.
35. *The Massachusetts Land Bankers of 1740* (Orono, 1959), 17-53.
36. John A. Schultz, *William Shirley: King's Governor of Massachusetts* (Williamsburg, 1961), 269.
37. The basic study of western attitudes is Robert J. Taylor, *Western Massachusetts in the Revolution* (Providence, 1954).
38. *Ibid.*; Lee Nathaniel Newcomer, *The Embattled Farmers: A Massachusetts Countryside in the American Revolution* (New York, 1953), 79-87; Benjamin W. Labaree, *Patriots and Partisans: The Merchants of Newburyport, 1764-1815* (Cambridge, 1962), 1-15; and David Syrett, "Town-Meeting Politics in Massachusetts, 1776-1786," *William and Mary Quarterly*, 3d ser., XXI (1964), 352-366.
39. *The Governor and the Rebel: A History of Bacon's Rebellion in Virginia* (Chapel Hill, 1957).
40. Bailyn, "Politics and Social Structure in Virginia," in *Seventeenth-Century America: Essays on Colonial History* (James Morton Smith ed., Chapel Hill, 1959), 90-115.
41. See Jack P. Greene, *The Quest for Power: The Lower Houses of Assembly in the Southern Royal Colonies 1689-1776* (Chapel Hill; 1963), 22-31.
42. *Gentleman Freeholders: Political Practices in Washington's Virginia* (Chapel Hill, 1952).
43. Thad W. Tate, "The Coming of the Revolution in Virginia: Britain's Challenge to Virginia's Ruling Class, 1763-1776," *William and Mary Quarterly*, 3d ser., XIX (1962), 323-343; David John Mays, *Edmund Pendleton 1721-1803: A Biography* (Cambridge, 1952).
44. Roy N. Lokken, *David Lloyd, Colonial Lawmaker* (Seattle, 1959), and

Frederick B. Tolles, *James Logan and the Culture of Provincial America* (Boston, 1957).

45. Frederick B. Tolles, *Meeting House & Counting House: The Quaker Merchants of Colonial Philadelphia* (Chapel Hill, 1948), 11-28; G. B. Warden, "The Proprietary Group in Pennsylvania, 1754-1764," *William and Mary Quarterly*, 3d ser., XXI (1964), 367-389.

46. Ketcham, "Conscience, War, and Politics in Pennsylvania, 1755-1757," *William and Mary Quarterly*, 3d ser., XX (1963), 416-439; John J. Zimmerman, "Benjamin Franklin and the Quaker Party, 1755-1756," *Ibid.*, XVII (1960), 291-313.

47. *Benjamin Franklin and Pennsylvania Politics* (Stanford, 1964), 201.

48. *In the Midst of a Revolution* (Philadelphia, 1963), 198.

49. Charles Page Smith, *James Wilson: Founding Father 1742-1798* (Chapel Hill, 1956).

50. *Robert Livingston 1654-1728 and the Politics of Colonial New York* (Chapel Hill, 1961).

51. Milton M. Klein, "Politics and Personalities in Colonial New York," *New York History*, XLVII (1966), 3-16.

52. Milton Klein, "Democracy and Politics in Colonial New York," *New York History*, XL (1959), 231, 238-240; Roger Champagne, "Family Politics versus Constitutional Principles: The New York Assembly Elections of 1768 and 1769," *William and Mary Quarterly*, 3d ser., XX (1963), 57-79; Don R. Gerlach, *Philip Schuyler and the American Revolution in New York 1733-1777* (Lincoln, 1964), xvii.

53. Bernard Bailyn, "The Beekmans of New York: Trade, Politics, and Families," *William and Mary Quarterly*, 3d ser., XIV (1957), 601-602.

54. *Pamphlets of the American Revolution 1750-1776* (Cambridge, 1965), I, 91, 188-189, 191.

55. The introduction to his recent edition of the *Pamphlets of the American Revolution* indicates that Bailyn does not now hold this view of the role of ideas in early American politics, though it was implicit in much of his earlier work.

56. *E Pluribus Unum: The Formation of the American Republic 1776-1790* (Boston, 1965).

57. Cecelia M. Kenyon "'An Economic Interpretation of the Constitution' after Fifty Years," *Centennial Review*, LXVII (1962), 338.

58. Pole, "Historians and The Problems of Early American Democracy," *American Historical Review*, LXVII (1962), 626-646, esp. 628-641.

59. "Democracy and the American Revolution: A Frame of Reference," *William and Mary Quarterly*, 3d ser., XXI (1964), 165-190.

60. Especially Miller, *The New England Mind: The Seventeenth Century* (Cambridge, 1939); Morgan, *Puritan Dilemma*; and Haskins, *Law and Authority in Early Massachusetts*.

61. Tolles, *Meeting House & Counting House*, and *James Logan*.

62. Fink, *The Classical Republicans: An Essay in the Recovery of a Pattern of Thought in Seventeenth-Century England* (Evanston, 1945); Robbins, *The Eighteenth-Century Commonwealthman: Studies in the Transmission, Development, and Circumstances of English Liberal Thought from the Restoration of Charles II until the War with the Thirteen Colonies* (Cambridge, 1959).

63. Pocock, "Machiavelli, Harrington, and English Political Ideologies in the Eighteenth Century," *William and Mary Quarterly*, 3d ser., XXII (1965), 547-583; H. Trevor Colbourn, *The Lamp of Experience: Whig History and the Intellectual Origins of the American Revolution* (Chapel Hill, 1965).

64. Bailyn, ed., *Pamphlets of the American Revolution*, 1-202, esp. 8, 20, 60; Wood, "Rhetoric and Reality in the American Revolution," *William and Mary Quarterly*, 3d ser., XXIII (1966), 31.

RECENT STUDIES

J. R. Pole, *Political Representation in England and the Origins of the American Republic* (New York: St. Martin's Press, 1966).

III

Rhetoric and Reality in the American Revolution

GORDON S. WOOD

If any catch phrase is to characterize the work being done on the American Revolution by this generation of historians, it will probably be "the American Revolution considered as an intellectual movement." For we now seem to be fully involved in a phase of writing about the Revolution in which the thought of the Revolutionaries, rather than their social and economic interests, has become the major focus of research and analysis. This recent emphasis on ideas is not of course new, and indeed right from the beginning it has characterized almost all our attempts to understand the Revolution. The ideas of a period which Samuel Eliot Morison and Harold Laski once described as, next to the English revolutionary decades of the seventeenth century, the most fruitful era in the history of Western political thought could never be completely ignored in any phase of our history writing.

It has not been simply the inherent importance of the Revolutionary ideas that has continually attracted the attention of historians. It has been rather the unusual nature of the Revolution and the constant need to explain what on the face of it seems inexplicable that has compelled almost all interpreters of the Revolution, including the participants themselves, to stress its predominantly intellectual character and hence

From *William and Mary Quarterly*, 3rd series, XXIII (January 1966), 3-32. Reprinted with abridged annotation by permission of the author.

its uniqueness among Western revolutions. Within the context of Revolutionary historiography the one great effort to disparage the significance of ideas in the Revolution—an effort which dominated our history writing in the first half of the twentieth century—becomes something of an anomaly, a temporary aberration into a deterministic social and economic explanation from which we have been retreating for the past two decades. Since roughly the end of World War II we have witnessed a resumed and increasingly heightened insistence on the primary significance of conscious beliefs, and particularly of constitutional principles, in explaining what once again has become the unique character of the American Revolution. In the hands of idealist-minded historians the thought and principles of the Americans have consequently come to repossess that explanative force which the previous generation of materialist-minded historians had tried to locate in the social structure.

Indeed, our renewed insistence on the importance of ideas in explaining the Revolution has now attained a level of fullness and sophistication never before achieved, with the consequence that the economic and social approach of the previous generation of behaviorist historians has never seemed more anomalous and irrelevant than it does at present. Yet paradoxically it may be that this preoccupation with the explanatory power of the Revolutionary ideas has become so intensive and so refined, assumed such a character, that the apparently discredited social and economic approach of an earlier generation has at the same time never seemed more attractive and relevant. In other words, we may be approaching a crucial juncture in our writing about the Revolution where idealism and behaviorism meet.

[1]

It was the Revolutionaries themselves who first described the peculiar character of what they had been involved in. The Revolution, as those who took stock at the end of three decades of revolutionary activity noted, was not "one of those events which strikes the public eye in the subversions of laws which have usually attended the revolutions of governments." Because it did not seem to have been a typical revolution, the sources of its force and its momentum appeared strangely unaccountable. "In other revolutions, the sword has been drawn by the arm of offended freedom, under an oppression that threatened the vital powers of society."[1] But this seemed hardly true of the American Revolution. There was none of the legendary tyranny that had so often driven desperate peoples into revolution. The Americans were not an oppressed people; they had no crushing imperial shackles to throw off. In fact, the Americans knew they were probably freer and less burdened with cumbersome feudal and monarchical restraints than any part of mankind in the eighteenth century. To its victims, the Tories, the Revolution was truly incomprehensible. Never in history, said Daniel Leonard, had there been so much rebellion with so "little real cause." It was, wrote Peter Oliver, "the most wanton and unnatural rebellion that ever existed." The Americans' response was out of all proportion to the stimuli. The objective social reality scarcely seemed capable of explaining a revolution.

Yet no American doubted that there had been a revolution. How then was it to be justified and explained? If the American Revolution, lacking "those mad, tumultuous actions which disgraced many of the great revolutions of antiquity," was not a typical revolution, what kind of revolution was it? If the origin of the American Revolution lay not in the usual passions and interests of men, wherein did it lay? Those Americans who looked back at what they had been through could only marvel at the rationality and moderation, "supported by the energies of well weighed choice," involved in their separation from Britain, a revolution remarkably "without violence or convulsion." It seemed to be peculiarly an affair of the mind. Even two such dissimilar sorts of Whigs as Thomas Paine and John Adams both came to see the Revolution they had done so much to bring about as especially involved with ideas, resulting from "a mental examination," a change in "the minds and hearts of the people." The Americans were fortunate in being born at a time when the principles of government and freedom were better known than at any time in history. The Americans had learned "how to define the rights of nature,—how to search into, to distinguish, and to comprehend, the principles of physical, moral, religious, and civil liberty," how, in short, to discover and resist the forces of tyranny before they could be applied. Never before in history had a people achieved "a revolution by reasoning" alone.

The Americans, "born the heirs of freedom," revolted not to create but to maintain their freedom. American society had developed differently from that of the Old World. From the time of the first settlements in the seventeenth century, wrote Samuel Williams in 1794, "every thing tended to produce, and to establish the spirit of freedom." While the speculative philosophers of Europe were laboriously searching their minds in an effort to decide the first principles of liberty, the Americans had come to experience vividly that liberty in their everyday lives. The American Revolution, said Williams, joined together these enlightened ideas with America's experience. The Revolution was thus essentially intellectual and declaratory: it "explained the business to the world, and served to confirm what nature and society had before produced." "All was the result of reason. . . ." The Revolution had taken place not in a succession of eruptions that had crumbled the existing social structure, but in a succession of new thoughts and new ideas that had vindicated that social structure.

The same logic that drove the participants to view the Revolution as peculiarly intellectual also compelled Moses Coit Tyler, writing at the end of the nineteenth century, to describe the American Revolution as "preeminently a revolution caused by ideas, and pivoted on ideas." That ideas played a part in all revolutions Tyler readily admitted. But in most revolutions, like that of the French, ideas had been perceived and acted upon only when the social reality had caught up with them, only when the ideas had been given meaning and force by long-experienced "real evils." The American Revolution, said Tyler, had been different: it was directed "not against tyranny inflicted, but only against tyranny anticipated." The Americans revolted not out of actual suffering but out of reasoned principle. "Hence, more than with most other epochs of revolutionary strife, our epoch of revolutionary strife was a strife of ideas: a long warfare of political logic; a succession of annual campaigns in which the marshalling of arguments not only preceded the marshalling of armies, but often exceeded them in impression upon the final result."[2]

[II]

It is in this historiographical context developed by the end of the nineteenth century, this constant and at times extravagant emphasis on the idealism of the Revolution, that the true radical quality of the Progressive generation's interpretation of the Revolution becomes so vividly apparent. For the work of these Progressive historians was grounded in a social and economic explanation of the Revolutionary era that explicitly rejected the causal importance of ideas. These historians could scarcely have avoided the general intellectual climate of the first part of the twentieth century which regarded ideas as suspect. By absorbing the diffused thinking of Marx and Freud and the assumptions of behaviorist psychology, men had come to conceive of ideas as ideologies or rationalizations, as masks obscuring the underlying interests and drives that actually determined social behavior. For too long, it seemed, philosophers had reified thought, detaching ideas from the material conditions that produced them and investing them with an independent will that was somehow alone responsible for the determination of events. As Charles Beard pointed out in his introduction to the 1935 edition of *An Economic Interpretation of the Constitution*, previous historians of the Constitution had assumed that ideas were "entities, particularities, or forces, apparently independent of all earthly considerations coming under the head of 'economic.' " It was Beard's aim, as it was the aim of many of his contemporaries, to bring into historical consideration "those realistic features of economic conflict, stress, and strain" which previous interpreters of the Revolution had largely ignored.[3] The product of this aim was a generation or more of historical writing about the Revolutionary period (of which Beard's was but the most famous expression) that sought to explain the Revolution and the formation of the Constitution in terms of socio-economic relationships and interests rather than in terms of ideas.[4]

Curiously, the consequence of this reversal of historical approaches was not the destruction of the old-fashioned conception of the nature of ideas. As Marx had said, he intended only to put Hegel's head in its rightful place; he had no desire to cut it off. Ideas as rationalization, as ideology, remained—still distinct entities set in opposition to interests, now however lacking any deep causal significance, becoming merely a covering superstructure for the underlying and determinative social reality. Ideas therefore could still be the subject of historical investigation, as long as one kept them in their proper place, interesting no doubt in their own right but not actually counting for much in the movement of events.

Even someone as interested in ideas as Carl Becker never seriously considered them to be in any way determinants of what happened. Ideas fascinated Becker, but it was as superstructure that he enjoyed examining them, their consistency, their logic, their clarity, the way men formed and played with them. In his *Declaration of Independence: A Study in the History of Political Ideas* the political theory of the Americans takes on an unreal and even fatuous quality. It was as if ideas were merely refined tools to be used by the colonists in the most adroit manner possible. The entire Declaration of Independence, said Becker, was calculated for effect, designed primarily "to convince a candid world that the colonies had a moral and legal right to separate from Great Britain." The severe indictment of the King did not spring from unfathomable passions but was contrived, conjured up, to justify a rebellion whose sources lay elsewhere. Men to Becker were never the victims of their thought, always the masters of it. Ideas were a kind of

legal brief. "Thus step by step, from 1764 to 1776, the colonists modified their theory to suit their needs."[5] The assumptions behind Becker's
1909 behaviorist work on New York politics in the Revolution and his
1922 study of the political ideas in the Declaration of Independence
were more alike than they at first might appear.

Bringing to their studies of the Revolution similar assumptions about
the nature of ideas, some of Becker's contemporaries went on to expose
starkly the implications of those assumptions. When the entire body of
Revolutionary thinking was examined, these historians could not avoid
being struck by its generally bombastic and overwrought quality. The
ideas expressed seemed so inflated, such obvious exaggerations of reality, that they could scarcely be taken seriously. The Tories were all
"wretched hirelings, and execrable parricides"; George III, the "tyrant
of the earth," a "monster in human form"; the British soldiers, "a
mercenary, licentious rabble of banditti," intending to "tear the bowels
and vitals of their brave but peaceable fellow subjects, and *to wash the
ground wtih a profusion of innocent blood.*"[6] Such extravagant language, it seemed, could be nothing but calculated deception, at best
an obvious distortion of fact, designed to incite and mold a revolutionary fervor. "The stigmatizing of British policy as 'tyranny,' 'oppression'
and 'slavery,' " wrote Arthur M. Schlesinger, the dean of the Progressive historians, "had little or no objective reality, at least prior to the
Intolerable Acts, but ceaseless repetition of the charge kept emotions
at fever pitch."[7]

Indeed, so grandiose, so overdrawn, it seemed, were the ideas that the
historians were necessarily led to ask not whether such ideas were valid
but why men should have expressed them. It was not the content of
such ideas but the function that was really interesting. The Revolutionary rhetoric, the profusion of sermons, pamphlets, and articles in the
patriotic cause, could best be examined as propaganda, that is, as a
concerted and self-conscious effort by agitators to manipulate and shape
public opinion. Because of the Progressive historians' view of the Revolution as the movement of class minorities bent on promoting particular
social and economic interests, the conception of propaganda was crucial
to their explanation of what seemed to be a revolutionary consensus.
Through the use of ideas in provoking hatred and influencing opinion
and creating at least "an appearance of unity," the influence of a minority of agitators was out of all proportion to their number. The Revolution thus became a display of extraordinary skillfulness in the manipulation of public opinion. In fact, wrote Schlesinger, "no disaffected
element in history has ever risen more splendidly to the occasion."[8]

Ideas thus became, as it were, parcels of thought to be distributed and used where they would do the most good. This propaganda was not of course necessarily false, but it was always capable of manipulation. "Whether the suggestions are to be true or false, whether the activities are to be open or concealed," wrote Philip Davidson, "are matters for the propagandist to decide." Apparently ideas could be turned on or off at will, and men controlled their rhetoric in a way they could not control their interests. Whatever the importance of propaganda, its connection with social reality was tenuous. Since ideas were so self-consciously manageable, the Whigs were not actually expressing anything meaningful about themselves but were rather feigning and exaggerating for effect. What the Americans said could not be taken at face value but must be considered as a rhetorical disguise for some hidden interest. The expression of even the classic and well-defined natural rights philosophy became, in Davidson's view, but "the propagandist's rationalization of his desire to protect his vested interests."[9]

With this conception of ideas as weapons shrewdly used by designing propagandists, it was inevitable that the thought of the Revolutionaries should have been denigrated. The Revolutionaries became by implication hypocritical demagogues, "adroitly tailoring their arguments to changing conditions." Their political thinking appeared to possess neither consistency nor significance. "At best," said Schlesinger in an early summary of his interpretation, "an exposition of the political theories of the antiparliamentary party is an account of their retreat from one strategic position to another." So the Whigs moved, it was strongly suggested, easily if not frivolously from a defense of charter rights, to the rights of Englishmen, and finally to the rights of man, as each position was exposed and became untenable. In short, concluded Schlesinger, the Revolution could never be understood if it were regarded "as a great forensic controversy over abstract governmental rights."[10]

[III]

It is essentially on this point of intellectual consistency that Edmund S. Morgan has fastened for the past decade and a half in an attempt to bring down the entire interpretive framework of the socio-economic argument. If it could be shown that the thinking of the Revolutionaries was not inconsistent after all, that the Whigs did not actually skip from one constitutional notion to the next, then the imputation of Whig frivolity and hypocrisy would lose its force. This was a central intention of Morgan's study of the political thought surrounding the

Stamp Act. As Morgan himself has noted and others have repeated, "In the last analysis the significance of the Stamp Act crisis lies in the emergence, not of leaders and methods and organizations, but of well-defined constitutional principles." As early as 1765 the Whigs "laid down the line on which Americans stood until they cut their connections with England. Consistently from 1765 to 1776 they denied the authority of Parliament to tax them externally or internally; consistently they affirmed their willingness to submit to whatever legislation Parliament should enact for the supervision of the empire as a whole."[11] This consistency thus becomes, as one scholar's survey of the current interpretation puts it, "an indication of American devotion to principle."[12]

It seemed clear once again after Morgan's study that the Americans were more sincerely attached to constitutional principles than the behaviorist historians had supposed, and that their ideas could not be viewed as simply manipulated propaganda. Consequently the cogency of the Progressive historians' interpretation was weakened if not unhinged. And as the evidence against viewing the Revolution as rooted in internal class-conflict continued to mount from various directions, it appeared more and more comprehensible to accept the old-fashioned notion that the Revolution was after all the consequence of "a great forensic controversy over abstract governmental rights." There were, it seemed, no deprived and depressed populace yearning for a participation in politics that had long been denied; no coherent merchant class victimizing a mass of insolvent debtors; no seething discontent with the British mercantile system; no privileged aristocracy, protected by law, anxiously and insecurely holding power against a clamoring democracy. There was, in short, no internal class upheaval in the Revolution.[13]

If the Revolution was not to become virtually incomprehensible, it must have been the result of what the American Whigs always contended it was—a dispute between Mother Country and colonies over constitutional liberties. By concentrating on the immediate events of the decade leading up to independence, the historians of the 1950's have necessarily fled from the economic and social determinism of the Progressive historians. And by emphasizing the consistency and devotion with which Americans held their constitutional beliefs they have once again focused on what seems to be the extraordinary intellectuality of the American Revolution and hence its uniqueness among Western revolutions. This interpretation, which, as Jack P. Greene notes, "may appropriately be styled neo-whig," has turned the Revolution into a rationally conservative movement, involving mainly a constitutional defense of existing political liberties against the abrupt and unexpected provocations of the British government after 1760. "The issue then, according to the neo-whigs, was no more and no less than separation from Britain and the preservation of American liberty." The Revolution has therefore become "more political, legalistic, and constitutional than social or economic." Indeed, some of the neo-Whig historians have implied not just that social and economic conditions were less important in bringing on the Revolution as we once thought, but rather that the social situation in the colonies had little or nothing to do with causing the Revolution. The Whig statements of principle iterated in numerous declarations appear to be the only causal residue after all the supposedly deeper social and economic causes have been washed away. As one scholar who has recently investigated and carefully dismissed the potential social and economic issues in pre-Revolutionary Virginia has concluded, "What remains as the fundamental issue in the coming of the Revolution, then, is nothing more than the contest over constitutional rights."[14]

In a different way Bernard Bailyn in a recent article has clarified and reinforced this revived idealistic interpretation of the Revolution. The accumulative influence of much of the latest historical writing on the character of eighteenth-century American society has led Bailyn to the same insight expressed by Samuel Williams in 1794. What made the Revolution truly revolutionary was not the wholesale disruption of social groups and political institutions, for compared to other revolutions such disruption was slight; rather it was the fundamental alteration in the Americans' structure of values, the way they looked at themselves and their institutions. Bailyn has seized on this basic intellectual shift as a means of explaining the apparent contradiction between the seriousness with which the Americans took their Revolutionary ideas and the absence of radical social and institutional change. The Revolution, argues Bailyn, was not so much the transformation as the realization of American society.

The Americans had been gradually and unwittingly preparing themselves for such a mental revolution since they first came to the New World in the seventeenth century. The substantive changes in American society had taken place in the course of the previous century, slowly, often imperceptibly, as a series of small piecemeal deviations from what was regarded by most Englishmen as the accepted orthodoxy in society, state, and religion. What the Revolution marked, so to speak, was the point when the Americans suddenly blinked and saw their society, its changes, its differences, in a new perspective. Their deviation from European standards, their lack of an established church and a titled aristocracy, their apparent rusticity and general equality, now became desirable, even necessary, elements in the maintenance of their society and politics. The comprehending and justifying, the endowing with high moral purpose, of these confusing and disturbing social and political divergences, Bailyn concludes, was the American Revolution.[15]

Bailyn's more recent investigation of the rich pamphlet literature of the decades before Independence has filled out and refined his idealist interpretation, confirming him in his "rather old-fashioned view that the American Revolution was above all else an ideological-constitutional struggle and not primarily a controversy between social groups undertaken to force changes in the organization of society." While Bailyn's book-length introduction to the first of a multivolumned edition of Revolutionary pamphlets makes no effort to stress the conservative character of the Revolution and indeed emphasizes (in contrast to the earlier article) its radicalism and the dynamic and transforming rather than the rationalizing and declarative quality of Whig thought, it nevertheless represents the culmination of the idealist approach to the history of the Revolution. For "above all else," argues Bailyn, it was the Americans' world-view, the peculiar bundle of notions and beliefs they put together during the imperial debate, "that in the end propelled them into Revolution." Through his study of the Whig pamphlets Bailyn became convinced "that the fear of a comprehensive conspiracy against liberty throughout the English-speaking world—a conspiracy believed to have been nourished in corruption, and of which, it was felt, oppression in American was only the most immediately visible part— lay at the heart of the Revolutionary movement." No one of the various acts and measures of the British government after 1763 could by itself have provoked the extreme and violent response of the American Whigs. But when linked together they formed in the minds of the Americans, imbued with a particular historical understanding of what constituted tyranny, an extensive and frightening program designed to enslave the New World. The Revolution becomes comprehensible only when the mental framework, the Whig world-view into which the Americans fitted the events of the 1760's and 1770's, is known. "It is the development of this view to the point of overwhelming persuasiveness to the majority of American leaders and the meaning this view gave to the events of the time, and not simply an accumulation of grievances," writes Bailyn, "that explains the origins of the American Revolution."[16]

It now seems evident from Bailyn's analysis that it was the Americans' peculiar conception of reality more than anything else that convinced them that tyranny was afoot and that they must fight if their liberty was to survive. By an empathic understanding of a wide range of American thinking Bailyn has been able to offer us a most persuasive argument for the importance of ideas in bringing on the Revolution. Not since Tyler has the intellectual character of the Revolution received such emphasis and never before has it been set out so cogently and completely. It would seem that the idealist explanation of the Revolution has nowhere else to go.[17]

[IV]

Labeling the recent historical interpretations of the Revolution as "neo-whig" is indeed appropriate, for, as Page Smith has pointed out, "After a century and a half of progress in historical scholarship, in research techniques, in tools and methods, we have found our way to the interpretation held, substantially, by those historians who themselves participated in or lived through the era of, the Revolution." By describing the Revolution as a conservative, principled defense of American freedom against the provocations of the English government, the neo-Whig historians have come full circle to the position of the Revolutionaries themselves and to the interpretation of the first generation of historians. Indeed, as a consequence of this historical atavism, praise for the contemporary or early historians has become increasingly common.

But to say "that the Whig interpretation of the American Revolution may not be as dead as some historians would have us believe" is perhaps less to commend the work of David Ramsay and George Bancroft than to indict the approach of recent historians.[18] However necessary and rewarding the neo-Whig histories have been, they present us with only a partial perspective on the Revolution. The neo-Whig interpretation is intrinsically polemical; however subtly presented, it aims to justify the Revolution. It therefore cannot accommodate a totally different, an opposing, perspective, a Tory view of the Revolution. It is for this reason that the recent publication of Peter Oliver's "Origin and Progress of the American Rebellion" is of major significance, for it offers us—"by attacking the hallowed traditions of the revolution, challenging the motives of the founding fathers, and depicting revolution as passion, plotting, and violence"—an explanation of what happened quite different from what we have been recently accustomed to.[19] Oliver's vivid portrait of the Revolutionaries with his accent on their vicious emotions and interests seriously disturbs the present Whiggish interpretation of the Revolution. It is not that Oliver's description of, say, John Adams as madly ambitious and consumingly resentful is any more correct than Adams's own description of himself as a virtuous and patriotic defender of liberty against tyranny. Both interpretations of Adams are in a sense right, but neither can comprehend the other because each is preoccupied with seemingly contradictory sets of motives. Indeed, it is really these two interpretations that have divided historians of the Revolution ever since.

Any intellectually satisfying explanation of the Revolution must encompass the Tory perspective as well as the Whig, for if we are compelled to take sides and choose between opposing motives—unconscious or avowed, passion or principle, greed or liberty—we will be endlessly caught up in the polemics of the participants themselves. We must, in other words, eventually dissolve the distinction between conscious and unconscious motives, between the Revolutionaries' stated intentions and their supposedly hidden needs and desires, a dissolution that involves somehow relating beliefs and ideas to the social world in which they operate. If we are to understand the causes of the Revolution we must therefore ultimately transcend this problem of motivation. But this we can never do as long as we attempt to explain the Revolution mainly in terms of the intentions of the participants. It is not that men's motives are unimportant; they indeed make events, including revolutions. But the purposes of men, especially in a revolution, are so numerous, so varied, and so contradictory that their complex interaction produces results that no one intended or could even foresee. It is this interaction and these results that recent historians are referring to when they speak so disparagingly of those "underlying determinants" and "impersonal and inexorable forces" bringing on the Revolution. Historical explanation which does not account for these "forces," which, in other words, relies simply on understanding the conscious intentions of the actors, will thus be limited. This preoccupation with men's purposes was what restricted the perspectives of the contemporaneous Whig and Tory interpretations; and it is still the weakness of the neo-Whig histories, and indeed of any interpretation which attempts to explain the events of the Revolution by discovering the calculations from which individuals supposed themselves to have acted.

No explanation of the American Revolution in terms of the intentions and designs of particular individuals could have been more crudely put than that offered by the Revolutionaries themselves. American Whigs, like men of the eighteenth century generally, were fascinated with what seemed to the age to be the newly appreciated problem of human motivation and causation in the affairs of the world. In the decade before independence the Americans sought endlessly to discover the supposed calculations and purposes of individuals or groups that lay behind the otherwise incomprehensible rush of events. More than anything else perhaps, it was this obsession with motives that led to the prevalence in the eighteenth century of beliefs in conspiracies to account for the confusing happenings in which men found themselves caught up. Bailyn has suggested that this common fear of conspiracy was "deeply rooted in the political awareness of eighteenth-century Britons, involved in the very structure of their political life"; it "reflected so clearly the realities of life in an age in which monarchical autocracy flourished, [and] in which the stability and freedom of England's 'mixed' constitution was a recent and remarkable achievement."[20] Yet it might also be argued that the tendency to see conspiracy behind what happened reflected as well the very enlightenment of the age. To attribute events to the designs and purposes of human agents seemed after all to be an enlightened advance over older beliefs in blind chance, providence, or God's interventions. It was rational and scientific, a product of both the popularization of politics and the secularization of knowledge. It was obvious to Americans that the series of events in the years after 1763, those "unheard of intolerable calamities, spring not of the dust, come not causeless." "Ought not the PEOPLE therefore," asked John Dickinson, "to watch? to observe facts? to search into causes? to investigate designs?" And these causes and designs could be traced to individuals in high places, to ministers, to royal governors, and their lackeys. The belief in conspiracy grew naturally out of the enlightened need to find the human purposes behind the multitude of phenomena, to find the causes for what happened in the social world just as the natural scientist was discovering the causes for what happened in the physical world. It was a necessary consequence of the search for connections and patterns in events. The various acts of the British government, the Americans knew, should not be "regarded according to the simple force of each, but as parts of a system of oppression." The Whigs' intense search for the human purposes behind events was in fact an example of the beginnings of modern history.

In attempting to rebut those interpretations disparaging the colonists' cause, the present neo-Whig historians have been drawn into writing as partisans of the Revolutionaries. And they have thus found themselves entangled in the same kind of explanation used by the original antagonists, an explanation, despite obvious refinements, still involved with the discovery of motives and its corollary, the assessing of a personal sort of responsibility for what happened. While most of the neo-Whig historians have not gone so far as to see conspiracy in British actions (although some have come close), they have tended to point up the blundering and stupidity of British officials in contrast to "the breadth of vision" that moved the Americans. If George III was in a position of central responsibility in the British government, as English historians have recently said, then, according to Edmund S. Morgan, "he must bear most of the praise or blame for the series of measures that alienated and lost the colonies, and it is hard to see how there can be much praise." By seeking "to define issues, fix responsibilities," and thereby to shift the "burden of proof" onto those who say the Americans were narrow and selfish and the empire was basically just and beneficent, the neo-Whigs have attempted to redress what they felt was an unfair neo-Tory bias of previous explanations of the Revolution; they have not, however, challenged the terms of the argument. They are still obsessed with why men said they acted and with who was right and who was wrong. Viewing the history of the Revolution in this judicatory manner has therefore restricted the issues over which historians have disagreed to those of motivation and responsibility, the very issues with which the participants themselves were concerned.

The neo-Whig "conviction that the colonists' attachment to principle was genuine" has undoubtedly been refreshing, and indeed necessary, given the Tory slant of earlier twentieth-century interpretations. It now seems clearer that the Progressive historians, with their naive and crude reflex conception of human behavior, had too long treated the ideas of the Revolution superficially if not superciliously. Psychologists and sociologists are now willing to grant a more determining role to beliefs, particularly in revolutionary situations. It is now accepted that men act not simply in response to some kind of objective reality but to the meaning they give to that reality. Since men's beliefs are as much a part of the given stimuli as the objective environment, the beliefs must be understood and taken seriously if men's behavior is to be fully explained. The American Revolutionary ideas were more than cooked up pieces of thought served by an aggressive and interested minority to a gullible and unsuspecting populace. The concept of propaganda permitted the Progressive historians to account for the presence of ideas but it prevented them from recognizing ideas as an important determinant of the Americans' behavior. The weight attributed to ideas and constitutional principles by the neo-Whig historians was thus an essential corrective to the propagandist studies.

Yet in its laudable effort to resurrect the importance of ideas in historical explanation much of the writing of the neo-Whigs has tended to return to the simple nineteenth-century intellectualist assumption that history is the consequence of a rational calculation of ends and means, that what happened was what was consciously desired and planned. By supposing "that individual actions and immediate issues are more important than underlying determinants in explaining particular events," by emphasizing conscious and articulated motives, the neo-Whig historians have selected and presented that evidence which is most directly and clearly expressive of the intentions of the Whigs, that is, the most well-defined, the most constitutional, the most reasonable of the Whig beliefs, those found in their public documents, their several declarations of grievances and causes. It is not surprising that for the neo-Whigs the history of the American Revolution should be more than anything else "the history of the Americans' search for principles."[21] Not only, then, did nothing in the Americans' economic and social structure really determine their behavior, but the colonists in fact acted from the most rational and calculated of motives: they fought, as they said they would, simply to defend their ancient liberties against British provocation.

By implying that certain declared rational purposes are by themselves an adequate explanation for the Americans' revolt, in other words that the Revolution was really nothing more than a contest over constitutional principles, the neo-Whig historians have not only threatened to deny what we have learned of human psychology in the twentieth century, but they have also in fact failed to exploit fully the terms of their own idealist approach by not taking into account all of what the Americans believed and said. Whatever the deficiencies and misunderstandings of the role of ideas in human behavior present in the propagandist studies of the 1930's, these studies did for the first time attempt to deal with the entirety and complexity of American Revolutionary thought— to explain not only all the well-reasoned notions of law and liberty that were so familiar but, more important, all the irrational and hysterical beliefs that had been so long neglected. Indeed, it was the patent absurdity and implausibility of much of what the Americans said that lent credence and persuasiveness to their mistrustful approach to the ideas. Once this exaggerated and fanatical rhetoric was uncovered by the Progressive historians, it should not have subsequently been ignored —no matter how much it may have impugned the reasonableness of the

American response. No widely expressed ideas can be dismissed out of hand by the historian.

In his recent analysis of Revolutionary thinking Bernard Bailyn has avoided the neo-Whig tendency to distort the historical reconstruction of the American mind. By comprehending "the assumptions, beliefs, and ideas that lay behind the manifest events of the time," Bailyn has attempted to get inside the Whigs' mind, and to experience vicariously all of what they thought and felt, both their rational constitutional beliefs and their hysterical and emotional ideas as well. The inflammatory phrases, "slavery," "corruption," "conspiracy," that most historians had either ignored or readily dismissed as propaganda, took on a new significance for Bailyn. He came "to suspect that they meant something very real to both the writers and their readers: that there were real fears, real anxieties, a sense of real danger behind these phrases, and not merely the desire to influence by rhetoric and propaganda the inert minds of an otherwise passive populace."[22] No part of American thinking, Bailyn suggests—not the widespread belief in a ministerial conspiracy, not the hostile and vicious indictments of individuals, not the fear of corruption and the hope for regeneration, not any of the violent seemingly absurd distortions and falsifications of what we now believe to be true, in short, none of the frenzied rhetoric—can be safely ignored by the historian seeking to understand the causes of the Revolution.

Bailyn's study, however, represents something other than a more complete and uncorrupted version of the common idealist interpretations of the Revolution. By viewing from the "interior" the Revolutionary pamphlets, which were "to an unusual degree, *explanatory*," revealing "not merely positions taken but the reasons why positions were taken," Bailyn like any idealist historian has sought to discover the motives the participants themselves gave for their actions, to re-enact their thinking at crucial moments, and thereby to recapture some of the "unpredictable reality" of the Revolution.[23] But for Bailyn the very unpredictability of the reality he has disclosed has undermined the idealist obsession with explaining why, in the participants' own estimation, they acted as they did. Ideas emerge as more than explanatory devices, as more than indicators of motives. They become as well objects for analysis in and for themselves, historical events in their own right to be treated as other historical events are treated. Although Bailyn has examined the Revolutionary ideas subjectively from the inside, he has also analyzed them objectively from the outside. Thus, in addition to a contemporary Whig perspective, he presents us with a retrospective view of the ideas—their complexity, their development, and their consequences—that the actual participants did not have. In effect his essay represents what has been called "a Namierism of the history of ideas," a structural analysis of thought that suggests a conclusion about the movement of history not very different from Sir Lewis Namier's, where history becomes something "started in ridiculous beginnings, while small men did things both infinitely smaller and infinitely greater than they knew."

In his *England in the Age of the American Revolution* Namier attacked the Whig tendency to overrate "the importance of the conscious will and purpose in individuals." Above all he urged us "to ascertain and recognize the deeper irrelevancies and incoherence of human actions, which are not so much directed by reason, as invested by it *ex post facto* with the appearances of logic and rationality," to discover the unpredictable reality, where men's motives and intentions were lost in the accumulation and momentum of interacting events. The whole force of Namier's approach tended to squeeze the intellectual content out of what men did. Ideas setting forth principles and purposes for action, said Namier, did not count for much in the movement of history.

In his study of the Revolutionary ideas Bailyn has come to an opposite conclusion: ideas counted for a great deal, not only being responsible for the Revolution but also for transforming the character of American society. Yet in his hands ideas lose that static quality they have commonly had for the Whig historians, the simple statements of intention that so exasperated Namier. For Bailyn the ideas of the Revolutionaries take on an elusive and unmanageable quality, a dynamic self-intensifying character that transcended the intentions and desires of any of the historical participants. By emphasizing how the thought of the colonists was "strangely reshaped, turned in unfamiliar directions," by describing how the Americans "indeliberately, half-knowingly" groped toward "conclusions they could not themselves clearly perceive," by demonstrating how new beliefs and hence new actions were the responses not to desire but to the logic of developing situations, Bailyn has wrested the explanation of the Revolution out of the realm of motivation in which the neo-Whig historians had confined it.

With this kind of approach to ideas, the degree of consistency and devotion to principles become less important, and indeed the major issues of motivation and responsibility over which historians have disagreed become largely irrelevant. Action becomes not the product of rational and conscious calculation but of dimly perceived and rapidly changing thoughts and situations, "where the familiar meaning of ideas

and words faded away into confusion, and leaders felt themselves peer-
ing into a haze, seeking to bring shifting conceptions somehow into
focus." Men become more the victims than the manipulators of their
ideas, as their thought unfolds in ways few anticipated, "rapid, irre-
versible, and irresistible," creating new problems, new considerations,
new ideas, which have their own unforeseen implications. In this kind
of atmosphere the Revolution, not at first desired by the Americans,
takes on something of an inevitable character, moving through a process of escalation into levels few had intended or perceived. It no longer
makes sense to assign motives or responsibility to particular individuals
for the totality of what happened. Men were involved in a complicated
web of phenomena, ideas, and situations, from which in retrospect escape seems impossible.[24]

By seeking to uncover the motives of the Americans expressed in
the Revolutionary pamphlets, Bailyn has ended by demonstrating the
autonomy of ideas as phenomena, where the ideas operate, as it were,
over the heads of the participants, taking them in directions no one
could have foreseen. His discussion of Revolutionary thought thus represents a move back to a deterministic approach to the Revolution, a
determinism, however, which is different from that which the neo-
Whig historians have so recently and self-consciously abandoned. Yet
while the suggested determinism is thoroughly idealist—indeed never
before has the force of ideas in bringing on the Revolution been so
emphatically put—its implications are not. By helping to purge our
writing about the Revolution of its concentration on constitutional
principles and its stifling judicial-like preoccupation with motivation
and responsibility, the study serves to open the way for new questions
and new appraisals. In fact, it is out of the very completeness of his
idealist interpretation, out of his exposition of the extraordinary nature
—the very dynamism and emotionalism—of the Americans' thought that
we have the evidence for an entirely different, a behaviorist, perspective
on the causes of the American Revolution. Bailyn's book-length introduction to his edition of Revolutionary pamphlets is therefore not only
a point of fulfillment for the idealist approach to the Revolution, it is
also a point of departure for a new look at the social sources of the
Revolution.

[v]

It seems clear that historians of eighteenth-century America and the
Revolution cannot ignore the force of ideas in history to the extent that

Namier and his students have done in their investigations of eighteenth-century English politics. This is not to say, however, that the Namier approach to English politics has been crucially limiting and distorting. Rather it may suggest that the Namier denigration of ideas and principles is inapplicable for American politics because the American social situation in which ideas operated was very different from that of eighteenth-century England. It may be that ideas are less meaningful to a people in a socially stable situation. Only when ideas have become stereotyped reflexes do evasion and hypocrisy and the Namier mistrust of what men believe become significant. Only in a relatively settled society does ideology become a kind of habit, a bundle of widely shared and instinctive conventions, offering ready-made explanations for men who are not being compelled to ask any serious questions. Conversely, it is perhaps only in a relatively unsettled, disordered society, where the questions come faster than men's answers, that ideas become truly vital and creative.[25]

Paradoxically it may be the very vitality of the Americans' ideas, then, that suggests the need to examine the circumstances in which they flourished. Since ideas and beliefs are ways of perceiving and explaining the world, the nature of the ideas expressed is determined as much by the character of the world being confronted as by the internal development of inherited and borrowed conceptions. Out of the multitude of inherited and transmitted ideas available in the eighteenth century, Americans selected and emphasized those which seemed to make meaningful what was happening to them. In the colonists' use of classical literature, for example, "their detailed knowledge and engaged interest covered only one era and one small group of writers," Plutarch, Livy, Cicero, Sallust, and Tacitus—those who "had hated and feared the trends of their own time, and in their writing had contrasted the present with a better past, which they endowed with qualities absent from their own, corrupt era."[26] There was always, in Max Weber's term, some sort of elective affinity between the Americans' interests and their beliefs, and without that affinity their ideas would not have possessed the peculiar character and persuasiveness they did. Only the most revolutionary social needs and circumstances could have sustained such revolutionary ideas.

When the ideas of the Americans are examined comprehensively, when all of the Whig rhetoric, irrational as well as rational, is taken into account, one cannot but be struck by the predominant characteristics of fear and frenzy, the exaggerations and the enthusiasm, the general sense of social corruption and disorder out of which would be born a new world of benevolence and harmony where Americans would become the "eminent examples of every divine and social virtue." As Bailyn and the propaganda studies have amply shown, there is simply too much fanatical and millennial thinking even by the best minds that must be explained before we can characterize the Americans' ideas as peculiarly rational and legalistic and thus view the Revolution as merely a conservative defense of constitutional liberties. To isolate refined and nicely-reasoned arguments from the writings of John Adams and Jefferson is not only to disregard the more inflamed expressions of the rest of the Whigs but also to overlook the enthusiastic extravagance—the paranoiac obsession with a diabolical Crown conspiracy and the dream of a restored Saxon era—in the thinking of Adams and Jefferson themselves.

The ideas of the Americans seem, in fact, to form what can only be called a revolutionary syndrome. If we were to confine ourselves to examining the Revolutionary rhetoric alone, apart from what happened politically or socially, it would be virtually impossible to distinguish the American Revolution from any other revolution in modern Western history. In the kinds of ideas expressed the American Revolution is remarkably similar to the seventeenth-century Puritan Revolution and to the eighteenth-century French Revolution: the same general disgust with a chaotic and corrupt world, the same anxious and angry bombast, the same excited fears of conspiracies by depraved men, the same utopian hopes for the constructions of a new and virtuous order. It was not that this syndrome of ideas was simply transmitted from one generation or from one people to another. It was rather perhaps that similar, though hardly identical, social situations called forth within the limitations of inherited and available conceptions similar modes of expression. Although we need to know much more about the sociology of revolutions and collective movements, it does seem possible that particular patterns of thought, particular forms of expression, correspond to certain basic social experiences. There may be, in other words, typical modes of expression, typical kinds of beliefs and values, characterizing a revolutionary situation, at least within roughly similar Western societies. Indeed, the types of ideas manifested may be the best way of identifying a collective movement as a revolution. As one student of revolutions writes, "It is on the basis of a knowledge of men's beliefs that we can distinguish their behaviour from riot, rebellion or insanity."[27]

It is thus the very nature of the Americans' rhetoric—its obsession with corruption and disorder, its hostile and conspiratorial outlook, and its millennial vision of a regenerated society—that reveals as nothing else apparently can the American Revolution as a true revolution with its sources lying deep in the social structure. For this kind of frenzied rhetoric could spring only from the most severe sorts of social strain. The grandiose and feverish language of the Americans was indeed the natural, even the inevitable, expression of a people caught up in a revolutionary situation, deeply alienated from the existing sources of authority and vehemently involved in a basic reconstruction of their political and social order. The hysteria of the Americans' thinking was but a measure of the intensity of their revolutionary passions. Undoubtedly the growing American alienation from British authority contributed greatly to this revolutionary situation. Yet the very weakness of the British imperial system and the accumulating ferocity of American antagonism to it suggests that other sources of social strain were being fed into the revolutionary movement. It may be that the Progressive historians in their preoccupation with internal social problems were more right than we have recently been willing to grant. It would be repeating their mistake, however, to expect this internal social strain necessarily to take the form of coherent class conflict or overt social disruption. The sources of revolutionary social stress may have been much more subtle but no less severe.

Of all of the colonies in the mid-eighteenth century, Virginia seems the most settled, the most lacking in obvious social tensions. Therefore, as it has been recently argued, since conspicuous social issues were non-existent, the only plausible remaining explanation for the Virginians' energetic and almost unanimous commitment to the Revolution must have been their devotion to constitutional principles. Yet it may be that we have been looking for the wrong kind of social issues, for organized conflicts, for conscious divisions, within the society. It seems clear that Virginia's difficulties were not the consequence of any obvious sectional or class antagonism, Tidewater versus Piedmont, aristocratic planters versus yeomen farmers. There was apparently no discontent with the political system that went deep into the social structure. But there does seem to have been something of a social crisis within the ruling group itself, which intensely aggravated the Virginians' antagonism to the imperial system. Contrary to the impression of confidence and stability that the Virginia planters have historically acquired, they seemed to have been in very uneasy circumstances in the years before the Revolution. The signs of the eventual nineteenth-century decline of the Virginia gentry were, in other words, already felt if not readily apparent.

The planters' ability to command the acquiescence of the people seems extraordinary compared to the unstable politics of the other colonies. But in the years before independence there were signs of increasing anxiety among the gentry over their representative role. The ambiguities in the relationship between the Burgesses and their constituents erupted into open debate in the 1750's. And men began voicing more and more concern over the mounting costs of elections and growing corruption in the soliciting of votes. . . . By the late sixties and early seventies the newspapers were filled with warnings against electoral influence, bribery, and vote seeking. . . . In this context Robert Munford's famous play, *The Candidates*, written in 1770, does not so much confirm the planters' confidence as it betrays their uneasiness with electoral developments in the colony, "when coxcombs and jockies can impose themselves upon it for men of learning." Although disinterested virtue eventually wins out, Munford's satire reveals the kinds of threats the established planters faced from ambitious knaves and blockheads who were turning representatives into slaves of the people.

By the eve of the Revolution the planters were voicing a growing sense of impending ruin, whose sources seemed in the minds of many to be linked more and more with the corrupting British connection and the Scottish factors, but for others frighteningly rooted in "our Pride, our Luxury, and Idleness. The public and private writings of Virginians became obsessed with "corruption," "virtue," and "luxury." The increasing defections from the Church of England, even among ministers and vestrymen, and the remarkable growth of dissent in the years before the Revolution, "so much complained of in many parts of the colony," further suggests some sort of social stress. The strange religious conversions of Robert Carter may represent only the most dramatic example of what was taking place less frenziedly elsewhere among the gentry. By the middle of the eighteenth century it was evident that many of the planters were living on the edge of bankruptcy, seriously overextended and spending beyond their means in an almost frantic effort to fulfill the aristocratic image they had created of themselves. Perhaps the importance of the Robinson affair in the 1760's lies not in any constitutional changes that resulted but in the shattering effect the disclosures had on that virtuous image. Some of the planters expressed openly their fears for the future, seeing the products of their lives being destroyed in the reckless gambling and drinking of their heirs.

The Revolution in Virginia . . . undoubtedly gained much of its force from this social crisis within the gentry. Certainly more was expected from the Revolution than simply a break from British imperialism, and it was not any crude avoidance of British debts. The Revolutionary reforms, like the abolition of entail and primogeniture, may have signified something other than mere symbolic legal adjustments to an existing reality. In addition to being an attempt to make the older Tidewater plantations more economically competitive with lands farther west, the reforms may have represented a real effort to redirect what was believed to be a dangerous tendency in social and family development within the ruling gentry. The Virginians were not after all aristocrats who could afford having their entailed families' estates in the hands of weak or ineffectual eldest sons. Entail, as the preamble to the 1776 act abolishing it stated, had often done "injury to the morals of youth by rendering them independent of, and disobedient to, their parents." There was too much likelihood, as the Nelson family sadly demonstrated, that a single wayward generation would virtually wipe out what had been so painstakingly built.[28] George Mason bespoke the anxieties of many Virginians when he warned the Philadelphia Convention in 1787 that "our own Children will in a short time be among the general mass."

Precisely how the strains within Virginia society contributed to the creation of a revolutionary situation and in what way the planters expected independence and republicanism to alleviate their problems, of course, need to be fully explored. It seems clear, however, from the very nature of the ideas expressed that the sources of the Revolution in Virginia were much more subtle and complicated than a simple antagonism to the British government. Constitutional principles alone do not explain the Virginians' almost unanimous determination to revolt. And if the Revolution in the seemingly stable colony of Virginia possessed internal social roots, it is to be expected that the other colonies were experiencing their own forms of social strain that in a like manner sought mitigation through revolution and republicanism.

It is through the Whigs' ideas, then, that we may be led back to take up where the Progressive historians left off in their investigation of the internal social sources of the Revolution. By working through the ideas —by reading them imaginatively and relating them to the objective social world they both reflected and confronted—we may be able to eliminate the unrewarding distinction between conscious and unconscious motives, and eventually thereby to combine a Whig with a Tory, an idealist with a behaviorist, interpretation. For the ideas, the rhetoric, of the Americans was never obscuring but remarkably revealing of their

deepest interests and passions. What they expressed may not have been
for the most part factually true, but it was always psychologically true.
In this sense their rhetoric was never detached from the social and
political reality; and indeed it becomes the best entry into an understanding of that reality. Their repeated overstatements of reality, their
incessant talk of "tyranny" when there seems to have been no real oppression, their obsession with "virtue," "luxury," and "corruption,"
their devotion to "liberty" and "equality"—all these notions were neither manipulated propaganda nor borrowed empty abstractions, but
ideas with real personal and social significance for those who used
them. Propaganda could never move men to revolution. No popular
leader, as John Adams put it, has ever been able "to persuade a large
people, for any length of time together, to think themselves wronged,
injured, and oppressed, unless they really were, and saw and felt it to
be so." The ideas had relevance; the sense of oppression and injury, although often displaced onto the imperial system, was nonetheless real.
It was indeed the meaningfulness of the connection between what the
Americans said and what they felt that gave the ideas their propulsive
force and their overwhelming persuasiveness.

It is precisely the remarkable revolutionary character of the Americans' ideas now being revealed by historians that best indicates that
something profoundly unsettling was going on in the society, that raises
the questions, as it did for the Progressive historians, why the Americans should have expressed such thoughts. With their crude conception of propaganda the Progressive historians at least attempted to
grapple with the problem. Since we cannot regard the ideas of the
Revolutionaries as simply propaganda, the question still remains to be
answered. "When 'ideas' in full cry drive past," wrote Arthur F. Bentley in his classic behavioral study, *The Process of Government*, "the
thing to do with them is to accept them as an indication that something is happening; and then search carefully to find out what it really
is they stand for, what the factors of the social life are that are expressing themselves through the ideas."[29] Precisely because they sought to
understand both the Revolutionary ideas and American society, the
behaviorist historians of the Progressive generation, for all of their
crude conceptualizations, their obsession with "class" and hidden economic interests, and their treatment of ideas as propaganda, have still
offered us an explanation of the Revolutionary era so powerful and so
comprehensive that no purely intellectual interpretation will ever replace it.

NOTES

1. [William Vans Murray], *Political Sketches, Inscribed to His Excellency John Adams* (London, 1787), 21, 48.
2. Moses Coit Tyler, *The Literary History of the American Revolution, 1763-1783* (New York, 1897), I, 8-9.
3. Charles A. Beard, *An Economic Interpretation of the Constitution* (New York, 1935), x, viii.
4. While the Progressive historians were attempting to absorb and use the latest scientific techniques of the day nonbehaviorists in government departments and others with a traditional approach to political theory—men like Andrew C. McLaughlin, Edwin S. Corwin, William S. Carpenter, Charles M. McIlwain, and Benjamin F. Wright—were writing during this same period some of the best work that has ever been done on Revolutionary constitutional and political thought. However, because most of them were not, strictly speaking, historians, they never sought to explain the causes of the Revolution in terms of ideas.
5. Carl L. Becker, *The Declaration of Independence: A Study in the History of Political Ideas* (New York, 1922), 203, 207, 133.
6. Quoted in Philip Davidson, *Propaganda and the American Revolution, 1763-1783* (Chapel Hill, 1941), 141, 373, 150.
7. Arthur M. Schlesinger, *Prelude to Independence: The Newspaper War on Britain, 1764-1776* (New York, 1958), 34.
8. Davidson, *Propaganda*, 59; Schlesinger, *Prelude to Independence*, 20.
9. Davidson, *Propaganda*, xiv, 46.
10. Schlesinger, *Prelude to Independence*, 44; Arthur M. Schlesinger, *New Viewpoints in American History* (New York, 1923), 179.
11. Edmund S. Morgan, "Colonial Ideas of Parliamentary Power, 1764-1766," *Wm. and Mary Qtly.*, 3d Ser., V (1948), 311, 341; Edmund S. and Helen M. Morgan, *The Stamp Act Crisis: Prologue to Revolution*, rev. ed. (New York, 1963), 396-370.
12. Jack P. Greene, "The Flight From Determinism: A Review of Recent Literature on the Coming of the American Revolution," *South Atlantic Quarterly*, LXI (1962), 257.
13. This revisionist literature of the 1950's is well known. See the listings in Bernard Bailyn, "Political Experience and Enlightenment Ideas in Eighteenth-Century America," *American Historical Review*, LXVII (1961-62), 341*n*.
14. Greene, "Flight from Determinism," 237, 257; Thad W. Tate, "The Coming of the Revolution in Virginia: Britain's Challenge to Virginia's Ruling Class, 1763-1776," *Wm. and Mary Qtly.*, 3d Ser., XIX (1962), 323-343, esp. 340.
15. Bailyn, "Political Experience and Enlightenment Ideas," 339-351.
16. Bernard Bailyn, ed., assisted by Jane N. Garrett, *Pamphlets of the American Revolution, 1750-1776* (Cambridge, Mass., 1965–), I, viii, 60, x, 20. The 200-page general introduction entitled, "The Transforming Radicalism of the American Revolution" has been expanded and published

separately as *The Ideological Origins of the American Revolution* (Cambridge, 1967).

17. For examples of the re-examination of traditional problems in Revolutionary political theory see Richard Buel, Jr., "Democracy and the American Revolution: A Frame of Reference," *Wm. and Mary Qtly.*, 3d Ser., XXI (1964), 165-190; and Bailyn's resolution of James Otis's apparent inconsistency in *Revolutionary Pamphlets*, I, 100-103, 106-107, 121-123, 409-417, 546-552.

18. Morgan, "Revisions in Need of Revising," 13.

19. Adair and Schultz, eds., *Peter Oliver's Origin*, ix.

20. Bailyn, *Revolutionary Pamphlets*, I, 87, ix.

21. Greene, "Flight From Determinism," 258; Morgan, *Birth of the Republic*, 3.

22. Bailyn, *Revolutionary Pamphlets*, I, vii, ix.

23. *Ibid.*, vii, viii, 17.

24. Bailyn, *Revolutionary Pamphlets*, I, 90, x, 169, 140.

25. See Sir Lewis Namier, *The Structure of Politics at the Accession of George III*, 2d ed. (London, 1961), 16; Sir Lewis Namier, "Human Nature in Politics," in *Personalities and Power: Selected Essays* (New York, 1965), 5-6.

26. Bailyn, *Revolutionary Pamphlets*, I, 22.

27. Bryan A. Wilson, "Millennialism in Comparative Perspective," *Comparative Studies in Society and History*, VI (1963-64), 108.

28. Emory S. Evans, "The Rise and Decline of the Virginia Aristocracy in the Eighteenth Century: The Nelsons," in Darrett B. Rutman, ed., *The Old Dominion: Essays for Thomas Perkins Abernethy* (Charlottesville, 1964), 73-74.

29. Arthur F. Bentley, *The Process of Government: A Study of Social Pressures* (Chicago, 1908), 152.

RECENT STUDIES

Bernard Bailyn, *The Ideological Origins of the American Revolution* (Cambridge: Harvard University Press, 1967).

Alan Heimert, *Religion and the American Mind: From the Great Awakening to the Revolution* (Cambridge: Harvard University Press, 1966).

Edmund S. Morgan, "The Puritan Ethic and the American Revolution," *William and Mary Quarterly*, 3rd ser., XXIV (January 1967), 3-43.

John Shy, *Toward Lexington: The Role of the British Army in the Coming of the American Revolution* (Princeton: Princeton University Press, 1965).

Jackson Turner Main, *The Social Structure of Revolutionary America* (Princeton: Princeton University Press, 1965).

IV

The Confederation Period and the American Historian

RICHARD B. MORRIS

Plautus tells us that "one eyewitness is worth ten hearsays," but I am not sure that he would have left us this counsel if he had lived during the Confederation period of American history. In this era the eyewitnesses themselves failed to see eye to eye. In fact, the two opposing views of the post-Revolutionary years which are held by historians of the twentieth century can be traced directly to the Founding Fathers. The first we might call the Washington-Madison-Hamilton approach, accepted by most historians of the post-Revolutionary generation, and developed by George Bancroft, John Fiske, John B. McMaster, and with some reservations by Andrew C. McLaughlin. The other is the approach of certain Antifederalist leaders, an approach adopted by Henry B. Dawson, by J. Allen Smith, by the early Charles A. Beard, and by the more recent Merrill Jensen.

If one could read the minds of the majority of the Founding Fathers in 1787—and an abundant and ever-increasing quantity of first-hand documentation makes this a less formidable effort than it seems on its face—he might be very much surprised indeed that any issue should have arisen in historiography about the years of the Confederation. The majority of the Founders saw a clear drift toward anarchy

From *William and Mary Quarterly*, 3rd series, XIII (April 1956), 139-156. Reprinted with permission of the author.

culminating in a crisis. Constantly needled by such correspondents as Henry Knox and David Humphreys, Washington's alarm at the weaknesses of the Confederacy was deepened as the disorders in Massachusetts in the fall of 1786 seemed to portend a crisis for the nation. "I predict the worst consequences from a half-starved, limping government, always moving upon crutches and tottering at every step," he wrote. On August 1, 1786, he asserted: "I do not conceive we can long exist as a nation without having lodged somewhere a power which will pervade the whole Union in as energetic a manner as the authority of the State governments extends over the several states." On October 22 he wrote David Humphreys: "But for God's sake tell me what is the cause of all these commotions? . . . I am mortified beyond expression that in the moment of our acknowledged independence we should by our conduct verify the predictions of our transatlantic foe, and render ourselves ridiculous and contemptible in the eyes of all Europe." Nine days later he wrote Henry Lee, "To be more exposed in the eyes of the world, and more contemptible than we already are, is hardly possible."[1] On November 5 he told James Madison, "We are fast verging to anarchy and confusion!"[2]

Others than the New England Federalists, who were closest to Shays' Rebellion and understandably perturbed, shared Washington's views about the state of the nation. Henry Lee declared: "We are all in dire apprehension that a beginning of anarchy with all its calamitys has approached, and have no means to stop the dreadful work."[3] In December of 1786 Madison wrote Jefferson of "dangerous defects" in the Confederation.[4] During the fall of 1786 John Jay kept writing Jefferson that "the inefficacy of our Government becomes daily more and more apparent," and intimated that the Shaysites had more "extensive" objectives than the immediate redress of grievances.[5] Edmund Randolph, who oscillated between Federalism and Antifederalism, wrote Washington in March of 1787, "Every day brings forth some new crisis"; and he expressed doubt whether Congress could survive beyond the current year.[6] No one at the Constitutional Convention was more explicit than Randolph in spelling out the defects of the government, which he considered "totally inadequate to the peace, safety, and security of the Confederation" and which he repeatedly denounced for its "imbecility."[7]

For the classic contemporary view of the alarming weaknesses of the Confederation we must turn to *The Federalist*. Therein Hamilton, a consistent viewer-with-alarm during this period, attacks the Confederation government as inefficient, asserts that the country had "reached almost the last stage of national humiliation," speaks disparagingly of "the present shadow of a federal government," views the Confederacy as dying, and urges ratification of the Constitution to prevent anarchy, civil war, and "perhaps the military despotism of a victorious demagogue."[8] It would be easy to pile up assertions in similar vein from the pens of Knox and the two Morrises.

These Federalist worthies were in general agreement that the weaknesses of the Confederation could be attributed to financial muddling by the states; to English dumping; to the loss of the British West Indian market; to paper money; to stay laws; to state tariffs; but, above all, to a lack of coercive power by a central authority. Observers in charge of foreign affairs, notably Jay and John Adams, felt that this was the most critical spot in the American system of government. "I may reason till I die to no purpose," declared Adams in June 1785. "It is unanimity in America which will produce a fair treaty of commerce."[9]

In eloquence, prestige, and even in numbers among the leadership the Federalist view of conditions had impressive support, but it was far from universally held. George Clinton, the bête noire of the nationalist leaders, was quoted as intimating that the calling of a Constitutional Convention was "calculated to impress the people with an idea of evils which do not exist."[10] At the Convention, Gunning Bedford of Delaware expressed a complacent view of the government of the Confederacy, and at the Pennsylvania ratifying convention Antifederalists under the leadership of William Findley, Robert Whitehill, and John Smilie asserted that the people along with the legislature had been frightened into consenting to a state convention by unfounded talk of impending anarchy.

Thus there was a division of opinion in 1787 about conditions in the Confederation, and there never has ceased to be down to the present day. More recent writers who look at the Confederation through Antifederalist spectacles are buoyed up by the fact that Franklin and Jefferson were not as disturbed about conditions as other contemporaries. Yet Jefferson, as he was passing through Boston on his way to France, found "the conviction growing strongly that nothing could preserve the confederacy unless the bond of union, their common council, should be strengthened."[11] It is perhaps especially significant that when Franklin, Jefferson, and Robert R. Livingston expressed in writing a more roseate view of conditions than other Founding Fathers, they were making these observations to foreigners—to Frenchmen or to Englishmen. They were seeking to reassure friends and well-wishers of America abroad that this country was not headed for a collapse. Such assertions must be discounted as skillful propaganda. In France, for example, Jefferson reassured Démeunier that the United States was in no danger of bankruptcy and that, with certain minor exceptions, "the Confederation is a wonderfully perfect instrument."[12] Similarly, when Franklin wrote to M. Le Veillard on March 6, 1786, that "America never was in higher prosperity,"[13] commodity prices had steadily dropped—they were to decline thirty per cent between 1785 and 1789; farm wages were shrinking and were to fall to a low of forty cents a day by 1787; mortgage foreclosures and judgments for debts in central and western Massachusetts had reached an all-time high; and in the Valley of Virginia, as Freeman Hart has pointed out, executions more than doubled between 1784 and 1788.[14] In fact, the only economic index that showed an upturn was that for foreign trade, for in commerce the worst of the depression set in a bit earlier than in other lines and showed a more complete recovery by 1788. Again, when Livingston wrote Lafayette in April 1787 that commodity prices and wages were higher than before the war, he was evading the real issue of how far they had dropped since the coming of the peace.[15]

This double standard of correspondence—one line for Americans, the other for foreign well-wishers—is revealed in the writings of that archpessimist, George Washington. It is true that he was somewhat more candid with his old friend Lafayette, whom he wrote on August 15, 1786, that he chose to remain silent on domestic affairs "since I could not disguise or palliate, where I might think them erroneous."[16] Yet two weeks earlier he had written two letters which are very nearly contradictory to each other. On August 1 he wrote the Chevalier de la Luzerne a reassuring letter to counteract reports of the American situation circulating in Europe. "In short," he concluded his picture of domestic America, "the foundation of a great empire is laid, and I please myself with a persuasion, that Providence will not leave its work imperfect." On the same day, however, he wrote John Jay, then Secretary for Foreign Affairs, expressing the doubt that the nation could exist much longer unless stronger powers were lodged with the central government.[17]

Even the younger generation, men who could scarcely be accused of strong Federalist attachments, accepted the Federalist view of the glaring weaknesses of the Confederation. Consider, for example, Andrew Jackson, who was admitted to practice law the year the Constitutional Convention met in Philadelphia. In his Proclamation against Nullification Jackson declared in 1832: "But the defects of the Confederation need not be detailed. Under its operation we could scarcely be called a nation. We had neither prosperity at home nor consideration abroad. This state of things could not be endured, and our present happy Constitution was formed, but formed in vain if this fatal doctrine prevails."[18]

Jackson's view of the Confederation period was the view of the nationalist commentators on the Constitution and of the nationalist historians. It was expounded by James Wilson and Nathaniel Chipman, by Nathan Dane, and most notably by Joseph Story and George Ticknor Curtis, who gave formal expression to the views of Daniel Webster. In his *History of the Origin, Formation, and Adoption of the Constitution*, first published in 1854, Curtis begins by declaring: "The Constitution of the United States was the means by which republican liberty was saved from the consequences of impending anarchy. . . ." Paraphrasing the Founding Fathers, Curtis saw the Confederation as "a great shadow without the substance of a government. . . ." He saw the whole period as replete with "dangers and difficulties," full of "suffering and peril."[19]

Curtis' view of the Confederation interlude was fully shared by the nationalist historians writing in the generation or two following the adoption of the Constitution. Most distinguished of this group, George Bancroft—whose literary career spans the period from the Age of Jackson to the Age of Chester A. Arthur—put off writing about the post-Revolutionary era until the closing years of his life. His *History of the Formation of the Constitution of the United States of America* was not published until 1882. As might be expected, Bancroft viewed the period from a nationalist or continental point of view. He stressed the "helplessness" of Congress, whose "perpetual failures" he considered "inherent and incurable." To Bancroft "no ray of hope remained" but from the convention summoned at Annapolis.[20] Nevertheless, he treats the Massachusetts debtors with sympathy and understanding, approves of Bowdoin's lenity toward the Shaysites, and reviews the economic decline which set in at the start of the period in sober language, in sharp contrast with the more intemperate treatment of the insurrection by his contemporary Richard Hildreth, who had surveyed the period many years earlier.[21]

Perhaps the historian who coined the term "critical period" to describe the Confederation interlude was William Henry Trescot. In his rather temperate and fair-minded *Diplomatic History of the Administrations of Washington and Adams*, published in 1857, he asserted: "Indeed, it would be more correct to say, that the most critical period of the country's history embraced the time between the peace of 1783 and the adoption of the constitution in 1788."[22] This point of view was adopted by Frothingham, by Schouler, and by von Holst. The last-named spoke of "the contemptible impotence of congress. . . ." This was strong language, but Washington had used it before him.[23]

The classic exposition of the Federalist approach is found in John Fiske's *The Critical Period of American History, 1783-1789*. His title has fastened upon an epoch in American history a popular nomenclature that dies hard. The first edition appeared in 1888, not too long after the appearance of Bancroft's *Last Revision*. The title and theme of the book were suggested by the fact of Tom Paine's stopping the publication of the "Crisis," on hearing the news of the treaty of peace in 1783. Now, Paine said, "the times that tried men's souls are over." Fiske does not agree with Paine. The next five years, he contends, were to be the most critical time of all. Fiske used the term "critical" first to settle the question whether there was to be a national government or a group of small city-states. Secondly, he used the term to describe what he regarded to be the utter incompetence of the states and the federal government to deal with the problem of postwar reconstruction. To Fiske the drift "toward anarchy" was only checked by the eleventh-hour ratification of the federal Constitution.[24]

It has become the fashion of latter-day historians to criticize Fiske's scholarship. McLaughlin concedes that "there are not many errors in fact in the book," but insists that "as an authority the work is altogether without scientific standing, because it is little more than a remarkably skilful adaptation of a very few secondary authorities, showing almost no evidence of first-hand acquaintance with the source."[25] Yet McLaughlin himself shows surprisingly little acquaintance with the sources when he describes economic conditions in the Confederation and gives the reader a string of generalizations entirely unsupported by statistical evidence or other business documentation. But the issue is not whether Fiske used first-hand sources, but whether he produced a valid synthesis. As one who has conducted graduate seminars for some time, I am not unaware of the fact that a good many people saturate themselves in the primary sources but are utterly unable to interpret them intelligently. Whether or not William Macdonald's appraisal of Fiske's book as "the best comprehensive account of the period"[26] still stands today, John Fiske's approach to the era had an enormous impact both upon the public and upon fellow historians. John Bach McMaster adopts it without reservations. In his *History of the People of the United States* he refers to the "disaffected," meaning the Shaysites, "associating for evil purposes," as opposed to "the better-minded," equally active in forming societies "for good purposes."[27] His treatment might well have been written by George R. Minot, clerk of the Massachusetts lower house, whose contemporary account of Shays' Rebellion betrays the fears of the conservative element as to the broader implications of the insurrection.[28] McMaster excoriates Clinton and New York for particularist tendencies. Save for Rhode Island, no state behaved worse than New York, McMaster contends.[29]

Other writers, while generally accepting the nationalist synthesis of the period, have approached the Confederation years in a somewhat more objective spirit than did Fiske and most of his predecessors. In the editor's introduction to Andrew C. McLaughlin's volume in the old *American Nation* series, Albert Bushnell Hart expresses doubt whether Fiske's "critical period" was "really a time of such danger of national dissolution as people then and since have supposed." He views the McLaughlin volume as showing "a more orderly, logical, and inevitable march of events than has commonly been described."[30] McLaughlin sees little or no justification for the constant lament about poverty in this period. "Some tribulation there was," he concedes, "but that the country was forlorn, destitute, and poverty-stricken is far from the truth." He sees indications of an upturn in trade by 1786. However, on the constitutional and diplomatic aspects of the period there is little difference between McLaughlin and Fiske. Referring to the humiliating relations with the Barbary states, McLaughlin asserts: "All this, like everything else one touches during the dismal period, discloses the helplessness of the confederacy." Toward the Shaysites he is far less sympathetic than Bancroft. "The vicious, the restless, the ignorant, the foolish—and there were plenty of each class—were coming together to test the strength of the newly established government of Massachusetts." The result, as he sees it, was "nothing short of civil war," but its virtue was that it disclosed the dangers, helped to bring about a reaction, discredited extreme democratic tendencies, and thereby aided the men who sought to inject vigor into the union.[31] Thus, those who were led by the editor of the series to believe that they were going to read a revisionist book were to find that it was essentially conventional in interpretation. Similarly, Edward Channing, in his *History of the United States*, published some years after McLaughlin, stresses the "helplessness" of the existing government and its failure to win respect either at home or abroad, but finds evidence of a business upthrust before the new Constitution went into operation.[32]

The Antifederalist or pro-democratic interpretation (and I need hardly say that the two terms are not necessarily equated) was perhaps first, among nineteenth-century historians, expounded by Henry B. Dawson, a learned military historian of the American Revolution, who also devoted himself to studying the role of the masses in that war, and had a penchant for picking controversial issues which he fought with relish and passion. In an article in the *Historical Magazine* in 1871, Dawson attempted to refute John Lothrop Motley, who, in a celebrated letter to the London *Times* written during the Civil War, had asserted that the Confederation was a period of "chaos," in which the absence of law, order, and security for life and property was "as absolute as could be well conceived in a civilized land." These were reckless and false accusations, Dawson charged. He traced their origin to distinguished men of the Confederation period who had spread them "for selfish or partisan motives." He accused these leaders of having "nullified the established law of the Confederacy and violently and corruptly substituted for it what they styled the Constitution of the United States." Dawson had made extreme and curiously unbalanced charges but failed to substantiate them. The significance of the attack, however, lies far less in the kind of evidence adduced than in its formulation of the notion that the Federalists conspired to falsify the true conditions of the period in a deliberate effort to create panic and undermine the government of the Confederation. Oddly enough, the criminal statistics Dawson cites for New York State not only are inconclusive regarding lawlessness, but point directly opposite to what Dawson believed. They indicate that in New York City and County there were almost twice as many indictments between 1784 and 1789 as there were for the first five years under the new federal government.[33] Concerning law and order, Dawson may very well have been on the right track, but somewhere along the path he lost the scent.

Despite the intemperate character of his attack, Dawson had touched on certain doubts as to the reportorial objectivity both of the Founding Fathers and of later historians. These were again raised in 1907, when J. Allen Smith, in his *The Spirit of American Government*, attacked on a second front, contending that the Constitution was the result of a counterrevolution. To him the Declaration of Independence spelled sweeping changes in the American form of government, changes manifest in an omnipotent legislature and the overthrow of the system of checks and balances which had been derived from the English constitution, with its characteristic blending of monarchical, aristocratic, and democratic elements. To Smith the chief feature of the Articles of

Confederation was the entire absence of checks and balances, the vesting of all power in a single legislative body, unchecked by a distinct executive or judiciary. The fact that the power which was vested in the continental legislature was ineffectual did not disturb him. His main point, though, was that such democratic changes had been wrought by radical forces and that the conservatives, once they had a chance to assess the situation, set about, in more or less conspiratorial fashion, to redress the balance. The Constitutional Convention was called, according to Smith, not only to impart vigor to the government but to institute an elaborate system of constitutional checks. The adoption of this system he calls a "triumph of a skillfully directed reactionary movement."[34] The idea that the adoption of the Constitution was the result of a struggle among interest groups was pressed by Arthur F. Bentley in *The Process of Government* (1908), in language which stemmed from Madison's *Federalist* 10, and in a more naked form by A. M. Simons' *Social Forces in American History* (1911).

The most significant amplification of the Smith-Bentley-Simons approach came in 1913 from the pen of Charles A. Beard. In his *An Economic Interpretation of the Constitution of the United States* Beard concedes that "interpretative schools seem always to originate in social antagonism," but he prefers the road which explains proximate or remote causes and relations to the so-called "impartial" history which surveys outward events and classifies and orders phenomena.[35] Beard was profoundly influenced by the Turnerian school, which substituted for the states'-rights interpretation of our history a recognition of social and economic areas, independent of state lines, which acted as units in political history. For the period of the Confederation the most important Turnerian contribution was Orin G. Libby's *Geographical Distribution of the Vote of the Thirteen States on the Federal Constitution*, an original and searching study published as far back as 1894. Beard found that nationalism cut across state lines, that it was created by a welding of economic interests of creditors, holders of personalty—especially public securities—, manufacturers, shippers, commercial groups, and speculators in western lands. While this majestic formula helped explain why people were Federalists, it has failed dismally in explaining differences between Federalists and Antifederalists. Recent studies by Robert Thomas of the property interests of members of the ratifying convention in Virginia have failed to turn up any significant differences between the two parties either in the kind and quantity of their property-holdings or in their relative status as creditors or debtors. On the other hand, Jackson T. Main asserts that the Virginians who favored greater centralization were found in pro-creditor areas, the Northern Neck and much of the Tidewater, while the opposition came from the debtor Piedmont. After 1785, Main contends, the Shenandoah Valley counties, which had previously voted with the Piedmont on most issues, now supported a grant to Congress of power over commerce. But the picture is at best hardly clean-cut or conclusive.[36]

Beard suggested that general social conditions were prosperous and that the defects of the Articles did not justify the "loud complaints" of the advocates of change. In short, Beard found that the "critical period" was really not so critical after all, but, drawing upon Dawson's article, "a phantom of the imagination produced by some undoubted evils which could have been remedied without a political revolution."[37] Save for a quotation from Franklin, Beard fails to document this crucial generalization.

Lest anyone should carry away with him the view that Beard opposed the Constitution, as did J. Allen Smith, it might be well to point out that in his *Supreme Court and the Constitution*, published the previous year, he praised the Constitution and furnished historical precedents for judicial review. In later years he drew further and further away from any monolithic economic interpretation of the period. Although his *Rise of American Civilization* adhered to the approach of his *Economic Interpretation*, as did Parrington's treatment in *Main Currents in American Thought*, Beard by 1935 completely repudiated economic determinism. In *The Republic* (1943) he considered the adoption of the Constitution as the alternative to military dictatorship. In his *Basic History of the United States* (1944) he defended checks and balances as curbs on despotic powers, whereas in his earlier *Rise of American Civilization* he insists that checks and balances dissolved "the energy of the democratic majority."[38] In *The Enduring Federalist*, published in 1948, he refers to the Congress of the Confederation as "a kind of debating society," and describes conditions in the Confederation period in language which would have gratified Fiske and perhaps shocked Bancroft.[39] In short, by the end of his career, Beard, the confirmed nationalist and isolationist, had moved a long way from the Beard of pre-World War I days.

But it is the unreconstructed Beard who still captures the imagination of our younger scholars. Today the chief disciple of J. Allen Smith and the early Beard is Merrill Jensen. In two significant books, *The Articles of Confederation*, published in 1940, and a more amplified treatment of the same problem, *The New Nation*, which appeared in 1950, Professor Jensen expounds learnedly and at length the argument that the Federalist party was organized to destroy the kind of democratic government and economic practice made possible by the Articles of Confederation.[40] Jensen sees the Articles as a constitutional expression of the philosophy of the Declaration of Independence, the Constitution as a betrayal of those principles. To Jensen the Articles were designed to prevent the central government from infringing upon the rights of the states, whereas the Constitution was designed to check both the states and the democracy that found expression within state bounds. As Jensen sees it, the Confederation government failed, not because it was inadequate, but because the radicals failed to maintain the organization they had created to bring about the American Revolution. He speaks of the radicals as having won *"their* war," but the fact remains that it was as much the war of the conservatives; probably a good deal more so.

Mr. Jensen finds conspiracy and betrayal at various levels. He suggests that the conservatives might well have betrayed the diplomatic objectives of the Revolution were it not for the integrity of Jay and Adams. He deplores the fact that radical leaders of the Thomas Burke-Richard Henry Lee-Sam Adams vintage quit the field and left it to what General Horatio Gates, scarcely an objective or disinterested patriot, called "the rapacious graspers of power and profit." Gates was one grasper of power who just missed the brass ring. Mr. Jensen sees this revolutionary group outnumbered by 1781, and worn down by defeat. Then from 1781 to 1783 the government revolved around Robert Morris and his satellites, for all practical purposes a dictatorship in Mr. Jensen's eyes. But when we look more closely at these counterrevolutionaries, the sharp line between radicals and conservatives seems to fade away. Who was more radical than Alexander McDougall in Sons-of-Liberty days? Yet it was he who headed a delegation of officers to Congress in the winter of 1783. Perhaps Hamilton was not far wrong when he defended the Morris faction as not only "the most liberal," but as "the men who think continentally." The issue does not seem to have been one between radicals and conservatives, but between particularists of the Clinton stripe and continental nationalists of varying shades and degrees.

Mr. Jensen is most effective in recounting the constructive steps taken in the Confederation period to repair federal and state finances. He points out that the Confederation actually managed to reduce the principal of its debt, and praises the states for their role in paying the national debt. Mr. Jensen points to the rapid amortization of state debts as evidence of the ability of the states to put their financial houses in order without much help from a central government. There is no doubt whatsoever that the states had now largely assumed the debt-funding function that the federal government had proven incapable of shouldering. Dr. E. J. Ferguson's studies of the assumption of the federal debts by the states reveal the considerable progress that was made in that direction in the Confederation period.[41] But, in terms of more recent ideas of economic planning, it would now seem that states like Massachusetts made the mistake of a too rapid amortization of the state debt, thereby initiating a sharp deflationary thrust. Even a conservative like Governor Bowdoin urged in 1786 a more gradual plan of amortization than that which the property-conscious legislature had enacted.

In short, the Beard-Jensen approach has served to present the Confederation period in a more constructive light, to give greater recognition to signs of economic expansion in the period and to the stabilizing role of the states, particularly in financial matters. As Allan Nevins has pointed out, when the new federal government went into effect, in no state was the debt appallingly high, and in some it was already low.[42] Mr. Jensen is doubtless correct in arguing that in most states the forces of law and order never lost the upper hand. In New York that arch-Antifederalist George Clinton personally led the troops of the state against the insurrectionary Shays. In most cases—and Maryland is an excellent example—the disgruntled elements confined their efforts to obtaining relief in a legal manner through legislative action.

In truth, the real difference between the nationalist and Antifederalist schools of historiography turns neither on the extent of the depression nor on the amount of anarchy in the "critical period," but springs from a deep divergence in interpreting the American Revolution and the issues for which it was fought. Mr. Jensen sees the radical party in the Revolution as comprising the town masses and the frontier groups. As he views it, the radicals fought for an internal revolution; those conservatives who reluctantly supported the war merely wanted independence from England. In fact, this school of historiography depicts the American Revolution as essentially a civil war among the Whigs. In this version there seems to be little or no room for Tories, for redcoats, or for Hessians. This formula fails to explain why New York City and Philadelphia were hotbeds of Loyalism, why the regulators of Carolina and the levelers of upstate New York were Tories, or why debtors and creditors, hard-money men and paper-money men, suffrage expansionists and suffrage restrictionists were arrayed on the same side. It fails to explain the prominent role of the Whig conservative elite in bringing about the Revolution or to lay the foundation for understanding why in so many areas the radicalism of the leadership was that of the Gironde, not the Mountain.[43]

In the last analysis the view that the course of the Confederation period was determined by a counterrevolutionary movement, which, through the instrumentality of the Constitutional Convention, nipped democracy in the bud, hinges upon one's ideas about the American Revolution. Unless one is ready to accept the thesis that the group that started the war were libertarians and democrats and were supplanted by a conservative authoritarian party, one cannot give uncritical adherence to the Smith-Beard-Jensen approach to the Confederation period. The facts simply will not support the argument that the democratic forces originally seized control of the movement in the states. Even in the short run, these forces were unsuccessful in every state save Pennsylvania and Georgia. In New Jersey, then as now hospitable to democracy, the Constitution, as Mr. McCormick has demonstrated,[44] was welcomed by all classes because it promised needed financial relief. In that state a western conservative coalition brought about deflationary policies, but not until the very end of the period under review. But the counterrevolution, if the halting of the leftward swing of the pendulum deserves that appellation, was gradual and mild. States like Delaware and Maryland, as John A. Munroe[45] and Philip Crowl[46] have shown us, did not have a counterrevolution, because there never was the kind of democratic upthrust that characterized the early Revolutionary years in Pennsylvania.

The failure of the so-called democratic forces, as Elisha P. Douglass has recently restated for us,[47] is a tribute to the vigorous Revolutionary leadership of the Whig conservative forces and their awareness of the fundamental issues at stake. It was the Whig conservatives, not the regulators in North Carolina or the back-country insurgents in Massachusetts, who took the lead in the movement toward independence. Only where the Whig elite seemed timorous and unwilling to move from protest to revolution did the democratic and back-country forces have any chance of seizing power. That was the case in Pennsylvania, where the conservatives had abdicated their political leadership, and to a lesser degree in Georgia, where the story still remains to be spelled out and where the democratic victory was by no means as clear-cut as in Pennsylvania.

The Burke-Bryan-Lee-Clinton forces that comprised the so-called "democratic" party in the Revolutionary years—just what did they stand for? What kind of democracy did they want? The touchstone of their democracy seems to have been an advocacy of a unicameral legislature, a popularly elected judiciary, and a weak executive—and very little else. In some respects the Whig conservatives held more advanced views than did the radicals. Judged by present-day standards the majoritarians were not always liberal. Back-country enthusiasts of the Great Awakening, they were by no means as ready to tolerate non-Protestant religious beliefs as were the deistically-minded Whig leaders. In fact, some of the most revealing evidence presented by Mr. Douglass is that which indicates that left-wing Protestants of Pietist or evangelical inclinations were fundamentalists in outlook and often basically conservative on political issues. It was they who tried to curb the political rights of non-Protestants, and in Pennsylvania it was the so-called radicals who enacted a law restricting freedom of expression. No, the majoritarians did not always act in democratic ways, nor did they seem always willing to abide by the will of the majority. Witness the shocking abuse of power by the radicals in Pennsylvania who established the state constitution by fiat and did not dare submit it to the people. In fact, they went so far as to require the people to take an oath to support the constitution as a prerequisite to exercising the franchise.

Much has been made of the distrust of the masses held by the Whig conservatives, of the views of men like Jay that "the mass of men are neither wise nor good." But many of the Antifederalists shared similar views. Take Samuel Chase, who, as Philip Crowl has shown us, was instrumental in framing Maryland's ultraconservative constitution, and is alleged to have been unstinting in his praise of the aristocratic features of that document, particularly of the electoral college for choosing senators. His desertion to the Antifederalist camp is perhaps best explained by his financial reverses, but he did not linger in it too long. In the federal Convention the Antifederalist John F. Mercer had opposed allowing the people to participate, declaring, "The people cannot know and judge of the characters of Candidates. The worst possible choice will be made."[48] Elbridge Gerry, who refused to sign the Constitution, asserted that "the evils we experience flow from the excess of democracy" and expressed concern at "the danger of the levilling [sic] spirit."[49] In New York the bulwark of Antifederalism was the landowner, with his rural isolation, his dread of the federal impost, and his jealousy of sharing political power. True, he was supported in his opposition to the Constitution by tenants and small farmers, but the Antifederalist leaders of that state had little faith in the people. At the New York Convention George Clinton criticized the people for their fickleness, their tendency "to vibrate from one extreme to another." It was this very disposition, Clinton confessed, against which he wished to guard.[50]

The Antifederalists were not poured out of one democratic mold,[51] any more than the Federalists represented a unitary point of view about how to strengthen the central government. As Robert East has demonstrated,[52] there was a wide breach between the Bowdoin-Adams kind of federalism in Massachusetts and the Cabot-Pickering stripe of particularism, with its strong sectional and anti-Southern overtones. There was an even wider gulf between the democratic nationalism of Franklin and the authoritarian nationalism of Hamilton.

On the pro-democratic side of the Federalist ledger must be credited the position of the Whig conservatives in support of certain basic human rights which they conceived as fundamental and not subject to change at the caprice of majority rule. Fortunately for the evolution of American democracy, the principles of the conservative revolutionaries and their so-called democratic opponents were largely complementary to each other. Although almost everywhere the radicals were defeated in their efforts to seize the machinery of Revolution, the liberative effects of the war proved a deterrent to the kind of social revolution which would have enshrined class hatreds and ensured violent reaction.[53]

Yes, the American Whigs were divided in the years of the Revolution on almost all issues except that of political independence from Great Britain. Since diverse and even divergent interests forged the Whig alliance, it was only to be expected that the victory of the patriots would settle no single social or economic issue except freedom from British mercantilist controls, hardly an unmixed blessing in the years of the Confederation. Despite the efforts of J. Franklin Jameson to consider the American Revolution as a social movement, the fact is that the great internal social reforms lay ahead. As Harrison Gray Otis once wrote to a friend of Revolutionary days: "You and I did not imagine when the first war with Britain was over that the revolution was just begun."[54] Similar sentiments were expressed by Dr. Benjamin Rush on an earlier occasion. In his "Address to the People of the United States on the Defects of the Confederation" Rush declared: "The American war is over; but this is far from being the case with the American Revolution."[55]

Indeed, the imposition of a vitalized federalism and the tightening of the bonds of union precipitated a greater revolution in American life than did separation from England. To those who view the adoption of a system of republican federalism as constituting a more thoroughgoing break with the political system of the past than did that earlier severing of the tenuous bonds of empire—and there is impressive evidence in the Confederation interlude of our history to substantiate this interpretation—the Federalists, not the Antifederalists, were the real radicals of their day.

NOTES

1. *The Writings of George Washington from the Original Manuscript Sources*, 1745-1799, ed. J. C. Fitzpatrick (Washington, 1931-44), XXVIII, 502; XXIX, 27, 34.
2. *Ibid.*, XXIX, 51.
3. Henry Lee to George Washington, Oct. 17, 1786, *Letters of Members of the Continental Congress*, ed. E. C. Burnett (Washington, 1921-33), VIII, 486.
4. *The Papers of Thomas Jefferson*, ed. Julian P. Boyd (Princeton, 1950—), X, 574.
5. *Ibid.*, p. 489.
6. *The Writings of George Washington* . . . , ed. Jared Sparks (Boston, 1834-37), IX, 243 n.
7. *Records of the Federal Convention of 1787*, ed. Max Farrand (New Haven, 1911-37), I, 19, 24, 25.
8. See especially *Federalist* 1, 15, 16, and 85.
9. Adams to Jay, June 26, 1785, *Works of John Adams*, ed. C. F. Adams (Boston, 1850-56), VIII, 276.
10. *Advertiser*, New York, July 21, 1787.
11. Jefferson to Madison, July 1, 1784, *Jefferson Papers*, VII, 356.
12. *Jefferson Papers*, X, 14 ff.
13. *Complete Works of Benjamin Franklin*, ed. John Bigelow (New York, 1887-88), IX, 300-301.
14. Freeman H. Hart, *The Valley of Virginia in the American Revolution* (Chapel Hill, 1942), pp. 123-125. For evidence from the court records of sharply mounting indebtedness in central and western Massachusetts, see R. B. Morris, "Insurrection in Massachusetts," in *America in Crisis*, ed. Daniel Aaron (New York, 1952), p. 24. On the steady upsurge of insolvency in Connecticut during the entire Confederation period, see *Public Records of the State of Connecticut* (1776-1796), eds. C. J. Hoadly and L. W. Labaree (Hartford, 1894-1951), VII, xv, xvi.
15. R. R. Livingston Papers, Bancroft Transcripts, New York Public Library.
16. Washington, *Writings*, ed. Fitzpatrick, XXVIII, 521.
17. *Ibid.*, pp. 501, 502.
18. *Compilation of the Messages and Papers of the Presidents*, 1789-1902, ed. J. D. Richardson (Washington, 1903), II, 643.
19. George Ticknor Curtis, *History of the Origin, Formation, and Adoption of the Constitution of the United States* . . . (New York, 1854), I, xi, 233, 234, 330.

20. George Bancroft, *History of the Formation of the Constitution of the United States of America* (New York, 1885), I, 262-266.
21. *Ibid.*, pp. 274-275; Richard Hildreth, *The History of the United States of America* (New York, 1848-51), III, 472-477.
22. William Henry Trescot, *The Diplomatic History of the Administrations of Washington and Adams: 1789-1801* (Boston, 1857), p. 9. Long before Trescot, however, Richard Henry Lee, a leading Antifederalist, wrote, Oct. 8, 1787: "I know our situation is critical, and it behoves us to make the best of it." "Letters of the Federal Farmer," Letter I, in *Pamphlets on the Constitution of the United States*, ed. P. L. Ford (Brooklyn, 1888), p. 280.
23. Richard Frothingham, *The Rise of the Republic of the United States* (Boston, 1910. First published in 1872), pp. 583 ff.; James Schouler, *History of the United States of America under the Constitution* (revised ed., New York, 1894), I, 13 ff.; H. von Holst, *The Constitutional and Political History of the United States*, trans. John J. Lalor and Alfred B. Mason (Chicago, 1889-92), I, 37.
24. John Fiske, *The Critical Period of American History, 1783-1789* (Boston and New York, 1888), pp. 55-57, and Chap. IV, *passim*.
25. Andrew C. McLaughlin, *The Confederation and the Constitution, 1783-1789*, in *The American Nation: A History*, ed. Albert Bushnell Hart, X (New York and London, 1905), 319-320.
26. William Macdonald, in *The Literature of American History: A Bibliographical Guide . . .* , ed. J. N. Larned (Boston, 1902), p. 156.
27. John Bach McMaster, *A History of the People of the United States, From the Revolution to the Civil War* (New York 1883-1913), I, 313.
28. *History of the Insurrection in Massachusetts in 1786 . . .* (Worcester, 1788).
29. *History*, I, 369-370.
30. McLaughlin, *The Confederation and the Constitution*, p. xv.
31. *Ibid.*, pp. 71, 107, 156, 161.
32. Edward Channing, *A History of the United States* (New York, 1916-26), III, 491, 414-415, 426-427.
33. Henry B. Dawson, "The Motley Letter," *Historical Magazine*, 2nd Ser., IX (Mar., 1871), 157 ff.
34. J. Allen Smith, *The Spirit of American Government: A Study of the Constitution, Its Origin, Influence, and Relation to Democracy* (Chautauqua, 1911), p. 37.
35. Charles A. Beard, *An Economic Interpretation of the Constitution of the United States* (New York, 1949), pp. 3-4.
36. Robert E. Thomas, "The Virginia Convention of 1788: A Criticism of Beard's *An Economic Interpretation of the Constitution*," *Journal of Southern History*, XIX (1953), 63-72. Jackson T. Main, "Sections and Politics in Virginia, 1781-1787," *William and Mary Quarterly*, 3rd Ser., XII (1955), 96-112.
37. Beard, *An Economic Interpretation of the Constitution*, pp. 47-48.
38. Charles A. Beard and Mary R. Beard, *The Rise of American Civilization* (New York, 1930. First published in 1927), I, 326.
39. Beard, *The Enduring Federalist* (New York, 1948), pp. 27-30.

40. *The Articles of Confederation: An Interpretation of The Social-Constitutional History of the American Revolution, 1774-1781* (University of Wisconsin, 1940. Second printing with additional foreword, 1948). *The New Nation: A History of the United States During the Confederation, 1781-1789* (New York, 1950).

41. E. J. Ferguson, "State Asumption of Federal Debt During the Confederation," *Mississippi Valley Historical Review,* XXXVIII (1951), 403.

42. Allan Nevins, *The American States During and After the American Revolution* (New York, 1927), p. 541.

43. For examples from New England, see Lee N. Newcomer, *The Embattled Farmers: A Massachusetts Countryside in the American Revolution* (New York, 1953); Oscar Zeichner, *Connecticut's Years of Controversy, 1750-1776* (Chapel Hill, 1949). Robert E. Brown, *Middle-Class Democracy and the Revolution in Massachusetts, 1691-1780* (Ithaca, N. Y., 1955), demonstrates that in Massachusetts the property qualification for voting did not bar the majority of adult males from taking part in elections. He opposes the view of an "international revolution" on the ground that democracy was already established. It is unlikely, however, that a re-examination of the nature and extent of the franchise and other so-called democratic indices in most of the remaining twelve states will support his concluding speculation that the "common man . . . had come into his own long before the era of Jacksonian Democracy."

44. Richard P. McCormick, *Experiment in Independence: New Jersey in the Critical Period, 1781-1789* (New Brunswick, 1950).

45. *Federalist Delaware, 1775-1815* (New Brunswick, 1954).

46. *Maryland During and After the Revolution* (Baltimore, 1942).

47. *Rebels and Democrats* (Chapel Hill, 1955).

48. *Records of the Federal Convention of 1787,* ed. Max Farrand (New Haven, 1911-37) II, 205.

49. *Ibid.,* I, 48.

50. *Debates in the Several State Conventions on the Adoption of the Federal Constitution, . . . Together with the Journal of the Federal Convention . . . ,* ed. Jonathan Elliot (Philadelphia, 1881), II, 359.

51. The reader is referred to the provocative article by Cecelia M. Kenyon, "Men of Little Faith: The Anti-Federalists on the Nature of Representative Government, *William and Mary Quarterly,* 3rd Ser., XII (1955), 3-43.

52. "The Massachusetts Conservatives in the Critical Period," in *The Era of the American Revolution,* ed. R. B. Morris (New York, 1939), pp. 349-391.

53. "Was there ever a revolution brought about, especially so important as this, without great internal tumults and violent convulsions!" Sam Adams asked rhetorically. *The Writings of Samuel Adams,* ed. H. A. Cushing (New York, 1904-08), III, 304.

54. Samuel Eliot Morison, *The Life and Letters of Harrison Gray Otis* (Boston and New York, 1913), I, 49.

55. Reprinted in H. Niles, *Principles and Acts of the Revolution in America* (Baltimore, 1822), p. 402.

RECENT STUDIES

Richard B. Morris, *The Peacemakers: The Great Powers and American Independence* (New York: Harper & Row, 1965).

E. James Ferguson, *The Power of the Purse: A History of American Public Finance, 1776-1790* (Chapel Hill: University of North Carolina Press, 1961).

Marion L. Starkey, *A Little Rebellion* (New York: Alfred A. Knopf, 1955).

V

The Founding Fathers: Young Men of the Revolution

STANLEY ELKINS AND ERIC MCKITRICK

The intelligent American of today may know a great deal about his history, but the chances are that he feels none too secure about the Founding Fathers and the framing and ratification of the Federal Constitution. He is no longer certain what the "enlightened" version of that story is, or even whether there is one. This is because, in the century and three quarters since the Constitution was written, our best thinking on that subject has gone through two dramatically different phases and is at this moment about to enter a third.

Americans in the nineteenth century, whenever they reviewed the events of the founding, made reference to an Olympian gathering of wise and virtuous men who stood splendidly above all faction, ignored petty self-interest, and concerned themselves only with the freedom and well-being of their fellow-countrymen. This attitude toward the Fathers has actually never died out; it still tends to prevail in American history curricula right up through most of the secondary schools. But bright young people arriving at college have been regularly discovering, for nearly the last fifty years, that in the innermost circle this was regarded as an old-fashioned, immensely oversimplified, and rather dewy-eyed view of the Founding Fathers and their work. Ever since J. Allen Smith and Charles Beard wrote in the early years of the twentieth

From the *Political Science Quarterly*, LXXVI (June 1961), pp. 181-216. Reprinted with permission.

century, the "educated" picture of the Fathers has been that of a group not of disinterested patriots but of hard-fisted conservatives who were looking out for their own interests and those of their class. According to this worldlier view, the document which they wrote—and in which they embodied these interests—was hardly intended as a thrust toward popular and democratic government. On the contrary, its centralizing tendencies all reflected the Fathers' distrust of the local and popular rule which had been too little restrained under the Articles of Confederation. The authors of the Constitution represented the privileged part of society. Naturally, then, their desire for a strong central government was, among other things, an effort to achieve solid national guarantees for the rights of property—rights not adequately protected under the Articles—and to obtain for the propertied class (their own) a favored position under the new government.

This "revisionist" point of view—that of the Founding Fathers as self-interested conservatives—has had immeasurable influence in the upper reaches of American historical thought. Much of what at first seemed audacious to the point of lèse majesté came ultimately to be taken as commonplace. The Tory-like, almost backward-turning quality which this approach has imparted to the picture of constitution-making even renders it plausible to think of the Philadelphia Convention of 1787 as a counter-revolutionary conspiracy, which is just the way a number of writers have actually described it. That is, since the Articles of Confederation were the product of the Revolution, to overthrow the Articles was—at least symbolically—to repudiate the Revolution. The Declaration of Independence and the Constitution represented two very different, and in some ways opposing, sets of aspirations; and (so the reasoning goes) the Philadelphia Convention was thus a significant turning-away from, rather than an adherence to, the spirit of the Declaration.

In very recent years, however, a whole new cycle of writing and thinking and research has been under way; the revisionists of the previous generation are themselves being revised. The economic ideas of the late Professor Beard, which dominated this field for so long, have been partially if not wholly discredited. And yet many of the old impressions, intermingled with still older ones, persist. Much of the new work, moreover, though excellent and systematic, is still in progress. Consequently the entire subject of the Constitution and its creation has become a little murky; new notions having the clarity and assuredness of the old have not as yet fully emerged; and meanwhile one is not altogether certain what to think.

Before the significance of all this new work can be justly assessed, and before consistent themes in it may be identified with any assurance, an effort should be made to retrace somewhat the psychology of previous conceptions. At the same time, it should be recognized that any amount of fresh writing on this subject will continue to lack something until it can present us with a clear new symbolic image of the Fathers themselves. The importance of this point lies in the function that symbols have for organizing the historical imagination, and the old ones are a little tired. The "father" image is well and good, and so also in certain respects is the "conservative" one. But we may suppose that these men saw themselves at the time as playing other rôles too, rôles that did not partake so much of retrospection, age, and restraint as those which would come to be assigned to them in after years. The Republic is now very old, as republics go, yet it *was* young once, and so were its founders. With youth goes energy, and the "energy" principle may be more suggestive now, in reviewing the experience of the founding, than the principle of paternal conservatism.

[1]

Charles A. Beard, who in 1913 published *An Economic Interpretation of the Constitution of the United States,* did more than any single figure to make of the Constitution something other than a topic for ceremonial praise. By calling it a product of economic forces, Beard established an alternative position and enabled the entire subject to become one for serious historical debate. He thus created the first real dialectic on the Constitution and Founding Fathers, and for that reason Beard's work must still be taken as the point of departure for any historical treatment of that subject.

For Beard, the reality behind the movement for a constitution in the 1780's was economic interest. The animating surge came from holders of depreciated Continental securities who were demanding that their bonds be paid at par, and from conservative elements throughout the Confederation who wanted a national bulwark against agrarian-debtor radicalism. Beard thus identified the Federalists as those who wanted protection for property, especially personal property. The Anti-Federalists, on the other hand, were the great mass of agrarian debtors agitating for schemes of confiscation and paper money inflation in the state legislatures. Their hard-earned taxes would go to support any new bonds that a stronger United States government might issue; conversely, further fiscal experimentation on their part would be checked by national power. The Anti-Federalists, those who opposed a new constitution, were therefore the radicals; the Federalists, who favored it, were the conservatives.

Beard's argument was immediately challenged and kept on being challenged, which helped it to retain the fresh attractiveness of an avart-garde position for many years. But the man's influence grew, and his work played a vital part in historical thinking until well after the Second World War. Historical thinking, however, has its own historical setting. Why should such a statement as Beard's not have been made until the twentieth century, more than 125 years after the event?

In the nineteenth century the American Constitution had operated as the central myth of an entire political culture. While that culture was still in the tentative stages of its growth, still subject to all manner of unforeseen menaces, and with very little that was nationally sacred, there reigned everywhere the tacit understanding that here was the one unifying abstraction, the one symbol that might command all loyalties and survive all strife. The Constitution thus served multiple functions for a society that lacked tradition, folk-memory, a sovereign, and a body of legend. The need to keep the symbol inviolate seems to have been felt more instinctively during its earlier history than later on. Public controversy of the bitterest kind might occur over the charter's true meaning; enemies might accuse each other of misconstruing the document; but one did not challenge the myth itself. Americans even fought a civil war with both sides claiming to be the true upholders of the Constitution. Thus it was natural that when the historians of the nineteenth century—Bancroft, Hildreth, Frothingham, Fiske, McMaster—came to describe the origins of the Constitution, they should reach for the non-controversial idiom and imagery of a Golden Age. The Supreme Law had been fashioned and given to the people by a race of classic heroes.[1]

America's veneration for its Constitution became steadily more intense in the years that followed the Civil War. Now it was the symbol not only of the Union, for which that generation had made such heavy sacrifices, but also of the unfettered capitalism which was turning the United States into one of the richest and most powerful nations in the world. The new material order—wasteful, disorderly, already acquainted with labor disturbances, yet immensely productive—was watched over by the benevolent and solicitous eye of the Constitution.

In 1888, in a setting darkened by portent of industrial warfare, John

Fiske published *The Critical Period of American History*, an account of the events leading to the Philadelphia Convention of 1787. It was an instant success; the notion of the Confederation interlude as a "critical period" was dramatically perfect. A time of trouble, political drift, threatening disunity, and irresponsible agitation provided the occasion at Philadelphia for a supreme act of disinterested statesmanship. There, an intrepid conclave of Old Romans rose above personal and local concerns and presented their countrymen with an instrument of vigorous and effective government.

By the opening of the twentieth century, the state of mind in which men could uncritically ascribe a sort of immaculateness to their political and legal arrangements had altered sharply. By then a profound economic and social crisis had been met and overcome, but with remnants of psychological crisis left unresolved in its wake. The ending of the depression and hard times of the 1890's, the defeat of Populism and Bryanism, the election of McKinley and return of Republican rule—these things were not enough to restore the old complacent innocence. The American public, now full of guilty misgivings, had begun to ask itself searching questions about the evils of the existing order and about the price it had allowed itself to pay for material progress. The answer which was hit upon by publicists and civic spokesmen was *vested interest*. The formula was not exactly new, but after the experience of the 1890's, when public rhetoric had abounded in sinister allusions to "Wall Street" and "the monopolies," it was no more than natural that the "vested interest" concept should have taken on an immensely new and widened range of application. The "interests" were the shadowy powers that manipulated things and made them run the way they did. Thus vested interest came to be seen in the Progressive Era—those years roughly from the turn of the century through the First World War—as the ultimate reality behind the life of affairs.

It was in that era, moreover, that "reality" itself first came to be a synonym for all the equivocal, seamy, and downright evil facts of life from which innocent and respectable people are normally sheltered. Few periods in American history have been so strikingly noted for civic awareness and the reforming spirit—and reform meant getting to the bottom of things. The most efficacious step in exorcising an evil was exposing it. Thus the literature of exposure, which claimed an enormous amount of journalistic and literary energy, did much to whet and sustain that generation's relish for reform. "Muckraking" meant dredging up heaps of grubby "reality" for all to behold. "Reality," as Richard Hofstadter has said, was the bribe, the rebate, the bought franchise, the sale of adulterated food. It was what one found in *The Jungle, The Octopus, Wealth against Commonwealth,* or *The Shame of the Cities.* . . . Reality was a series of unspeakable plots, personal iniquities, moral failures, which, in their totality, had come to govern American society. . . .

The sheer excitement of discovery tended to leave people's perceptions of appearance and reality somewhat unbalanced. It is perhaps too much to say that anything hidden was taken as bad (though there were certainly strong presumptions); yet one of the great unspoken dogmas of American thought, implanted in this period, was that the "facts of life" had to be hidden in order to qualify as "real."

In academic precincts, meanwhile, such thinkers as Roscoe Pound, John Dewey, Thorstein Veblen, Arthur Bentley, and J. Allen Smith had begun to challenge the older static and formalist theories of law, philosophy, economics, and government. They were no longer so interested in the formal outlines which enclosed, say, government or the law; they were much more concerned to locate the dynamic forces inside these realms—to identify the powers that made them really work. Thus "economic interest" as a kind of *élan vital,* a basic prime mover, came to be given greater and greater emphasis. "Wherever we turn," wrote E. R. A. Seligman as early as 1902, ". . . we are confronted by the overwhelming importance attached by the younger and abler scholars to the economic factor in political and social progress." Here was "reality" being given an intellectual and scholarly sanction.

In view of this mounting preoccupation with "interests," one might be led to conclude that significant numbers of intelligent people were approaching a "class" theory of society not unlike that of Marx—a theory in which classes and class interests contended more or less frankly with each other for advantage. Yet by and large this did not happen; these were not the terms in which most people thought about society. For one reason, there was very little evidence to support such a theory. But a more important reason was that, to a people saturated in democratic prejudices, "class" habits of thought were fantastically difficult to understand, let alone imitate. To the Progressive mind, the way vested interest worked was not so much through class as through *conspiracy.*

Vested interest and conspiracy were concepts so closely related that they were almost synonymous. The interests worked in secret; their power rested on stealthy understandings and was exercised through the pulling of invisible strings. Hidden from view, they might freely cir-

cumvent the law and gain their ends by corrupting and manipulating
the agencies of government. The Marxian view that a man openly and
automatically reflected the interests of his class, doing this even in the
name of ideals and justice, was incomprehensible to most Americans.
The mediating term between economic interest and political action had
to be something both simpler and more disreputable, and the techniques such as could not bear daylight. One important source of this
attitude was the Progressive faith in the essential honesty of the people.
Only the few, acting in secret, would set their interests against those of
the nation. They achieved their aims not by consulting the majority
will but by thwarting and evading it. Thus when writers of the Progressive period tried to weigh the importance of economic factors in
any political development, the imagery they slipped into was almost
invariably that of a conspiracy against the people. Such a mode of con-
ceiving reality would even be brought to bear upon the origins of the
United States Constitution.

Two of Charles Beard's immediate precursors in that realm were
J. Allen Smith and Algie Simons. They were, for their own purposes,
innovators; yet in a broader sense their minds followed a typical Progressive pattern. In J. Allen Smith's *Spirit of American Government,
A Study of the Constitution* (1907), the myth of the Philadelphia
convention as a forum of disinterested statesmen came under sharp
attack. Claiming that "it was the property-owning class that framed
and secured the adoption of the Constitution," Smith seemed to be
feeling his way toward an economic interpretation based on class. But
this tentative theme was quickly overshadowed by the central idea, that
of a conspiracy against democratic rule:

> Democracy . . . was not the object which the framers of the
> American Constitution had in view, but the very thing they
> wished to avoid. . . . Accordingly the efforts of the Constitu-
> tional Convention were directed to the task of devising a system
> of government which was just popular enough not to excite pop-
> ular opposition and which at the same time gave the people as
> little as possible of the substance of political power.

Algie Simons, who was a convinced socialist and should therefore
have hewed more consistently to the doctrine of class interest, fell into
much the same sort of reasoning. In *Social Forces in American History*
(1912), Simons' words seemed at first full of cool detachment when
he said that it was not necessarily bad for the Constitutional Convention to have been virtually a committee of the propertied class, because

that class "represented progress." But the lures of "conspiracy" in the end proved too much for him. Simons' closing rhetoric almost sweats with rural superstition as he tells his readers that

> the organic law of this nation was formulated in secret session by a body called into existence through a conspiratory trick, and was forced upon a disfranchised people by means of dishonest apportionment in order that the interests of a small body of wealthy rulers might be served.

But it was Charles A. Beard, taking up the "class interest" formula in his famous *Economic Interpretation* the following year, who succeeded to all intents and purposes in making it stick. Whereas neither Smith nor Simons had made any secret of their reforming passions (they denied that the Constitution was a sacred document, so their fellow-citizens should feel free to change it if they wished), Beard disclaimed any intention of writing a political tract. He would simply be the observer of historical events, impassively examining the facts. All he wanted to do was discover whether in fact economic forces had played a significant part in the drafting and ratification of the Constitution. Early in his book Beard insisted that it was not his purpose "to show that the Constitution was made for the personal benefit of the members of the Convention," but merely to determine whether the Fathers represented "distinct groups whose economic interests they understood and felt in concrete, definite form, through thir own personal experience with identical property rights. . . ." Then, setting in motion an impressive system of scholarly apparatus, he proceeded to answer his own questions.

Beard's ostensible argument—that the Fathers were pursuing class rather than personal interests and that there was a real distinction between them—had a certain Marxian subtlety, but he would not have made his case with very many Progressive readers if he had actually stuck to it. Instead, in the course of his book that side of the case, the "class" side, slipped entirely out of sight while the personal side, the one that really engaged Beard's mind, just grew and grew. The distinction was impossible to maintain; even to him it was probably not very serious. At any rate, the reason he was able to create his sensation was that the things he showed the Fathers doing were of exactly the sort that the muckraking magazines had, in other connections, made all too familiar.

Beard's basic research materials were a batch of old Treasury records which had never previously been opened ("reality"), and in them he found the names of a number of the Federalist leaders, members of the Philadelphia Convention as well as delegates to ratifying conventions in the various states. These men held substantial amounts of Continental securities which—Beard reasoned from later developments—would rise sharply in value with the establishment of a strong central government. This seemed to explain the energy with which they worked to bring such a government into being, and this was just the sort of evidence that impressed Beard's contemporaries most. Beard himself, for all his disclaimers, sums up his argument in language whose dominant theme is *direct personal interest*. Here, three of his thirteen conclusions are quite explicit:

(1) The first firm steps toward the formation of the Constitution were taken by a small and active group of men immediately interested through their personal possessions in the outcome of their labors.

(2) The members of the Philadelphia Convention who drafted the Constitution were, with a few exceptions, immediately, directly, and personally interested in, and derived economic advantages from, the establishment of the new system.

(3) The leaders who supported the Constitution in the ratifying conventions represented the same economic groups as the members of the Philadelphia Convention; and in a large number of instances they were also directly and personally interested in the outcome of their efforts.

Accompanying the principal theme of personal interest were several sub-themes:

(1) The Constitution was essentially an economic document based upon the concept that the fundamental private rights of property are anterior to government and morally beyond the reach of popular majorities.

(2) [The entire process, from the calling of the Philadelphia Convention to the ratifying of the Constitution, was unrepresentative and undemocratic; there was no popular vote on calling the convention; a large propertyless (and therefore disfranchised) mass was not represented at Philadelphia; and only a small minority in each state voted for delegates to the ratifying conventions.][2]

(3) [Where battles did occur over ratification], the line of cleavage . . . was between substantial personalty interests on the one hand and the small farmers and debtor interests on the other.

Beard thus managed in the end to have it both ways; he charged the Fathers, as members of a class, with things of which he had said he was not going to accuse them as individuals. But the distinction was too fine to matter a great deal; the response to the book, both favorable and hostile, was based on the secrets Beard had unearthed about the Fathers as individuals. Few of his readers had paid much attention to the subtle relationship which he had tried to establish between class interest and political ideology, so few could have noticed when the relationship began to dissolve. Actually, few had had any real quarrel with capitalism in the first place; the Progressive mentality was simply frightened by *big* capitalism—that is, by the vested interests. Beard himself was nothing if not a Progressive, fully immersed in his times. It was the interests and their inside doings that caught the Progressive imagination; it was this that the Progressives longed to befool and discomfit by public exposure. If Beard was to show that the Federal Constitution was not a product of abstract political theory but of concrete economic drives, there was no happier way of doing it than to paint the Founding Fathers in the familiar image of the vested interests—the small group of wealthy conspirators hostile to, even contemptuous of, the majority will, and acting for clear, "practical" reasons such as rigging the value of public securities.

Despite the bursts of pained protests which *An Economic Interpretation* initially drew from many older academics (who either thought that Beard could comprehend no motives other than base ones, or else concluded that he must be a socialist), it also drew plenty of praise from academic as well as non-academic quarters. Not only did the book do well for a scholarly monograph, it did better and better as time went on. In the 1920's the reforming side of Progressivism had lost its popularity, but this was not true of the debunking side. Meanwhile the success of Vernon L. Parrington's *Main Currents in American Thought* (which owed much to Beardian influences), as well as of Beard's own *Rise of American Civilization*, served to keep Beard's views before the public.

The *Economic Interpretation* came fully into into own in the New Deal era. The times by then required a conception of the Constitution that would stress the flexible, rather than the rigid and immutable aspects of the document. Former President Hoover, and even the Supreme Court, were apparently insisting in the face of all enlightened opinion that social and economic experimentation of any kind was ruled out by the spirit of the Constitution. Yet it would be reasonable enough to expect that the Constitution should respond to the economic

needs of the present, if there were convincing historical proof that its
very birth had been in response to the economic needs of its framers.
American intellectuals, moreover, had by this time become a good deal
more accustomed to ideas of class conflict than formerly. To significant
numbers of them the image of class struggle was now appealing enough
that they had begun applying it in a spirit of experimentation to a
great variety of problems. Business groups of every sort had fallen into
bad odor. This was the setting in which prophetic insights came to be
ascribed to the writings of Charles A. Beard. Those writings by the late
1930's had become voluminous, and the Master had acquired a legion
of followers.

And the Master himself could still have it both ways. Marxist and
quasi-Marxist interpretations of society could, and did for a season,
draw much historical sanction from his pages. At the same time Beard
had bequeathed to American historical method something far more
pervasive, a technique of explanation which could take "class" interpretations or leave them alone. This was the "reality" technique, which
assumes that the most significant aspects of any event are those concealed from the eye. Men's true intentions are to be judged neither
from the words we hear them speak nor the deeds we see them do, and
the "real" forces behind historical change will turn out, more often
than not, to be those of conspiracy.

[II]

In 1940 certain new and interesting corollaries were added to the mode
of approach which, due so largely to Beard's example, had come to influence historical thinking on the formation of the Constitution. In
that year Merrill Jensen published *The Articles of Confederation: An
Interpretation of the Social-Constitutional History of the American
Revolution, 1774-1781*. Jensen's own approach was consistent with
most of the general principles which had been laid down by Beard.
But whereas Beard's primary interest had been with the Federalists—
the men who led and supported the campaign for a new constitution
—Jensen turned his attention to the Anti-Federalists, those who had
opposed the constitutional movement. What, he asked, was the nature
of the political system which the Constitution displaced, and what
were the aims and intentions of the men who had created that system?

In the face of most prior opinions to the contrary, Jensen found in
the Confederation just the sort of loose arrangement most favorable to
democratic self-rule on the local and state level, inasmuch as the pri-

mary authority was located in the state legislatures. It was for achieving exactly this object, he thought, that the Confederation's strongest sup-porters—such leaders as Samuel Adams, Patrick Henry, Thomas Burke, and Richard Henry Lee—had pushed the Colonies into the Revolution in the first place. Conversely, those who opposed the Confederation were the men who had at first been reluctant to support the Revolu-tion. They had feared the consequences of a break with England be-cause that would remove the one central power strong enough to re-strain the forces of local democracy. These men did, to be sure, join the Patriot forces after the break had become inevitable. Yet almost at once they began working for a continental government which might supply the stabilizing and conservative force previously maintained by the Crown. Their eventual triumph would come, of course, at Phila-delphia in 1787.

In a second book, *The New Nation* (1950), Jensen considered the accomplishments of the Confederation, together with the social and economic conditions of the period from 1781 to 1789. He concluded that the "critical period" was really not so critical after all. American ships were not excluded from many foreign ports; tariff wars between states were the exception rather than the rule; the Confederation gov-ernment had solved the problem of western lands and was well on the way to settling the outstanding boundary disputes. By 1786 the eco-nomic depression which had struck the country in 1784 was coming to an end. Even the problem of national credit was not so serious as the Federalists wanted people to believe, since a number of the states had assumed responsibility for portions of the Continental debt held by their own citizens. Had the states been brought to accept a national impost—a tariff duty on incoming foreign goods levied solely and ex-clusively by Congress, the revenue of which would be reserved for the support of the government—the Confederation would have been fully capable of surviving and functioning as a true federal establishment.

The collapse of the Confederation, Jensen argued, was not the logical outcome of weakness or inefficiency. It was the result of a determined effort by a small but tightly-organized group of nationalists to impose a centralized government upon the entire country despite the contrary desires of great majorities everywhere:

> Most of these men were by temperament or economic interest believers in executive and judicial rather than legislative control of state and central governments, in the rigorous collection of taxes, and, as creditors, in strict payment of public and private debts. . . . They deplored the fact that there was no check upon

the actions of majorities in state legislatures; that there was no
central government to which minorities could appeal from the
decisions of such majorities, as they had done before the Revolution.

These were the men who conspired to overthrow the Confederation
and who masterminded the triumph of the Constitution.

There were points at which Jensen had not seen eye to eye with
Beard. He was more impressed, for instance, by the Fathers' general
outlook and ideology than by their property holdings; unlike Beard,
moreover, he denied that the Confederation era was a time of serious
economic difficulty. Yet he had actually strengthened the Beardian
logic at more than one point, and the differences were minor in the
light of the convictions which united the two in spirit and intention.
The work of Merrill Jensen, like that of Beard and Parrington and
J. Allen Smith before him, still balanced on the assumption that the
energy behind the American Constitution was conspiratorial energy,
and that the Constitution came into being by means of a *coup d'état*
—through the plotting of a well-disciplined Toryish few against the interests of an unvigilant democratic majority.

Indeed, Merrill Jensen's *The New Nation*—published two years after
the death of Charles Beard—was the last major piece of Constitution
scholarship to be done in the Progressive tradition, and represented the
end of an era. By that time, 1950, Beard's own notions had begun to
arouse not the admiration, but the suspicion, of a new generation of
postwar intellectuals.

[III]

A few modest little articles, case studies of ratifying conventions held
in individual states in 1788, had begun appearing here and there in
the regional quarterlies. In 1947 there was one by Philip Crowl on
Maryland, another on North Carolina by William Pool in 1950, still
another on Virginia by Robert Thomas in 1953. Such fragments, of
course, could not be expected to cause much immediate stir. But these
studies carried implications, similar in each case, that would prove in
the long run profoundly damaging to the whole structure of Beardian
scholarship and Beardian reasoning.

A major item in that reasoning had been Beard's assumption that
the principle which differentiated Federalists from Anti-Federalists was
the principle of class and property interests—that the Federalists as a
group were upholding one kind of class interest and defending one

form of property while the Anti-Federalists, presumably, represented something else, something basically opposed. For some reason, Beard had never taken the trouble to check the Anti-Federalist side of his equation. Thomas, in his study of the delegates to the Virginia ratifying convention (where the fight had been unusually bitter), discovered that the members of both sides held property of essentially the same kind, in approximately the same amounts, and represented the same social class—the planting gentry. The other studies showed a similar pattern. In short, the conflict over ratification was apparently fought out not between classes, but between cliques of the same ruling class within these states, and whatever the conflict's "real" basis, it was not a struggle over property rights as such. Beard's "class" and "property" formula was simply indeterminate; the story had to be found elsewhere.

By 1956, Beard's *Economic Interpretation* had been set up for the *coup de grâce*. The executioner was Robert E. Brown, a professor at Michigan State who had been at work for some time implacably compiling a catalogue of the Master's offenses. In his *Charles Beard and the Constitution*, published that year, Brown tracked Beard through every page of the latter's masterpiece and laid the ax to virtually every statement of importance that Beard had made in it. There was absolutely no correlation between the Philadelphia delegates' property holdings and the way they behaved on the question of a constitution. It was not true that large numbers of adult males were disfranchised; the suffrage was remarkably liberal everywhere. Farmers as a class were by no means chronically debtors; many were creditors and many others were both. The supporters of Shays' Rebellion (the debtors' uprising in western Massachusetts which occurred during the fall and winter of 1786-1787) were certainly not united against the Constitution; if they had been, it could never have been ratified, since the Shaysites had a clear majority at the time of the Massachusetts convention. Nor did the Philadelphia delegates know that the Continental debt would be funded at par. If they had, the banker Robert Morris, for one, would never have speculated in western lands with the thought of paying for them in depreciated Continental paper.

Not only was Beard's evidence inconclusive at all points, Brown insisted, but there were even occasions when the Master had not been above doctoring it. He edited Madison's Federalist No. 10 to eliminate all but its economic emphasis; he quoted only those passages of the Philadelphia debates that made the Fathers look least democratic; he arranged his treatment of the ratification process in an order that violated chronology, centered unjustified attention on states where hard struggles did occur, overlooked the ease with which ratification was achieved in other states, and thus created a wildly exaggerated picture of the opposition at large.

Brown's book was respectfully received; there was little inclination to dispute his arguments; no champions arose to do serious battle for the departed Beard. Some of the reviewers were a little dismayed at Brown's tone; they thought it need not have been quite so ferocious. And the book did seem to bear out the principle that any work of destruction in the realm of discourse, however necessary, must be executed within restrictions that make for a certain stultification. Richard Hofstadter remarked in this connection that Brown was "locked in such intimate embrace with his adversary that his categories are entirely dictated by Beard's assertions." Even Brown, in his way, had toyed with the "reality" theme. He had exonerated the Fathers of conspiratorial intentions but convicted Charles Beard in their place: Beard had cooked the evidence, had conspired to hide the truth.

The first effort in recent years to view the Constitution all over again in a major way, shaking off the Beardian categories and starting as it were from scratch, has been undertaken by Forrest McDonald. We The People, published in 1958, was the first of a planned trilogy whose design was to survey anew the entire story of how the Constitution was brought into existence. Although McDonald, like Brown, felt it necessary to show the inadequacy of Beard's conclusions, his strategy was quite different from Brown's; it was undertaken less to discredit Beard than to clear the way for his own projected treatment of the great subject. In the Economic Interpretation, Beard had made a number of proposals for research which he himself had not performed—and never did perform—but which would, Beard felt, further corroborate his own "frankly fragmentary" work. McDonald began by undertaking the very research which Beard had suggested, and its results convinced him that Beard had simply asked all the wrong questions.

One of the things McDonald investigated in We The People was an assumption upon which Beard had put a great deal of stress, the notion of a fundamental antagonism between "personalty" and "realty" interests at the time of the Philadelphia Convention. ("Personalty" was wealth based on securities, money, commerce, or manufacturing; "realty" was landed property whose owners' outlook tended to be primarily agrarian.) He found that there was no such split in the Convention. The seven men who either walked out of the Convention or else refused to sign the completed document were among the heaviest security-holders there, and represented "an all-star team of personalty interests." In state after state, moreover, there was no appreciable difference between the property holdings of Federalists and Anti-Federalists. Finally, the three states that ratified the Constitution unanimously —Delaware, New Jersey, and Georgia—were overwhelmingly dominated by agrarian interests.

Unlike Brown, McDonald was quite unwilling to write off the possibility of an economic analysis (his book's subtitle was *The Economic Origins of the Constitution*); it was just that Beard's particular economic categories led nowhere. Beard's sweeping "personalty" and "realty" classifications were meaningless, and he had deceived himself profoundly in supposing that the Federalists' property interests "knew no state boundaries" but were "truly national in scope." On these two points of difference McDonald set up an entirely new and original research scheme, and in so doing effected a really impressive conceptual maneuver. He was quite ready, in the first place, to find "economic forces" behind the movement for a constitution, but these must be sought not in "classes" or in broad categories of property but rather in the specific business interests of specific groups in specific places. The other organizing category would be the individual states themselves. The political framework within which any group had to operate was still that imposed by the state; the states were, after all, still sovereign units, and the precise relationship between economic forces and political action depended almost entirely on the special conditions within those states, conditions which varied from one to the other.

By abandoning Beard's "national" framework and recasting the entire problem on a state-by-state basis, McDonald made it possible to see with a sudden clarity things which ought to have been obvious all along. The states where ratification was achieved most readily were those that were convinced, for one reason or another, that they could not survive and prosper as independent entities; those holding out the longest were the ones most convinced that they could go it alone. The reasons for supporting ratification might vary considerably from state to state. For Georgia, an impending Indian war and the need for military protection could transcend any possible economic issue; New York, at one time imagining for itself an independent political and economic future, would finally ratify for fear of being isolated from a system which already included ten states and which might soon be joined by a seceded New York City.

The single problem of the Continental debt took different forms in different states. New Jersey, Massachusetts, and New York had each assumed portions of the debt held by their own citizens, but New

Jersey and Massachusetts found their obligations intolerably burdensome while New York did not. Massachusetts had put an excessively
heavy load on its direct property and poll-tax system; thus any possibility of the debt's being funded by a new Federal government should
have found both the Boston security-holder and the Shaysite debtor
more than willing to support such a government—and this, it appears,
is about what happened. In New York and New Jersey an additional
key to the debt issue was the question of a national tariff. New York
had a state tariff, which was part of a financial system worked out to
service the debt, and for that reason the state had been reluctant to
accept a national import in 1786. New Jersey, on the other hand, with
no ocean trade of any account and having to receive most of its imports through New York, had no such revenue, was hard pressed to
maintain interest payments on its debt, and thus had everything to
gain from both a national impost and a national funding system. New
Jersey was one of the first to ratify, and did so unanimously.

Recognizing the importance of specific location made it also easier
and more natural to appreciate the way in which particular interests in
particular places might be affected by the question of a stronger national government. Boston shipping interests, for example, seem to
have been less concerned in the 1780's over class ideology or general
economic philosophy than over those conditions of the times which
were especially bad for business. The British would not let them into
the West Indies, the French were excluding their fish, and their large
vessels were no longer profitable. A strong national government could
create a navy whose very existence would reduce high insurance rates;
it could guarantee an orderly tariff system that would remove all pressure for higher and higher state tariffs; and it could counter British and
French discrimination by means of an effective navigation act. Manufacturing interests would also tend to favor the Constitution, though
not necessarily on principle; the vigor of their support would depend
on the size of their establishments and the extent to which they competed with England. Support from Pennsylvania iron and Connecticut
textiles would be particularly energetic. So also with the wheat and
tobacco farmers of the Connecticut Valley, though not for the same
reason. They had to pay import taxes to New York for the goods they
bought (their crops were sold there); they were heavily taxed, at the
same time, to support a state-funded debt which they would be only
too glad to see removed by a central government. Farmers in the Kentucky area, on the other hand, could be very suspicious of a Constitution under which northeastern shipping interests might influence the

government to surrender free navigation on the Mississippi in return for a favorable trade treaty with Spain.

Forrest McDonald's work, according to him, has only just begun; years of it still lie ahead. But already a remarkable precision of detail has been brought to the subject, together with a degree of sophistication which makes the older economic approach—"tough-minded" as it once imagined itself—seem now a little wan and misty. The special internal conditions of the several states now seem fully valid as clues to the ratification policies of those states, each in its separate turn. And there is a credibility about the immediate needs and aspirations of particular groups, and the way they varied from place to place, that Beard's "interests" never quite possessed—or if they did, they had long since lost their hold on the modern mind.

And yet there are overtones in McDonald's work—for all its precise excellence, perhaps partly because of it—that have already succeeded in creating a new kind of "reality" spell. McDonald is very open-minded about all the manifold and complex and contradictory forces that converged upon the movement for a constitution. But somehow the ones he takes most seriously—the "real" forces behind the movement—were specific, particular, circumscribed, hard, and immediate. They were to be looked for mostly on the local level, because that is where one really finds things. A state—the largest permissible "reality" unit—was an agglomeration of specific, particular, immediate localities. There were interests to be served, political or economic, and they were *hard*. They were pursued rationally and without sentimentality; men came down where they did because their hard, immediate, specific interests brought them there. But are we prepared to say that the final result was just the sum—or extension—of these interests?

No doubt large enough numbers of people were convinced of the economic advantages they would gain under a new federal government that we may, thanks to Professor McDonald, account for a considerable measure of the support which the Constitution received. In places where there was a balance to tip, we have a much better idea of just how it happened. Still, Merrill Jensen pointed out some time ago that the economic situation was already somewhat on the mend by 1786. There were, moreover, certain powerful states such as Virginia and New York that might very well have thrived either as independent units or in coalitions with their immediate neighbors. And conditions in general could not have been so desperate that a national government was absolutely required for solving economic problems, let alone for staving off economic collapse. The steps actually taken were not the only ones possible; there were certainly alternatives, and it is hard to believe that they would all have led to disaster.

The new approach is extremely enlightening and useful. But has it yet taken on life? When will it fully engage the question of initiative and energy? How do we account for the dedication, the force and éclat, of Federalist leadership? When all is said and done, we do not exactly refer to the "interests" of a James Madison. We wonder, instead, about the terms in which he conceives of personal fulfillment, which is not at all the same. What animates him? The nationalist movement *did* have a mystique that somehow transfigured a substantial number of its leaders. What was it like, what were its origins?

[IV]

The work of Merrill Jensen, done in the 1930's and 1940's, has suffered somewhat in reputation due to the sweep and vehemence of the anti-Beardian reaction. Yet that work contains perceptions which ought not to be written off in the general shuffle. They derive not so much from the over-all Beardian traditions and influences amid which Jensen wrote, as from that particular sector of the subject which he marked off and preëmpted for his own. Simply by committing himself—alone among Beardians and non-Beardians—to presenting the Confederation era as a legitimate phase of American history, entitled to be taken seriously like any other and having a positive side as well as a negative one, he has forced upon us a peculiar point of view which, by the same token, yields its own special budget of insights. For example, Jensen has been profoundly impressed by the sheer force, determination, and drive of such nationalist leaders as Hamilton, Madison, Jay, Knox, and the Morrises. This energy, he feels, created the central problem of the Confederation and was the major cause of its collapse. He deplores this, seeing in the Confederation "democratic" virtues which it probably never had, finding in the Federalists an "aristocratic" character which in actual fact was as much or more to be found in the Anti-Federalists, smelling plots everywhere, and in general shaping his nomenclature to fit his own values and preferences. But if Professor Jensen seems to have called everything by the wrong name, it is well to remember that nomenclature is not everything. The important thing—what does ring true—is that this driving "nationalist" energy was, in all probability, central to the movement that gave the United States a new government.

The other side of the picture, which does not seem to have engaged

Jensen's mind half so much, was the peculiar sloth and inertia of the Anti-Federalists. Cecelia Kenyon, in a brilliant essay on these men,[3] has shown them as an amazingly reactionary lot. They were transfixed by the specter of power. It was not the power of the aristocracy that they feared, but power of any kind, democratic or otherwise, that they could not control for themselves. Their chief concern was to keep governments as limited and as closely tied to local interests as possible. Their minds could not embrace the concept of a national interest which they themselves might share and which could transcend their own parochial concerns. Republican government that went beyond the compass of state boundaries was something they could not imagine. Thus the chief difference between Federalists and Anti-Federalists had little to do with "democracy" (George Clinton and Patrick Henry were no more willing than Gouverneur Morris to trust the innate virtue of the people), but rather in the Federalists' conviction that there was such a thing as national interest and that a government could be established to care for it which was fully in keeping with republican principles. To the Federalists this was not only possible but absolutely necessary, if the nation was to avoid a future of political impotence, internal discord, and in the end foreign intervention. So far so good. But still, exactly how did such convictions get themselves generated?

Merrill Jensen has argued that the Federalists, by and large, were reluctant revolutionaries who had feared the consequences of a break with England and had joined the Revolution only when it was clear that independence was inevitable. The argument is plausible; few of the men most prominent later on as Federalists had been quite so hot for revolution in the very beginning as Patrick Henry and Samuel Adams. But this may not be altogether fair; Adams and Henry were already veteran political campaigners at the outbreak of hostilities, while the most vigorous of the future Federalists were still mere youngsters. The argument, indeed, could be turned entirely around: the source of Federalist, or nationalist, energy was not any "distaste" for the Revolution on these men's part, but rather their profound and growing involvement in it.

Much depends here on the way one pictures the Revolution. In the beginning it simply consisted of a number of state revolts loosely directed by the Continental Congress; and for many men, absorbed in their effort to preserve the independence of their own states, it never progressed much beyond that stage even in the face of invasion. But the Revolution had another aspect, one which developed with time and left a deep imprint on those connected with it, and this was its character as a continental war effort. If there is any one feature that most unites the future leading supporters of the Constitution, it was their close engagement with this continental aspect of the Revolution. A remarkably large number of these someday Federalists were in the Continental Army, served as diplomats or key administrative officers of the Confederation government, or, as members of Congress, played leading rôles on those committees primarily responsible for the conduct of the war.

Merrill Jensen has compiled two lists, with nine names in each, of the men whom he considers to have been the leading spirits of the Federalists and Anti-Federalists respectively. It would be well to have a good look at this sample. The Federalists—Jensen calls them "nationalists"—were Robert Morris, John Jay, James Wilson, Alexander Hamilton, Henry Knox, James Duane, George Washington, James Madison, and Gouverneur Morris. Washington, Knox, and Hamilton were deeply involved in Continental military affairs; Robert Morris was Superintendent of Finance; Jay was president of the Continental Congress and minister plenipotentiary to Spain (he would later be appointed Secretary for Foreign Affairs); Wilson, Duane, and Gouverneur Morris were members of Congress, all three being active members of the war committees. The Anti-Federalist group presents a very different picture. It consisted of Samuel Adams, Patrick Henry, Richard Henry Lee, George Clinton, James Warren, Samuel Bryan, George Bryan, George Mason, and Elbridge Gerry. Only three of these—Gerry, Lee, and Adams—served in Congress, and the latter two fought consistently against any effort to give Congress executive powers. Their constant preoccupation was state sovereignty rather than national efficiency. Henry and Clinton were active war governors, concerned primarily with state rather than national problems, while Warren, Mason, and the two Bryans were essentially state politicians.

The age difference between these two groups is especially striking. The Federalists were on the average ten to twelve years younger than the Anti-Federalists. At the outbreak of the Revolution George Washington, at 44, was the oldest of the lot; six were under 35 and four were in their twenties. Of the Anti-Federalists, only three were under 40 in 1776, and one of these, Samuel Bryan, the son of George Bryan, was a boy of 16.

This age differential takes on a special significance when it is related to the career profiles of the men concerned. Nearly half of the Federalist group—Gouverneur Morris, Madison, Hamilton, and Knox—quite literally saw their careers launched in the Revolution. The remaining five—Washington, Jay, Duane, Wilson, and Robert Morris—though established in public affairs beforehand, became nationally known after 1776 and the wide public recognition which they subsequently achieved came first and foremost through their identification with the continental war effort. All of them had been united in an experience, and had formed commitments, which dissolved provincial boundaries; they had come to full public maturity in a setting which enabled ambition, public service, leadership, and self-fulfillment to be conceived, for each in his way, with a grandeur of scope unknown to any previous generation. The careers of the Anti-Federalists, on the other hand, were not only state-centered but—aside from those of Clinton, Gerry, and the young Bryan—rested heavily on events that preceded rather than followed 1776.

As exemplars of nationalist energy, two names in Professor Jensen's sample that come most readily to mind are those of Madison and Hamilton. The story of each shows a wonderfully pure line of consistency. James Madison, of an influential Virginia family but with no apparent career plans prior to 1774, assumed his first public rôle as a member of the Orange County Revolutionary Committee, of which his father was chairman. As a delegate from Orange County he went to the Virginia convention in 1776 and served on the committee that drafted Virginia's new constitution and bill of rights. He served in the Virginia Assembly in 1776 and 1777 but failed of re-election partly because he refused to treat his constituents to whisky. (He obviously did not have the right talents for a state politician.) In recognition of Madison's services, however, the Assembly elected him to the Governor's Council, where he served from 1778 to 1780. Patrick Henry was then Governor; the two men did not get on well and in time became bitter political enemies. At this period Madison's primary concern was with supplying and equipping the Continental Army, a concern not shared to his satisfaction by enough of his colleagues. It was then, too, that he had his first experience with finance and the problems of paper money. He was elected to the Continental Congress in 1780, and as a member of the Southern Committee was constantly preoccupied with the military operations of Nathanael Greene. The inefficiency and impotence of Congress pained him unbearably. The Virginia Assembly took a strong stand against federal taxation which Madison ignored, joining Hamilton in the unsuccessful effort to persuade the states to accept the impost of 1783. From the day he entered politics up to that time, the energies of James Madison were involved in continental rather than state problems—problems of supply, enlistment, and finance—and at every point his chief difficulties came from state parochialism, selfishness, and lack of imagination. His nationalism was hardly accidental.

The career line of Alexander Hamilton, *mutatis mutandis*, is functionally interchangeable with that of James Madison. Ambitious, full of ability, but a young man of no family and no money, Hamilton arrived in New York from the provinces at the age of 17 and in only two years would be catapulted into a brilliant career by the Revolution. At 19 he became a highly effective pamphleteer while still a student at King's College, was captain of an artillery company at 21, serving with distinction in the New York and New Jersey campaigns, and in 1777 was invited to join Washington's staff as a lieutenant-colonel. He was quickly accepted by as brilliant and aristocratic a set of youths as could be found in the country. As a staff officer he became all too familiar with the endless difficulties of keeping the Continental Army in the field from 1777 to 1780. With his marriage to Elizabeth Schuyler in 1780 he was delightedly welcomed into one of New York's leading families, and his sage advice to his father-in-law and Robert Morris on matters of finance and paper money won him the reputation of a financial expert with men who knew an expert when they saw one. He had an independent command at Yorktown. He became Treasury representative in New York in 1781, was elected to Congress in 1782, and worked closely with Madison in the fruitless and discouraging effort to create a national revenue in the face of state particularism. In the summer of 1783 he quit in despair and went back to New York. Never once throughout all this period had Alexander Hamilton been involved in purely state affairs. His career had been a continental one, and as long as the state-centered George Clinton remained a power in New York, it was clear that this was the only kind that could have any real meaning for him. As with James Madison, Hamilton's nationalism was fully consistent with all the experience he had ever had in public life, experience whose sole meaning had been derived from the Revolution. The experience of the others—for instance that of John Jay and Henry Knox—had had much the same quality; Knox had moved from his bookstore to the command of Washington's artillery in little more than a year, while Jay's public career began with the agitation just prior to the Revolution and was a story of steady advancement in continental affairs from that time forward.

The logic of these careers, then, was in large measure tied to a chronology which did not apply in the same way to all the men in public life during the two decades of the 1770's and 1780's. A significant proportion of relative newcomers, with prospects initially modest, happened to have their careers opened up at a particular time and in such a way that their very public personalities came to be staked upon the national quality of the experience which had formed them. In a number of outstanding cases energy, initiative, talent, and ambition had combined with a conception of affairs which had grown immense in scope and promise by the close of the Revolution. There is every reason to think that a contraction of this scope, in the years that immediately followed, operated as a powerful challenge.

[v]

The stages through which the constitutional movement proceeded in the 1780's add up to a fascinating story in political management, marked by no little élan and dash. That movement, viewed in the light of the Federalist leaders' commitment to the Revolution, raises some nice points as to who were the "conservatives" and who were the "radicals." The spirit of unity generated by the struggle for independence had, in the eyes of those most closely involved in coördinating the effort, lapsed; provincial factions were reverting to the old provincial ways. The impulse to arrest disorder and to revive the flame of revolutionary unity may be pictured in "conservative" terms, but this becomes quite awkward when we look for terms with which to picture the other impulse, so different in nature: the urge to rest, to drift, to turn back the clock.

Various writers have said that the activities of the Federalists during this period had in them a clear element of the conspiratorial. Insofar as this refers to a strong line of political strategy, it correctly locates a key element in the movement. Yet without a growing base of popular dissatisfaction with the status quo, the Federalists could have skulked and plotted forever without accomplishing anything. We now know, thanks to recent scholarship, that numerous elements of the public were only too ripe for change. But the work of organizing such a sentiment was quite another matter; it took an immense effort of will just to get it off the ground. Though it would be wrong to think of the Constitution as something that had to be carried in the face of deep and basic popular opposition, it certainly required a series of brilliant maneuvers to escape the deadening clutch of particularism and inertia. An Anti-Federalist "no" could register on exactly the same plane as a Federalist "yes" while requiring a fraction of the energy. It was for this reason that the Federalists, even though they cannot be said to have circumvented the popular will, did have to use techniques which in their sustained drive, tactical mobility, and risk-taking smacked more than a little of the revolutionary.

By 1781, nearly five years of intimate experience with the war effort had already convinced such men as Washington, Madison, Hamilton, Duane, and Wilson that something had to be done to strengthen the Continental government, at least to the point of providing it with an independent income. The ratification of the Articles of Confederation early in the year (before Yorktown) seemed to offer a new chance, and several promising steps were taken at that time. Congress organized executive departments of war, foreign affairs, and finance to replace unwieldy and inefficient committees; Robert Morris was appointed Superintendent of Finance; and a 5 per cent impost was passed which Congress urged the states to accept.

By the fall of 1782, however, the surge for increased efficiency had lost the greater part of its momentum. Virginia had changed its mind about accepting the impost, Rhode Island having been flatly opposed all along, and it became apparent that as soon as the treaty with England (then being completed) was ratified, the sense of common purpose which the war had created would be drained of its urgency. At this point Hamilton and the Morrises, desperate for a solution, would have been quite willing to use the discontent of an unpaid army as a threat to coerce the states out of their obstructionism, had not Washington refused to lend himself to any such scheme. Madison and Hamilton thereupon joined forces in Congress to work out a revenue bill whose subsidiary benefits would be sufficiently diffuse to gain it general support among the states. But in the end the best that could be managed was a new plan for a 5 per cent impost, the revenues of which would be collected by state-appointed officials. Once more an appeal, drafted by Madison, was sent to the states urging them to accept the new impost, and Washington wrote a circular in support of it. The effort was in vain. The army, given one month's pay in cash and three in certificates, reluctantly dispersed, and the Confederation government, with no sanctions of coercion and no assured revenues, now reached a new level of impotence. In June, 1783, Alexander Hamilton, preparing to leave Congress to go back to private life, wrote in discouragement and humiliation to Nathanael Greene:

> There is so little disposition either in or out of Congress to give solidity to our national system that there is no motive to a man

to lose his time in the public service, who has no other view than to promote its welfare. Experience must convince us that our present establishments are Utopian before we shall be ready to part with them for better.

Whether or not the years between 1783 and 1786 should be viewed as a "critical period" depends very much on whose angle they are viewed from. Although it was a time of economic depression, the depressed conditions were not felt in all areas of economic life with the same force, nor were they nearly as damaging in some localities as in others; the interdependence of economic enterprise was not then what it would become later on, and a depression in Massachusetts did not necessarily imply one in Virginia, or even in New York. Moreover, there were definite signs of improvement by 1786. Nor can it necessarily be said that government on the state level lacked vitality. Most of the states were addressing their problems with energy and decision. There were problems everywhere, of course, many of them very grave, and in some cases (those of New Jersey and Connecticut in particular) solutions seemed almost beyond the individual state's resources. Yet it would be wrong, as Merrill Jensen points out, to assume that no solutions were possible within the framework which then existed. It is especially important to remember that when most people thought of "the government" they were not thinking of Congress at all, but of their own state legislature. For them, therefore, it was by no means self-evident that the period through which they were living was one of drift and governmental impotence.

But through the eyes of men who had come to view the states collectively as a "country" and to think in continental terms, things looked altogether different. From their viewpoint the Confederation was fast approaching the point of ruin. Fewer and fewer states were meeting their requisition payments, and Congress could not even pay its bills. The states refused to accept any impost which they themselves could not control, and even if all the rest accepted, the continued refusal of New York (which was not likely to change) would render any impost all but valueless. Local fears and jealousies blocked all efforts to establish uniform regulation of commerce, even though some such regulation seemed indispensable. A number of the states, New York in particular, openly ignored the peace treaty with England and passed discriminatory legislation against former Loyalists; consequently England, using as a pretext Congress' inability to enforce the treaty, refused to surrender the northwest posts. Morale in Congress was very low as members complained that lack of a quorum prevented them most of the time from transacting any business; even when a quorum was present, a few negative votes could block important legislation indefinitely. Any significant change, or any substantial increase in the power of Congress, required unanimous approval by the states, and as things then stood this had become very remote. Finally, major states such as New York and Virginia were simply paying less and less attention to Congress. The danger was not so much that of a split with the Confederation—Congress lacked the strength that would make any such "split" seem very urgent—but rather a policy of neglect that would just allow Congress to wither away from inactivity.

These were the conditions that set the stage for a fresh effort—the Annapolis Convention of 1786—to strengthen the continental government. The year before, Madison had arranged a conference between Maryland and Virginia for the regulation of commerce on the Potomac, and its success had led John Tyler and Madison to propose a measure in the Virginia Assembly that would give Congress power to regulate commerce throughout the Confederation. Though nothing came of it, a plan was devised in its place whereby the several states would be invited to take part in a convention to be held at Annapolis in September, 1786, for the purpose of discussing commercial problems. The snapping-point came when delegates from only five states appeared. The rest either distrusted one another's intentions (the northeastern states doubted the southerners' interest in commerce) or else suspected a trick to strengthen the Confederation government at their expense. It was apparent that no serious action could be taken at that time. But the dozen delegates who did come (Hamilton and Madison being in their forefront) were by definition those most concerned over the state of the national government, and they soon concluded that their only hope of saving it lay in some audacious plenary gesture. It was at this meeting, amid the mortification of still another failure, that they planned the Philadelphia Convention.

The revolutionary character of this move—though some writers have correctly perceived it—has been obscured both by the stateliness of historical retrospection and by certain legal peculiarities which allowed the proceeding to appear a good deal less subversive than it actually was. The "report" of the Annapolis meeting was actually a call, drafted by Hamilton and carefully edited by Madison, for delegates of all the states to meet in convention at Philadelphia the following May for the purpose of revising the Articles of Confederation. Congress itself transmitted the call, and in so doing was in effect being brought to by-pass its own constituted limits. On the one hand, any effort to change the

government within the rules laid down by the Articles would have required a unanimous approval which could never be obtained. But on
the other hand, the very helplessness which the several states had imposed upon the central government meant in practice that the states
were sovereign and could do anything they pleased with it. It was precisely this that the nationalists now prepared to exploit: this legal paradox had hitherto prevented the growth of strong loyalty to the existing
Confederation and could presently allow that same Confederation,
through the action of the states, to be undermined in the deceptive
odor of legitimacy. Thus the Beardian school of constitutional thought,
for all its errors of economic analysis and its transposing of ideological
semantics, has called attention to one element—the element of sub-
version—that is actually entitled to some consideration.

But if the movement had its plotters, balance requires us to add that
the "plot" now had a considerable measure of potential support, and
that the authority against which the plot was aimed had become little
more than a husk. Up to this time every nationalist move, including
the Annapolis Convention, has been easily blocked. But things were
now happening in such a way as to tip the balance and to offer the
nationalists for the first time a better-than-even chance of success. There
had been a marked improvement in business, but shippers in Boston,
New York, and Philadelphia were still in serious trouble. Retaliatory
measures against Great Britain through state legislation had proved
ineffective and useless; there was danger, at the same time, that local
manufacturing interests might be successful in pushing through high
state tariffs. In the second place, New York's refusal to reconsider a
national impost, except on terms that would have removed its effectiveness, cut the ground from under the moderates who had argued that,
given only a little time, everything could be worked out. This did not
leave much alternative to a major revision of the national government.
Then there were Rhode Island's difficulties with inflationary paper
money. Although that state's financial schemes actually made a certain
amount of sense, they provided the nationalists with wonderful propaganda and helped to create an image of parochial irresponsibility.

The most decisive event of all was Shays' Rebellion in the fall and
winter of 1786-1787. It was this uprising of hard-pressed rural debtors
in western Massachusetts that frightened moderate people everywhere
and convinced them of the need for drastic remedies against what
looked like anarchy. The important thing was not so much the facts of
the case as the impression which it created outside Massachusetts. The
Shaysites had no intention of destroying legitimate government or of

redistributing property, but the fact that large numbers of people could very well imagine them doing such things added a note of crisis which was all to the Federalists' advantage. Even the level-headed Washington was disturbed, and his apprehensions were played upon quite knowingly by Madison, Hamilton, and Knox in persuading him to attend the Philadelphia Convention. Actually the Federalists and the Shaysites had been driven to action by much the same conditions; in Massachusetts their concern with the depressed state of trade and the tax burden placed them for all practical purposes on the same side, and there they remained from first to last.

Once the balance had been tipped in enough states, to the point of a working consensus on the desirability of change, a second principle came into effect. Unless a state were absolutely opposed—as in the extreme case of Rhode Island—to any change in the Articles of Confederation, it was difficult to ignore the approaching Philadelphia Convention as had been done with the Annapolis Convention: the occasion was taking on too much importance. There was thus the danger, for such a state, of seeing significant decisions made without having its interests consulted. New York, with strong Anti-Federalist biases but also with a strong nationalist undercurrent, was not quite willing to boycott the convention. Governor Clinton's solution was to send as delegates two rigid state particularists, John Yates and Robert Lansing, along with the nationalist Hamilton, to make sure that Hamilton would not accomplish anything.

We have already seen that nineteenth century habits of thought created a ponderous array of stereotypes around the historic Philadelphia conclave of 1787. Twentieth century thought and scholarship, on the other hand, had the task of breaking free from them, and to have done so is a noteworthy achievement. And yet one must return to the point that stereotypes themselves require some form of explanation. The legend of a transcendent effort of statesmanship, issuing forth in a miraculously perfect instrument of government, emerges again and again despite all efforts either to conjure it out of existence or to give it some sort of rational linkage with mortal affairs. Why should the legend be so extraordinarily durable, and was there anything so special about the circumstances that set it on its way so unerringly and so soon?

The circumstances *were*, in fact, special; given a set of delegates of well over average ability, the Philadelphia meeting provides a really classic study in the sociology of intellect. Divine accident, though in some measure present in men's doings always, is not required as a part of this particular equation. The key conditions were all present in a pattern that virtually guaranteed for the meeting an optimum of effectiveness. A sufficient number of states were represented so that the delegates could, without strain, realistically picture themselves as thinking, acting, and making decisions in the name of the entire nation. They themselves, moreover, represented interests throughout the country that were diverse enough, and they had enough personal prestige at home, that they could act in the assurance of having their decisions treated at least with respectful attention. There had also been at work a remarkably effective process of self-selection, as to both men and states. Rhode Island ignored the convention, and as a result its position was not even considered there. There were leading state particularists such as Patrick Henry and Richard Henry Lee who were elected as delegates but refused to serve. The Anti-Federalist position, indeed, was hardly represented at all, and the few men who did represent it had surprisingly little to say. Yates and Lansing simply left before the convention was over. Thus a group already predisposed in a national direction could proceed unhampered by the friction of basic opposition in its midst.

This made it possible for the delegates to "try on" various alternatives without having to remain accountable for everything they said. At the same time, being relieved from all outside pressures meant that the only way a man could expect to make a real difference in the convention's deliberations was to reach, through main persuasion, other men of considerable ability and experience. Participants and audience were therefore one, and this in itself imposed standards of debate which were quite exacting. In such a setting the best minds in the convention were accorded an authority which they would not have had in political debates aimed at an indiscriminate public.

Thus the elements of secrecy, the general inclination for a national government, and the process whereby the delegates came to terms with their colleagues—appreciating their requirements and adjusting to their interests—all combined to produce a growing *esprit de corps*. As initial agreements were worked out, it became exceedingly difficult for the Philadelphia delegates not to grow more and more committed to the product of their joint efforts. Indeed, this was in all likelihood the key mechanism, more important than any other in explaining not only the peculiar genius of the main compromises but also the general fitness of the document as a whole. That is, a group of two or more intelligent men who are subject to no cross-pressures and whose principal commitment is to the success of an idea, are perfectly capable—as in our scientific communities of today—of performing what appear to be prodigies of intellect. Moving, as it were, in the same direction with a specific purpose, they can function at maximum efficiency. It was this that the historians of the nineteenth century did in their way see, and celebrated with sweeping rhetorical flourishes, when they took for granted that if an occasion of this sort could not call forth the highest level of statesmanship available, then it was impossible to imagine another that could.

Once the Philadelphia Convention had been allowed to meet and the delegates had managed, after more than three months of work, to hammer out a document that the great majority of them could sign, the political position of the Federalists changed dramatically. Despite the major battles still impending, for practical purposes they now had the initiative. The principal weapon of the Anti-Federalists—inertia— had greatly declined in effectiveness, for with the new program in motion it was no longer enough simply to argue that a new federal government was unnecessary. They would have to take positive steps in blocking it; they would have to arouse the people and convince them that the Constitution represented a positive danger.

Moreover, the Federalists had set the terms of ratification in such a way as to give the maximum advantage to energy and purpose; the key choices, this time, had been so aranged that they would fall right. Only nine states had to ratify before the Constitution would go into effect. Not only would this rule out the possibility of one or two states holding up the entire effort, but it meant that the Confederation would be automatically destroyed as an alternative before the difficult battles in New York and Virginia had to be faced. (By then, Patrick Henry in Virginia would have nothing but a vague alliance with North Carolina to offer as a counter-choice.) Besides, there was good reason to believe that at least four or five states, and possibly as many as seven, could be counted as safe, which meant that serious fighting in the first phase would be limited to two or three states. And finally, conditions were so set that the "snowball" principle would at each successive point favor the Federalists.

As for the actual process of acceptance, ratification would be done through state conventions elected for the purpose. Not only would this circumvent the vested interests of the legislatures and the ruling coteries that frequented the state capitals, but it gave the Federalists two separate chances to make their case—once to the people and once to the conventions. If the elected delegates were not initially disposed to do the desired thing, there was still a chance, after the convention met, of persuading them. Due partly to the hampering factor of transportation and distance, delegates had to have considerable leeway of choice and what amounted to quasi-plenipotentiary powers. Thus there could be no such thing as a fully "instructed" delegation, and members might meanwhile remain susceptible to argument and conversion. The convention device, moreover, enabled the Federalists to run as delegates men who would not normally take part in state politics.

The revolutionary verve and ardor of the Federalists, their resources of will and energy, their willingness to scheme tirelessly, campaign everywhere, and sweat and agonize over every vote meant in effect that despite all the hairbreadth squeezes and rigors of the struggle, the Anti-Federalists would lose every crucial test. There was, to be sure, an Anti-Federalist effort. But with no program, no really viable commitments, and little purposeful organization, the Anti-Federalists somehow always managed to move too late and with too little. They would sit and watch their great stronghold, New York, being snatched away from them despite a two-to-one Anti-Federalists majority in a convention presided over by their own chief, George Clinton. To them, the New York Federalists must have seemed possessed of the devil. The Federalists' convention men included Alexander Hamilton, James Duane, John Jay, and Robert Livingston—who knew, as did everyone else, that the new government was doomed unless Virginia and New York joined it. They insisted on debating the Constitution section by section instead of as a whole, which meant that they could out-argue the Anti-Federalists on every substantive issue and meanwhile delay the vote until New Hampshire and Virginia had had a chance to ratify. (Madison and Hamilton had a horse relay system in readiness to rush the Virginia news northward as quickly as possible.) By the time the New York convention was ready to act, ten others had ratified, and at the final moment Hamilton and his allies spread the chilling rumor that New York City was about to secede from the state. The Anti-Federalists, who had had enough, directed a chosen number of their delegates to cross over, and solemnly capitulated.

In the end, of course, everyone "crossed over." The speed with which this occurred once the continental revolutionists had made their point, and the ease with which the Constitution so soon became an object of universal veneration, still stands as one of the minor marvels of American history. But the document did contain certain implications, of a quasi-philosophical nature, that make the reasons for this ready consensus not so very difficult to find. It established a national government whose basic outlines were sufficiently congenial to the underlying commitments of the whole culture—republicanism and capitalism—that the likelihood of its being the subject of a true ideological clash was never very real. That the Constitution should mount guard over the rights of property—"realty," "personalty," or any other kind—was questioned by nobody. There had certainly been a struggle, a long and exhausting one, but we should not be deceived as to its nature. It was not fought on economic grounds; it was not a matter of ideology; it was not, in the fullest and most fundamental sense, even a struggle between nationalism and localism. The key struggle was between inertia and energy; with inertia overcome, everything changed.

There were, of course, lingering objections and misgivings; many of the problems involved had been genuinely puzzling and difficult; and there remained doubters who had to be converted. But then the perfect bridge whereby all could become Federalists within a year was the addition of a Bill of Rights. After the French Revolution, anti-constitutionalism in France would be a burning issue for generations; in America, an anti-constitutional party was undreamed of after 1789. With the Bill of Rights, the remaining opponents of the new system could say that, ever watchful of tyranny, they had now got what they wanted. Moreover, the Young Men of the Revolution might at last imagine, after a dozen years of anxiety, that *their* Revolution had been a success.

NOTES

1. Richard B. Morris has pointed out that in Henry Dawson there was at least one exception to this universal veneration for the Constitution. Dawson in 1871 published an article wherein he deplored the ancestor-worship which already wreathed the Fathers and their work. See Morris, "The Confederation and the American Historian," *William and Mary Quarterly*, XIII, 3rd ser. (April 1956), pp. 139-56; Dawson, "The Motley Letter," *Historical Magazine*, IX, 2nd ser. (March 1871), pp. 157 *et seq.*
2. Not a direct quotation but a summary of four of the thirteen conclusions.
3. "Men of Little Faith: The Anti-Federalists on the Nature of Representative Government," *William and Mary Quarterly*, XII, 2rd ser. (January 1955), pp. 3-43.

RECENT STUDIES

Jackson Turner Main, *The Anti-Federalists, Critics of the Constitution, 1781-1788* (Chapel Hill: University of North Carolina Press, 1961).

Linda Grant De Pauw, *The Eleventh Pillar: New York State and the Federal Constitution* (Ithaca: Cornell University Press, 1966).

Broadus Mitchell, *Alexander Hamilton, The National Adventure 1788-1804* (New York: The Macmillan Company, 1962).

Adrienne Koch, *Madison's "Advice to My Country"* (Princeton: Princeton University Press, 1965).

Dumas Malone, *Jefferson and the Ordeal of Liberty* (Boston: Little, Brown and Co., 1962).

David Hackett Fischer, *The Revolution of American Conservatism: The Federalist Party in the Era of Jeffersonian Democracy* (New York: Harper & Row, 1965).

VI

Andrew Jackson versus the Historians

CHARLES SELLERS

Andrew Jackson's masterful personality was enough by itself to make him one of the most controversial figures ever to stride across the American stage. "It can hardly be expected that the present generation will do justice to the character of Jackson," complained the compiler of his funeral eulogies in 1846, for "his opponents have ever been most bitter enemies, and his friends almost his worshippers."[1] And when James Parton sat down fifteen years later to attempt the first impartial biography of Old Hickory, he despairingly concluded from the mountain of conflicting sources before him that his subject "was a patriot and a traitor. He was one of the greatest of generals, and wholly ignorant of the art of war. A writer brilliant, elegant, eloquent, without being able to compose a correct sentence, or spell words of four syllables. The first of statesmen, he never devised, he never framed a measure. He was the most candid of men, and was capable of the profoundest dissimulation. A most law-defying, law-obeying citizen. A stickler for discipline, he never hesitated to disobey his superior. A democratic autocrat. An urbane savage. An atrocious saint."[2]

Such radical opposites could not be reconciled simply by splitting the difference; Parton and all who followed him on this difficult terrain

From *The Mississippi Valley Historical Review*, XLIV (March 1958), pp. 615-34. Reprinted with annotated notes by permission.

have been forced pretty substantially either into the Jackson camp or into the camp of Jackson's enemies. Indeed, Parton's lament could almost stand today as the conclusion to a review of Jacksonian historiography.

The reasons for such continuing disagreement run far deeper than the individual characteristics of any historical personality. Andrew Jackson was intimately identified with the full flowering of American democracy; and as long as democracy remains pre-eminently the distinguishing feature of our society, the period and symbol of its triumph will remain controversial.

While American democracy emerged victorious on the plane of political ideology around 1776 or 1800, and on the plane of political practice around 1828, it did not achieve respectability in American historiography (for all George Bancroft's efforts) until about 1900. From the Jacksonian era to the end of the nineteenth century the writing of American history was dominated, as Charles H. Peck observed in 1899, by men "who were educated under the sway of the Whiggish culture of the country."[3] This "Whig" school of Jacksonian historiography included the first two important Jackson biographers, James Parton and William Graham Sumner; the authors of the first two detailed American histories extending to the Civil War, Hermann E. von Holst and James Schouler; and Moisei Ostrogorski, author of the enormously influential study of *Democracy and the Organization of Political Parties*.

These writers, in effect, stamped the partisan fulminations of Jackson's political enemies with the cachet of scholarly authority. If Henry Clay had pronounced Old Hickory "ignorant, passionate, hypocritical, corrupt, and easily swayed by the base men who surround him," von Holst could similarly pronounce him an "arrogant general" whose "mind was as untrained as his passions were unbridled" and who was "like wax in skillful hands." Sumner thought him a "barbarian" who "acted from spite, pique, instinct, prejudice or emotion"; Schouler flatly declared him "illiterate"; Ostrogorski expatiated on his "autocratic policy"; and Parton, despite a grudging admiration for some aspects of Jackson's character, lamented "the elevation to the presidency of a man whose ignorance, whose good intentions, and whose passions combined to render him, of all conceivable human beings, the most unfit for the office."[4]

Yet it was not fundamentally Jackson's personality that turned the Whig historians against him, nor was it the general policies he pursued as president. These writers were all liberals of the nineteenth-century stripe and actually approved the laissez-faire tendencies of most of the

Jacksonian measures. Sumner was outraged that Jackson had "unjustly, passionately, ignorantly, and without regard to truth assailed a great and valuable financial institution," for the Yale economist was a stout champion of sound money and vested interests. But Sumner was an even more strenuous champion of Herbert Spencer's doctrine of unfettered individual enterprise, and his philosophy compelled him to admit that "it came in Jackson's way to do some good, to check some bad tendencies and to strengthen some good ones." Parton went further in approval of Jackson's policies, defending not only the objectives but also the aggressive tactics of the Jacksonian assault on the national bank. An admirer of Jefferson, Parton was also one of the earliest American Spencerians, and he considered Jackson an instinctive disciple of both his ideological heroes.[5] And all the Whig historians were ardent nationalists and applauded Jackson's bold stand against the South Carolina nullifiers.

How, then, could Parton say that "notwithstanding the good done by General Jackson during his presidency, his election to power was a mistake"? How could von Holst speak of "the frightful influence . . . which he exercised during the eight years of his presidency"? A clue may be found in the abhorrence with which the Whig historians uniformly treated Jackson's policy of removing his political enemies from federal office and replacing them with his friends. Indeed, for these scholarly mugwumps, the institution of the spoils system on a large scale became almost the distinguishing feature of Jackson's administration. "If all his other public acts had been perfectly wise and right," said Parton, "this single feature of his administration would suffice to render it deplorable."[6]

Yet the spoils system was only a symptom of the real disease—the new system of democratic politics that both Jackson and the spoils system symbolized. "Popular sovereignty," said von Holst, would be "a dreadful condition of things"; and Schouler lamented the fact that, all too often, "the great body of our American democracy . . . slips back unconsciously into the mire whence the poverty-stricken millions emerge and falls too easy a prey to vice and ignorance." Ostrogorski got to the heart of the Whig historians' case against Jacksonian Democracy when he complained that it "excluded men of sterling worth and high principles from public life." Von Holst similarly argued that since Jackson "the people have begun to exchange the leadership of a small number of statesmen and politicians of a higher order for the rule of an ever increasing crowd of politicians of high and low degree, down even to the pothouse politician and the common thief, in the protecting mantle of demagogism." And as a result, said Parton, "the public affairs of the United States have been conducted with a stupidity which has excited the wonder of mankind."[7]

It is important to remember that the Whig historians all came from eastern or European middle-class or upper-middle-class families with traditions of education, prestige, and public service, the kind of families that had claimed social and political leadership as their natural right during the early days of the republic. By the time these men began to write the history of Jacksonian Democracy, however, their kind had been largely ousted from political leadership by the professional politicians and new-style parties that had arisen as the institutional embodiments of the Jacksonian democratic revolution. They were writing, moreover, in the era of Grantism in national politics and Tweedism in local politics, when the least lovely aspects of democracy were most conspicuous. Whig historiography, indeed, was a facet of "patrician liberalism," the movement that sought to restore the pristine purity of American politics by destroying the spoils system, breaking the bosses' power, ending the unholy alliance between government and business, and placing gentlemen in public office. What could be more natural, then, than for the Whig historians to find in Jacksonian Democracy the origin of the features of American life they most deplored? These scholars displayed, in short, the class bias of an elite displaced from leadership by a vulgar and frequently corrupt democracy.

By the 1890's patrician liberalism was giving way to the broader movement which under the name Progressivism was soon to effect a profound shift in the mood and direction of American life. A corresponding shift in the mood of American historiography was signaled in 1893, when the young Wisconsin historian, Frederick Jackson Turner, read his famous paper emphasizing "The Significance of the Frontier in American History." Yet Turner's real significance lies less in his controversial frontier thesis than in his influence as leader of the massive shift of American historiography to a pro-democratic orientation. A whole new generation of young historians—men like Woodrow Wilson, William E. Dodd, John Spencer Bassett, Charles A. Beard, and Vernon L. Parrington—stood ready to echo Turner's vibrantly sympathetic description of democracy emerging "stark and strong and full of life, from the American forest."[8]

Two facts should be especially noted about these young scholars who were to transform the writing of American history. One is that nearly all of them came from rural or small-town backgrounds in the West or South, and this in itself brought a new point of view into a field previously dominated by the urban Northeast. The second significant fact is that though they came from substantial middle-class families, they lived in a period when middle-class Americans, and particularly middle-class intellectuals, were being swept into the current of reform. The Progressive campaign to preserve the traditional values of American society in the threatening new contest of industrialism and urbanism was made possible by a revival of faith in the possibilities of the whole people, and the Progressives characteristically devoted much of their energy to making the democratic process work more effectively. Small wonder, then, that the young scholars of the Progressive era responded enthusiastically to Turner's reaffirmation of the long-tarnished democratic faith of an earlier day.

Andrew Jackson and his Democracy were naturally among the leading beneficiaries of the new pro-democratic orientation of American historiography. Out of the "frontier democratic society" of the West, said Turner, "where the freedom and abundance of land in the great Valley opened a refuge to the oppressed in all regions, came the Jacksonian democracy which governed the nation after the downfall of the party of John Quincy Adams." This Jacksonian Democracy was "strong in the faith of the intrinsic excellence of the common man, and in his capacity to share in government."[9]

Turner's contemporaries quickly took up the refrain. John W. Burgess enthusiastically acclaimed Jackson as "the noblest Roman of them all"; while William E. Dodd thought of the "brave and generous" Old Hickory as "a second Jefferson," whose mission it was "to arouse the people to a sense of their responsibility." In the eyes of that rather romantic nationalist, Woodrow Wilson, Jackson represented the "forces of health" that were to "nationalize the government." Though Jackson's policies "temporarily ruined the business of the country" and "permanently demoralized our politics," Wilson nevertheless regarded his election as "a great democratic upheaval," which "did the incalculable good of giving to the national spirit its first self-reliant expression of resolution and of consentaneous power."[10]

The earliest major product of the democratic school of Jacksonian historiography was John Spencer Bassett's *Life of Andrew Jackson*, published in 1911. Bassett was the first scholar since Parton to work thoroughly through the extant Jacksonian sources, which now seemed to reveal "a man who was great, spite of many limitations." Bassett was generally sympathetic to Jackson's purposes and policies, but he was not uncritical, and his final chapter remains the most successful attempt to appraise Jackson's baffling character. Jackson had plenty of shortcomings—"lack of education, his crude judgments in many affairs, his occasional outbreaks of passion, his habitual hatred of those enemies with whom he had not made friends for party purposes, and his crude ideas of some political policies"—yet, for Bassett, "all lose some of their infelicity in the face of his brave, frank, masterly leadership of the democratic movement which then established itself in our life. . . . Few American Presidents have better lived up to the demands of the movement which brought them into power."[11]

The transitional indecision of a few scholars was best represented by William MacDonald, whose volume on the Jackson period for the American Nation Series fell squarely between the Whig and Democratic positions. Though MacDonald described Jackson as "an untrained, self-willed, passionate frontier soldier," he admonished his readers that "It was as idle then as it is now to bemoan" his election, for "this predominance of the masses" is "the price of popular government." It almost seems that MacDonald was unconsciously making the same accommodation to democracy as a Whig historian in 1906 that Daniel Webster had made as a Whig politician in 1840.[12]

But most American historians embraced the democratic orientation with only slight hesitation, and even the Spencerians capitulated to Jackson. The anti-democratic Whiggery that had made Parton and Sumner so critical of Old Hickory, despite their sympathy for his laissez-faire policies, had little effect on their fellow Spencerian, John Fiske. Though Fiske boggled a bit at the spoils system, he concluded that Jackson's "sounder instincts prompted him to a course of action quite in harmony with the highest political philosophy," as contained in the works of Herbert Spencer. For Jackson had checked "a tendency toward the mollycoddling, old granny theory of government, according to which the ruling powers are to take care of the people, build their roads for them, do their banking for them, rob Peter to pay Paul for carrying on a losing business, and tinker and bemuddle things generally."[13]

What a dramatic shift in interpretation the democratic orientation could effect was demonstrated even more strikingly when Carl Russell Fish, writing in 1904, almost made a Jacksonian virtue of the spoils system in his study of *The Civil Service and the Patronage*. By careful scholarship Fish showed that the civil service had needed some ventilation in 1829, and that the irresistible pressures for the spoils system must have triumphed regardless of who was president. But it was Fish's democratic frame of reference rather than his research that produced his most startling conclusions. "The spoils system paid for the party organization . . . which established a 'government of the people' in the United States in 1829," he declared, and in so doing, "it served a purpose that could probably have been performed in no other way, and that was fully worth the cost."[14]

While the new democratic orientation was winning converts, another influence was finally making itself felt in Jacksonian historiography: the cult of objectivity. In 1903 Ralph C. H. Catterall produced a study of the Second Bank of the United States that was a masterpiece. Though Catterall's personal sympathies were unquestionably Whiggish—he regretted, for example, that the influence of "enlightened business men" and other members of "the intelligent class" on public affairs "has always been inconsiderable, partly because they are not interested in politics, partly because they are themselves objects of suspicion to the democratic masses"—he nevertheless granted Jackson's complete sincerity and reported his position fully and fairly.[15]

The desire for objectivity had less fortunate results in the case of John Bach McMaster, whose habits of quoting copiously from the contemporary arguments on both sides of every question, while scrupulously withholding his own judgments and interpretations, made an arid waste of his multi-volume history. Yet the reader can discern that by 1900, when he reached the Jackson period, he had gone over to the democratic camp, for he described in great detail the democratic reform movements of the era, he relieved Jackson from responsibility for the spoils system, and he acclaimed Old Hickory's victory of 1828, with unwonted enthusiasm, as "indeed a great uprising of the people, a triumph of democracy, another political revolution the like of which the country has not seen since 1800."[16]

The pro-democratic orientation that transformed Jacksonian historiography at the turn of the century has continued to be the dominant influence on writings about the Jackson period ever since. It permeated Marquis James's impressive Jackson biography of the 1930's, as well as the extensive studies of the Jackson period by Claude G. Bowers in the 1920's and Arthur M. Schlesinger, Jr., in the 1940's. More significantly, it has controlled the interpretations of Jacksonian Democracy to be found in nearly all the general works on American history written in the twentieth century, from the widely influential accounts of Vernon L. Parrington and Charles and Mary Beard to the most obscure textbooks. Political scientists have joined in the chorus of approval, with such writers as John W. Burgess, Wilfred E. Binkley, and Leonard D. White praising Jackson and his followers for strengthening the presidency and developing the new-style political party as an indispensable democratic institution.[17]

Despite this widespread acceptance, the twentieth-century democratic school of Jacksonian historiography has attained neither the unchallenged hegemony nor the unity of outlook that the Whig school enjoyed in the nineteenth century. For one thing, the Whig interpretation would not play dead.[18] Most embarrassing to the democratic view of Andrew Jackson has been the interpretation of Old Hickory's role in early Tennessee politics advanced by Thomas P. Abernethy. Abernethy presents Jackson as a frontier nabob who took sides against the democratic movement in his own state. Actually, this leader of the democratic movement in national politics was a demagogic aristocrat, says Abernethy, an "opportunist" for whom "Democracy was good talk with which to win the favor of the people and thereby accomplish ulterior objectives."[19]

The Whig interpretation has received its fullest modern application to the Jackson movement as a whole in Charles M. Wiltse's impressive biography of Calhoun. Wiltse sees the reality of Jacksonian politics as a selfish struggle for office and federal subsidy. Jackson was in many respects "a frontier bully," and "in a growing, expanding, gambling, ebullient country like the United States of the 1820's and 30's, the frontier bully was a national hero."[20]

Yet the democratic historians have suffered less from these dissenting views than from their own inability to make clear just what they mean by "democracy." The men of Turner's generation who originated democratic historiography conceived of the democratic process in a characteristically middle-class, Progressive way. Hating monopoly and plutocracy, they rejoiced in the egalitarian, anti-monopolistic tradition that stemmed from Jacksonian Democracy. But hating the class consciousness of Populism and Socialism as much or more, they shrank from any interpretation of the American past that smacked of social conflict. Their enthusiasm for democracy rested on an essentially romantic faith in the whole people, whom they saw as an undifferentiated mass, virtually free of inequalities and conflicts. Democracy, in the view which informed both Progressive politics and Turnerean historiography, was the process by which the whole people's fundamentally virtuous impulses were translated into public policy.

Thus Turner was careful to assert that "classes and inequalities of fortune played little part" in frontier democracy. It "did not demand equality of condition," he declared, for it believed that the "self-made man had a right to his success in the free competition which western life afforded." Mere inequality of condition was a negligible considera- tion to Turner, alongside the more spiritual brand of equality that the frontier process had guaranteed. "Mere success in the game . . . gave to the successful ones no right to look down upon their neighbors," he insisted, and he clung passionately to his conviction that the abundance of free land made it impossible for "the successful ones . . . to harden their triumphs into the rule of a privileged class."[21]

However plausible this view of democracy may have been for the early nineteenth century, the free land was undeniably gone by Turner's day, while inequality of condition had become so gross that its danger to democracy could no longer be ignored. The successful ones now threatened either to harden their triumphs into the rule of a privileged class, or to provoke a bitter class struggle, and both possibilities dis- turbed middle-class Americans. It was this apparent crisis of democracy that produced both the Progressive movement and the democratic school of historians.

Turner mirrored one mood of his generation in his desperate efforts to believe that there was no crisis, that the great monopolists them- selves were products of the democratic West and, by a quasi-Lamarck- ian inheritance of acquired characteristics "still profess its principles."[22] But the more typical response of the democratic historians was to rely upon a revival of democracy, a movement of the whole people; and they were in effect supplying a historical tradition for Progressivism when they described the democratic upheaval of Jackson's day as an amorphous force, arising with no specific cause or particular pro- gram from the creative western forest, and spreading over the East by contagion.

The democratic historians' aversion to social conflict was a major factor in causing them to supplement the frontier thesis with a heavy emphasis on sectionalism. Conflict was simply too obvious in the Jack- son era to be ignored, but Turner and his followers muted the dis- cordant note of class struggle by transposing it into conflict between distinct geographical sections. Thus, alongside the Jacksonian rise of the whole people, we find in their writings a three-way contest among the democratic West (epitomized by Jackson), the capitalist North- east, and the planting and increasingly aristocratic South. Beard and Parrington, to be sure, made social conflict central to their interpreta- tions. But even their dramas of struggle against privileged minorities were grounded on the same Rousseauistic concept of the whole people as the conventional democratic interpretation; and more often than not they, too, fell back upon oversimplified sectional categories.

This vague conception of democracy remained prevalent in Jacksonian historiography until 1945, when Arthur M. Schlesinger, Jr., published *The Age of Jackson*. Schlesinger's thesis was that "more can be understood about Jacksonian democracy if it is regarded as a problem not of sections but of classes." Defining the central theme of American political history to be the efforts "on the part of the other sections of society to restrain the power of the business community," he interpreted Jacksonian Democracy as a movement "to control the power of the capitalistic groups, mainly Eastern, for the benefit of noncapitalist groups, farmers and laboring men, East, West, and South." Schlesinger traced the movement to the economic hardships of the 1820's, and he saw the East and the workingmen as playing the crucial roles in the Jacksonian coalition.[22]

Schlesinger not only provided a sharper definition of the democratic movement and a clearer explanation of its origins, but he also stirred up a warm debate which prompted other historians to offer alternative definitions. The attack on *The Age of Jackson* was launched by a scholarly official of the Federal Reserve Board, Bray Hammond, who was irritated in the first instance by Schlesinger's failure to appreciate the central banking functions that the national bank had exercised so beneficially before it was attacked by Jackson. Emphasizing the role of the state banks in fomenting the Jacksonion assault on the national bank, Hammond insisted that the real animus of Jacksonian Democracy was not against business but against the exclusion of new entrepreneurs from business opportunities. Schlesinger "represents the age of Jackson as one of triumphant liberalism," he complained, "when it was as much or more an age of triumphant exploitation."[23]

Hammond was quickly joined in his criticism of Schlesinger by a group of historians at Columbia University. Joseph Dorfman argued that the "labor" spokesmen whom Schlesinger had emphasized did not represent a genuine labor movement, and that their views were far from anti-business.[24] Richard B. Morris contended that Jackson was anti-labor rather than pro-labor,[25] while several of Morris' students attempted, with questionable success, to demonstrate that workingmen did not vote for Jackson.[26]

These historians showed a considerable affinity for the Whig view of Jackson personally, especially in the version advanced by Thomas P. Abernethy. Their own interpretation of the Jackson movement was expressed best, perhaps, by Richard Hofstadter, who described it as "a phase in the expansion of liberated capitalism," and as "closely linked to the ambitions of the small capitalist."[27]

Thus the recent historiography of Jacksonian Democracy has been dominated by the debate over Schlesinger's "class-conflict" or "labor" thesis on the one hand and the "entrepreneurial" thesis put forward by Schlesinger's critics on the other. Schlesinger and his supporters picture the democratic impulse largely as a movement of protest against the unfair privileges claimed by an exploitative business elite, while the Columbia historians defend the diametrically opposed view that the democratic movement was itself strongly capitalist in spirit and objected only to any limitation on free entry into the game of capitalist exploitation.

Yet closer examination reveals some significant affinities between the two interpretations. They share, for one thing, a common origin. It was the socialist publicist Algie M. Simons who staked the first effective claim of real significance for Jacksonian labor. Using data first turned up by John B. McMaster, Simons argued that the labor movement not only was an important part of the democratic upsurge of Jackson's day, but "measured by the impress it left, was the most important event in American history."[28]

After John R. Commons and his associates published their monumental *Documentary History of American Industrial Society*, labor's importance in the Jackson era could no longer be ignored. Even Turner gave the eastern workingmen a minor place in the Jackson movement, and a few scholars went further. In 1913 a textbook writer, Willis Mason West, assigned labor equal weight with the West and asserted that for some years the Democratic party "remained in large degree a workingmen's party." Ten years later Arthur M. Schlesinger, Sr., used West's treatment as the basis for an essay on Jacksonian Democracy that dealt briefly with many of the points subsequently developed in the younger Schlesinger's *Age of Jackson*.[29]

Labor historians were following the same line, but general American historians remained largely unshaken in their devotion to the frontier-sectional interpretation set by Turner. It is rather remarkable, in fact, that the growing vogue of economic interpretation did not produce a greater emphasis on economic class interests in the Jackson period. Even Charles and Mary Beard treated the Jacksonian conflicts as mainly sectional in their *Rise of American Civilization*, an approach which belied their chapter title, "Jacksonian Democracy—A Triumphant Farmer-Labor Party," as well as their over-all interpretation of American history.[30]

The entrepreneurial thesis, like the labor thesis, found its first full statement in the socialist tracts of Algie Simons, where it appeared as a gloss on Turner's frontier thesis. "The 'frontier' which is spoken of as being in the ascendent under Jackson was distinctly individualistic and small capitalistic in its instincts, rather than proletarian," Simons declared. Jacksonian Democracy was "neither frontier, nor wageworking, or even purely capitalist in its mental make-up." It was the "democracy of expectant capitalists." Throughout Simons' account there runs a note of Marxian distaste for this greedy democracy of "petit bourgeois," an attitude which, at one remove from its Marxian roots, may be detected in later expositions of the entrepreneurial thesis.[31]

The striking fact that both the labor thesis and the entrepreneurial thesis found their first full development in Simons invites a further examination of their affinities. Both, it is clear, are indebted to Marxian analysis and represent a "realistic" approach to history, the one maintaining a detached, analytical attitude, which occasionally betrays an implicit distaste for the middle-class norms of American democratic capitalism, and the other viewing democratic liberalism as being perennially sustained and advanced by antibusiness elements in American society, class-conscious and organized for social and political struggle. This "realism" explains the hostility of both to the diffuse Turnerean conception of democracy, but it does not account for the fact that writers of both schools are consistently critical of agrarian elements and seek to deemphasize their importance in our history. These latter facts, when correlated with the personal origins and sympathies of the writers involved, suggest the belated emergence of the city as a major influence on American historical scholarship.

Thus we are reminded once again of the profound influence of frames of reference. Indeed the historians of Jacksonian Democracy might best be classified by the social and intellectual environments that seem so largely to control their interpretations. In place of the simple categories of a Whig school and a democratic school, we might distinguish three main groups.

First, a "patrician" school of historians, drawn from eastern or European upper-middle-class backgrounds, dominated Jacksonian historiography until the end of the nineteenth century. Resenting the vulgar democracy and the equally vulgar plutocracy that were displacing their kind of social and intellectual elite from leadership, these men spoke for the conservative, semi-aristocratic, mugwumpish liberalism of the Gilded Age.

Around 1900 the patrician historians were displaced by an "agrarian democratic" school, drawn from western and southern middle-class backgrounds and reflecting the revival of old-fashioned democratic dogmas in the Progressive era. Fearful of both class antagonism and monopoly capitalism, these men effected a reorientation of American historiography around the concept of an agrarian-derived democracy of the whole people.

Finally, in recent years, we have seen the emergence of a school of "urban" scholars, drawn from eastern cities, who find the agrarian democratic theme naïve or otherwise unsatisfactory. Most of these urban historians came to maturity during the New Deal years, and they often manifest a greater sympathy for industrial labor than for farmers and middle-class businessmen. Their stance seems to be that of self-conscious intellectuals and critics, expressing through their detached, "scientific," faintly ironic, "realistic" analysis an alienation from the middle-class mainstream of American life that is reminiscent of the patrician school. The entrepreneurial thesis is the most characteristic product of this group, though the labor thesis grows out of many of the same influences.

Actually, Arthur M. Schlesinger, Jr., the leading proponent of the labor thesis, emphasizes entrepreneurial elements in Jacksonian Democracy far more than his critics appear to realize; indeed, he sees the western Jacksonians as almost wholly entrepreneurial in spirit. Basically, however, his *Age of Jackson* seems to represent a marriage of the agrarian democratic and the urban points of view, in much the same way that Simons seemed to mix Populism with Marxism. Schlesinger's semi-Marxist "realism" is solidly urban, but the democratic idealism with which he combines it is clearly in the tradition of Turner.

But what of Old Hickory himself and Jacksonian Democracy? What are we to conclude when, after a century of scholarship, historians still squarely contradict each other about the essential nature of both the man and the movement? Has the frame of reference cut us off from the past as it actually was? Do historical writings tell us more about their authors than they do about their purported subjects?

Before accepting these disheartening conclusions, it may be well to remind ourselves that an interpretation is not necessarily wrong merely because a writer seems to have been impelled toward that interpretation by a particular frame of reference. The conclusions of honest men, working within limits set by an abundance of reliable and relatively unmalleable evidence, must have some basis in the reality of the past they seek to interpret. This may suggest that each school of Jacksonian historiography has been correct up to a point, and that the real problem of interpreting Jacksonian Democracy is to define the proper relationship among the various elements emphasized by the different schools.

Several recent writers, in attempting to do just this, have concluded that the Jacksonian movement was essentially paradoxical. Louis Hartz describes the American democrat of the Jackson era as a hybrid personality—both a class-conscious democrat and an incipient entrepreneur—at once the "man of the land, the factory, and the forge . . . who has all the proletarian virtues that Marx was forever contrasting with the pettiness of the petit-bourgeois," and "an aggressive entrepreneur, buying 'on speculation,' combining 'some trade with agriculture,' making 'agriculture itself a trade'." He had "a certain smallness of entrepreneurial preoccupation which has never been glamorous in Western thought," Hartz concludes, but at the same time he was involved in "two heroic dramas, the covered wagon drama of the American frontier and the strike-ridden drama of a rising labor movement, so that when we come to men like Jackson and Leggett we are never quite sure whether we are dealing with a petty hope or a glorious dream."[32]

Another scholar has defined the paradox of Jacksonian Democracy somewhat differently. Judging from Jackson's own public papers, says Marvin Meyers, the Jacksonians appealed "not to some workingman's yearning for a brave new world; not to the possibilities of a fresh creation at the western limits of civilization; not to the ambitions of a rising laissez-faire capitalism—not to any of these so much as to a *restoration* of old virtues and a (perhaps imaginary) old republican way of life." Meyers states the paradox thus: "The movement which in many ways cleared the path for the triumph of laissez-faire capitalism and its culture in America, and the public which in its daily life acted out that victory, held nevertheless in their conscience an image of a chaste republican order, resisting the seductions of risk and novelty, greed and extravagance, rapid motion and complex dealings." Still another scholar, John W. Ward, has found confirmation for this mood of Old Republican restorationism in the symbolic uses to which Jackson was put by his generation.[33]

If these scholars are right about the paradoxical character of the Jacksonian democratic impulse, then it is easy to see why historians, in emphasizing different elements of the paradox, have reached such different interpretations. Viewed in this light, the frame of reference has served a valuable purpose after all, by leading historians to the different elements of the complex Jacksonian past out of which an over-all synthesis must eventually be constructed.[34]

Yet the succession of frames of reference and the multiplication of hypotheses can distort as well as amplify the past, and our current wealth in hypotheses about the Jackson period suggests that we are poor in the data by which our hypotheses must be checked. The sources, moreover, can force upon our notice factors to which our frames of reference might never lead us. But the melancholy truth is that from Parton's day to our own, hardly more than a half-dozen scholars have worked thoroughly through the available Jackson material. Consequently few phases of American history offer historians a greater challenge to research and synthesis.

Looking back over a century of scholarship, students of Jacksonian Democracy may well rejoice that their subject has been so central to defining the American experience as to become a major focus for each succeeding reorientation of historical interpretation. New frames of reference have steadily yielded new insights, and the critical spirit in which frames of reference are increasingly used is itself a momentous advance in historical technique. The course from Parton to Turner to our present indecision between labor thesis and entrepreneurial thesis may not look like a straight-line approach to Truth. "Objective reality" we know we can never altogether reach, but we need not apologize for assuming it is there, or for believing that our zigzag course brings us swinging in on a circle of ever closer vantage points for discerning its salient features.[35]

NOTES

1. Benjamin M. Dusenbery (comp.), *Monument to the Memory of General Andrew Jackson: Containing Twenty-five Eulogies and Sermons Delivered on Occasion of His Death* (Philadelphia, 1846), 32.
2. James Parton, *Life of Andrew Jackson* (3 vols., New York, 1861), I, vii.
3. Charles H. Peck, *The Jacksonian Epoch* (New York, 1899), 328.
4. Hermann E. von Holst, *The Constitutional and Political History of the United States* (8 vols., Chicago, 1876-1892), II, 2, 3, 30; William Graham Sumner, *Andrew Jackson as a Public Man: What He Was, What Chances He Had, and What He Did with Them* (Boston, 1882), 25, 278-79; James Schouler, *History of the United States of America under the Constitution* (Rev. ed., 6 vols., New York, 1894-1904), II, 439; M. Ostrogorski, *Democracy and the Organization of Political Parties* (2 vols., New York, 1902), II, 46, 65; Parton, *Jackson*, III, 694-700.
5. Sumner, *Jackson*, 279, 339; Parton, *Jackson*, III, 693-94.
6. Parton, *Jackson*, II, 692, 694; von Holst, *History*, II, 29-31.

7. Von Holst, *History*, II, 77-79; Schouler, *History*, III, 198-99; Ostrogorski, *Democracy and Political Parties*, II, 50, 69-70; Parton, *Jackson*, II, 149-50, 698, 700.
8. Frederick Jackson Turner, *The Frontier in American History* (New York, 1920), 216.
9. *Ibid.*, 192, 302.
10. John W. Burgess, *The Middle Period, 1817-1858* (New York, 1905), 135; William E. Dodd, *Expansion and Conflict* (Boston, 1915), 3, 36; Woodrow Wilson, *Division and Reunion, 1829-1909* (New York, 1910), 25, 115.
11. John Spencer Bassett, *The Life of Andrew Jackson* (2 vols., Garden City, 1911), I, xi; II, 750.
12. William MacDonald, *Jacksonian Democracy 1829-1837* (New York, 1906), 42, 311-12.
13. John Fiske, *Essays Historical and Literary* (2 vols., New York, 1902), I, 286, 310-11.
14. Carl Russell Fish, *The Civil Service and the Patronage* (Cambridge, 1904), 75-78, 155-57.
15. Ralph C. H. Catterall, *The Second Bank of the United States* (Chicago, 1903), 168 and *passim*.
16. John B. McMaster, *A History of the People of the United States from the Revolution to the Civil War* (8 vols., New York, 1883-1913), V, 518, 522, and V-VI *passim*.
17. See, for example, Marquis James, *The Life of Andrew Jackson* (2 vols. in 1, Indianapolis, 1938), 720-24 and *passim*; Claude G. Bowers, *The Party Battles of the Jackson Period* (Boston, 1922); Arthur M. Schlesinger, Jr., *The Age of Jackson* (Boston, 1945); Vernon L. Parrington, *Main Currents in American Thought: An Interpretation of American Literature from the Beginnings to 1920* (3 vols., New York, 1927-1930), II, 146; Charles A. and Mary R. Beard, *The Rise of American Civilization* (2 vols., New York, 1927), I, 557; Burgess, *Middle Period*, 282-83; Wilfred E. Binkley, *The Powers of the President: Problems of American Democracy* (Garden City, 1937), 67-88; Wilfred E. Binkley, *American Political Parties: Their Natural History* (2nd ed., New York, 1954), 141; Leonard D. White, *The Jacksonians: A Study in Administrative History, 1829-1861* (New York, 1954), 17, 48-49, 566.
18. Jackson's most inveterate scholarly foe in the twentieth century has been Richard R. Stenberg. Stenberg's point of view gained some currency through a series of articles: "The Texas Schemes of Jackson and Houston, 1829-1836," *ibid.*, XV (December, 1934), 229-50; "Jackson, Buchanan, and the 'Corrupt Bargain' Calumny," *Pennsylvania Magazine of History and Biography* (Philadelphia), LVIII (January, 1934), 61-85; "Jackson's 'Rhea Letter' Hoax," *Journal of Southern History* (Baton Rouge), II (November, 1936), 480-96; "The Jefferson Birthday Dinner, 1830," *ibid.*, IV (August, 1938), 334-45.
19. For Abernethy's view of Jackson see: "Andrew Jackson and the Rise of Southwestern Democracy," *American Historical Review* (New York), XXXIII (October, 1927), 64-77; *From Frontier to Plantation in Tennessee: A Study in Frontier Democracy* (Chapel Hill, 1932), especially 238-49.

Abernethy's interpretation of Jackson's role in Tennessee politics is criticized in Charles G. Sellers, Jr., "Banking and Politics in Jackson's Tennessee, 1817-1827," *Mississippi Valley Historical Review* (Cedar Rapids), XLI (June, 1954), 61-84.

20. Charles M. Wiltse, *John C. Calhoun* (3 vols., Indianapolis, 1944-1951), II, 234-35 and *passim*.

21. Turner, *Frontier*, 302-303, 342-43.

22. Schlesinger, Age of Jackson, 208-209, 263, 505.

23. Bray Hammond, "Jackson, Biddle, and the Bank of the United States," *Journal of Economic History* (New York), VII (May, 1947), 1-23. See also his review of the *Age of Jackson, ibid.*, VI (May, 1946), 79-84.

24. Joseph Dorfman, *The Economic Mind in American Civilization* (3 vols., New York, 1946-1949), II, 601; Joseph Dorfman, "The Jackson Wage-Earner Thesis," *American Historical Review*, LIV (January, 1949), 296-306.

25. Richard B. Morris, " 'Old Hickory' Jackson Was No FDR," *Labor and Nation* (New York), V (May-June, 1949), 38-40; Morris, "Andrew Jackson, Strikebreaker," *American Historical Review*, LV (October, 1949), 54-68.

26. William A. Sullivan, "Did Labor Support Andrew Jackson?" *Political Science Quarterly* (New York), LXII (December, 1947), 569-80; Edward Pessen, "Did Labor Support Andrew Jackson? The Boston Story," *ibid.*, LXIV (June, 1949), 262-74; William A. Sullivan, *The Industrial Worker in Pennsylvania, 1800-1840* (Harrisburg, 1955), 159-207. These studies are criticized in Robert T. Bower, "Note on 'Did Labor Support Jackson? The Boston Story,' " *Political Science Quarterly*, LXV (September, 1950), 441-44.

In a recent article Pesson has retreated from some of the positions formerly maintained by the Columbia historians. Edward Pessen, "The Workingmen's Movement of the Jacksonian Era," *Mississippi Valley Historical Review*, XLIII (December, 1956), 428-43.

27. Richard Hofstadter, *The American Political Tradition and the Men Who Made It* (New York, 1954), 58; Harold C. Syrett, *Andrew Jackson: His Contribution to the American Tradition* (Indianapolis, 1954).

28. A. M. Simons, *Social Forces in American History* (New York, 1911), 188.

29. Turner, *Frontier*, 216, 303; Willis Mason West, *The Story of American Democracy, Political and Industrial* (Boston, 1922), 438; Arthur M. Schlesinger, *New Viewpoints in American History* (New York, 1922), 200-19.

30. Beard, *Rise of American Civilization*, I, 542-57.

31. Simons, *Class Struggle* (1903 ed.), 10; Simons, *Social Forces*, 210.

32. Louis Hartz, *The Liberal Tradition in America: An Interpretation of American Political Thought since the Revolution* (New York, 1955), 89-138, especially 115-16.

33. Marvin Meyers, "The Jacksonian Persuasion," *American Quarterly* (Philadelphia), V (Spring, 1953), 3-15; John W. Ward, *Andrew Jackson: Symbol for an Age* (New York, 1955).

34. It was Vernon L. Parrington—so wrong about so many things—who first described the contradictory character of the American democrat in the Jackson period. . . . Inspired by both Turner and Simons, Parrington

found in Jacksonian Democracy a growing, and to him fatal, entrepreneurial spirit on the one hand, and a delaying action by an anti-aristocratic, anti-business alliance of farmers and workingmen on the other. *American Thought*, II, v, 137-52.

35. Unfortunately, two major contributions to Jacksonian historiography have appeared barely too late for discussion here: Bray Hammond, *Banks and Politics in America from the Revolution to the Civil War* (Princeton, 1957), and Marvin Meyers, *The Jacksonian Persuasion: Politics and Belief* (Stanford, 1957).

RECENT STUDIES

Bray Hammond, *Banks and Politics in America from the Revolution to the Civil War* (Princeton: Princeton University Press, 1957).

Richard P. McCormick, "New Perspectives on Jacksonian Politics," *American Historical Review*, LXV (January 1960), 288-301.

Walter Hugins, *Jacksonian Democracy and the Working Class: A Study of the New York Workingmen's Movement* (Stanford: Stanford University Press, 1960).

Lee Benson, *The Concept of Jacksonian Democracy: New York as a Test Case* (Princeton: Princeton University Press, 1961).

Frank Otto Gatell, "Money and Party in Jacksonian America: A Quantitative Look at New York City's Men of Quality," *Political Science Quarterly*, LXXXII (June 1967), 235-52.

Richard P. McCormick, *The Second American Party System: Party Formation in the Jacksonian Era* (Chapel Hill: University of North Carolina Press, 1966).

William W. Freehling, *Prelude to Civil War: The Nullification Controversy in South Carolina, 1816-1836* (New York: Harper & Row, 1966).

Robert V. Remini, *Andrew Jackson* (New York: Twayne, 1966).

Daniel J. Boorstin, *The Americans: The National Experience* (New York: Random House, 1965).

Marvin Meyers, *The Jacksonian Persuasion: Politics and Belief* (Stanford: Stanford University Press, 1957).

VII

Ante-Bellum Reform

DAVID BRION DAVIS

Although American historians have generally subscribed to a liberal
ideology and have shown a favorable attitude toward change, material
improvement, and the extension of human rights, they have long displayed a certain uneasiness and awkwardness in their treatment of ante-
bellum reform. Like Ralph Waldo Emerson . . . they have usually
applauded the *goals* of the early reformers; yet, they have been put off
by the same reformers' extremism, fanaticism, eccentricity, and conten-
tiousness. As a result, even in our best textbooks and general histories of
the period, discussions of reform seem curiously equivocal and dis-
jointed. And while we profit from an increasing number of excellent
studies of individual reforms and reformers, we still lack a satisfactory
overall treatment of the subject.

There are a number of reasons why ante-bellum reform has been un-
congenial to twentieth-century scholars. Most of the early reformers
were devout Protestants whose public expressions of piety have appeared sanctimonious to an age that, at least until the 1960s, has
equated social progress with secular, rational thought. If the distinctive
traits of ante-bellum reform were its moral fundamentalism and radical

From *Ante-Bellum Reform*, New York: Harper and Row, 1967, pp. 1-10,
with omissions. Copyright © 1967 by David Brion Davis. Reprinted by permission of Harper & Row, Publishers.

comprehensiveness, as Henry Steele Commager has observed, then it has been all the more alien to a society which is inclined to dismiss ethical arguments as subjective "value judgments," and which places a high premium on pragmatic solutions to limited and concrete problems. Then, too, the sentimental romanticism and tender sensitivity to human suffering, which permeated the writings of early reformers, have been unpalatable to men suspicious of emotion and hardened to human atrocity. Since the antislavery movement came to dominate all other reforms, and was inextricably linked with the coming of the Civil War, the subject of reform has unavoidably been tied to questions of guilt and responsibility for our greatest national trauma. The failure of the Eighteenth Amendment and a resulting consensus that alcoholism is an individual problem have created still another barrier to understanding the host of ante-bellum reformers who saw temperance as the grand route to national virtue and happiness. We still live in the wake of the great rebellion against the Genteel Tradition, which reflected the full flush of early New England idealism only as a sickly afterglow. We are still repulsed by the sour and cramped spirit of latter-day "reformers" who have sought to outlaw sex, art, and liquor. And if these more recent censors and moralists have differed markedly from their spiritual ancestors of the 1830s and 1840s, they have shared a sense of irrepressible outrage over personal sin. To a society at once permissive and tough-minded, no traits appear more offensive and dangerous than sentimental piety and moral self-righteousness.

Yet it is difficult to deny the importance of the social ferment and agitation, the utopian hopes and profound dissatisfaction that swept over America in the decades before the Civil War. The main issues raised by the reformers are still very much alive. We have by no means solved the problems of racial and sexual discrimination. We still dream of extending the intimate love of the private family to a wider circle of social relationships, and yet debate, as did the ante-bellum reformers, the justifications for monogamous marriage, the proper role of woman, and the best methods of child-rearing. We are still perplexed by the discrepancy between our penal institutions and our ideal of reforming and rehabilitating criminals. We argue endlessly over the most effective methods for redeeming what Theodore Parker called "the dangerous classes of society" and what we now term "the culturally deprived." If we are usually more cynical than the ante-bellum reformers, we have not abandoned their dream of a world without war. Indeed, the radical protest movements of the 1960s have hauntingly echoed the ante-bellum ideal of nonresistance, the "come-outer" spirit of disengagement from a sinful society, and the reliance on individual conscience as opposed to all forms of corporate and bureaucratic power.

In short, we continue to believe that without social criticism a nation is doomed to complacency, stultification, and hardening injustice. We like to think that American history is something more than a record of diverse groups and interests struggling for power. And if we are to find in our heritage some trace of the unfolding of an ideal, some evidence, however imperfect, of a continuing tradition of discontent, of repudiating the status quo, of insisting that things can and should be better, then we must see the ante-bellum reformers in part as they saw themselves: as the legitimate heirs of the American Revolution, as champions of the ideals of the Declaration of Independence.

This was the dominant view of the abolitionists, at least, among the nineteenth-century nationalistic historians who sought to justify the North's victory in the Civil War. But these same historians made the abolitionists appear as the mere vehicles of inevitable progress, which was identified with the broad forces of nationalism and increasing liberty. This not only obscured the reformers' role as social critics, but tended to associate them with the new status quo and its conservative defenders, and made them appear as the precursors of Grantism and the betrayers of Jeffersonian democracy. It is true that the temperance and feminist movements, which gained renewed vigor in the early twentieth century, stimulated a certain interest in the first leaders of such reforms. But as reform itself became more pragmatic and institutional in approach, it was often necessary to repudiate the supposedly naïve and visionary methods of the past.

Serious study of early reform movements required a degree of detachment that could come only with the passage of time. It also required a broadened view of the proper subject matter of history, which until the 1920s was largely conceived in terms of political, economic, and constitutional development. It was in the 1920s and 1930s that such scholars as Arthur M. Schlesinger, Merle Curti, Carl Russell Fish, Gilbert H. Barnes, and John Allen Krout wrote their pioneering accounts of social movements, and elevated social history to a high level of academic respectability. By and large their studies were objective and, if negative toward what Allan Nevins has termed the "extravagances" of many reformers, were sympathetic in their general evaluations.

In these same decades the image of ante-bellum reform was darkened by an intensifying debate over the causes and implications of the Civil

War. This is not the place to review the vast controversial literature on this subject. It is sufficient to note that a group of extremely able and persuasive historians, many of whom were of Southern origin, developed the thesis that the Civil War had not been an inevitable conflict between two incompatible civilizations, that it had not been desired by the people in either the North or South, that it had nothing to do with slavery, which was a benign and dying institution, and that it had solved no problems. This view of the Civil War as an unmitigated and avoidable tragedy had great appeal to a generation that had come to see the First World War as a similar tragedy caused by malicious propaganda, mass hysteria, and the plotting of politicians and munitions makers. And in the eyes of Frank L. Owsley, Charles W. Ramsdell, Arthur Y. Lloyd, James G. Randall, and Avery Craven, the abolitionists were irresponsible fanatics who, along with the Southern "fire-eaters," helped to drive the nation to madness.

This so-called "revisionist" picture of abolition agitators drew much support from Gilbert H. Barnes's *The Antislavery Impulse, 1830-1844* (1933), one of the first studies to explore both the psychology of antebellum reform and its basis in revivalistic religion. Barnes himself was by no means an apologist for the South or its peculiar institution, and his pioneering book contributed some of our most prevalent ideas concerning the antislavery movement. It was Barnes (who oddly enough was an economist himself) who helped to divert historians' attention from economic interest to the effects of religious revivalism, who established a dichotomy between New England and Midwestern abolitionism, and who popularized a distinction between supposedly practical and conscientious abolitionists such as Theodor D. Weld and James G. Birney, and the irresponsible fanatics such as Garrison.

The first modern attempt to relate all the ante-bellum reform movements to the social and religious developments of the age was Alice Felt Tyler's *Freedom's Ferment* (1944). In Mrs. Tyler's view, religious revivalism, Transcendentalism, Jeffersonian rationalism, and frontier democracy all merged to create an era of ferment, of restlessness, and of exuberant confidence in man's ability to perfect human institutions. Unfortunately, these concepts acquired little precision as Mrs. Tyler applied them to specific movements, and for the most part she was content with a textbookish survey of popular cults, utopias, and reform movements. A more successful integration of reform movements with the economic and social history of a limited region was Whitney Cross's *The Burned-Over District* (1950), which related the religious revivals of Charles Grandison Finney and the subsequent social fervor to economic dislocations and denominational competition in upstate New York.

By the 1940s and 1950s ante-bellum reform began attracting the attention of some of America's most eminent historians, such as Allan Nevins, Merle Curti, and Arthur M. Schlesinger, who sought to find common themes and characteristics in the seemingly diverse movements. Their interpretations have helped to crystallize the image of early reform as it is found in standard textbooks and survey courses in American history. However successful these new syntheses were in listing common traits of the various movements, they were distressingly ambiguous on a number of crucial matters such as the sources of reform ideology, the motives of reformers, the relative radicalism or conservatism of the movements, and their ultimate effect on public opinion and legislation. It is well to give brief consideration to each of these questions.

In his *The American as Reformer* (1950), Arthur M. Schlesinger pictured all American reform as part of a liberal tradition derived from the philosophy of the Enlightenment and from the Protestant concern for public welfare and individual moral responsibility. According to Merle Curti, in *The Growth of American Thought* (1943), the main "roots" of American reform were to be found first in the Enlightenment's faith in the goodness of man and his capacity for progressing through the use of reason toward a heavenly city on earth; and second, in a liberal, humanitarian religion which also preached the goodness of man and his capacity for perfection by following the example of Christ. In an effort to show how ideas interacted with changing social conditions, Curti suggested that the new faith in change and improvement was related to the needs of a rising middle class seeking release from commercial and political restraints. The ideas of progress and perfectibility were instruments well-adapted to the fluid conditions of American life. There was a natural fit between the needs of America in an era of westward expansion and urban growth and the newer currents of imported doctrine, such as romanticism, Transcendentalism, and utilitarianism.

As plausible as this functionalist approach might seem, especially to a generation that thought of ideas as instruments or weapons tooled to the needs of particular classes, it left much unexplained. To describe all reform as part of the widening spirit of democracy leads to a blurring of important distinctions and makes it extremely difficult to account for the large number of reformers who believed in man's inherent depravity, or for the radical abolitionists who repudiated majority rule, or for anti-slavery champions like Beriah Green who called for "Heaven-anointed" leaders who would rule by "divine right." Obviously reformers drew on ideas and beliefs that we associate with the Enlightenment or with evangelical revivalism; but why did these "streams" or "roots" converge when they did? Charles and Mary Beard, in their *The Rise of American Civilization* (rev. ed., 1940), pointed out that the abolitionists had no monopoly on evangelical religion or the Declaration of Independence. Not only were there thousands of Americans who never supported a reform movement but who drew moral and intellectual nourishment from the supposed "roots" of reform; there were also deeply conservative elements to both the Enlightenment and the revivals. In fact, the great object of American revivalists from Jonathan Edwards to Billy Graham has not been to perfect society but to save men's souls by arousing them to a full awareness of their involvement in sin. Insofar as the Enlightenment encouraged respect for balance, order, and rational moderation, it led to a frame of mind that could only be repelled by the uncompromising moralism of most reformers of the ante-bellum period. Moreover, traditional institutions could be defended as well as condemned by the principle of utility or the philosophy of natural rights. If one agreed with some eighteenth-century thinkers that men were governed by self-interest and that maximum wealth and harmony depended on minimum interference with individual desires and actions, it would appear that most reformers were upsetting the balance of nature and working to extinguish basic liberties. The harshest critics of reform were frequently devout Christians or good disciples of the Enlightenment.

Since the moral and intellectual sources seem inadequate to explain the emergence of reform at a particular time, it is reasonable to look at the motives of the reformers themselves. But here historians have faced a formidable problem. By and large the ante-bellum reformers could not be likened to an oppressed group struggling for economic security; they seldom had vested material interests in their causes. The Beards, who usually emphasized the economic basis of historical change, were frank in admitting their bafflement. In two massive volumes by Edward Westermarck on the history of moral ideas they could find no clue to the inspiration of such a crusade as abolitionism. They stressed the context of sectional struggle and the fact that the North had no slaves to lose, and yet finally concluded that devotion to the abolitionist creed arose from "sentiments of a moral nature." Merle Curti suggested that receptivity to reform ideas was related to social structure; because of its own mobility, the middle class was prepared to think in terms of social improvement. But Curti did not show that reformers came from more mobile groups than did nonreformers, and he ultimately stated that historians could not really know the motives behind reforms.

Nevertheless, as early as 1906 Frank T. Carlton tried to find a more precise relationship between the motives of reformers and a specific social situation. In an article of "Humanitarianism, Past and Present," in the *International Journal of Ethics,* Carlton proposed the theory that ante-bellum reform was essentially the protest of a declining ruling class against the ruthless, competitive world of business. As the old leaders and old families lost power and became isolated from the dynamic social and business currents of the 1820s and 1830s, they struck out desperately against the evil consequences of profit-seeking and laissez-faire capitalism. Carlton did not imply that humanitarianism was a mere screen concealing ignoble motives, nor, apparently, did he think of reform as the attempt of displaced leaders to regain social status. Indeed, it was the remoteness and isolation of the old ruling class which provided a relatively objective view of social problems: ". . . no golden stream was flowing into their pockets to obscure and blur their vision as to past and present conditions." Their value as social critics arose from their independence of economic pressures and their commitment to values and ideals of the past.

More recently several imaginative historians have refined these concepts with respect to radical antislavery. The thesis that abolitionists were responding not so much to slavery as to social and economic dislocations in their own society has been skillfully employed by revisionist historians like Avery Craven. . . . David Donald, in an influential essay in *Lincoln Reconsidered* (1956), maintained that the abolitionists were so violently aggressive and uncompromising that they must have been affected by some profound social or psychological dislocation, and consequently seized upon antislavery as an outlet for irrational needs and fears. After carefully analyzing the social and economic background of 106 key abolitionists, and finding that their families had been linked with the rural social order which began to disintegrate in the 1820s and 1830s, Donald concluded that the antislavery crusade was the protest of "a displaced social elite" against the new industrial world. Abolitionists found self-fulfillment in a cause that offered a chance for moral leadership and a reassertion of traditional values. A somewhat similar approach was taken by Stanley M. Elkins in his seminal work, *Slavery: A Problem in American Institutional and Intellectual Life* (1959). Though less interested in motives than in why ante-bellum Americans were incapable of dealing with slavery in a flexible and realistic manner, Elkins was struck by the abolitionists' excessive individualism, their hostility toward all institutions, their rigidity and abstractness of thought, and their inclination to reduce complex problems to simple, moral absolutes. These traits, he argued, were the product of America's amorphous social structure. Because of the lack of tradition and of truly national institutions, intellectuals and reformers were cut off from sources of power and thus from a sense of responsibility. There were no established channels through which reform could flow. There were no moderating influences which would make protest more flexible, concrete, and effective.

Future studies of American reform will be heavily indebted to the new approaches taken by Donald and Elkins. Nevertheless, in recent years the ante-bellum reformers have appeared in a somewhat different light as modern radicals have grown increasingly skeptical about flexible, pragmatic methods and about working within the framework of established institutions. It has also become apparent that we have little evidence of how ante-bellum reformers differed from other segments of the population. . . . there is reason to doubt broad generalizations about the motives and psychology of such groups as the abolitionists when our knowledge is limited to a few leaders who were perhaps unrepresentative, and when psychological theory is itself in a state of flux.

When we turn to the question of the relative conservatism or radicalism of reform, we again encounter considerable confusion. In 1950 Arthur M. Schlesinger drew a bland picture of American reform. Because American society lacked the "impediments" of an aristocracy or established church, and was continually stimulated by the arrival of restless immigrants, the desire for improvement could flow freely in safe, middle class channels, without challenging private property or other basic institutions. It should be noted that Stanley Elkins derived almost opposite conclusions from America's lack of institutional restraints. On the other hand, Allan Nevins, in his *Ordeal of the Union* (1947), affirmed that American reform was distinctive not in its fanaticism or eccentricity but in the fact that it was a "pragmatic growth in a pragmatic society." The practicality of American reformers was especially evident in such causes as the amelioration of prisons and asylums, and the abolition of flogging in the Navy. Although Nevins considered men like Garrison narrow-minded fanatics, he applauded the practicality and entrepreneurial skill of the Midwestern abolitionists and spoke of the "conservative wisdom" of James G. Birney. He was bothered by the irresponsibility of many social critics and by a frequent failure to penetrate to the roots of social ills. Nevertheless, he found ante-bellum reform "an inspiring force and a powerful agency" in shaping America's future.

Merle Curti presented a sharper dichotomy between liberal and conservative factions. In the decades after the Revolution, American history was essentially a struggle between forces which on one side represented patrician privilege, reactionary religion, and the East; and on the other, the heritage of the Enlightenment, science, "democratic" religion, and the West. This dualism, though frequently adopted in general texts, has raised increasing problems. The division between democratic and undemocratic religion makes it difficult to account for abolitionists who believed in original sin and eternal damnation, or for pro-slavery theorists who embraced scientific rationalism. The evangelical crusade to save the West for Protestant Christianity, which Curti classes as part of the patrician reaction, was in reality the seedbed of later reforms. It is clear that ante-bellum reform spanned a wide spectrum from utopian anarchism to an obsessive quest for social order. But the subject is so complex that the conventional meanings of "conservative," "liberal," and "radical" have proved inadequate as modes of classification. Few subjects in American history are in such need of rigorous analysis as the interrelationship of specific reform movements and the transition from an evangelical drive for social control to a romantic and humanitarian crusade for liberty, uplift, and social justice.

Perhaps the vaguest of all answers concerning ante-bellum reform pertains to its ultimate effects. According to Curti, the reformers served an important function, though they had, in the last analysis, little popular appeal. The Beards tell us that the influence of abolitionists outran their poor showing at the polls. Nevins seems to credit the reformers with a more positive effect in shaping opinion both at home and abroad. Alice Felt Tyler affirms that the movements flowed into the mainstream of American life and contributed to our later democratic philosophy To the revisionist historians the abolitionists bear much of the blame for the Civil War. According to Stanley Elkins, the abolitionists contributed to America's failure to deal imaginatively and realistically with the problem of slavery and race relationships. Few questions are so difficult to answer as those of influence and responsibility. Hopefully we will acquire more precise criteria for measuring the impact of ante-bellum reformers, but as our own experience changes our perspective on the problems they faced and the methods they adopted, it seems probable that we will continue to alter our views of their significance and accomplishment.

. . . Recent studies which build upon the research, the hypotheses, and the controversies just described, reflect a growing interest in motivation, social structure, and intellectual history, and succeed in moving beyond many of the clichés and conventional labels of earlier histories. If the emerging picture is rather smudged and lacking in clear and simple shapes, the student should be reassured by knowing that we have gone beyond the superficial level of categorizing people as progressives and reactionaries, as puritans and liberals, as crackpots and saints. Though few questions have yet been answered, at least many of the right questions have been asked. . . .

We should not conclude without briefly noting some of the blankest areas in our present knowledge of reform. In addition to the need for more detailed information on the psychology of reformers, there is an almost total lack of evidence on the differences between what might be called the verbalizers—the lecturers, journalists, and pamphleteers—and the activists or organizers. Little is known of the rank and file members, to say nothing of the passive supporters, of a single reform movement. Yet there is presumably important evidence in petitions, memorials, records of contributions, and membership lists, which might be subject to reasonably sophisticated quantification. It seems futile to talk about the social composition of reform movements until such data has been rigorously analyzed. We are virtually ignorant of the dynamics of reform organizations, of the relations between leaders and followers. Although sociologists and social psychologists have learned much about the workings of small groups, their generalizations have not been applied or tested by historians of reform. We also need to know much more about the relation of secular reform to the sectarian and perfectionist traditions. Despite the strong anarchistic and primitivistic strains within ante-bellum reform, these aspects of the subject have not been systematically studied. The whole relationship of reform propaganda to popular literature has been surprisingly neglected. Finally, we must ultimately ask whether the Civil War represents an abrupt terminus to an entire cycle of reform. Is it valid, in other words, to speak of ante-bellum reform as a self-contained phenomenon, or have we overlooked significant continuities between the first so-called "age of reform" and the later emergence of Reform Darwinism, the Social Gospel, and Progressivism?

RECENT STUDIES

John L. Thomas, "Romantic Reform in America, 1815-1865," *American Quarterly* XVII (Winter 1965), 656-81.

Louis Filler, *The Crusade Against Slavery, 1830-1860* (New York: Harper & Row, 1960).

C. Vann Woodward, "The Antislavery Myth," *American Scholar*, XXXI (Spring 1962), 312-28.

John Demos, "The Antislavery Movement and the Problem of Violent 'Means'," *New England Quarterly*, XXXVII (December 1964), 501-26.

Martin Duberman (ed.), *The Antislavery Vanguard: New Essays on the Abolitionists* (Princeton: Princeton University Press, 1965).

Bertram Wyatt-Brown, "William Lloyd Garrison and Antislavery Unity: A Reappraisal," *Civil War History*, XIII (March 1967), 5-24.

Donald G. Mathews, "The Abolitionists on Slavery: The Critique Behind the Social Movement," *Journal of Southern History*, XXXIII (May 1967), 163-82.

VIII

The Kansas-Nebraska Act: A Century of Historiography

ROY F. NICHOLS

The process of federal lawmaking can be very intricate, and correspondingly baffling to the historian. Few acts of Congress have had a passage more difficult to trace accurately than that of Kansas-Nebraska fame, and few have received more attention from historians. The historiography of the measure has been the more difficult because of the sectional conflict in which it was a significant episode. Historical thinking about it has been colored by the emotional overtones produced by the historians, conditioned by their several geographical and cultural backgrounds. Despite the hundred years which have elapsed since the episode occurred, historians are still of several minds about it and there is cause to doubt whether the full story has yet been told. A century of historiography has produced an extensive bibliography, a variety of interpretations, much argument, and certain questions yet unanswered.

Historical thinking and writing about the bill began very shortly after its enactment. The subsequent struggle to make the territory of Kansas into a state, and the political fortunes of Senator Stephen A. Douglas, the sponsor of the bill, called forth frequent reference to the circumstances of its passage in various famous political campaigns involving his senatorial and presidential ambitions. Two very divergent

From *The Mississippi Valley Historical Review*, XLIII (September 1956), pp. 187-212. Reprinted with annotation abridged by permission.

views concerning the nature of the bill and the motivation of its supporters became current almost immediately. The friends of Douglas
described the bill in terms of his own committee report as designed to
advance "certain great principles, which would not only furnish adequate remedies for existing evils, but, in all time to come, avoid the
perils of similar agitation, by withdrawing the question of slavery from
the halls of Congress and the political arena, committing it to the
arbitration of those who were immediately interested in, and alone responsible for, its consequences."[1] Another and much more numerous
company, including Douglas' foes, found something akin to their views
in "An Appeal of the Independent Democrats in Congress," which
appeared twenty days after Douglas presented his own statement. These
opponents of the measure thundered forth in print: "We arraign this
bill as a gross violation of a sacred pledge; as a criminal betrayal of
previous rights; as part and parcel of an atrocious plot."[2]

These views, so wide apart in their implications, provided the ideas
basic to the two schools of thought which have been dominant ever
since, and much of what has been written on the subject has been conditioned either by one of these ideas or by the other. The second view
was almost the only one prevalent in the historical literature which
appeared during the Civil War. This writing was highly colored by the
conflict and when the popular authors who were chronicling the battles
and campaigns alluded to the Act they generally characterized it as a
move of southern aggression, part of the plot, a thing which was evil,
and by statement or implication Douglas was an evildoer.

The next phase of the historiography of the bill was supplied by
writers of reminiscences, such as Joshua R. Giddings, Ohio congressman, Horace Greeley, famous editor of the New York *Tribune*, and
Henry S. Foote, sometime senator from Mississippi. They supplied
some scattered details designed to belittle Douglas and to demonstrate
the idea of a southern conspiracy. Practically all of this writing was
northern in origin and sympathy.[3] This disparagement of Douglas was
soon followed by an effort on the part of his brother-in-law to glorify
his leadership in the matter. In a book consisting of a series of statements which he said had been dictated to him by the Senator, J. Madison Cutts presented an extended account of Douglas' efforts to open
Nebraska, pointing out the pressure of the population on the frontier
and the absolute necessity of making concessions to southern legislators
who had the power of blocking the measure indefinitely. Douglas was
said to have boasted: "I passed the Kansas-Nebraska Act myself. I had
the authority and power of a dictator throughout the whole controversy

in both houses. The speeches were nothing. It was the marshaling and directing of men and guarding from attacks, and with a ceaseless vigilance preventing surprise."[4]

The climax of this phase of the bill's historiography came with the publication, beginning in 1872, of the *History of the Rise and Fall of the Slave Power in America*, written by Henry Wilson, vice-president under Grant and formerly a leading Free-Soiler. Wilson made an extensive effort to gather facts by consulting his contemporaries. His own viewpoint was well illustrated by the title of his work and by the following quotation:

> No event in the progress of the great conflict stands out more prominently than the abrogation of the Compromise of 1820. As both effect and cause it defies competition and almost comparison with any single measure of the long series of aggressions of the Slave Power. . . . No single act of the Slave Power ever spread greater consternation, produced more lasting results upon the popular mind, or did so much to arouse the North and to convince the people of its desperate character.[5]

Thus the verdict of these participants—practically all of them pro-Union and antislavery—as they penned their memoirs was largely in agreement with the theory that there had been a conspiracy against the best interests of the nation, though there was no clear outline of who had conspired or how. And there was no agreement as to the part Douglas had played or about his motivation. Was he a statesman, a conspirator, or a tool?

At this point a new element entered into the historiography of the bill. This was provided by men who had not participated in the scenes of conflict, but who were now coming forward to examine the records and write from them in a fashion which began to be called scientific. The first of these was a trained German historian, Professor Hermann E. von Holst of the University of Freiburg. During political exile in the United States he had begun thinking about its history and when he returned to Germany he wrote a multi-volume work. That which included the Kansas-Nebraska episode appeared in English in 1885 and in it he devoted some two hundred pages to a very detailed account of the Act.[6] He had read little but the official documents, yet he was the only writer so far to grasp the influence of the complexities of American politics upon the shaping of the bill. Nevertheless, he was content with the simple conclusion natural to a liberal who hated slavery, that the rivalry of Douglas and Pierce for southern support for the presidency

was the prime motivation. At the same time, he effectively destroyed
the constitutional pretensions of Douglas' arguments, though he failed
to grasp the realistic value of the Senator's planning. His work did
much to strengthen the current northern or Republican theory of an
evil thing done at the behest of the slave power.

While von Holst's volumes were appearing, two wealthy men, turned
historians, were engrossed in similarly extensive works. In 1891, the
fifth volume of James Schouler's *History of the United States under
the Constitution* appeared,[7] and in the next year James Ford Rhodes
began the publication of his *History of the United States from the
Compromise of 1850*. Both used much more source material than did
von Holst but they reached much the same conclusion. The Kansas-
Nebraska bill was the reprehensible creation of Douglas, the demagogic
aspirant for the presidency.[8]

Hardly had this canon of Republican interpretation been "scientifically" established by this trio of historians when a measure of reaction
set in and efforts were made in the direction of the rehabilitation of
Douglas. In 1897, Professor John W. Burgess of Columbia University
published a volume entitled *The Middle Period*, which covered the
Kansas-Nebraska situation. Professor Burgess was a Tennessee Unionist,
veteran of the Civil War. He had the prevailing German concepts of
scientific history and was a nationalistic liberal. He was closely associated with his most brilliant student, William A. Dunning, whose father
had been a war Democrat. Burgess pictured Douglas as a sincere representative of the West sharing with his fellow citizens a keen sense of
the importance of local autonomy. He defended him for declaring his
principles and pointed out that men often identify themselves and
their ambitions with principles which they believe essential for the
peace and welfare of their country.[9]

At the turn of the century, younger scholars, products of the bur-
geoning graduate schools, began to take up the problem. A young Columbia graduate student, Allen Johnson, had been within the range of
Burgess's influence although taking his doctorate in European history.
When he settled down to teach in Grinnell College, Iowa, he chose as
his next work a study of Stephen A. Douglas, who had been waiting
forty years for a scholarly and comprehensive biographer. Johnson explored vigorously, turned up a certain amount of new source material
including what few fragments the Douglas framily then seemed to have
preserved, and produced a scholarly, well-written biography which appeared in 1908.

His was a well-rounded account of Douglas and the bill. He had a more comprehensive grasp of the part which the needs of the West played in creating this measure. He discounted the immediate presidential ambitions of Douglas and pictured him as a sincere believer in popular sovereignty as the solution of the problem of the peaceable opening up of new territories. His effort to maintain a judicial attitude is illustrated by his verdict that the effort of the Senator to repeal the Missouri Compromise by "subtle" indirection was the "device of a shifty politician." Douglas, nevertheless, was the dominant figure, the resourceful statesman to whom the responsibility for the measure was due.[10]

In the next year after the publication of Johnson's *Douglas*, P. Orman Ray's Cornell doctoral dissertation, *The Repeal of the Missouri Compromise*, was published.[11] This work represented an intensive, unprejudiced recanvass of the evidence and the discovery of significant new material. Ray challenged the theory of Douglas' exclusive agency and emphasized the idea suggested by the memoir writers and von Holst that various political situations, particularly the bitterness of Missouri local politics, were the controlling factors.[12] As some reviewers of this book pointed out, probably Ray claimed too much, the evidence which he marshaled was not altogether conclusive, the Missouri question was only one of a series of factors in a complex situation.

One of the reviewers was Professor Frank H. Hodder of the University of Kansas. He had been long at work on the history of the bill, in fact as early as 1899 he had published an almost unnoticed article defending Douglas as a sincere statesman laboring for western development. Hodder was developing a theory regarding the bill, which he presented before the State Historical Society of Wisconsin in 1912.[13]

Hodder's perspective was much broader than Ray's and he played up an idea which he had not advanced in his earlier article. He was impressed by the part played in western development by railroad promoters, particularly those seeking to construct a line to the Pacific. It was Hodder's conclusion that the chief interest at work in opening up Nebraska was the promoters' desire to secure a right of way for this transcontinental line. He saw Douglas as the railroad promoter motivated by this role rather than by his political ambitions. Though he had some complimentary things to say about Ray's work, he brusquely dismissed his main thesis as "untenable."

Ray replied at the annual meeting of the American Historical Association in 1914 by describing Hodder's thesis as unproven and untenable.[14] Some years later, Hodder devoted his presidential address before the Mississippi Valley Historical Association, in 1925, to providing further evidence of Douglas' railroad interest.[15]

While we applaud the zeal of these protagonists we may also comment on the inflexibility which controversy develops. The truth probably would have been more nearly attained had each recognized that the other had made a contribution and had they united their points of view. This, in fact, was done by Albert J. Beveridge in his *Abraham Lincoln* in 1928. In this fragment in which interestingly enough Douglas was the hero, Beveridge, in an elaborate account of the Kansas-Nebraska bill, recanvassed all the evidence and brought back Douglas as the glamorous leader dealing with and influenced by the combination of forces developed by Hodder and Ray.[16]

The 1930's produced at least two additions to the growing corpus of analysis and interpretation. The author of this essay and George Fort Milton re-examined the roles of two of the prominent figures in the action, Franklin Pierce and Stephen A. Douglas. Since the work of Henry Wilson, various allusions had been made to the part played by the President under pressure either of ambition or of expediency. Not until the publication of *Franklin Pierce* in 1931 had any comprehensive attempt been made to explain the President's situation and the practical motivation which led him to make the bill an administration measure. The factional strife in the Democratic party was explored, and with it the President's need of regaining the support of important elements in his party, particularly in the Senate. The success of his administration depended upon congressional endorsement of his patronage program, his domestic legislative plans, and particularly of his ambitious foreign policy. Without the support of the Senate leaders he would be helpless and discredited. Therefore, when the leading bloc of senators demanded his endorsement of the measure, he felt he must acquiesce.[17]

George Fort Milton, in the meantime, had conceived of a comprehensive trilogy of volumes to embrace the whole period from 1850 to 1869. He had finished the last one, *The Age of Hate*, and he then turned to the first. As in the last he had chosen a central figure, Andrew Johnson, so in the first he would concentrate on Douglas. He turned to the problem with great ingenuity and enterprise and shortly discovered what had always been thought to be lost, namely, the papers of Douglas in great quantity. Mining this great treasure and working indefatigably in repositories all over the land he produced a very comprehensive biography. In his consideration of the Kansas-Nebraska bill, he recognized the inadequacy of simple explanations of complex phenomena and brought together in a comprehensive synthesis the fruits of his own labors and of those of his many predecessors. He showed calm judgment and capacity to evaluate many of the controversial factors in the situation. For much of Douglas' career, his work will be definitive. But he did not deal with the chief historiographical problem connected with Kansas-Nebraska, namely, the influences, external and internal, which produced the various drafts of the bill; nor did he provide a systematic reconstruction of what Douglas personally went through in his connection with the legislative process which produced the law. To Milton, Douglas more than ever was the dominant courageous statesman, the master of the situation. Milton's work, published in 1934, placed the capstone on the structure of Douglas' rehabilitation; von Holst, Rhodes, *et id genus omne* had been revised.[18]

But revision does not stay put and there is ever a yearning for new and more satisfying synthesis and interpretation. Allan Nevins of Columbia determined to rewrite Rhodes completely and in the course of this work made a thorough recanvass of the circumstances attending the enactment of the Kansas-Nebraska bill. In 1947 his first volumes appeared containing his findings.[19] He was impressed by the inadequacy of the various specialized interpretations and prepared an inclusive and complicated narrative designed to retell and resynthesize the story. While he still maintained Douglas in the central position, he took much of the heroic statesman away from him. He showed him as a powerful and ruthless opportunist, playing by ear, with little respect for logic or truth, determined above all things to carry his bill and demonstrate his leadership. Despite his exhaustive studies, Nevins found enigma and mystery in the framing of the bill. Why did a man of Douglas' experience behave in such a curious, complex, and heedless fashion?

Six years later, another thoughtful historian, Avery Craven, published the results of his mature judgment. He had given some of his findings in *The Coming of the Civil War* in 1942,[20] but his further thought was presented in *The Growth of Southern Nationalism*, published in 1953.[21] His special contribution was a penetrating analysis of public opinion in the South, tracing in enlightening detail the way in which northern attack changed indifference into united support on the part of the South. This change of opinion in turn gave birth to the northern idea of southern aggression which did so much to furnish the stereotype of an aggressive and wicked South. He painted a most realistic picture of Douglas and showed how his turgid character made him either loved or feared and made him so easy to hate. Like Nevins, Craven alluded to an elusive element. On the question of the motivation for the peculiar metamorphosis of the bill, he wrote, "Who and what were responsible for this remains a mystery."[22]

Finally, the latest in the chapters of the historiography of the bill, written by James C. Malin, *The Nebraska Question, 1852-1854*, likewise appeared in 1953.[23] Malin, a disciple of Hodder, returned to the theme of Douglas the great statesman. Douglas, in his opinion, was fighting the tendency toward centralization which the mechanical revolution was advancing. His doctrine of popular sovereignty or local self-government was designed to restore the balance and preserve democracy. Malin has made a minute analysis of as much of public opinion as he could find recorded in western Missouri to show that Douglas was but reflecting ideas current on the Missouri-Kansas frontier. However, as he has not yet fully investigated the problem of the congressional action on the bill, he has not penetrated the depths of its "mysteries."

The fact that both Craven and Nevins made mention of unsolved problems in the historiography of the Kansas-Nebraska bill presents a convenient opportunity to join with them in expressing the belief that something is still lacking in the complete history of the bill. Despite all this great labor and highly intelligent consideration, historians have been studying Hamlet with Hamlet either left out or incorrectly identified. For Stephen A. Douglas was not Hamlet. This situation has arisen because of what appears to be the historian's principal intellectual difficulty. He is, speaking generally, an excellent reporter but he frequently leaves something to be desired as an interpreter. This does not mean that he does not sense the working of the forces that shape events but rather that the nature of the process by which these forces influence human behavior eludes him. He fails to trace adequately the connections between antecedent situations and accomplished fact, the process of becoming.

This is the difficulty with the historiography of the Kansas-Nebraska bill. We now very clearly understand the various forces making it inevitable but we have contented ourselves with thinking of Douglas as the agency through which they worked to shape the bill. This is not an adequate consideration of the extremely complex process by which the bill took its peculiar shape and was enacted into law. This process of becoming is the Hamlet which has been left out.

This key to the whole matter, this process of becoming, can only be discovered by exploring some of the intricate processes of American political behavior connected with our party system and lawmaking mechanism. Such an exploration may help to clear up the mystery, to identify Hamlet.

The growth of the nation and the expansion of its population had reached a point in the early 1850's when the passage of a bill opening up the Nebraska territory had become inevitable, and whether Douglas was interested in it or not probably in the end did not much matter. As far as the achievement of the object of the bill was concerned, states were going to be organized between the Missouri and the Rockies regardless of any man or men. In the short session of the Thirty-second Congress, a simple bill organizing a territory called Nebraska had passed the House. The territory was given limits approximately those of the present state of Kansas and no reference was made to slavery. It had failed in the Senate in its last hours for lack of four southern votes.

True understanding of what happened next can be best secured by reference to the disorganized state of American politics of that particular time. In 1853-1854 there was prevalent a feeling of political uneasiness, probably symptomatic of the process of disintegration going on within existing political combinations, an uneasiness which ordinarily precedes the reintegration of a series of political elements into a new party. In the United States in the nineteenth century there were such periods of disintegration and reintegration in politics every twenty years or thereabouts just as there were financial panics. Democrats and Whigs had crystallized about 1834-1836 and now a new combination was about to form as the Republican party in 1854-1856.

The chief indication of this disintegration-reintegration process was the prevalence of a factionalism in both major parties which was producing a growing sense of insecurity among the leaders. This insecurity produced a tendency among politicians to grasp any possible advantage which might arise from current interests and to push it to extreme length. It was above all else a period of political expediency and sometimes of desperate expedients.

The factionalism current at the close of the 1840's seemed to have very dangerous implications. A split in the ranks of the Jacksonians had lost them the presidency in 1848. In the fight over the organization of the Mexican Cession both Democrats and Whigs had been so fragmentized in 1850 that it had been extremely difficult to reorganize them for the campaign of 1852. The force of traditional combat and the lure of spoils and power, however, had temporarily restored an uneasy unity within each party. In an election which careful analysis showed to be very close, the Democrats won by only a small margin in the popular vote. They had won only to fall into a more complex factionalism which bore the promise of even greater demoralization than that of 1848, and their executive leadership showed itself incompetent to deal with the situation.

The Whig party which the election returns showed to have a great political voting strength, was plagued by the fact that in combatting the usually victorious Democrats on the state level its two wings had supported policies that nationally were irreconcilable. In the South the Whigs had become very southern, in the North, very northern; so extreme had been their expressions that it was more than ever difficult to get them together on any platform of national agreement. How could they escape this dilemma?

Two other developments added to the disorganized state of politics. During the turmoil over Texas, the Mexican War, and the Compromise of 1850, three resourceful men, John P. Hale of New Hampshire, Salmon P. Chase of Ohio, and Charles Sumner of Massachuetts, had gained places in the Senate by skillful maneuvering in badly divided state legislatures. But without regular party support, these Free-Soilers were now faced with private life. They were men of desperate fortunes and likely to undertake disruptive policies. And a final disturbing force in the politics of the time was a revival of antagonism to foreigners and to Catholicism.

Politics, it can be seen, were thus in such confusion that a maximum number of politicos were disturbed and disoriented by it. An unusual number were uncertain of their proper roles and were confusedly groping for new alignments which would insure some greater security and more certain prospect of victory. Under such circumstances, any legislation which offered opportunity for political controversy and advantage would be seized upon. For this purpose the Nebraska question was ideal. It was obvious that some bill must be passed and soon, therefore, each faction and individual was alert to gain the greatest possible advantage from the inevitable.

Most observers, including probably Douglas, thought that the chief reason why the Nebraska bill had failed in March, 1853, was because the arbitrary limits of the short session did not give enough time to complete the measure. And there is reason to believe that Douglas thought that in the next session it would go through with little trouble. Certainly no one seems to have foreseen the terrific explosion which developed. The reasons why these unforeseen developments were precipitated in the disturbing fashion which so aroused the nation can be better understood if we examine a series of situations which were cumulating during the summer of 1853 and which had little to do with the ostensible purpose of this legislation, with territorial organization, railroad projects, or anything else but politics.

The first of these were the personal difficulties of Douglas, which were many. In 1852, as a relatively young man, not yet forty, he had challenged his elders and made a strenuous effort to secure the Democratic nomination for the presidency. In doing so, he had stepped out of line and had, therefore, gained the ill will of many of his party associates, particularly those of more advanced years. The friends of Lewis Cass were particularly ill-disposed toward him. Largely as a result of this precocity, Pierce had given him no part or influence in the new administration, a snub which was all too obvious. Added to these political difficulties, he had suffered great personal sorrow in the death of his wife.

Thus beset, Douglas literally fled from the scene of his griefs and disappointments and spent some six months between sessions in Europe. From the middle of May until the end of October he was out of the country and largely out of touch with American politics. He traveled widely and talked with monarchs and statesmen. There were indications that he was planning to take up foreign affairs and to seek a new role in the Senate as a leader in shaping foreign policy. It might enable him to recover lost ground and give him a new means of forging ahead in popular esteem for, as the Democrats had discovered, foreign affairs were sometimes more effective politically than domestic affairs—and safer.

But while Douglas was far away that summer of 1853, the game of politics in the Democratic party was becoming intense and bitter. The Pierce administration had realized that the Democrats were in power only because the Barnburners, the bolters of 1848, had returned to the fold; and the returning group had been admitted to the patronage. But many party members were not forgiving and bitterly opposed their readmission to good standing. One group in New York who were called Hard-shells, a current term for believers in closed communion, fought this policy of Pierce so hard that the Democrats lost the state in 1853.[24] In the South, radical followers of Calhoun displayed equal bitterness as they battled to regain control of the Democratic party in their section. In several southern states "soft" men had accepted the Compromise of 1850 and had come to power on coalition Union tickets dedicated to sectional peace, a policy endorsed by Pierce in his distribution of patronage.[25] The heirs of Calhoun and the Hard-shells were likely to make trouble when the Senate took up the confirmation of Pierce's Barnburner and "Soft-shell" appointees.

A final issue which created dissention within the party had appeared during the summer, when the President and members of his cabinet made a ceremonial excursion to New York City to open the Crystal Palace Exhibition. On the journey, James Guthrie, secretary of the treasury, and Jefferson Davis, secretary of war, had spoken in support of federal aid for a transcontinental railroad to the Pacific. There were important elements in the Democratic party, notably in Virginia, who were opposed to the exercise of such powers by the federal government as well as to the appropriation of such sums of money.[26] So there was dissatisfaction on this count.

All these tangled relationships increased distrust of Pierce as a political chief. His policies were considered demoralizing, his platform inadequate. The party was thought to be falling apart under his incompetent leadership. Certain influential people became convinced that it had been a mistake to choose a leader so young and untried. Some more experienced party tacticians, it was believed, must come forward to repair the damage before it was too late. They must provide some new platform on which the party might once again unite.

A move in this direction appears to have started rather early that summer in an obscure way in Virginia. The so-called national party organ, the Washington *Union*, had been supporting Pierce's patronage recognition of the rebels of 1848. Its editor, Robert Armstrong of Tennessee, who never wrote a line, had reorganized his staff and had fired a Virginian, Roger A. Pryor, replacing him with John W. Forney of Pennsylvania. This act may not have been unrelated to the next journalistic development. In September, a new Democratic newspaper, *The Sentinel*, appeared in Washington. This sheet was edited by a Virginian, Beverly Tucker, who undertook to combat the "free-soil" tendencies of the Pierce administration.

Whether this journalistic venture was a part of a wider plan for supplying the leadership which Pierce had failed to produce is not altogether clear. But it is obvious that as Congress was assembling there was a movement in that direction in the Senate under leadership very definitely southern. The chairmen of the three principal committees—foreign relations, finance, and judiciary—Senators James M. Mason and Robert M. T. Hunter of Virginia and Andrew P. Butler of South Carolina, together with David R. Atchison of Missouri, president pro tempore and acting vice-president, were congenial spirits who kept house together on F Street near the Patent Office. Politically they were the heirs of Calhoun and they were among those who were distressed at Pierce's "weakness" and the seeming disintegration of their party. They liked Pierce personally but they realized that he needed help. They could hardly have been said to approve of his patronage recognition of Barnburners, but they did not want to revolt against him this early by refusing to confirm his "free-soil" appointees. They were the most powerful men in the Senate, but they were burdened by a sense of responsibility and they were looking for a way out.[27]

Atchison's political situation in Missouri may have given them a suggestion as to the means, particularly as events in the early days of the new session were especially irritating to them. When Congress assembled in December 1853, Forney, of the *Union*, was elected clerk of the House. Hardly had he entered office than he dismissed a Virginian, John A. Parker, the librarian of the House. The clannish and powerful Virginians liked this no better than the dismissal of Pryor. They did not find it difficult, therefore, to join with the Whigs and some Hard-shell Democrats in arranging an obvious snub to the President. They joined in defeating the plan of the administration to assign the Senate printing to Armstrong of the *Union*, and instead chose Beverley Tucker for the contract.

At the same time the members of the F Street Mess were planning a more aggressive step in the direction of taking over party leadership. They seem to have determined to reinterpret the party platform and to prescribe it as a test which the Barnburners must accept before the Senate would approve certain of the President's principal New York appointees. The Hard-shell press mentioned this possibility with enthusiasm.

In the shaping of this new test Atchison's needs could be used as a convenient instrument. The Senate was about to resume consideration of the Nebraska bill which had so nearly passed during the last session. In a bitter campaign which Atchison had been fighting with Thomas H. Benton that summer in Missouri for re-election to the Senate, he had promised to secure the organization of the new territory without the exclusion of slavery or else withdraw. These messmates seemed now to have become convinced that they could use the Nebraska question as a means to prescribe a new test, and incidentally to help their colleague retain his seat in the face of Benton's onslaught. The basic tenet in Pierce's political creed was acceptance of the Compromise of 1850, which prescribed self-government in the territories and popular sovereignty, particularly regarding the existence of slavery. To this general creed the Barnburners had subscribed. But if popular sovereignty was good for some territories, it must be good for all. Therefore, the logical implication of this policy was that it should be extended to all territories, even those dedicated to freedom by the Missouri Compromise. The party must now recognize this logic by extending popular sovereignty to Nebraska, and the Barnburners must demonstrate their sincerity by accepting it.

Behind this brief for consistency was southern feeling, particularly among those with speculative interests, that if great railroad and real estate operations were to be undertaken, the South must be allowed to participate; its leaders would no longer submit to the humiliation of exclusion. Some among the southern leadership appear to have become convinced that if they could produce a measure which would organize Nebraska along the lines of the Compromise of 1850 and "requiring a distinct vote now either for or against . . . this would compel honorable gentlemen to show their hands and let the country know what they understand by the administration phrase 'acquiesce in the compromise measures.' "[28] They were in truth the heirs of Calhoun.

Douglas, as chairman of the committee on territories, must of course be dealt with. There was no political love lost between the Calhounites and the opportunistic and pushing young Illinoisan. He might be described as a boon companion of Atchison and his name might be coupled with Hunter's in political and business enterprises, but they did not think of him as one of them and his power was frequently a threat to theirs. The Senate managers, who included Jesse D. Bright of Indiana, lieutenant of Cass and Douglas' rival for the dominant role in the Northwest, were busy with a plan to enlarge the membership of the Senate committees by adding another Democrat to each of the major groups. Whether they were ready to deprive Douglas of his cherished post if he proved recalcitrant is not known, though they did take it from him five years later. Bright was busy with this reshuffling and Atchison perhaps found it an opportune time to approach Douglas, who could not fail to recognize him as a member of the Mess.

Atchison, according to his own testimony, which Douglas never categorically and unequivocally denied, reminded Douglas that he needed at least four southern votes for the Nebraska bill. These he could not have unless some way were found to permit slaveholders to go with their property into the new territory at its opening. The bill of the previous session, which ignored this question, would not do. Atchison further told Douglas that if he did not want to father this new bill, he, Atchison, would resign as vice-president de facto and assume the chairmanship of the committee on territories. Douglas realized he must heed Atchison's "suggestions"; he was helpless and he knew it. Without the votes of the Mess he could secure no bill, and the pressures for its enactment were mounting.

But he would do it in his own way, for he knew he had taken on no easy assignment. He had canvassed the possibility of abandoning the Missouri Compromise a year before this but had discarded it as too hazardous and had nearly succeeded in getting through a bill which ignored the issue. Now he must face the slavery question in some fashion, but under real difficulties. Contrary to the accepted belief, Douglas did not have comfortable control of his own committee. It had been reconstructed by some of his senatorial enemies, either by accident or design in a way embarrassing to him. He was associated with three Democrats and two Whigs; but one of the Democrats was Sam Houston. The Texas senator had his own ideas about Nebraska, and in the last session he had voted against the simple bill then under discussion. Now he delayed coming to Washington for a month and upon arriving would not attend committee meetings. Douglas could do nothing until Houston agreed, and it turned out that Houston would accept nothing outside the framework of the Compromise of 1850. So in the end Douglas copied the phraseology of the act organizing Utah with an explanatory stipulation that the design of the Nebraska bill was to leave all questions pertaining to slavery in this new territory "to the decision of the people residing therein, through their appropriate representatives." Nothing was said about the Missouri restriction; it was just ignored. The new bill embraced not the small area of the previous bill but all the remainder of the Louisiana Purchase.

The presentation of Douglas' revision of the 1853 bill on January 4, 1854, gave other interests ideas about political uses to which they might put the measure. Senator William H. Seward, a leader of the Whig party, shrewdly grasped some rather intricate possibilities. He urged some of his northern Whig associates to lead in attacks upon Democrats by encouraging public meetings of protest and sponsoring legislative resolutions demanding that northern senators and congressmen oppose the bill. In after years he described the more Machiavellian role he played. He suggested that southern Whigs place their Democratic opponents at a disadvantage by assailing them for dodging repeal, and at the same time to proclaim the Whigs as true friends of the South by opposing the dodge or by offering a repeal amendment to the act. Beyond this, Seward had an even more subtle intent. He wished to make the bill as obnoxious as possible to northern voters, for this would help northern Whigs discredit the Democrats. Although Whig Senator Archibald Dixon of Kentucky offered the repeal amendment, he claimed many years later that he could not remember Seward's influence.

Dixon's move gave the cue to a third group to engage in the politics of the bill. The Free-Soil senators and representatives moved much more directly than the subtle Seward. Sumner offered an amendment reaffirming the Missouri exclusion and the Ohio men, led by Giddings and Chase, drafted the "Appeal of the Independent Democrats," arraigning the bill as "a gross violation of a sacred pledge." This manifesto was designed to and did set off a chain reaction which gave northern leaders their desired opportunity to mobilize the anti-southern voting strength of the more populous North.

While the Whigs and Free-Soilers were planning these moves, elements in the Democratic party had become increasingly dissatisfied with Douglas' dodge. Some Calhounite lawyers thought it would not admit slavery to Nebraska. Then, too, the repeal amendment of Dixon further embarrassed southern Democrats because it served to expose them to a charge that they were acquiescing in a subterfuge and so gave advantage to their Whig opponents. Simultaneously, doubts were rising in the minds of certain northern Democrats like Cass and members of the administration, none too friendly with Douglas, that the matter was being badly handled in a fashion that might easily split the party again. Therefore, various Democrats, including Pierce and his cabinet, began seeking a new formula which might insure united Democratic supports and the passing of the much desired bill.

The Calhounites, Douglas, and the President finally achieved a formula to which they got the rather unstable Pierce committed in writing. They would open Nebraska to slavery by declaring that the Missouri Compromise had been "superseded" by the Compromise of 1850 and "declared inoperative." Also, two territories were created instead of one, one west of a slave state and the other west of a free state. This division, reminiscent of the arrangement of 1820, gave the measure more of an air of compromise, and Pierce agreed to give the bill his support.

The second revision of the bill and the "Appeal" were launched almost simultaneously on January 23 and 24 and they brought immediate results. Such a wave of indignation swept through the North at this blow to liberty that the possibility of support from northern Democrats was threatened; and if there were to be a serious revolt among them, the seemingly overwhelming majorities in the Senate and House might disappear, for in both bodies there were more Democrats from the North than from the South.

A further matter for concern was the discovery by the Calhounites of a great and seemingly unexpected indifference to the measure in the South. Many in that region just did not believe that climate would permit any more slave states, and they were not interested in efforts to open territories that would only create more free states. Furthermore, they did not trust Douglas' popular sovereignty. To many it implied that a host of free state people unhampered by any slave property might move right in and elect a territorial legislature which would immediately exclude slavery. Such a proposition was a tricky device to get more free states with no possible advantage to the South. Many so-called Compromise or Union Democrats in the South held these views.

Thus the Democratic strength seemed to be melting away, north and south. The fate of the bill, therefore, hung on selling the idea to the South, particularly by appealing to the southern Whigs, and on whipping northern Democrats into line behind an administration bill. For these purposes, the second revision—the January 23 bill—was proving unsatisfactory, so a series of partisan and bipartisan senatorial caucuses was organized to hammer out another formula which would really insure repeal without using the word and which would overcome southern suspicions of popular sovereignty.

In this series of caucuses in which the leadership was now definitely southern and bipartisan, and in which Douglas by the nature of things could have only a restricted part, a new formula was achieved. The Missouri Compromise was at last specifically declared "void." Recent immigrants were excluded from voting in the territorial elections, an idea attractive to the revived nativism which was becoming popular among southern Whigs. The question of the legality of slave property in the territories was by peculiar language assigned to the Supreme Court. By these caucus actions southern Democrats and southern Whigs were brought to agreement and persuaded to present an almost completely united front. The force behind the caucus procedure was not Douglas but the increasing violence of the attacks against the bill as an act of aggression on the part of the slave power. This insult roused the latent southern nationalism which had been slowly taking shape and for the first time the South presented a united front. Such a combination had a leadership which included not only Douglas, but the members of the Mess and the fiery Whig, Robert Toombs of Georgia. Douglas had the spectacular floor leadership but these others dominated the caucuses that supplied the votes. The bill in this shape finally secured a very comfortable margin in the Senate—37 to 14. But it still had to pass the House.[29]

The heated contest in the Senate had been simple compared with the complex situation that was developing among the representatives. The historian finds that little critical attention has been given over the century to this phase of the struggle and, what is more damaging to the cause of truth, little evidence regarding the contest remains beyond the official record and scattered partisan newspaper comment. Personal correspondence, diary, and memoir material seems not to have survived in any significant quantity. Most historians, absorbed in Douglas and the Senate contest, have expended their pages liberally on that phase of the problem, and have then passed quickly over the struggle in the House. Von Holst, who treated it most extensively, failed to grasp the principal problems of strategy.

The bill ran into trouble in the House from the start. The principal reason was the political hazard which it provided for so many of the representatives. Most members were concerned by the fact that they were in the midst of or on the eve of their re-election campaigns. The rising tide of indignation in the North was frightening to many Democrats who would have to face angry voters, indignant at contrivers or supporters of this measure. Furthermore, the nature of the Democratic majority in the House provided a problem. On paper it was so huge, 159 to 75, that there might seem to have been no conceivable trouble. But the difficult hurdle was that 92 of the 159 Democrats, by far the greater part, came from northern constituencies. So there was trouble, even in the House Committee on the Territories. The chairman of this group was one of Douglas' most loyal associates, William A. Richardson of Illinois, who presided over a committee made up of four southern Democrats, another from Missouri, a second Democrat from a free state—William H. English of Indiana—and two Whigs. The original plan had been to report out a duplicate of Douglas' January 23 version on that day, but English and the Whigs objected and delayed the report until January 31, and with it English then filed a minority pronouncement.

The discussion in the House committee defined the strategy of the contest which was to ensue. English represented a large proportion of the ninety-two northern Democrats. These men resented the semantic gymnastics used to deal with the slavery question. They wanted a forthright statement of the doctrine of popular sovereignty, of self-government in the territories, acknowledging the complete control of the slave question by the territorial governments. They felt they would have a chance in the coming election if they were fighting a positive battle to extend democracy, whereas if they were forced on the defensive by charges of destroying the Missouri Compromise they were in grave danger.

The final version of the bill as it came from the Senate put them at the greatest disadvantage. This version—the revision of the January 23 bill—not only declared the Missouri Compromise void, but it gave no specific authority to the territorial governments over the admission of slavery. To make matters worse for some of the congressmen, the bill excluded unnaturalized foreign immigrants from political participation in the organization of the territories. Not only did this provision exclude numerous potential free state voters but it aroused foreign-born voters against the Democrats in various districts.

A group of northern Democrats, therefore, planned some embarrassing strategy which, if successful, would for the time being at least take the bill out of the control of the administration leaders. Sixty-six of the ninety-two northern Democrats revolted and successfully completed this maneuver. The administration was defeated, 110 to 95. Of the thirteen delegations which the northern Democrats "controlled," only Pennsylvania, Illinois, and California showed any real loyalty. New England, New York, and New Jersey failed utterly. Even Michigan and Indiana, bailiwicks of Cass and Bright, fell away. Ohio and Wisconsin would have little of the measure.

This defeat was a blow which challenged all the ingenuity which the administration, Douglas, and the bipartisan southern coalition could muster. Probably few of the sixty-six wanted to prevent the organization of the territories but many either wanted a different bill or hoped to get something for themselves out of the measure's passage. In fact the revolting northern Democrats were fighting not so much to defeat the bill as to change it. They wanted a return to Douglas' first bill of January 4 or else to have English's popular sovereignty amendment or something like it inserted. Furthermore, they wanted to strike out the immigrant-exclusion amendment.

So three forces girded themselves for final efforts. The opposition sought to enlist the revolting sixty-six Democrats in the final defeat of the bill. The administration and the congressional managers were trying to get them to return to regularity. The revolters themselves were battling to get their terms accepted. Here history draws the curtain. The evidence of what went on in the minds and emotions of the sixty-six still remains hidden, if it exists. What experiences these sixty-six had, what pressures were exerted on them, how they reacted, what they wanted and either got or did not get, whether some reasoned it out or reacted to pressure from home, how many were moved by moral indignation or were swayed by party loyalty, remains hidden. Answers to these questions would supply the real history of this phase of the bill's passage, yet these answers are not known.

It was, of course, obvious that the President and his cabinet made some efforts with patronage promises, offers of administrative favors, and persuasive arguments, but they were handicapped by the fact that much of their patronage had been used up. Furthermore, the unstable President and the administration newspaper, the Washington *Union,* blew hot and cold. Some effort was made to re-form the ranks by appeals to party loyalty, and Douglas sought to persuade, to order, to overawe; in fact he used all the tactics his ingenious mind and dynamic personality could contrive. Who was promised what, and why shifts were made is still almost wholly unknown. We have only the bare results. No change was made in the bill save the restoring of political privilege to unnaturalized settlers and the bill passed.

On one occasion before final passage of the bill, some eighteen Democrats were persuaded to return to the ranks of regularity and on one other strategic roll-call, when a two-thirds vote was required, a second eighteen, who on no other occasion supported the bill, contributed their votes. Even then the final victory was won, not by Douglas and his Democratic cohorts, but by a bipartisan coalition marshaled by the Georgia Whig, Alexander H. Stephens, who devised the slick maneuver which in the end put the bill over. The eighteen Democratic rebels who had been persuaded to change and vote "aye" were not enough. Had it not been for the support of thirteen southern Whigs, the now impotent Democratic majority could not have carried the bill.[30]

Thus the act came into being. It bore little resemblance to the bill for which Douglas had struggled in the short session of the preceding Congress. The Calhoun faction, southern and northern Whigs, Free-Soilers, the administration, and certain Hard-shell Democrats had all made use of this measure in one way or another and the final bill was the work of many hands and the fruit of much strategic planning. Its real history is the analysis of how a bill ostensibly to organize a territory had been made an instrument of the fundamental political reorganization that the disintegration of the old parties had made inevitable. The story of these political maneuvers is the neglected element in the history of the bill; it is the so-called mystery, the Hamlet which has been hitherto either omitted or only very sketchily treated.

In this fateful legislative session a new plank had been added to the

Democratic platform, the President and the principal Barn-burner and Soft-shell officeholders had accepted it, the appointments had been confirmed. Douglas himself had lost an essential portion of his northern support without improving his position in the South. A significant segment of the northern Democracy had left the party. Likewise, a real anti-southern coalition which could capitalize the voting superiority of the more populous North was insured; the seed of the Republican party had been planted. Finally, and not usually noted, was the fact that in this winter of political discontent, the southern members of Congress for the first time organized and presented a well-nigh solid political front and among them traditional party divisions were largely laid aside. It was but a few steps onward to secession, the Confederacy, and the Solid South.

The great volcano of American politics was in a state of eruption. In the midst of the cataclysm, one sees Douglas crashing and hurtling about, caught like a rock in a gush of lava. When the flow subsided, old landmarks were found to be either greatly altered or obliterated. Two new masses were prominent on the political landscape, the Republican party and the Solid South. Douglas had disappeared.

NOTES

1. *Senate Reports*, 33 Cong., 1 Sess., No. 15.
2. *Cong. Globe*, 33 Cong., 1 Sess., 281.
3. Joshua R. Giddings, *History of the Rebellion, Its Authors and Causes* (New York, 1864), 364; Horace Greeley, *The American Conflict* (2 vols., Hartford, 1864-1866), I, 224; Henry S. Foote, *War of the Rebellion* (New York, 1866), 182-84, and *Casket of Reminiscences* (Washington, 1874), 93.
4. J. Madison Cutts, *A Brief Treatise upon Constitutional and Party Questions* (New York, 1866), 122.
5. Henry Wilson, *History of the Rise and Fall of the Slave Power in America* (3 vols., Boston, 1872-1877), II, 378.
6. Hermann E. von Holst, *Constitutional and Political History of the United States* (7 vols., Chicago, 1876-1892), IV, 256-461.
7. James Schouler, *History of the United States of America under the Constitution* (7 vols., Boston, 1880-1913), VI, 285.
8. James Ford Rhodes, *History of the United States from the Compromise of 1850* (7 vols., New York, 1892-1906), I, 420-98. For Rhodes's motivation see Frank H. Hodder, "Propaganda as a Source of American History," *Mississippi Valley Historical Review*, IX (June, 1922), 3-18.
9. John W. Burgess, *The Middle Period, 1817-1858* (New York, 1897).
10. Allen Johnson, *Stephen A. Douglas* (New York, 1908).
11. P. Orman Ray, *The Repeal of the Missouri Compromise* (Cleveland, 1909).

12. John A. Parker, "The Secret History of the Kansas-Nebraska Bill," *National Quarterly Review*, XLI (July, 1880), 105-18.
13. Frank H. Hodder, "Stephen A. Douglas," *Chautauquan*, XXIX (August, 1899), 432-37; Hodder, "The Genesis of the Kansas-Nebraska Act," State Historical Society of Wisconsin, *Proceedings*, 1912, 69-86.
14. Ray, "The Genesis of the Kansas-Nebraska Act," American Historical Association, *Annual Report*, 1914 (2 vols., Washington, 1916), I, 259-80.
15. Hodder, "The Railroad Background of the Kansas-Nebraska Act," *Mississippi Valley Historical Review*, XII (June, 1925), 3-22.
16. Albert J. Beveridge, *Abraham Lincoln, 1809-1858* (4 vols., Boston, 1928), III, 165-217.
17. Roy F. Nichols, *Franklin Pierce* (Philadelphia, 1931).
18. George Fort Milton, *Eve of Conflict: Stephen A. Douglas and the Needless War* (New York, 1934).
19. Allan Nevins, *Ordeal of the Union* (2 vols., New York, 1947), II, 43-159.
20. Avery Craven, *The Coming of the Civil War* (New York, 1942).
21. Craven, *The Growth of Southern Nationalism, 1848-1861* (Baton Rouge, 1953), 172-205.
22. *Ibid.*, 180.
23. James C. Malin, *The Nebraska Question, 1852-1854* (Lawrence, Kan., 1953).
24. Roy F. Nichols, *Democratic Machine, 1850-1854* (New York, 1923), *passim*, and *Franklin Pierce*, 241-58, 276-93; Craven, *Growth of Southern Nationalism*, 172-77; Nevins, *Ordeal of the Union*, II, 69-77.
25. This southern political complex has never been given adequate attention. We are in particular need of a closer analysis of Virginia politics during the 1850's.
26. Nichols, *Franklin Pierce*, 279-80.
27. Ray, *Repeal of the Missouri Compromise*, 229-33.
28. New York *Herald*, January 4, 1854.
29. The final draft of the bill, written in a clerk's hand, is in the Senate Files (National Archives). That its wording received close attention up to the last minute is illustrated by the fact that in a sentence concerning "The principle of non-intervention by Congress with slavery in the States and Territories, as established by the legislation of 1850 . . ." the word "established" was crossed out and "recognized," written in another hand, substituted.
30. The final affirmative vote was 113 to 100, with only 100 of the 159 Democrats voting aye. Of the northern Democrats who voted, forty-four were favorable and forty-three opposed. Eight southern Democrats and five northern Democrats did not vote; from their own statements and previous votes the last five seem certainly to have been opposed to the measure. Full Democratic support for the bill can be reckoned as 108, which was not enough to carry it.

RECENT STUDIES

Frederick Merk, *The Monroe Doctrine and American Expansion, 1843-1849* (New York: Alfred A. Knopf, 1966).

Charles Sellers, *James K. Polk: Continentalist, 1843-1846* (Princeton: Princeton University Press, 1966).

William H. Goetzmann, *When the Eagle Screamed: The Romantic Horizon in American Diplomacy, 1800-1860* (New York: John Wiley, 1966).

Norman A. Graebner, "1848: Southern Politics at the Crossroads," *The Historian*, XXV (November 1962), 14-35.

Holman Hamilton, *Prologue to Conflict: The Crisis and Compromise of 1850* (Lexington: University of Kentucky Press, 1964).

Robert R. Russel, "The Issues in the Congressional Struggle Over the Kansas-Nebraska Bill, 1854," *Journal of Southern History*, XXIX (May 1963), 187-210.

IX

The Profitability of Slavery: A Historical Perennial

HAROLD D. WOODMAN

Abolitionists and their proslavery antagonists in the ante bellum period argued hotly over the profitability of slavery. Since the Civil War, historians and economists have continued the argument, less acrimoniously but no less vehemently. In part, solution of the problem of the profitability of slavery has been blocked by a lack of agreement as to how the problem is to be defined. Either implicitly or—as is more often the case—explicitly, contemporaries and modern scholars alike have begun their discussion of the profitability of slavery by posing the question: Profitable for whom? For the slave? For the slaveowner? For the South as a section? For the American economy as a whole? Answers to the general question, of course, depend upon how the question is posed. As a result, conflicting conclusions often reflect differing definitions of the problem as well as different solutions. What seem to be clashing opinions often do not clash at all but pass each other in the obscurity created by a lack of an agreed upon definition of the problem.

When a writer answers the question, "Profitable for whom?" by limiting himself to the planter or slaveholder, he is dealing with the question of profitability in terms of a business or industry. He is concerned with such questions as: Did the planters make money? Did *all*

From *The Journal of Southern History*, XXIX (August 1963), pp. 303-25. Copyright 1963 by the Southern Historical Association. Reprinted by permission of the Managing Editor.

planters make money? Did planters make as much on their investment in slaves as they would have made had they invested elsewhere? Staple production with slave labor is regarded as a business enterprise much as automobile manufacture is seen as a business enterprise today. Profitability relates only to the success or failure of slave production as a business and ignores the broader questions of the effect of this type of enterprise on the economy as a whole.

If, on the other hand, a writer answers the question, "Profitable for whom?" by discussing the effect of slavery on the South, he is treating slavery as an economic system rather than as a business enterprise. The issue of profits earned by individual planters is subordinated to the larger problems of economic growth, capital accumulation, and the effect of slavery on the general population.

Debate over the years has ranged on both aspects of the topic, with most writers emphasizing one or the other aspect and an occasional writer dealing with both. Despite the many contributions which have been made—and are still being made—historians and economists have not been able to reach a consensus on this vexing problem. The debate rages undiminished and, except for greater subtlety of method and sophistication of presentation, often rests today on substantially the same ground that it did a hundred years ago.

If we trace the development of this continuing controversy through the works of its most able participants, we can discern some reasons for the lack of substantial progress in solving the problem and suggest certain lines of approach which may lead to a more satisfactory solution.

Dispute on the profitability of slavery in the ante bellum period was confined almost solely to the question of slavery as a system rather than a business. This is not surprising. Proslavery writers could hardly be expected to defend the peculiar institution on the ground that it made the planters rich. In the face of obvious Southern economic backwardness and poverty, such a position would be tantamount to an argument for abolition in the eyes of anyone other than the favored planters. On the other hand, the antislavery or abolitionist group would have a weak argument indeed if they confined it to the contention that slaveowners made a profit. The right to make a profit was uniformly accepted in the United States, and to point out that planters made a profit by using slave labor was no indictment of them. The nature of the situation, then, led prewar commentators to deal with slavery primarily as an economic and social system rather than as a form of business enterprise and to argue its merits on the basis of its effects on the well-being of the whole population.

This did not mean, however, that the contenders clashed directly. Specific arguments seldom met with specific rebuttal. Rather, the antislavery group picked out those aspects of the question they felt most damaging and most to be condemned; defenders answered by pointing to what they considered to be the beneficial features of the peculiar institution. The antagonists, of course, were directly involved. Their aim was most often not to convince their opponents by scholarly argument but to attack or defend slavery within the larger context of the sectional controversy.

The essence of the antislavery economic argument was that the slave system caused Southern economic backwardness. The words of Hinton Rowan Helper, the North Carolina white farmer, summarize this position and at the same time show the intense feeling which the argument generated in the ante bellum South:

> . . . the causes which have impeded the progress and prosperity of the South, which have dwindled our commerce, and other similar pursuits, into the most contemptible insignificance; sunk a large majority of our people in galling poverty and ignorance, rendered a small minority conceited and tyrannical, and driven the rest away from their homes; entailed upon us a humiliating dependence on the Free States; disgraced us in the recesses of our own souls, and brought us under reproach in the eyes of all civilized and enlightened nations—may all be traced to one common source, and there find solution in the most hateful and horrible word, that was ever incorporated into the vocabulary of human economy—*Slavery!*[1]

The burden of Helper's argument was that even in the area of the South's touted superiority, agriculture, the North was far ahead. Using figures from the 1850 consus, Helper argued that the value of agricultural products in the free states exceeded that of the slave states and that the value of real and personal property in the free states topped that of the slave states (when the value of slaves was excluded). Helper adduced figures for commercial and industrial development which told the same story. His contention that slavery was the cause of this economic inequality came from a process of elimination rather than from a direct analysis of the operation of the slave system. At the close of the eighteenth century the South stood in an equal or superior position to the North in all aspects of economic development. Since then the South had fallen further and further behind. Wherein lay the differences between North and South which could account for this? Slavery, obviously, was the culprit.[2]

The Kentucky editor, Cassius M. Clay, regularly condemned slavery in his newspaper, the Lexington *True American*. Slavery, he argued, was economically destructive. Because it degraded labor, whites refused to do physical work, thereby fostering idleness. Those who would work were faced by the competition of slave labor, and their wages never exceeded the subsistence level which was the pay accorded slaves. When whites did not work and slaves were kept ignorant, skill or excellence could not develop. In addition, slave labor was economically expensive for the South because capital was tied up or frozen in the form of labor:

> The twelve hundred millions of capital invested in slaves is a dead loss to the South; the North getting the same number of laborers doing double the work, for the interest on the money; and sometimes by partnerships, or joint operations, or when men work on their own account, without any interest being expended for labor.[3]

Finally, slavery hindered the development of a home market for local industry and thereby retarded economic development:

> Lawyers, merchants, mechanics, laborers, who are your consumers; Robert Wickliffe's two hundred slaves? How many clients do you find, how many goods do you sell, how many hats, coats, saddles, and trunks, do you make for these two hundred slaves? Does Mr. Wickliffe lay out as much for himself and his two hundred slaves, as two hundred freemen do . . .? Under the free system the towns would grow and furnish a home market to the farmers, which in turn would employ more labor; which would consume the manufactures of the towns; and we could then find our business continually increasing, so that our children might settle down among us and make industrious, honest citizens.[4]

Clay's arguments, written in the 1840's, attempted to *explain* the economic consequences of the slave system rather than to *describe* them as did Helper a decade later. Clay's three main points—slavery degrades labor and keeps it ignorant, thereby hindering the development of skills; slavery freezes capital in the form of labor, thereby making it unavailable for other enterprises; slavery limits the home market—were recurring themes in the economic attack on slavery. A pamphlet by Daniel Reaves Goodloe, written about the same time that Clay's articles appeared, raised the same arguments.[5] George Tucker, in a general economic treatise written a decade earlier, gave major stress to the problem of idleness which he felt was a result of the degradation of labor induced by slavery.[6]

The most detailed economic indictment of the slave system in the ante bellum period—published just after the outbreak of the war— was made by a British economist. J. E. Cairnes stressed the detrimental effects of slavery as a form of labor and as a form of capital. The weaknesses of slave labor, he maintained, stemmed from three characteristics: "It is given reluctantly; it is unskillful; it is wanting in versatility." Soil exhaustion necessarily followed from the use of such labor. Scientific agriculture was impossible; slaves who worked reluctantly and in ignorance were incapable of learning and applying new farming techniques. Only the best lands, therefore, were used and, losing their fertility, were left desolate.[7]

Slave labor also hindered industrial and commercial development, Cairnes continued. Slaves were kept in ignorance and were thus unable to cope with machinery. If educated and brought to the cities as industrial workers, the danger of their combining to better their conditions or of their engaging in insurrection was increased. Commerce likewise was impossible. The dangers of mutiny on the high seas or of desertion in free ports would deter slaveowners from using their property in this work.

Cairnes agreed with Clay and Goodloe that slave capital was economically expensive because it involved a larger capital outlay than free labor. Available capital was tied up in slaves and therefore unavailable for manufacturing and commerce. As manufacturing and commerce were important sources for the accumulation of capital, the lack of these enterprises hindered accumulation in the South. This completed a vicious circle, accentuating the shortage of capital and making nonagricultural pursuits even more difficult to begin.[8]

Ante bellum defenders of slavery, for the most part, did not meet these economic criticisms head on. Except for those who charged that Helper manipulated his figures to produce the desired result,[9] upholders of slavery shifted the ground of controversy.

Slavery was defended as an economic good because it transformed ignorant and inferior African savages into productive workers. "There is nothing but slavery which can destroy those habits of indolence and sloth, and eradicate the character of improvidence and carelessness, which mark the independent savage," wrote Thomas R. Dew.[10] Another defender, Albert Taylor Bledsoe, after his sketch of the horrors of life in Africa, concluded that "No fact is plainer than that the blacks have been elevated and improved by their servitude in this

country. We cannot possibly conceive, indeed, how Divine Providence could have placed them in a better school of correction."[11]
William J. Grayson versified the same argument:

> Instructed thus, and in the only school
> Barbarians ever know—a master's rule,
> The Negro learns each civilising art
> That softens and subdues the savage heart,
> Assumes the tone of those with whom he lives,
> Acquires the habit that refinement gives,
> And slowly learns, but surely, while a slave,
> The lessons that his country never gave.
>
> .   .   .   .
>
> No better mode can human wits discern,
> No happier system wealth or virtue find,
> To tame and elevate the Negro mind.[12]

Thus slavery was not only an economic good but a social and humanitarian blessing as well.

Slavery, according to its defenders, was economically beneficial in other ways. It was said to mitigate the class conflict which existed in every society.[13] "It is impossible to place labor and capital in harmonious or friendly relations, except by the means of slavery, which identifies their interests," George Fitzhugh wrote.[14] His *Cannibals All!* also stressed the well-being of the slave. Because capital and labor were united in the slave he was better cared for and suffered none of the privations visited upon the wage slave of the North for whom freedom was a condition of dubious value. Grayson employed his heroic couplets to make this point:

> If bound to daily labor while he lives,
> His is the daily bread that labor gives;
> Guarded from want, from beggary secure,
> He never feels what hireling crowds endure,
> Nor knows like them in hopeless want to crave,
> For wife and child, the comforts of the slave,
> Or the sad thought that, when about to die,
> He leaves them to the cold world's charity,
> And sees them slowly seek the poor-house door—
> The last, vile, hated refuge of the poor.[15]

Proslavery writers, virtually ignoring the view of slavery as economically debilitating to the South, argued instead that it strengthened the nation's economy.[16] They pointed to the products of slave labor, tracing their importance to the country as a whole. Upon slavery and slave labor, in fact, rested the economic well-being of the nation and the world. David Christy, writing that slavery was not "a self-sustaining system, independently remunerative," contended that "it attains its importance to the nation and to the world, by standing as an agency, intermediate, between the grain growing states and our foreign commerce." Taking the products of the North, slavery "metamorphoses them into cotton, that they may bear export." To the world it supplied cotton for manufacture into cloth and clothing, stimulating commerce and industry. For the United States it provided the largest cash exports (cotton and tobacco); it comprised a market for manufactured goods, supplied food and other groceries, and helped to pay for foreign imports.[17] Northern profits depended upon Southern wealth, argued Thomas Kettell in 1860; the North, therefore, should do everything in its power to keep the South, with its peculiar institution, in the Union.[18]

Whatever advantages did accrue to the South came, ironically, to those who did not own slaves, according to the editor J. D. B. De Bow. Not only did the nonslaveowning merchants benefit from slavery because they handled the goods produced by slave labor, but the white worker in the South also benefited. He had status by virtue of being a white man; he was not forced to work in unhealthy shops as was his white brother in the North; and most important of all, he had the opportunity of becoming a slaveholder and by so doing relieving himself and his wife of drudgery in the fields.[19]

Although ante bellum disputants thus came to opposite conclusions regarding the profitability of the slave system, not all of their arguments were mutually exclusive. This observation is most clearly illustrated by the manner in which Ulrich B. Phillips, re-examining the question in the twentieth century, was able to incorporate a large part of both ends of the argument into his economic analysis of the slave system. He accepted many of the conclusions of slavery's defenders while at the same time maintaining that the slave system was detrimental to the economic development of the South. He was able to unite the two points of view by clearly differentiating between the plantation system and slavery. At the same time he considered another factor in his discussion, that of slavery as a business enterprise.

While slavery existed, for the most part, within the plantation system, the two, Phillips maintained, were not inseparable. Indeed, the plantation regime "was less dependent upon slavery than slavery was upon it." The plantation system was a means of organizing labor; slavery, on the other hand, was a means of capitalizing labor.

The plantation system had definite advantages both economic and social. By routinizing labor, dividing different tasks rationally, and instituting strict supervision, while at the same time caring for the health of the workers (slaves), the plantation made for efficient methods of production.[20] Such methods were required because of the crude labor used. In effectively organizing ignorant and savage labor into efficient production it was economically advantageous; and "in giving industrial education to the laboring population, in promoting certain moral virtues, and in spreading the amenities" it was socially advantageous. The plantation was "a school constantly training and controlling pupils who were in a backward state of civilization."[21]

But the ante bellum plantation system hampered the economic development of the South. Its weakness stemmed less from its role as an organizer of labor and more from its close tie-in with slavery as an economic system. If the plantation was a school, the slave system prevented the apt students from ever being graduated. Laborers whose abilities transcended crude field work were yet harnessed to it and could not establish themselves as independent farmers. Unskilled labor was what was required and planters found it economically wasteful to train many skilled laborers despite any ability they might exhibit.[22]

Slavery, then, was harmful to the South because it prevented full utilization of the potential skills and abilities in the labor force. But the detrimental effects of slavery went deeper than this, according to Phillips. The central economic disadvantage of slavery was that it required that the entire life's labor of the worker be capitalized. Under a free labor system, wages are paid as work is done, and income from the sale of products can be used to pay future wage bills as they arise. The planter, however, was forced to buy his labor; that is, his wage bill became a long-term capital investment. Thus the slave system absorbed available capital. "Individual profits, as fast as made, went into the purchase of labor, and not into modern implements or land improvements."[23]

Because capital tended to be absorbed by the slave system, its availability was at a premium and planters were forced to look to outside sources for credit: "Circulating capital was at once converted into fixed capital; while for their annual supplies of food, implements, and luxuries the planters continued to rely upon their credit with the local merchants, and the local merchants to rely upon their credit with northern merchants and bankers." The result was a continuous economic loss as capital was drained from the South.[24]

The capital shortage stunted Southern economic development by hindering diversification in the economy, thereby keeping the South dependent upon the North. While Ohio benefited New York by becoming a market and a supplier of food and raw materials, Alabama had no such reciprocal relationship with Virginia or South Carolina. On the contrary, the Southwest competed with the Southeast to the detriment of the older regions because it could produce cotton more cheaply on the better lands and because increased production and labor needs drove the prices of slaves up. Economic benefits accrued to the North where manufactured goods and services had to be purchased; the Southeast was prevented from opening mills because all available capital was absorbed in slaves.[25]

Phillips introduced another dimension to his discussion of the economics of slavery—the question of the profitability of slavery to the individual slaveholder.[26] Matching the continual public loss as capital left the South was the private loss in the form of interest payments on borrowed capital. Profits were absorbed by the need to capitalize labor, a situation which was greatly aggravated in the 1850's when prices of slaves skyrocketed. As a result, Phillips declared, by the end of the 1850's only those plantations on the best lands, under the most efficient supervision, could make a profit for their owners.[27]

For Phillips, then, the plantation system was often economically beneficial to the South.[28] Its weakness stemmed from the fact that it was inextricably bound to slavery. It was slavery as an economic system which hindered and warped Southern development and kept the South backward in the prewar period. And it was slavery which made staple production in the ante bellum period an unprofitable enterprise for all but the most favorably situated planters. Phillips concluded that slavery was "an obstacle to all progress." He had to explain the continued existence of a personally and socially unprofitable system on noneconomic grounds. Slavery, he wrote, was initially introduced as a means of labor control and at first had proved to be profitable. As the number of slaves continued to rise, slavery became essential as an instrument of race control. It became the means to police an inferior race, to keep the Negroes' "savage instincts from breaking forth, and to utilize them in civilized industry." For the moment private gain and social gain were united. But as time went on the question of race control became most important—and an end to be attained only "at the expense of private and public wealth and of progress."[29]

Phillips' work was immensely influential. In the 1920's and 1930's a series of state studies were published which tended to support his conclusions. Perhaps because they were local studies and not concerned with overall Southern development, these monographs gave major emphasis to slavery as a form of business enterprise rather than as an economic system. The question posed was simply whether the planters made money on their investment in slaves. Rosser Howard Taylor, basing his conclusions on the testimony of travelers and on extant plantation records, concluded that in North Carolina "slaveholding was not generally profitable."[30] Ralph B. Flanders, in his study of Georgia slavery, found that although some planters were able to amass a fortune, many others made but a marginal living. He found much evidence showing that ante bellum Georgia planters bemoaned the unprofitability of the peculiar institution.[31] Slavery in Mississippi was investigated by Charles S. Sydnor. He found that free labor was much cheaper than slave and would have been more profitable for the planter to use. A thirty-slave plantation required a $40,000 investment, while if free labor had been used only $10,000 would have been needed. The greater the capital investment, he concluded, the greater the interest costs which had to be charged against profits. Furthermore, the large investment in labor the slaveowner was forced to make "added nothing to the productivity of the soil or to the betterment of the farm equipment," and it was doubtful whether the increased efficiency gained by slavery justified the "enlarged investment of capital." After calculating the costs of production on a typical fifty-slave Mississippi plantation, Sydnor concluded that profits were low. Only by spending the interest and other hidden charges (interest on capital invested in slaves, depreciation of slave property, land, and equipment) and by not calculating their own wages as supervisors of the business could planters seem to make a profit. A similar situation prevailed in Alabama, according to the historian of the cotton kingdom in that state, Charles S. Davis. Even with cotton selling at eight cents per pound, production by slave labor "was a fair business and nothing more." While some planters did make a great deal of money, "for the great majority the planting profession meant only a living."[32]

Further support for Phillips' views came from an influential article by Charles W. Ramsdell in 1929. Ramsdell maintained that slavery could be profitable only on the very best lands and since these lands, by the late 1850's, had been almost completely settled, slavery would have gradually become more and more decadent until, finally, economic causes would have required emancipation. He pointed out that high cotton prices of the 1850's could not last and, in fact, had already shown evidence of decline by 1860. As good lands were taken up and cotton prices declined, slave prices would drop also and Eastern states would no longer have the Western slave market in which to dispose profitably of excess slaves. In the meantime, with no new land available, more slaves would be on hand than could be used. Owners of large slave forces would find the expense of maintaining them too high to make cotton production by slave labor profitable. Slaves would become an economic handicap and slaveowners would look for a way to free their slaves and thereby relieve themselves of the burden of supporting them.[33]

While Phillips and his followers were amassing a formidable array of economic reasoning and statistical data to prove that slavery was unprofitable both as an economic system (because of its effects on the South) and as a business enterprise (because slaveowners made little profit), other historians were challenging this thesis on all levels. Some sought to show that Southern backwardness was not the fault of slavery, others stoutly maintained that planters on the whole made very substantial profits. The beginnings of this anti-Phillips or revisionist school can be traced back as far as the first decade of the twentieth century, but most of the revisionist work was done in the period beginning in the 1930's. It is this school which seems to be most active at the present time; nevertheless, there are still strong adherents to the traditional point of view.

The Mississippi planter and historian, Alfred Holt Stone, writing in the first decade of the century, relied heavily on Phillips but came to different conclusions. Stone's central argument was that it was the Negro and not slavery which retarded the ante bellum South. The Negro, according to Stone, was an inferior being incapable of advancing whether free or slave: "The negro was a negro before he was a slave and he remained a negro after he became free. I recall no sound economic argument against slave negro labor per se . . . which is not today equally as sound against free negro labor per se." Had white free labor been used in Southern production, the foundation of Southern economic life would have been sounder. Some form of the plantation system would have undoubtedly developed, "but it would have been based upon free white labor, and would have served as a great training school for the production of small farmers."[34] The innate inferiority of Negroes prevented them from reaching this level.

But the most telling of the earlier blows struck in the revisionist cause were the works of Robert R. Russel and Lewis C. Gray written in the 1930's. Neither sought to reverse completely Phillips' point of view, but both aimed at changing the emphasis of his analysis.

Russel made no effort to deny that the ante bellum Southern economy was backward; he did deny, however, that slavery was responsible. Rather, the South was hamstrung by its "climate, topography, natural resources, location with respect to the North and to Europe, means of transportation, and character of the white population."[35] The fact that population in the North was less dispersed led to more concentrated markets for Northern manufacturers and lessened the problems of transportation to and from these markets. Household manufacture was more firmly entrenched in the Northeast from the start, and, as Northwestern agricultural regions opened up, Easterners were forced to leave the countryside—they were no longer able to compete—and were thus available as operatives in industry. In the South, the profitability of staple agriculture and the fact that slaves "were certainly not as well adapted to mechanical employments as to agriculture" prevented the development of this same pattern. The central weakness in the South was not simply that slave labor was used but that it was primarily an area of commercial agriculture. Planters lived on future earnings and borrowed from Northern and British sources, thereby incurring an expense which limited the amount of capital accumulation in the region. Overproduction of the staples forced prices down and cut into profits and, therefore, into savings. But these were phenomena of agricultural production and had little to do with the use of slave labor. Furthermore, the argument that slavery absorbed Southern capital was incorrect: "Slavery did not absorb Southern capital in any direct sense; it affected the distribution of capital within the section. The mere capitalization of the anticipated labor of a particular class did not destroy or diminish any other kind of property."[36]

The central element in Lewis C. Gray's revisionist argument was that slavery was a highly profitable form of business enterprise. Slave labor, when used for staple production, would always supplant free labor because it was cheaper and more efficient. The employer of slave labor had a guaranteed labor supply; women as well as men could be used in the fields; child labor could be used extensively; labor troubles such as strikes and lockouts were unknown. The slaveowner could appropriate every bit of surplus created by the slave over and above bare subsistence. Thus, slaveowners had to give their slaves only just enough to keep them alive; wage laborers could not offer their services for less.[37] The high prices of slaves in the 1850's, Gray wrote, reflected accurately the profitability of such labor, and it was profitability that accounted for its continued use.[38]

Although Gray disputed the contention that all of the South's ills could be traced to slavery, he did argue that the "ultimate influence"

of slavery "upon the economic well-being of the South was pernicious."
Slavery was most profitable on the richest and most favorably situated
lands; other lands were left to the free population which lived at a
subsistence level. This free population provided a very small market
and exerted little pressure for the construction of roads, canals, schools,
and other necessary social improvements. Because slavery was profitable,
all available capital that was accumulated went into expansion of
staple production using slave labor and, hence, was unavailable to industry or trade. The South remained, therefore, "a predominantly
agricultural country" and was "consequently subject to the disadvantages characteristic" of such an economy. The fundamental disadvantage was the slow accumulation of local capital which further
intensified the problems of expansion, diversification, and economic
growth. "Hence," he concluded, "we have the near-paradox of an economic institution competitively effective under certain conditions, but
essentially regressive in its influence on the socio-economic evolution
of the section where it prevailed."[39]

The work of Gray and Russel opened up a double-barreled assault
on the Phillips point of view. Russel had questioned the allegation that
slavery was the main cause of Southern backwardness, and Gray had
disputed the contention that slaveowning was not a profitable business enterprise. Further revisionist work proceeded along these two
lines, although most of the succeeding work gave major emphasis to
the problem of slavery as a business rather than as an economic system.

Thomas P. Govan subjected the bookkeeping methods used by
Phillips and his followers to critical scrutiny. The central problem in
determining profitability, according to Govan, was simply to decide
whether planters made money on their investment. He criticized the
work of Phillips, Sydnor, Flanders, and others on two counts: They
failed to consider all possible sources of profit in making their calculations, and they considered as an expense an item which should have
been considered as part of the profit. Services received from household slaves, food and other provisions grown on the plantation and
used by the owner, and the increase in the value of land and slaves
must all be considered as part of profit; yet, Govan charged, these
items were ignored in figuring income. Furthermore, interest on investment, which Sydnor and others listed as an expense, was, in reality,
a profit item. According to the classical economists, profit is made up
of interest on investment, payment for supervision, and payment for
risk. Accountants usually do not separate the first and last of these,
but they do include them in the profit column. When these adjust-

ments in bookkeeping methods are made, Govan concluded, slave-ownership emerges as a highly profitable business.[40]

The bookkeeping problem was approached somewhat differently by Robert Worthington Smith. It is a mistake, he insisted, to consider capital investment on the basis of current prices on slaves. While slave prices were extremely high in the 1850's, it would be incorrect to use the appreciated value of slaves owned from an earlier period (or those born and raised on the plantation) as the capital investment in figuring profit. If, Smith concluded, profit is calculated upon the "capital actually invested in slaves" rather than upon current prices, "a very good return seems to have been paid to the majority of owners."[41]

The most all-inclusive revisionist work on the question of American slavery is Kenneth M. Stampp's *The Peculiar Institution*, published in 1956. Disagreeing with Phillips about almost every aspect of slavery in the United States, Stampp differed with him, too, over the economics of slavery. But while Phillips gave major emphasis to the problem of slavery as an economic system, Stampp was mainly concerned with slavery as a business: ". . . allowing for the risks of a laissez-faire economy, did the average ante-bellum slaveholder, over the years, earn a reasonably satisfactory return from his investment?"[42] Stampp's answer was unequivocal: "On both large and small estates, none but the most hopelessly inefficient masters failed to profit from the ownership of slaves." Slave labor was cheaper and could be more fully exploited; this made up for any loss due to inefficiency. Capital invested in slaves was not an added expense but merely a payment in advance for work which would be performed over a period of years. Hidden sources of profit, such as food produced on the plantation, sale of excess slaves, natural increase of slaves, appreciation of land values because of improvements—all, when added to the income from the sale of the staple, served to increase profits.[43] Stampp concluded that there is no evidence that slavery was decadent, no evidence that it would soon have died had not the war brought it to an abrupt end.[44]

Two Harvard economists added their voices to the chorus of revisionist argument in a paper published in 1958. Their purpose, declared Alfred H. Conrad and John R. Meyer, was to take the argument over profitability out of the realm of accounting and, instead, measure profitability according to economic concepts.[45] They constructed an economic model of a Southern cotton plantation for the years 1830 to 1860 and then computed the return on investment on the basis of a Keynesian capital-value formula.[46] Their calculations showed that returns on cotton production varied from 2.2 per cent on low-yield land to 13.0 per cent on very fertile land, with returns of 4¼ to 8 per cent encompassing "the majority of ante bellum cotton operations." Profits on the raising and selling of slaves were considered separately. Their calculations for this part of the slave industry showed returns varying from 7.1 per cent to 8.1 per cent depending on the number of children produced. These figures, the authors maintained, showed not only that profits were made in slaveowning, but that this form of investment was as good as an investment elsewhere in the economy. This was true throughout the South and not only on the best lands. Where lands were good, profits came from cotton production; where lands were poor, profits came from the raising and selling of slaves.[47]

Up to this point Conrad and Meyer centered their argument on the question of slavery as a business. They then turned to the broader question of slavery and its effect on the South. Slavery, they concluded, did not hamper Southern economic growth. Available capital was not used for industrialization and diversification simply because it could be more profitably used in agricultural production. The economic problems of the South were the product of an agricultural community and not a result of the existence of slavery.[48]

Two recent works, in dealing with the question of profitability, show the influence of Conrad and Meyer's findings. Stanley M. Elkins in his study of slavery wrote that the economists, by dropping accounting methods and substituting "the economic . . . concept of profit" have made a "conceptual breakthrough" on the question of profitability. Paul W. Gates, in his discussion of slavery in The Farmer's Age, leaned heavily on Conrad and Meyer's analysis in concluding that slavery was profitable.[49] It is clear, however, that Conrad and Meyer's work will not find universal acceptance. It was almost immediately challenged, briefly but cogently, by Douglas F. Dowd.[50]

More recently another economist, Robert Evans, Jr., has published his findings on the question of profitability. Assuming a classical market, he calculated returns on investments in slave capital on the basis of profits earned through the hiring out of slaves during the three decades before the Civil War. He found that the rate of return on slaves varied from 9.5 per cent to 18.5 per cent, figures which were usually higher than those which could be earned in possible alternate areas of investment.[51]

Almost all the writers whose work has been discussed in these pages, whether economists or historians, have, to one degree or another, influenced the conclusions of writers of more general works, who show some of the same diversity of opinion as do the specialists.[52]

It would be folly to assume that this vexing question will ever be resolved to everyone's satisfaction. In part, the difficulty in arriving at a satisfactory solution stems from varying definitions of the problem. Contemporaries argued vociferously, but they were arguing about two very different things. They could agree that slavery had to be considered in its relation to the Southern economy, but there was no agreement as to the particular issues this consideration involved. Ulrich B. Phillips in his analysis gave major stress to slavery as an economic system, but he also introduced what to him apparently was a secondary question, the profitability of slavery as a business enterprise. It was this question which his followers, and the revisionists as well, have emphasized down to our own day.[53] Thus, a subtle shift in emphasis has taken place through the years in the discussion of slavery's profitability, a shift which is obvious if one compares not the conclusions but the central problem posed by Phillips early in the century with that considered by Conrad and Meyer several decades later.

Some light at least could be shed on the problem if there could be agreement as to what the problem is. In reality, two distinct topics have been discussed over the years, and they are not necessarily related. At least, their relationship has to be proved before they can be considered related. Even if every slaveowner were able to realize a twenty-five per cent return on his investment, it does not necessarily follow that slavery as a system was economically profitable. The real question is neither one of bookkeeping nor one of economic profit. It is a problem of economic history.

To deal with the question of slavery as an economic system, one must clearly distinguish those elements in the Southern economy which existed because of slavery and those which were unrelated to slavery. Those who argue that Southern backwardness arose, for the most part, because the South was primarily agricultural must first show that this would have been true whether or not the institution of slavery existed. Conversely, those who argue that slavery prevented diversification must prove (1) that economic diversification did take place in nonslave agricultural areas and (2) that it was slavery and not other factors which prevented diversified investment in the South. Furthermore, if slavery is to be called the cause of any given phenomenon in the Southern economy, the exact dynamics of the influence of slavery must be shown. It is not enough to juxtapose the results with the existence of slavery to establish a causal relationship. A final methodological question must be posed: Can the economics of slavery be discussed adequately in purely economic terms?

Some work has already been done along the lines suggested here. Two decades ago Fabien Linden considered the effect of slavery on the development of manufacturing in the prewar South. Treating slavery as a political and social as well as an economic institution, Linden traced the dynamics of the opposition to a move to establish widespread manufacturing establishments in the South in the 1840's.[54] More recently Eugene D. Genovese has, in a similar manner, investigated the problem of slavery in relation to the home market in the ante bellum South.[55]

A different line of approach has been taken by Douglas Dowd, who made a comparative analysis of economic development in the South and West. Further work in this direction, including comparisons with underdeveloped countries, might yield significant results. Dowd also suggested ways in which the economic question had to be broadened: "The nature and extent of resources are of course meaningless apart from the social context within which they exist."[56]

Certainly new lines of thought and research can be explored. If scholars are mindful of the complexities of the question of profitability, and cognizant of the nature of the work already accomplished, we can expect the writings of the future to increase our knowledge of the South and its peculiar institution. The prospect is of more than academic interest. Not only could further work in this field deepen our understanding of nineteenth-century American economic history. It might also give valuable insights into the dynamics of economic growth and development.

NOTES

1. Hinton Rowan Helper, *The Impending Crisis of the South* . . . (New York, 1859), 25.
2. *Ibid.*, 1-25, 33, 39, 66, 69, 72, 81, 283-86, esp.
3. Cassius Marcellus Clay, *Writings*, Horace Greeley, ed. (New York, 1848), 204-205, 224.
4. *Ibid.*, 227, also 346-47.
5. [Daniel Reaves Goodloe], *Inquiry into the Causes Which Have Retarded the Accumulation of Wealth and Increase of Population in the Southern States: In Which the Question of Slavery Is Considered in a Politico-Economical Point of View* (Washington, 1846), *passim*. Goodloe added that the degradation of labor served to keep immigrants away from the South, thus depriving the section of the skills and capital which new arrivals brought to the North.
6. George Tucker, *The Laws of Wages, Profits, and Rent, Investigated* (Philadelphia, 1837), 46-48. Tucker argued that as the number of slaves in-

creased, the cost of raising them would be greater than the gain from their use, and emancipation would result. *Ibid.*, 49.

7. J. E. Cairnes, *The Slave Power: Its Character, Career, and Probable Designs: Being an Attempt to Explain the Real Issues Involved in the American Contest* (2nd ed., London, 1863), 44, 54-56, 81.

8. *Ibid.*, 70-72, 74-75.

9. See Samuel M. Wolfe, *Helper's Impending Crisis Dissected* (Philadelphia, 1860); Elias Peissner, *The American Question in Its National Aspect, Being Also an Incidental Reply to Mr. H. R. Helper's "Compendium of the Impending Crisis of the South"* (New York, 1861). Obviously in response to Helper were two other works, Thomas Prentice Kettell, *Southern Wealth and Northern Profits . . .* (New York, 1860) and J. B. D. De Bow, *The Interest in Slavery of the Southern Non-Slaveholder* (Charleston, 1860). While Kettell presented figures which would dispute Helper, his main point was not to contend with Helper. De Bow was attempting to argue against Helper's contention that non-slaveholders were dupes of the planters. These two works will be discussed below.

10. Thomas R. Dew, *Review of the Debate in the Virginia Legislature, 1831-32*, as reprinted in *The Pro-Slavery Argument . . .* (Charleston, 1852), 328. Chancellor William Harper echoed these sentiments but in a more general way. Slavery, he wrote, is the only road to civilization. "If any thing can be predicated as universally true of uncultivated man, it is that he will not labor beyond what is absolutely necessary to maintain his existence. . . . The coercion of slavery alone is adequate to form man to habits of labor. . . . Since the existence of man upon the earth, with no exception whatever, either of ancient or modern times, every society which has attained civilization, had advanced to it through this process." Harper, "Slavery in the Light of Social Ethics," in E. N. Elliott (ed.), *Cotton Is King, and Pro-Slavery Arguments* (Augusta, Ga., 1860), 551-52.

11. Albert Taylor Bledsoe, "Liberty and Slavery; or, Slavery in the Light of Moral and Political Philosophy," *ibid.*, 413-16.

12. William J. Grayson, *The Hireling and the Slave . . .* (Charleston, 1856), 34-35. See also [Stephen Colwell], *The South: A Letter from a Friend in the North, with Special Reference to the Effects of Disunion upon Slavery* (Philadelphia, 1856), 14.

13. "It is the order of nature and of God, that the being of superior faculties and knowledge, and therefore of superior power, should control and dispose of those who are inferior. It is as much in the order of nature, that men should enslave each other, as that other animals should prey upon each other." Harper, "Slavery in the Light of Social Ethics," 559-60.

14. George Fitzhugh, *Cannibals All! or, Slaves Without Masters* (Richmond, 1857), 48. Governor James Henry Hammond of South Carolina, while admitting that economically speaking "slavery presents some difficulties" and that it was more expensive than free labor, nevertheless concluded that it was economically beneficial. There was no overpopulation in the South, he argued, no group of men so hungry that they would work for next to nothing. He concluded self-righteously, "We must, therefore, content ourselves with our dear labor, under the consoling reflection that

what is lost to us, is gained to humanity; and that, inasmuch as our slave costs us more than your free man costs you, by so much is he better off." Hammond, "Slavery in the Light of Political Science," in Elliott (ed.), *Cotton Is King*, 646-47.

15. Grayson, *The Hireling and the Slave*, 43-44.

16. Southern backwardness could not be ignored. The tariff, rather than slavery, was frequently pointed to as the cause. See Thomas Dew, *Review of the Debate*, 486. J. D. De Bow, in *De Bow's Review*, regularly called for the introduction of manufacturing in the South and the establishment of direct trade to Europe to solve the section's economic problems.

17. David Christy, *Cotton Is King* . . . (New York, 1856), 78-82, 163.

18. Kettell, *Southern Wealth and Northern Profits, passim.*

19. De Bow, *The Interest in Slavery of the Southern Non-Slaveholder.*

20. Ulrich B. Phillips, "The Decadence of the Plantation System," American Academy of Political and Social Science, *Annals*, XXXV (January 1910), 37-38, and "The Origin and Growth of the Southern Black Belts," *American Historical Review*, XI (July 1906), 803-804.

21. Phillips, "Decadence," 39; Ulrich B. Phillips, *American Negro Slavery* (New York, 1918), 291, 313-14, 342.

22. *Ibid.*, 343; Phillips, "Decadence," 40.

23. Ulrich B. Phillips, "The Economic Cost of Slaveholding in the Cotton Belt," *Political Science Quarterly*, XX (June 1905), 271-72; Phillips, *American Negro Slavery*, 395-96.

24. Phillips, "Economic Cost," 272; Phillips, *American Negro Slavery*, 397, 399.

25. Phillips, "Decadence," 39; Phillips, *American Negro Slavery*, 396.

26. This was not the first time this aspect of the problem was raised. Complaints by ante bellum planters that they made little money were common, and newspapers (especially during a crisis period) carried notices of sheriffs' sales of lands and slaves lost by planters. Slavery itself was seldom seen as the root cause of such difficulties. Low cotton prices, the closing of the slave trade, the tariff, the machinations of the middlemen, and other such factors were usually adduced as the reasons for poor return with slave labor. Antislavery disputants sometimes touched on the question also, but the emphasis was on the detrimental effects on the South in general. "Slavery *is* profitable to the few," Daniel Goodloe wrote to Frederick Law Olmsted, "because it is simply a privilege of robbing the many." Frederick Law Olmsted, *The Cotton Kingdom*, Arthur M. Schlesinger, ed. (New York, 1953), xxix.

27. Phillips, "Economic Cost," 271, 274; Phillips, *American Negro Slavery*, 391-92.

28. Writing soon after the turn of the century, Phillips concluded that the continued backwardness of the South was due to the *absence* of the old plantation system. The problem of ignorant labor remained, Phillips argued, and its utilization in small-scale farming (through small land-owning, tenantry, renting, or share-cropping) was inefficient. Restore the order, the discipline, the direction, and the large-scale methods which characterized the ante bellum plantation, and the South, relieved of the burden of slavery, would prosper. All of the advantages of the ante

bellum situation would be present with none of the disadvantages associated with slavery. Ulrich B. Phillips, "The Economics of the Plantation," *South Atlantic Quarterly*, II (July 1903), 231-36; Phillips, "Decadence," 40-41; Ulrich B. Phillips, "Conservatism and Progress in the Cotton Belt," *South Atlantic Quarterly*, III (January 1904), 1-10; Ulrich B. Phillips, "Plantations with Slave Labor and Free," *American Historical Review*, XXX (July 1925), 738-53.

29. Phillips, "Economic Cost," 259, 275. See also his "The Slave Labor Problem in the Charleston District," *Political Science Quarterly*, XXII (September 1907), 416-39, and "The Central Theme of Southern History," *American Historical Review*, XXXIV (October 1928), 30-43. In a more expansive mood, Phillips found the slave less socially useful for its benefits in building Southern character: ". . . In the large it was less a business than a life; it made fewer fortunes than it made men." *American Negro Slavery*, 401.

30. Rosser Howard Taylor, *Slaveholding in North Carolina, an Economic View* (Chapel Hill, 1926), 94-98.

31. Ralph Betts Flanders, *Plantation Slavery in Georgia* (Chapel Hill, 1933), 221-30. As Phillips had done earlier, Flanders found the continued existence of a largely unprofitable business to be explained by noneconomic factors. The planters, he wrote, confused the plantation system, slavery, and the race question. "This confusion made it difficult for anti-slavery critics to understand the tenacity with which slave-owners clung to a social and economic system they despised, and which seemed to them unprofitable." *Ibid.*, 231.

32. Charles Sackett Sydnor, *Slavery in Mississippi* (New York, 1933), 196-200; Charles S. Davis, *The Cotton Kingdom in Alabama* (Montgomery, 1939), 180. In a brief analysis of the economics of slavery during the last decade before the Civil War, James D. Hill concluded that the business of production by slave labor was in general unprofitable. Many planters, he admitted, became rich, "but these cases were more than likely due to peculiar advantages in location, fertility of soil or individual administrative ability; on the whole, in spite of slavery rather than because of it." Hill, "Some Economic Aspects of Slavery, 1850-1860," *South Atlantic Quarterly*, XXVI (April 1927), 161-77.

33. Charles W. Ramsdell, "The Natural Limits of Slavery Expansion," *Mississippi Valley Historical Review*, XVI (September 1929), 151-71. Ramsdell's conclusion, of course, was that slavery would have disappeared within a generation, and therefore the Civil War had been unnecessary.

34. Alfred Holt Stone, "Some Problems of Southern Economic History," *American Historical Review*, XIII (July 1908), 791; Alfred Holt Stone, "The Negro and Agricultural Development," American Academy of Political and Social Science, *Annals*, XXXV (January 1910), 13.

35. Robert R. Russel, "The General Effects of Slavery upon Southern Economic Progress," *Journal of Southern History*, IV (February 1938), 54.

36. *Ibid.*, 47-52. See also Robert R. Russell, "The Effects of Slavery upon Nonslaveholders in the Ante-Bellum South," *Agricultural History*, XV (April 1941), 112-26, and *Economic Aspects of Southern Sectionalism, 1840-1861* (Urbana, 1924), 55-64.

37. Lewis Cecil Gray, *History of Agriculture in the Southern United States*

to 1860 (2 vols., Washington and New York, 1933-41), I, 448, 462, 470-74. Gray disputed the contention that the planter's need to buy his labor supply was an added expense when figured in terms of the entire life of the slave: "When capitalization was accurately effected, the series of successive incomes as they became available actually were equivalent to interest and replacement; for interest and replacement would have been allowed for in the relatively low value that the owner paid for the services of the slave, capitalized on a terminable basis." In other words, Gray was arguing that the alleged extra cost in the form of interest and depreciation on the slave as a form of capital investment was not an extra cost at all but was a surplus which could be appropriated by the planter by virtue of his ownership of the slave over the entire period of his life. *Ibid.*, 473-74.

38. *Ibid.*, 448, 476-77; II, 933-34, 939.
39. *Ibid.*, 933-34, 940-42.
40. Thomas P. Govan, "Was Plantation Slavery Profitable?" *Journal of Southern History*, VIII (November 1942), 513-35.
41. Robert Worthington Smith, "Was Slavery Unprofitable in the Ante-Bellum South?" *Agricultural History*, XX (January 1946), 62-64.
42. Kenneth M. Stampp, *The Peculiar Institution* (New York, 1956), 390. Stampp denied that slavery kept the planters in debt. This problem arose from poor management and extravagance, a product, not of slavery, but of "the southern culture that required these extravagances." *Ibid.*, 391. The charge that slavery absorbed capital and retarded industrialization was also false, according to Stampp: "It is doubtful . . . that slavery in any decisive way retarded the industrialization of the South. After the African slave trade was legally closed, the southern labor system absorbed little new capital that might have gone into commerce or industry. . . . The domestic slave trade involved no further investment; it merely involved the transfer of a portion of the existing one between individuals and regions." *Ibid.*, 397. Another historian, George R. Woolfolk, in a study attacking what he called the Helper-Phillips thesis, argued that slavery did not freeze great wealth in slaves. On the contrary, he wrote, slave capital was easily converted into liquid capital because of the great facility with which slaves could be sold. Woolfolk, "Cotton Capitalism and Slave Labor in Texas," *Southwestern Social Science Quarterly*, XXXVII (June 1956), 43-52.
43. Stampp, *Peculiar Institution*, 400-11, 414. It is clear that Stampp relies heavily on Gray, Govan, and Smith. His footnotes give recognition of his debt to these earlier revisionist scholars.
44. ". . . If the slave-holder's economic self-interest alone were to be consulted, the institution should have been preserved. Nor is there any reason to assume that masters would have found it economically desirable to emancipate their slaves in the foreseeable future." *Ibid.*, 417-18.
45. Alfred H. Conrad and John R. Meyer, "The Economics of Slavery in the Ante Bellum South," *Journal of Political Economy*, LXVI (April 1958), 96.
46. "Investment returns are properly computed by using the capital-value formula $y = x_t/(1 + r)^t$, where y is the cost of the investment, x_t is realized return t years hence, and r is the internal rate of return of what

Keynes called the marginal efficiency of capital. . . . The criterion for a profitable investment is that the marginal efficiency exceeds the interest rate (in the Keynesian terminology)." *Ibid.*, 98. The authors calculated the longevity of slaves (assuming on the basis of available figures that a 20-year-old field hand had a 30-year life expectancy), the cost of investment (average cost of slaves, land, equipment, and average annual maintenance costs over the period, 1830-1860), the annual average yield per hand, and the average annual price for cotton. Using 6 per cent as the rate of return slaveowners could earn in other investments outside of slavery, the authors applied these figures to the formula and solved for r. *Ibid.*, 99-107.

47. *Ibid.*, 106-107, 109-14, 120-22. Their explanation of how figures were calculated (and the assumptions they were forced to make in the absence of adequate figures) may be found on pp. 106-108.

48. *Ibid.*, 119-20. A brief article by John E. Moes suggested that the capitalization of labor "does of itself most probably have a detrimental effect on economic growth." But, Moes wrote, this is a problem only when a society "is dependent upon its own capital resources." Such was not the case in the South, for the section was able to import large amounts of capital, a situation which would tend to overcome the detrimental effects of slavery on economic growth. He concluded by questioning the generally accepted assertion that "investment (and development) in the Ante Bellum [South] lagged behind that of the North." John E. Moes, "The Absorption of Capital in Slave Labor in the Ante-Bellum South and Economic Growth," *American Journal of Economics and Sociology*, XX (October 1961), 535-41.

49. Stanley M. Elkins, *Slavery* (Chicago, 1959), 234; Paul W. Gates, *The Farmer's Age: Agriculture, 1815-1860* (New York, 1960), 154-55. Gates also cited as his sources the work of Gray and Stampp, but his argument parallels most closely that of Conrad and Meyer.

50. Douglas F. Dowd, "The Economics of Salvery in the Ante Bellum South: A Comment," *Journal of Political Economy*, LXVI (October 1958), 440-42.

51. Robert Evans, Jr., "The Economics of American Negro Slavery, 1830-1860," in National Bureau of Economic Research, *Aspects of Labor Economics* (Princeton, 1962), 185-243. Evans indicated that he used "the net rent received by owners of slaves when they rented them out as the estimate of the income earned by the capital good" (p. 191) and assumed "that the hired slave labor market was classical rather than Keynesian in character . . ." (p. 194n). Evans' method and his approach to the problem were immediately attack by a historian (Thomas P. Govan) and an economist (John E. Moes). See "Comments" by these scholars, *ibid.*, 243-56. Govan wrote that he agreed with Evans' conclusion but added that the economist's evidence had "little relevance to this conclusion" (p. 243).

52. Avery Craven questioned whether slavery could be blamed for Southern backwardness. Southern values and ideals rather than slavery accounted for a lack of diversified economic life in the ante bellum South. "The South often deliberately chose rural backwardness." Avery Craven, *The Coming of the Civil War* (New York, 1942), 90-91. Allan Nevins came

to exactly opposite conclusions. The South did not choose rural backwardness, according to Nevins; it was forced upon the section by the institution of slavery, which "discouraged industrialism," kept immigrants from the region, discredited "the labor of the white artisan," and "tied the South to a slovenly and wasteful staple-crop system." Allan Nevins, *Ordeal of the Union* (2 vols., New York, 1947), I, 493-94. Two prominent Southern historians, Francis Butler Simkins and Clement Eaton, tend to straddle the fence in their textbooks. They recognize that the slave system was in many ways disadvantageous to the Southern economy, but they do not put the entire blame for Southern backwardness on the peculiar institution. Climate, improvidence, and, most important, the fact that the South was primarily agricultural must share the blame with slavery, according to these two. Simkins, *A History of the South* (New York, 1953), 129-32; Eaton, *A History of the Old South* (New York, 1949), 273-78. Economic historians seem to be more united in their opinions. Louis M. Hacker argued that only those few planters on the very best land could make money; most could not. Hacker, *The Triumph of American Capitalism* (New York, 1940), 317-21. The authors of current popular economic histories agree in general with this and also agree that slavery was responsible for retarding Southern economic development. Ernest L. Bogart and Donald L. Kemmerer, *Economic History of the American People* (New York, 1947), 386-410; Edward C. Kirkland, *A History of American Economic Life* (New York, 1951), 170-73; Herman E. Kroos, *American Economic Development* (Englewood Cliffs, N. J., 1956), 129-32; Gilbert C. Fite and Jim E. Reese, *An Economic History of the United States* (Boston, 1959), 164-65.

53. The works of Russel and, in part, Gray are the most noteworthy exceptions to this.

54. Fabien Linden, "Repercussions of Manufacturing in the Ante Bellum South," *North Carolina Historical Review*, XVII (October 1940), 313-31.

55. Eugene D. Genovese, "The Significance of the Slave Plantation for Southern Economic Development," *Journal of Southern History*, XXVIII (November 1962), 422-37.

56. Douglas F. Dowd, "A Comparative Analysis of Economic Development in the American West and South," *Journal of Economic History*, XVI (December 1956), 558-74.

RECENT STUDIES

Alfred H. Conrad and John R. Meyer, *The Economics of Slavery and other Studies in Econometric History* (Chicago: Aldine Publishing Co., 1964).

Eugene D. Genovese, *The Political Economy of Slavery: Studies in the Economy and Society of the Slave South* (New York: Pantheon, 1965).

Herbert S. Klein, *Slavery in the Americas: A Comparative Study of Cuba and Virginia* (Chicago: University of Chicago Press, 1966).

David Brion Davis, *The Problem of Slavery in Western Culture* (Ithaca: Cornell University Press, 1966).

Robert W. Fogel and Stanley L. Engerman, "The Economics of Slavery," in Fogel & Engerman, *The Reinterpretation of American Economic History* (New York: Harper & Row, 1968).

Stanley L. Engerman, "The Effects of Slavery Upon The Southern Economy: A Review of the Recent Debate," *Explorations in Entrepreneurial History*, 2nd Series, Vol. 4 (Winter 1967).

X

Civil War Historians and the "Needless War" Doctrine

THOMAS N. BONNER

Few students of American History are unaware that the historiography of the Civil War has been strongly affected in the past two decades by a body of writing and interpretation of such importance as to constitute a "school" in the eyes of some historians. What the writers of this persuasion seem to have in common, among other things, is a conviction that the political, economic, constitutional and moral factors previously adduced to explain the war's coming are insufficient causes of a catastrophe so shattering as the Civil War. It was, therefore, not inevitable, but in the various terms used by the revisionists, a "needless war," a "repressible conflict," or the folly of a "blundering generation." . . .

Historians in general . . . use the term "cause" as if it had definite and precise meaning. Does causation mean to them only regularity of sequence? Or does it imply the predictability of events? Does it mean that like causes have like effects? What does it mean when one speaks of the causes of the Civil War? . . .

Most writers on the Civil War have not troubled to define terms in describing the background and causes of that struggle. This has been

From *The Journal of the History of Ideas*, XVII (April 1956), pp. 193-216. Reprinted with deletions of text and abridged annotation by permission.

true even of the recent revisionists, who have dramatically echoed the denial of the Peace Democrats that slavery was a morally irrepressible force in causing war. No critical attention has been given even to such key concepts as causation and inevitability. The growth of this idea of the needlessness of the Civil War, at first broached only hesitantly by scholars, is one of the fascinating chapters in twentieth-century American historiography. When Jesse Macy suggested in 1900 that slavery was "in no proper sense the cause of the national tragedy" and that the nation "might have escaped the scourge of civil war," he was in an insignificant minority, at least among northern historians. Yet his views seem familiar a half-century later when he blamed statesmen for failing to compromise differences, and concluded that the war was due to the breakdown of the democratic process.[1]

In the immediate aftermath of World War I several authors expressed their doubts about the historic necessity for the Civil War. One of these, Nathaniel Stephenson, saw the war's coming as a problem in applied psychology: "Granted the emotions of 1860, the way in which our country staggered into war has all the terrible fascination of a tragedy on the theme of fate."[2] Another historian, Max Farrand, speculated over the outcome had the Missouri Compromise line been extended to the Pacific Ocean in 1850, and suggested that through its adoption "the Civil War might . . . have been avoided, for slavery would have been doomed before long through economic forces."[3] In 1921 Mary Scrugham, observing that there was indifference toward slavery and abolition as late as 1860, queried: "Who then willed that the 'irrepressible conflict' should begin in 1861? Absolutely, there is no evidence that the American people . . . expressed themselves in favor of fighting as the method of their choice for settling the condition of four million uneducated Africans."[4] There was sufficient doubt in the mind of Frederick Jackson Turner the year following the publication of Scrugham's views that he cautioned that it was no longer "certain that the Civil War was inevitable. Probably the majority of Americans . . . were astonished when secession was followed by war instead of by a reconciliation of differences."[5]

By the middle 1920's even New England's Edward Channing, indulging his penchant for second-guessing, hypothesized that if Bell and Everett had been elected in 1860, secession and war would have been averted for another decade and perhaps forever.[6] For Philip Auchampaugh, the sectional conflict was "a needless and heartless 'Brothers' War' followed by a cruel reconstruction."[7] Toward the end of the decade, Robert R. Russel, a keen student of the complex economic and social problems of the antebellum South, summarized the attitude of a growing minority of Civil War historians when he charged that "Statesmanship failed" in not making "the compromises, concessions, and adjustments necessary to prevent conflicting interests and ambitions from resulting in an attempted dissolution of the Union." Because secession and war were permitted to come, warned Russel, "we are not entitled to lay the flattering unction to our souls that the Civil War was an inevitable conflict."[8]

It is instructive to note the evolution of the views on this subject of William E. Dodd, whose students, along with those of William A. Dunning, were to play an important rôle in the later growth of the revisionist ideas. In Dodd's seminar or classroom at one time or another sat Avery Craven, Frank L. Owsley, Laura White and H. Clarence Nixon. As early as 1913 Dodd himself deplored the useless sacrifice of the Civil War; two years later he declared in his *Expansion and Conflict* that it was "the business of politics" to resolve sectional hatreds.[9] He charged Chase and the anti-Nebraska Democrats with exploiting the Kansas controversy for narrow political reasons. It was politics again that kept the stiff-necked Republicans from compromising in 1861, and they proved "unwilling to throw away the results of a victory constitutionally won, even to avoid a long and bloody war." Again in 1927 Dodd anticipated the "political agitation" theory of inciting the nation to war, and went further the following year to refer flatly to the war as "one of those great and needless conflicts from which both parties emerged losers. . . ."[10]

But it was the work of Charles and Mary Beard, also appearing in 1927, which did most to set the stage for the modern "repressible conflict" school of interpretation. This may seem strange since the Beards themselves did not challenge the unavoidable character of the war. For them it was still an "irrepressible conflict," as they entitled their chapter on the 1850's, but one between clashing economic systems rather than one of freedom versus slavery. To them the pressure of economic circumstances seemed as ineluctable as the moral issue had to their predecessors.

Significantly, however, they dismissed slavery as too simple a factor, at least in its moral dimensions alone, to account for the coming of the war. The antislavery party was not opposed to slavery for moral reasons but to gain political ascendancy in order to fasten the economic stranglehold of northern capitalism upon the South. Historians who had already challenged the traditional interpretation, such as Dodd and Russel, applauded this new impetus to shift attention from moral to economic factors. Southern scholars in particular, long faced with the dilemma of explaining the sectional warfare by an outdated constitutional thesis or an unpalatable moral interpretation borrowed from the North, turned with relief to the school of economic determinism. Thus, in 1930, Professor Coulter said of the southern independence movement: "The agricultural régime seeing that it could never secure itself against the industrial North . . . decided that it could maintain itself only through political independence."[11] Others like Walter Webb wrote now of slavery as only a symbol of the more basic differences which produced "two distinct cultures, two civilizations."[12]

The eager acceptance of the Beard thesis marked the half-way stage in the evolution of the "needless war" doctrine. The defensive interpretation of Davis and Stephens, which Beard was only the last to subject to logical scrutiny, was exchanged for the idea of economic irrepressibility, which ascribed responsibility to impersonal economic forces beyond the control of either section. This idea was to be in turn cast aside in favor of the even more appealing concept that the war might have been averted altogether by patient understanding and skilled statesmanship on both sides, with its corollary that equal or (as some were to feel) greater blame should go to the North which had tried to hold an unwilling South in a forced union prejudicial to that section's interests.[13]

The emergence of the "avoidable conflict" doctrine as a full-blown interpretation of the war's coming, supported by an extensive body of scholarly writings, may be traced to the early 1930's and the work of Avery Craven at the University of Chicago. As early as 1930 he published an article containing a skeletal outline of the views which were later to be extended to monograph length. Here may be found such familiar features of Craven's later writing as his emphasis on the economic and cultural diversity of the pre-war South; and his separation of the three factors which identified the South as a section: the old world country-gentleman ideal, the presence of the Negro, and the ruralness of the South, the last rather than slavery being responsible for the area's backwardness. In this article Craven made the distinction since stressed by the revisionists between the Negro and slavery as a cause of the South's troubles. "The Negro," he wrote, "must always be thought of as a laborer who produced a race question by his presence; slavery must be looked at as a method of solving a labor problem and a means of making white society safe. . . ." Finally, the South became politically united only "when other sections, or politicians or reformers in them, stirred enough of emotion or resentment within such diversity as to compel co-operation."[14]

In his biography of Edmund Ruffin, two years later, Craven repeated these same observations in more specific detail. The force from outside which rendered a naturally diversified South into a unit was the zeal of the abolitionists, compounded by the politicians who exploited the slavery and expansion issues and hopelessly entangled them. In this book Craven also leaned strongly toward the view that Lincoln had maneuvered the South into firing the first shot at Sumter.[15] His rejection of the idea of irrepressibility, implicit in these first writings, became explicit in 1933 in his review of Gerald Johnson's popular revisionist volume on southern secession. With approval he quoted Johnson's charge that "Farcical statesmanship precipitated the Civil War." He asserted further that despite the abolitionists and hate-mongers, the situation could still have been saved by high statesmanship in the 1850's "to offset sanctimonious emotion and pious rationalizing."[16]

By the middle 1930's, Craven was declaring confidently that "The conflict was the work of politicians and pious cranks."[17] He pictured a South constantly on the defensive after 1830, the victim of politicians and agitators who had transformed local resentments of New England and the Northwest into a burning hostility to the southern planter. Disclaiming that any deterministic forces operated to shape events, the historian began to place greater stress on chance factors of human personality and decision. In his Louisiana State lectures of 1938, Professor Craven reduced still further the rôle of basic sectional differences as forces leading toward war. Without equivocation he declared that there were no "inherent differences great enough to make war 'inevitable' or 'irrepressible' between [the South] and other sections within the nation." Slavery was relatively insignificant as a source of difference until taken up by the politicians in their struggle for place and advantage in the expanding nation. Though never expressly stated, Craven's thesis demanded a corollary, to which he alluded only briefly, that slavery would eventually have come to its natural end without abolitionism and war.[18]

In 1942 Craven published his volume on The Coming of the Civil War which represented his ripest contribution to Civil War revisionism. His conclusions on the war were couched in the sharpest terms he had employed to that time. Full responsibility for "the tragedy of the nation in bloody strife from 1861 to 1865" he assigned "to a generation of well-meaning Americans, who . . . permitted their shortsighted politicians, their over-zealous editors, and their pious reformers to emotionalize real and potential differences and to conjure up distorted impressions of those who dwelt in other parts of the nation."[19]

Another important figure in the revisionist camp of the 1930's was George Fort Milton, whose political biography of Stephen Douglas marked a milestone on the way to a new interpretation of the war. Milton concluded that to the summer of 1860 and possibly later the Civil War was not inevitable.[20] Ten years of research, said Milton, led him to the conclusion that Douglas had found in popular sovereignty a formula for sectional adjustment which if embraced would have postponed and probably have averted the Civil War. The "persistent fallacy" of historians, in Milton's words, was "the assumption that because a certain event did occur, it was inevitable."[21]

Ranking with Craven in influence and importance as a pioneer in the revisionist movement was the distinguished Lincoln biographer and Civil War specialist, James G. Randall. His future views on the Civil War were already apparent in 1932 when he gave enthusiastic approval to Roy Nichols' sympathetic, though discriminating, biography of Franklin Pierce. "As the war was due," argued Randall, "largely to extremists on both sides, it would seem that the times called for moderates such as Pierce."[22] In December, 1934, Randall told the American Historical Association that one of the tests of integrity of the Lincoln biographer was the way he treated "conciliatory efforts to avoid the Civil War, for he will be tempted to assume that the war was 'inevitable', that the Union could not have been saved without a struggle."[23] By 1937 Randall was quite definite in his conviction that the Civil War had not been proven inevitable. Wars were not understood, he said, by noting differences; historians should study unfought wars and they would find that differences as great as those between North and South had existed "without breaking down the processes of statesmanship and producing the débâcle of war."[24]

Randall published three articles in 1940 dealing with the question of the war's coming.[25] In the best known of these he explained the onset of the war completely in terms of psychological causes, emotional upset, irrationality and blundering. In a frequently-quoted paragraph, he concluded: "Let one take all the factors—the Sumter maneuver, the election of Lincoln, abolitionism, slavery in Kansas, cultural and economic differences—and it will be seen that only by a kind of false display could any one of these issues, or all of them together, be said to have caused the war if one omits the elements of emotional unreason and overbold leadership. If one word or phrase were selected to account for the war, that word would not be slavery, or states-rights, or diverse civilizations. It would have to be such a word as fanaticism (on both sides), or misunderstanding, or perhaps politics."[26]

Certain differences in the outlook and argument of Professors Randall and Craven were already apparent by 1940. Craven had tended to stress more consistently the importance of sectional economic differences, though denying they had to provoke war; while Randall asked in reply why agricultural and industrial sections did not complement rather than antagonize one another. Toward Lincoln's policy Randall was likely to be more sympathetic and approving, while Craven criticized Randall's "stereotyped treatment" of the Lincoln program and chided him for ignoring the work of scholars who had pointed to Lincoln's war guilt at Sumter.[27] Though less susceptible of proof, it seemed further that Craven's motivation came more from sympathies for the South drawn from a North Carolina family background, while Randall's views reflected a deep rational distrust of emotion and an almost pacifistic aversion to the slaughter and uselessness of war.

In 1945 there appeared in print the first two volumes of Professor Randall's long-awaited study of Lincoln's presidential career. His earlier views on the background of the war were repeated in unequivocal terms in the larger work. Again heavy responsibility was placed upon the "politicians and agitators" and the "whipped-up crisis" of the 1850's.[28] Throughout the biography, Randall tended to minimize the strength of Lincoln's antislavery views. The Lincoln volumes pointed up Randall's own paradox: he respected and greatly admired Lincoln, yet Lincoln was associated with a party which believed slavery was a great moral issue requiring an unflinching stand even at the risk of disunion. Randall resolved his dilemma by emphasizing Lincoln's moderate views vis-à-vis the Republican party, even though that meant making Republicanism indistinguishable from abolitionism at times. Thus, alternative explanations more favorable to Randall's own outlook were provided for Lincoln's trenchant antislavery speeches; the meaning of the 1860 campaign; the Lincoln-Douglas debates; and Lincoln's post-election silence. Similarly, the historian played down the importance of Lincoln's motives and part in the emancipation program later. He dissociated Lincoln thereby, at least in part, from the opprobrium which he must personally have felt for the sectional party which stirred up agitation and controversy on abstract issues affecting slavery, and then beat down attempts at compromise once elected to office.

Professor Randall made much of the fact that Lincoln himself regarded the war as avoidable. It may be coincidence only that Randall,

Milton and Roy Nichols were all biographers of men who felt the Civil War might have been averted. Though Nichols' important book on *The Disruption of American Democracy* was warmly received by the revisionists, it is difficult to classify his writings with those of the "needless war" school. Like the revisionists, he noted the important rôle played by emotion, political irresponsibility, agitation, lack of statesmanship and psychological factors in precipitating the crisis, but he denied that the war was avoidable. The emotionalism and political failures of the 1850's did not disprove the inevitability of war but simply demonstrated how, when unchecked by patriotic and national considerations, these forces could constitute in themselves a kind of inevitability.[29] This accounts for the seeming contradiction in reviewers such as Craven, Randall and Milton welcoming Nichols to the revisionist camp in 1948, while Nichols himself was being quoted as remarking that he had concluded in his book "that the Civil War was an irrepressible conflict."[30]

Looking at the revisionist writings as a whole, some of the tenets of the revisionist doctrine may now be identified. Despite considerable differences, historians of this school have shared certain attitudes, opinions or conclusions about the Civil War: (1) The war might have and presumably should have been averted. (2) It was not averted because of the failures of politicians and statesmen, and the hyper-emotionalism incited by agitators of the stump, press and pulpit. (3) In this failure the responsibility of the abolitionist was heavy. (4) Abolitionist extremism had been originally the provocation for the pro-slavery movement in the South. (5) The statesmen of compromise and moderation, such as Stephen Douglas, deserved greater praise and credit than they have received. (6) Contrariwise, the anti-compromise stand of the Republicans was crucial in tipping the scales toward war. (7) The rôle of slavery and the moral resentment of its opponents was of small significance as a fundamental cause of the war.

In the conclusion that the Civil War was due to avoidable human failures, most writers of the revisionist persuasion have concurred. A majority of these writers, however, have ignored the significant question as to when, if ever, the time came when war was no longer avoidable. As late as April, 1861, according to Randall, Lincoln's policy at Sumter alienated the Upper South which "constituted Lincoln's best chance of saving the Union without war."[31] Most historians, further, have not made clear the historical evidence upon which their conclusions in this regard rest. They simply reject on rational or critical grounds the traditional explanations as inadequate. Allan Nevins, sympathetic to portions of the revisionist thesis, expressed a typical opinion that if the bungling statesmen of the 1850's could "have glimpsed for one minute the reeking field of Chancellorsville or Gettysburg, they would have acted far more responsibly" and secession "would never have occurred had Americans realized what a great war meant."[32]

One tenet of the revisionist interpretation upon which there has been virtually unanimous agreement is the totally negative contribution of the abolitionist reformers to American life. . . . For Randall, abolitionism was "an agent of destruction and disturbance," while Craven felt that if Garrison were alive today, he "could profitably consult a psychiatrist."[33] Frank Owsley, then of Vanderbilt University, complained in 1940 that the abolitionists threatened "the existence of the South as seriously as the Nazis threaten the existence of England . . . their language was so violent, obscene, and insulting that even Dr. Goebbels in all his flights has seldom equaled and never surpassed it."[34]

Of the other tenets of revisionist doctrine, the rôle of slavery in the southern economy and social life, and its importance as a moral factor in spurring the North toward war, deserves further examination. Revisionist historians have been almost unanimous in denying that slavery was important either as the backbone of southern civilization or as a cause of the war. The rôle of the yeoman farmer in southern economic life rather than the large slaveholder has been recently stressed; the limits of slavery expansion have been held up as evidence that slavery restrictionists were disingenuous; the irrelevance of an abstract territorial issue has been continually cited; the relative benevolence of American slavery has been praised, particularly when laid side by side with conditions in northern mills and factories; its economic unprofitableness as a labor system has been claimed by some; and slavery has been viewed in general as a decaying institution on the road to eventual extinction without war.

A quarter-century has passed since Charles Ramsdell summed up brilliantly his arguments that slavery had reached its natural boundaries by 1860.[35] The implications of Ramsdell's work were carried to their logical conclusion by Professor Randall and others. Randall saw the importance of the slavery extension issue "not as a thing to settle, but as a thing to agitate."[36] In his eyes, the Kansas-Nebraska Act was as reasonable as Stephen Douglas proclaimed it to be. Indeed, it was "difficult to see how any more reasonable bill could have passed Senate and House. . . ." Professor Randall was brought to the rational conclusion that slavery in the territories, like the fugitive slave question, was "utterly inadequate" as a *casus belli*."[37]

The conviction that slavery would have disappeared eventually without war is essential to the general argument of the "needless war" school. Yet the implications of this have been ignored by most revisionists. Typical of revisionist treatment of the matter was the optimistic belief of George Milton that "given time, the South would abandon slavery because it did not pay," and the vague reference of Randall to slavery in 1945 as "an institution which in fact was crumbling and declining in the presence of nineteenth century tendencies."[38] Many historians have found themselves in something of a logical contradiction by agreeing that slavery was on its last legs, yet disputing Helper's claim that slavery was responsible for any of the major ills of the antebellum South. Avery Craven, like others on the horns of this dilemma, never met head-on the problem of when, how, or especially why a profitable and useful institution like slavery, as he believed it to be, would have begun to disappear of its own accord.[39] Certainly not from moral suasion, which Craven assured his readers was precisely the thing against which the South reacted in the pious abolitionists.

As for the treatment of the slaves, the varying interpretations of the revisionists unite in stressing the kindness of the masters, the insensitivity of the Negro, and the comparable lot of the northern wage-earner. In his sardonic analysis of the "disadvantages" of slavery, Professor Craven revealed in 1942 a representative attitude toward the institution of slavery. The slave, he commented, "had surrendered, with his physical freedom, the right to drift about from employer to employer. . . . He was robbed of the dignity of responsibility and the stimulation of worry. . . . Even . . . his life partner was often selected for him. His plight in this respect was as bad as that of European royalty. . . ."[40]

There are other aspects of the war's coming which are matters of dispute among the revisionists themselves. Not all exponents of the "needless war" doctrine, for example, would agree that there is serious need for historical rehabilitation of President Buchanan. Professor Randall notably has seconded the efforts of Philip Auchampaugh in his attempts to defend Buchanan's crisis policy as one which represented the will of the people against the extremists on both sides, but others have disagreed. There has been disagreement, too, on the distribution of property and wealth in the antebellum South and on the stature of General McClellan later on. On the question of Lincoln's handling of the Fort Sumter episode, the range of revisionist interpretation was described by one sympathetic historian recently as "whether Lincoln was the marplot and bungler or the cunning villain and provocateur; whether he stumbled into war at Sumter or whether he planned it."[41]

The pattern of reaction among historians to the "needless war" doctrine has been an interesting one. To the question as to whether the "avoidable conflict" idea belongs to a "southern school" of interpretation, an affirmative answer can with considerable assurance be given. Most of the leading spokesmen for revisionism—Dodd, Craven, Ramsdell, Milton, Johnson—were born or had a major part of their education in the former Confederate states. Only James Randall among historians of northern birth has been clearly identified with leadership in spreading the "needless war" idea. . . .

The idea that the Civil War might have been averted met at first with a rather cool reception from historians, North and South alike. When Milton's *Eve of Conflict* was published in 1933, for example, reviewers were almost unanimous in their skepticism. . . . Between 1933 and 1936, however, several new converts were won over to the cause of revisionism. In the former years, Richard Shryock decried the "nationalistic tradition" of interpreting the Civil War and answered negatively his own question as to whether "After all, *was* it so glorious a thing that the Union was saved by means of civil war."[42] . . . By 1936 Ramsdell had reversed his stand, now asserting that conflict was not inevitable as late as March, 1861. He forecast confidently that historians would finally agree on emotional disturbance rather than moral conviction or economic rivalry as the basic cause of war, with the politicians exploiting these emotional forces for their own ends.[43]

Though northern historians remained unaffected for the most part by the rising tide of revisionism in the 1930's, there were indications of a significant stirring of interest, North and South, by the close of the decade. In 1939 alone six books bearing on the problem were published. Aside from Craven's volume of lectures on "The Repressible Conflict," a new biography of John Tyler and a history of the slavery controversy bore witness to the increasing strength of the revisionist thesis among southern scholars. Tyler's biographer suggested that if the Virginia president's principles had been followed, there would have been no war; while Arthur Lloyd placed full responsibility upon insincere abolitionists and their allies for fomenting the sectional differences leading to war.[44] Opposed to this view of the abolitionists was a study by Ohio-born Dwight Dumond who argued flatly that slavery caused the war, that abolitionists waged a moral crusade, and that their animadversion to the "peculiar institution" was largely justified.[45] The northern-born authors of the last two books both expressed sympathy for the slavery interpretation of the war's causes and in one case for the concept that the conflict was inevitable.[46]

During the early years of World War II, the influence and favor of revisionist ideas rose remarkably, while the voices of opposition were fewer in number. Craven's *Coming of the Civil War* was hailed in 1942 by a large majority of historians, North and South, most of whom failed to qualify their approval with any reservations about the central thesis. . . . Of the few critics of the book, Henry Commager remained most consistent in his long-standing opposition to the revisionist trend in Civil War historiography. "The unwary reader" of Craven's volume, he cautioned, might "need to be reminded that there were happier states than that of slavery and that no free Negro was ever known to run the other way. . . ."[47]

Two other studies which accepted in general the revisionist thesis appeared simultaneously with Craven's book. Like Craven, David Potter asserted that emphasis by historians on North-South differences had obscured their essential similarity, and he questioned why "chronic antagonism" between the sections had to become "open war" in 1861. He concluded, though curiously denying he had done so, that the conflict was repressible. Indeed, if Potter's judgment was accurate, Lincoln's later forbearance toward the South may have been due in part to the "conviction that if the [secession crisis] had been handled differently . . . the conflict might have been averted."[48] . . . The conclusions of Henry Simms on the causes of the war in his *Decade of Sectional Controversy* left less doubt. Simms felt that "sound statesmanship might have found some solution for questions of such little practical significance" was those concerning fugitive slaves and the territories.[49] By the close of 1942, Avery Craven could claim with confidence that "most Southern writers hold that the War between the States was not 'an irrepressible conflict.' They are certain it might have been avoided . . . they are of the opinion that it is the statesman's business to compromise issues until a people have grown to higher levels where problems solve themselves."[50]

The influence of revisionism by the close of World War II began to be reflected in the work of other northern scholars beside Professor Randall. One Columbia University historian, born and educated within the confines of New York City, declared in 1944 that not slavery, but the Republican exploitation of the psychological and emotional factors surrounding it, was responsible for the rise and success of Republicanism.[51]

Since 1945, the revisionist thesis has been subject to increasing scrutiny and criticism. The first sharp censure came from Bernard De Voto, who used two of his "Easy Chair" columns in *Harper's Magazine* to analyze the "avoidable conflict" doctrine presented in Randall's introductory volumes of the Lincoln biography.[52] The Republican administration, he pointed out, was elected by constitutional means and had no power to interfere with any Southern right "except the arrogated right of a minority to control the government." The revisionists, De Voto chided, had refused to give full weight to this central fact, which made for "bad history" since it was "history by ellipsis." Revisionism had filled the void with the "nonsensical speculation" that somehow it was the duty of statesmanship to appease a South which refused to accept the results of a valid election. As for the fact that debate had centered on "abstract issues" and not on the morality of slavery itself, it was the duty of historians, De Voto charged, to explain and not to ignore the relation of the territorial question to the central moral problem. He scored heavily the historical relativism which forebade the revisionists, on the one hand, to cast any preconceived moral judgments on slavery, yet which permitted them to castigate the abolitionists for their views and behavior on the other.

Several books sympathetic to certain of the revisionist insights were published in the late 1940's, but by this time the historical tide had begun to sweep noticeably in the other direction. Arthur Schlesinger Jr. summed up a growing feeling of impatience on the part of many historians, particularly in the North, in a significant article in the *Partisan Review*.[53] Schlesinger attributed the vogue of revisionism to an "optimistic sentimentalism" characteristic of the times which provided "an escape from the severe demands of moral decision." Because the revisionists themselves felt no moral urgency regarding slavery, they deplored as fanatics the reformers who did. It was the moral question which gave the territorial and fugitive slave questions the importance which Randall and others had not been able to understand. These were the only frontiers on which the moral conflict, screened from open discussion by constitutional limitations, could be fought out. Professor Schlesinger concluded that the problem of inevitability was devoid of meaning. Revisionist criticism entailed a sentimental concept of man and history, in which evils like slavery would somehow become "outmoded" by the invincible march of progress. Men sometimes worked themselves into "logjams" involving great social issues where the necessity for moral choice was inescapable; this, he believed, was the case with human slavery in the antebellum South. "Nothing exists in history," he warned, "to assure us that the great moral dilemmas can be resolved without pain."

Since 1949, there have been notably few unqualified re-statements of the chief tenets of the Craven-Randall interpretation. When Professor Coulter published his volume on the Confederate States in 1950, for example, he offered an eclectic recipe for the war's origins compounded chiefly of Beards' "Two Civilizations" idea and Phillips' "central theme," but which included a sizeable dose of slavery, and only a pinch of aroused emotions and designing politicians.[54] A number of historians, on the other hand, have placed renewed stress upon the moral basis of antislavery, the significance of slavery itself as the nexus of sectional difference, and the insolubility of the question of inevitability. Russel Nye and Benjamin Thomas have both emphasized recently what the latter has called the "rich humanity" of the abolitionists and "the tremendous impact of the moral convictions they avowed."[55] Both Thomas and Kenneth Stampp have denied the possibility of proving or disproving the Civil War inevitable. Stampp found that there were "deep and fundamental causes" including slavery and economic contrasts which lay under the propaganda of the agitators and made insurmountable the problems of statesmanship.[56]

Further evidence of this shift in opinion can be found in the later writings of Avery Craven. Though he has never openly recanted his earlier views, there is much less attention given to the war's inevitability, crazed abolitionists, the beneficence of slavery, and the rôle of emotional and psychological factors *per se* in leading to conflict. The shift in his interpretation has been toward what he now terms the "breakdown of the democratic process" as explaining what happened in 1861. As early as 1947 Craven began to insist that he took for granted that slavery was a great moral evil which inspired a sharp reaction of principle by the 1850's.[57] He agreed, too, that it was the opposition of the South to the slavery restriction principle which provoked that section into secession. Gone were the scheming politicians, Lincoln's duplicity at Sumter, the identification of Republicanism with abolitionism, and the suggestion that the war might have been averted.

By 1950 Craven could comment on Stampp's book with its implicit correction of revisionism as one of "the most scholarly and provocative books" on the period.[58] The following year he explained his new approach to the Civil War in an article which concluded that the American democratic process worked all right in dealing with all problems except those involving "morals or the basic structure of society." A state of controversy was reached in American politics by 1860-61 when the talk went to morals, then to force. Sometimes it was wise to drop these moral and legal attitudes and face problems practically, but there were other "times when progress or the sound evolution of society requires of men that they stand by their guns and perish for the sake of a cause."[59] To some, this sounded very much like the old idea of the moral irrepressibility of the slavery crisis. Even more recently, Craven went one step further to admit that it was "probably true" that "Negro slavery was the fundamental factor in producing the American Civil War," and that there would have been no war without it.[60]

In his last book on the subject, Professor Craven revealed his present uncertainty about the revisionist thesis. The contrast with his earlier study of the same period was sharp in numerous details and the conclusions showed his gradual adjustment to the criticisms leveled at the main tenets of the "needless war" interpretation. But he was still unwilling to admit that a change in his views had taken place or that his own relation to the revisionist doctrine had become steadily more ambiguous. In his final "generalizations" he begged the questions of whether the war was inevitable and whether slavery was its cause, though he had clearly answered them in the text of his book.[61]

The attitude of Allan Nevins, who has made perhaps the most detailed study of the pre-Civil War period, deserves special attention. Before 1947, when his important volumes on *The Ordeal of the Union* appeared, there were already indications that Nevins was sympathetic to certain of the revisionist insights. As early as 1930, Nevins had philosophized that "Had all, North and South, possessed half the moderation of Lincoln, the war might have been averted. . . . As we regard the States' eighty-odd years of common history, it seems that the war should have been avoided."[62] . . .

The reception given *The Ordeal of the Union* told much about Nevins' position in the "needless war" controversy in 1947, for the revisionists in general attacked him for his northern bias, while many northern historians placed him squarely in the revisionist camp. . . .

Certainly there were aspects of Nevins' treatment of the 1840's and 1850's which displeased the revisionists. Without hesitation he recognized the moral basis of much of northern antagonism toward the South, and concluded that slavery was "the greatest misery, the greatest wrong, the greatest curse . . . that America has ever known." Professor Nevins described the revisionist hero Douglas as "a man of dim moral perceptions." Furthermore, his picture of Garrison was sympathetic and fair; he denied that the proslavery argument had its origins in a reaction to abolitionism; he found that *Uncle Tom's Cabin* did not overstate the case against slavery, but did overstate the case for slavery; he questioned the revisionist assumption that a majority of bondsmen were contented with their lot; he sympathized with the North in the Kansas struggle; and he found the Democratic presidents Pierce and Buchanan to be weak and hopelessly inadequate. But while admitting the strength of underlying moral and economic forces in conditioning the politics of the period, Nevins nevertheless stressed the final crucial rôle played by statesmanship in the years preceding the war. The task of statesmanship for this era he defined as the finding of "a workable adjustment between the two sections, while offering strong inducements to the Southern people to regard their labor system not as static but evolutionary, and equal persuasions to the Northern people to assume a helpful rather than scolding attitude."[63]

By 1950, however, Nevins had moved much closer to the revisionist fold. The clear identification of the moral factor as basic to the sectional conflict was missing in *The Emergence of Lincoln*. More attention was given in the later work to the rôle of propaganda and aroused emotions in magnifying every incident of the late 1850's. The abolitionists were treated with more bitterness than any other group, not excepting the southern extremists. This caused one critic to protest that Nevins did not recognize the "difference between being a fanatic for freedom and being a fanatic for slavery."[64] On the question of averting the war, Nevins stated flatly that as late as 1857 the hope of peaceful adjustment was reasonable.[65]

A study of recent Civil War historiography ought to yield at least some conclusions on the whole matter of revisionism and its central doctrine. It may be suggested first that the revisionist school has sought to revise opinion not so much on the causes of the Civil War as on the responsibility for the war. Not only their writings but their own declarations of lack of interest in causation lead to this conclusion. The leading revisionists, moreover, have all expressed dissatisfaction or disillusionment with the immediate or long-term results of the conflict. The professional reaction to the "needless war" doctrine shows that hereditary, family or sectional bias still prevades historical thinking on the "war guilt" question, and is one important cause of revisionism. As in the case of war revisionism in general, the Civil War revisionists have made the arguments and course of action of those opposed to the war seem more attractive in retrospect. Finally, the new findings and research of members of the "needless war" school have been more effect than cause of their revised interpretation of the conflict.

A comparison of recent historiography of the Civil War and of American entry into World War I reveals a number of remarkable similarities. Both schools of revisionism had their origins about 1930, found their first complete expression and popular support by the middle 1930's, and then grew increasingly stronger among scholars and laymen alike to the beginning of American involvement in World War II. During the course of the war, a reaction against revisionism began to set in, to be followed in the post-war period by a considerable degree of indecision and confusion concerning the historical status of both questions. This pattern suggests that recent revisionism concerning wars in general owes something to pressures other than those arising from new findings and a clearer perspective. Perhaps the answer lies in the feeling of disillusionment and futility regarding war which overtook Americans in the 1920's, followed by the economic collapse, wars, and threats of wars in the 1930's and 1940's. One spokesman for revisionism, in writing of the evitability of the Civil War in 1940, remarked pointedly that one reason for his article was "the obvious importance today of restating the needlessness of the quarrels and irritations that produced the Civil War."[66] Three of his most significant papers accusing the Civil War generation of blundering into war were read or published between the outbreak of European war in September, 1939, and the fall of France the following June.

A further observation arising from this study is that the continuing quarrel among historians and laymen over the causes of the war, especially over the importance of slavery, is the best possible argument for the irrepressibility of the moral question as the fundamental cause of the war. Almost a century after the event, the sectional division even among scholars is testimony to the depth of feeling which finds reflection in their books and essays, whether directly or indirectly, subtly or bluntly, consciously or unconsciously. Southern historians, it seems, have always leaned strongly toward that current interpretation of the war which is least unflattering to the motives of the defeated South, yet consistent with good scholarship and academic respectability. The same has been true, though less self-consciously, of the North. One wonders whether the "needless war" champions might not be in the other section today if the South had won its independence.

The revisionist argument that slavery was not important as a war cause because emancipation was not the center of debate in the 1850's or because it was not a war aim of the Republicans, is clearly specious. The fugitive slave and territorial issues aroused all the fury that would have been directed against slavery itself in a different legal and constitutional setting. To measure the actual number of fugitive slaves is not important. . . . In the same way, the question of slavery in the territories is not understood by counting the number of slaves in Kansas. Why was it that a whole generation worked itself into frenzied excitement over a matter that in the coldly rational light of a century later seemed pure abstraction? The weakness of the Randall-Craven argument on the unimportance of the territorial question is that it makes too much of the geographical limits of slavery, the impossibility of Kansas becoming a slave state, and the fact that there were only two slaves in Kansas in 1860: all things which could not be confirmed in the heated controversies of the 1850's. They do not stress the obvious fact that the North was not likely to be convinced of the geographical limits of slavery while men like Senator Atchison were exulting that "Southern men" with their slaves could take "every acre of timber" in Kansas, then sweep on to "carry slavery to the Pacific Ocean."

As for the idea that the war resulted from a "failure of statesmanship," this is a non-historical concept devoid of all meaning. Ultimately, the only alternative to weakness is strength, to appeasement, resolution. Buchanan was elected by a united Democratic party only because he did not believe in a strong policy, in coercion, or in majoritarianism. The weakness in executive leadership in this period was not due to any weakness in the democratic process, as Nichols and recently Craven have contended, or to weakness of personality or character, as Nevins has said, but because only a policy of appeasement under an ambivalent leader could hold for long the one remaining national party together.

Finally, emotionalism alone, as the revisionists themselves have lately recognized, can scarcely be assigned as the cause or even the precipitating agent of war. Every emotional response must have a stimulus, real or imagined. Is it more reasonable to assign the emotion or its object as the motivating force in human behavior? Some of the early revisionists might have replied that it was a *baseless* emotionalism incited by the exaggerations of editors and politicians. But then other questions must be answered. Why did the editors and politicians act so irresponsibly? Why did the people respond to this irrational incitement? Perhaps most important, what are the implications of all this for a democracy based upon a faith in the reason of the people? Unfortunately, the so-called psychological approach raises more questions than it answers.

It may be concluded that the waning attack of the revisionists is based at bottom upon differences in emphasis and semantics to accord with the natural aversion of Southerners for a moral interpretation of the Civil War, and of us all for a view which exposes human helplessness in a web of our own making.

NOTES

1. Jesse Macy, *Political Parties in the United States 1846-1861* (New York, 1900), 269-72.
2. Nathaniel W. Stephenson, *Abraham Lincoln and the Union*, The Chronicles of America Series, XXIX (New Haven, 1918), 81.
3. Max Farrand, *The Development of the United States; from Colonies to a World Power* (New York, 1918), 213.
4. Mary Scrugham, *The Peaceable Americans of 1860-1861* (New York, 1921), pp. 13-14.
5. Frederick J. Turner, *The Significance of Sections in American History* (New York, 1932), 318-19; an essay reprinted from the *Yale Review* (October, 1922).
6. Edward Channing, *A History of the United States* (New York, 1925), VI: 252-53.
7. Philip G. Auchampaugh, *James Buchanan and His Cabinet on the Eve of Secession* (Lancaster, Pa., 1926), 201.
8. Robert R. Russel, "A Revaluation of the Period before the Civil War: Railroads," *The Mississippi Valley Historical Review*, XV (December, 1928), 354.
9. William E. Dodd, "History and Patriotism," *The South Atlantic Quarterly*, XII (April, 1913), 109-10; *Expansion and Conflict* (New York, 1915), 205-06.
10. Dodd, "The Rise of Abraham Lincoln," *The Century Magazine*, 113 (March, 1927), 571.
11. E. Merton Coulter, "Southern Agriculture and Southern Nationalism before the Civil War," *Agricultural History*, IV (July, 1930), 91.
12. Walter P. Webb, *Divided We Stand* (New York, 1937), 9.
13. Frank L. Owsley in 1930 followed Beard in rejecting moral irrepressibility. But by the 1940's he was himself ridiculing the whole concept of irrepressibility. See F. L. Owsley, "The Irrepressible Conflict," *I'll Take My Stand* (New York, 1930), 73; *The Mississippi Valley Historical Review*, IX (February, 1943), 119-20.
14. Avery O. Craven, "The South in American History," *The Historical Outlook*, XXI (March, 1930), 105-09.
15. Craven, *Edmund Ruffin, Southerner* (New York, 1932), 96-104, 211-12.
16. *New York Herald Tribune Books* (December 3, 1933), 30.
17. Craven, "Coming of the War between the States: an Interpretation," *The Journal of Southern History*, II (August, 1936), 305.
18. Craven, *The Repressible Conflict 1830-1861* (Louisiana State University, 1939), 63-97.
19. Craven, *The Coming of the Civil War* (New York, 1942), 1-2.
20. George Fort Milton, *The Eve of Conflict; Stephen A. Douglas and the Needless War* (Boston, 1934), 519.

21. Milton, "Stephen A. Douglas' Efforts for Peace," *The Journal of Southern History*, I (August, 1935), 262.
22. *The Mississippi Valley Historical Review*, XIX (June, 1932), 120.
23. This paper was published as J. G. Randall, "Has the Lincoln Theme Been Exhausted?" *The American Historical Review*, XLI (January, 1936), 293.
24. Randall, *The Civil War and Reconstruction* (New York, 1937), vi-vii.
25. Randall, "When War Came in 1861," *The Abraham Lincoln Quarterly*, I (March, 1940), 3-42; "The Blundering Generation," *The Mississippi Valley Historical Review*, XXVII (June, 1940), 3-28; "The Civil War Restudied," *The Journal of Southern History*, VI (November, 1940), 439-57.
26. Randall, "The Blundering Generation," *The Mississippi Valley Historical Review*, XXVII (June, 1940), 15.
27. *The Mississippi Valley Historical Review*, XXIV (September, 1937), 264.
28. Randall, *Lincoln the President* (2 vols., New York, 1945), I, 75-76.
29. Roy F. Nichols, *The Disruption of American Democracy* (New York, 1948), 513-17.
30. *Current Biography* (1949), 455.
31. Randall, *Civil War and Reconstruction*, 258.
32. Allan Nevins, *The Emergence of Lincoln* (2 vols., New York, 1950), I, 20.
33. Randall, *Civil War and Reconstruction*, 148; Craven, "Coming of the War between the States," *The Journal of Southern History*, II (August, 1936), 312.
34. *The Journal of Southern History*, VI (November, 1940), 559.
35. Charles W. Ramsdell, "The Natural Limits of Slavery Expansion," *The Mississippi Valley Historical Review*, XVI (September, 1929), 151-71.
36. Randall, *Lincoln the Liberal Statesman* (New York, 1947), 19.
37. Randall, *Lincoln the President*, I, 81, 237.
38. Milton, "Stephen A. Douglas' Efforts for Peace," *The Journal of Southern History*, I (August, 1935), 266; Randall, *Lincoln the President*, I, 86.
39. See, for example, his *Repressible Conflict*, 57-59, and *The Coming of the Civil War*, 118.
40. Craven, *Coming of the Civil War*, 82.
41. E. Merton Coulter, *The Confederate States of America 1861-1865*, A History of the South, VII (Louisiana State University, 1950), 37.
42. Richard H. Shryock, "The Nationalistic Tradition of the Civil War; a Southern Analysis," *The South Atlantic Quarterly*, XXXII (July, 1939), 294ff.
43. Charles W. Ramsdell, "The Changing Interpretation of the Civil War," *The Journal of Southern History*, III (February, 1937), 18-20.
44. Oliver P. Chitwood, *John Tyler* (New York, 1939), 457; Arthur Y. Lloyd, *The Slavery Controversy 1831-1860* (Chapel Hill, N. C., 1939), 100-1.
45. Dwight L. Dumond, *Antislavery Origins of the Civil War in the United States* (Ann Arbor, Mich., 1939).
46. Roger W. Shugg, *Origins of Class Struggle in Louisiana* (Louisiana State University, 1939), 174-75; Burton J. Hendrick, *Statesmen of the Lost Cause* (Boston, 1939), 54-55.

47. *New York Times Book Review*, May 42, 1942.
48. David M. Potter, *Lincoln and His Party in the Secession Crisis* (New Haven, 1942), viii, 375, 385, *passim*.
49. Henry H. Simms, *A Decade of Sectional Controversy 1851-1861* (Chapel Hill, N. C., 1942), viii.
50. A Craven, "Southern Attitudes toward Abraham Lincoln," Illinois State Historical Society, *Papers in Illinois History and Transactions for the Year 1942* (Springfield, 1944), 13-14.
51. Reinhard H. Luthin, *The First Lincoln Campaign* (Cambridge, 1944), 221-22.
52. Bernard De Voto, "The Easy Chair," *Harper's Magazine*, 192 (February, March, 1946), 123-26, 234-37.
53. Arthur M. Schlesinger Jr., "The Causes of the Civil War: a Note on Historical Sentimentalism," *Partisan Review*, XVI (October, 1949), 969-81.
54. E. Merton Coulter, *The Confederate States*, 8-13.
55. Russel B. Nye, *Fettered Freedom* (East Lansing, Mich., 1949); Benjamin P. Thomas, *Theodore Weld* (New Brunswick, N. J., 1950), vi.
56. Kenneth M. Stampp, *And the War Came* (Louisiana State University, 1950), vii, 1-3.
57. A. Craven, "The Civil War and the Democratic Process," *The Abraham Lincoln Quarterly*, IV (June, 1947), 269-92.
58. *The Saturday Review of Literature*, XXXIII (Dec. 2, 1950), 40; see too Craven's article on "The 1840's and the Democratic Process," *The Journal of Southern History*, XVI (May, 1950), 161-76.
59. Craven, "The South and the Democratic Process," *The Alabama Review*, IV (July, 1951), 212-13.
60. Craven, "The Price of Union," *The Journal of Southern History*, XVIII (February, 1952), 5.
61. Craven, *The Growth of Southern Nationalism 1848-1861*, A History of the South, VI (Louisiana State University, 1953).
62. Allan Nevins, "Lincoln's Plans for Reunion," *Abraham Lincoln Association Papers*, 1930 (Springfield, 1931), 63.
63. Nevins, *Ordeal of the Union* (2 vols., New York, 1947), I: 144-48, 408, 461, 543; II: 78-121, 108, 451.
64. Oscar Handlin in *The Nation*, 171 (Dec. 2, 1950), 513.
65. Nevins, *The Emergence of Lincoln*, I, 21.
66. J. G. Randall, When War Came in 1861," *The Abraham Lincoln Quarterly*, I (March, 1940), 40-41.

RECENT STUDIES

Harry V. Jaffa, *Crisis of the House Divided: An Interpretation of the Issues in the Lincoln-Douglas Debates* (Garden City: Doubleday & Co., 1959).
Robert W. Johannsen, "Stephen A. Douglas and the South," *Journal of Southern History*, XXXIII (February 1967), 26-50.
Don E. Fehrenbacher, "The Origins and Purpose of Lincoln's 'House-Divided' Speech," *Mississippi Valley Historical Review* (March 1960), 615-43.

David M. Potter, "The Historians' Use of Nationalism, and Vice Versa," *American Historical Review*, LXVII (July 1962) 924-50.

David Donald, "An Excess of Democracy: The American Civil War and the Social Process," Chapter Eleven of *Lincoln Reconsidered* (2nd ed., New York: Vintage Books, 1961).

Alexander E. Campbell, "An Excess of Isolation: Isolation and the American Civil War," *Journal of Southern History*, XXIX (May 1963), 161-74.

Avery Craven, *An Historian and the Civil War* (Chicago: University of Chicago Press, 1964).

George M. Frederickson, *The Inner Civil War: Northern Intellectuals and the Crisis of the Union* (New York: Harper & Row, 1965).

XI

Negro Suffrage and Republican Politics: The Problem
of Motivation in Reconstruction Historiography

LAWANDA AND JOHN H. COX

Republican party leadership of the 1860's was responsible for establishing the legal right of Negro citizens to equal suffrage, first in the
defeated South by act of Congress and then throughout the nation by
constitutional amendment.[1] Whether historians have condemned or
applauded the grant of suffrage to Negroes in the post-Civil War years,
they have more often than not viewed the motives behind this party
action with considerable cynicism. The purpose of this article is to
review their treatment and to raise for re-examination the question of
what moved Republicans in Congress to such far-reaching action.

The earliest study of the origins of the Fifteenth Amendment was
prepared by a scholarly lawyer from western Virginia, Allen Caperton
Braxton, for presentation to the state bar association in 1903. The work
is still cited, and a new edition was printed in the 1930's.[2] Braxton
held that Negro suffrage was the result of "gratitude, apprehension and

From *The Journal of Southern History*, XXXIII (August 1967), pp. 303-30.
Copyright © 1967 by the Southern Historical Association. Reprinted by permission of the Managing Editor.

Mrs. Cox is professor of history at Hunter College of the City University of
New York, and Mr. Cox is professor of history at the City College of the
City University of New York.

politics—these three; but the greatest of these was politics."[3] To Radical leaders of the Republican party, enfranchisement early appeared "a promising means of party aggrandisement"; it soon became "essential to the perpetuation of their power." In the struggle with President Andrew Johnson over Reconstruction, they had alienated "the entire white race of the South" for at least a generation to come. Once the Southern states were restored to the Union and the white vote of the South added to the Democratic vote of the North, the Republican party would face hopeless defeat; the only means of escape lay through the Southern Negro. In the legislation of March 1867 Radicals effected "a *coup d'etat* of the first magnitude," but it was not a stable foundation on which to build future political power. The law might be rescinded by Congress, overturned by judicial decision, or defied by the Southern states after their readmission. Only a constitutional amendment could provide security. It would also mean votes from an increasing Negro population in the North as a potential balance of power in close elections.[4] A few footnotes and quotations, notably one from Charles Sumner, appear as illustrative, and there is a flat assertion that debates in Congress on the Fifteenth Amendment "leave no room to doubt" its political inspiration.[5] It is clear, however, that the author felt no need either to scrutinize or to document his interpretation; a primary relationship between Negro suffrage and party expediency appeared to him self-evident.

Braxton did examine in detail a thesis and the historic contradiction that it implied. "One may well question," he wrote in conclusion, "whether the popular will was executed or thwarted when negro suffrage was written into the fundamental law of this nation."[6] No reader would doubt that the author's answer was "thwarted." Despite some overstatement and minor distortions of fact, this thesis is sound history. The national guarantee of an equal vote to the Negro did not reflect a popular consensus, even in the North.[7] Braxton's attempt to explain how an unwanted policy became the fundamental law of the land, though less convincing, raised an important historical problem.

Despite his emphasis upon political expediency as the impelling causal element behind equal suffrage, the Virginia attorney might have considered Republican leaders who had imposed this result upon the nation, at least a few of their number, men sincerely concerned with the Negro's right to vote. References to "fanaticism," "bigotry," and "negrophiles" suggest that he did, though obviously without sympathy. This implication, however, is explicitly disavowed and with specific reference to Senator Sumner. Braxton found "shocking" evidence of insincerity in the fact that men who argued for the inalienable right of the Negro to vote agreed to exclude Indians and Chinese from the franchise.[8] He considered leaders of the party to be distinguished from the rank and file of Northerners neither by principle nor by lack of prejudice. Unlike their constituents, congressmen were removed from personal competition with the Negro, and their national perspective made them aware of the dependence of Republican party power upon Negro enfranchisement. Braxton's indictment of Republican motivation showed charity on just one count. He granted that some leaders were moved neither by "malice toward the South" nor by "heartless political ambition." They had come to equate the life of the Republican party with the life of the nation and honestly feared a Democratic victory as a national disaster.[9]

The second study of the Fifteenth Amendment, by John M. Mathews, appeared in 1909 and was to remain the standard historical account for more than half a century. Originally prepared as a paper for a seminar in political science at Johns Hopkins University, it is a most unhistorical history in the sense that its author was more concerned to analyze concepts than men or events. He narrowly delimited the chronology and substance of his "legislative history" and showed special interest in the judicial interpretation of the amendment.[10] Neither the historic problem posed by Braxton's study nor the question of men's motives as individuals or as party leaders presented a challenge to Mathews; he did not even consider it important to identify with particular congressmen or with political parties the four elements in his analysis—the humanitarians, the nationalists, the politicians, and the local autonomists. Indeed, he explicitly stated that "These forces were primarily principles, rather than men or groups of men. They were not always separable except in thought, for the same senator or representative was often influenced by more than one of them at the same time."[11]

Yet the Mathews monograph does carry certain implications in respect to motivation. The statement that "There was little real difference of opinion among the leaders in Congress as to the desirability of enlarging the sphere of political liberty for the negro race" might be read as an assumption of genuine concern for the Negro on the part of the lawmakers. On the other hand, a quite different interpretation could be given to statements that "The politician was the initiator and real engineer of the movement," that he labored for a concrete objective "fraught with definite, practical results," and that he was not altogether satisfied with the final form of the amendment "because it did not directly and specifically guarantee the African's right to vote" and hence might be evaded.[12] In this study so long considered authoritative, there is nothing to confirm Braxton's identification of equal suffrage with partisan advantage, but neither is there anything that would cause its readers to question that assumption.

The writings of William A. Dunning and of James Ford Rhodes, the two most influential scholars with accounts of Reconstruction published during the first decade of the twentieth century, did sound a warning.[13] To Southerners it had been "inconceivable," Dunning pointed out, that "rational men of the North should seriously approve of negro suffrage *per se*"; hence they assumed that the only explanation was "a craving for political power."[14] Dunning was implying a fallacy in their understanding. Yet he himself attributed Republican sponsorship of Negro suffrage in the First Reconstruction Act of 1867 to the "pressure of party necessity and of Sumner's tireless urging." In writing of the Fifteenth Amendment, Dunning assumed that he had established the motivation behind it. He cited an earlier paragraph as support for the statement: "We have already seen the partisan motive which gave the impulse to the passage of the Fifteenth Amendment." Any reader who took the trouble to turn back the pages would find a passage which, far from proving the contention, did not necessarily imply it. Dunning had written that after the presidential election of 1868 in which Democrats gained majorities in Georgia and Louisiana through the use of violence, moderate Republicans had no uncertainty as to "the policy of maintaining what had been achieved in enfranchising the blacks."[15]

Rhodes was more explicit in his warning and more direct in crediting to humanitarian feelings within Republican party ranks an influence in "forcing negro suffrage upon the South." He cautioned readers not to lose sight of the high motives involved "for it would be easy to collect a mass of facts showing that the sole aim of congressional reconstruction was to strengthen the Republican party."[16] Neither the statement quoted nor his account as a whole would stir to skepticism anyone who had assumed with Braxton the predominance of political expediency. He did not analyze or criticize the Braxton assumption but rather supplemented it. In Rhodes's view, there were men with "intelligence and high character" who were "earnest for the immediate enfranchisement of the freedmen," but they were "numerically small."[17] His writing at times carried an unintended innuendo. For example, he stated that the majority of Republicans in Congress when they reassembled after the Christmas holidays of 1866 did not favor the imposition of Negro suffrage upon the South, a policy which they sustained by a two-thirds vote a few weeks later. The explanation lay in "The rejection of the Fourteenth Amendment by the South, the clever use of the 'outrages' argument, the animosity to the President . . . which was increased to virulence by his wholesale removals of Republicans from office," factors that "enabled the partisan tyranny of Stevens and the pertinacity of Sumner to achieve this result."[18]

The ambivalence in Rhodes's treatment arose primarily from his strong conviction that the grant of suffrage to the Negro during Reconstruction was a major mistake in policy. This judgment was evident in a paper which he delivered before the Massachusetts Historical Society while writing his account of Reconstruction[19] and also in the volumes of his *History of the United States* which appeared two years later. Suffrage had been an abysmal failure which "pandered to the ignorant negroes, the knavish white natives and the vulturous adventurers who flocked from the North" and "neutralized the work of honest Republicans. . . ."[20] Experience in the North, in his opinion, also discredited the grant of equal suffrage to the Negro—he had shown little political leadership, rarely identified himself "with any movement on a high plane," such as civil service, tariff reform, honest money, or pure municipal government, and "arrogantly asserts his right to recognition" because he is "greedy for office and emolument." All this had not been the Negro's fault; he had been "started at the top" despite "all the warnings of science and political experience."[21] Rhodes believed that the findings of science were clear and that they had been available to Sumner and his fellow advocates of Negro enfranchisement through the distinguished Harvard scientist Louis Agassiz, who was Sumner's friend.[22] He did not place all blame on Sumner, however, but indicated that the fault lay in our national character. "I think that England or Prussia would have solved the negro problem better"; they would have "studied the negro scientifically"; in the "age of Darwin and Huxley" Americans had made no attempt to do so.[23]

In discussing the problem with fellow historians, Rhodes revealed more sharply than in his writings his personal assessment of motivation: "From a variety of motives, some praiseworthy and others the reverse, we forced negro suffrage upon the South. . . . Party advantage, the desire of worthless men at the North for offices at the South, co-operated with a misguided humanitarianism."[24] The warning which he sounded, and the less explicit one from Dunning as well, reflected a conscientious desire on the part of these distinguished historians to be fair, restrained, and judicious. The assumption that most

Republican members of Congress who voted for equal Negro suffrage did so primarily, if not solely, for reasons of political expediency, was an assumption they accepted; it apparently did not occur to either man that there was need for any careful scrutiny to establish the validity of this accusation.

For three decades, until the post-World War II years, few historians handled the question of Republican motivation with as much fairness as had Rhodes and Dunning. Ellis P. Oberholtzer, in his multivolume *History of the United States Since the Civil War*, wrote that "Just as the war had not been waged to free the negro from bondage" so the postwar strife "except to a few minds, had little enough to do with the improvement of the lot of the black man." He continued: "The project to make voters out of black men was not so much for their social elevation as for the further punishment of the Southern white people—for the capture of offices for Radical scamps and the intrench-ment of the Radical party in power for a long time to come in the South and in the country at large."[25] The small but influential volume in the Yale *Chronicles of America* series written by Dunning's fore-most student, Walter L. Fleming, made the indictment specific. The election of 1868, Fleming wrote, showed that Democrats could com-mand more white votes than could Republicans "whose total included nearly 700,000 blacks." This prompted the Radicals to frame the Fifteenth Amendment which, as it appeared to them, would not only "make safe the negro majorities in the South" but also add strength from Negroes previously denied the ballot in the North, thus assuring "900,000 negro voters for the Republican party."[26]

During the late 1920's and the 1930's, a period in Reconstruction historiography which saw the "canonization" of Andrew Johnson,[27] little charity was shown to those who had been Johnson's opponents. Claude G. Bowers developed the "conspiracy" approach to Negro suf-frage, seeing it as the culmination of a plot hatched by Sumner and a few Radicals and dating back at least to the early days of 1865.[28] He quoted approvingly the Georgian, Benjamin H. Hill, who charged that Negro suffrage was a matter of knaves using fools "to keep the Radi-cal Party in power in the approaching presidential election, . . . to retain by force and fraud the power they are losing in the detection of their treason in the North.' "[29] George Fort Milton recognized that "The Radicals had mixed motives in this insistence on negro suffrage," but his lack of sympathy for the "old Abolitionists" led him to gibe at Sumner. From a letter of the Senator, he quoted, " 'We need the votes of all,' " then observed, "Could it be that practical political necessities moved him as well as lofty idealistic views?"[30] Milton did little more than mention the Fifteenth Amendment but could not resist using the opportunity to belittle its Republican sponsors: ". . . one or two Senators shamefacedly admitted that perhaps an intelligent white woman had as much right as an ignorant negro plow-hand to determine the destinies of the nation. But there seemed little political advantage in women suffrage. . . ."[31] James G. Randall, whose substantial volume on the Civil War and Reconstruction served as a standard college textbook from the 1930's to the 1960's, handled the subject of Negro suffrage with restraint; yet in substance he accepted a mild version of Bowers' conspiracy thesis. Randall's variant was that "the importance of the Negro vote to the Republican party North and South caused leading Radicals to keep their eye upon the issue" although Northern sentiment would not support nationwide Negro suffrage. Gradually, as the power of the Radicals increased, they moved toward their goal. "Step by step they were able to enact laws promoting Negro suffrage without an amendment, and finally to carry the suffrage amendment itself in the first year of Grant's administration."[32] This account was allowed to stand without modification when the volume was revised in 1961 by David Donald.[33]

The chronological limits of Howard K. Beale's study of the election of 1866, perhaps the most influential scholarly product of the pro-Johnson historiography, precluded an examination of the Reconstruction Acts of 1867 and the Fifteenth Amendment. However, there is a chapter devoted to Negro suffrage as a general issue.[34] Beale divided its Radical proponents into four groups—old abolitionists, who believed in the principle of equal suffrage; friends of the Negro, who saw the ballot as his only means of defense; men hostile to racial equality, who would use Negro suffrage to humiliate the defeated South; and, lastly, "a more numerous group" to whom "expediency was the motive."[35] Curiously, his classification had the same weakness as Mathews' disembodied analysis; it offered the reader no evidence that any one of the four "groups" was identifiable in terms of specific individuals. In fact, despite a deep personal commitment to Negro equality and intensive manuscript research, Beale added little new except to link the suffrage issue with his general thesis that Radical leaders were motivated by economic as well as political ends. "If the South could be excluded, or admitted only with negro suffrage," he wrote, "the new industrial order which the Northeast was developing, would be safe."[36]

Yet Beale did not dismiss the suffrage issue as summarily as had the Republicans in the 1866 campaign. His treatment suggests his interest in the subject, and particularly in the claim made during 1865 and after that the Negro would never be safe unless protected by the ballot. Beale considered it "a powerful [argument]" even though he looked with sympathy upon those who mistrusted a grant of unqualified suffrage to naïve and uneducated freedmen. After struggling with the argument for several pages, he concluded that no one could say with certainty whether without the ballot the status of the newly freed slave among white Southerners would have been shaped by "the fair-minded" or "the vicious." Then he added: "Few cared to know. Extreme Radicals wanted negro suffrage; outrages against the negroes, and an exaggeration of cruel codes would reconcile Northerners to it."[37] In other words, the "powerful argument" was essentially a propaganda device; its prevalence in the 1860's would not lighten the charges against the Republican Radical leadership.

Another election study, Charles H. Coleman's analysis of the Grant-Seymour campaign of 1868, was published in the 1930's and at once took its place as the standard, perhaps definitive, account. Coleman's discussion of the Negro suffrage issue in the elections of 1867 and 1868 is exceptionally fair and informative. Without raising the question of motivation or passing judgment, it yet provides considerable material pertinent to the problem.[38] Also, Coleman, like Walter Fleming, was interested in the importance of the Negro vote. He estimated that it had provided Grant with 450,000 of his total, without which the Republicans would not have gained a popular majority.[39] While Coleman believed that a majority of the white voters of the country favored the Democratic party in 1868 and implied that this remained true until 1896, unlike Fleming, he did not point to any connection between the 1868 election results and the movement immediately thereafter for an equal-suffrage amendment. The omission may have been due to his clear recognition that Grant's victory in the electoral college would have been secure without any Negro votes. The Democrats with better leadership, according to Coleman, might have contended with the Republicans on almost equal terms in 1868, but they did not lose the election "through the operation of the reconstruction acts."[40] Despite a generally careful and balanced presentation, in his opening paragraphs Coleman made reference incidentally and uncritically to "Republican ascendancy" as the motive behind the Fifteenth Amendment.[41] He had not given thought to the relationship between his findings and the time-honored charges of Braxton and Fleming.

By the 1950's a new direction was evident in historical writings dealing with the Negro in nineteenth-century America, one that rejected the assumption of racial inferiority and cherished the quest for racial equality.[42] This trend, which reached major proportions in the 1960's, drew stimulus and support both from the contemporary social and intellectual climate and from interior developments within historical research. During the thirties revisionist articles dealing with so-called "Black" Reconstruction in the South had anticipated postwar attitudes toward race relationships and had upset the negative stereotypes of "scalawags," "carpetbaggers," and "Radical" regimes.[43] In the forties the National Archives provided material for new departures in Reconstruction scholarship by making available the manuscript records of the Freedmen's Bureau with a useful checklist.[44] The extremes to which vindication of Andrew Johnson had been carried in the thirties, together with a program to assemble and publish his papers, led to re-examination of his record and that of his opponents.[45] Military confrontation with Hitler stimulated a challenge to the "needless war" interpretation of the American civil conflict, redirecting attention to slavery as a moral issue.[46] Antislavery agitators became the focus of renewed interest and sympathy, the latter reinforced by a growing sophistication in the historian's borrowings from psychology and sociology.[47] Leadership of Negroes in the contemporary struggle for equality found a counterpart in an increased recognition of the role of Negro leadership during the nineteenth century.[48] Through new biographies and analytical articles, a beginning was made in reassessing the record and motives of leading Radicals.[49] Finally, the coincidence of the Civil War centennial with the great public civil rights issues of the 1960's quickened the pace of historical writings concerned with the status of the Negro.[50]

Out of these recent studies has come a new perspective on the post-Civil War grant of suffrage to the Negro, once widely regarded with dismay. The Fifteenth Amendment is now seen as a "momentous enactment." It included Negroes within "the American dream of equality and opportunity," gave the United States distinction as being the first nation committed to the proposition that in a "bi-racial society . . . human beings must have equal rights," and established an essential legal substructure upon which to build the reality of political equality.[51]

There has also emerged an explanation of political Radicalism during Reconstruction, even of Republicanism generally, in terms of ideas and idealism. The case has been subtly argued and dramatically summarized by Kenneth M. Stampp: ". . . radical reconstruction ought to be viewed in part as the last great crusade of the nineteenth-century romantic reformers." If anything, Radicals were less opportunistic and more candid than the average politician. "To the practical motives that the radicals occasionally revealed must be added the moral idealism that they inherited from the abolitionists."[52] The case for Radicalism has also been persuasively presented by the English historian William Ranulf Brock, who has written that the cement binding together the Radicals as a political group was "not interest but a number of propositions about equality, rights, and national power."[53] In fact, Brock does not limit this generous interpretation of motive to the Radicals, but includes moderate Republicans as well. He has gone even further and identified "the great moving power behind Reconstruction" with "the conviction of the average Republican that the objectives of his party were rational and humane."[54] The study by the present authors led to the conclusion that the moderates in Congress broke with the President in 1866 primarily because of their genuine concern for equal civil rights short of suffrage.[55]

With the ferment and new direction of Reconstruction historiography, the old Braxton-Rhodes-Fleming assumption of party expediency as the controlling motive behind support for Negro suffrage by Republican congressmen might reasonably be expected to meet one of three fates: it might be quietly replaced by the opposite assumption that congressional votes reflected in large measure the strain of idealism in Republicanism; it could be dismissed on the ground that there had been a fusion of principle and expediency so intimate and indivisible as to preclude further inquiry; or it could be subjected to an incisive, detailed, and comprehensive examination. At the present writing neither the first nor third alternative appears at all likely. As for the second, the problem of motivation deserves a better resolution, for it is important both to our understanding of the past and to our expectations of the future.

The "practical" view of Republican motivation is too casually accepted in historical writings and too consonant with prevailing attitudes toward politicians and parties to be in danger of just disappearing. Leslie H. Fishel, Jr., Emma Lou Thornbrough, and Leon F. Litwack in their sympathetic pioneering studies of Negroes in the North all assume that Republican politicians had little interest in the Negro except to obtain his vote.[56] In staking out the well-merited abolitionist claim of credit for having championed the cause of Negro equality during the Civil War and Reconstruction, James M. McPherson perpetuates the traditional attitude toward Republicans: the abolitionists provided moral justification, but party policies "were undertaken primarily for military or political reasons."[57] Indeed, McPherson condemns the whole North for a failure of conscience and belittles the public support given to equal rights as "primarily a conversion of expediency rather than one of conviction."[58] David Donald has attempted to bypass the "difficulty of fathoming . . . motives" by disregarding individuals in favor of "objective behavior patterns" and "quantitatively measurable forces." His procedures and logic, however, start with the assumption that politicians wish either re-election or higher office and that this fact is controlling in presidential policy and congressional voting.[59] It is startling to read that Lincoln's policies could have been arrived at by "A rather simple computer installed in the White House, fed the elementary statistical information about election returns and programed to solve the recurrent problem of winning re-election. . . ."[60]

Even Stampp, who restates the old hostile arguments regarding the political motivation of Radicals in order to challenge them, replies directly only with the observation that conservatives as well were thinking how best to keep the Republican party in power—to them Negro suffrage simply appeared an obstacle rather than an instrument of party unity and control. Stampp also strikes a disparaging note evident elsewhere in recent scholarship. This is the charge of "timidity" and "evasion" leveled against Republican politicians on the question of Negro suffrage.[61] There is irony in the shifting basis of attack upon the reputation of Republican politicians. Once berated from the right for plots and maneuvers to thwart the popular will and establish Negro suffrage, these whipping boys of history are now in danger of assault from the left for having lacked the boldness, energy, and conviction neded for an earlier and more secure victory.

There finally appeared in 1965 to supersede the Mathews monograph an intensive, scholarly work by a young historian, William Gillette, on the passage and ratification of the Fifteenth Amendment. Reflecting the modern temper in its rejection of caste and commitment to equality, the new study nevertheless represents a vigorous survival of the Braxton-Fleming tradition.[62] Gillett's thesis transfers to the North the emphasis formerly placed on the South, but political expediency remains the heart of the matter: "The primary object of the Amendment was *to get the Negro vote* in the North. . . ."[63] As revealed by the election results of 1868, "prospects for both northern and southern Republicans were not bright" and, according to Gillette, "Republicans had to do something." They were pessimistic about reliance upon the Negro vote in the South but alert to its potential in the North. This prospect motivated the framing of the amendment and accounted for ratification in the face of widespread opposition since it "made political sense to shrewd politicians. . . ."[64] In effect, Gillette accepts as his thesis the judgment pronounced in 1870 by the Democratic party-line newspaper, the New York *World*, that Republican leaders " 'calculated that the Negro vote in the doutbful Northern states would be sufficient to maintain the Republican ascendancy in those states and, through them, in the politics of the country. It was with this in view that they judged the Fifteenth Amendment essential to the success of their party.' "[65]

In challenge to the dominant pattern of interpretation from Braxton through Gillette, we should like to suggest that Republican party leadership played a crucial role in committing this nation to equal suffrage for the Negro not because of political expediency but *despite* political risk. An incontestable fact of Reconstruction history suggests this view. Race prejudice was so strong in the North that the issue of equal Negro suffrage constituted a clear and present danger to Republicans. White backlash may be a recently coined phrase, but it was a virulent political phenomenon in the 1860's. The exploitation of prejudice by the Democratic opposition was blatant and unashamed.

The power base of the Republican party lay in the North. However much party leaders desired to break through sectional boundaries to create a national image or to gain some measure of security from Southern votes, victory or defeat in the presidential elections of the nineteenth century lay in the Northern states. With the exception of the contested election of 1876, electoral votes from the South were irrelevant—either nonexistent or unnecessary—to Republican victory. It was the loss of Connecticut, Indiana, and New York in 1876 and 1884, and of those states plus Illinois in 1892, which was critical; had they remained in the Republican column, Democrats would have waited until the twentieth century to claim residence for one of their own in the White House.[66]

What has been charged to timidity might better be credited to prudence. The caution with which Republicans handled the Negro suffrage issue in 1865, 1866, and again in 1868 made political sense. Had the elections of 1866 and 1868 been fought on a platform supporting equal suffrage, who could say with certainty, then or now, that Republicans would have maintained their power?[67] In the state elections of 1867, when Negro suffrage was a major issue, the party took a beating in Connecticut, New York, Pennsylvania, and New Jersey, suf

fered losses in local elections in Indiana and Illinois, and came within
0.4 per cent of losing the Ohio governorship despite the personal political strength of their candidate Rutherford B. Hayes. In Ohio the
issue was clearly drawn, for, in addition to the nationwide commitment
to Negro suffrage in the South made by the First Reconstruction Act
of March 1867, the Republican party bore responsibility for a state-
wide referendum on behalf of equal suffrage at home. The proposed
suffrage amendment to the state constitution went down to defeat
with less than 46 per cent of the votes cast. Democrats gained control of both houses of the state legislature, turning a comfortable Republican margin of forty-six into a Democratic majority of eight. Even
judged by the gubernatorial vote, Republicans suffered a serious loss
of support, for the popular Hayes gained 50.3 per cent of the vote as
compared to 54.5 per cent won by the Republican candidate for secretary of state in 1866.[68]

There was nothing exceptional about Ohioans' hostility to Negro
suffrage. In Republican Minnesota and Kansas equal-suffrage amend-
ments also went down to defeat in the fall elections of 1867, with a
respectable 48.8 per cent of the vote in the former but with less than
35 per cent in the latter despite the fact that Kansas Republicans in
the 1860's constituted 70 per cent of the electorate. From 1865
through 1869 eleven referendum votes were held in eight Northern
states on constitutional changes to provide Negroes with the ballot;
only two were successful—those held during the fall of 1868 in Iowa
and Minnesota. The Minnesota victory, gained after two previous defeats, has been attributed to trickery in labeling the amendment.[69]
The issue was never placed before the white voters of Illinois, Indiana, Pennsylvania, or New Jersey; and this fact probably indicated a
higher intensity of race prejudice than in Connecticut, New York, and
Ohio, where equal suffrage was defeated.[70] These seven were marginal
states of critical importance to the Republicans in national elections.
The tenacity of opposition to Negro enfranchisement is well illustrated
in New York, where one might have expected to find it minimal since
Negroes had always voted in the state although subjected to a discriminatory property qualification since 1821. After a Republican legislature ratified the Fifteenth Amendment in April 1869, New Yorkers
defeated a similar change in the state constitution, swept the Republicans out of control at Albany and returned a Democratic majority of
twenty, which promptly voted to rescind New York's ratification.[71]

In short, Republican sponsorship of Negro suffrage meant flirtation
with political disaster in the North, particularly in any one or all of

the seven pivotal states where both the prejudice of race and the Democratic opposition were strong. Included among them were the four most populous states in the nation, with corresponding weight in the electoral college: New York, Pennsylvania, Ohio, and Illinois. Negroes were denied equal suffrage in every one of these critically important seven, and only in New York did they enjoy a partial enfranchisement. If Negroes were to be equally enfranchised, as the Fifteenth Amendment directed, it is true that Republicans could count upon support from an overwhelming majority of the new voters. It does not necessarily follow, however, that this prospect was enticing to "shrewd politicians." What simple political computation could add the number of potential Negro voters to be derived from a minority population that reached a high of 3.4 per cent in New Jersey and 2.4 per cent in Ohio, then diminished in the other five states from 1.9 to 1.1 per cent, a population already partially enfranchised in New York and to be partially disenfranchised in Connecticut by the state's nondiscriminatory illiteracy tests; determine and subtract the probable number of white voters who would be alienated among the dominant 96.6 to 98.9 per cent of the population; and predict a balance that would ensure Republican victory?

The impact of the Negro suffrage issue upon the white voter might be softened by moving just after a national election rather than just before one; and this was the strategy pursued in pushing through the Fifteenth Amendment.[72] Yet risk remained, a risk which it is difficult to believe politicians would have willingly assumed had their course been set solely, or primarily, by political arithmetic. Let us, then, consider the nature of the evidence cited to show that Republican policy sprang from narrow party interests.

Since the days of Braxton, historians have used the public statements of public men, straight from the pages of the *Congressional Globe*, not only to document the charge of party expediency but also to prove it by the admission of intent. The frequency with which either Senator Charles Sumner or Thaddeus Stevens has been quoted on the arithmetic of Negro enfranchisement might well have suggested caution in using such oral evidence for establishing motivation. As craftsmen, historians have been alerted against a proclivity to seize upon the discovery of an economic motive as if, to quote Kenneth Stampp, they then were "dealing with reality—with something that reflects the true nature of man." Stampp cites Sumner as an example of the fallacy: ". . . when he argued that Negro suffrage was necessary to prevent a repudiation of the public debt, he may *then* have had a concealed motive—that is, he may have believed that this was the way to convert bondholders to his moral principles."[73] An equal sophistication is overdue in the handling of political motivation. With reference to the Reconstruction legislation of 1867, Sumner did state—frankly, as the cynically inclined would add—that the Negro vote had been a necessity for the organization of "loyal governments" in the South. He continued with equal forthrightness: "It was on this ground, rather than principle, that I relied most. . . ."[74] A man remarkably uncompromising in his own adherence to principle, Sumner obviously did not believe it wise to rely upon moral argument alone to move others. Thaddeus Stevens' belief in the justice of equal suffrage and his desire to see it realized were as consistent and genuine as Sumner's own, but Stevens was a much shrewder practitioner of the art of politics. It is worth noting, then, that Negro suffrage was not the solution to which he clung most tenaciously in order to guarantee "loyal governments" in the South; he looked more confidently to the army and to white disfranchisement. In the last critical stage of battle over Reconstruction policy, it was the moderate Republicans who championed an immediate mandate for Negro suffrage in the South, while Stevens led the fight to delay its advent in favor of an interlude of military rule.[75]

All this suggests the need for a detailed analysis of who said what, when, in arguing that Negro suffrage, South or North, would bring Republican votes and Republican victories. Did the argument have its origin with the committed antislavery men or with the uncommitted politician? Was it used to whet an appetite for political gain or to counter fear of losses? Such a study might start by throwing out as evidence of motivation all appeals to political expediency made after the Fifteenth Amendment was sent to the states for ratification. By that time Republicans were tied to the policy and could not escape the opprobrium it carried; a leadership that used every possible stratagem and pressure to secure ratification in the face of widespread opposition could be expected to overlook no argument that might move hesitant state legislators, particularly one that appealed to party loyalty and interest.

It has been implied that election results in the 1870's and 1880's were evidence of political motivation behind the Fifteenth Amendment. The logic is faulty. Consequences are not linked causally to intentions. Favorable election returns would not constitute proof that decision making had been dependent upon calculation, nor would election losses preclude the existence of unrealistic expectations. Yet it would be of interest to know the effect of the enfranchisment of Negroes upon Republican fortunes, particularly in the marginal Northern states. Election returns might serve to test the reasonableness of optimistic projections of gain by adding black voters, as against the undoubted risk of losing white voters. If the end result of Negro enfranchisement in the North was one of considerable advantage to Republicans, we may have overestimated the element of political risk. If enfranchisement brought the Republicans little benefit, the case for a careful re-examination of Republican motivation is strengthened. Inquiry can reasonably be restricted to the results of presidential and congressional contests, since these were of direct concern to the Republicans in Congress responsible for the Fifteenth Amendment.[76]

Negro votes in the critical Northern states were not sufficient to ensure victory in three of the six presidential elections following ratification of the Fifteenth Amendment in 1870.[77] For purposes of comparing the "before" and "after" vote, the election of 1872 is unfortunately of no utility. Horace Greeley proved so weak a Liberal Republican-Democratic candidate that in every one of the critical seven states Grant would have won without a single Negro ballot.[78] In the 1876 contest, which affords the best comparison with 1868, the Republican percentage of the vote dropped in every one of the marginal states, four of which were lost to the Democrats. Comparison of the number of Republican losses in the seven states for the three elections before 1872 with those for the three elections after 1872, shows four losses in the earlier period as against nine losses after Negro enfranchisement.[79] Of course, it could be argued that Republicans would have done even worse without the Negro vote and the politicians in 1869 could not have anticipated the depression of 1873. Politicians would have known, however, that Negroes in the North, outside the border states, were too few to constitute a guarantee of victory in the face of any major adversity. In 1880 and 1888, years of success, Republicans might have lost Indiana without the Negro, but they would not have lost the Presidency. The only presidential contest in the nineteenth century in which Negro voters played a critical role was that of 1876, and the voters lived not in the North but in the South. Analysis of ballots in the 1870's and 1880's does not confirm the reasonableness of expectations for a succession of Republicans in the White House as the result of Negro enfranchisement.

As to Congress, Republicans could hope to gain very little more than they already held in 1869. Of thirty-six Democrats seated in the House of Representatives from the seven marginal states, only four came from districts with a potential Negro electorate large enough to turn the Republican margin of defeat in 1868 into a victory.[80] Of the four, Republicans gained just one in 1870, in Cincinnati, Ohio. Their failure to profit from the Negro vote in the Thirteenth District of Illinois, located at the southern tip of the state, is of particular interest. The district had gone Republican in 1866 and had a large concentration of Negro population. In 1868 the Republican share of the vote had been a close 49.1 per cent; in 1870 it actually decreased with the Democratic margin of victory rising from 503 to 1,081. In the two counties with the highest proportion of Negroes to whites, over 20 per cent, a jump in the Republican percentage plus an increase in the actual number of Republican votes cast—unusual in a nonpresidential year—indicate that Negroes exercised their new franchise. However, this apparently acted as a stimulus for whites to go to the polls and vote Democratic. In three of the five counties in the district where Negroes constituted over 5 per cent of the population, more Democratic votes were recorded in 1870 than in 1868.[81]

The Republicans did better in holding seats won by slim margins in 1868 than in winning new ones. Eighteen congressional districts in the critical seven states had gone to Republicans by a margin of fewer than five hundred votes. Of these, Republicans retained fourteen and lost four to the Democrats in 1870.[82] Three of the four districts lost had a potential Negro electorate large enough to have doubled the Republican margins of 1868. The record of voting in congressional elections from 1860 through 1868 in the fourteen districts retained suggests that half might have remained Republican without any benefit of the Fifteenth Amendment.[83] It is doubtful whether three of the other seven, all districts in Ohio, would have been placed in jeopardy had Negro suffrage not been raised as an issue in 1867 both at home and in Washington, for the margin of victory dropped sharply from 1866 to 1868.[84] One of the remaining four, the Second District in Connecticut, consisted of two counties, Middlesex with a Negro population of 372 and New Haven with 2,734, the largest concentration of Negroes in the state. New Haven had gone Democratic in 1869 (Connecticut elected its congressmen in the spring) by 62 votes, though the Republican won the district; two years later, with Negroes enfranchised, the Democratic margin in New Haven actually increased to 270! Middlesex saved the day for the incumbent, who barely survived by 23 votes. This suggests that the district remained Republican not because of Negro enfranchisement, but despite it. Two seats, one in Pennsylvania and the other in New Jersey, were retained by an increase in the margin of victory larger than the number of potential Negro voters.[85] The last of the fourteen districts, the Eleventh of New York, consisting of Orange and Sullivan counties, may have been saved by Negro voters, although the election results there are particularly difficult to interpret.[86]

If we consider the total picture of the 1870 congressional races, we find that the Republican share of the vote decreased in five of the seven critical states, remained practically constant in Ohio, and increased in New Jersey. The party did best in the two states with the highest percentages of Negroes in their population, Ohio and New Jersey, netting one additional seat in each. However, in the seven states as a whole Republicans suffered a net loss of nine representatives. Democrats gained most in New York and Pennsylvania, almost doubling their congressional delegation in the latter from six to eleven out of a total of twenty-four. Republicans retained control in Congress but with a sharply reduced majority. In short, results of the Northern congressional elections of 1870 suggest that Negro voters may have offset to some extent the alienation of white voters by the suffrage issue, that they did little, however, to turn Republican defeats into Republican victories, and that the impact of the Fifteenth Amendment was in general disadvantageous to the Republican party.

Election returns blanket a multitude of issues, interests, and personalities. In an effort to relate them more precisely to the impact of Negro enfranchisement, we have identified all counties in the seven marginal states in which Negroes constituted a higher-than-average percentage of the population. Using 5 per cent, we found thirty-four such counties.[87] An analysis of the number of Republican voters in 1868 as compared with 1870 and of the changing percentage of the total vote won by Republicans in 1866, 1868, 1870, and 1876 would indicate that Negroes did go to the polls and vote Republican in numbers which more than offset adverse white reaction, but this appears to have been the case in less than half the counties.[88] The net effect upon Republican fortunes was negligible, if not negative. Thus, in the first congressional election after Negroes were given the ballot, three of the thirty-four counties shifted from Democratic to Republican majorities, but another three went from the Republicans to the Democrats. The record was no happier for Republicans in the 1876 presidential election. Again, only six counties changed political alignment as compared with the 1868 balloting. Two were added to the Republican column, and four were lost!

From whatever angle of vision they are examined, election returns in the seven pivotal states give no support to the assumption that the enfranchisement of Northern Negroes would help Republicans in their struggle to maintain control of Congress and the Presidency. This conclusion holds for all of the North. Any hope that may have been entertained of gaining substantial strength in the loyal border states was lacking in realism. It failed to take into account the most obvious of facts—the intensity of hostility to any form of racial equality in communities recently and reluctantly freed from the institution of Negro slavery. Only Missouri and West Virginia had shown Republican strength in 1868; of the ten congressional seats which Republicans then won, half were lost in the elections of 1870. Kentucky had the largest Negro population in the North, but in seven of its nine congressional districts the Democratic margin of victory was so overwhelming that the state could not possibly be won by the Republican opposition, and, in fact, all nine seats remained Democratic in 1870. Although no Republican had won a seat from Maryland in 1868, there the odds were better. The outcome, however, was only a little more favorable. In 1870 Republicans failed to make any gain; in 1872 they were victors in two of the six congressional districts; these they promptly lost in 1874. The pattern of politics in Delaware was similar, consistently Democratic except in the landslide of 1872.

The lack of political profit from the Negro vote in pivotal states of the North reinforces the contention that Republican sponsorship of Negro suffrage in the face of grave political risk warrants a reexamination of motive. There is additional evidence which points to this need. Circumstances leading to the imposition of unrestricted Negro suffrage upon the defeated South are not consistent with an explanation based upon party expediency. Two detailed accounts of the legislative history of the Reconstruction Act of March 2, 1867, have recently been written, one by Brock and the other by David Donald; in neither is there any suggestion that the men responsible for the Negro suffrage provision, moderates led by John A. Bingham, James G. Blaine, and John Sherman, placed it there as an instrument of party advantage.[89] They were seeking a way to obtain ratification of the Fourteenth Amendment, which the Southern states had rejected, and to restore all states to the Union without an indefinite interval of military rule or the imposition of more severe requirements.

The nature of the Fifteenth Amendment also suggests the inadequacy of the view that its purpose was to make permanent Republican control of the South. The amendment did not constitute a guarantee for the continuance of Radical Republican regimes, and this fact was recognized at the time. What it did was to commit the nation, not to universal, but to *impartial* suffrage. Out of the tangle of legislative debate and compromise there had emerged a basic law affirming the principle of nondiscrimination. A number of Republican politicians, South and North, who measured it in terms of political arithmetic, were not happy with the formulation of the amendment. They recognized that under its provisions the Southern Negro vote could be reduced to political impotence by literacy tests and other qualifications, ostensibly equal.[90]

If evidence of Republican concern for the principle of equal suffrage irrespective of race is largely wanting in histories dealing with Negro enfranchisement, it may be absent because historians have seldom considered the possibility that such evidence exists. With the more friendly atmosphere in which recent scholarship has approached the Radicals of Reconstruction, it has become apparent that men formerly dismissed as mere opportunistic politicians—"Pig Iron" Kelley, Ben Wade, Henry Wilson—actually displayed in their public careers a genuine concern for the equal status of the Negro.[91] It is time to take a fresh look at the Republican party record as a whole. For example, let us reconsider the charge that Republicans were hypocrites in forcing equal suffrage upon the South at a time when Northern states outside New England did not grant a like privilege and were refusing to mend their ways. Aside from disregarding the sequence of events which led to the suffrage requirement in the legislation of 1867, this accusation confuses Republicans with Northerners generally. In the postwar referendums on Negro suffrage, race prejudice predominated over the principle of equality but not with the consent of a majority of Republican voters. Thus the 45.9 per cent of the Ohio vote for Negro suffrage in 1867 was equivalent to 84.6 per cent of the Republican electorate of 1866 and to 89 per cent of the Republicans who voted in 1867 for Rutherford B. Hayes as governor.[92] In truth, Republicans had fought many lost battles in state legislatures and in state referendums on behalf of Negro suffrage.[93] What is surprising is not that they had sometimes evaded the issue but that on so many occasions they had been its champion. Even the most cynical of observers would find it difficult to account for all such Republican effort in terms of political advantage. What need was there in Minnesota or Wisconsin or Iowa for a mere handful of potential Republican voters? In these states, as in others, the movement to secure the ballot for Negroes antedated the Civil War and cannot be discounted as a mere maneuver preliminary to imposing Negro suffrage upon a defeated South.

Historians have not asked whether Republicans who voted for the Fifteenth Amendment were acting in a manner consistent with their past public records. We do not know how many of these congressmen had earlier demonstrated, or failed to demonstrate, a concern for the well-being of free Negroes or a willingness publicly to support the unpopular cause of Negro suffrage.[94] The vote in the House of Representatives in January 1866 on the question of Negro suffrage in the District of Columbia offers an example of neglected evidence. The issue was raised before a break had developed between President Johnson and Congress; it came, in fact, at a time when an overwhelming majority of Republicans accepted the President's decision not to force Negro suffrage upon the South, even a suffrage limited to freedmen who might qualify by military service, education, or property holding. In other words, this vote reflected not the self-interest but the conscience of Republicans. They divided 116 for the measure, 15 against, and 10 recorded as not voting.[95] In the next Congress, which passed upon the Fifteenth Amendment, support for that measure came from seventy-two representatives elected from Northern states which had not extended equal suffrage to Negroes. Were these men acting under the compulsion of politics or of conscience? More than half, forty-four in all, had served in the House during the previous Congress. Every one of the forty-four had voted in favor of Negro suffrage for the District of Columbia. Why can they not be credited with an honest conviction, to use the words of a New York *Times* editorial, "that a particular color ought not of itself to exclude from the elective franchise . . . ?"[96]

The motives of congressmen doubtless were mixed, but in a period of national crisis when the issue of equality was basic to political contention, it is just possible that party advantage was subordinated to principle. Should further study rehabilitate the reputation of the Republican party in respect to Negro suffrage, it would not follow that the 1860's were a golden age dedicated to the principle that all men are created equal. During the years of Civil War and Reconstruction, race prejudice was institutionalized in the Democratic party. Perhaps this very fact, plus the jibes of inconsistency and hypocrisy with which Democrats derided their opponents, helped to create the party unity that committed Republicans, and through them the nation, to equal suffrage irrespective of race.

NOTES

1. The First Reconstruction Act, passed over President Andrew Johnson's veto March 2, 1867, and the Fifteenth Amendment, passed by Congress February 26, 1869, and declared ratified March 30, 1870. In 1860 the only states with equal suffrage for Negroes were Maine, New Hampshire, Vermont, Massachusetts, and Rhode Island. New York permitted Negroes with a $250 freehold estate to vote. By 1869 the following Northern states had been added to the above list: Nebraska, Wisconsin, Minnesota, and Iowa.

2. A. Caperton Braxton, *The Fifteenth Amendment: An Account of Its Enactment* (Lynchburg, Va., n.d.). The foreword is dated April 30, 1934.

3. *Ibid.*, 7.

4. *Ibid.*, 16-17, 24, 33-38, 41, 47.

5. *Ibid.*, 56-57, 58.

6. *Ibid.*, 78.

7. *Ibid.*, 46.

8. *Ibid.*, 59.

9. *Ibid.*, 47-48.

10. John Mabry Mathews, *Legislative and Judicial History of the Fifteenth Amendment* (Baltimore, 1909).

11. *Ibid.*, 35.

12. *Ibid.*, 12, 22, 32, 36.

13. For recent comment on their treatment of Reconstruction, see Bernard A. Weisberger, "The Dark and Bloody Ground of Reconstruction Historiography," *Journal of Southern History*, XXV (November 1959), 446-47; Alan D. Harper, "William A. Dunning: The Historian as Nemesis," *Civil War History*, X (March 1964), 54-66; Kenneth M. Stampp, *The Era of Reconstruction, 1865-1877* (New York, 1965), 3-23.

14. William Archibald Dunning, *Reconstruction, Political and Economic, 1865-1877* (New York and London, 1907), 111.

15. *Ibid.*, 94, 174, 135.

16. James Ford Rhodes, *History of the United States from the Compromise of 1850 to the Final Restoration of Home Rule at the South in 1877* (7 vols., New York, 1907-1910), VI (c. 1906), 200-201.

17. *Ibid.*, V (c. 1904), 522.

18. *Ibid.*, VI, 30.

19. The paper was not published, but an abstract, together with some indication of the discussion that followed, appeared in Massachusetts Historical Society, *Proceedings*, 2d Ser., XVIII (Boston, 1905), 465-67; XIX (Boston, 1906), 34-37.

20. Rhodes, *History*, VII, 168.

21. *Ibid.*, 170.

22. Abstract of paper on "Negro Suffrage and Reconstruction," Massachusetts Historical Society, *Proceedings*, 2d Ser., XVIII, 466-67.

23. *Ibid.*, XIX, 37; Rhodes, *History*, VII, 174.

24. Abstract of paper on "Negro Suffrage and Reconstruction," Massachusetts Historical Society, *Proceedings*, 2d Ser., XIX, 37.

25. Ellis Paxson Oberholtzer, A History of the United States Since the Civil War (5 vols., New York, 1917-1937), I, 484-85.
26. Walter Lynwood Fleming, Sequel of Appomattox: A Chronicle of the Reunion of the States (New Haven, 1919), 169-70.
27. We borrow the phrase from Willard Hays's study in historiography, "Andrew Johnson's Reputation," East Tennessee Historical Society, Publications, No. 32 (1960), 18.
28. Claude G. Bowers, The Tragic Era: The Revolution After Lincoln (Cambridge, 1929), 7, 13-15, 99, 151-54.
29. Ibid., 214-15.
30. George Fort Milton, The Age of Hate: Andrew Johnson and the Radicals (New York, 1930), 216, 219, 225; quotations are from pages 216 and 225.
31. Ibid., 649-50.
32. J. G. Randall, The Civil War and Reconstruction (Boston, 1937), 799.
33. J. G. Randall and David Donald, The Civil War and Reconstruction (2d ed., Boston, 1961), 641.
34. Howard K. Beale, The Critical Year: A Study of Andrew Johnson and Reconstruction (New York, 1930), 173-95.
35. Ibid., 173-74.
36. Ibid., 146-47.
37. Ibid., 187, 194-95.
38. Charles H. Coleman, The Election of 1868: The Democratic Effort to Regain Control (New York, 1933), 18-24, 48-54.
39. Ibid., 369-70.
40. Ibid., 363, 377-78.
41. Ibid., 13.
42. Important were the unpublished Harvard doctoral dissertation (1954) of Leslie H. Fishel, Jr., parts of which appeared as "Northern Prejudice and Negro Suffrage, 1865-1870," Journal of Negro History, XXXIX (January 1954), 8-26, and "The Negro in Northern Politics, 1870-1900," Mississippi Valley Historical Review, XLII (December 1955), 466-89; Emma Lou Thornbrough, The Negro in Indiana: A Study of a Minority (Indianapolis, 1957); Louis Ruchames, "Race, Marriage, and Abolition in Massachusetts," Journal of Negro History, XL (July 1955), 250-73; C. Vann Woodward, "Equality: America's Deferred Commitment," American Scholar, XXVII (Autumn 1958), 459-72.
43. John Hope Franklin's Reconstruction: After the Civil War (Chicago, 1961) consolidates and extends this revisionism. For an earlier summation, see Howard K. Beale, "On Rewriting Reconstruction History," American Historical Review, XLV (July 1940), 807-27.
44. For examples, see John and LaWanda Cox, "General O. O. Howard and the 'Misrepresented Bureau,'" Journal of Southern History, XIX (November 1953), 427-56; John A. Carpenter, "Atrocities in the Reconstruction Period," Journal of Negro History, XLVII (October 1962), 234-47.
45. LeRoy P. Graf, "Andrew Johnson and the Coming of the War," Tennessee Historical Quarterly, XIX (September 1960), 208-21; Eric L. McKitrick, Andrew Johnson and Reconstruction (Chicago, 1960); LaWanda and John H. Cox, Politics, Principle, and Prejudice, 1865-1866: Dilemma of Reconstruction America (New York, 1963).

46. Two germinal and widely reprinted articles were those by Bernard De Voto, "The Easy Chair," *Harper's Magazine*, CXCII (February 1946), 123-26, and by Arthur Schlesinger, Jr., "The Causes of the Civil War: A Note on Historical Sentimentalism," *Partisan Review*, XVI (October 1949); 969-81.

47. For present-day sympathy with the abolitionists, see Martin Duberman (ed.), *The Antislavery Vanguard: New Essays on the Abolitionists* (Princeton, 1965); and for a criticism of overly simplified approaches to motivation, see Duberman's own essay, "The Northern Response to Slavery," *ibid.*, 406-13.

48. This is evident in Charles H. Wesley, "The Participation of Negroes in Anti-Slavery Political Parties," *Journal of Negro History*, XXIX (January 1944), 32-74; Leon F. Litwack, *North of Slavery: The Negro in the Free States, 1790-1860* (Chicago, 1961); Howard H. Bell, "Negro Emancipation in Historic Retrospect: The Nation: The Condition and Prospects of the Negro as Reflected in the National Convention of 1864," *Journal of Human Relations*, XI (Winter 1963), 221-31; and August Meier, *Negro Thought in America, 1880-1915: Racial Ideologies in the Age of Booker T. Washington* (Ann Arbor, 1963).

49. Particularly noteworthy were Hans L. Trefousse, "Ben Wade and the Negro," *Ohio Historical Quarterly*, LXVII (April 1959), 161-72, and Ira V. Brown, "William D. Kelley and Radical Reconstruction," *Pennsylvania Magazine of History and Biography*, LXXXV (July 1961), 316-29.

50. For example, see the emancipation centennial issue of the Illinois State Historical Society, *Journal*, LVI (Autumn 1963).

51. The quotations and paraphrase are from Carl N. Degler, *Out of Our Past* (New York, 1959), 211; W. R. Brock, *An American Crisis: Congress and Reconstruction, 1865-1867* (London and New York, 1963), 302-303; Stampp, *Era of Reconstruction*, 12-13, 214-15.

52. Stampp, *Era of Reconstruction*, 98-102; quotations are on pages 101 and 102.

53. Brock, *An American Crisis*, 75.

54. *Ibid.*, 62, 180-81; the quotation is on page 62.

55. Cox and Cox, *Politics, Principle, and Prejudice*, especially Chapter 10.

56. Fishel, "Northern Prejudice and Negro Suffrage," 11; Fishel, "Negro in Northern Politics," 466; Thornbrough, *Negro in Indiana*, ix-x, 251-52; Litwack, *North of Slavery*, 62, 80, 90-91.

57. James M. McPherson, *The Struggle for Equality: Abolitionists and the Negro in the Civil War and Reconstruction* (Princeton, 1964), viii.

58. *Ibid.*, 430-31.

59. David Donald, *The Politics of Reconstruction, 1863-1867* (Baton Rouge, 1965), 12, 26-28, 82; quotations are from pages 28 and 82. The first part of the assumption is explicitly stated as a hypothesis; the second part is implicit throughout.

60. *Ibid.*, 17.

61. Stampp, *Era of Reconstruction*, 92-94, 141-42. The most striking example is Edgar A. Toppin, "Negro Emancipation in Historic Retrospect: Ohio: The Negro Suffrage Issue in Postbellum Ohio Politics," *Journal of Human Relations*, XI (Winter 1963), 232-46.

62. Revisions in the manuscript made after its completion as a doctoral dis-

sertation softened the original statement of the author's views but did not materially alter them. Compare *The Right to Vote: Politics and the Passage of the Fifteenth Amendment* (Baltimore, 1965) with "The Power of the Ballot: The Politics of Passage and Ratification of the Fifteenth Amendment" (unpublished Ph.D. dissertation, Princeton University, 1963), especially the preface and the first and last chapters.

63. Italics ours. Gillette, *Right to Vote*, 165.

64. *Ibid.*, 41-43, 89-90, 160, 163; quoted passages are on pages 43 and 160.

65. *Ibid.*, 115, quoting *World* editorial of April 1, 1870.

66. For the election of 1868, see Coleman, *Election of 1868*, p. 363. Calculations for the other years are based upon the electoral vote as given in W. Dean Burnham, *Presidential Ballots, 1836-1892* (Baltimore, 1955), 888-89. In 1872 Republicans had 286 electoral votes and would have held a substantial majority without the six Southern states and the two border states which were included in the total. Republicans could have won in 1876 without the 19 contested votes of Florida, Louisiana, and South Carolina had they retained either New York (35 votes) or both Connecticut (6) and Indiana (15). In the elections of 1880, 1884, 1888, and 1892, the Republican candidate gained no electoral votes from any former slave state. In 1884, as in 1876, either the New York vote or a combination of those of Indiana and Connecticut would have won the election for the Republicans. In 1892 the electoral count was 277 Democratic, 145 Republican, and 22 Populist. Republicans needed an additional 78 votes for a majority, which could have come from New York (36), Illinois (24), Indiana (15), and Connecticut (6). The party kept Pennsylvania and Ohio (except for one vote); it had not held New Jersey (10 votes) since 1872.

67. More than a simple majority would have been necessary to retain control of Reconstruction in the face of President Johnson's vetoes and to pass the Fifteenth Amendment. Johnson supporters welcomed Negro suffrage as an issue on which they expected to redress their 1866 defeat. Doolittle to Browning, November 8, 1866, quoted in Cox and Cox, *Politics, Principle, and Prejudice*, 230.

68. All local and state election returns, except presidential votes, are from the *Tribune Almanac*. Some percentages are there given; more have been calculated. We are indebted to Stuart Horn, doctoral candidate at the City University of New York, for his assistance in compiling statistical data.

69. Fishel, "Northern Prejudice and Negro Suffrage," 24.

70. The other two states where equal suffrage was defeated were Wisconsin and Michigan.

71. Dixon Ryan Fox, "The Negro Vote in Old New York," *Political Science Quarterly*, XXXII (June 1917), 252-72; Litwack, *North of Slavery*, 80-84. Fishel has also linked the defeat of the suffrage proposal and the Democratic victory in New York. "Northern Prejudice and Negro Suffrage," 20. See also, Gillette, *Right to Vote*, 115, n. 18.

72. Aaron M. Powell's report of Senator Henry Wilson's statement, *National Anti-Slavery Standard*, June 13, 1868, cited in McPherson, *Struggle for Equality*, 421. Senator Oliver Morton wished the amendment passed and ratified quickly because he feared its effect if the issue hung over the

elections of 1870 and 1872. Henry Wilson estimated that the struggle to make the Negro an equal citizen had cost the Republican party a quarter of a million votes. In an eloquent reply to the charge that the amendment was only an effort to maintain power and the spoils of office, Wilson pointed out that there was "not to-day a square mile in the United States where the advocacy of the equal rights and privileges of those colored men has not been in the past and is not now unpopular. . . . The public man or the political party that honestly and zealously espouses their cause will continue to be misunderstood, misrepresented, and maligned. . . . I fear it will be so in some portions of the country for years to come." *Cong. Globe,* 40 Cong., 3 Sess., 672 (January 28, 1869), quoted in part in Braxton, *Fifteenth Amendment,* 55.

73. Stampp, *Era of Reconstruction,* 106-107.

74. Sumner to Bright, May 27, 1867, in Edward L. Pierce, *Memoir and Letters of Charles Sumner* (4 vols., Boston, 1894), IV, 319.

75. Brock, *American Crisis,* 192-95; Donald, *Politics of Reconstruction,* 73-75.

76. Local elections did, of course, have consequences for senators, who were elected by state legislatures; and a shift of political fortune in a critical state was always of national interest. However, the Fifteenth Amendment was not generated from local politics. The argument of political expediency implies political profit in national elections.

77. See footnote 66 above and footnote 79 below.

78. The percentage of Negroes in the population as compared with the percentage margin of victory in 1872 follows: Connecticut, 1.8 per cent with 2.4; New York, 1.2 per cent with 3.1; Pennsylvania, 1.9 per cent with 12.1; New Jersey, 3.4 per cent with 4.4; Ohio, 2.4 per cent with 3.2; Indiana, 1.5 per cent with 3.2; Illinois, 1.1 per cent with 6.2. The Negro percentage is from Gillette's convenient chart, *Right to Vote,* 82; the percentage of the Republican vote was calculated from the election figures in Burnham, *Presidential Ballots,* as was that of 1868 and 1876.

79. Before 1872: New Jersey in 1860 (in part), 1864, and 1868, and New York in 1868. After 1872; Connecticut, New York, and Indiana in 1876 and 1884; New Jersey in 1876, 1880, and 1884.

80. The four were the Second District in New Jersey, the First in Ohio, the Sixth in Indiana, and the Thirteenth in Illinois. This conclusion is based upon an inspection of election returns as reported in the *Tribune Almanac,* comparing the margin of victory for Democratic winners in 1868 with an approximation of the number of potential Negro voters estimated as one-fifth of the Negro population in the counties comprising each district. Population figures were taken from the *Ninth Census of the United States,* 1870 (Washington, 1872). Districts where Republican candidates were seated as the result of ·a contest were not counted as Democratic even though a Democratic majority was shown in the *Tribune Almanac* election returns.

81. That Negroes were responsible for the increase in the Republican vote cannot, of course, be proved but appears highly probable; similarly, the explanation for the larger Democratic vote is inference. The Republican vote in Alexander County with a Negro population of 21.73 per cent rose from 656 to 804 (37.8 to 45.6 per cent); in Pulaski with a Negro population of 27.4 per cent from 543 to 844 (46 to 55.59 per cent). The three

counties showing an increase in the number of Democratic votes were Jackson (Republican votes increased there also), Massac, and Pulaski.

82. Districts lost were the Sixteenth Pennsylvania, the Third and Fourth Ohio, and the Seventh Indiana. Districts retained were the Second Connecticut, the Eleventh and Twelfth New York, the Third, Fifth, Tenth, and Thirteenth Pennsylvania, the Fourth New Jersey, the Second, Sixth, Seventh, Fourteenth, and Sixteenth Ohio, and the Fourth Indiana.

83. This tentative conclusion is based upon Republican victories in at least four of the five congressional elections before 1870. The winner in 1860 had to be estimated on the basis of the county vote because district boundaries were changed in 1862. In only one of the seven had the margin of Republican victory in 1866 been less than five hundred. This district, the Fifth in Philadelphia, may have needed Negro votes for victory in 1870 despite its Republican record. Together with it, the Thirteenth in Pennsylvania and the Fourth in Indiana had slim majorities in 1870. In the latter two, however, the margin decreased as compared with 1868, making it unlikely that Negro enfranchisement helped more than it hurt the Republican candidates.

84. In every one of the seven close Ohio districts, the majority vote had been against the state's Negro suffrage amendment in 1867. Their congressmen, however, supported Negro suffrage, all having voted for the First Reconstruction Act of March 1867, and also for Negro suffrage in the District of Columbia on January 18, 1866, and again on December 14, 1866. These men, each of whom served both in the Thirty-ninth and Fortieth Congresses (1865-1869) were Rutherford B. Hayes, Robert C. Schenck, William Lawrence, Reader W. Clarke, Samuel Shellabarger, Martin Welker, and John A. Bingham.

85. The Tenth District in Pennsylvania, made up of Lebanon and Schuylkill counties, had a Negro population of 458, or about 90 potential voters. The Republican margin increased by 404 votes. The Fourth District in New Jersey had a larger Negro population, but the incumbent's margin jumped from 79 to 2,753.

86. The Republican incumbent lost in 1868 by 322 votes but contested the outcome and was seated. In 1870 another Republican won by 500 votes. There were 2,623 Negroes, somewhat more than 500 possible voters, of whom some would have qualified under the old freehold requirement.

87. One in New York (Queens); three in Pennsylvania (Chester, Delaware, Franklin); eight in New Jersey (Cape May, Cumberland, Salem, Camden, Mercer, Monmouth, Somerset, Bergen); ten in Ohio (Meigs, Gallia, Pike, Ross, Brown, Clinton, Fayette, Clark, Greene, Paulding); five in Indiana (Clark, Floyd, Spencer, Vanderburgh, Marion); and seven in Illinois (Alexander, Jackson, Gallatin, Massac, Pulaski, Randolph, Madison). The three urban centers with the largest aggregate number of Negroes in 1870 did not meet the 5-percent criterion and are not included. Leslie Fishel has compiled a revealing table showing Negro and foreign-born urban population. Table II, Appendix III-B, "The North and the Negro, 1865-1900: A Study in Race Discrimination" (unpublished Ph.D. dissertation, Harvard, 1954), For the three cities with over 5,000 Negroes, the comparative figures in 1870 were:

	Colored	Foreign-born	Total
Philadelphia	22,147	183,624	674,022
New York	13,072	419,094	942,292
Cincinnati	5,900	79,612	216,239

88. Twelve counties showed an increase in both the number and percentage of Republican votes in 1870 as compared with 1868; in nine of these, Republicans also made a better showing than in 1866. In 1876 twelve counties had a higher percentage of Republican votes than in 1868. Of these, eight were identical with counties showing marked gains in 1870. The eight, with an indication of their pre-1870 party record, are: in New Jersey, Camden (R), Mercer (D/R), and Somerset (D); in Ohio, Pike (D) and Ross (D/R); in Indiana, Clark (D); in Illinois, Alexander (D) and Pulaski (D/R). The two clear instances of contested counties turning Republican in 1870 and remaining Republican were Mercer in New Jersey and Pulaski in Illinois, the former with a Negro population of 5.1 per cent and the latter with 27.3 per cent.

89. Brock, *American Crisis*, Chapter V; Donald, *Politics of Reconstruction*, Chapter III.

90. Gillette, *Right to Vote*, 50, 57-58, 71, 77; Mathews, *Legislative and Judicial History*, 36, 44-46.

91. Brown, "William D. Kelley and Radical Reconstruction"; Hans L. Trefousse, *Benjamin Franklin Wade: Radical Republican from Ohio* (New York, 1963); Ernest A. McKay, "Henry Wilson and Reconstruction: The Anatomy of a Radical," an unpublished paper prepared for a graduate seminar at Hunter College and preliminary to a biography in process as a doctoral dissertation at New York University.

92. Republican support in Kansas was the weakest, with the 1867 referendum gaining only 54.3 per cent of the vote for the party's candidate for governor the previous year. In the 1867 defeat for Negro suffrage in Minnesota, the proposal had the support equal to 78.7 per cent of those voting for the Republican governor. The 1865 vote on the constitutional proposal in Connecticut amounted to 64 per cent of the vote for the Republican candidate for governor; that in Wisconsin, to 79 per cent of the Republican gubernatorial vote. New York rejected equal suffrage in 1869 with supporters equaling 60 per cent of the 1868 Republican vote for governor and 80 per cent of the party's 1869 vote for secretary of state.

93. For the pre-1860 record, see Emil Olbrich, *The Development of Sentiment on Negro Suffrage to 1860* (Madison, Wis., 1912). Recent state studies of outstanding merit are Leslie H. Fishel, Jr., "Wisconsin and Negro Suffrage," *Wisconsin Magazine of History*, XLVI (Spring 1963), 180-96, and Ira V. Brown, "Pennsylvania and the Rights of the Negro, 1865-1887," *Pennsylvania History*, XXVIII (January 1961), 45-57.

94. The technique recently used by Edward L. Gambill, Glenn M. Linden, and David Donald to identify Radicals and Moderates on the basis of their voting records in Congress could be adapted to clarify the position of Republicans with respect to the Negro. See Donald, *Politics of Reconstruction*, Appendix; Gambill, "Who Were the Senate Radicals?" *Civil War History*, XI (September 1965), 237-44; Linden, " 'Radicals' and

Economic Policies: The Senate, 1861-1873," *Journal of Southern History*, XXXII (May 1966), 189-99. Conventional sources and methodology have not been exhausted. A number of recent scholarly biographies shed little light on motivation because they have not sharply defined the problem and analyzed their subject's attitude toward the Negro and racial equality.

95. *Cong. Globe*, 39 Cong., 1 Sess., 311 (January 18, 1866); Edward McPherson, *Hand Book of Politics for 1868* (Washington, 1868), 115. The total vote was 116 yeas, 54 nays, and 12 not voting.

96. New York *Times*, September 27, 1865.

RECENT STUDIES

Rembert W. Patrick, *The Reconstruction of the Nation* (New York: Oxford University Press, 1967).

XII

The Turner Thesis—A Problem in Historiography

GENE M. GRESSLEY

When Frederick Jackson Turner quietly announced his frontier thesis 60 years ago, it caused little more than a ripple in historical circles. Thirty years later, not only was it widely accepted as the primary explanation of American growth, but American historiography had benefited from thousands of monographs, articles and other historical tomes which emerged in a steady flow.

The fact that the frontier thesis produced little immediate reaction is not surprising. The current vogue was the "germ" school, best fostered and developed in the seminars of Herbert Baxter Adams at Johns Hopkins University. However, no school or theory was well set: American historiography was in a period of rapid change and ferment. American history as an academic discipline was in its incipient stages. . . . Yet within a generation, due to the tremendous accomplishments of pioneer universities and early historians, American history was well established at the graduate level.

The new scholar-historian had several traditions which were conveniently at hand for his use. The romantics, in the immediate background, used a different fabric than the "scientific" historian to weave their historical tale; in many instances they were just as careful in the use of their sources. A second tradition was what Harry Stevens has

From *Agricultural History*, XXXII (October 1958), pp. 227-49. Reprinted with permission of the author.

chosen to call the "ethical and spiritual" approach, introduced by Andrew Dixon White at Michigan.[1] White, who, Carl Becker said, "probably had a greater influence on the history of higher education in the United States in the nineteenth century than anyone else," matriculated at the Collège de France and the Sorbonne. He also attended the University of Berlin for a short time. White returned to the United States in 1857 and was hired as a professor of history at Michigan. He began implementing his vision of an academic program in the History and Political Science Department. Lectures, accompanied by liberal dosages of wide collateral reading, were White's prescription for all "worthy young men."

Evolution as a method in approaching historical thought was sliding into the historical scene at nearly the same time White was at work in Michigan.[2] Comtian positivism sought to apply the natural sciences to ferret out laws of historical development which could provide the sign posts for a study of direct evolution. While the social evolutionist sent reverberations down many a historical spine, it is hard to find a historian before James Harvey Robinson who used evolution as the central theme of his work.

It was in this evolutionary and nationalistic milieu that the new "scientific" historian emerged in the latter quarter of the nineteenth century. The new professionals were faced with two main alternatives. They could either convert history into a sociological and evolutionary science or they could apply "scientific" methods to the writing of history. Their German training influenced the professional historian and finally swayed him to the "scientific" approach.

Charles Kendall Adams was one of the first to drift toward the "scientific" procedure. A former student of White, Adams followed his mentor as professor of history at the University of Michigan in 1869. . . . By 1882, with the establishment of a School of Political Science (due largely to Adams' efforts) his seminar had developed into something akin to present-day graduate form. . . .

In 1876, John W. Burgess was appointed to a professorship of history, political science and international law at Columbia University. Burgess, a graduate of Amherst College, had studied at Leipzig, Göttingen and Berlin. Four years after his arrival at Columbia, Burgess persuaded the trustees to establish a School of Political Science. He originated a program of three years' study, which ultimately culminated in a doctorate of philosophy.[3]

In the same year that Burgess became a professor at Columbia, Herbert Baxter Adams—age 26—received a fellowship from the Johns Hopkins University. As were many of the "scientific" historians, Adams was trained in German universities. Quickly Adams developed a historical seminar that was copied by universities all over the country. . . .[4]

In Adams' seminars the Teutonic hypothesis was developed to its fullest extent. Adams espoused the belief in the idea that the United States had been the recipient of Teutonic "seeds" brought over from England, just as originally these "seeds" were brought to England from the German forest by the Anglo-Saxons. . . . His endorsement of the Teutonic hypothesis was put in an article on the "Germanic Origins of New England Towns."[5] Adams wrote that in the German forest were "planted the seeds of Parliamentary or Self-Government of Commons and Congresses. Here lay the germs of religious reformation and of popular revolutions, the ideas which have formed Germany and Holland, England and New England, the *United States* in the broadest sense of that old Germanic institution."

In 1889, a student enrolled in Adams' seminar. Born and raised in the frontier community of Portage, Wisconsin, Frederick Jackson Turner found the "germ" theory wanting in explaining American institutional growth. Turner was emotionally and intellectually interested in the American scene; the remote "seed" of the Teutonic theorist stood in a poor second place in his ideas on the American development.[6] . . .

Turner was looking for a historical summit from which to view American history and by 1893, when he delivered his address in Chicago, he had discovered that vantage point. In one famous sentence, Turner outlined the next stage in American historiography: "The existence of an area of free land, its continuous recession, and the advance of American settlement westward, explain American development." Turner then stated that the emerging political institutions in America were due to environmental conditions and not to race as the Teutonists claimed.

That most important "area of free land" provided the atmosphere wherein the individual frontiersman unchained himself from the European social rigidity and bounded forth to enjoy economic equality, social mobility and democracy. In a word, wrote Turner, "free lands mean free opportunity." From the impact of the frontier on the individual was forged the American character. For Professor Turner this meant the pioneer was nationalistic yet individualistic and that above all he had a passionate belief in democracy.[7]

With the passing of the frontier, Turner discerned the advancement of a social homogeneity which in turn launched him on his next search for factors explaining this phenomenon. Finally, he settled on the section as the agent which would aid in the comprehension of the forces at work on the closing of the frontier.[8]

Two major questions have received much attention from scholars in American historiography: One, into what magic barrel or barrels did Turner dip for his ideas? Two, what are the reasons for three decades of almost unqualified acceptance of Turner's theories? . . . Turner did what his precursors did not do: he unified and dramatized the material on the frontier. One might list a host of names whose ideas can be found somewhere in Turner's writings. To attempt to link Turner in direct historiographic line with these names is neither fruitful nor pertinent. This is not to say that the study of the frontier concept before Turner is not profitable. Indeed, it may be extremely worthwhile, as the Mood and Benson studies have demonstrated.[9] . . .

Why Turner's ideas were so widely adopted by the historical profession has caused much speculation, and so far no one diagnosis has proven completely valid.[10] A myriad of explanations are readily apparent. At the time that Turner announced his thesis, American history was dominated by two principle themes: the Teutonic hypothesis and the obsession with the slavery controversy.[11] The Age was ripe for a nationalistic explanation of America's growth. Young historians who were casting about for something more "American" than the Teutonic school adopted the thesis for a solution to the uniqueness of American history. By following Turner one could be in the yeast of the Progressive movement but still not be labelled a Marxist. The thesis was in the mold of the Jeffersonian democracy of a century earlier. . . .

Besides the frontier thesis, the attention of local historians was focused on the frontier by the revolutionary changes occurring in the last quarter of the nineteenth century.[12] Lee Benson outlined these as (1) the communication revolution which riveted the attention of Americans on the public domain of the West and (2) the general belief in the inexhaustibility of public lands. There was a general feeling that one could always go West. Turner's calm announcement of the Superintendent of Census' observation that the frontier was gone jolted many scholars into revising their attitudes.[13]

Another reason for the endorsement of the frontier school is often overlooked, the stream of graduate students whom Turner taught over the years. There is ample testimony that Turner's graduate seminars became laboratories for testing the ideas of master and student. . . . A high percentage of them devoted their lives to exploring the unknowns of the "hither edge." If Turner had never written a word his concepts would have been well-known through the publicizing powers of his students. . . .

The early criticism of Turner and the frontier thesis was sketchy, ill-defined and usually directed at one or two points of the thesis, which points the critics, from their personal experience, believed to be inaccurate.[14] Curiously enough, the first published criticism of the frontier thesis came from a Turner student, Edmond S. Meany, at the University of Washington. In a paper published in the *Annual Report* of the American Historical Association for 1909, Meany took exception to Turner's statement that "The trading posts became the nuclei of later settlement; the trader's trails grew into the early roads, and their portages marked out the location for canals. Little by little the fur-trade was undermining the Indian society and paving the way for the entrance of civilization."[15] Meany conceded the validity of this evolution when used east of the divide, but he stated that it could not be employed for the Pacific Northwest. Professor Meany demonstrated that the nuclei for early settlement in the Pacific Northwest were usually sawmills, available water power, a mine or a crossroad. Meany's criticism made little impression on the historical profession.[16]

Twelve years elapsed before the next attack on Turner. Charles A. Beard directed his assault on the frontier thesis along four lines. First, the Agrarian West, slavocracy, labor and capitalism together explained American development, but certainly not free land and the Westward Movement alone. Second, Beard objected to the reasoning that the frontier is the most effective factor in the process of Americanization. Beard admitted that there was a certain plausibility to the thesis, but he proceeded to cite the cohesiveness of the frontier Germans of Pennsylvania who clung tenaciously to their customs long after the frontier was passed. Third, Beard took exception to the phrase that legislation was conditioned by the frontier. He maintained that legislation was "influenced" but not "conditioned" by the frontier. Fourth, Beard found little evidence to support Turner's contention that loose construction of the constitution increased as the nation marched Westward. Beard said there was no period more loose than that between 1789 and 1795, and furthermore, a hundred years later Western capitalists in Colorado and California were a long way from loose construction when it came to income tax legislation. Beard climaxed his argument by invoking the historical profession to pay more attention to the conflict between capital and labor.[17]

The same year that Beard first registered his dissent with the Turner thesis, Clarence W. Alvord rejected one aspect of the frontier thesis.

Alvord's particular pique was with the famous sentence in which Turner describes the migration from the East. "Each passed in successive waves across the continent. Stand at Cumberland Gap and watch the procession of civilization, marching single-file—the buffalo following the trail to the salt springs, the Indians, the fur trader and hunter, the cattle-raiser, the pioneer farmer—and the frontier has passed by."[18] Professor Alvord expressed the opinion that the division of classes was not as distinct as this sentence would lead one to think. Did not Richard Henderson accompany Daniel Boone? Alvord believed that frontier migration would be characterized by a flood—not by successive waves. In the same article, Alvord observed what later critics were to hammer at—that Turner ignored the role of the land speculator.[19]

Four years later, John C. Almack published one of the first general discordances with the whole thesis. After writing that the Turner thesis was not based upon facts, Almack stated that he did not believe that the frontier was the motivating force behind such governmental reforms as free tax supported schools, direct legislation, civil service reform and primary nominations. Almack noted that labor was the prime mover behind many of these reforms, and ended by saying that the frontier was not unique.[20]

John Carl Parish focused his criticism on the frontier thesis in another quarter. Writing in *Yale Review* in 1926, Parish offered the hypothesis that the Westward Movement persisted after the 1890's. New frontiers of conservation, intensive farming, banking, manufacturing and cultural arts continued to advance in progression after 1890. Parish held the opinion that the "ancient spirit" of the frontier would be kept alive by the twin tendencies of culture to change as it migrates and the continued strength of sectionalism.[21]

With the advent of the 1930's, criticism of Turner and the frontier thesis increased in force. . . . The intellectual vogue was for blanket condemnation of the "robber barons" and malefactors of great wealth. The country at large was demanding a "new deal." . . .

How would a thesis that extolled the benefits of America's past, the uniqueness of the American way of life, individualism and equal opportunity stand up against this onslaught? Yet the depression element in the criticism can be over-emphasized. Had there been no depression, the frontier thesis would still have come under searching and minute examination in the light of gigantic strides being made in industrialization, organization of labor and urbanization.

The 1930's disputations opened with a professor of government at Harvard University, Benjamin F. Wright, questioning the growth of democracy on the frontier. Wright thought that the greatest short-coming of the frontier interpretation was "its tendency to isolate the growth of American democracy from the general course of Western Civilization." Wright questioned whether democracy came out of the American forest; he thought a better truism would be that it came from the East and found in the West a congenial atmosphere upon which to nurture.

In a succeeding essay, Wright developed another area of dissent. He was not concerned with institutional growth as found in the constitutional history of the new West. So far as Wright was able to determine there was no considerable desire on the part of the men who framed the early Western constitutions to differ from those already long established in the East. From his research, Wright found that the frontiersmen were imitative, not creative. Furthermore, he wanted a better definition of the frontier than Turner had provided; had not Turner over-emphasized the geographic factors and minimized ethnic and cultural factors?[22]

Differing from Wright, Louis Hacker approached the Turner interpretation from essentially a Marxian angle. Hacker saw "amazing errors" in the frontier thesis. Of the uniqueness of the frontier experience and the continuity of sectional differences, Hacker said, "Merely to mention these rather naive ideas, as I have is enough to refute them." In agreement with Wright, Hacker claimed that excessive stress on the uniqueness of American experience and sectional development had turned American historiography inward upon itself, whereas "all eyes should have been on events going on beyond the country's borders." Hacker enunciated that agriculture of the Western region was really the "catspaw" of industry; once having served to develop the nation's capital, it could be abandoned both politically and economically. Finally, Hacker expressed adherence to the safety-valve theory and its evil effect on American labor. By continuing to draw off workingmen to free lands the American labor movement was robbed of preserving a continuous revolutionary tradition.[23]

Charles Beard renewed his charges in the year that saw the beginning of Franklin D. Roosevelt's second term. Again he was perplexed by the neglect of the Turnerians to deal with the "democratic impulses in Eastern idealism" of the labor movement. Beard asserted that co-operation, as much as individualism, was in evidence on the frontier. Beard did not believe that the frontier had as much influence as Turnerians imagined, but he was desirous in knowing just what kind and how much influence the frontier did have.[24]

When the migrants were trekking across Southwestern United States in the middle 'thirties, there occurred the most important and thorough research that has been done by the critics of frontier on American development. These scholars concentrated their intellectual diligence on the safety-valve theory. The concept was not an integral part of the Turner thesis, although George Pierson commented that a good deal of the charm and optimism of the frontier thesis was derived from the notion that the Golden West was a land of opportunity.[25]

The opening salvo in the safety-valve controversy was fired by Professors Carter Goodrich and Sol Davison of Columbia University. In their study, Davison and Goodrich made little use of the manuscript census of the General Land Office records.[26] The methodological difficulties encountered with these two sources were that the Census did not show where the worker first practiced his occupation and the Homestead entries were of little use since the information contained on occupations was mentioned only occasionally. Their chief source of information was the files of contemporary newspapers.

On the basis of availability of newspaper files, Goodrich and Davison chose Fall River, Massachusetts, for their pilot study. They discovered that a number of workers went West. But of the emigrants that went West, seven out of ten returned to the East. After quickly surveying the town records of Lowell and Springfield, Massachusetts, the investigators offered their conclusion. First, the most serious obstacle to Western migration was the lack of capital; second, there was a definite move to overcome this handicap by group colonization enterprises, which on occasion were supported by philanthropic funds. While migration projects may have raised the percentage of industrial workers traveling West, Goodrich and Davison conclude that, "the movement of Eastern wage earners to the Western lands was surprisingly small." Too few industrial workers reached the frontier to attract notice in the amounts of settlements. What is more striking, too few wage-earners left the industrial centers to exert any marked effect on the labor situation. Having stated this conclusion, Goodrich and Davison emphasized that there was nothing in the present study that would throw doubt upon the doctrine that the growth of industrial America was delayed by the presence of the frontier. Their analysis confirmed that many potential wage-earners left for the Western lands. Hence, there was a safety-valve for the farmer rather than the wage-earner which seemed to operate best from states contiguous to the frontier land.[27]

The Goodrich and Davison study touched off a fast and furious race among scholars to present their varied findings. In July, 1936, just three months after the Goodrich-Davison study, Fred A. Shannon[28] discovered that because of the many weaknesses in the Homestead Act, the Act failed to aid the emigrant. Second, Shannon said that the West was merely beginning to fill up by 1890. In addition, if any movement occurred, it was from farm to farm or from farm to city, but rarely from city to farm.

Murray Kane presented a statistical analysis of selected counties in Michigan and Massachusetts. Kane ascertained that in times of depression there was an increase in the population of these states and simultaneously a decline in industrial employment. This led Kane to deduce that a minor part of the workers returned to the agricultural communities, from which they had been recruited, but that they did not migrate to free land on the frontier. Usually when the cities captured the farm laborers, they manifested a remarkable tendency to hold them.[29]

A reply to these detractors of the safety-valve was made by a Turner student, Joseph Schafer, in a series of three articles between December, 1936 and December, 1937.[30] In answer to Goodrich and Davison, he pointed out that even they admitted that the frontier tended to hold up the level of industrial wages. He took issue with them on the methodology of their research. . . . Why had Davison and Goodrich not made use of county histories? Schafer's major point was the psychological effect the frontier land had. These lands were an omnipresent threat to employers, a hope for the unemployed and a constant agent in the minds of the general public. So whether the people migrated or not to free land in the West was not as important as the fact that they thought they could.

A year and a half after Schafer finished his rebuttal, Goodrich and Davison wrote a rejoinder. They still disagreed over the use of the manuscript census. Second, they were interested in eastern migration, not the immigrant from abroad. Third, they accepted Schafer's point on the psychological effect of the frontier, but commented that this element was not measurable.[31]

Seven years later, Fred A. Shannon endeavored to nail the coffin lid shut on the "safety-valve myth."[32] After a detailed statistical inquiry, Shannon wrote that 20 farmers moved to urban centers for every industrial worker that went to the farm. In addition, 10 sons of the agricultural hewers went to the city for every son that became the proud owner of a new farm. Shannon debated the conclusion that immigrants moved on to the farms after serving a tenure under the smokestacks.

More often, Shannon reported, they stayed on, becoming a drag on the labor market. Shannon attested to the fact that when industrial violence was reaching its peak during the 1870's and 1880's the safety-valve was supposedly blowing its optimum steam; he wondered whether this labor unrest would have come about if wages had been buoyed up by a scarcity of labor? Shannon generalized that if there were any safety-valve, it was the city.

In spite of Shannon's efforts to bury the safety-valve, the lid on the coffin blew off in 1958. Norman J. Simler believed that critics as well as the advocates of the safety-valve had overlooked a major point in the whole controversy.[33]

Utilizing economic theory, Simler argued that more germane than whether the safety-valve performed perfectly was whether it operated at all. Simler believed that an economic safety-valve was certainly at work. He was willing to agree with the social safety-valve adherents' viewpoint that "the West, by and large, offered no easy avenue of escape for propertyless wage-earners."

However, Simler stated this did not deny that an economic safety-valve of some type was functioning. Indeed, his work with economic theory definitely showed the operation of some economic safety-valve. Simler pointed out that after all the West was populated and "it clearly did not get that way by spontaneous generation."

The next criticism shifted from the Middle West to the South Atlantic section. Thomas Abernethy of the University of Virginia wrote that the frontier did not give birth to democracy but to opportunism, crudity and aristocracy. The land speculator-politician dominated the frontier scene. Abernethy saw the speculator as the originator of separatist movements. "So closely did democracy cling to its leaders and so tenaciously were voting habits and political traditions, that we find the strange phenomenon of men voting against their own economic interests without regard to changing issues."[34]

The disapprobations on the frontier thesis during the 1940's and 1950's in some measure formed a continuous line with those voiced in the 1930's. A general trend may be noted—the vehemence of the arguments declined. Instead of just criticizing the frontier thesis, the dissenters started offering a thesis of their own to supplant the frontier thesis. The urban-industrial thesis received increasing examination over the next two decades. This had the beneficial result of providing the historical profession with new pockets of unmined data.

Arthur M. Schlesinger, Sr., an apostle of urbanism, initiated the criticism of the 1940's.[35] Schlesinger enunciated that American history was long overdue for a new interpretation. . . . The most forceful exposition of his views was presented in an article in the *Mississippi Valley Historical Review*. Schlesinger said that by 1820 the migration to the cities was faster than to the frontier. And by 1860, one out of every six persons in the United States was living in population centers of 8,000 or more. Schlesinger stated that in the pre-Civil War period most humanitarian impulses centered in the cities. Furthermore, the cultural lag between city and rural areas highlighted the differences between the two ways of life. Between 1790 and 1890, the population growth of the nation as a whole was 16-fold, contrasted with the urban population which had grown 139-fold. In light of this, Schlesinger wrote that the historic announcement in the 1890 census was less a prophecy of an end to an old civilization than a long overdue admission of the arrival of a new one.

Shortly after Schlesinger's article was published, Murray Kane launched his disagreement with the frontier thesis. Kane found Turner's historical interpretation dominated by anthropological and geographical determinism. Not only does Turner misplace the anthropological and geographical elements but he over-accentuates them in his historical structure. According to Kane, this has the consequence of making Turner's theories a statistical interpretation of history rather than a historical interpretation of statistics. Kane registered agreement with Turner for stressing economic factors, but felt that he traded the terminology of the economist for that of the geographer.[36]

George W. Pierson . . . undertook a broad-gauge overhauling of Turner and the frontier thesis. First, Pierson wondered why Turner had neglected . . . climate, crops, animals and disease. Second, Turner over-stressed the freehold phase of the frontier. Third, Turner exaggerated the uniformity of the frontier experiences. Fourth, Pierson was disturbed by the lack of a consistent definition of key terms— "frontier" and "democracy."[37] Pierson concluded:

> . . . it would already seem reasonable to recognize that Turner's "frontier" was hazy and a shifting concept, riddled with internal contradictions, overlaid with sectional bias, and saturated with nationalistic emotion.[38]

A year later Pierson presented his maturing ideas in the *New England Quarterly*. Pierson conceded that the frontier offered novel problems, but its influence was strengthened by repetition—copying became easy. What happens to originality? Was the social and democratic legislation of the Populists and progressive reformers to be ascribed to the frontier? What about the evolution of Parliament, colonial legislatures, New England town meetings and self-government of Congregational churches? Pierson thought Turner was deterministic—almost fatalistic. Pierson does not credit Turner with inventing the "escape concept" that Pierson sees inherent in the safety-valve. "Yet if today our leaders still hitch our star to a covered wagon, the frontier theory may share the responsibility." Pierson ended by writing that the frontier theory in its "full development" does not hang together. Nationalism contradicts sectionalism, innovations are secured by repetition, materialism winds its way into idealism. "In what it proposes, the frontier hypothesis needs painstaking revision. By what it fails to mention, the theory disqualifies itself as an adequate guide to American development."[39]

In 1945, Arthur M. Schlesinger, Jr. provided lucid exposition of the urban-industrial thesis. Schlesinger, Jr. expounded his theories in the Pulitzer-prize winning volume, *The Age of Jackson*. Schlesinger sought to prove two main theses: Jacksonian democracy was better understood in terms of classes than sections and liberalism in the United States has most commonly been a movement of other "sections of society to restrain the power of the business community." Schlesinger's tome had not been published long before criticism appeared. These critics will be treated later in this paper.[40]

In the same year that *The Age of Jackson* was published, Carlton J. H. Hayes presented his presidential address to the American Historical Association. Hayes entitled his remarks, "The American Frontier—Frontier of What?" Actually Hayes' title summarized his address. He believed that the obsession of the American People with sectional and local history had led to an extreme self-centeredness and isolationism. Hayes thought this was "unrealistic, contrary to basic historical facts, and highly dangerous for our country at the present and in the future." What was demanded of American scholars and citizens was a broader knowledge of Europe.[41]

James C. Malin, a year after Hayes' address, presented a tightly reasoned case, which Thomas Le Duc has called Malin's "ideas to action" analysis.[42] Malin based his disagreement with Turner on what he chose to designate as Turner's "peculiar absorption" with the closed space doctrine. Malin declared that if mobility is the true answer to opportunity for the individual, there should be no occasion to worry about a substitute for the frontier. For so long as the communication revolution continues indefinitely, mobility in space is assured. Malin hastened to point out that he was not sure that either of the above points were valid.[43]

David M. Potter, a colleague of Pierson's at Yale, found the frontier thesis of little help in explaining the American character. Potter, in a series of provocative lectures delivered at the University of Chicago in 1953 (the Charles G. Walgreen Lectures), delved into the effect of abundance on the American character.

Concerning the Turner thesis Potter had several objections: (1) Turner, by his over-emphasis on the benefits of the frontier, had induced apprehension and pessimism as to the state of society in the post-frontier era; (2) Turner's obsession with the beneficial effects of agrarian milieu caused him to overlook the circumstances in the American environment which were operating for constant change and experimentation; (3) "Turner did not recognize that the attraction of the frontier was simply as the most accessible form of abundance, and therefore he could not conceive that other forms of abundance might replace it as the lodestone to which the needle of American aspirations would point."[44]

In concluding his comments on the Turner thesis, Potter was willing to admit that Turner's geographical determinism had some validity. In support of his viewpoint, he cited Walter P. Webb's *The Great Frontier*. However, Potter diverged from Webb when the latter claimed for the frontier an exclusive domain in the production of American abundance. This, wrote Potter, was not taking cognizance of technology. After all, hadn't technological revolutions historically preceded periods of discovery and experience?

Contemporary with Potter, two historians, Henry Nash Smith and Richard Hofstadter, were writing about what they believed to be basic discrepancies in Turner's theories. Smith interpreted Turner as believing the highest social values were to be found in "the relatively primitive society just within the agricultural frontier." Smith reasoned that Turner, in juxtaposition, held the opinion that society evolved through various stages to an eventual industrial civilization. Smith saw Turner as wavering between these two judgements. Smith then took cognizance of a second inconsistency. The frontier has nourished an "agrarian myth" which has tended to divert the attention from American industrialization and promote a one sided view of American development. The "agrarian myth" has had a pronounced effect on American politics. Distrust of the city has impeded co-operation and abetted ignorance on the part of both urban and rural population. Reiterating Carlton J. H. Hayes' contention, Smith argues that the agrarian tradition has made it difficult for Americans to think of themselves as effective members of a world community. But the foremost difficulty of the agrarian tradition is "that it accepted the paired contradictory ideas of nature and civilization as a general principle of historical and social interpretation. A new intellectual system was requisite before the West could be adequately dealt with in literature or its social development could be fully understood."[45]

The "agrarian myth" was also explored by Richard Hofstadter. Hofstadter wrote that the triumph of commercial agriculture had spelled the doom of the "agrarian myth," but at the same time the victory of commercial agriculture revealed the idea of the self-made man.

> The same forces in American life that had made Jacksonian equalitarianism possible and had given to the equalitarian theme in agrarian romance its most compelling appeal had also unleashed in the nation an entrepreneurial zeal probably without precedent in history, a rage for business, for profits, for opportunity, for advancement.[46]

The next stage was the land speculator. The increasing land values in the new areas incited quick liquidation and frequent migration casting the small entrepreneur in the role of a land speculator. According to Hofstadter, the huge public domain did more to create a gambling spirit than a freeholding idea. The agricultural society became attracted to land values instead of to the soil *per se*. Hofstadter gathered his perceptions into one generalization: the United States did not produce a distinctively rural culture (if you take as your criterion a pre-capitalist soil centered viewpoint). This observation led Hofstadter to weave his analysis into interpreting agriculture discontent and the Populist movement. He found that Populism can be best understood not as a product of the frontier, but as "an effort on the part of a few important segments of a highly heterogeneous capitalistic agriculture to restore profits in the face of much exploitation and under unfavorable market and price conditions."[47]

A Swiss student, Roland H. Beck, discerned relationships between the Turner writings and the romantics' outpouring of the early nineteenth century, along with an undercurrent of scientific and evolutionary concepts of the latter part of the century. Beck was critical of Turner's concepts in general, but was willing to concede some usefulness might result from applying the frontier thesis to the period 1775-1830 of our history.[48]

In tracing the historiographical trends of the frontier school I have chosen to include personal observations of Turner and his methodology (since both criticism and defense have been based on this), charges against the urban-industrial interpretation and specific rebuttals. Much of the defense of the frontier thesis centered around the personality of Turner rather than around the thesis itself. Just as much of the attack concerned the progenitor of the thesis. As a whole, Turner's students were devoted to their teacher and many became highly incensed over the nature of the criticisms. Unfortunately, emotionalism on the part of both skeptics and disciples has colored and distorted many phases of the controversy.

The early criticisms of the frontier thesis aroused few attempts at refutation. It is possible that many advocates felt the way their master did when Almack's article was published. A former student of Turner's informed the writer that one day Turner walked into his seminar and passed out copies of Almack's essay. His students indignantly queried Professor Turner as to when he was going to issue his rebuttal. Turner replied to the effect that he saw no reason to answer Almack.

One of the first important men of the frontier school was Frederic L. Paxson. While he cannot be classed as defending it in his main works, he used the frontier thesis and wrote one of the first scholarly and important histories of the frontier. In his *Last American Frontier*, which described the Westward Movement beyond the Mississippi, Paxson wrote, "The influence of the frontier has been the strongest single factor in American history. . . ." Fourteen years later, Paxson, in the *History of the American Frontier, 1763-1893* said, "The first century of American independence was dominated by the influence of the frontier; its second seems likely to be shaped by industry and pressure of the outside world." This sentence illustrates a point that has often been overlooked when discussing Paxson's work. He can definitely be considered a part of the frontier school, but Paxson had some qualifications and reservations about the frontier thesis.[49]

The first specific rejoinder to the critics came in an appreciation of Turner by Carl Becker. In a beautifully written tribute, Professor Becker emphasized traits which later defenders were to repeat. Becker said that Turner's explanatory and descriptive style should not cloud over the knowledge that he conducted exhaustive research. Becker stressed the lack of dogmatism on the part of Turner and that if Turner displayed any bias, it was Americanism. As a scholar, Becker thought Turner's approach was basically to understand rather than to judge institutions. Becker ended his appraisal with the following, "And his pupils understand it better than any others, because his pupils know, better than any others, that the man is more than his work. And so I end as I began—with 'that man Turner,' who laid upon all the spell of his personality."[50]

Merle Curti, in his essay on the methodological concepts of Turner, stressed, as Becker had, Turner's lack of dogmatism toward his research. "It is the essence of his method that he works as though his wiser successor would correct, reconstruct, and be reconstructed." Turner's methodology resembled the natural scientist in that he consistently used the multiple hypothesis to test his observations. In his method of using the physiographic map to correlate political and cultural behavior, Turner was especially careful in applying the multiple hypothesis. Curti also had a reply for those who felt that Turner had given industrial capitalism an inadequate place in his thesis. Curti pointed out that Turner recognized the importance of industrial capitalism as was illustrated by his 1910 presidential address before the American Historical Association.[51] But Turner was primarily concerned with the United States in its agricultural era; after all, industrial capitalism has only recently invaded wide regions of the country.[52]

Joseph Schafer, in 1933 and 1934, wrote in answer to some of Frederic Paxson's detractions. Schafer echoed the same points that Curti and Becker had underlined—namely, that Turner did not consider Western expansion as the only explanation of American history, but as the most important single process.[53]

Benjamin Stolberg differed from the former supporters in that he was not as much concerned with defending the frontier thesis as with refuting Hacker's Marxian polemics. Writing in the *Nation*, a month before President Roosevelt's quarantine speech in Chicago, Stolberg censured Hacker for the latter's conception of frontier agriculture as the tool of industrialism. To say this, said Stolberg, was to ignore the "tremendous psychological effects of the frontier upon our nation's mentality." Stolberg declared that after our frontier was closed the spirit of individualism was carried over into finance, labor and industry.[54]

One of the most vocal and influential of Turner's students is Avery Craven. Although Craven disagrees with Turner on some features of the frontier thesis, the overwhelming balance of his comments are on the side of buttressing the thesis. Four years after Hacker's article appeared in the *Nation*, Craven replied.[55] In contrast to Hacker, Craven claimed that exposure of institutions to free land was a unique experience. Furthermore, to assert completely the urban-industrial perspective over the agricultural interpretation would be to deny the effect of 200 years of rural dominance. Craven, dispensing with Hacker, turned his attention to the contradictions, generalizations and apparent inaccuracies that detractors kept forging to the front of the controversy. Craven readily admitted that there were apparent contradictions and that it was impossible to remove all contrarieties, for those "who knew the man and his work at first hand were seldom conscious of contradictions." Turner abhorred generalizations, wrote Craven, but his kind of history required generalizations. Craven reflected that Turner's whole emphasis was on change in general, not specifically. "The approach [Craven insisted on the term approach instead of thesis] was the important thing, not some exact pattern which might appear in its application."[56] . . .

A year after the turn of mid-century, Craven again came forward to testify for Turner at a symposium on the frontier held at the University of Kansas City.[57] Craven still had faith in the frontier approach. Nevertheless, some of the main canons of his faith were shaken by modern day scholarship. What Craven had staunchly defended in previous years was now open to question. He told his audience, "In the light of present day scholarship, it seems quite apparent that Turner overstressed the comparative influence of the frontier in producing both nationalism and democracy. Other influences certainly had a hand in this. He recognized but he did not always properly evaluate the contradictions inherent in his approach. The West was both national and provincial in its temper; it was both materialistic and idealistic; it was both radical and conservative; it was both individualistic and cooperative. Turner also applied his findings to the Old West and he lent his findings to other wests where they won't work."

Differing in outlook from Craven, John D. Hicks has preferred to walk the middle ground. Although describing himself as a reasonably orthodox Turnerian, Hicks feels that frontier historians have neglected the industrial era. In an article labelled, "The 'Ecology' of the Middle Western Historians," Hicks takes historians to task for endeavoring to write about unfamiliar regions and institutions.[58] Hicks cites a reviewer of Frederic L. Paxson's description of the "long drive" saying, "The Author simply does not know his cows." Comments Hicks, "how could he? One might about as well try to explain agriculture without ever having lived on a farm." Hicks saw the current tendency to break away from the frontier thesis as a natural historical phenomenon. After all, Turner had written his essay from the background of his environment; was it not conceivable that today's historians would approach history from the urban-industrial environment?

From another perspective, the frontier thesis was defended in 1941. Gilbert J. Garraghan thought more attention should be placed on the non-economic features in the frontier movement. Dr. Garraghan summarized his assertions in three propositions: (1) the most significant phenomenon in American History was the frontier; (2) the most "tangible and effective factor" in causing the movement was the free land in the West; (3) the movement cannot be explained entirely on an economic basis—non-economic factors such as religion and education share the responsibility.[59]

As noted previously, the year 1945 saw the publication of Arthur M. Schlesinger, Jr.'s *Age of Jackson*. No more than a year had passed before the volume, and especially the urban-industrial thesis, came under heavy criticism. These animadversions are included here because some of the most prominent criticism of Turner and the frontier school has come from advocates of the urban-industrial interpretation. The following comments can by no stretch of the imagination be considered a defense of the frontier thesis *per se*, but only as a critique of the urban-industrial theorists' explanations, which they seek to substitute for the frontier as a causal factor.

The first dissent from Schlesinger, Jr.'s findings was registered by Bray Hammond.[60] After reprimanding Schlesinger for not making use of the standard authorities on the United States Bank, Hammond agreed with the pre-eminence given in the *Age of Jackson* to the concept that Eastern forces as well as frontier forces were at work for democracy in the Jacksonian period. But Hammond said this was only part of the story; what were the Eastern business interests doing at this time? How did these business interests influence democratization? . . .

Joseph Dorfman, in a peppery analysis, took up the fight against the wage-earner thesis.[61] First of all, Dorfman was quick to take on the proponents of the Jackson wage-earner thesis, who emphasized the demand of the Democratic Party for the alleviation of imprisonment for debt. Professor Dorfman denied that amelioration for debtors was the sole concern of the working class. The small businessman and often the large entrepreneur was just as concerned. Dorfman agreed that the Jacksonians were in favor of monetary reform, but the purpose of this was to create better business conditions and diminish panics—not to help labor. The advocates of the wage-earner thesis have fallen into the common trap of definition. The term "workingman" did not include merely the manual laborer, but every man who, in the words of George Evans, earns his bread by "useful exertion, whether mental or physical." When understood in this broad concept, the so-called labor organizations became anti-aristocratic rather than anti-capitalistic. Dorfman reasons this is why the labor movement has frequently had within it both humanitarian and business elements. At times the humanitarian element advanced the impetus towards reform, but was decidedly paled by the business aims. Dorfman states, "after all the Age of Jackson was an age of expansion, a great age of business enterprise."

Ten months after Professor Dorfman's critique, Arthur Schlesinger, Jr., replied. Schlesinger said the *Age of Jackson* did not pronounce a class conflict between the large capitalist and the mass of property-less wage-earners. But he would contend there was a real struggle between non-business groups and business domination. Concerning the connection between the Jacksonian era and later reform movements, Schlesinger, Jr., maintained that the *Age of Jackson* claimed no more than a trace of psychological and political similarity. He asserted that altogether, Dorfman's reflections did not alter the main thesis of the *Age of Jackson*, "that more can be understood about Jacksonian democracy if it is regarded as a problem not of sections but of 'classes' and 'Liberalism' in America has been ordinarily the movement on the part of the other sections of society to restrain the power of the business community."[62] . . .

Beginning with Ray A. Billington's *Westward Expansion* in 1949,[63] the next seven years saw the frontier thesis rigorously applied and tested. Billington, with the collaboration of James B. Hedges, sought to present the whole sweep of American expansion from colonial days to 1896. In his preface, Billington left no doubt as to the master plan of his work. Billington desired to use Turner's geographical premises plus "specific suggestions left behind in his writings." The outline of his work was to follow Turner's seminar in the history of the frontier at Harvard. Billington and Hedges' history soon became a standard work. One of the most valuable features of the entire work was the extensive bibliography.[64]

Different in area of application of the Turner thesis from Billington was Walter P. Webb's *The Great Frontier*.[65] Webb undertook the gigantic task of using the frontier thesis to interpret all of Western Civilization since 1500. In his previous works, *The Great Plains* and

Divided We Stand, Webb has indicated the direction of his thinking.[66] Webb in *The Great Plains* contrasted the civilization of the Great Plains (characterized by level land surface, treeless region and sub-humid climate) to Eastern United States. Webb pictured an "institutional fault" roughly following the 98th meridian. "Practically every institution that was carried across it was either broken and remade or else greatly altered." East of the Mississippi, proclaimed Webb, civilization had stood on the three legs of water, land and timber. West of the Mississippi there remained but one leg. The key word was contrast. "The salient truth, the essential truth is that the West cannot be understood as a mere extension of things Eastern."

According to Webb in *Divided We Stand*, the closing of the frontier in 1890, together with the rise of corporations, spelled a crisis for American democracy and individualism. A laissez-faire policy had abetted the rise of corporations, but with the depression of the 'thirties corporations were subjected to governmental regulation. New types of relief were substituted for the old ones of the frontier. Webb closed his argument with a plea for the end of sectionalism, which he believes would be accomplished only by a political party on a national rather than sectional basis.

Following some of the main premises enunciated in the *Great Plains* and *Divided We Stand*, Webb plunged into suggesting the frontier thesis for Western Civilization in *The Great Frontier*. As the age of discovery dawned in the Metropolis (Webb's term for western Europe), the poverty-stricken population was crowded onto the Metropolis' land mass at the ratio of 26.7 per square mile. A hundred and fifty years after the year 1500, the ratio of man to land in Europe plus the frontier had dropped to 4.8. Then the deluge of wealth created a business boom such as the world had not known before.

Webb was convinced this "boom" had far-reaching effects. By 1930 the population had increased over 1500 by 625 percent, gold and silver by 18,308 percent and "things, goods or commodities" by an indeterminable ratio. This climate of abundance provided man with unlimited opportunities for development; capitalism flourished, democracy and individualism were fostered, international and commercial law arose, literature bloomed, democratic churches contested authoritarian dogmas and the arts were given a practical and democratic touch.

However, by the end of four centuries, the Great Frontier rapidly diminished. By 1930 the population had increased till the ratio per square mile had surpassed the 1500 mark. Webb saw the same thing happening that he had described in *Divided We Stand*. With cheap goods and land vanishing, man began to construct controls needed to deal with a larger society. What is Webb's prognosis?

> Society as it thickens will become more closely intergrated and its members more interdependent. Governments will tend to become stronger, using more compulsion in order to meet their obligations. There will be a tendency toward socialization as exhibited in the United States and Great Britain or toward absolutism as exhibited by the fascist states and by Russia. The individual will become relatively less important and will tend to lose his identity in a growing corporate life.[67]

Webb is not entirely pessimistic about the future;[68] the challenge today is whether we can manage the products of the Great Frontier.

In 1953, a year after *The Great Frontier* appeared, John D. Barnhart's *Valley of Democracy* was published.[69] The scope, approach and intention of Barnhart's volume was radically different from *The Great Frontier*. Barnhart chose "a testing of the Turner interpretation by an application to a specific area and time." The specific area was the Ohio Valley—the time, 1775-1818. Barnhart admitted that certain factors such as land speculation and the plantation were not adequately handled by Turner. But Barnhart held the opinion that the main opportunity for historians lay in "supplementing and completing Turner's work rather than in trying to refute it."

Barnhart saw the basic issue as one of tracing the struggle of the Ohio Valley Peoples for a political democracy. With this aim in mind, he meticulously analyzed the early constitutions of the Valley. He kept in mind such general questions as causes of the constitutional conventions, factionalism in the state as a whole and then in the conventions, backgrounds of the delegates and the origin of specific sections of the constitutions. Barnhart discerned an ever-present trend in all of the early governments: yeoman against planter, frontier against tidewater and democratic elements against aristocratic. The pioneer governments of Watauga, Monongahela-Ohio region, Cumberland and the State of Franklin represented only slight tendencies towards political democracy. From these early communities, Barnhart turned his attention to the political evolution in Kentucky, Tennessee, Ohio, Indiana and Illinois. He considered Kentucky had won a substantial victory in loosening the control of the Tidewater aristocracy. Of the five methods of aristocratic control in Virginia (property qualifications, inequality of representation, well established church, large land holdings and slavery) "only the last two crossed the mountains." The story in Tennessee was much the same. The frontier forces managed to have some democratic features embodied in the constitution, but the conservative features of property qualifications and life tenure for the justices of the peace remained undefeated.

Turning north of *la belle rivière*, Barnhart discovered that when democracy was unhampered by the inequitable distribution of land and slavery, significant gains were made toward laying the foundation of future democratic procedures.[70] . . .

How did all this conform to Frederick Jackson Turner's views? The last chapter of *Valley of Democracy* was assigned to a discussion of the findings in relation to the Turner thesis. Barnhart concluded that his results closely followed Turner's interpretations, observing that there was ample evidence of the democratic influence on the frontier, and that Turner did not claim that democracy originated on the frontier, "merely those characteristics which distinguished it from European democracy." The pioneers of the Ohio Valley had contributed a great deal to the democratic ideals of America.

Following closely the Barnhart study, Stanley Elkins and Eric McKitrick, sought "A Meaning for Turner's Frontier."[71] The two scholars decided that Turner's critics should be allowed all concessions, with the exception of "political democracy as a habit and the American as a unique political creature." They felt that Turner had stated an indisputable fact—that there was an organic connection between American democracy and this country's frontier. The problem to these University of Chicago professors was how to test this belief in a conceptual framework.

They knew that sociologist Robert K. Merton had discovered, from research on two housing developments, that whenever a new community faces a multitude of problems without a structured leadership the community is forced into co-operative democratic participation in their government. McKitrick and Elkins decided to apply Merton's theory to new communities on three American frontiers: the Old Northwest, the Southwest frontier of Alabama and Mississippi and the Puritan frontier of Massachusetts Bay.

Their findings based on research of new communities in each of these frontiers proved to Elkins and McKitrick's satisfaction that practical democracy was strong in both the Old Northwest and Massachusetts Bay, but somewhat less in evidence in the South where imported leadership structured the colonists' lives.

The author concluded:

Yet Turner, after all, has been preempting the frontier long past his time. It should no longer be necessary to force literal meaning from his texts, now that they have entered our cultural metaphor. At the same time a host of problems may be examined with fresh interest if we put in testable terms facts which he knew by instinct: the fact that the experience forced by the frontier was unique—that in a century of westward expansion it was repeated over and over, that in a multitude of forms it found its way into the daily habits of the people, making Americans truly and profoundly different from anyone else in the world.[72]

Merle Curti has gone about as far from Webb's spatiality as it is possible to go. Curti used a small region in Wisconsin—Trempealeau County—to examine the Turner thesis at the grass roots level. In a preliminary report to the Newberry Conference on American Studies, Curti wrote

> The plan was to study an actual frontier and to see what the records and other evidence still at hand did show about democratic practices on that frontier—about individualism, widespread participation in the making of decisions about the common life, and equality of economic and cultural opportunity. As far as we know, no one has yet examined microscopically a given area that experienced transition from wilderness to a settlement community with the purpose of determining how much democracy, in Turner's sense, did exist initially, in the first phase of settlement during the process of settlement itself, and in the period following settlement.[73]

In carrying out his research project, it was Curti's aim to use quantitative methods in hopes that such employment would contribute to the further development of these methods as historical tools.

Curti's choice of Trempealeau County was dictated more on the basis of the availability of public records than on any other consideration. For comparative purposes, Curti and his staff chose 11 contiguous townships in northern Vermont. The townships were principally rural areas from which many Trempealeaunians had migrated. Using quantitative methods, the staff thoroughly investigated all householders and gainfully employed persons who were listed in the unpublished manuscript censuses of 1850, 1860, 1870 and 1880. The researchers discovered that the main ground for political democracy in Trempealeau was the tailor-made county government imposed by the State of Wisconsin and was not due to particular frontier attitudes.

Then the investigators attacked the problem of whether or not there was economic equality in Trempealeau County. Was there a progression for national origin groups up the agricultural ladder from farm hand to farm owner? Curti's research disclosed that in general there was progress up the ladder for those who stayed in the county. Did a few men dominate the agricultural life of the community? Curti answered with a resounding "No." When Trempealeaunians needed capital (and often they did need it), they borrowed it from a neighbor, merchant or businessman. Usually, they gave a mortgage for $50 to $200—rarely more than $200 was ever borrowed. Furthermore, this year's debtor might be next year's creditor. Curti thought this was significant. "The Democratic implications of this tendency are obvious, and the natural assumption, common today, that the lending of money and the taking of mortgages in turn is apt to be centered in a few well-to-do men, did not hold for pioneer Trempealeau."[74]

Curti, et. al., were interested in the educational opportunities that were open to the citizen of Trempealeau County. The results showed that though the foreign-born children had a lower attendance record at schools, they did not encounter anti-democratic or hostile attitudes. From this preliminary report, Curti and his colleagues state, "Whatever the economic, political and social inequalities, and there were indeed more than the Turner thesis would lead one to expect, the statistical picture we have drawn is not in itself a refutation." Curti's opinion seems to be that though the Turner thesis is in need of qualification and revision, in most aspects the frontier thesis holds true.[75]

The focus of Turner defense shifted from the United States to England in 1957 with the publication of an essay by H. C. Allen,[76] Commonwealth Fund Professor of American History at the University of London, who was ready and willing to defend fervently almost any of Turner's concepts. . . . That the frontier fostered democracy, individualism, nationalism and idealism, were accepted by Allen with little qualification. Equally well received by the British professor were Turner's thoughts on the importance of free land in American development and the frontier as a line of rapid and effective Americanization. Blaming Turner's followers for most of the exaggerations and falsifications in the frontier thesis, Allen noted that Turner's ideas "contained a very small proportion of dross."

In summary, there have been a number of main criticisms of the frontier thesis. The frontier as an explanation of American development has been over-stressed. The urban-industrial factors have not been given enough consideration. Land speculation on the frontier has too often been ignored by frontier theorists. Democracy was not originated on the frontier but was imported there. Terms such as "frontier" and "democracy" are hazy and conflicting; better definitions are needed. Geographical and anthropological elements have generally been emphasized beyond their merit. The thesis should have been modified with the discovery of new material. The frontier thesis is full of contradictions, frontiersmen were both materialistic and idealistic, nationalistic and provincial, individualistic and co-operative, democratic and autocratic. Finally, Turner's methodology was "loose" and poorly constructed.

Defenders of the frontier thesis claim that many critics have been picayunish, attacking the minor points and giving too little attention to the over-all value of the thesis. Turner did not claim that democracy originated on the frontier, but only those aspects which differentiated it from European democracy. How is one able to apply the urban-industrial thesis to a rural-dominated first century of our history? The frontier thesis was a gigantic step forward in American historiography and should be judged in this light. Contradictions will inevitably appear in a thesis of this general nature, but these contradictions should not diminish its value as a guide-post to the understanding of American history. Finally, Turner's history demanded the narrative style, and one should remember that hours of exhaustive and meticulous research were behind each interpretative sentence.

In what repute is the frontier thesis held today? One fact easily discerned is that few historians today would whole-heartedly embrace the thesis or unilaterally discount the frontier in American history. Most historians would find themselves in the position of echoing John D. Hicks, rather than Joseph Schafer or George W. Pierson. . . .

Cumulatively the past seven decades have been an era of immense productivity and growing maturity for historians in their search for the explanation of the American character. Only the most unimaginative mind could fail to be intrigued by what possible findings will result from seven more decades of research on the interpretative theories of American civilization.

Whether one agrees or not with Fulmer Mood that, "the main professional obligation of the times"[77] is resolving the frontier issue, no one has yet completely ascertained the many-faceted effects of the frontier on American civilization.

NOTES

1. Harry R. Stevens, "Cross Section and the Frontier," *The South Atlantic Quarterly*, 52:446 (July, 1953).
2. Richard Hofstadter, *Social Darwinism in American Thought* (Boston, 1955), 3-122; Merle Curti, *The Growth of American Thought* (New York, 1951), 574-575.
3. John W. Burgess, *Reminiscences of An American Scholar* (New York, 1934), 191-244.
4. For Turner's and Adams' relationship see Fulmer Mood, "The Historiographic Setting of Turner's Frontier Essay," *Agricultural History*, 17:154 (July, 1943).
5. Herbert B. Adams, "Germanic Origins of New England Towns," *The Johns Hopkins University Studies in Historical and Political Science*, 1:5-38 (1883).
6. In his formative years Turner did not reject the Teutonic theory entirely. He was very much interested in the social evolutionary approach throughout his life. See the review by Turner of Theodore Roosevelt's *Winning of the West* in *Dial*, 10:71-73 (August, 1889); two articles by Fulmer Mood provide a brilliant backdrop for understanding Turner's formative period. Fulmer Mood, "Turner's Formative Period," in the *Early Writings of Frederick Jackson Turner* (Madison, 1938), 3-39; Fulmer Mood, "The Development of Frederick Jackson Turner as a Historical Thinker," in the *Proceedings of the Colonial Society of Massachusetts*, 34:281-352 (1943).
7. Frederick J. Turner, *The Frontier in American History* (New York, 1921), 259-260, 358.
8. How Turner evolved the sectional approach is given in Max Farrand's introduction to Turner's *The Significance of Sections in American History* (New York, 1932), iii-v; Fulmer Mood, "Origin, Evolution and Application of the Sectional Concept, 1750-1900," in *Regionalism in American History*, edited by Merrill Jensen (Madison, 1952), 5-98.
9. Lee Benson, "Historical Background of Turner's Frontier Essay," *Agricultural History*, 25:59-82 (April, 1951).
10. Sveaas Anderson, *Westward Is the Course of Empires* (University of Oslo Press, 1956).
11. For Turner and slavery see Thomas J. Presley, *Americans Interpret Their Civil War* (Princeton, 1954), 163-192.
12. Earle D. Ross, "A Generation of Prairie Historiography," *Mississippi Valley Historical Review*, 33:391-410 (December, 1946).
13. Lee Benson, "Historical Background of Turner's Frontier Essay," *Agricultural History*, 25:59-82 (April, 1951).
14. Two short and general treatments which survey the literature on the critics of the frontier school are R. L. Lokken, "The Turner Thesis: Criticism and Defense," *Social Studies*, 32:356-358 and 363-365 (December, 1941) and J. A. Burkhart, "The Turner Thesis: A Historian's Controversy," *Wisconsin Magazine of History*, 31:70-83 (September, 1947).
15. Frederick Jackson Turner, *Rise of the New West, 1819-1829. The American Nation: A History* (28 vols., New York, 1904), 14:113-114.

16. Edmond S. Meany, "The Towns of the Pacific Northwest Were Not Founded on the Fur Trade," *Annual Report* of the American Historical Association, 1909 (Washington, 1911), 165-172.

17. Charles A. Beard, "The Frontier in American History," *New Republic*, 25: 349-350 (February 16, 1921); Charles A. Beard, "Culture and Agriculture," *Saturday Review of Literature*, 5:272-273 (October 20, 1928).

18. Frederick J. Turner, "The Significance of the Frontier in American History," *The Frontier in American History* (New York, 1947), 12.

19. C. W. Alvord, "Review of Frederick J. Turner's *Frontier in American History*," *Mississippi Valley Historical Review*, 7:403-407 (March, 1921).

20. John C. Almack, "The Shibboleth of the Frontier," *Historical Outlook*, 16:197-201 (May, 1925).

21. John Carl Parish, "The Persistence of the Westward Movement," *Yale Review*, 5:461-477 (April, 1926).

22. Benjamin F. Wright, "American Democracy and the Frontier," *Yale Review*, 20:349-365 (December, 1930); Benjamin F. Wright, "Political Institutions and the Frontier," *Sources of Culture in the Middle West*, edited by Dixon R. Fox (New York, 1934), 15-38.

23. Louis M. Hacker, "Sections or Classes," *The Nation*, 137:108-110 (July, 1933).

24. Charles A. Beard, "The Frontier in American History," *New Republic*, 97:359-362 (February, 1939).

25. George W. Pierson, "Recent Studies of Turner and the Frontier Doctrine," *Mississippi Valley Historical Review*, 34:453-458 (December, 1947).

26. Carter Goodrich and Sol Davison, "The Wage-Earner in the Westward Movement," *Political Science Quarterly*, 50:161-185 (June, 1935) and 51:61-116 (March, 1936).

27. One of the best works on internal migration is Lewis D. Stilwell, *Migration from Vermont* (Montpelier, 1948).

28. Fred A. Shannon, "The Homestead Act and the Labor Surplus," *American Historical Review*, 41:637-651 (July, 1936). See also Fred A. Shannon, *The Farmer's Last Frontier* (New York, 1945), 53-58.

29. Murray Kane, "Some Consideration on the Safety-Valve Doctrine," *Mississippi Valley Historical Review*, 23:169-188 (September, 1936).

30. Joseph Schafer, "Some Facts Bearing on the Safety-Valve," *Wisconsin Magazine of History*, 20:216-232 (December, 1936); Joseph Schafer, Concerning the Frontier as a Safety-Valve," *Political Science Quarterly*, 102:407-420 (September, 1937); Joseph Schafer, "Was the West a Safety-Valve for Labor?" *Mississippi Valley Historical Review*, 24:299-314 (December, 1937).

31. Carter Goodrich and Sol Davison, "The Frontier as a Safety-Valve: A Rejoinder," *Political Science Quarterly*, 53:268-271 (June, 1938).

32. Fred A. Shannon, "A Post Mortem on the Labor-Safety-Valve Theory," *Agricultural History*, 19:31-38 (January, 1945).

33. Norman J. Simler, "The Safety-Valve Doctrine Reevaluated" (Presented to the Fifty-first Annual Meeting of the Mississippi Valley Historical Association, April, 1958). I am indebted to Dr. Simler for sending me a copy of his paper, which appears in this issue of *Agricultural History*.

34. Thomas P. Abernethy, *Frontier to Plantation* (Chapel Hill, 1932), 362;

Thomas P. Abernethy, *Western Land and the American Revolution* (New York, 1937), 367; Thomas P. Abernethy, *Three Virginia Frontiers* (Baton Rouge, 1940); Thomas P. Abernethy, "Democracy and the Southern Frontier," *Journal of Southern History*, 4:3-13 (February, 1938).

35. Arthur M. Schlesinger, "The City in American History," *Mississippi Valley Historical Review*, 27:43-67 (June, 1940).
36. Murray Kane, "Some Considerations on the Frontier Concept of Frederick Jackson Turner," *Mississippi Valley Historical Review*, 27:379-400 (December, 1940).
37. George W. Pierson, "American Historians and the Frontier Thesis in 1941," *Wisconsin Magazine of History*, 26:36-60 and 170-185 (September, December, 1942).
38. George W. Pierson, "The Frontier and the Frontiersmen of Turner's Essays," *Pennsylvania Magazine of History and Biography*, 64:478 (October, 1940).
39. George W. Pierson, "The Frontier and American Institutions—A Criticism of the Turner Theory," *New England Quarterly*, 15:224-255 (June, 1942); see also George W. Pierson, "Recent Studies of Turner and the Frontier Doctrine," *Mississippi Valley Historical Review*, 24:452-458 (December, 1947).
40. Arthur M. Schlesinger, Jr., *The Age of Jackson* (Boston, 1945).
41. Carlton J. H. Hayes, "American Frontier—Frontier of What?" *American Historical Review*, 51: 199-210 (January, 1946). For a discussion similar to Hayes' see William A. Williams, "The Frontier Thesis and American Foreign Policy," *Pacific Historical Review*, 24:379-395 (November, 1955).
42. Thomas Le Duc, "An Ecological Interpretation of Grasslands History," *Nebraska History*, 31:226-233 (September, 1950).
43. James C. Malin, *Essays On Historiography* (Lawrence, Kansas, 1946), 1-44.
44. David M. Potter, *People of Plenty* (Chicago, 1954), 158.
45. Henry Nash Smith, *Virgin Land* (Cambridge, 1950), 260; Henry N. Smith, "The West as an Image of the American Past," *The University of Kansas City Review*, 18:29-40 (Autumn, 1951).
46. Richard Hofstadter, *The Age of Reform* (New York, 1955), 39.
47. Material on the "agrarian myth" and Hofstadter may be located in Richard Hofstadter, *The Age of Reform* (New York, 1955); and "Turner and the Frontier Myth," *American Scholar*, 18:433-443 (Autumn, 1949).
48. Roland H. Beck, *Die Frontier Theorie von Frederick Jackson Turner* (Zurich, 1955).
49. Frederic L. Paxson, *The Last American Frontier* (New York, 1910); Frederic L. Paxson, *The History of the American Frontier, 1763-1893* (Boston, 1924).
50. Carl Becker, "Frederick Jackson Turner," in *American Masters of Social Science*, edited by Howard W. Odum (New York, 1927), 317.
51. Frederick Jackson Turner, "Social Forces in American History," *American Historical Review*, 16:217-233 (January, 1911).
52. Merle Curti, "The Section and the Frontier in American History: The Methodological Concepts of Frederick Jackson Turner," *Methods in Social Science*, edited by Stuart A. Rice (Chicago, 1931), 353-367. For

a later statement on Turner see, Merle Curti, "Frederick Jackson Turner," *Historiadores de Americana, II, Instituto Panamericano de Geografia e Historia* (Mexico, D. F., 1949).

53. Joseph Schafer, "Turner's Frontier Philosophy," *Wisconsin Magazine of History*, 16:451-469 (June, 1933); Joseph Schafer, "Turner's America," *Wisconsin Magazine of History*, 17:447-465 (June, 1934).

54. Benjamin Stolberg, "Turner, Marx and the A. F. of L.," *Nation*, 137:302-303 (September, 1933).

55. Avery Craven, "Frederick Jackson Turner," *Marcus W. Jernegan Essays in American Historiography*, edited by William T. Hutchinson (Chicago, 1937), 252-270.

56. Avery Craven, "Turner Theories and the South," *Journal of Southern History*, 5:295 (August, 1939).

57. Avery O. Craven, "Frederick Jackson Turner and the Frontier Approach," *University of Kansas City Review*, 18:3-17 (Autumn, 1951).

58. John D. Hicks, "The 'Ecology' of the Middle-Western Historians," *Wisconsin Magazine of History*, 24:377-384 (June, 1941).

59. Gilbert J. Garraghan, "Non-Economic Factors in the Frontier Movement," *Mid-America*, 13:263-271 (October, 1941).

60. Bray Hammond, "Public Policy and National Banks," *Journal of Economic History*, 6:79-84 (May, 1946).

61. Joseph Dorfman, "The Jackson Wage-Earner Thesis," *American Historical Review*, 54:296-306 (January, 1949).

62. Arthur M. Schlesinger, Jr., "To the Editor of the American Historical Review," *American Historical Review*, 64:785-786 (April, 1947).

63. Ray A. Billington and James B. Hedges, *Westward Expansion* (New York, 1949).

64. Nine years after the appearance of *Westward Expansion*, Professor Billington answered some of Turner critics; Ray A. Billington, "How the Frontier Shaped the American Character," *American Heritage*, 9:4-9, 86-89 (April, 1958).

65. Walter P. Webb, *The Great Frontier* (Boston, 1952).

66. Walter P. Webb, *The Great Plains* (New York, 1931); Walter P. Webb, *Divided We Stand* (Austin, 1944).

67. *Ibid.*, 415.

68. For essays on the application of the Turner thesis to world frontiers see Walker D. Wyman and Clifton Kroeber, eds., *The Frontier in Perspective* (University of Wisconsin Press, 1957).

69. John D. Barnhart, *Valley of Democracy* (Bloomington, Indiana, 1953).

70. John D. Barnhart, *Valley of Democracy*, 214.

71. Stanley Elkins and Eric McKitrick, "A Meaning for Turner's Frontier," *Political Science Quarterly*, 69:321-353: 565-602 (September, December, 1954).

72. *Ibid.*, 602.

73. Merle Curti, "Democracy in a Wisconsin Frontier Community: Trempealeau County," Sixth Newberry Library Conference on American Studies (Chicago, May 21, 1955), 1.

74. *Ibid.*, 9.

75. For more of Curti's ideas on the frontier and democracy, see Merle Curti,

"The Democratic Theme in American Historical Literature," *Mississippi Valley Historical Review*, 39:3-28 (June, 1952): Merle Curti, *Probing Our Past* (New York, 1955), *passim.*

76. H. C. Allen, "F. J. Turner and the Frontier in American History," in *Essays in American History*, edited by H. C. Allen and C. P. Hill (New York, 1957).

77. Fulmer Mood, "Frontier Concept, 1871-1898," *Agricultural History*, 19: 24-30 (January, 1945).

RECENT STUDIES

Arthur K. Moore, *The Frontier Mind: A Cultural Analysis of the Kentucky Frontiersman* (Lexington: University of Kentucky Press, 1957).

Dietrich Gerhard, "The Frontier in Comparative View," *Comparative Studies in Society and History*, I (March 1959), 205-229.

Rush Welter, "The Frontier West as Image of American Society," *Mississippi Valley Historical Review*, XLVI (March 1960), 593-614.

T. Scott Miyakawa, *Protestants and Pioneers: Individualism and Conformity on the American Frontier* (Chicago: University of Chicago Press, 1964).

Gilbert C. Fite, *The Farmers' Frontier, 1865-1900* (New York: Holt, Rinehart and Winston, 1966).

Ray Allen Billington, *America's Frontier Heritage* (New York: Holt, Rinehart and Winston, 1966).

XIII

The Robber Baron Concept in American History

HAL BRIDGES

Widespread in American historical writing is the idea that business leaders in the United States from about 1865 to 1900 were, on the whole, a set of avaricious rascals who habitually cheated and robbed investors and consumers, corrupted government, fought ruthlessly among themselves, and in general carried on predatory activities comparable to those of the robber barons of medieval Europe. Such at any rate appears to be the content of the idea when put into plain language. As actually used by historians, the concept tends to become more suggestive than precise. In this study it will be referred to as the idea of the robber barons, and an effort will be made to trace the broad outlines of its historical development after the Civil War, to point out historical interpretations at variance with it, and to appraise its value for present-day historians.

In the post-Civil War era, some relatively early expressions of the idea of the robber barons can be found. In 1869 E. L. Godkin in *The Nation* denounced Cornelius Vanderbilt's extortionate ways and called the Commodore "a lineal successor of the medieval baron that we read about. . . ."[1] In the early seventies the Grangers adopted resolutions comparing American railroad corporations to oppressive "feudal barons of the Middle Ages."[2] In the eighties and nineties cries of rob-

From *Business History Review*, XXXII (Spring 1958), pp. 1-13. Reprinted with permission.

bery came from Greenbackers and Populists. Matthew Josephson states that he drew the title of his book *The Robber Barons* from "the folklore of the Kansas Greenbackers and Populists of the 1880's."[3]

With the publication in 1894 of Henry Demarest Lloyd's *Wealth against Commonwealth*, the idea of the robber barons gained new importance for American intellectuals. Lloyd, an independently wealthy journalist, was an Emersonian religious thinker and a social reformer who almost but never quite joined the Socialist party.[4] The impassioned rhetoric of his book was aimed not only at the Standard Oil monopoly but at an even bigger target—business, the capitalistic system as it then existed. "Business," he wrote, "colors the modern world as war reddened the ancient world." And, anticipating somewhat a later theme of Thorstein Veblen, he declared that if civilization was destroyed it would not be by Macaulay's "barbarians from below" but by "barbarians . . . from above," the "great money-makers" who now exercised "power kings do not know." Among these moneyed barbarians were the rulers of Standard Oil. The record of the Standard corporation, which Lloyd set forth in detail, illustrated his thesis that "Monopoly is Business at the end of its journey."[5]

Allan Nevins has called *Wealth against Commonwealth* propaganda rather than history; Chester M. Destler has defended the book as essentially accurate, and the most recent study of the rise of the Standard monopoly supports Nevins' judgment.[6] But if there is controversy over Lloyd's accuracy, there is general agreement that his book strongly influenced public opinion. More, probably, than *Chapters of Erie, and Other Essays*, or *Progress and Poverty*, or such relatively mild novels as *The Gilded Age, Looking Backward*, and *A Traveler from Altruria*, it served to fasten a robber baron portrait of the postwar businessman into the American mind.

This portrait was etched more deeply as the century waned and Populism broadened into Progressivism. The intellectual preoccupations of the Progressive Era—the national debate over controlling the trusts, the muckrakers' revelations, Socialist agitation, and the novels of big business by naturalists like Frank Norris and Theodore Dreiser—created a climate of suspicion and hostility toward American business leaders. Business chicane was held up to the public by a host of writers, including Lincoln Steffens, whose *Shame of the Cities* exposed corrupt politics and corporate privilege more fully than had James Bryce's *American Commonwealth*; Gustavus Myers, whose Socialist *History of the Great American Fortunes* was to become a source book for future writers of robber baron history; Thorstein Veblen, who began in the

Theory of the Leisure Class and the *Theory of Business Enterprise* a series of attacks on predatory businessmen; E. A. Ross, whose *Sin and Society* denounced corporate amorality; and Ida Tarbell, who retraced Lloyd's steps more thoroughly and objectively in her *History of the Standard Oil Company*.

Two eminent American historians whose work reflected the Progressive ideology were Vernon Louis Parrington and Charles A. Beard. Both made zestful use of the idea of the robber barons. Parrington, whose Progressive cast of mind was reinforced by a Jeffersonian agrarian bias against businessmen, seems to have accepted the idea with little reservation, though he expressed it in maritime metaphors. When in the last volume of his *Main Currents in American Thought* he presents his "Figures of Earth," the outstanding personages of the Gilded Age, he discusses "ruthless, predatory" business leaders, "the raw materials of a race of capitalistic buccaneers." Within the space of three more sentences he remarks that "Pirate and priest issued from the common source. . . ." And again in the next sentence, "The romantic age of Captain Kidd was come again. . . ." Plainly this master of metaphors loved to take his figures of earth to sea aboard a pirate ship; and it is perhaps not unfair to say that few if any of his metaphors, either in his description of the Gilded Age or in his artistic narrative of the Progressive Era, convey other than a predatory image of the American businessman.[7]

To the mind of Charles Beard, historical patterns were not so clear-cut. His analysis of post-Civil War business leaders in *The Rise of American Civilization*, written with Mary Beard, emphasized the historical importance of the businessman in successive civilizations from ancient times to modern America. The Beards not only pointed out the creative results of American business expansion, but held Ida Tarbell "partly responsible for the distorted view" of the Standard Oil Company to be found "in the popular mind." Her history they dismissed as "a drama with heroes and villains, rather than a cold and disinterested summary by an impartial student." And yet, for all their interest in objectivity, the Beards made extended use of the idea of the robber barons. Phrases like "barons of business," and "the new capitalist baronage" run through a narrative that presents a generally negative analysis of the methods and motives of business consolidation. The following passage is typical: "If the barons of capitalism did not themselves put on armor and vanquish the possessors of desirable goods in mortal combat . . . they did sometimes hire strong-arm men. . . . Usually, however, they employed less stereotyped means to attain their ends; namely, stock manipulation, injunctions, intimidation, rate cutting, rebates, secret agreements, and similar pacific measures."[8]

Why did Beard and Parrington so freely employ the idea of the robber barons? The answer to this question, to the extent that it can be provided, would seem also to help us understand the meaning and uses of the idea for Progressive writers in general, and for the many later-day historians who have been influenced by Beard and Parrington.[9] A number of factors must be considered.

First, it seems proper to place both Beard and Parrington within the general category of Richard Hofstadter's discontented professoriat of the Progressive Era, those members of a rising academic profession who were critical of American business civilization, resentful of being controlled by boards of trustees dominated by conservative businessmen, and troubled by academic-freedom cases.[10] Parrington and Beard knew from personal experience how conservative pressure could affect college faculties. In 1908 Parrington lost his position as professor of English at the University of Oklahoma during the controversy that arose when President David R. Boyd of the university was replaced by a political supporter of the governor of the state, C. N. Haskell, who was soon to be accused of improper affiliations with the Standard Oil Company.[11] In 1917 Beard resigned from Columbia University after he became convinced that conservative trustees were trying to purge the faculty of liberals on the pretext that they were disloyal Americans. Max Lerner has described this resignation as basically "a protest against business control of university educational policy." Such unpleasant experiences may well have influenced Parrington and Beard toward a readier acceptance of what Hofstadter and Walter Metzger call the "potent academic stereotype" of "the businessman as a malefactor."[12]

Another probable influence upon Beard and Parrington is the Progressive concept of reality. The Progressives, according to Hofstadter, conceived of reality as something akin to what the muckrakers revealed. Basically it was "rough and sordid . . . hidden, neglected, and . . . off-stage . . . essentially a stream of external and material events. . . ."[13] The relation of the robber baron idea to this kind of reality is obvious. When Beard and Parrington wrote of the rough, sordid, hidden and off-stage methods by which a Jay Gould manipulated railroads, they could sincerely feel that they were describing the basic reality of business in Gould's time. Parrington also reflects the fascination with brute strength that Alfred Kazin has emphasized as a facet of the Progressive mind. His business leaders of the seventies were vital, "primitive souls . . . never feeble . . . never given to puling or whining," men of the bold buccaneer or robber baron breed.[14]

Also pertinent to this inquiry is the Marxian economic approach to history that has influenced Beard and Parrington and other Progressive writers,[15] and indeed the entire American historical profession, which has made much fruitful use of economic interpretation while rejecting other aspects of Marxism. The idea of the robber barons fits nicely into economic interpretation: the very imagery of it tends to exclude non-economic analysis. Moreover, the idea affords a convenient means of classifying a lot of individualistic businessmen, plus an opportunity for interesting, colorful writing. The business buccaneers, though wicked, were "picturesque in their rascality."[16] Nor, finally, should it be forgotten that at the time *Main Currents* and *The Rise of American Civilization* were written historians knew relatively little about post-Civil War business expansion, aside from the more sensational and sordid events. The Beards, is fact, carefully pointed out that the methods that brought about this expansion had "never been subjected to scientific analysis."[17]

Readily available to other writers, then, in the history of Parrington and Beard, the idea of the robber barons flourished in the debunking twenties and took on fresh vitality in the thirties. During the Great Depression, businessmen were more suspect than ever. Intellectuals quoted the Brookings Institution on America's wasted capacity to produce, Keynes on the "secular stagnation" of capitalism, and Berle and Means on the future dangers of corporate growth. Businessmen were blamed for America's entry into the First World War, and also, after a brief NRA honeymoon, for the continuing depression. Some former Progressives, and young intellectuals who might once have been Progressive, embraced Communism.[18]

The nation was in a mood receptive to a number of new books that embodied the idea of the robber barons, such as Lewis Corey's *The House of Morgan*, Frederick Lewis Allen's *The Lords of Creation*, and Josephson's *The Robber Barons*. Josephson, who dedicated his book to Charles and Mary Beard, traveled further down the road of Marxian determinism than the Beards had gone. His barons, though touched with an aura of glamor, were essentially grim, amoral figures, furthering the Marxian process of expropriation and consolidation of property. Their activities were making the masses of workers dissatisfied with the old business system and "the fearful sabotage practiced by capital upon the energy and intelligence of human society."[19] In the stricken nation of the thirties, epitomized in John Dos Passos' *U. S. A.*, Josephson's book read convincingly enough. Perhaps more than any other single volume it served to disseminate the phrase, "the robber barons," through American historical writing. It was, in a sense, the culmination of the idea expressed in its title.

Now let us consider some views of American business leaders that, taken all together, might be termed the revisionist approach to the idea of the robber barons. Edward C. Kirkland has called attention to Charles Francis Adams, Jr., E. L. Godkin, and Andrew Carnegie as conservatives of the Gilded Age whose "conclusions that the business order of their day was not all evil, loss, and hypocrisy should contribute to a more balanced judgment of the era."[20] Adams considered the robber baron metaphor, as applied by the Grangers to railroad corporations, "a grotesque absurdity."[21] However it should be noted that in 1869, the year he wrote "Chapters of Erie," Adams remarked in a private letter that Daniel Drew, Cornelius Vanderbilt and Jay Gould made "the old robber barons" appear like "children in the art of thieving. . . ."[22] Actually Adams seems to have entertained toward the American business world ambivalent attitudes that reflect his personal aspirations and experiences as railroad reformer, railroad president, and victim of Jay Gould.[23]

If Adams did not wholly accept the idea of the robber barons, neither did a major American historian, Frederick Jackson Turner. Turner was certainly no apologist for industrial wrongdoing, yet his complex approach to the past led him to see aspects of American industrial expansion that did not fit into the robber baron mold. In an essay first published in 1926 he distinguished Western builders of new industry from Eastern speculative investors in old enterprises, and characterized John D. Rockefeller, Cyrus McCormick, J. O. Armour, and Jay Cooke, among others, as creative sons of Middle Western pioneers.[24] Earlier, at a time when trust-busting ideas were in the air, he had stressed the complexities involved in historical analysis of the two decades of industrial expansion from 1890 to 1910. The occasion was his presidential address of 1910 to the American Historical Association. He noted that the two decades in question were "peculiarly the era when competitive individualism" in America changed into monopoly, but quoted E. H. Harriman to the effect that industrial combination and expansion were in keeping with the speculative pioneer spirit that had developed the nation. He then pointed out that American ideals and moral standards were changing. The squatter ideal of "individual freedom to compete unrestrictedly for the resources of a continent" was yielding to an increasing use of government in order that Americans might preserve another ideal—democracy. Violations of land laws that were formerly condoned by the public and defended in Congress now resulted in jail sentences. "That our great industrial enterprises developed in the midst of these changing ideals," Turner concluded, "is important to recall when we write the history of their activity."[25]

In this same address Turner reminded his fellow historians that among the "complex of forces" molding the past were individual leaders, who were shaped by their own creative genius and by the psychology, moral tendencies, and ideals of their time and place.[26] His words, which thirty-nine years later would be echoed by historians seeking greater understanding of American business leaders,[27] might well serve as a general criterion for biographical writing, and biographers who have studied American businessmen in this spirit have produced works that seriously challenge the idea of the robber barons. A number of non-robber baron biographies appeared in the antibusiness thirties, contrasting markedly with the general tenor of popular thought. Among these were works by John T. Flynn, Burton J. Hendrick, William T. Hutchinson, Allan Nevins, and Henrietta M. Larson.[28] All wrote with varying degrees of sympathy, and re-created business leaders too multisided to be dismissed simply as predatory money seekers. In each business career examined, negative and positive means and ends seemed inseparably bound togther. With this duality in mind, N. S. B. Gras in his introduction to Larson's *Jay Cooke* declared that businessmen are generally "above the average in creative work" and complained that a "recent national pastime" had been to judge them without studying them.[29]

The dual nature of business careers was one of several theses advanced in Allan Nevins' *John D. Rockefeller*, which appeared in 1940. Nevins as early as 1927 had published a balanced account of post-Civil War business, and in 1934 had demurred at Josephson's sweeping use of the robber baron metaphor.[30] In the Rockefeller biography, he followed the English economist Alfred Marshall in ascribing the Standard Oil Trust to "a combination of exceptional constructive ability and astute destructive strategy." He held that Rockefeller and his associates had often used methods that were morally wrong as well as unlawful, but like Charles R. Van Hise he argued that the kind of monopoly control they effected was a natural and even inevitable response to the cutthroat competition of the times, in Europe as well as in the United States. Like Turner, he stressed the changing business ethics of Rockefeller's era. And like Joseph Schumpeter he drew attention to the complexity of the motives of entrepreneurs. The chief motive of leaders like Rockefeller, Nevins asserted, was not greed but "competitive achievement, self-expression, and the imposition of their wills on a given environment." Schumpeter had distinguished entrepreneurial activities in which financial gain was secondary, and "economic action becomes akin to sport." Nevins wrote: "In business . . . Americans of the nineteenth century found the Great Game." This analysis contrasts somewhat with that of Werner Sombart, who conceded that entrepreneurs have nonacquisitive motives, but argued that since profit is the measure of capitalistic success all other motives in capitalistic enterprise become "subordinate to profit making."[31]

When Nevins in 1953 published a second biography of Rockefeller, he adhered essentially to his earlier interpretation, but advanced a more elaborate hypothesis of business leadership after the Civil War. The constructive aspects of this leadership were in the long run, he declared, more important than the destructive. American historians should follow the English example and correct their national industrial history—too long based mainly on legislative investigations of business chicane—to show the constructive side. America's industrial revolution had "cost less than Germany's, much less than England's, and infinitely less than Russia's." Further, and most important, the rapid expansion of American industry after the Civil War had come just in time to insure victory for "the free world" in the two World Wars. But had better ways been available for building national industrial strength? Nevins did not inquire. His broad hypothesis, which of course did not escape challenge, probably represents the culmination to date of the revisionist approach to the idea of the robber barons.[32]

Yet business history of all types, biographical and otherwise, offers numerous other studies of a nonrobber baron nature, some of them quite recent. James Blaine Hedges, Richard C. Overton, Edward C. Kirkland and Thomas C. Cochran, among others, have emphasized the constructive work of certain railroad leaders of the Gilded Age.[33] Fritz Redlich has redefined Schumpeter's "entrepreneur" as "creative entrepreneur" and analyzed the creative achievement of American business leaders in banking and the iron and steel industry.[34] Ralph and Muriel Hidy, restudying the rise of the Standard Oil monopoly, have portrayed Rockefeller as only one member of a business team that mistakenly tried to apply previously learned small business mores to giant industry, and responded somewhat involuntarily to the "prods and pressures" of a changing political and legal climate.[35] Other writers have produced biographies of secondary business leaders who were not robber barons,[36] while statistical studies have thrown new light on the American business elite.[37]

The American business mind is a fruitful field of present-day investigation for entrepreneurial historians who utilize the concepts of social role, social sanctions, and cultural codes of conduct. Notably, Thomas Cochran has demonstrated that Social Darwinism and the Gospel of Wealth are, though certainly important, not the whole story of the business mind, and that certain American railroad leaders of the period 1845-1890 could be influenced quite as often by their view of their proper social role in a given situation as by predatory motives.[38]

Thus, although historians like Josephson and Destler continue vigorously to defend the idea of the robber barons,[39] the current trend in American historiography is away from this concept. Michael Kraus has written that the idea is fading, the 1954 report of the Committee on Historiography of the Social Science Research Council views it skeptically, Thomas Cochran calls it legend.[40] All this may be in part a manifestation of present-day conservatism, but this writer regards it primarily as the logical reaction of historians to the cumulative evidence contained in the studies that have been designated here as the revisionist approach to the idea of the robber barons. Of course the revisionist views are not flawless. As a summary critique of them it can be said that the naturalness or inevitability of monopoly at any time in the United States is a moot question;[41] that both Turner and Nevins have been accused of ignoring important aspects of the American economy;[42] that all biographers are open to the charge of being too sympathetic toward their subjects; and that the company records with which business historians work make it difficult for them to avoid a board-of-directors bias. Yet when all discounts have been made for possible error, there does seem to be enough truth left in the revisionist views to reveal the inadequacy of the idea of the robber barons. In an emotional, romanticized way, this concept sums up the business activities of Jay Gould and his kind and expresses the predatory side of the careers of many other business leaders of the post-Civil War era. But it grants insufficient recognition to the creative aspects of such careers or to business leaders of habitually high moral standards. It tends to deny to business leaders through thirty-five years of American life that basic capacity for doing good as well as evil which historians freely concede to other members of the human race. Born apparently of a desire for denunciation rather than objective analysis, the idea of the robber barons seems destined to fall into increasing disuse, as historians seek to apply ever more precise thinking to the complex American past.

NOTES

1. "The Vanderbilt Memorial," *The Nation*, Vol. IX (Nov. 18, 1869), pp. 431-432; quoted in Edward C. Kirkland, *Business in the Gilded Age: The Conservatives' Balance Sheet* (Madison, Wisconsin, 1952), p. 37.
2. Charles Francis Adams, Jr., *Railroads: Their Origin and Problems* (New York, 1893), pp. 128-129.
3. Allan Nevins and Matthew Josephson, "Should American History Be Rewritten?" *The Saturday Review*, Vol. XXXVII (Feb. 6, 1954), p. 10. H. D. Lloyd in "The Political Economy of Seventy-Three Million Dollars," *The Atlantic Monthly*, Vol. L (1882), pp. 69-81, compared Jay Gould to an assassin. Inspired by this article, Carl Schurz referred to contemporary business leaders as "the robber barons" in a Phi Beta Kappa oration at Harvard University. Also, in *The Chicago Tribune* "of the early eighties" Lloyd editorials "made repeated comparisons between the great railroad magnates and the nobility of the Medieval Rhine." See Chester M. Destler, "Entrepreneurial Leadership Among the 'Robber Barons': A Trial Balance," *The Tasks of Economic History* (Supplemental Issue of *The Journal of Economic History*), Vol. VI (1946), p. 28, n. 1.
4. Daniel Aaron, *Men of Good Hope: A Story of American Progressives* (New York, 1951), pp. 150, 158, 169.
5. Henry Demarest Lloyd, *Wealth against Commonwealth* (New York, 1902 ed.), pp. 509, 510.
6. For the Nevins-Destler debate over Lloyd's accuracy see Chester McA. Destler, "Wealth against Commonwealth, 1894 and 1944," *American Historical Review*, Vol. L (Oct., 1944), pp. 49-69, and Allan Nevins, Letter to the Editor, *American Historical Review,*, Vol. L (April, 1945), pp. 676-689. Ralph W. Hidy and Muriel E. Hidy, *Pioneering in Big Business, 1882-1911* (New York, 1955), p. 644, supports Nevins' judgment.
7. Vernon Louis Parrington, *Main Currents in American Thought* (New York, 1930 ed.), Vol. III, pp. 10-12, 405-413.
8. Charles A. Beard and Mary R. Beard, *The Rise of American Civilization* (New York, 1934 ed.), Vol. II, pp. 166-210; for quoted portions see pp. 187, 201.
9. Richard Hofstadter has called attention to the Progressive bent of Beard and Parrington and their wide appeal to other writers. See his "Charles Beard and the Constitution," in Howard K. Beale, ed., *Charles A. Beard: An Appraisal* (Lexington, Kentucky, 1954), p. 88. That there is high professional regard for *Main Currents* and *The Rise of American Civilization* is clearly shown in John Walton Caughey, "Historians' Choice: Results of a Poll on Recently Published American History and Biography," *Mississippi Valley Historical Review*, Vol. XXXIX (Sept., 1952), p. 209.
10. Richard Hofstadter, *The Age of Reform: from Bryan to F. D. R.* (New York, 1955), pp. 154-155.
11. Parrington called this controversy a "political cyclone." George Harvey Genzmer, "Vernon Louis Parrington," *Dictionary of American Biography*, Vol. XIV (1934), ed. by Dumas Malone, p. 253. Along with President Boyd, some dozen members of the Oklahoma faculty were fired. The con-

troversy arising from these dismissals and the accusations of improper relationships with Standard Oil that led in the fall of 1908 to Governor Haskell's resignation as treasurer of the Democratic National Committee can be followed in a series of unsigned editorial articles in *The Outlook*, Vol. XC (1908), Sept. 5, pp. 15-17, Oct. 4, pp. 233, 235-237, 242-244, 249-251, Oct. 17, pp. 325-326. It might also be noted that Parrington's good friend and colleague at the University of Washington, J. Allen Smith, was fired from Marietta College for publishing liberal monetary views and supporting William Jennings Bryan in the election of 1896. Richard Hofstadter and Walter P. Metzger, *The Development of Academic Freedom in the United States* (New York, 1955), pp. 423-424.

12. Investigations by the trustees and summary dismissals of faculty members preceded Beard's resignation. See Charles A. Beard, "A Statement," *The New Republic*, Vol. XIII (Dec. 29, 1917), pp. 249-250. Lerner's interpretation can be found in his *Ideas Are Weapons: The History and Uses of Ideas* (New York, 1939), p. 158. Additional details are given in Hofstadter and Metzger, *Academic Freedom*, pp. 501-502. The reference to the academic stereotype of the businessman is on page 420 of this work; in Chapter IX, "Academic Freedom and Big Business," Hofstadter and Metzger show how the stereotype developed in the Populist and Progressive Eras, and how it does not always fit the facts of academic-freedom cases prior to the First World War.

13. Hofstadter, "Charles Beard and the Constitution," p. 87.

14. Alfred Kazin, *On Native Grounds: An Interpretation of Modern American Prose Literature* (New York, 1942), p. 93; Parrington, *Main Currents*, Vol. III, p. 12.

15. Hofstadter, "Charles Beard and the Constitution," pp. 81-82.

16. Parrington, *Main Currents*, Vol. III, p. 12.

17. C. A. and Mary Beard, *The Rise of American Civilization*, Vol. II, p. 198.

18. A. D. H. Kaplan, *Big Enterprise in a Competitive System* (Washington D.C., 1954), pp. 27-29; Eric F. Goldman, *Rendezvous with Destiny* (New York, 1953), pp. 353-367; Aaron, *Men of Good Hope*, pp. 295-297.

19. Matthew Josephson, *The Robber Barons: The Great American Capitalists 1861-1901* (New York, 1934). The quoted portion is from p. 453.

20. Kirkland, *Business in the Gilded Age*, p. 59.

21. Adams, *Railroads*, pp. 128-129; Kirkland, *Business in the Gilded Age*, p. 12.

22. Joseph Dorfman, *The Economic Mind in American Civilization*, Vol. III, 1865-1918 (New York, 1949), p. 23.

23. In his autobiography, Adams set forth his often quoted view of American big businessmen as "mere money-getters . . . essentially unattractive and uninteresting," but also confessed that as his life's achievement he "would like to have accumulated—and ample and frequent opportunity for so doing was offered me—one of those vast fortunes of the present day, rising up into the tens and scores of millions . . ." so that he could have donated a fortune to Harvard. *Charles Francis Adams 1835-1915: An Autobiography* (Boston, 1916), pp. 190, 210.

24. Frederick Jackson Turner, *The Significance of Sections in American History* (New York, 1932), pp. 262-264. Compare the strong emphasis on the creative achievement of post-Civil War industrial capitalists in Louis

M. Hacker, *The Triumph of American Capitalism* (New York, 1940), pp. 427-435.

25. Frederick Jackson Turner, *The Frontier in American History* (New York, 1920), pp. 317-321, 328.

26. *Ibid.*, p. 322.

27. There is a striking similarity between the approach to the past advocated here by Turner and the modern methods for understanding business leaders that are set forth, much more fully, of course, and in more technical language, in *Change and the Entrepreneur: Postulates and Patterns for Entrepreneurial History* [Research Center in Entrepreneurial History, Harvard University], (Cambridge, Massachusetts, 1949), pp. 108-175.

28. John T. Flynn, *God's Gold: The Story of Rockefeller and His Times* (New York, 1932); Burton J. Hendrick, *The Life of Andrew Carnegie* (Garden City, New York, 1932), 2 vols.; William T. Hutchinson, *Cyrus Hall McCormick: Harvest, 1856-1884* (New York, 1935); Allan Nevins, *Abram S. Hewitt: With Some Account of Peter Cooper* (New York 1935); Henrietta M. Larson, *Jay Cooke: Private Banker* (Cambridge, Mass., 1936).

29. Larson, *Jay Cooke*, p. xiv.

30. *The Emergence of Modern America 1865-1878* (New York, 1927), pp. 42, 397-400; review of *The Robber Barons* in *The Saturday Review of Literature*, Vol. X (March 3, 1934), p. 522. But in *Grover Cleveland: A Study in Courage* (New York, 1933), p. 607, Nevins in summarizing the social unrest of the nineties mentioned only the sordid side of the Standard Oil record and favorably described Lloyd's *Wealth against Commonwealth* as a "searching exposure" and the parent of later muckraking literature.

31. Allan Nevins, *John D. Rockefeller: The Heroic Age of American Enterprise* (New York, 1940), Vol. I, pp. 603-622, Vol. II, pp. 707-714; Charles R. Van Hise, *Concentration and Control: A Solution of the Trust Problem in the United States* (New York, 1912); Joseph A. Schumpeter, *The Theory of Economic Development*, trans. Redvers Opie (Cambridge, Mass., 1934), p. 93; Werner Sombart, "Capitalism," *Encyclopedia of the Social Sciences*, ed. by Edwin R. A. Seligman and Alvin Johnson, Vol. III (1930), p. 200.

32. Allan Nevins, *Study in Power: John D. Rockefeller* (New York, 1953), Vol. I, p. viii, Vol. II, pp. 426-436. See also Allan Nevins, "New Lamps for Old in History," *The American Archivist*, Vol. XVII (Jan., 1954), pp. 3-12. Josephson opposes this hypothesis in Nevins and Josephson, "Should American History be Rewritten?", pp. 9-10, 44-46.

33. James Blaine Hedges, *Henry Villard and the Railways of the Northwest* (New Haven, 1930); Richard C. Overton, *Burlington West: A Colonization History of the Burlington Railroad* (Cambridge, Mass., 1941); Edward Chase Kirkland, *Men, Cities and Transportation: A Study in New England History 1820-1900*, 2 vols. (Cambridge, Mass., 1948); Thomas C. Cochran, *Railroad Leaders 1845-1890: The Business Mind in Action* (Cambridge, Mass., 1953).

34. Fritz Redlich, *History of American Business Leaders: A Series of Studies*, Vol. I, *Theory, Iron and Steel, Iron Ore Mining* (Ann Arbor, Michigan, 1940), Vol. II, *The Molding of American Banking: Men and Ideas, Part*

I, 1781-1840 (New York, 1947), *Part II*, 1840-1910 (New York, 1951).

35. Hidy and Hidy, *Pioneering in Big Business*, pp. xxviii, 3-8, 201-232, 715-717.

36. For example, Hal Bridges, *Iron Millionaire: Life of Charlemagne Tower* (Philadelphia, 1952); Philip Dorf, *The Builder: A Biography of Ezra Cornell* (New York, 1952).

37. For example, Francis W. Gregory and Irene D. Neu, "The American Industrial Elite in the 1870's: Their Social Origins," in William Miller, ed., *Men in Business: Essays in the History of Entrepreneurship* (Cambridge, Mass., 1952), pp. 193-211. See also Sidney Ratner, ed., *New Light on the History of Great American Fortunes: American Millionaires of 1892 and 1902* (New York, 1953), in which Ratner in his introduction criticizes various statistical studies of American business leaders.

38. Cochran, *Railroad Leaders*, pp. 1-16, 92-93, 172, 182-183, 200-228. For another interesting approach to the business mind of the Gilded Age see Edward C. Kirkland, "Divide and Ruin," *Mississippi Valley Historical Review*, Vol. XLIII (June, 1956), pp. 3-17. See also, by Kirkland, *Dream and Thought in the Business Community, 1860-1900* (Ithaca, N. Y., 1956).

39. Josephson, "Should American History Be Rewritten?", pp. 9-10, 44-46; Destler, "Entrepreneurial Leadership," pp. 28, 38, and "The Opposition of American Businessmen to Social Control During the 'Gilded Age,'" *The Mississippi Valley Historical Review*, Vol. XXXIX (March, 1953), pp. 641-672.

40. Michael Kraus, *The Writing of American History* (Norman, Okla., 1953), p. 337; *The Social Sciences in Historical Study: A Report of the Committee on Historiography Bulletin 64* (New York, 1954), p. 154; Thomas C. Cochran, "The Legend of the Robber Barons," *The Pennsylvania Magazine of History and Biography*, Vol. LXXIV (July, 1950), pp. 307-321.

41. Vigorous arguments against the inevitability of monopoly are presented in Walter Adams and Horace M. Gray, *Monopoly in America: The Government as Promoter* (New York, 1955).

42. On Turner see for example Louis M. Hacker, "Sections—Or Classes?" *The Nation*, Vol. CXXXVII (July 26, 1933), pp. 108-110. On Nevins see for example Lewis Galantière, "John D.: An Academy Portrait," *The New Republic*, Vol. CIII (Dec., 9, 1940), pp. 795-797.

RECENT STUDIES

John Tipple, "The Anatomy of Prejudice: Origins of the Robber Baron Legend," *Business History Review*, XXXII (Winter 1959), 510-23.

Alfred D. Chandler, Jr., "The Beginnings of 'Big Business' in American Industry," *Business History Review* XXXII (Spring 1959), 1-31.

Rendigs Fels, *American Business Cycles, 1865-1897* (Chapel Hill: University of North Carolina Press, 1959).

Robert W. Fogel, *The Union Pacific Railroad: A Case Study in Pre-*

mature Enterprise (Baltimore: Johns Hopkins University Press, 1960).

Edward C. Kirkland, *Industry Comes of Age: Business, Labor, and Public Policy, 1860-1897* (New York: Holt, Rinehart and Winston, 1961).

Morton Keller, *The Life Insurance Enterprise, 1885-1910: A Study in the Limits of Corporate Power* (Cambridge: Harvard University Press, 1963).

H. Wayne Morgan (ed.), *The Gilded Age: A Reappraisal* (Syracuse: Syracuse University Press, 1963).

XIV

The "New South"

PAUL M. GASTON

In 1893, in a pioneer attempt to probe the meaning of the "New South," Amory Dwight Mayo, a northern exponent of new developments below the Potomac, found that there was "a good deal of unnecessary friction in the heated discussion of the question whether there really is a new South." Doubting his own ability to produce a definitive picture, Mayo offered little encouragement to the historians of the future. "Probably the time will never come," he predicted, "when the journalist, or even the average statesman, will be able to take an all-around view of a theme so large that it may be compassed only by many observations of many minds."[1] Since Mayo's time a good many historians, though not so many as one might wish, have set out to "compass" the "New South," but we today are likely to agree that they have yet to produce the "all-around view" with which our guild can be permanently satisfied.

Part of the difficulty—and it is a problem that grows with the passage of time—lies in the extraordinary ambiguity of the term itself. C. Vann Woodward, for example, feels that it has caused so much "mischief" that, if possible, it ought to be abandoned entirely.[2] Most of the con-

From *Writing Southern History: Essays in Historiography in Honor of Fletcher M. Green*, Arthur S. Link and Rembert W. Patrick, eds. (Baton Rouge: Louisiana State University Press, 1966). Reprinted with abridged annotation by permission.

fusion stems from the fact that "New South" has customarily implied at least two quite different things. One the one hand, it denotes a particular ideology—thus the "New South School," referring to the Henry Gradys who were prophets of a "New South." On the other hand, it is used with equal, if not greater, frequency to mark off various, and vaguely defined, periods of southern history. It may signify the South since 1865; since 1877; from 1877 to 1913; since 1900, or simply the South of the present. Moreover, many writers who use the term to denote a particular period are not careful to state that "New South" has no connotative meaning. Or, conversely, the term may be implicitly invested with a vague meaning, stemming from the Grady ideology, and the progress of the region measured against achievement of those ideals. In this case one finds, in almost any post-Civil War period one investigates, that the "New South" is emerging, or must be resisted, or has triumphed, or, as Harry S. Ashmore put it a few years ago, is now "coming to reluctant maturity."[3] Finally, diverse groups have taken the term to describe themselves and their particular periodicals. Among these we find nineteenth-century journals devoted to industrialization and reconciliation, the familiar theme; a twentieth-century communist periodical; and the monthly publication of the Southern Regional Council, advocating a South free of racial discrimination.

Clearly, then, before one can discuss the historiography of the "New South," some definitions and limitations must be established. As for the term itself, the position taken here is that it should be used almost exclusively as an adjective and seldom as a noun; and in its adjectival form it will be restricted largely to modification of the men of the post-Reconstruction years who first worked out in detail an ideology which was enthusiastically preached throughout the region. In addition, it will be used to describe the point of view of historians of a later period whose interpretations reflected the ideas of the original New South crusaders. As for periodization, the discussion will be restricted largely to the period from the end of Reconstruction to the Populist Revolt, the era in which the New South movement had its largest following and made its greatest impact.

There is only one genuinely historiographical essay on this period, a recent paper published by Professor Jacob E. Cooke. Actually, his "New South" extends from 1877 to 1914, and he finds that this period "does not readily lend itself to historiographical discussion" because, he explains, "few historians have presented a monistic interpretation which gives unity and meaning to the varied facts of Southern experience." Historians, he declares, have tended to emphasize different aspects of the region's history—economic development, political practices, race relations—and "few have argued that any single interpretive key would unlock the door of this vast storehouse of historical material."[4] Perhaps, as a comment on recent studies, this judgment has merit. But there was a time when, under the spell of the New South magic, historians found a central theme for most of the period and developed it with great enthusiasm, conviction, and oftentimes elaborate documentation. If, by a "school" of historians we mean a group of scholars all writing more or less toward the same end, there was in the years between 1900 and the Great Depression a group, composed mostly of Southerners, deserving to be called the New South school of historians.

Albert Bushnell Hart, the Harvard historian, confronted one of the principal characteristics of this group when he wrote, in 1910, that the southern tendency toward exaggeration had to be understood before one could properly evaluate southern writings. In the hands of southern writers, he declared, "the clever but no-wise distinguished professor of Latin is 'Probably the greatest classical scholar in the United States,' the siege of Vicksburg was 'the most terrific contest in the annals of warfare'; the material progress of the South is 'the most marvelous thing in human history.'" Later in the same volume, Hart exposed a critical truth when he explained that the exaggerated statements of southern material growth were widely believed in the region. "In every discussion of Southern affairs," he declared, "an important thing to reckon with is a fixed belief that the South is the most prosperous part of the country, which fits in with the conviction that it has long surpassed all other parts of the world in civilization, in military ardor, and in the power to rise out of the sufferings of a conquered people."[5]

The themes of prosperity and power which Hart noted were rapidly becoming the stock-in-trade of writers on the South's recent history. Guy Carleton Lee, in the preface to Philip Alexander Bruce's *The Rise of the New South*, found the "subject of the South since the Civil War" to be an "inspiring one." Actually, he continued, the years since the war offered "such examples of heroic effort, such persistent struggle, such triumphant results, that the historian finds himself tending to an exaltation of the mind." Bruce's volume, praised by Lee as an authentic and comprehensive study of recent southern history, was "a vital narration of the progress of a mighty people, who, from adversity such as no other section of North America has ever experienced," had brilliantly "won the race with adverse fate and become the pride of the Union."[6]

Bruce's history stands as the capstone of the New South crusade itself; in fact, the New South school of historians, of which Bruce was the first major representative, had its origins in the promotional literature of the New South editors and publicists of the 1880's and 1890's. During these years the New South propagandists flooded the nation with an insistent literature in which historians of our generation find an astonishing mixture of fact and fancy, wish and reality. Few observers from the North were unimpressed by what they read. To cite a typical example, Charles Dudley Warner, writing in 1886, was persuaded that the South was in the throes of a mighty "economical and political revolution" whose story "will be one of the most marvellous the historian has to deal with."[7]

The marvel lies not so much in the history with which one must deal as in the descriptions that appeared in the eighties and nineties from the pens of the New South promoters. A New South creed, born in the seventies, nurtured in the early eighties, and brought to maturity with Grady's address before the New England Society of New York in 1886, was compounded of two distinct parts, the blending of which by the New South spokesmen accounts for numerous historiographical difficulties. On the one hand was the doctrine that the South was poor, frustrated, and despised because it had, by decree of history, become entangled in wrong policies; the road to the future lay in abandoning one-crop agriculture, militant sectionalism, and outright repression of the Negro, and adopting instead a diversified industrial economy, a spirit of reconciliation, and a program of education providing separate independence for the Negro. The dream which they created was essentially a promise of American life for the South. It proffered all the glitter and glory and freedom from guilt that inhered in the American ideal. Sloughing off those characteristics which had marked him as poor, quarrelsome, unprogressive, guilt-ridden, and unsuccessful, the Southerner would—if he heeded the New South prophets—become a true heir of his heritage: prosperous, successful, confident of the future.

Before long, however, the promotional literature of the New South spokesmen included wondrous descriptions of a people who had already achieved, or were on the verge of achieving, all that had been promised as fruits of long toil. Testimony to the achievements of the new order was produced in copious quantity. From his headquarters in Baltimore, Richard Hathaway Edmonds, editor of the *Manufacturers' Record*, ground out statistics to substantiate his claim that the region was "throbbing" with industrial activity and that capitalists of the North and Europe were "looking to the South as the field for investment."[8] Henry Watterson thanked God that, at last, one could say of the South, "it is simply a geographic expression."[9] And, finally, a Vanderbilt professor declared that the "New South," which had first showed itself in 1880," had by 1886 "proved its name by evidences so powerful and convincing that only the blindest can fail to see them."[10]

Proclaiming the reality of an affluent and triumphant South, these spokesmen were equally fervent in depicting a South innocent of racial injustice. "Each has his own place," Grady declared of white and black, "and fills it, and is satisfied."[11] The program of paternalism, education, regulated franchise, and increasing segregation was advanced as the final solution to the conundrum presented by the demands of Negro freedom and the American tradition of equality. The New South image thus underwent in a short period a metamorphosis. Emerging from a program of action to save a despondent region from ruin, it evolved into a declaration of triumph. Uncritically it could be assumed that, because "facts" proved it, affluence and power were at hand and that the Negro lived in the best of all possible worlds, righteously separated from, but nurtured by, his white brethren. This was the intellectual tradition which historians of the twentieth century inherited; and with certain exceptions, it was this tradition which dominated southern historical writing until the 1930's when the revisionist erosion set in.

Before that era of devastating reappraisal, however, a pattern of history was established which was comprehensive in scope and appealing in tone. The New South school of historians developed, as the central theme of their works, the concept of triumph over adversity, of steel will and impeccable character overcoming staggering problems, often against what seemed impossible odds. The South that was depicted in most of these early histories rose from the extraordinary devastation of the Reconstruction to a glorious plateau of achievement. Viewed from the plateau, the story was one of hope and inspiration. Holland Thompson, the first academic historian to write a general history of the period, opened his work with the declaration that "somehow, somewhere, sometime, a new hopefulness was born and this spirit—evidence of new life —became embodied in 'the New South.' "[12] To optimism and cheerfulness was added the element of daring and romance. Broadus Mitchell, in *The Rise of the Cotton Mills in the South*, enticed his readers with the assurance that his story, properly understood, was "not only an industrial chronicle, but a romance, a drama as well."[13] Here, then, were powerful romantic elements to compete with the more popular and more numerous histories of the gallant South that had fallen at Appomattox. And the histories of the new regime had the one virtue denied chronicles of the Old South: they were success stories.

An essential ingredient was the element of strong moral fiber. While the New South historians agreed that the new order differed from the old in innumerable ways, few were willing to concede that the peculiar moral superiority of the Southerner had perished with the Lost Cause. As Bruce put it, the war and Reconstruction had shattered the South's economic structure and visited economic ruin on the region; but they had not detroyed the extraordinary "moral qualities of the people." These, in fact, were strengthened in adversity and were the principal weapons available to Southerners to meet new challenges.[14] Ironically coupled with this sense of moral superiority was the common belief that the war and Reconstruction had emancipated the white South from the shackles of an old order that had barred material progress and prosperity. "The Civil War," Mitchell wrote, "brought into glaring view the absence of Southern economic self-sufficiency," and its outcome freed "not just the slaves, but the South as a whole." The "emancipated" whites, no longer fettered by the economic chains of the past but still endowed with the ancient traits of their forebears, were required to rebuild on new foundations. Driven by "moral incitement" and "civic piety," Southerners undertook the task of creating a prosperous industrial society. In response to a "moral stimulus," their leaders built cotton mills that provided work for impoverished poor whites and, one is almost led to believe, gave little thought to self-enrichment.[15]

It is important to remember that, almost without exception, New South historians wrote as confirmed nationalists and interpreted southern development within the context of national trends. Reconciliation and conversion to national ways and values were central to their histories. To Paul Herman Buck, the historian of reconciliation and, in many ways, a characteristic representative of the New South school, "the central theme of American life after the war . . . is not to be found in . . . sectional divergence. It was national integration which marked every important development in the years that followed."[16] This theme of national reconciliation is likely to be deceptive, and one should observe that it was never meant to imply a surrender of southern will to northern superiority. It signified, rather, a recognition in the South that the road to affluence and power led to the adoption of those national patterns which had accounted for American greatness. This is what Edwin Mims meant when he wrote, in his biography of Sidney Lanier that southern progress had been made possible by the "adoption of the national point of view.";[17] it is what Burton J. Hendrick, the biographer of Walter H. Page, had in mind when he declared that the new nationalism was the essential force underlying the South's resurgence, that "above all," the period of Page's crusading "was an era that witnessed the transformation of the backward Civil War South into a progressive part of a united country."[18] A generation of New South historians was vindicated in 1937 when Buck concluded that, by 1900, "a union of sentiment based upon integrated interests had become a fact."[19]

New South historians, in stressing the theme of nationalism, were particularly careful to emphasize two complementary aspects. In the first place, they argued that the primary force binding the sections was the adoption by the South of what E. L. Godkin once called "the industrial stage of social progress."[20] To Buck, the South's new departure had brought about an "interlocking of economic dependence" which promoted similarity and destroyed particularism.[21] Broadus and George Mitchell, in *The Industrial Revolution in the South*, argued that the industrialization of the South destroyed "separatism" and invited "national consciousness."[22] In 1908, their historian father, Samuel C. Mitchell, attempted to place the movement toward American nationalism in a universal context, concluding of the South, "We have simply found out God's plan in our generation, and have fallen in line. . . . Whatever tends to equalize economic conditions in different sections of our country," he explained, "promotes similarity of view and identity of purpose."[23] Bruce also concluded that the industrial revolution in the South was the major factor in producing a republic "united in all its parts," free of debilitating antagonism.[24]

In the second place, these historians were convinced that the resurgent southern economy had brought into existence a South of affluence, power, and independence which fully vindicated the New South spokesmen who had called the movement into being. As early as 1885, according to Mims, "factories were prospering, farm products were becoming more diversified, more farmers owned their own places, . . . the national spirit was growing, and . . . [a] day of hope, of freedom, of progress, had dawned." By the end of the century, Mims believed, the South was assured of a "brilliant future."[25] To other historians brilliance did not have to await future developments. Bruce was struck by a "recuperative power in the Southern people" which was "perhaps unsurpassed in history."[26] The Mitchells believed that there "arrived nearly overnight an Industrial Revolution as swift and as vigorous as that in England."[27] Buck pronounced the "economic revolution" to have been both "remarkable" and "sensationally rapid."[28] Reenforcing this sense of material greatness was the common belief that the South had been master of its own destiny, achieving its eminence virtually unaided. Moreover, nothing is so striking to the historian of today as the common absence of suggestions that the region was in any sense a colony of the North. Bruce, for example, noted the prominence of northern financiers in southern railroad development, but his analysis did not lead him to attach any special significance to the fact.[29] Buck, summing up the matter, could declare: "Thirty years after Appomattox there remained no fundamental conflict between the aspirations of North and South. The people of the United States constituted at last a nation integrated and united in sentiment."[30]

It would have been paradoxical in the extreme had these historians coupled their accounts of a pioneering, progressive, and energetic industrial leadership with an interpretation of political development which conceded the truth of the occasional northern charge that "Bourbon" politicians in the South stubbornly held to the past, refusing to adapt to the changing conditions of a new order. The truth is, such concessions were seldom made. . . . On the contrary the early historians believed that the role played by the political leaders of the South was essentially the same as that played by the industrial leaders. Just as the latter had redeemed the South from economic error, so the former had redeemed the region from political error and, in addition, had assured conditions which facilitated sectional reconciliation and material progress.

To understand this favorable interpretation of the "Redeemers," one must recapture something of the perspective from which the New South historians wrote. To them the experience of Reconstruction was a horror unique in American history and for this reason doubly noxious and degrading. Against this background, the Redeemers appeared virtually as knights in shining armor. Their primary task—indeed, their knightly duty—was to cut away the "poisonous growth," as Bruce put it, planted by a band of alien bandits and desecrators.[31]

Thus the image of the Redeemers is a relatively uncomplicated one. They began their careers in glory, especially those who participated in the noble act of securing definitive home rule as a result of the "Wormley House Bargain." They were, in contrast to the "aliens" who had ruled the South before redemption, the "natural" leaders of the region, men who had distinguished themselves during the Civil War. This is not to say that they were the old plantation aristocracy. Several New South historians recognized that many of the leaders came from the new commercial-industrial urban class rather than from the older planter class. In either case, however, they were *natural* leaders, men born to the region.

Their achievement, in the view of the New South historians, amply justified the trust that the masses confided in them. Responsible men, they reversed the corrupt and fraudulent practices of Reconstruction. Holland Thompson pronounced their administrations free from scandal of any kind. "No governments in American history," he wrote, "have been conducted with more economy and more fidelity."[32] Impeccable honesty was coupled with a high sense of fiscal responsibility. The ruinous taxes and extravagant appropriations of the carpetbag regimes were abolished as the Redeemers faced up realistically to the demands of recovery. Expenses were diminished by scaling down dishonest debts, eliminating unnecessary governmental positions, and lowering salaries. A new tax structure released capital for investment. In brief, an atmosphere was created in which business could thrive and men could exercise their initiative without fear of retaliation by a capricious government.

Moreover, none of these achievements would have been secured had the Redeemers not guaranteed freedom from political instability and resumption of Negro-Republican rule. It is in this sense that the New South historians generally applauded the Redeemer creation of a one-party, solid South. Taking the explanations of the political leaders more or less at face value, the historians gave credence to the simple formula that the South's suffering had come as a consequence of Republican domination resulting in "Negro rule." Bruce was convinced that, even after home rule, "an enormous number of black voters" continued to threaten "the stability of Southern institutions."[33] The threat could have become a reality, however, only if the Republican party had found support among native whites, and this could have occurred only if the whites had divided. Patriotism, loyalty to race and region, demanded, then, unswerving support of the Democratic party. The permanence of a "redeemed" South, in short, depended upon the maintenance of a "solid" South.

Thus it was that one-partyism, white supremacy, patriotism, morality in government, and the industrial revolution were all part of one pattern. Finding this connection, the historians of the early part of the century discovered much of which to be proud in the "New South": Reconstruction had been successfully undone, and a superior southern will had charted a prosperous, successful course for the once defeated and occupied land.

Reaction to this felicitous interpretation of the Redeemer era was bound to occur, and signs of dissent began to appear in the 1920's.[34] But it was not until the Depression that full scale revision began to take shape. The glowing picture of a prosperous and triumphant South made little sense to a region soon to be accurately, if somewhat undip-lomatically, labeled the nation's "economic problem no. 1." The ex-cruciating plight of the South provided new perspectives that helped to provide new interpretations of the Redeemer era.

The most eloquent and heated, if not the most thoroughly re-searched, interpretation emanated primarily from Nashville and is as-sociated with the Vanderbilt Agrarian movement. The Nashville Cru-saders, in their manifesto, *I'll Take My Stand*, wrote charmingly of an ordered, conservative, soil-oriented style of life, presumably character-istic of the Old South, which had been betrayed by the New South promoters.[35] Lamenting the seduction of younger Southerners by the industrial gospel, the Agrarians called for a critical examination of the "advantages of becoming a 'new South' which," they insisted, would "be only an undistinguished replica of the usual industrial commu-nity."[36] Concerned with the present, wishing to launch the counter-revolution which they believed still had chances of success, they charged the New South historians with perpetuating original errors by failing to write genuinely critical history. What should be written, declared Donald Davidson in *The Attack on Leviathan*, was that America's need in 1900 was "to set off the tendencies that were leading the country straight into overindustrialization and social degeneracy." This could have been accomplished most effectively, he concluded, by "strengthen-ing the conservative culture of the South, to the virtues of which [Wal-ter Hines] Page and his followers were blind."[37]

Despite their appeal to traditional values rooted deeply in southern history, the Agrarians produced no historical studies of the Redeemer era, apart from occasional essays such as those by John Donald Wade on Henry Grady and Joel Chandler Harris.[38] Frank Lawrence Owsley, the most distinguished historian in the group, rediscovered the plain people of the Old South, but he did not investigate the social and eco-nomic history of this class after the Civil War. The significance of the Agrarians, then, lies primarily in the fact that they heightened aware-ness of an anti-New South tradition in the region and suggested to historians the profitability of exploring the patterns of conflict and antagonism in modern southern history.

The theme of conflict soon appeared in several works. Benjamin B. Kendrick and Alex M. Arnett, in *The South Looks at Its Past* (1935), found that "the quarter-century that followed the restoration of native white rule in the South was marked by a conflict between those who looked to the past and those who looked to the future." The Redeemer era could be described as a conflict between an Old South party of agrarianism and a New South party of industrialism, with the former fighting a rear-guard action.[39] A similar interpretation was included in William B. Hesseltine's general history of the South, first published in 1936.[40] To him, the South was beset by a conflict between the values of the Old South, embodied in Jefferson Davis, and the New South, embodied in Robert E. Lee, which left a lasting mark on the South. Hesseltine's conflict thesis was developed in more detail in his *Confederate Leaders in the New South*.[41]

However, the new views of conflict between an agrarian and an industrial tradition—a conflict that presumably reached its point of greatest intensity during the Redeemer era—resulted in relatively few serious monographic studies of that period. Commenting on the paucity of such studies, Judson C. Ward suggests that "the slower evolutionary processes of economic and social reconstruction carried on under one-party domination have not possessed for historians the dramatic appeal of the more spectacular period of the Civil War and Reconstruction which preceded this period or the Populist revolt which followed it."[42] Here Ward raises a point that is crucial in understanding the nature of the revisionism of the 1930's and 1940's. To many scholars of the Depression era, the Populist period held very special attraction. As C. Vann Woodward has pointed out, the two periods had much in common. There was, first of all, the common setting of depression and economic dislocation, coupled with a common antagonism toward the dominant business interests of the country. In addition, a sense of urgently and desperation infected large elements of the population. And, for Southerners, agricultural problems were among the most pressing and agrarian reform was at the center of much political and economic discussion.[43]

Southern scholars began asking themselves why the New South historians had almost uniformly passed over the Populist revolt, as though it were some form of temporary aberration, best neglected and forgotten. Could it be that, in minimizing the significance of southern populism, previous historians had missed a key element in post-Reconstruction history? More important, could it be true that the harmonious structure of New South historiography, based on a general concept of unity, absence of conflict, and progress and reconciliation, might be dismantled by studies that exposed the proportions of the revolt against the New South regimes? Was the seething discontent of the nineties a reflection of agrarians struggling to maintain an old order, or did it represent a much more fundamental and comprehensive indictment of the power structure of the South? These and other questions were raised with increasing frequency in a decade in which thoughtful men found much to condemn in their own generation.

The point here is that the most searching revisionist studies of the Redeemer era—the ones upon which our present view of the period has been built—were primarily studies of Populism and not of the Redeemer era itself. It is true, of course, that some important studies of Populism were written before the Depression. Alex M. Arnett's *The Populist Movement in Georgia* (New York, 1922) is a good example. And John D. Hicks's standard work, *The Populist Revolt*, was published in 1931 at the very beginning of the Depression. But the most important works, which fundamentally challenged the New South view of the Redeemers, appeared after the onset of the Depression. A selective listing of these studies would include Roscoe C. Martin, *The People's Party in Texas* (Austin, 1933); Daniel M. Robison, *Bob Taylor and the Agrarian Revolt in Tennessee* (Chapel Hill, 1935); William D. Sheldon, *Populism in the Old Dominion* (Princeton, 1935); articles by James A. Sharp on Populism in Tennessee, published in 1937 and 1938; and articles by Kathryn T. Abbey on Florida, published in 1938;[44] Woodward, *Tom Watson* (1938); Francis B. Simkins, *Pitchfork Ben Tillman* (Baton Rouge, 1944); and Stuart Noblin, *Leonidas LaFayette Polk* (Chapel Hill, 1949).

The full impact of the revisionist departure was not apparent until 1951 when Professor Woodward, building on the new monographs and his own extensive research, published his *Origins of the New South*. It was the first general history of the post-Reconstruction South since Holland Thompson's brief volume of 1919 and the first detailed study since Bruce's work of 1905.[45] Resemblances between the new and older works were difficult to find. Not only, of course, had Woodward written from a different perspective, but his skeptical, ironic approach to the materials was in direct contrast to the relatively uncomplicated and uncritical studies of the New South school. The results were generally devastating to the old tradition.

A significant clue to Woodward's approach was offered in a shorter book published earlier in the same year, *Reunion and Reaction*, a study of the Compromise of 1877 and the inauguration of the Redeemer regime. Its Beardian interpretation attacked the "Wormley House Bargain" legend and suggested that reunion was built, in large part, on a community of economic interests, with the Redeemers pledging support of nationalistic economic policies in return for economic aid to the South. Implicit in the settlement was an alliance of capitalists of the South and Northeast to preserve the status quo. Ironically agreeing with the New South historians that reunion was premised on the marriage of southern and northern capitalists, Woodward's revisionism lay in his assertion of the opportunistic and shortsighted motives that underlay the union.

Incorporating this interpretation in *Origins of the New South*, Woodward analyzed in detail the character of the Redeemer leadership, concluding that a high percentage of the new leaders were prewar Whigs, forced into the Democratic party because of the exigencies of white supremacy politics. Few, he found, came from the old planter class; nearly all, including most of those with agrarian connections, were oriented toward the commercial and industrial interests of the region. Redemption, then, was not a restoration of the old order but, rather, "a new phase of the revolutionary process begun in 1865. Only in a limited sense can it be properly called a 'counter-revolution.' "[46]

In describing the policies of the Redeemers, Woodward differed in almost every respect from the New South historians. Retrenchment, hailed by the earlier scholars as an indication of realism, was regarded by Woodward as an abdication of social responsibility. But perhaps a more permanent injury, he wrote, "was the set of values imposed upon the Southern mind by the rationalization of this neglect."[47] Equally devastating to the Redeemer reputation was the lengthy documentation of thievery in official places that marked the careers of many state administrations. Although finding that the stealing was less extensive than during the Reconstruction era, Woodward's history nonetheless tarnished another of the major claims made for the service of the Redeemers to their region.[48]

In dissecting the anatomy of the "Solid South," Woodward cut away the shibboleths of white supremacy to reveal a politics of class and interest that cleverly exploited race and tradition to perpetuate its hold over the region. Detailing the mounting grievances of various anti-Redeemer elements within the South, he attributes the success of the one-party machines to Machiavellian techniques that had been perfected in the fight against the carpetbaggers. The result, at least until the Populist revolt, was political apathy and despair, "a period of political torpor more stultifying, perhaps, than any in . . [the South's] long history."[49]

But the New South promoters and the historians who followed in their tradition had not built their image of a triumphant South on a basis of political achievement alone. Political leaders, honest and loyal though they might have been, were regarded as benefactors of the region chiefly because they created the order and the atmosphere in which an industrial revolution could take place. Here Woodward does not equivocate in challenging completely the New South point of view. While conceding that the South, in many respects, did hold its own in rates of relative growth, he finds that, in absolute terms, the economic disparity between North and South increased, rather than decreased, during the period 1880-1900. Moreover—and here was the unkindest cut of all—the economy of the South became increasingly controlled by northern and other outside capitalists. The South, Woodward concluded, "was limited largely to the role of a producer of raw materials, a tributary of industrial powers, and an economy dominated by absentee owners." The unhappy result was "low wages, lack of opportunity, and poverty."[50]

By 1951, then, the revisionist movement had found its spokesman in a brilliant work, at once original and yet reflective of two decades of new thought. In conclusion, one ought to ask where we stand today. Have we reached a new consensus? Are counterrevisions of a major nature in progress? Or, is the whole subject being neglected?

There is still much that we do not know. Woodward was struck by the absence of adequate monographs when he wrote *Origins of the New South*, and anyone who reads his "Critical Essay on Authorities" may find that complaint documented in suggestions for numerous studies. Other periods of southern history, it appears, are more inviting to the profession. Some years ago David Potter made a study of articles appearing in the *Journal of Southern History* from 1935 through 1949. Of those articles which he could classify by period, he found that 48.8 percent had been written on the period 1830-1865 while only 16.3 percent were devoted to the entire period since 1877.[51] During the period 1950-1963, the proportion on the period since 1877 has gone up slightly, to 21.9 percent of the total classifiable by period, but studies of the Redeemer era itself are disappointingly scarce.

We still lack, for example, good studies of the Redeemer era in most southern states despite an obvious need and the example of a few pioneer volumes of merit. Albert D. Kirwan's splendid analysis of Mississippi (which is not restricted to the Redeemer years) is a model to be emulated by students of other states. Works more limited in time span, such as Allen Going's monograph on Alabama, reveal what can be done to enrich our understanding of the period.[52] The Kirwan and Going volumes, both published in the same year that *Origins of the New South* appeared, largely support Woodward's revisionist generalizations. Should we have good studies of all the other states, however, the picture might become more complex, if not basically different. An analysis of South Carolina, for example, might well qualify the thesis that the conservative political regimes were dominated by commercial and industrial interests. In addition to the paucity of good state studies, another deficiency is in biography. Since 1951 good biographies of a few significant figures, such as James S. Hogg and George W. Cable, have been published, but equally important men still await biographers or invite reinterpretation by modern students.[53]

For the most part, the work done in recent years has tended to support, rather than to challenge, the principal revisionist findings. There are exceptions. Nash K. Burger and John K. Bettersworth's *South of Appomattox* (New York, 1959) seems blithely unaware of revisionist findings and describes the Redeemers as highly motivated patriots, rescuers of an oppressed people. Thomas B. Alexander's study of Whiggery in the postwar South offers a more serious challenge to Woodward's view of the Redeemers. Examining the Hayes papers, where Woodward located much of the evidence for his economic interpretation of the Compromise of 1877, Alexander found "surprisingly few" items referring to economic matters. He does not press the point but suggests that "a more detailed study of the individual oldline Whigs in Congress might well establish the conclusion that the southern bloc would have acted as it did in 1877 had there been no railroad lobby involved."[54] On the other hand, Alexander's statistical study of former southern Whigs amply confirms the revisionist position that Whiggery was the dominant element in the Democratic party during the Redeemer era.

Alexander's careful study of political backgrounds has been matched by few other studies. We do not have a major general study of Redeemer politics, such as V. O. Key's pioneer masterpiece on twentieth-century politics, nor do we have sufficient monographs on the structure and process of politics to ease the burden of one undertaking such a task. Two recent interpretive books by T. Harry Williams and Dewey W. Grantham, both quite brief on the period, make stimulating reading but do not depart from the revisionist construction.[55] Indeed, Grantham's excellent account of the forging of the Solid South underscores the extent to which the revisionist position has triumphed. Williams expresses reservations about some parts of the revisionist interpretation, arguing that Woodward erred in describing Redeemer politics as a politics of race and tradition, largely devoid of realistic concerns. Actually, the real difference between the two is slight.[56] The most notable recent advance of political history has resulted from two excellent studies of the Republican party and the South by Vincent

P. DeSantis and Stanley P. Hirshson.[57] These works emphasize the continuing influence and importance of the GOP throughout the period, thus correcting occasional careless generalizations about the disappearance of the party in the South after Reconstruction. At the same time, they contribute to a fuller understanding of Redeemer opposition and the perfection of one-party politics.

Studies of race relations . . . were pioneered by Vernon L. Wharton and George B. Tindall.[58] Woodward's *Strange Career of Jim Crow* (New York, 1955) added a new dimension to the subject by advancing the thesis that segregation laws came fairly late and by reemphasizing the degree to which the Redeemers were willing to forestall movements for proscription of Negro rights. Charles E. Wynes and Frenise A. Logan have tested the "Woodward thesis" for Virginia and North Carolina (with positive findings, in the main) and students of other states could follow suit with profit.[59] These recent studies accelerated the dismantling of the image of harmonious racial adjustment, predicated on subordination, given us by the New South school and, at the same time, revealed greater complexity in the political and economic aspects of race relations.

In the area of economic development one finds occasional echoes of the earlier writings. For example, John S. Ezell, though generally in agreement with Woodward, asserts one older view. He declares that the "crowning glory of the Bourbon era was its sensational success in attracting manufacturing to the South," adding that "the progress of Southern industrialization was little short of a miracle."[60] More commonly, however, scholars have tended to the revisionist position on this as well as on other subjects. Typical is the statement by Thomas D. Clark that the years between 1865 and 1914 were "lean and barren";[61] and revealing is William H. Nicholls' acceptance of the fact of industrial lethargy in the late nineteenth century and his attempt to explain continued economic backwardness in noneconomic terms.[62] Relatively little has been done with the problem of economic colonialism, raised poignantly by Woodward, but studies such as John F. Stover's *The Railroads of the South, 1865-1900* (Chapel Hill, 1955) show how it can be approached through a single industry. Stover's conclusion, in keeping with the revisionist finding, is that northern men and money extended their influence over virtually the entire railroad complex of the South.

The whole field of southern economic growth badly needs attention, for many current generalizations rest on shaky foundations. Robert S.

Smith's study of Danville cotton mills, though concerned primarily with the twentieth century, is an example of the kind of meticulous company history required in quantity.[63] Anthony Tang's study of economic development in the southern Piedmont, though, like Smith's work, largely devoted to the twentieth century, reveals what can be done by careful analysis.[64] Another welcomed approach would be a study within the framework of economic theory along the lines of Conrad and Meyer's essay on the profitability of slavery.[65] For the time being, as we await both the theoretical and empirical studies, an extraordinarily useful compendium of economic data to be exploited is Everett S. Lee and others, *Population Redistribution and Economic Growth: The United States, 1870-1950* (Philadelphia, 1957).

Tracing the shifting interpretations of the Redeemer era, as attempted in this essay, raises a number of intriguing questions. Studying the original New South idea leads one to wonder why it had such appeal and persistence, what gave its spokesmen their persuasiveness and ability to deceive others as well as themselves, and why it aroused such enduring partisanship and antagonisms in contemporaries as well as in their descendants.

In trying to understand the New South historians, one feels almost as though they were looking through a powerful telescope. The background against which their histories were written heightened the contrasts and exaggerated the images they saw. They saw southern economic achievements against a scene of grinding poverty, increasing political power and self-determination against an experience of galling powerlessness, attempts at reconciliation against the legacy of hatred and mistrust, and concessions to the Negro against a backdrop of slavery and black codes. It is not surprising that in describing their region's attempt to don the mantle of the American heritage they were lured into admiring the emperor's new clothes. Today, the South's more cosmopolitan historians see the region's history silhouetted against American and world experience; and bitter southern memories are no longer so potent. The most thoroughgoing of the revisionists reveal New South claims in all their factitiousness and find the era that gave birth to them barren and stultifying. Like the child in Andersen's fairy tale, they look at the emperor and exclaim, "But he has got nothing on!"

It is thus clear that New South historians and revisionists alike have shared a fundamental moral concern, a sense of the responsibility to judge, not simply describe, the past. In large measure, the "facts" upon which the changing interpretations have rested have not changed, but values have undergone a revolution. Thus, within the framework of their own value judgments, the earlier historians created an image of inspiration; later historians replaced it with a picture of near degradation. The trend of the future is uncertain. Increasing demand for detailed and impartial testing of current generalizations suggests that the next stage may involve less attention to ultimate meaning. On the other hand, the potent paradoxes and contrasts of the period itself will continue to confront historians with the perennial task of explaining the mentality of the era and the inheritance that it bequeathed.

NOTES

1. Mayo, "Is There a New South?" *Social Economist*, V (October, 1893), 200.
2. Woodward, *Origins of the New South, 1877-1913* (Baton Rouge, 1951), ix-x.
3. Ashmore, *An Epitaph for Dixie* (New York, 1958), 14.
4. Cooke, "The New South," in Donald Sheehan and Harold C. Syrett (eds.), *Essays in American Historiography, Papers Presented in Honor of Allan Nevins* (New York and London, 1960), 50-80.
5. Hart, *The Southern South* (New York, 1910), 73-74, 218.
6. Lee in Bruce, *The Rise of the New South* (Philadelphia, 1905), v-vi.
7. Warner, "Society in the New South," *New Princeton Review*, I (January, 1886), 1.
8. Edmonds, *Facts About the South* (Baltimore, 1907), 60-61, and *The South's Redemption From Poverty to Prosperity* (Baltimore, 1890), 5.
9. Watterson, *The Compromises of Life* (New York, 1903), 289.
10. Wilbur Fisk Tillett, "The White Man of the New South," *Century Magazine*, XXXIII (March, 1887), 769-70.
11. Joel Chandler Harris (ed.), *Life of Henry W. Grady, Including His Writings and Speeches* (New York, 1890), 303.
12. Thompson, *The New South* (New Haven, 1919), 7.
13. Mitchell, *The Rise of the Cotton Mills in the South* (Baltimore, 1921), vii.
14. Bruce, *The Rise of the New South*, 4.
15. Mitchell, *The Rise of the Cotton Mills*, 53-54, 81, 153.
16. Buck, *The Road to Reunion*, 1865-1900 (Boston, 1937), vii.
17. Mims, *Sidney Lanier* (Boston, 1905), 275.
18. Hendrick, *The Training of an American: The Earlier Life and Letters of Walter H. Page, 1855-1913* (Boston, 1928), v.
19. Buck, *The Road to Reunion*, viii.
20. Godkin, "The White Side of the Southern Question," *Nation*, XXXI (August 19, 1880), 126.
21. Buck, *The Road to Reunion*, 298.
22. Broadus and George Mitchell, *The Industrial Revolution in the South* (Baltimore, 1930), ix.
23. Samuel C. Mitchell, "The Nationalization of Southern Sentiment," *South Atlantic Quarterly*, VII (April, 1908), 110.

24. Bruce, "Social and Economic Revolution in the Southern States," *Contemporary Review*, LXXVIII (July, 1900), 72-73.
25. Mims, *Sidney Lanier*, 279.
26. Bruce, *The Rise of the New South*, 279, 342.
27. Mitchell and Mitchell, *The Industrial Revolution*, 294.
28. Buck, *The Road to Reunion*, 178.
29. Bruce, *The Rise of the New South*, Chap. 19.
30. Buck, *The Road to Reunion*, 298.
31. Bruce, *The Rise of the New South*, 3.
32. Thompson, *The New South*, 25.
33. Bruce, *The Rise of the New South*, 446-47.
34. See for example, William H. Skaggs, *The Souther Oligarchy: . . .* (New York, 1924).
35. Twelve Southerners, *I'll Take My Stand: The South and the Agrarian Tradition* (New York, 1930).
36. *Ibid.*, x-xi.
37. Davidson, *The Attack on Leviathan: Regionalism and Nationalism in the United States* (Chapel Hill, 1938), 278.
38. See, for example, Wade, "Henry W. Grady," *Southern Review*, III (Winter, 1938), 479-509, and "Profits and Losses in the Life of Joel Chandler Harris," *American Review*, I (April, 1937), 17-35.
39. Kendrick and Arnett, *The South Looks at Its Past* (Chapel Hill, 1935), 105-108.
40. Hesseltine, *A History of the South, 1607-1936* (New York, 1936).
41. Hesseltine, *Confederate Leaders in the New South* (Baton Rouge, 1950), 41.
42. Ward, "The New Departure Democrats of Georgia: An Interpretation," *Georgia Historical Quarterly*, XLI (September, 1957), 227.
43. Woodward, *The Burden of Southern History* (Baton Rouge, 1960), 141-42.
44. Sharp, "The Entrance of the Farmers' Alliance into Tennessee Politics," East Tennessee Historical Society *Publications*, No. 9 (1937), 77-92, and "The Farmers' Alliance and the People's Party in Tennessee," East Tennessee," Historical Society *Publications*, No. 10 (1938), 91-113; Abbey, "Florida Versus the Principles of Populism, 1896-1911," *Journal of Southern History*, IV (November, 1938), 462-75.
45. For an earlier formulation worked out for one state, consult C. Vann Woodward, "Bourbonism in Georgia," *North Carolina Historical Review*, XVI (January, 1939), 22-35.
46. Woodward, *Origins of the New South*, 22.
47. *Ibid.*, 61.
48. *Ibid.*, 66-74.
49. *Ibid.*, 106.
50. *Ibid.*, 311.
51. Potter, "An Appraisal of Fifteen Years of the *Journal of Southern History*, 1935-1949," *Journal of Southern History*, XVI (February, 1950), 25-32.
52. Kirwan, *Revolt of the Rednecks: Mississippi Politics, 1876-1925* (Lexington, 1951); Going, *Bourbon Democracy in Alabama, 1874-1890* (University, Alabama, 1951).
53. Robert C. Cotner, *James Stephen Hogg: A Biography* (Austin, Texas,

1959); Arlin Turner, *George W. Cable: A Biography* (Durham, 1956).

54. Alexander, "President Whiggery in the Confederate South, 1860-1877," *Journal of Southern History*, XXVII (August, 1961), 324-25.

55. Williams, *Romance and Realism in Southern Politics* (Athens, Georgia, 1961); Grantham, *The Democratic South* (Athens, Georgia, 1963).

56. Williams declares that Woodward was "led to conclude that the politics of Redemption was the romantic type, emphasizing tradition and demanding the subjection of all other issues to one while ignoring the future and denying issues of economics and self-interest." According to Williams, this interpretation is partly wrong, for the Redeemers "placed economics and power above questions of race." As proof of this point, Williams notes that the ruling whites did not disfranchise the Negro but manipulated his vote in order to preserve their own political power and enhance their own economic positions. Williams, *Romance and Realism*, 47-49. In fact, Woodward has developed this point in detail, but he would disagree with the implication that Redeemer opportunism belied a nonrational politics rooted in an appeal to race and tradition. Rather, the two are part of the same pattern.

57. DeSantis, *Republicans Face the Southern Question: The New Departure Years, 1877-1897* (Baltimore, 1959); Hirshson, *Farewell to the Bloody Shirt: Northern Republicans and the Southern Negro, 1877-1893* (Bloomington, Indiana, 1962).

58. Wharton, *The Negro in Mississippi, 1865-1890* (Chapel Hill, 1947); Tindall, *South Carolina Negroes, 1877-1900* (Columbia, South Carolina, 1952).

59. Wynes, *Race Relations in Virginia, 1870-1902* (Charlottesville, 1961); Logan, *The Negro in North Carolina, 1876-1894* (Chapel Hill, 1964).

60. Ezell, *The South Since 1865* (New York, 1963), 136, 152.

61. Clark, *The Emerging South* (New York, 1961), 35.

62. Nicholls, *Southern Tradition and Regional Progress* (Chapel Hill, 1960).

63. Smith, *Mill on the Dan: A History of Dan River Mills, 1882-1950* (Durham, 1960).

64. Tang, *Economic Development in the Southern Piedmont, 1860-1950, Its Impact on Agriculture* (Chapel Hill, 1958).

65. Alfred H. Conrad and John R. Meyer, "The Economics of Slavery in the Ante Bellum South," *Journal of Political Economy*, LXVI (April, 1958), 95-130.

XV

Populism: Its Significance in American History

EVERETT WALTERS

Along with reinterpretations of earlier democratic movements, such as that of the Jacksonian period, the political movement in the United States termed Populism has been the subject of reappraisal by historians, economists, and others. What was the significance of this turbulent and dramatic phenomenon of American politics that flared up in the latter part of the nineteenth century, carrying repercussions into the twentieth century?

Past and recent interpretations fall into two main categories. Historians, economists, and others have viewed the Populist movement on the one hand as socialistic and on the other extreme as old-fashioned pioneer doctrine. Other judgments usually range within these extremes. The present essay seeks to summarize these varied interpretations, to indicate their major trend, and also to venture a brief personal conclusion.

That a similarity existed between Populism and Socialism was emphasized in a study in the early nineties made by Frank L. McVey.[1] McVey's slender volume, published in 1896 before the political campaign of that year, reflected the conservative economic views then prevailing. McVey had little sympathy with the Populists. He exam-

From *Essays in American Historiography* . . . Donald Sheehan and Harold C. Syrett, eds., (New York: Columbia University Press, 1960), pp. 217-30. Reprinted with permission.

ined their platform tenets and concluded that the Populist party was not a party of constructive principles but was a movement merely of protest against the existing economic system. The party failed to state any basic views on the large national problems. McVey attacked all the main beliefs of the Populists: ownership of railroads, free silver, the abolition of national banks, the subtreasury scheme, and curtailment of the existing mortgage and loan procedures. He censured the leaders for their failure in the Omaha Platform to say anything about the tariff. Many of their demands, he claimed, were merely efforts to secure political allies. The call for a shorter working day and the restriction of immigration—sops offered to please the labor unions—were not popular with the farmer of Kansas, since he worked many more than eight hours and an increased population would mean additional consumers for his products.

McVey implied that, if the silver advocates were not so powerful in the party, the similarity between Populism and Socialism would be even closer. "Its whole tone is socialistic," he declared of the Omaha platform. To support this contention he prepared a chart to show the similarity in the demands of the Socialist and Populist parties. Although he admitted that there was the great difference of common ownership and equality of income, he believed that "national ownership of the railroad and telegraph, coupled with a demand for increased state action, can only characterize the platform as socialistic in its tendency."[2] He held that the party's hope lay in casting aside halfway measures and following the logic of its underlying tendencies, boldly announcing itself as the Socialist party in America, confessing paternalism as its principle of constitutional interpretation, advocating the socialization of industry as its economic doctrine, and ignoring politics as its political program. "Thus it may become a party of principle, and possess all the elements of a great one; but it must rest with the future to say whether such a party, however great, can be right."[3]

Apparently believing that the future would prove the party to be wrong, McVey concluded that its existence was transient; a party must be based on more lasting qualities than mere discontent. It had added nothing "but variety to our political life."[4]

The view that Populism was an old-fashioned pioneer phenomenon found impressive presentation by the renowned historian and creator of the frontier theory, Frederick Jackson Turner.[5] So great was his prestige that his interpretation had general acceptance for many years. The Populist was "a survival of the pioneer, striving to adjust present conditions to his old ideas. The ideals of equality, freedom of opportunity, faith in common man." The task of the Middle West, the home of the Populist, was "that of adapting democracy to the vast economic organization of the present [1901]."[6] Always conscious of the role of the West in what has been "distinctive and valuable in America's contributions to the history of the human spirit," Turner contended that "Populism is a manifestation of the old pioneer ideals of the native American, with the added element of increasing readiness to utilize the national government to effect its ends."[7] Many of the Populists, he went to considerable lengths to show, were native Americans "of the New England and New York current." They were of the breed who had fought at Concord Bridge. As they went West they had taken their ideals with them. Mary Ellen Lease might sound raucous to the New Englander, but she was an echo of the Revolutions of '76—and, indeed, of "the leaders and sectaries of Cromwell's army."[8] Later, Turner stressed that the Grangers and the Populists were prophets of the reform movement of the early twentieth century. Their emphasis on the need for "governmental regulation of industrial tendencies in the interest of the common man" was reflected in "Mr. Bryan's Democracy, Mr. Debs' Socialism, and Mr. Roosevelt's Republicanism."[9]

"The disappearance of the frontier, the closing of an era," Turner wrote, convinced the Western radical that he "must sacrifice his ideals of individualism and free competition in order to maintain his ideal of democracy." "The former safety valve of abundant resources" had brought on a "new national development." The Populist came to believe that government was the people and that the powers of the various governments must be extended to preserve "his historic ideal of democratic society." Capital, labor, and the Western pioneer had abandoned competitive individualism in order to organize their interests in more effective combinations.[10] Of course, it was the Westerner who began the movement.

Turner's interpretation was largely accepted by John D. Hicks in his scholarly volume *The Populist Revolt*,[11] which, published in 1931, frequently has been termed the definitive history of the movement. Sparing in interpretation, Hicks presented the history of the agrarian movement of the last decades of the nineteenth century from its frontier background and initial grievances to the national election of 1908. As he summarized their doctrines, the Populists insisted that American laborers, farmers, and factory workers were entitled to a decent living in return for their labors. When farm prices fell and their economic situation became critical, farmers began to find fault with the existing order, the prevailing economic and political conditions, especially such factors as the power of the railroads, the grasping practices of loan companies, and the widespread corruption in government. Like Turner, Hicks declared that, since there was no frontier with available lands where they might begin life anew, the farmers turned to the government for assistance. "Now with the lands all taken and the frontier gone, this safety valve was closed. The frontier was turned back on itself. The restless and the discontented voiced their sentiments more and fled from them less."[12] When they found the government in the hands of the plutocrats, they felt compelled to obtain control. The two fundamental propositions of Populist philosophy, Hicks indicated, are, "one, that the government must restrain the selfish tendencies of those who profited at the expense of the poor and needy; the other, that the people, not the plutocrats, must control the government."[13] He observed that many of the Populist demands, "while despised and rejected for a season, won triumphantly in the end." Thanks to this triumph, "one may almost say that, in so far as political devices can insure it, the people now rule." Granted the existence of some corruption, "on the whole the acts of the government have come to reflect fairly clearly the will of the people." Hicks admitted that to the radicals of 1931 the Populists' reforms seem totally inadequate. Indeed, he concluded, in view of the proposed drastic changes of the dark days of the great depression, the demands of the Populists seem quite conservative; they have been accepted, in the main, by both political parties.[14]

But Turner's frontier theory was not to remain undisturbed; it was increasingly attacked as a whole and in many of its applications. Among the critics was Chester McArthur Destler, who found fault with Turner's interpretation of the rise of Populism. In his book on American radicalism, 1865-1901, Destler developed a new appraisal of the Populist movement.[15] He attacked frontally the idea that Populism was "exclusively the product of repetitive sociological and economic processes at work on the frontier which found expression in a somewhat emotional discontent or in a patchwork of remedial proposals that lacked any philosophical basis other than a desire to restore the working prosperity of a small entrepreneur, rural economy."[16] To secure a better understanding of Western radical thought, he used a concept taken from social anthropology, cultural diffusion. This, he believed, would test "the possibility of ideological transmission between rural and urban areas in both directions, not only of single concepts as culture traits, but of an entire complex of ideas."[17] Destler examined the intercourse between urban and agrarian radicals from the Locofocoism of the Jackson era to the free silver victory of 1896. His conclusion was that Populism was a "re-elaboration of the Jeffersonian tradition in an attempt to meet the problems produced by corporate monopoly and the urban-industrial age," and that its basic concepts (antimonopolism, insistence on equal rights, labor-cost theory of wealth, hostility to finance capitalism and the money power, and the assertion of a community of interest between rural and urban producers) were foreshadowed in the writings of John Taylor of Caroline and of William Leggett. "Grafted into this radical ideology," he asserted, "were other concepts and proposals that re-orient it from political negation to positive but limited state intervention in the economic field."[18]

Destler also stressed at some length the importance of the farmer-labor alliance, a "neglected aspect of the Populist movement." His contention was that the "greatest problem of ideological conflict and adaptation produced by the attempted coalition did not develop out of a conflict between Populism and the half-formulated philosophy of a shattered trades unionism . . . [but] from the clash of indigenous Populism, produced by decades of cross-fertilization between urban and agrarian radical movements with an imported, proletarian Socialism which made its first great appeal to English-speaking wage earners in America in the depression-ridden nineties." The clash, he pointed out, was partly responsible for the People's party declaration for free silver at the St. Louis convention in 1896.[19] Destler's examination of the agrarian labor alliance deserves the careful attention of the student of Populism. His detailed articles on the Labor-Populist alliance in Illinois during the election of 1894 do indeed point out a "neglected aspect of the Populist movement." Earlier writers, such as Turner, Buck, and Hicks, barely mention the significance of the labor groups.

Destler's emphasis on the influence of "imported, proletarian Socialism" on the rise of Populism drew replies from other students of the period. Hicks, writing eighteen years after the publication of his magnum opus on the Populist revolt, conceded the effectiveness of liberal humanitarianism and "imported socialism." He hastened, however, to reaffirm his belief that "American radicalism would simply never have been what it was but for its long and sturdy line of Granger-Greenback-Populist progenitors." In support of this view he traced at length the influence of Populism on such early twentieth-century leaders as Robert La Follette, Albert B. Cummins, John A. Johnson, Joseph W. Folk, and even Theodore Roosevelt.[20] Several years later Hicks insisted that the "middle western agrarians were not socialists; on the contrary, they were, or at least aspired to be, small capitalists." Their antimonopoly views, he added, were developed naturally from their long-existent hatred of monopolies, especially the railroads, and their interest in government regulation and control was a logical consequence.[21]

Other historians have examined the relation of Populism and Socialism during recent years and in general conclude that the influence of Socialism was slight. George Harmon Knoles pointed out, in his analysis of the political campaign of 1892, that Socialism and Populism were basically antithetical although they had a common opposition to industrial capitalism; the former expressed radical views concerning individualism, whereas the latter represented radical agrarianism. "Populists, as a rule," he declared, "did not recognize the fundamental cleavage dividing the two; the radical socialists did." As Knoles saw it, the differences between the two proved irreconcilable. Populism had its roots deep in that distinct social entity, the American farmer, who could not become a proletarian, and who, when his way of life was seriously invaded, turned to familiar remedies—managed currency, control of monopolies, and land legislation. Socialism, a new development in America, "drew upon Marx for its theory and upon European and American labor strife for its experience." "Populism was the natural expression of farmer protest; Socialism was the natural expression of the dissent of industrial labor."[22]

In his recent examination of the roots of American Communism, Theodore Draper reiterates the thesis that Populism and Socialism were poles apart. Populism, he claimed, was an expression of "a dream of recapturing an imaginary idyllic past of independent freeholders," but one which never threatened the foundations of private property. "The demand for government ownership and control that came out of the Populist tradition was not a step toward collectivism, Socialism, or Communism," he stated, but "a peculiar American device to defend the capitalism of the many against the capitalism of the few." Although Populism and Socialism "spurned each other," Draper concluded, the latter could take over from the former. Some Populist leaders, such as Eugene Debs, became Socialist leaders; indeed, in 1909 former Populists accounted for fifteen percent of the Socialist party members, and many popular Socialist songs of the West were Populist in origin.[23]

Another recent trend of interpretation has been the stress placed on the democratic nature of Populism or, conversely, on its antidemocratic nature. A. Whitney Griswold, in his *Farming and Democracy*, published in 1948, pointed out that the Populists sought "to enforce through direct legislation the classic democratic principles of individual liberty, equal opportunity, and popular sovereignty." In this, Griswold held, they were indeed conservative. Their radicalism, he added, "consisted largely in their militancy and in their rejection of laissez-faire tactics for a deliberate use of government and public policy as means to their ends."[24]

Grant McConnell, writing in 1953, extends this view, contending that the subsequent decline of agrarianism brought on a decline in democracy.[25] The farm movements of the late nineteenth century, including Populism, were a protest "against the system of power growing out of the raw and turbulent capitalism of the era. The protest was made not merely against injustices to farmers but against injustice to all men. Agrarianism spoke in the name of all." This voice of democracy, McConnell charged, has lately been lost because a power structure (the American Farm Bureau Federation and other farm organizations) has developed and sharpened class lines so that there now exists an elite in agriculture.

In commenting on the books by Griswold and McConnell, as well as books by other writers who stressed the theme of democracy in Populism, Charles M. Hardin expresses doubt that Populism was a real democratic mass movement for all men. First, he points out that, because of its political and economic demands, the movement would have required a formidable organization of power, which was certainly not democratic. Second, he contends that its prejudices against aliens, townspeople, and, in many areas, Negroes were inimical to democracy. Finally, Hardin claims, the Populist demand for a scapegoat (Wall Street, bankers, and the railroads) "must be considered inhospitable to democracy."[26]

Although not a historian of the period, the literary critic Irving Howe has offered a picture of Populism that reflects a popular antidemocratic theme. He asserts that in Populism there was an "insistently programmatic mindlessness, a mindlessness that was sometimes its only program; a xenophobic scorn of city slickers and intellectual 'long hairs' . . . an occasional stereotyped identification of the Jew with the odious Wall Street banker; a sentimental glorification of mere solidarity at the expense of thought . . . it comprises an authoritarian tendency buried deep within a certain kind of plebeian revolt."[27] It would appear that, in striving so earnestly for rhetorical effect, Howe has failed to understand the real issues of Populism.

Most Southern historians have stressed the unusual sectional aspects of Populism. They have examined in considerable detail the economic appeal of the movement in the South, but they always emphasize the influence the Populists had on the established parties, especially the Democratic party.[28] Thus Populism in many areas of the South represented a certain wing of Democrats that broke away in an effort to split the tight machine or "ring" control of the Democratic leaders who had gained political dominance in the last decades of the nineteenth century. Although the pattern varied from state to state, the Populists usually used the Negro problem to their own advantage. John B. Clark, writing in 1927, maintained that the Negro was a "tool, a pawn for which white parties contested, and that the negro, more than other factors, was responsible for the Populist party in Alabama. Economic questions fell into the background." C. Vann Woodward, in summarizing the role of the Populists, points out that the leaders openly spoke of the conflict of class and section and "ridiculed the clichés of Reconciliation and White Solidarity." Some of the leaders, he added, attacked the cult of racism and stressed the hope of common action by farmers and workers from both classes.[29] Thus in many parts of the South the movement challenged the one-party system as well as white solidarity. All writers agree, however, that with few exceptions, the Populist leaders assumed that the South would continue to be controlled by the white class even if the new party attained political power.

Since the era of Roosevelt and the New Deal, historians generally have come to interpret Populism as one of the first steps in the modern American reform movement, a movement culminating in the New Deal. Only the reaction of the twenties interrupted the movement from Populism to Progressivism to New Dealism. One of the most colorful historians of this movement is Eric Goldman, whose *Rendezvous with Destiny* pictures the stream of reformers, contrasting Populism with the liberalism of the eighties and nineties.[30] While Populists and liberals had a common desire for reforms in existing governmental procedures, the former were much too extreme for the latter. The "obvious socialism" of the Populist demands, he points out,"brought the most anguished of all cries from liberals." The liberals of the period emphasized "liberty, the freedom of the individual in political, economic, and social relations, either with another individual or with the government." The Populists, on the other hand, considered liberty to be "the freedom to escape poverty and to rise in economic and social status." They stressed economic opportunity rather than political liberty.[31]

Goldman brings out the interesting fact that both Populists and liberals found their hero in Thomas Jefferson. The Populists looked to him as the man who despised capitalist groups as the greatest enemy of the people, and the liberals saw him as the great political thinker who feared centralized power.[32]

A recent illuminating analysis of Populism has been offered by Richard Hofstadter in his excellent volume *The Age of Reform.* Despite his urban, somewhat cynical, attitude toward the agrarian group as a whole, Hofstadter presents effectively an interpretation of Populism from the perspective of today. In his examination of the three great reform movements of the past sixty-five years, he characterizes Populism as an intense expression of the first movement, the agrarian uprising of the latter part of the nineteenth century. Hofstadter discusses two other movements for reform, the Progressive movement from 1900 to 1914 and the New Deal, "whose dynamic phase was concentrated in a few years of the 1930's."[33]

Hofstadter views Populism as a heightened expression of the discontent of the farmers and others with the economic changes that were taking place. He believes that this dissatisfaction has persisted, and is now expressed "partly as an undercurrent of provincial resentments, popular and 'democratic' rebelliousness and suspiciousness, and nativism." He admits that, in reexamining the chief tenets of the Populists and Progressives, he found much that was "retrograde and delusive, a little that was vicious, and a good deal that was comic." By his critical examination he hopes to stimulate "safeguards against the political misuse" of some of the alleged values of these ideas and to salvage the real values that are still meaningful.[34] Hofstadter constructs what he calls the "agrarian myth"—the dominance of the Jeffersonian concept of the self-reliant, independent yeoman who could satisfy virtually all his needs on his own farm, and the belief that only an agricultural society was perfect. Then he shows how illusory was this myth, since the independent yeoman had virtually disappeared by 1860 and had been supplanted by the commercial farmer. Thus, because of its peculiar development, American rural society neither preserved the Jeffersonian farmer nor gave rise to the European type of farm village community. Rather, it developed a "harassed little country businessman who worked very hard, moved all too often, gambled with his land, and made his way alone."[35]

The Turnerian explanation of Populism is rejected by Hofstadter. The notion that Populism was the logical product of the frontier spirit, he contends, is "a deceptive inheritance from the Turnerian school." To justify his refutation, Hofstadter describes the decisive role of the South, the limited support Populism received from the West as a whole, the influence of the world agrarian movement, and the weakness of the so-called valve theory of the Turner school.

In his essay on "The Folklore of Populism," Hofstadter describes the dominant themes in Populist ideology that were nurtured by the tradition of the agrarian myth. As he sees it, these themes were the dream of a golden agricultural community, the concept of the natural harmony of interests among the productive classes, the dualistic version of social struggles, the idea that history was a conspiracy working against the farmer, and the doctrine of the primacy of money.[36] Inevitably, these motifs reflect what he calls the delusive aspect of Populism, the general view of society in which the Populists were held to be "most credulous and vulnerable." He dwells upon what he believes to be neglected aspects of the movement—its provincialism as revealed in the stress on nativism and nationalism and "its tincture of anti-Semitism." Another neglected aspect is the jingoism of the 1890s that arose concurrently with Populism.[37] In his essay "From Pathos to Parity," Hofstadter examines the People's Party as a political movement and explains why it failed.[38] Its failure derived from its basic limitations: its inability to capture the vote of the laboring classes, its meager following among farmers east of Indiana, its inability to obtain sufficient financial backing, and, finally, its championing of free silver. But although it failed politically, the successes of Populism are impressive; plank after plank of its platforms has been adopted, not through its own efforts but through the efforts of the major parties.

Perhaps Hofstadter's most important contribution to our understanding of Populism is his account of the "soft" side of agrarianism, which gave way to the "hard" side. In other words, the farmer of the agrarian myth was replaced by the farmer of commercial actuality. Fortunately for the farmer, this change, which had been developing slowly and came to a climax sharply in 1896, was accompanied by the great prosperity of the era that preceded World War I.

For the student of American history, Populism remains an ever fascinating movement, open for fresh speculation and for reinterpretation. It had, and it retains, political and historical significance. Whether it is viewed as a farmers' protest against a changing society, as a native socialist expression, as a reactionary, even totalitarian, demonstration, or simply as a senseless revolt of a benighted farming group, the blunt truth remains that many of the demands made by the Populists have become accepted in our tradition and have become law. Theirs was not an intellectual movement; it was emotional, pragmatic—and effective!

Populists were leaders in the fight for reforms needed in American democracy; although their movement failed to acquire political acceptance, yet what they sought for themselves and others has been widely accepted in the years that followed. More than fifty years later Populism may be viewed as a movement of protest against injustice and inequality, a protest typical of Americans since pre-Revolutionary War days.

NOTES

1. Frank L. McVey, *The Populist Movement* (American Economic Association, Economic Studies, Vol. I, No. 3; New York, 1896).
2. *Ibid.*, p. 184.
3. *Ibid.*, p. 190.
4. *Ibid.*, p. 195.
5. Frederick Jackson Turner, *The Frontier in American History* (New York, 1920).
6. *Ibid.*, p. 155.
7. *Ibid.*
8. *Ibid.*, pp. 239-40.
9. *Ibid.*, p. 281.
10. *Ibid.*, pp. 280, 305-6.
11. John D. Hicks, *The Populist Revolt* (Minneapolis, 1931). James C. Malin, a careful student of agrarianism, sharply criticizes this volume, especially the author's failure to deal with the international economic situation of the nineties, to give a comprehensive survey of United States agriculture of the period, and to investigate Populism in Kansas and several other states. Malin also comments briefly on other early writers on Populism. "Notes on the Literature of Populism," *Kansas Historical Quarterly*, I, No. 2 (1932), 160-64. Solon J. Buck's *The Agrarian Crusade* (New Haven, Conn., 1920), a slender history of the agrarian movement with virtually no interpretation, remains a brief and useful account.
12. *Ibid.*, p. 95.
13. *Ibid.*
14. *Ibid.*
15. Chester McArthur Destler, *American Radicalism, 1865-1901: Essays and Documents* (New London, Conn., 1946).
16. *Ibid.*, p. 2.
17. *Ibid.*
18. *Ibid.*, p. 222.
19. *Ibid.*, p. 30.
20. John D. Hicks, "The Legacy of Populism in Middle West," *Agricultural History*, XXIII (1949), 235-36.
21. Theodore Saloutos and John D. Hicks, *Agrarian Discontent in the Middle West, 1900-1930* (Madison, Wis., 1951), p. 30.
22. George Harmon Knoles, "Populism and Socialism, with Special Reference to the Election of 1892," *Pacific Historical Review*, XII (1943), 295-304.
23. Theodore Draper, *The Roots of American Communism* (New York, 1957), pp. 36-39. Another Midwesterner who gave up Populism for So-

cialism after 1896 was Julius A. Wayland. See Howard H. Quint, "Julius A. Wayland, Pioneer Socialist Propagandist," *Mississippi Valley Historical Review*, XXXVI (March, 1949), 585-606.

24. A. Whitney Griswold, *Farming and Democracy* (New York, 1948), pp. 145-46.
25. Grant McConnell, *The Decline of American Democracy* (Berkeley, Calif., 1953), p. 1.
26. Charles M. Hardin, "Farm Politics and American Democracy," *Journal of Politics*, XVII (1955), 655.
27. Irving Howe, *Sherwood Anderson* (New York, 1951), pp. 87-88. The quotation appears in Howe's comment on Anderson's *Marching Men*, an account of the restlessness of the nineties and the attempts made to organize labor.
28. Alex M. Arnett, *The Populist Movement in Georgia* (Columbia University Studies in History, Economics, and Public Law, No. 235; New York, 1922); John B. Clark, *Populism in Alabama* (Auburn, Ala., 1927); Roscoe C. Martin, *The People's Party in Texas: a Study in Third Party Politics* (University of Texas Bureau of Research in the Social Sciences Study, No. 4; Austin Texas, 1933); William DuBose Sheldon, *Populism in the Old Dominion: Virginia Farm Politics, 1885-1900* (Princeton, N.J., 1935).
29. C. Vann Woodward, *Origins of the New South, 1877-1913* (Baton Rouge, La., 1951), Chap. IX.
30. Eric F. Goldman, *Rendezvous with Destiny* (New York, 1953).
31. *Ibid.*, p. 51.
32. *Ibid.*, pp. 51-52.
33. Richard Hofstadter, *The Age of Reform; from Bryan to F. D. R.* (New York, 1955), p. 3.
34. *Ibid.*, pp. 5-11.
35. *Ibid.*, p. 46.
36. *Ibid.*, p. 62.
37. *Ibid.*, pp. 85-93.
38. *Ibid.*, pp. 94-109.

RECENT STUDIES

Allan G. Bogue, *From Prairie to Corn Belt: Farming on the Illinois and Iowa Prairies in the Nineteenth Century* (Chicago: University of Chicago Press, 1963).
J. Rogers Hollingsworth, *The Whirligig of Politics: The Democracy of Cleveland and Bryan* (Chicago: University of Chicago Press, 1963).
Harold U. Faulkner, *Politics, Reform, and Expansion, 1890-1900* (New York: Harper & Row, 1959).
C. Vann Woodward, "The Populist Heritage and the Intellectual," *American Scholar*, XXIX (Winter 1959-60), 55-72.
Martin Ridge, *Ignatius Donnelly: The Portrait of a Politician* (Chicago: University of Chicago Press, 1962).

Norman Pollack, *The Populist Response to Industrial America* (Cambridge: Harvard University Press, 1962).

Walter T. K. Nugent, *The Tolerant Populists: Kansas Populism and Nativism* (Chicago: University of Chicago Press, 1963).

Paul W. Glad, *McKinley, Bryan, and the People* (Philadelphia: Lippincott, 1964).

Robert F. Durden, *The Climax of Populism: The Election of 1896* (Lexington: University of Kentucky Press, 1965).

XVI

Theodore Roosevelt in American Historical Writing, 1945-1960

DEWEY W. GRANTHAM, JR.

During recent years Theodore Roosevelt has acquired a new vogue. The centennial observance of his birth, in 1958, seemed to reveal a new appreciation for the controversial Rough Rider. . . . Recent historical writing in America has reflected the revival of interest in the nation's twenty-sixth President.[1] Indeed, Roosevelt has become a rival of such heroic figures as Jackson, Wilson, and Franklin D. Roosevelt in attracting the attention of American historians." During the last decade and a half at least eight biographical studies of Roosevelt have been published and others are in progress.[2] No less than forty articles and essays, ranging from a discussion of his ancestry to an analysis of his rhetoric,[3] have appeared during the same period, as well as a superb eight-volume selection from his letters, several unpublished Ph.D. dissertations, and scores of collateral work.

Of course, the irrepressible "Teddy" has long fascinated students of the American past, but this hardly explains the new interest in him. A part of the answer is the peculiar attraction the progressive movement has come to have for historians in this country. Roosevelt was so intimately associated with American progressivism that the subject can

From *Mid-America*, XLIII (January 1961), pp. 3-35. This essay is reprinted in abridged version by permission of the author.

scarcely be considered without giving attention to his involvement in it. Another reason historians have focused attention on Roosevelt and the era he dominated is the renewed interest in his foreign policy, which has taken on new meaning when examined in the light of two world wars and recent international developments. No doubt more subtle influences manifested in the nation's dominant mood of late are also involved. It is possible, for instance, that the homogenizing forces so apparent in modern American society, and especially the desire to avoid social conflict, have found confirmation and inspiration in Theodore Roosevelt's basic attitudes.

In one respect recent Rooseveltian historiography has been curiously unproductive. There has been no full-length biography of Roosevelt during the last fifteen years, a circumstance which provides remarkable testimony to the powerful influence and durability of Henry F. Pringle's brilliantly-written biography.[4] One of the centennial studies, Edward Wagenknecht's *The Seven Worlds of Theodore Roosevelt* (New York, 1958), attempts to distill the essence of Roosevelt's thought and to delineate the character of his leadership. Although it is well-written and assimilates many of the new interpretations, it is lacking in critical judgment and its topical organization allows one to appreciate neither the fascinating story of Roosevelt's over-all growth nor the vital relationship between the man and his times. Another recent volume, Hermann Hagedorn's *The Roosevelt Family of Sagamore Hill* (New York, 1954), is a warm and entertaining account of the Roosevelt family at its Long Island home, but it is not much concerned with politics or Roosevelt's public career. . . .

The most detailed study yet made of Theodore Roosevelt's youth and early career is the first volume of Carleton Putnam's projected four-volume biography.[5] Putnam's readable and well-documented work limns the first twenty-eight years of the New Yorker's life in rich detail. Putnam emphasizes the influence of Theodore's father in the formation of the future President's character and ideals, describes "Teedie's" youthful enthusiasm for naturalism, discusses the physical regimen he prescribed for himself, brings the shadowy Alice Lee to life, does a workmanlike job in covering Roosevelt's legislative career, and deals effectively and at length with his ranching and hunting experiences.[6] He stresses Roosevelt's understanding of politics, his sense of *noblesse oblige*, his passion for law and order, his belief in individual self-responsibility, and the courage and determination he showed in developing his mind and body. But Putnam's portrait of the young Roosevelt is unduly flattering. If Pringle overemphasized the adolescent and foolish in Roosevelt's character, Putnam goes too far in depicting him as a responsible, mature, and purposeful young man. His volume is also open to other criticisms. It is largely descriptive, the space given to some topics to the relative neglect of others is open to question, and the author is not always critical in his use of sources. Nevertheless, *The Formative Years* provides for the first time a fairly complete and reliable factual account of Roosevelt's youth and early career. Nowhere outside of his own papers can one find so comprehensive a reconstruction of his early life.

Several recent articles and essays treat various aspects of Roosevelt's career before his elevation to the presidency in 1901. Elwyn B. Robinson and Robert W. Sellen have written perceptive articles on Roosevelt the historian;[7] Ari Hoogenboom, in an enlightening analysis of the effect the Pendleton Act had on the civil service, advances convincing proof of the New Yorker's genuine contributions to civil service reform;[8] and Clifford P. Westermeier's book on the cowboy volunteers of 1898 contains an appraisal of the war feats of Roosevelt and the Rough Riders.[9] . . .

As might be expected, Roosevelt's presidency has been one of the principal attractions for modern Roosevelt scholars. Although no one has written an over-all appraisal of Roosevelt's presidential years as comprehensive as Pringle's, the period has been dealt with extensively in monographs, articles, and biographies of other major figures. Three studies are particularly significant: George E. Mowry, *The Era of Theodore Roosevelt, 1900-1912* (New York, 1958), Howard K. Beale, *Theodore Roosevelt and the Rise of America to World Power* (Baltimore, 1956), and John Morton Blum, *The Republican Roosevelt* (Cambridge, 1954). Mowry's book is the best general account of Roosevelt's administration.[10] It contains an excellent appraisal of Roosevelt. Beale's study, vigorously written and based on exhaustive research, is a comprehensive and critical examination of Roosevelt's policies in the international sphere. Beale clearly demonstrates Roosevelt's skill in handling foreign relations but questions the wisdom of his major policies. Blum, who prepared himself well for undertaking an interpretative study of Roosevelt during his years as associate editor of *The Letters of Theodore Roosevelt*, has written an exciting essay that clarifies "the purposes and methods" of Roosevelt's career. It has probably done more than any other publication since 1945 to rehabilitate Roosevelt as an important and able leader. Blum pictures Roosevelt as a skillful conservative more concerned with the processes than with the ends of government; but a conservative who accepted change as the only means of preserving his nation's most cherished institutions.

Another interpretative essay is Richard Hofstadter's sketch in *The American Political Tradition and the Men Who Made It* (New York, 1948). This piece, which gives evidence of Hofstadter's interest in psychology, reminds one of Pringle in its skeptical approach and caustic characterization. Hofstadter refers to Roosevelt as the "stabilizer of the status quo," the "master therapist of the middle classes." He emphasizes the tension, the penchant for violence, the uneasiness over radicalism, and the tendency to straddle in Roosevelt's life, while minimizing his reform accomplishments as President and suggesting that his militarism and imperialism had much in common with recent authoritarianism.[11] . . .

An indirect but significant contribution to recent Rooseveltian historiography is the increasing number of able biographies of Roosevelt's political associates and contemporaries. The most impressive biographical studies have been those devoted to the lives of leading congressional figures, particularly Senators. The best of these are John A. Garraty's *Henry Cabot Lodge: A Biography* (New York, 1953). which throws light on the thirty-five-year political collaboration between Lodge and Roosevelt and on Massachusetts politics but fails to elaborate Lodge's attitude toward the Square Deal and his role during the troubled years 1910-1912;[12] Everett Walters' *Joseph Benson Foraker: An Uncompromising Republican* (Columbus, Ohio, 1948), a good study of a conservative who differed with the President over railroad regulation, patronage, administration policies in the Caribbean, and the Brownsville affray;[13] Belle Case and Fola La Follette, *Robert M. La Follette, June 14, 1855-June 18, 1925* (2 vols., New York, 1953), a detailed and sympathetic account of the Wisconsin progressive's long career which views the latter years of Roosevelt's administration from the perspective of a man whose experiences with the Rough Rider were disillusioning; Oscar Doane Lambert, *Stephen Benton Elkins* (Pittsburgh, 1955); Leland L. Sage, *William Boyd Allison: A Study in Practical Politics* (Iowa City, 1956); and Thomas Richard Ross, *Jonathan Prentiss Dolliver: A Study in Political Integrity and Independence* (Iowa City, 1958). The last three volumes are helpful in understanding the railroad regulatory legislation of the Roosevelt period, and the studies of the Iowans are especially valuable because of the way in which they relate Iowa politics to national developments. Although there is still no adequate study of Joseph G. Cannon's public career, Blair Bolles' sprightly-written *Tyrant from Illinois* contributes to an understanding of his speakership and his relations with Roosevelt.[14]

The members of Roosevelt's Cabinet have not attracted recent biographers. Since 1945 only one such study has appeared: Richard W. Leopold's *Elihu Root and the Conservative Tradition* (Boston, 1954).[15] Leopold deals incisively with Root's important work in the Cabinet and stresses his contribution to the conservative tradition in America. But his book contains few references to politics and fails to do justice to Root's views on the Square Deal. Other recent biographies that should be mentioned are Ira V. Brown's *Lyman Abbott, Christian Evolutionist: A Study in Religious Liberalism* (Cambridge, 1953), which is helpful for its discussion of the relations between Roosevelt and a high-minded reformer whose independent journal consistently supported Rooseveltian policies, and Merlo J. Pusey's *Charles Evans Hughes* (2 vols., New York, 1951), a lengthy but uncritical biography of the inscrutable New York reformer and jurist.[16] Walter Johnson's sparkling biography of William Allen White presents a vivid account of the Emporia editor's long association with Roosevelt and some valuable material on politics in Kansas during the Roosevelt era.[17]

No one has made a more penetrating analysis of Roosevelt's presidential politics than John M. Blum, who graphically demonstrates that the Rough Rider's proficiency in the processes of politics, administration, and legislation stamped him as "professional." By 1900, writes Blum, the New Yorker's party regularity had become "convincingly habitual," his utilization of the mechanics of power "smoothly effectual," and his standards of executive efficiency "refreshingly rigorous." Blum illuminates the course T.R. followed in transforming the party of Hanna and McKinley into the party of Roosevelt,[18] and shows how Roosevelt, with an intuitive understanding of politics and an "absolute sense of political pitch," captured the loyalty of the people as had no incumbent President since Andrew Jackson. Although Roosevelt sought to control rather than to change the American political system, his vivid performance and his success in persuading the people that he had "a conscience and would be fair" gave a powerful impetus to the reform movements of the early part of the twentieth century and provided "an irrepressible force" for the mandate of 1904.

Theodore Roosevelt's role in the revivification of the presidency has been described by Arthur S. Link as "the most significant political development of the time."[19] Several scholars have shown how Roosevelt's "stewardship theory" of the presidency, his role as a policy determiner in the legislative field, and his assertion of national leadership through control of public opinion contributed to the strengthening of the American presidency.[20] Blum's *The Republican Rosoevelt* provides the best analysis of that contribution. Blum's brilliant dissection of Roosevelt's quest for and use of power, and his treatment of T.R.'s approach to his party and to the people, of the methods he employed in dealing with Congress, and of the concerts of power he worked to establish in the international sphere constitute a series of instructive case studies.

In a superb chapter on the enactment of the Hepburn Act, Blum illustrates Roosevelt's facility in dealing with Congress and the nature of his approach to governmental control over industrial operations.[21] He was given to moral solutions and the dimensions of his morality, Blum says, involved practicality, popularity, and especially preoccupation with process. Having defined the tariff as a matter of expediency and the regulation of railroad rates as a matter of conduct (and morality for him was largely a matter of conduct), Roosevelt used "the specter of tariff agitation" to threaten the Old Guard and create a controlled environment within his party conducive to rate reform. He brought "a new respectability" to demands that went back to Populist days, and by mobilizing the full powers of his office he won an outstanding victory. Blum effectively refutes an interpretation that once had a good deal of currency which held that Nelson W. Aldrich outmaneuvered Roosevelt in the Hepburn fight.[22] Leland L. Sage's *William Boyd Allison* and Thomas R. Ross's *Jonathan Prentiss Dolliver* support Blum's interpretation and help to clear up the complicated maneuverings in the struggle between Roosevelt and Aldrich that preceded the Senate passage of the Hepburn bill.

Another aspect of Roosevelt's approach to the problem of industrial control—trustbusting—has been the focal point of considerable historical attention since 1945. Richard Hofstadter suggested in *The American Political Tradition* that antitrust action for T.R. was partly a means of satisfying the popular demand to see the government punish big business, but chiefly a threat to hold over business to compel it to accept regulation, which was really Roosevelt's solution for the trust problem.[23] In his volume in the New American Nation Series, George E. Mowry agrees substantially with this interpretation. With the path to effective control blocked by a stubborn, conservative Congress, Roosevelt was forced to bring "the arrogant capitalists to heel" through the judicious use of the antitrust laws.[24] Hans B. Thorelli's comprehensive study of the formative period of antitrust policy, *The Federal Antitrust Policy: Origination of an American Tradition* (Baltimore, 1954), while emphasizing the point that Theodore Roosevelt brought "executive initiative and leadership" to this area of public policy-making, insists that there was no well-defined and coherent Roosevelt plan during the early years of his presidency. Before 1903, declares Thorelli, there was nothing in Roosevelt's program *per se* "that is in conflict with the anti-monopoly tradition, although it is implied that the antitrust policy might need reinforcement or supplementation."[25]

Intrigued by the possibilities of federal power, Roosevelt moved toward a system of orderly control, first by establishing the Bureau of Corporations in the Department of Commerce and Labor to discipline consolidation. The power thus granted to an agency under the control of the Chief Executive was potentially very great and, though Roosevelt intended to rely upon experts in carrying on the work of the Bureau, John M. Blum has suggested that the open environment provided by the legislative or judicial processes might have been a more equitable approach to the problems of competition, consolidation, and control.[26] An important article by Arthur M. Johnson on Roosevelt's role in the establishment and early work of the Bureau lends support to Blum's reservations about the Rough Rider's solution to this problem.[27] Johnson concludes that the agency proved useful to Roosevelt in publicizing corporate abuses and in helping to prosecute offenders, but that its performance was uneven and its susceptibility to influence by the President constantly invited arbitrary distinctions between "good" and "bad" combinations. Such an arrangement, he says, was "too patently inconsistent with sound public policy to be institutionalized." In another recent article Robert H. Wiebe has shown how the House of Morgan negotiated "gentlemen's agreements" with the Roosevelt administration and thereby removed the United States Steel Corporation and the International Harvester Company from the scourge of antitrust prosecution.[28]

Several books and articles published since 1945 have clarified other features of Roosevelt's Square Deal. Robert J. Cornell, *The Anthracite Coal Strike of 1902* (Washington, 1957), a monograph based on extensive research, provides an excellent account of the strike and of Roosevelt's part in forcing a settlement. *The Health of a Nation: Harvey W. Wiley and the Fight for Pure Food* (Chicago, 1958), a carefully-prepared study by Oscar E. Anderson, Jr., concentrates on Wiley but also deals with Roosevelt's role in the fight for pure-food and drug legislation. Anderson shows Roosevelt to have been a "late convert" to the crusade for pure-food legislation, but his book does not underestimate the President's sustantial contribution to the passage of the Pure Food and Drugs Act of 1906.

Although there is still no adequate treatment of Roosevelt and the conservation movement, his policies in that field have not been altogether neglected during the last few years. Gifford Pinchot's *Breaking New Ground* (New York, 1947), while particularly concerned with the story of forest conservation in the United States, describes the various elements in Roosevelt's comprehensive conservation program.[29] An article by Whitney R. Cross on "The Conservation Policies of the Two Roosevelts" thoughtfully analyzes the first Roosevelt's conservation ideas.[30] Cross points out that Theodore Roosevelt's support of conservation was a congenial commitment on his part because it allowed him to stress convictions of honesty and efficiency that were firmly fixed in the American tradition. Cross contends that specific conservation problems "on their own merits" gradually led originally individualistic predispositions to evolve in "the collectivist direction," that through his conservation program Roosevelt came to assume a consistent and pervasive antimonopoly position, and that the inadequacy of simple righteousness in dealing with complicated and highly technical violations promoted the development of a comprehensive theory of resource management. Thus was Roosevelt led along the road to the New Nationalism and an elementary stage of the welfare state, says Cross. A somewhat different view is presented in a survey of Roosevelt's conservation activities by E. C. Blackorby, who emphasizes the western sources of the Rough Rider's conservation ideas and asserts that Roosevelt's policies derived from his interpretation of the powers of the presidency and his conception of the government's function as that of a steward for later generations of Americans.[31]

The most significant work on the conservation movement to appear in recent years is Samuel P. Hays, *Conservation and the Gospel of Efficiency: The Progressive Conservation Movement, 1890-1920* (Cambridge, 1959), which is based on extensive use of primary materials. Hays challenges those scholars who have emphasized the democratic features and the antimonopoly spirit of the conservation movement and advances the thesis that conservation was primarily a scientific movement, concerned with rational planning to promote the efficient development and use of all natural resources.[32] He argues that instead of being a great moral struggle between the virtuous "people" and the evil "interests," the movement was primarily the work of a limited group of people with a particular set of goals. Far from involving a reaction against large-scale corporate business, asserts Hays, conservation in fact shared its views in a mutual revulsion against unrestrained competition and undirected economic development. Hays' emphasis on the concept of efficiency in resource management is a significant contribution to a fuller understanding of the conservation movement, and it suggests a side of the progressive movement that needs further investigation. But the interpretation is too monolithic to explain the conservation crusade or the progressive movement entirely.

Hays is more successful in fitting the conservation policies of the Roosevelt administration into his conceptual framework. Stressing the close connection between the various elements in the larger conservation movement, he demonstrates how the Roosevelt administration expanded its public land policies and gradually broadened its early reclamation work into a full-fledged water development program and a single, coherent approach to conservation. But the administration had difficulty in adjusting the conflicts that arose over resource decisions. Encountering increasing opposition from Congress, which could not appreciate the conservationists' passion for efficiency and which sought to protect its own role in the making of resource decisions, Roosevelt and his conservation friends endeavored to overcome legislative restraints by devising new administrative concepts and practices, by expanding the interpretation of resource laws, and finally, by making a bid for popular support. At this point, Hays contends, middle- and upper-class urban dwellers, with little appreciation for rational and comprehensive planning, joined the conservation crusade.

Theodore Roosevelt's extraordinary energy, his passion for stability, his practicality and willingness to compromise, his fascination with processes rather than ends, and his devotion to the gospel of righteousness, all suggest why he should have demonstrated a flair for administration. Leonard D. White has said that as an administrator Roosevelt stood "head and shoulders above his predecessors since the days of James K. Polk."[33] . . . An illuminating case study is Alfred D. Chandler, Jr.'s essay on "Theodore Roosevelt and the Panama Canal: A Study in Administration," which appeared as an appendix to *The Letters of Theodore Roosevelt*.[34] Chandler points out that Roosevelt's administrative abilities lay less in the realm of theory than in the field of practice. As a practical executive his talents were three-fold: first, he made decisions rapidly and on the basis of the best advice available; second, he understood the necessity of choosing capable men for important administrative positions, of supporting them fully, and of convincing them of the value of their work; and finally, he had learned from experience "not only that authority and responsibility must be centralized but that authority to act must be commensurate with the responsibility exacted." Civil service reform, another element in the strenuous President's administrative work, has received extensive coverage in Paul P. Van Riper's history of the civil service.[35] Under Roosevelt's "stimulating guidance," says Van Riper, the public service first began to reflect the influence of the drive for "administrative and organizational reform."

Elting E. Morison has pointed out that Theodore Roosevelt was one of those Americans who first discerned that the country's future lay "within the whole world and not in some insulated corner."[36] His efforts to equip the nation for international maturity was a major part of his leadership and has been recognized as such by American historians. Roosevelt was unusually well-equipped to deal with foreign problems, as Howard K. Beale makes clear in his important study of Roosevelt's diplomacy. His travels abroad, his extensive reading, his friendships at home and abroad, and the sense of security and of *noblesse oblige* that he got from an aristocratic background were all important in his approach to international questions. Beale notes that the Roosevelts, unlike most of their predecessors, accepted living in the White House as "completely natural." They had the aristocrats' concern for good breeding but they blended regard for proprieties with simplicity in taste and freedom from ostentation. This facilitated Roosevelt's man-to-man diplomacy.[37]

In discussing Roosevelt's part in the rise of American imperialism, Beale places emphasis on the Rough Rider's moral rectitude, his belief in Anglo-Saxon superiority,[38] and his special brand of national honor; he observes that in his ignorance of modern war Roosevelt romanticized war, and that while he valued the blessings of peace he craved the excitement of war. Beale shows that Roosevelt's desire to have his country act as a great power was intimately related to his concern for the qualities of character he prized and his feeling that expansion would help develop those qualities in his fellow-citizens. This point is examined in an interesting article by John P. Mallan on "The Warrior Critique of the Business Civilization," which argues that the "little imperialist elite" composed of such men as Brooks Adams, Homer Lea, and Theodore Roosevelt made the only serious attempt during America's brief history as a world power to develop a genuinely conservative position on foreign policy.[39] In his study of the conflict between ideals and self-interest in the international life of the United States, Robert Endicott Osgood asserts that a group of "American Realists," motivated by "an aggressive national egoism and a romantic attachment to national power," briefly captured popular leadership under the banner of a missionary imperialism.[40] One of these realists, Theodore Roosevelt, found it easy to lead the nation to its most active participation in international affairs since the days of the French alliance; but this was not, according to Osgood, the result of any "sudden burst of realism" in the popular attitude toward world politics. Rather it should be attributed to Roosevelt's political genius, "his consummate skill in tapping the resources of aroused nationalism and directing them into new channels."

To understand Theodore Roosevelt's views on foreign policy, one must comprehend his belief in the oneness of American and British interests and his conviction that together they could dominate the world, to the advantage of civilization. Howard K. Beale's *Theodore Roosevelt and the Rise of America to World Power* contains an excellent account of Roosevelt's British policies. Beale does not make the mistake of interpreting Roosevelt as "an unqualified Anglophobe," but he shows how T.R. and his friends gradually developed a full-fledged foreign policy based on the belief that the two countries shared common interests. He reviews the conflicts and misunderstandings whose ultimate resolution led to the consummation of the entente, throws new light on Roosevelt's handling of the Alaskan boundary dispute, and suggests that the President and his associates desired but never quite dared to advocate publicly an Anglo-American alliance.[41] For all Roosevelt's prophetic insights, writes Beale, he failed to foresee the inevitable resentment of the colonial people whose domination was a major objective of the Anglo-American understanding.[42] Beale also criticizes Roosevelt and his colleagues for seeking in combination with Britain to preserve "an unstable balance" among the nations he considered civilized, and for their failure to inform the American people of the commitments they had made.[43]

As John M. Blum's penetrating essay makes clear, Roosevelt's foreign policy was governed (as were his policies at home) by his quest for order and his faith in power.[44] Roosevelt's first objective was the self-interest of the United States and this helps account for his interest in strategic considerations and his determination to develop the American navy.[45] His quest for order and his faith in power were perhaps most apparent in his Caribbean policies. But this area has received relatively little attention since World War II, in part perhaps because the subject had earlier been given elaborate treatment.[46] Even Beale slights Roosevelt's Caribbean diplomacy.

Most American diplomatic historians have been highly suspicious of Roosevelt's claim that he used the presence of Admiral Dewey's fleet in the Caribbean and sent a personal ultimatum to the Kaiser to force Germany's acceptance of American arbitration proposals during the

Venezuelan crisis of 1902-1903. In an article published in 1946, Seward W. Livermore challenged some of the conventional conclusions with regard to this episode.[47] Livermore concedes that Roosevelt might have embellished his recollection of his activities in the crisis, but the historian's examination of naval records convinced him that there exists "a substantial factual basis" for Roosevelt's statements. He thinks the key to the problem lies in the careful preparation the navy made in 1902 to defend the interests and security of the United States in the Caribbean, and in the way Roosevelt made use of American naval maneuvers in that area during the crisis for diplomatic purposes. In a fascinating exploration of the whole historiographical problem that has developed over this question, Beale goes further than Livermore in defending Roosevelt's claims. He views the affair as a notable example of Roosevelt's personal diplomacy and as important in its bearing on his "reputation for veracity."[48] He takes issue with Dexter Perkins and other historians and introduces considerable evidence to prove that "the substance" of Roosevelt's account is true.

Mowry's *The Era of Theodore Roosevelt* has a good brief account of Roosevelt's Far Eastern policies, but the most comprehensive study of Rooseveltian diplomacy in the Orient is contained in Beale's volume. In his chapter on Roosevelt and China, Beale examines T.R.'s handling of such problems as the dispute over the American China Development Company, shows how he miscalculated in the arrangements he made with Japan for the maintenance of the Open Door in China, and explores the implications of American imperialism with respect to that country. He is critical of Roosevelt for failing to formulate a foreign policy which would help resolve China's basic problems, and expresses the opinion that the United States missed a great opportunity during the Roosevelt era when it failed to become the friend and guide of the "new spirit" in China.[49] In another chapter Beale reviews in great detail Roosevelt's mediation in the Russo-Japanese War and his major policies designed to maintain the balance of power in the Far East. He probably overemphasizes Roosevelt's responsibility for the ultimate failure of the balance of power and Open Door arrangements he worked so hard to perfect in the Far East.

Although Roosevelt's role in European diplomacy was smaller than it was in the Far East, he was vitally interested in preserving the balance of power on that continent. He sought to avoid the outbreak of a war in Europe (which he suspected would become a general war) and in the first Moroccan crisis he played a useful part in avoiding an open conflict.[50] In his lengthy discussion of Roosevelt and the balance of power in Europe, Beale illuminates some of the hidden corners of the twenty-sixth President's notions about war and peace, and provides an especially discerning treatment of his position vis-à-vis Germany and the Kaiser.[51] Although Roosevelt generally turned a friendly countenance toward the Prince of Wilhelmstrasse, a recently published article by Seward W. Livermore shows how he made use of a pattern of naval-diplomatic activity to indicate American preference for the Anglo-French Entente and thus tip the balance against Germany in the precarious international situation.[52]

Several historians have pointed out the relationship between Roosevelt's domestic reforms and his purposes in the international sphere. For example, George E. Mowry has noted how the nationalist and collectivist impulse that encouraged one wing of progressivism to rely upon the federal state for the solution of internal problems also reflected itself in foreign affairs.[53] In an influential article published in 1952, William E. Leuchtenburg advanced the thesis that the progressives, with few exceptions, ardently supported imperialism or at the very least proved "agreeably acquiescent."[54] Although Leuchtenburg and other recent American specialists have clearly shown the affinity one branch of the progressives had for an imperialistic foreign policy, other historians have insisted that progressivism, especially in the Midwest and the South, was basically hostile to imperialism and the ambitious foreign policies of Theodore Roosevelt.[55]

Much of recent Rooseveltian scholarship has been concerned with Roosevelt and the progressive movement, with major emphasis on the years 1910-1912. The most significant volume on this subject is George E. Mowry's *Theodore Roosevelt and the Progressive Movement* (Madison, 1946), the first important work to be published on Roosevelt following World War II. The result of extensive research in manuscript sources and other records, Mowry's book is a perspicacious and well-written treatment of Roosevelt's influence on the progressive movement and the influence of the movement on the man. Mowry stresses the midwestern origins of the movement and asserts, in his evaluation of T.R.'s presidential constributions to the incipient reform wave, that "Roosevelt was the best publicity man progressivism ever had." He makes a detailed examination of the Taft administration, the various phases of insurgency,[56] and the gathering progressive storm in the West. He is much more critical of William Howard Taft, whom he views as a conservative and as a bungling politician, than was Henry F. Pringle.[57] He follows Roosevelt closely after his return from abroad and does much to clarify his motivations and behavior in the campaign of

1910; he discusses the gradual cleavage between the ex-President and Taft, the evolution of the New Nationalism, the organization of the Progressive party, and the election of 1912. His brief account of the decline of the Progressive party is a masterly treatment. Mowry has probably overemphasized Roosevelt's role in the progressive movement, especially in his thesis that he killed progressivism in the Republican party by leading the progressives out of the party in 1912, only to abandon them in 1916. He concentrates too closely upon domestic politics and is understandably limited in his handling of the relationship between far-flung local and state activities and national developments. But his book is indispensable for an understanding of Roosevelt and the progressive movement.

During the years since 1945 the election of 1912 has continued to be a central attraction for research on progressivism. Few American elections have been studied at the grass-roots level so intensively.[58] One aspect of this interest has been the origins of Roosevelt's New Nationalism. Eric F. Goldman, George E. Mowry, and other historians have stressed the role of Herbert Croly as the theoretician if not the originator of the New Nationalism.[59] Two scholars who have been most critical of Theodore Roosevelt in recent years—Daniel Aaron and Arthur A. Ekirch, Jr.—have concentrated their fire upon Roosevelt's well-advertised progressive doctrine. In *Men of Good Hope*, Aaron characterizes Roosevelt as a leader of "comic vanity and inveterate opportunism," a late-comer to reform whose progressivism was of the "most dubious sort."[60] He emphasizes the elite strain in the New Yorker's make-up and pictures the real Roosevelt as a militarist and a disciplinarian. According to Aaron, the Croly-Roosevelt program was a kind of "pseudo-progressive makeshift," engendered more from "a fear of social revolution than a dream of fulfillment."[99] It is at this point in particular that Aaron seeks to show that Brooks Adams greatly influenced Roosevelt's thinking.

Arthur A. Ekirch maintains that the progressive movement, while supporting some liberal causes and opposing many domestic abuses, was not primarily a liberal movement and that it abandoned almost completely the philosophy of natural rights for a kind of political instrumentalism.[61] As President, says Ekirch, Theodore Roosevelt emphasized to a "superlative degree" the nationalistic side of progressivism. Ekirch stresses the Hamiltonian notions of the progressives, the influence of collectivist and statist views from abroad on the evolution of American progressivism, the *rapport* between business and progressive tenets, and the intimate relationship between "the aggressive foreign policy of

the progressives and their emphasis on nationalism in home affairs."
Ekirch's interpretation is suggestive, but it errs in its emphasis and dis-
torts the meaning of American progressivism by characterizing the
movement as a whole largely in terms of the ideas of such eastern exponents of the New Nationalism as Herbert Croly, George W. Perkins,
and Theodore Roosevelt. As George E. Mowry has acutely observed of
Roosevelt in 1912, "He was supported in the West not because of his
New Nationalism but in spite of it."[62] The character of the progressive
movement can be accurately determined only when enough studies of
its manifestation at the state and local levels have been made to permit
authoritative generalizations. Such studies as Russel B. Nye's *Midwestern Progressive Politics* (which emphasizes the midwestern character
of progressivism and vividly contrasts the liberalism of Croly and Roosevelt with that of Midwesterners like La Follette),[63] Mowry's *The California Progressives* (Berkeley and Los Angeles, 1951), and Robert
S. Maxwell, *La Follette and Rise of the Progressives in Wisconsin*
(Madison, 1956) suggest how diversified a lot American progressives
were and how untenable a monolithic interpretation of the progressive
movement would be.

Three or four recent memoirs are important as sources for an understanding of Theodore Roosevelt and the progressive movement. Of
these, *The Autobiography of William Allen White* (New York, 1946)
is most notable. White, who was one of those who stood with Roosevelt at Armageddon, has written a graphic account of Republican insurgency and the Progressive party, and his magnificent evocation of
the spirit that animated the Roosevelt Progressives helps make his book
a classic in recent American history. Henry L. Stimson's *On Active
Service in Peace and War* offers a revealing example of how Roosevelt
attracted able young men to government service, throws light on New
York politics,[64] and provides a case study of a Roosevelt man who
stayed with the Taft administration in 1912. Important for its illumina-
tion of the conflict within the Progressive party during the years 1912-
1916 is Amos Pinchot's *History of the Progressive Party*, which has
been skillfully edited by Helene M. Hooker.[65] Pinchot, who was almost
from the first a "Cassandra to the Colonel," wrote a highly subjective
and selective account, but one that is valuable for the light it throws on
the abandonment of La Follette's candidacy by the Pinchots and others
early in 1912, the differences between the "radical nucleus" of the party
and Roosevelt over the trust question and the role of George W.
Perkins in the party's management, and the decline and collapse of the
organization.

Roosevelt's activities following his defeat in 1912 have not yet received adequate treatment. In addition to Mowry's account of the Progressive party's decline . . . Osgood uses Roosevelt as a symbol in the conflict between ideals and self-interest in American foreign relations during the first two decades of the twentieth century. He makes a notable contribution in his brilliant exegesis of Roosevelt's motivations in his fight for American public opinion. The ex-President feared that his country's position in the world would be destroyed if Germany won the war, but Osgood doubts that considerations of national security had a direct influence upon his desire for intervention. It was the inhumanity and humiliation inflicted by the submarine campaign and not its threat to the Western Hemisphere that aroused his passionate feelings. Wilson's apparent success in winning popular backing for his milk-and-water ideals, for which Roosevelt had the utmost contempt and which he sincerely believed would lead the country down the road to disaster, exacerbated his fears. Osgood uses Nietzche's distinction between the Warrior and the Priest to depict the positions of the two leaders, whose differences, he thinks, were more than personal and partisan, involving also a struggle between contrasting philosophies of international relations.[66] In some respects Roosevelt was a realist in his attitude toward foreign affairs; but Osgood's volume demonstrates that in others he was "a militant idealist and something of an aggressive national egoist as well."

No evaluation of recent Rooseveltian historiography would be complete without special reference to the eight-volume edition of Roosevelt's letters published during the early 1950's. A distinguished contribution to Roosevelt literature in its own right, this superbly-edited work has proven an extraordinary stimulus to historians and biographers interested in the Roosevelt era. Everyone will not agree with the editors' selection of letters and the specialist will still find it ncessary to use the Roosevelt manuscripts. Nevertheless, *The Letters of Theodore Roosevelt* is a magnificently documented record of Roosevelt's life and career.

A review of the impressive body of historical literature devoted to Roosevelt and his times prompts a few general observations. For one thing, despite the extensive work accomplished during the last fifteen years, there are striking gaps in the biographical and historical coverage of the Roosevelt era. In the case of Roosevelt himself, there is still no full-scale biography based on a familiarity with all of the Roosevelt manuscripts and other relevant sources. Nor have all phases and aspects of the Rough Rider's career received adequate treatment in monographic studies and articles. As for the Roosevelt period, one might suggest the need for biographies of such men as George B. Cortelyou, Philander C. Knox, and Nicholas Murray Butler, not to mention numerous congressional figures and state and local leaders. There is as yet no good treatment of important features of Roosevelt's presidency, including his conservative program, the Panic of 1907, the Country Life Commission, and his antitrust program. There are exciting possibilities for studies of reform on the local, state, and regional levels; for an investigation of American conservatism during this period; for the impact of technological advances and the organizational revolution upon American social and political life; and for new approaches to American foreign policy.

One of the notable characteristics of Rooseveltian historiography since World War II is the change in attitude of historians toward Roosevelt. . . . In many respects this is a desirable development. The older views of Roosevelt associated with Pringle's interpretation and the 1930's surely went too far in picturing the Rough Rider as a political opportunist, a man lacking in principle, and a pseudo-progressive who failed to comprehend the nature of the fundamental problems of his day, evaded issues, and in many ways actually hindered genuine reform. Yet it is a cause for wonder and perhaps concern that, with some important exceptions, most Roosevelt writers since 1945 have not paid proper tribute to the critical side of Clio's craft. Many of these authors have been amateurs, but the lack of critical judgment has also characterized the work on Roosevelt by some professional historians. One need not oppose a proper recognition of Roosevelt's constructive work and prophetic insights to feel that historians and biographers have swung too far away from the skeptical approach of the prewar scholars.

Roosevelt continues to be a controversial figure. His interpreters have not agreed, for example, whether to call him a conservative or a liberal. Although most recent writers have been inclined to accept John M. Blum's characterization of him as an enlightened conservative, two of the leading Roosevelt students—Howard K. Beale and George E. Mowry—have entered dissents and argue that Roosevelt falls within the American liberal tradition. It may well be, as Samuel P. Hays has suggested, that Roosevelt's biographers and historians of the progressive period have been overly concerned with the traditional theme of liberal-conservative conflict. Hays believes that Roosevelt is difficult to characterize because historians have asked the wrong question about him. They have insisted on interpreting the significance of his career as primarily in its role in the social conflict of the late nineteenth and

early twentieth centuries between the business community and the
farmer-labor groups. Actually, Hays declares, Roosevelt sought to avoid
social struggle, refused to become identified with either side, and is
chiefly significant for the attempt he made to supplant this conflict
with a "scientific" approach to social and economic questions. Whether
or not Theodore Roosevelt was a progressive, it is difficult to disagree
with Henry F. May's conclusion that he was "the greatest spokesman
of practical idealism in America" and "a compelling symbol of the
country's regeneration."[67]

There is much to be said for the historical writing on Theodore
Roosevelt during the years 1945-1960. Far better than was true before
1945, recent scholars, most notably John M. Blum, have illuminated
the roots of Roosevelt's career and the sources of his convictions. There
is now, after George E. Mowry's excellent work, a new understanding
of the impetus the twenty-sixth President gave to progressive politics in
the United States, and of his own evolving progressivism. His skill in
the game of politics, his contribution to the revivification of the presidency, his awareness of the implications of America's new industrial
society and his efforts to work out policies for adjusting to it, his understanding of the fact that the United States was, inexorably, a part of
the world and her foreign policy must be shaped with that in mind—all
of these things about Roosevelt have become much clearer during the
last decade and a half. Meanwhile, scores of historians not directly concerned with Roosevelt have helped to fill in the historical interstices of
his period. And, finally, recent Rooseveltian historiography has suggested, even if it has not adequately explained, those defects in Roosevelt's character and those limitations in his policies which prevented
him from being an even greater American.

NOTES

1. Some of this work was sponsored or inspired by the centennial commission
   and the Theodore Roosevelt Association.
2. At the time this essay was completed, in the fall of 1959, Howard K. Beale,
   William H. Harbaugh, and Carleton Putnam were engaged in writing
   biographies of Roosevelt. The untimely death of Professor Beale late in
   1959 interrupted a long and thorough preparation for the writing of what
   promised to be the definitive biography of Theodore Roosevelt. . . .
3. At least two of these articles proved too esoteric for the author to make
   anything of: Nora E. Cordingley's "Extreme Rarities in the Published
   Works of Theodore Roosevelt," *Papers of the Bibliographical Society of
   America*, XXXIX (1945), 20-50, and Dick Spencer, III, "Teddy Roosevelt's Saddle," *Western Horseman*, January, 1958.

4. *Theodore Roosevelt: A Biography*, New York, 1931. Even at the time of its publication, Pringle's biography had certain obvious limitations. The treatment of the post-presidential years, for which Pringle did not have access to the Roosevelt Papers, was thin and some aspects of the earlier period were inadequately developed. The book's great merit lay in its appraisal of Roosevelt's presidency and in its attempt to explain the man. Pringle could never quite bring himself to regard Roosevelt as anything more than a "violently adolescent person."

5. *Theodore Roosevelt: The Formative Years, 1858-1886*, New York, 1958.

6. Several recent articles have also illuminated some of the obscure features of Roosevelt's experiences in the Badlands. Significant for the light it throws on his experience in the open-range cattle industry is Ray H. Mattison, "Roosevelt and the Stockmen's Association," *North Dakota History*, XVII (April, 1950), 73-95, and *ibid.* (July, 1950), 177-209.

7. Robinson, "Theodore Roosevelt: Amateur Historian," *North Dakota History*, XXV (January, 1958), 5-13; Sellen, "Theodore Roosevelt: Historian with a Moral," *Mid-America*, XLI (October, 1959), 223-240.

8. "The Pendleton Act and the Civil Service," *American Historical Review* (AHR hereinafter), LXIV (January, 1959), 301-318. For an extremely critical estimate, see A. Bower Sageser, *The First Two Decades of the Pendleton Act: A Study of Civil Service Reform* (Lincoln, 1935), 141-142.

9. *Who Rush to Glory, the Cowboy Volunteers of 1898: Grigsby's Cowboys, Roosevelt's Rough Riders, Torrey's Rocky Mountain Riders*, Caldwell, Idaho, 1958.

10. Among general books on the period a good supplement to *The Era of Theodore Roosevelt* is Harold U. Faulkner, *The Decline of Laissez Faire, 1897-1917*, New York, 1951, which concentrates on economic institutions and their development. Matthew Josephson, *The President Makers: The Culture of Politics and Leadership in An Age of Enlightenment, 1896-1919*, New York, 1940, is also useful.

11. "Theodore Roosevelt: The Conservative as Progressive," *The American Political Tradition*, 203-233; in *The Age of Reform: From Bryan to F.D.R.*, New York, 1955, Hofstadter was much less critical of Roosevelt (pp. 13, 232-238, 243-251).

12. Karl Schriftgiesser, *The Gentleman from Massachusetts: Henry Cabot Lodge*, Boston, 1944, presents a sharply critical view of Lodge.

13. For two important articles on the Brownsville episode and its political repercussions, see James A. Tinsley, "Roosevelt, Foraker, and the Brownsville Affray," *Journal of Negro History*, XLI (January, 1956), 43-65, and Emma Lou Thornbrough, "The Brownsville Episode and the Negro Vote," *MVHR*, XLIV (December, 1957), 469-493.

14. *Tyrant from Illinois: Uncle Joe Cannon's Experiment with Personal Power*, New York, 1951.

15. Although less interpretative than Leopold's book, Philip C. Jessup, *Elihu Root*, 2 vols., New York, 1938, is more revealing in the light it throws on domestic issues and on Root's relations with Roosevelt.

16. The small volume by Dexter Perkins in the Library of American Biography —*Charles Evans Hughes and American Democratic Statesmanship*, Boston, 1956—makes out a case for Hughes as a farsighted middle-of-the-road

leader, but it does not achieve the interpretative excellence of Leopold's study of Root in the same series.

17. *William Allen White's America*, New York, 1947.
18. *The Republican Roosevelt*, 22, 37-72.
19. *Wilson: The New Freedom*, Princeton, 1956, 146-147.
20. Edward S. Corwin, *The President, Office and Powers, 1787-1957: History and Analysis of Practice and Opinion.* 4th rev. ed., New York, 1957, 120, 137, 152-153, 265-268; Wilfred E. Binkley, *President and Congress*, New York, 1947, 191-198.
21. *The Republican Roosevelt*, 73-105.
22. Nathaniel Wright Stephenson, *Nelson W. Aldrich: A Leader in American Politics*, New York, 1930, 280-318.
23. *The American Political Tradition*, 222.
24. *The Era of Theodore Roosevelt*, 132-134.
25. *The Federal Antitrust Policy*, 411-431, 528-554, 560-561, 592-593.
26. *The Republican Roosevelt*, 6, 116-121.
27. "Theodore Roosevelt and the Bureau of Corporations," *MVHR*, XLV (March, 1959), 571-590.
28. "The House of Morgan and the Executive, 1905-1913," *AHR*, LXV (October, 1959), 49-60; Wiebe, "Business Disunity and the Progressive Movement, 1901-1914," *MVHR*, XLIV (March, 1958), 664-685.
29. See also M. Nelson McGeary, *Gifford Pinchot: Forester-Politician*, Princeton, 1960.
30. "Ideas in Politics: The Conservation Policies of the Two Roosevelts," *Journal of the History of Ideas*, XIV (June, 1953), 421-438. For a general comparison of the two Roosevelts that is critical of T.R., see R. G. Tugwell, "The Two Roosevelts," *Western Political Quarterly*, V (March, 1952), 84-93.
31. "Theodore Roosevelt's Conservation Policies and Their Impact upon America and the American West," *North Dakota History*, XXV (October, 1958), 107-117.
32. A more traditional interpretation is found in J. Leonard Bates, "Fulfilling American Democracy: The Conservation Movement, 1907 to 1921," *MVHR*, XLIV (June, 1957), 29-57.
33. "The Public Life of 'T.R.,'" *Public Administration Review*, XIV (Autumn, 1954), 281.
34. Morison, *Letters*, VI, 1547-1557. This essay first appeared in *Explorations in Entrepreneurial History*, IV, Cambridge, 1951, 103-111.
35. *History of the United States Civil Service*, Evanston, Ill., 1958, 176-207, 540-541.
36. *Letters*, V, xviii.
37. Beale, *Roosevelt and World Power*, 1-13; Nelson Manfred Blake, "Ambassadors at the Court of Theodore Roosevelt," *MVHR*, XLII (September, 1955), 179-206.
38. *Roosevelt and World Power*, 14-80.
39. "Roosevelt, Brooks Adams, and Lea: The Warrior Critique of the Business Civilization," *American Quarterly*, VIII (Fall, 1956), 216-230.
40. *Ideals and Self-Interest in America's Foreign Relations: The Great Transformation of the Twentieth Century*, Chicago, 1953, especially 27-28.

41. *Roosevelt and World Power*, 81-171; Charles S. Campbell, Jr., *Anglo-American Understanding, 1898-1903*, Baltimore, 1957.
42. See David H. Burton, "Theodore Roosevelt and Egyptian Nationalism," *Mid-America*, XLI (April, 1959), 88-103.
43. *Roosevelt and World Power*, 151, 153, 159-171, 457-458. In a paper on "Theodore Roosevelt and the British Empire," Max Beloff challenges Beale on several of these points. See *The Great Powers: Essays in Twentieth Century Politics*, London, 1959, 215-232.
44. *The Republican Roosevelt*, 126.
45. Gordon Carpenter O'Gara, *Theodore Roosevelt and the Rise of the Modern Navy*, Princeton, 1943; Arthur M. Johnson, "Theodore Roosevelt and the Navy," *United States Naval Institute Proceedings*, LXXXIV (October, 1958), 76-82.
46. Howard C. Hill, *Roosevelt and the Caribbean*, Chicago, 1927.
47. "Theodore Roosevelt, the American Navy, and the Venezuelan Crisis of 1902-1903," *AHR*, LI (April, 1946), 452-471.
48. *Roosevelt and World Power*, 395-431.
49. *Roosevelt and World Power*, 172-252.
50. A colorful account of an earlier Rooseveltian gambit in Morocco is Barbara W. Tuchman, " 'Perdicaris alive or Raisuli dead,' " *American Heritage*, X (August, 1959), 18-21, 98-101.
51. *Roosevelt and World Power*, 335-447.
52. "The American Navy as a Factor in World Politics, 1903-1913," *AHR*, LXIII (July, 1958), 863-879.
53. *The Era of Theodore Roosevelt*, 144-146.
54. "Progressivism and Imperialism: The Progressive Movement and American Foreign Policy, 1898-1916," *MVHR*, XXXIX (December, 1952), 483-504.
55. See Foster Rhea Dulles, *America's Rise to World Power, 1898-1954*, New York, 1954, 83-85, and Arthur S. Link, *Woodrow Wilson and the Progressive Era, 1910-1917*, New York, 1954, 180-186.
56. Kenneth W. Hechler, *Insurgency: Personalities and Politics of the Taft Era*, New York, 1940.
57. *The Life and Times of William Howard Taft: A Biography*, 2 vols., New York, 1939.
58. For Roosevelt's abortive effort to win electoral support in the South, see George E. Mowry, "The South and the Progressive Lily White Party of 1912," *Journal of Southern History*, VI (May, 1940), 237-247; Arthur S. Link, "Theodore Roosevelt and the South in 1912," *North Carolina Historical Review*, XXIII (July, 1946), 313-324.
59. Goldman, *Rendezvous with Destiny: A History of Modern American Reform*, New York, 1952, 188-207; Mowry, *Theodore Roosevelt and the Progressive Movement*, 146. For a perceptive analysis of Croly's famous book, see Byron Dexter, "Herbert Croly and the Promise of American Life," *Political Science Quarterly*, LXX (June, 1955), 197-218.
60. "Theodore Roosevelt and Brooks Adams: Pseudo-Progressives," *Men of Good Hope: A Story of American Progressives*, New York, 1951, 245-280.
61. *The Decline of American Liberalism*, New York, 1955, 171-194.
62. *Theodore Roosevelt and the Progressive Movement*, 280.
63. *Midwestern Progressive Politics*, 181-296.

64. Henry L. Stimson and McGeorge Bundy, *On Active Service in Peace and War*, New York, 1947. See Elting E. Morison, *Turmoil and Tradition: A Study of the Life and Times of Henry L. Stimson*, Boston, 1960.

65. Helene Maxwell Hooker (ed.), *History of the Progressive Party, 1912-1916*, by Amos R. E. Pinchot, Washington Square, N.Y., 1958.

66. Osgood, *Ideals and Self-Interest*, 88-91, 96, 102-103, 112, 135-153, 202-203, 245, 249, 271-273.

67. *The End of American Innocence: A Study of the First Years of Our Own Time, 1912-1917*, New York, 1959, 17, 107.

RECENT STUDIES

G. Wallace Chessman, *Governor Theodore Roosevelt: The Albany Apprenticeship, 1898-1900* (Cambridge: Harvard University Press, 1965).

John Braeman, "Seven Progressives," *Business History Review*, XXXV (Winter 1961), 581-92.

J. Joseph Huthmacher, "Urban Liberalism and the Age of Reform," *Mississippi Valley Historical Review*, XLIX (September 1962), 231-41.

Roy Lubove, *The Progressives and the Slums: Tenement House Reform in New York City, 1890-1917* (Pittsburgh: University of Pittsburgh Press, 1962).

James H. Timberlake, *Prohibition and the Progressive Movement, 1900-1920* (Cambridge: Harvard University Press, 1963).

Gabriel Kolko, *Railroads and Regulation, 1877-1916* (Princeton: Princeton University Press, 1965).

Kenneth McNaught, "American Progressives and the Great Society," *Journal of American History*, LIII (Dec. 1966), 504-20.

William Henry Harbaugh, *The Life and Times of Theodore Roosevelt*. Rev. ed. (New York: Collier Books, 1963).

XVII

National Interest and American Intervention, 1917

DANIEL M. SMITH

In the two decades since 1945 several significant studies have been published on American involvement in World War I. These works have advanced beyond the revisionist debates of the 1930s to a more balanced consideration of economic, psychological, and political factors. Also they study the causes of hostilities within the context of developments in the principal European belligerent countries. An important aspect has been the investigation of considerations of the national interests in the decision of the United States to enter the great conflict in 1917. The purpose of this essay is to examine these recent studies, with an special concentration on the theme of the national interest and its influence on American foreign policy makers.

In 1950 Richard W. Leopold published a stimulating article on the historiography of the American involvement in World War I.[1] He pointed out that scholars had not achieved a consensus on the problem and that a general study had not been published since 1938. Until then the historical debate that began almost with President Woodrow Wilson's war message could be categorized into two schools. One was the "submarine" school, best represented by Charles Seymour, which contended that the nation had entered the war primarily because of violations of neutral rights and international law and morality by the ruth-

From *Journal of American History*, LII (June 1965), 5-24. Reprinted with abridged annotation by permission.

less German submarine campaigns. Another school comprised the unneutrality group, with Charles C. Tansill as the latest spokesman, that emphasized the patent American unneutrality in favor of the Allied Powers.[2]

During World War II, Leopold noted, a new interpretation emerged that the basic motive for intervention in 1917 had been to protect the nation's security against the menace of possible German victory and a disturbance to the balance of power, and to preserve Anglo-American domination of the North Atlantic. In 1943 Walter Lippmann maintained that the submarine issue had been merely the formal occasion for war, while "the substantial and compelling reason . . . was that the cutting of the Atlantic communications meant the starvation of Britain and, therefore, the conquest of Western Europe by imperial Germany."[3] While acknowledging that Wilson officially had justified hostilities on the basis of submarine violations of American neutral rights, Lippmann contended that this would not have sufficed as a rationalization if most Americans had not realized, intuitively or consciously, that a German victory would imperil American security. In another wartime book the newspaperman Forest Davis advanced a similar explanation.[4] As Leopold observed, however, scholars remained skeptical of these interpretations that seemed to project the fears of 1941 into the 1917 era, and at most viewed them as insights requiring extensive research and study. Diplomatic historian Thomas A. Bailey, for example, commented that there had been no rushing into war to redress the power balance and save the Allies in 1917, as seemingly they were winning; only after it was in the war did America realize the dire Allied plight.[5]

The diplomat and historian, George F. Kennan, published in 1950 a volume of essays on recent American diplomacy in which he recognized that there had been high American officials in World War I cognizant of the need to preserve a favorable balance of power against the disturbing possibility of a German triumph. Kennan concluded, however, that such a realistic approach had not been shared by the great majority of citizens; instead, the nation plunged into war on the narrow grounds of defending neutral rights and then turned the struggle into a moralistic-legalistic crusade to remold the world order.[6] The more detailed, study, *Ideals and Self-Interest in American Foreign Relations*, published in 1953 by Robert Endicott Osgood, in general substantiated that interpretation.[7]

Osgood acknowledged the plausibility of the Lippmann thesis and in his study, based on printed materials, he recorded similar views held

by a number of Americans in 1914-1917.[8] As a *New Republic* editor
Lippmann had written several articles contending that American security was involved in the continuation of the existing balance of power,
as had the American diplomat Lewis Einstein in 1913 and 1914. Other
prominent Americans publicly advanced arguments that vital national
interests would be threatened by a German victory. Theodore Roosevelt mixed with such views a type of belligerent moralism that advocated hostilities in 1916 in order to uphold national honor and save
civilization from the new barbarians.[9]

Several of Wilson's advisers, Osgood wrote, analyzed the meaning of
the war to America from a balance-of-power view. The list included
Colonel Edward M. House; Robert Lansing, Counselor and then Secretary of State in mid-1915; the ambassador to Britain, Walter Hines
Page; and James W. Gerard, ambassador to Germany. These men envisioned a German conquest in Europe as a threat to American security
in the western hemisphere and analyzed the war in terms of the national interest in Anglo-American naval predominance in the Atlantic.
Yet such considerations, though increasing their willingness to support
neutrality policies favorable to the Allies, did little more than quicken
events which led the United States into the war. That was because the
advisers did not really expect Germany to win and therefore their rec-
ommendations to the President did not advocate intervention on the
grounds of an endangered security. Events did not seem to pose the
clear alternative of fighting Germany or confronting a nearly certain
later attack by that power, so it was easier to follow the line of submarine violations of honor and morality and to enter the war on that
popular basis.[10] In any case, Osgood concluded, it would be difficult
to prove that these advisers had any appreciable influence on the idealistic Wilson, for the President was in nearly complete control of foreign
affairs and was unusually independent of counselors.[11]

Osgood thus seemed reluctant to accept the implications of his own
findings, that presidential assistants had taken a realistic approach toward the European war. Furthermore, Osgood tended to concentrate
on the question of immediate security. These advisers saw the national
interest in a broader sense as embracing not only security but economic
interests and a favorable postwar position. Osgood's own reasoning
strongly suggests that House, Lansing, and others might not have recommended to Wilson considerations of honor, morality, and ideology
as justifications for belligerency if they had not viewed Germany as a
menace to broadly defined national interests. Later studies also have
revealed that Wilson was capable of a more realistic approach to the

war and that he was far more receptive to advice and dependent on counselors than previously assumed.

Osgood and Kennan undoubtedly have been correct that there was little evidence of popular apprehensions of a direct German threat in 1914-1917. Much evidence exists, however, that an influential minority viewed imperial Germany askance. Since 1898 American military and naval leaders increasingly envisioned Germany as offering a threat to American security in the western hemisphere. . . . In testimony before the House Naval Affairs Committee in 1914, Admiral Charles Vreeland justified naval expansion as needed to cope with Germany and Japan.[12] A Navy General Board estimate of 1910, recirculated in February 1915, concluded that only Germany, driven by population pressures and rivalries in Latin America and the Far East, could undertake singlehandedly war on the United States and was therefore the most probable potential enemy. The War Department also had defensive war plans drawn with Germany as the theoretical opponent. A lengthy War College paper, 1909-1910, by Captain Paul B. Malone, described Germany as the most serious economic competitor of the United States, in contact and conflict with America both in Latin America and China. Although the author did not flatly predict hostilities he commented that, in the past, war had been the virtually inevitable result of such conflicting interests.

The historian Alfred Vagts has attempted to explain the fact that navalists in Germany and the United States, from the late 1890s to 1914, viewed each other as a probable opponent on the grounds that each needed an excuse to justify large naval expansion programs.[13] He concluded that actual commercial competition between the two states was small and that each power lacked coaling stations and naval cruising range for an attack on the other. Talk of rivalry in both countries primarily reflected the propaganda efforts of big navy advocates. No doubt a degree of validity must be accorded Vagts' interpretation, but the evidence indicates that the apprehensions were genuine and were shared by many leading civilians. On the other hand, apparently there were no official interchanges in the 1910-1917 period between the two defense departments and State in regard to American national interests in the outcome of a general Europe war. Officials in all three departments apparently shared similar appraisals of the situation, and perhaps informally discussed it, but no effort was made to plan and coordinate policy to cope with the danger.[14]

The decade before World War I witnessed a slowly maturing conviction among informed Americans that Germany was a potential enemy and Great Britain a natural ally of the United States. Editorials in the New York *Times* envisioned Germany as hostile, thus requiring an American navy of at least comparable size, and repeatedly expressed confidence in an enduring Anglo-American community of interest. From 1898 the American periodical press also occasionally printed articles expressing distrust of Germany's expansionist tendencies. . . . Articles from English journals on the theme of German naval threats to the United States were reprinted in American publications. Comparisons of the American and German navies were drawn and parity was strongly recommended. A 1909 article in *The Independent* by Amos S. Hershey, professor of Political Science and International Law at Indiana University, depicted Germany as menacing both world peace and American interests in the Far East and Latin America. To meet that danger Hershey advocated a defensive Anglo-American alliance. He wrote prophetically: "the people of the United States could hardly remain neutral in a war between Germany and Great Britain which might possibly end in German naval supremacy. . . . A blockade of the British Isles by German cruisers and submarine mines, or the loss involved in the danger to contraband trade would be severely felt in this country."[15]

Understandably, the general conflagration which began in 1914 increased the conviction of a number of Americans that Germany was in fact a menace and that American interests could best be secured through an Allied triumph. In the 1916 annual volume of the American Academy of Political and Social Science well-known scholars and pundits presented several papers that emphasized that United States security was involved in the preservation of British sea power. To help focus the widespread interest in 1916 in the preparedness question, the editors of *The Independent* printed an outline of pro and con arguments, prepared by Preston William Slosson, entitled: "Resolved: That the United States should enter the Great War on the side of the Entente Allies." The affirmative side asserted among other arguments that a Teutonic victory would endanger the future security of the American people.

These references to public opinion do not indicate that a majority of citizens in 1917 supported intervention on the grounds of vital national concerns. However, the evidence does reveal that for over a decade a number of educated and informed persons were exposed repeatedly to warnings that Germany challenged the security and the economic welfare of the nation. The existence of these attitudes probably made it inestimably easier to condemn Germany on moral and ideological grounds after 1914 and facilitated eventual war entry on the basis of a defense of neutral rights.

Edward H. Buehrig, as Osgood a political scientist, made an important contribution to the "national interest" school in a subtle study entitled *Woodrow Wilson and the Balance of Power*.[16] Based largely on printed sources and a few manuscript collections, the volume explained the American intervention in the war in 1917 as resulting from the German challenge to Britain's position as the dominant sea power. If Americans had been accustomed to viewing foreign relations in terms of practical power issues the ultimate war entry possibly might have been based squarely on considerations of security and economic connections. As it was, Germany and the United States were soon entrapped in complicated questions of neutral rights and drifted into war because of different attitudes toward British control of the seas. The United States accepted the British role as beneficial to its interests; Germany felt compelled to challenge it with every available weapon. Consequently, even though a bilateral German-American war was highly improbable, an Anglo-German struggle which threatened to alter drastically Britain's position posed serious questions to America's trans-Atlantic connections and created tensions culminating in war.[17]

The submarine issue was a point of departure for an evolving American policy toward the war. Without it, of course, German-American relations would have been smoother. American neutrality was in practice favorable to the Allies, but Germany decided to use fully the submarine weapon in 1917 because it alone seemed to promise victory. Probably no other course by the United States, short of cooperation with Germany to challenge the British blockade in order to renew substantial American trade with the Central Powers, could have averted unrestricted U-boat warfare. Germany naturally resented the American munitions trade with the Allies but, except as a moral justification, it played no important role in German decisions. What really was sought was to reverse British control of the seas and markets. To have satisfied the Berlin government by effecting a major change in neutral trade would have harmed important American economic interests and would have meant a disturbing replacement of British power with German.[18]

Wilson in 1915 adopted the policy of holding Germany fully accountable for losses of American lives and ships by submarine attacks around the British Isles in order to defend the traditional American concept of neutral rights and "freedom of the seas." He chose to uphold international law, and thereby to defend a conception of the national interest, for Americans had long believed that the nation's security was closely connected with the preservation of the world legal structure. In speeches advocating defensive military preparations in 1916, Wilson clearly developed that theme: the United States had to defend legal principles and support the international community. Germany's lawless methods of warfare affected American security, the President implied, dependent as it was on maintenance of national honor and rights and the preservation of the structure of international law and morality.[19]

When the *Sussex* controversy in 1916 made imminent the prospect of entering the war over the submarine issue, Wilson turned to diplomatic intervention in hopes of avoiding hostilities. The House-Grey Memorandum, negotiated earlier by Colonel House with British Foreign Secretary Sir Edward Grey, provided that at a time propitious for the Allies Wilson was to propose a conference to terminate the war; if Germany declined or rejected a "reasonable" peace, the United States "probably" would enter the struggle on the Allied side. The refusal of Britain and France to invoke the plan, which Wilson had hoped would end the war before America should be forced in, compelled the President to seek other means for mediation.[20]

In May 1916 President Wilson addressed the League to Enforce Peace and advocated a universal association of nations that would accord with America's national interest by preserving world free trade and access to markets ("freedom of the seas") and would protect all nations through territorial guarantees. This global organization, said Wilson, could prevent future wars by substitution of conferences for force, and the United States could facilitate the transition by making it known that its power would be thrown onto the international scales in behalf of peaceful means of adjustment. Buehrig analyzed the address as revealing not only Wilsonian idealism but also his interest in maintaining a stable world balance of power. Clear indications that the British government would not aid in promoting a negotiated peace caused Wilson in late 1916 to turn to other avenues for peace.[21] Wilson moved beyond considerations of a balance of power to a community of power when in December 1916 he requested statements of belligerent war aims and early in 1917 appealed for "peace without victory." The President thereby completed a shift from the initial policy of defense of maritime neutral rights to mediation efforts and a just peace on which to build a new community of nations. When Germany subsequently launched unrestricted submarine warfare and abolished not only all neutral rights but also made clear the determination to dictate a conqueror's peace, Wilson took the nation into war. He had no real choice, Buehrig concluded, either from the standpoint of maritime legal rights or of future world peace and stability.[22]

In Buehrig's view, Wilson in shaping American policy lacked neither astuteness nor an appreciation of balance-of-power concepts. The idealistic element in his policy finally received the major emphasis, over realistic considerations, because the President's temperament so required. The need to adjust policies to the requirements of an American public not trained to appraise world affairs in practical terms was also a probable factor.[23]

The Buehrig study has made at least two important contributions. In contrast to Osgood he defined the American concept of the national interests as comprising not only immediate but long-term security, economic interest in freedom of the seas, and the desire for world order and safety through preservation of an international regime of law. Buehrig also has carefully analyzed the elements of Wilsonian policies and thereby detected, along with idealistic elements, indications of a realistic consciousness of the balance of power and concrete American interests involved in the war.[24]

In an early volume in the New American Nation series, *Woodrow Wilson and the Progressive Era*, Arthur S. Link subscribed to the "submarine" school in interpreting the entry of the United States into World War I.[25] He recognized that House and Lansing had viewed realistically the European struggle, but he maintained that the two advisers "had only an incidental influence" on the President. In the ultimate analysis it was Wilson who, influenced by public opinion, had determined the American course. To mid-1916 Wilson had followed a neutrality course benevolent toward the Allies because of his moralistic appraisal of the war, German violations of international law, and the apparent greater readiness of Great Britain to make a reasonable peace. When he became convinced that the Allies in fact did not desire a fair settlement but sought, as Germany, a conclusive victory, he moved toward a genuinely impartial position. If Germany had not violated the *Sussex* pledge by unrestricted submarine warfare early in 1917, there would have been no war between the two countries. Considerations of finance, economic ties, ideology, or security were not involved in the presidential decision. War finally came because the submarine assaults on American lives and shipping left Wilson no feasible alternative.[26]

As he continued his multi-volume study of Wilson, Link seemed to modify his views of the causes of American intervention. In 1957 his Albert Shaw Lectures on Diplomatic History were published as *Wilson the Diplomatist.*[27] The interpretation generally followed that of the earlier volume: a genuinely neutral America adjusted to British measures, but the U-boat campaigns were opposed for legal and moral reasons.[28] By early 1917, however, after failure of efforts to halt the war short of total victory for either side and thereby to preclude American involvement and establish the basis for a stable postwar world, Wilson apparently decided to effect a diplomatic withdrawal. Continuation of the war, he foresaw, would cause further deterioration of neutral rights. The President seemingly was willing to retreat on strict accountability and perhaps would have accepted a new U-boat campaign against armed merchantmen or all belligerent vessels except passenger liners. The German decision to attack all shipping, neutrals included, forced Wilson to break diplomatic relations.[29]

Link thus considered the submarine issue to have been the immediate cause of hostilities, but he concluded that the agonized Wilson reluctantly accepted full hostilities in 1917, as opposed to armed neutrality or a limited naval war, only because of other factors. One of the most important of these, though supported by little direct evidence, was Wilson's "apparent fear that the threat of a German victory imperiled the balance of power and all his hopes for the future reconstruction of the world community."[30] Wilson seems not to have apprehended a serious German danger to the United States nor did he seek to preserve the old balance of power. Yet the Allies appeared to be on the verge of losing the war and that would mean German conquest and the end of Wilsonian hopes for a new world order. He remarked to Colonel House that Germany seemed to be a madman who required restraining —and he apparently thought that only through American armed intervention could a Central Power victory be avoided and American prestige among the Allies enhanced so that a just peace could be achieved. The President undoubtedly also was affected in the war decision by an aroused American public and by the reiterated counsel of his close advisers.[31]

In the preface of the third volume in the Link biography, *Wilson: The Struggle for Neutrality*,[32] the author expressed the hope that in this study of the first fifteen months of neutrality he had purged his mind of preconceived interpretations and could let the men and events speak for themselves. He would appear to have succeeded admirably in this exhaustively researched volume. Realistic appraisals of the war by House and Lansing had an important effect on Wilson's mind. House, as Lansing, was favorably inclined toward the Allies and feared the militaristic and expansionist tendencies of Germany. As a result, the Colonel advised Wilson to acquiesce in Allied war measures and to oppose those of Germany. Yet House did not want a sweeping Allied victory, only one sufficient to check Teutonic ambitions and still leave Germany powerful enough to block Russian imperialism.[33] President Wilson, after initial sympathy for the Allies, achieved a large degree of impartiality on the question of war guilt. As the war continued, Wilson was increasingly persuaded that the greatest opportunity for a just and lasting peace would come from an indecisive conclusion of the war. As he told a newspaperman, however, while "I cannot regard this [a sweeping Allied triumph] as the ideal solution, at the same time I cannot see now that it would hurt greatly the interests of the United States if either France or Russia or Great Britain should finally dictate the [peace] settlement."[34] Wilson thus indicated, by the close of 1914, a realistic view that the preferable result of the war would be a deadlock which would preserve the existing power structure and facilitate a just peace, but that American interests would not be adversely affected by a decisive Allied triumph. As far as American policy was concerned, however, both moral and practical considerations required maintenance of neutrality.

The fourth volume in Link's series, *Wilson: Confusions and Crises*, necessarily lacks the unifying themes present in the earlier volumes. Among other topics, domestic and foreign, it narrates America's relations with the belligerents through the *Sussex* crisis. The section on the House-Grey Memorandum, based on heretofore unexploited sources including French materials which the author could not directly quote or cite, is particularly valuable. Link depicts the divergence of motives behind the scheme: House, believing that intervention in the war was almost inevitable, was prepared to go far in assuring the Allies of American backing, whereas the President apparently contemplated only peaceful mediation. He believes Grey did not take his "understanding" with the Colonel very seriously, as he doubted the possibility of American intervention, and was aware that the Allied governments were adverse to a negotiated peace and sought a decisive triumph over the Central Powers.[35]

These interpretations reveal that Link is constantly reevaluating the materials as he continues his biography of Wilson. Wilson is now seen as not only the moralist and idealist, but also as aware of balance-of-power arguments, responsive to the advice of realistically-inclined counselors, and to a considerable degree framing the American course on the basis of practical considerations of the national interest. Completion of the biography and the concluding judgment of Link can only be awaited with great interest.

The centennial of Wilson's birth in 1956 occasioned a number of commemorative essays and books. Osgood and Buehrig restated their evaluations of Wilsonian neutrality;[36] Charles Seymour reiterated the submarine thesis,[37] and William L. Langer concurred.[38] Two short and unfootnoted but well-researched biographies were published by John A. Garraty and John M. Blum. Garraty described American neutrality as decidedly pro-Ally, because of Wilson's biases, but the President's views and emotions precluded him from either accepting a German victory or intervening in the war. Wilson eventually lost much of his faith in the Allies and attempted to mediate in late 1916, but was forced into the conflict by the submarine issue.[39] Blum believed that Wilson lacked a realistic appraisal of the war's meaning for American interests and that the country entered the conflict only because of unrestricted U-boat warfare.[40] A generally persuasive and solidly-based psychological study, *Wilson and Colonel House*, was published by Alexander L. and Juliette L. George, that pointed out that while Wilson undoubtedly was familiar with the balance-of-power concept, his psychological aversion to frank considerations of power and self-interest made it difficult for him to frame policies clearly based on such grounds.[41] Two years after the centennial, Arthur Walworth published a two-volume biography of Wilson that, while well-researched, hewed to the Seymour interpretation and made little new contribution to understanding the causes of involvement.[42]

The first extensive exploration of the formulation of German policy toward the United States appeared in Karl E. Birnbaum's *Peace Moves and U-Boat Warfare*.[43] His book, concentrating on the *Sussex* crisis and after, does not focus on American policy making but it does have important implications for American diplomatic historians. He found that not only did German policy oscillate between peace moves and intensification of submarine warfare, but that a third course was also pursued of trying to manage issues with the United States so that even full underseas warfare would not lead to hostilities.

In the *Lusitania* and *Arabic* crises full compliance with Wilson's demands was precluded by official skepticism of the President's impartiality and by German public opinion, which was embittered at the American war trade and hopeful of the power of submarine warfare.[44] As 1915 ended, Chancellor Theobald von Bethmann-Hollweg came under great military and public pressures for full underseas warfare.

Bethmann, deeply fearful of the dire consequences of hostilities with America, was hampered in resistance by the weakness of Kaiser Wilhelm II and by his own lack of energy and will.[45] The *Sussex* pledge, therefore, was only a temporary triumph over the U-boat enthusiasts.[46]

The Chancellor initiated a peace move in late 1916 in the hope of either forcing a general peace conference or of creating an atmosphere of reasonableness that would prevent hostilities with the United States when more drastic submarine warfare began. The overture failed and when Wilson asked on December 18 for a statement of belligerent war goals, the Berlin government gave it an evasive, negative reply because both the military and civilian officials distrusted the President's motives and suspected collusion with the Allies. Unfortunately, in Birnbaum's view, the quick reply to Wilson's overture doomed the policy of trying to create a rapport sufficiently strong to avoid hostilities over a new underseas campaign. This was the final failure of Germany's American policy.[47] At the decisive conferences at Pless on January 9, 1917, the military and naval leaders unanimously insisted on unrestricted underseas warfare as the best hope for victory, whereas the Chanlellor merely recited his past objections before deferring to the military view. Birnbaum believes that even at this date a more vigorous objection by Bethmann, analyzing the probable results of unrestricted warfare and the effects of an American entry, might have swayed the Kaiser and have postponed the decision at least long enough to try to cushion its impact on Wilson.

German vacillation between peace efforts and the submarine panacea finally broke down in a decision for the latter because of doubts over Wilson's neutrality and goals, and the growing primacy of the short-sighted military voice within the German government. Although the author disavowed in the preface any intention of answering the question of whether German-American hostilities were avoidable, in his conclusions he attributed considerable weight to German skepticism of Wilson engendered by the pro-Ally nature of American neutrality and the different attitudes of Washington toward Allied as opposed to German infractions of international law.[48] In that sense Birnbaum suggests a partial answer to the question if a more impartial American neutrality would not have strengthened the hands of German moderates in resisting pressures for unrestricted U-boat warfare.

The latest one-volume study of the neutrality period is Ernest R. May's *World War and American Isolation*.[49] Utilizing multi-archival research in Europe and the United States, May has examined the evolution of policies from the British and German perspectives as well as the American. He pointed out that in both Great Britain and Germany questions of policy toward neutral America were intertwined in domestic politics. In comparison with the Birnbaum study, May developed in greater detail the story of domestic German political pressures on foreign policy.

British Foreign Secretary Grey successfully shaped the English course in the first six months of the war by proceeding cautiously and considerately in applying maritime measures so that Anglo-American friendship would be preserved and strengthened. Even when Grey had lost the ability to control events because of mounting public pressures in England for a more drastic blockade, he had helped establish a moral basis of friendship capable of surviving a more trying period.[50]

In Germany Bethmann "fought long and hard against reckless opponents, only in the end to fail."[51] May thus gave a more favorable appraisal than did Birnbaum and Link, who portrayed the Chancellor in less flattering terms as failing to make a serious effort either to comprehend Wilson's peace objectives in 1916, to develop a reasonable German peace move, or to subject Admiralty claims for the submarine to close scrutiny and refutation.[52] May depicted the harried Chancellor as convinced that the submarine could not defeat England and that war with the United States would be disastrous for Germany. He could not force abandonment of the U-boat weapon, however, because of the fanatical attitude of the navy admirals, the submarine enthusiasm of the German public, and the pressures of the conservative political parties and press. Caught in a dilemma, complicated by reliance on the vacillating Kaiser, the Chancellor temporized and delayed, making enough concessions to the United States to avoid war in the *Lusitania, Arabic,* and *Sussex* crises and yet endeavoring to permit the navalists use of the submarine just short of that point. At best, therefore, Bethmann could only postpone a decision for war with America.[53] By the fall of 1916 the new supreme army command of Field Marshal Paul von Hindenburg and General Erich F. W. Ludendorff had come to dominate Wilhelm, and Bethmann could no longer control the Reichstag. Hence when the army leaders joined the admirals in insistence on unrestricted underseas warfare as the one reliable hope for victory, the Chancellor was compelled to acquiesce. Any other course would have meant his immediate political demise.[54]

In concurrence with Buehrig and other writers, May described American neutrality as generally benevolent toward the Allies. Yet permission of belligerent loans and the arms trade were not deliberately unneutral but merely reflected America's view of international law and its trade interests. Legal and moral factors also were involved in the different American policies toward the British blockade and the submarine zone, but "the central difference in the two cases was a matter of national interest and not of either law or morality." Wilson could be satisfied that he had complied with the requirements of international law and morality and had served the national interests.[55]

May agreed with previous writers that House and Lansing viewed a triumphant Germany as a future threat to American security. House repeatedly warned Wilson in late 1914 and after that Germany would never forgive America for its pro-Ally attitude and if it won the war would hold the United States accountable and might challenge the Monroe Doctrine in South America. The Colonel did not desire a smashing Allied victory, however, for that would leave Russia free to expand.[56] As for Wilson, May stated that "He does appear, however, to have shared the view of Lansing and House that Germany was an enemy. He hoped that she might be too exhausted by the European war to turn immediately upon the United States, but he was not sanguine."[57] Wilson in late 1915 admitted to House that a victorious Germany might well take the western hemisphere as its next target, and his speeches for military preparedness in 1916 revealed a deep apprehension for the future security of the Americas. The President differed from these advisers primarily in his emotional attachment to peace. Consequently, although Wilson accepted the judgments of House and Lansing for a firm policy toward Germany, caution and pacifist inclinations caused him to follow a course of patience and delay, hoping for a "miraculous deliverance" from his dilemma. Additionally, Wilson's caution reflected his consciousness of the divided state of American public opinion, military weaknesses of the United States, and the hope of playing a role of peacemaker in the European war.[58]

Ruthless use of the submarine was the only kind of German action that could have engendered German-American hostility, as Germany lacked other means to affect directly American interests. Wilson could have accepted German underseas warfare in early 1915, just as he had British actions, but he instead chose to condemn it. Other alternatives were rejected apparently because the U-boat campaign violated international law and morality, and because it endangered important American economic interests in the war trade with the Allies.[59] After the *Lusitania* crisis American national prestige was fully committed to the strict accountability policy and diplomatic flexibility was greatly circumscribed. If only moral principles and economic interests had been involved, some possibility of compromise would have remained; what prevented Wilson and his advisers from considering such, however, was apprehension that prestige would be lost by a retreat or a compromise. House conceived of prestige in reference to the diplomatic influence of the American government. Lansing saw it also as closely connected to domestic public confidence in the administration, while Wilson thought of prestige as affecting national pride and involving moral purposes.[60] To the American leaders the concept of national interests thus included not only security but legal, economic, and prestige factors as well.

The unrestricted submarine campaign in 1917 caused Wilson to respond with a decision for war apparently in large part because of his concern for the nation's prestige and moral influence as a great power. Acceptance of the new U-boat war would have been a surrender in the light of past American declarations and seemed impossible to Wilson, not so much now on the grounds of immediate economic or security considerations, but because of the damaging blow American prestige and influence would have suffered. Each succeeding crisis with Germany had seen American prestige more deeply committed; and the submarine issue had become a symbol of Wilson's dedication to uphold international law and the rights of humanity.[61] Full belligerency, rather than armed neutrality, was chosen because of the President's growing distrust of Germany, his desire to unite the American people, and his belief that the nation's role in the war would be limited militarily. May concluded that Wilson had held balance-of-power ideas but that they were subsidiary to his idealistic desire for a just and lasting world peace. Although Wilson has been criticized by some historians for not taking the nation into war to protect its security, May believes it difficult to find fault with Wilson's statesmanship. Not perceiving an immediate danger to America from a German victory in the war, Wilson realistically coped with the only endangered national interests, economic and prestige, and idealistically sought to promote world peace through a new international order.[62]

The problem of the role of the national interests in the neutrality period receives at least a partial answer in the studies by Buehrig, Link, and May. The evidence that Wilson was more realistic than portrayed in the past, and that he was aware of and held to some degree balance of power and national interest concepts, is too extensive to be dismissed as a mere selection of isolated statements from the larger corpus of Wilsonian materials. Contrary to previous interpretations, the works of Buehrig, Link's recent volumes, and May reveal that Wilson often was influenced by his realistic counselors, and that he shared much of their evaluations of the meaning of the European war. Secretary Lansing had the clearest conviction that American security would be menaced by a German victory and might require intervention to avert that possibility. House and Wilson generally believed that the outcome of the war most favorable to American and world interests would be a peace short of total victory for either side. May pointed out that both the Colonel and Wilson foresaw that a victorious Germany would probably threaten the position of the United States in South America. Yet as Buehrig, Link, and May agree, balance of power and other considerations caused Wilson and House in 1915 and 1916 to try to mediate the war and thus to avoid American involvement and to preserve the existing equipoise. When the President finally did take the nation into the conflict in 1917, it was not because he feared an immediate German menace to American security.

How, then, were concepts of the national interest involved in the American war entry? Buehrig saw the answer in a Wilsonian balance of power concern being transformed into reliance on a community of power concept to protect American interests and preserve a just future peace. The unrestricted submarine announcement of 1917 precipitated war because of past policy stands, and because Germany was seen as a menace to the new world order envisioned by Wilson. Link portrayed Wilson as driven into acceptance of full hostilities over the submarine issue because of fear of a German victory endangering the balance of power and precluding realization of his idealistic and moralistic hopes for world reconstruction. May placed the emphasis on the prestige factor, which in a sense combined both national interests (security, economic, and diplomatic influence) and moralistic ideas of national honor and duty.

The more simplistic explanations of American involvement in the European war, current in the 1920s and 1930s, whether on the narrow grounds of a defense of legal neutral rights or of unneutral economic ties with the Allies, no longer suffice. The Buehrig, Link, and May studies make that conclusion abundantly clear. Just as clearly, the hypothesis that the United States went to war in 1917 to protect its security against an immediate German threat lacks persuasiveness. It appears that a complex of factors, including legitimate economic interests, some fear of a German victory and long-term threat to the western hemisphere, moral and legal reactions to the submarine, a very sensitive awareness of the involvement of American prestige, and especially Wilson's determination to promote a just and enduring postwar system, underlay American policies and the war entry in 1917. Defined as meaning more than immediate security needs, the authors reviewed agreed that the concept of involved American national interests had a large place in Wilsonian policies and war entry. At least as important, however, if not more so, were moral and idealistic factors.

NOTES

1. Richard W. Leopold, "The Problem of American Intervention, 1917: An Historical Retrospect," *World Politics*, II (1950), 405-25. Richard L. Watson, Jr., in "Woodrow Wilson and His Interpreters, 1947-1957," *Mississippi Valley Historical Review*, XLIV (Sept. 1957), 207-36, examines recent literature.
2. Charles Callan Tansill, *America Goes to War* (Boston, 1938); Charles Seymour, *American Diplomacy During the World War* (Baltimore, 1934) and *American Neutrality, 1914-1917* (New Haven, 1935). Harley Notter, *The Origins of the Foreign Policy of Woodrow Wilson* (Baltimore, 1937). Also see Barbara W. Tuchman, *The Zimmermann Telegram* (New York, 1958).
3. Walter Lippmann, *U. S. Foreign Policy: Shield of the Republic* (Boston, 1943), 33-37.
4. Forest Davis, *The Atlantic System: The Story of Anglo-American Control of the Seas* (New York, 1941), 240-46.
5. See Thomas A. Bailey, *Woodrow Wilson and the Lost Peace* (New York, 1944), 12-13, and *A Diplomatic History of the American People* (6th ed., New York, 1958), 594n.
6. George F. Kennan, *American Diplomacy, 1900-1950* (Chicago, 1951), 64-66, 70-74.
7. Robert Endicott Osgood, *Ideals and Self-Interest in American Foreign Relations* (Chicago, 1953). Approximately one third of this study is devoted to the Wilson period.
8. *Ibid.*, 115-34.
9. Osgood, *Ideals and Self-Interest*, 135-53. Also see Howard K. Beale, *Theodore Roosevelt and the Rise of America to World Power* (Baltimore, 1956).
10. Osgood, *Ideals and Self-Interest*, 154-71.
11. *Ibid.*, 172-75.
12. Harold and Margaret Sprout, *The Rise of American Naval Power, 1776-1918* (Princeton, 1942), 311-13.
13. Alfred Vagts, "Hopes and Fears of an American-German War, 1870-1915," *Political Science Quarterly*, LIV (Dec. 1939), 514-35, and LV (March 1940), 53-76. Fritz T. Epstein, "Germany and the United States: Basic Patterns of Conflict and Understanding," G. L. Anderson, ed., *Issues and Conflict* (Lawrence, Kansas, 1959), 284-314, concludes that German-American friction prior to 1914 reflected psychological differences rather than actual clashes of interest.
14. Fred Greene, "The Military View of American National Policy, 1904-1940," *American Historical Review*, LXVI (1961), 354-77; J. A. S. Gren-

ville, in "Diplomacy and War Plans in the United States, 1890-1917," *Transactions of the Royal Society*, 5th Series, XI (London, 1961), 1-21. Also see Ernest R. May, "The Development of Political-Military Consultation in the United States," *Political Science Quarterly*, LXX (June 1955), 161-80.

15. Amos S. Hershey, "Germany—The Main Obstacle to the World's Peace," *Independent*, LXVI (May 20, 1909), 1071-76. For a similar analysis by a well-known English journalist, writing for *Fortnightly Review*, see Sydney Brooks, "Great Britain, Germany and the United States," reprinted in *Living Age*, CCLXII (July 31, 1909), 259-66.

16. *Woodrow Wilson and the Balance of Power* (Bloomington, 1955).

17. *Ibid.*, viii-ix, 16-17.

18. *Ibid.*, 79-84, 90, 102-05.

19. *Ibid.*, 106-08, 117-21, 149.

20. *Ibid.*, 172-73, 228, 230-35.

21. *Ibid.*, 238-46.

22. *Ibid.*, 260-66.

23. *Ibid.*, 274-75.

24. Buehrig noted that Robert Lansing held balance-of-power concepts about the war, but he asked to what degree this was submerged by an ideological view of the struggle. *Ibid.*, 135-37. That question was answered, at least partially, by Daniel M. Smith's *Robert Lansing and American Neutrality, 1914-1917* (Berkeley, 1958).

25. Arthur S. Link, *Woodrow Wilson and the Progressive Era 1910-1917* (New York, 1954).

26. *Ibid.*, 279-81.

27. *Wilson the Diplomatist: A Look at His Major Foreign Policies* (Baltimore, 1957).

28. *Ibid.*, 32-35, 40-54.

29. *Ibid.*, 70, 80-82.

30. *Ibid.*, 88.

31. *Ibid.*, 89-90.

32. Arthur S. Link, *Wilson: The Struggle for Neutrality, 1914-1915* (Princeton, 1960).

33. *Ibid.*, 45-48.

34. *Ibid.*, 49-56.

35. Arthur S. Link, *Wilson: Confusions and Crises, 1915-1916* (Princeton, 1964), 111-13, 130, 138-40.

36. Edward H. Buehrig, "Idealism and Statecraft," *Confluence*, V (Oct. 1956), 252-63; Robert E. Osgood, "Woodrow Wilson, Collective Security, and the Lessons of History," *ibid.*, (Jan. 1957), 341-54.

37. Charles Seymour, "Woodrow Wilson in Perspective," *Foreign Affairs*, XXXIV (Jan. 1956), 175-86.

38. William L. Langer, "From Isolation to Mediation," Arthur P. Dudden, ed., *Woodrow Wilson and the World of Today* (Philadelphia, 1957), 22-46.

39. John A. Garraty, *Woodrow Wilson: A Great Life in Brief* (New York, 1956), 96-97, 99, 112, 116-17.

40. John Morton Blum, *Woodrow Wilson and the Politics of Morality* (Boston, 1956), 96, 100, 129.

41. Alexander L. and Juliette L. George, *Woodrow Wilson and Colonel House: A Personality Study* (New York, 1956), 159-60.
42. Arthur Walworth, *Woodrow Wilson* (2 vols., New York, 1958).
43. Karl E. Birnbaum, *Peace Moves and U-Boat Warfare* (Stockholm, 1958).
44. *Ibid.*, 28-32, 36-37, 39.
45. *Ibid.*, 51-53, 58-61.
46. *Ibid.*, 78-79, 86.
47. *Ibid.*, 270.
48. *Ibid.*, 31, 336-38.
49. *The World War and American Isolation, 1914-1917* (Cambridge, 1959).
50. *Ibid.*, 18-19, 21-25, 32-33.
51. *Ibid.*, [vii].
52. Link, *Wilson the Diplomatist*, 79-80.
53. May, *World War and American Isolation*, 197-205.
54. *Ibid.*, 288-89, 413-15.
55. *Ibid.*, 45-53.
56. May, *World War and American Isolation*, 77-78.
57. *Ibid.*, 169.
58. *Ibid.*, 167-78.
59. *Ibid.*, 137-42.
60. *Ibid.*, 156-59.
61. *Ibid.*, 426-27.
62. *Ibid.*, 433-37. Richard W. Leopold, *The Growth of American Foreign Policy* (New York, 1962), has usefully synthesized recent scholarship on the neutrality era. See also Leopold's "The Emergence of America as a World Power: Some Second Thoughts," John Braeman and others, eds., *Change and Continuity in Twentieth-Century America* (Columbus, 1964).

RECENT STUDIES

Seward W. Livermore, *Politics Is Adjourned: Woodrow Wilson and the War Congress, 1916-1918* (Middletown: Wesleyan University Press, 1966).

Sigmund Freud and William C. Bullitt, *Thomas Woodrow Wilson, Twenty-eighth President of the United States: A Psychological Study* (Boston: Houghton Mifflin, 1967).

XVIII

The Twenties: A New Historiographical Frontier

BURL NOGGLE

"The Twenties" is an entrenched concept in American historiography, but the precise beginning and end of this period, and evaluations of it, vary from writer to writer. Rare, however, is the historian who fails to conceptualize American history, about 1919-1929, as a distinct unit, sharply set off from (and usually in unfavorable contrast to) the history which preceded and followed it.[1] Even before the end of the 1920s historians had begun to write the history of the decade and to offer characterizations that have lingered ever since. In 1926, John Spencer Bassett wrote of the nation's recent "weariness of reforms and reformers." "Exhausted by the emotions produced by the World War," the country craved rest.[2] No concept has endured longer or been more pervasive among historians than the one which views the 1920s as a time of reaction and isolationism induced by the emotional experience of World War I. Historians alone did not originate this concept; old prewar progressives themselves gave expression to it in the mid-1920s. In fact, historians have more than once reaffirmed the analyses and findings made during the 1920s by journalists and other students of the contemporary scene. And it was a "retrospective journalist," Frederick Lewis Allen, who in *Only Yesterday* first blocked out the 1919-1929 decennary as a unit of study, portraying it as a unique segment of American life with a style all its own.[3]

From *Journal of American History*, LIII (September 1966), 299-314. Reprinted with abridged annotation by permission.

Almost as soon as the 1920s crashed on Black Thursday, Allen began writing *Only Yesterday*. Ever since its appearance in 1931, when it was a Book-of-the-Month Club choice, his book has been a popular success and has been frequently reprinted. Whatever its appeal or its qualities, Allen's account, published within a year of the end of the decade, has deeply shaped historical recall of the 1920s.

Roger Butterfield suggested in 1957 that none of the studies published since the appearance of *Only Yesterday* had "essentially changed the over-all picture that Allen gave us."[4] But for historians who read through the work done on the 1920s over the past fifteen years, it soon becomes evident that Allen has not been revised so much as he has been transcended. Historians are not finding Allen wrong (indeed, he was remarkably accurate and discerning). Rather, they are moving beyond him, asking questions that he never considered, finding issues and themes and patterns that he never explored or formulated.

Most of this new activity has developed since 1950. Little of it appeared in the two decades following the publication of Allen's book. Instead, the approach to the 1920s throughout the 1930s continued for the most part to be one of breezy surveys in the Allen tradition; at best, there was an occasional detailed analysis of some isolated subject that Allen had outlined in cursory fashion.[5] In the Great Depression—and probably because of it—the economy of the 1920s did capture much attention, but mostly from economists, not from historians.[6]

A study of dissertation listings indicates that graduate students in the 1930s produced more studies of the 1920s than did their mentors. Whether the latter would themselves have published more if not burdened with direction of these studies is a conjecture. Less conjectural is the predominance of economic topics relevant to the 1920s shown in the list of dissertations accepted in American colleges and universities during the 1930s. Perhaps economists, if not economic historians, tend to concentrate on the present or the recent past; it seems significant that the economy of the 1920s was the subject of proportionately more dissertations in the decade that followed than in the two succeeding ones and that subjects such as diplomacy or social history, which were minimized or neglected in the 1930s, became more and more popular in the 1940s and 1950s. Apart from those specializing in economics, it is clear that few graduate students (or for that matter, established historians) in the 1930s had discovered, or at least chosen, the 1920s as a field for research.

The domestic political history of the 1920s was neglected in the 1930s and continued to be neglected until the late 1950s.[7] As Henry

F. May has suggested, by the early 1930s historians were already making the 1920s "an unfortunate interregnum" between progressivism and the New Deal.[8] Malcolm Cowley once recalled that the 1920s had been "an easy, quick, adventurous age, good to be young in; and yet on coming out of it one felt a sense of relief, as on coming out of a room too full of talk and people into the sunlight of the winter streets."[9] Evidently political historians in the 1930s felt this same sense of relief (or perhaps release). The emphasis of political historiography in the 1930s was upon progressives, Populists, Jacksonians—men whose programs had, it seemed, been preludes to the New Deal.

In the 1930s the domestic New Deal may have drawn historians away from domestic politics of the 1920s, but foreign policy issues of the 1930s, if they did anything, stirred up an increased interest in the diplomatic history of the preceding decade. Selig Adler has written of an "isolationist tornado" in the 1930s, during which Americans, including historians, sought safety from world conflict through economic nationalism, neutrality legislation, and other maneuvers usually labeled "isolationist."[10] Although a few revisionist histories of World War I (histories criticizing America's entry into the war) began to appear in the 1920s, not until the mid-1930s did many professional historians begin to produce such studies. Whether this was due to the presumed "tornado" of the 1930s is a moot question; but however they felt about World War I in that third decade American historians simply did not then form a monolithic bloc of isolationists in their approach to foreign policy of the 1920s. Most of them did declare the existence of isolationism during this decade, but as often as not they deplored it and saw it as contributing to those war tensions of the 1930s they were trying to avoid.[11]

From any perspective and to whatever purpose, neither diplomatic studies nor what may be loosely termed "social history" of the 1920s flourished in the 1930s. Although Allen, and before him Preston Slosson, had shown the potential in such a subject, only tentative appraisals appeared before 1960.[12] In the wartime and postwar 1940s, historians brought little if any more depth or perception to the 1920s than they had brought during the depression years. Much of the historical work on the 1920s done during and immediately after World War II might have been produced in the 1930s for all it differed from the studies coming out of that depressed decade. The same superficial appraisals, the same pale imitations of *Only Yesterday*, continued to find a market.[13]

Yet, just as they had in the 1930s, more cautious scholars in the

1940s added a few notable volumes to the small shelf of worthwhile studies made of the 1920s. Economists and economic historians continued to build up imposing mounds of evidence, although they often touched upon the 1920s only indirectly or as part of a larger theme. The National Bureau of Economic Research, as it had during the 1930s, published several formidable volumes. From such statistics and other quantitative material, George Soule was able to publish an economic history that showed, as he saw it, "the main currents of the economy of the 'New Era' more fully than at any previous period of American history."[14]

Among doctoral studies on the 1920s, economic themes outnumbered all the rest during the 1940s, although diplomatic history made a striking gain. Here, no doubt, World War II had effect, arousing interest in international relations and suggesting questions to pursue in the diplomacy of the 1920s. Not until the 1950s would the political historiography of the 1920s begin to thrive but already in the 1940s some excellent dissertations had been written.[15] The intellectual history of the 1920s also began to attract more attention.[16]

Meantime, at the annual meetings of the American Historical Association and the Mississippi Valley Historical Association, the professionals made several tentative approaches to the 1920s and presented a few pioneering essays. Infrequent though they were, these papers about the decade indicated a slowly growing interest that would soon quicken at mid-century.

A few excellent essays on domestic and international politics appeared during the 1940s, as did biographies of politicians prominent in the 1920s. By the mid-1940s old political figures out of the decade were publishing their recollections, some of which were to be useful to the historian. At the very end of the 1940s Samuel Eldersveld wrote an important analysis of the presidential elections of the period from 1920 through 1948, demonstrating the shift taking place in metropolitan areas away from the Republican and into the Democratic party after 1920. Within a few years, this shift of urban areas into the Democratic column was given a brilliant analysis by Samuel Lubell, and by the late 1950s historians began to find more and more of value in a study of the urban-rural tensions and conflicts of the 1920s that lay behind, or resulted from, this shift in the voting pattern.[17]

Intellectual historians of the 1920s did such significant work in the 1940s as appraisals of Freud's impact upon American thought and literature, the life of the expatriate intellectual in Paris, the critique of American society by the American intellectual, the Sacco-Vanzetti case, and the response of American liberals to the Russian revolution.[18] These and other themes of the decade's intellectual history have still not received an authoritative synthesis, but studies done in the 1940s clarified some of the categories which that synthesis must include.

By 1950, then, some largely discursive pioneer probing had been made into the period of the 1920s. But among historians the image of the decade had changed little from the brilliant panorama offered by Allen in 1931. After mid-century a massive analysis got under way, one which continues to take on greater depth, complexity, and intensity. By comparison with what has appeared since the early 1950s, studies on the 1920s before then were negligible in scope, meager in detail, and artless in analysis.

Doctoral studies of the 1920s showed a spectacular increase after 1950 with diplomatic history in clear ascendancy, followed closely by studies of domestic politics. At the annual meetings of the two major historical associations between 1950 and 1963, historians presented some thirty-five papers dealing with the 1920s. Many of these papers, or versions of them, were subsequently published. And since 1950 books and articles have all but deluged the student of the 1920s who hopes to stay afloat in this new wave of scholarship.

The Ku Klux Klan, that perennial symbol of the decade's intolerance, is now receiving close and documented study. Historians are not merely describing the Klan's bigotry and violence but are studying its place in local and national politics; they are correlating it with prohibitionist, rural, and fundamentalist elements in the population and are viewing it as a symptom of the social tensions that permeated the 1920s.[19] This emphasis on tensions in the decade—brought on by a conflict between an older, rural, Anglo-Protestant America and a newer, urban, and cosmopolitan one—may well be the most revealing and comprehensive concept that historians of the 1920s have recently brought to the period. The Klan, the Scopes trial at Dayton, Tennessee, the National Origins Act of 1924, and the defeat of Alfred E. Smith in 1928 are among the subjects that have gained new meaning when viewed within a rural-urban context.[20]

Other standard themes of the 1920s have also either assumed new dimensions or have been viewed from new perspectives. Ideas and outlooks on and by the business community have begun to be charted, and as a result some old views about the businessman of the 1920s have been weakened and others strengthened; in both cases the intellectual history of the decade has been expanded. Morrell Heald, studying business leadership in the 1920s, has found that even the most ardent defenders of profit-making stressed that "management must think more than ever before of the social implications of its policies." "Far from being completely immobilized in adulation of the status quo," in the 1920s business leaders recognized that drastic changes were occurring in American society and they had begun to explore "new solutions for new, or recently recognized problems." On the other hand, Otis Pease, who analyzed "the extent to which concepts of public responsibility existed in the national advertising industry [between 1920 and 1940]," writes with irony and an implied distaste for the work of the advertising men who talked the cant of "responsibility" while perfecting new ways of appealing to the American consumer.[21]

James W. Prothro's *Dollar Decade* is also unflattering to the businessmen of the 1920s. Prothro found six recurrent themes expressed by business leaders in the decade: "elitism, materialism, economic pre-eminence, stability, antipopulism, individualism." Men with such an outlook had so much concern for "the immediate and narrow interests of the economic elite" that they were "blind to the most urgent needs of the public at large." But John P. Gleason, while not denying the self-interest that business displayed in the 1920s, has found that debate and publicity on the McNary-Haugen plan among businessmen was "decidedly beneficial" to the American farmer. Although most businessmen opposed the plan, they did begin to realize that something must be done about the farm problem. The McNary-Haugen campaign "helped to prepare the business community for [New Deal farm] legislation of the 1930s."[22]

The literary life of the 1920s continues to provoke quality work. The American intellectual's encounter with Paris in the 1920s shows no signs of losing favor as a subject for study. This is evidenced by the continued appearance of memoirs by those who lived in Paris at the time and by the steady publication of works by intellectual historians. In a recent memoir Matthew Josephson, one of the more famous expatriates of the 1920s, has challenged the "fallacy of the Lost Generation." Granted that the impact of World War I upon Americans was immense, Josephson nevertheless thinks it "nonsense to hold that a generation of American youth were 'lost' or driven to despair as a result of that brief war."[23] But however they may be described, a swarm of Americans moved into or through Paris in the 1920s, there to write, to live, and often to find a "second country." Appraising the lure of Paris, Warren Susman has demonstrated why it was Paris, and Paris in the 1920s, that attracted the American expatriate.[24] And Louise Cowan's study of the Fugitive poets at Nashville in the 1920s has served as a reminder that literary colonies of the period were not limited to those of New York and Paris.[25]

Politics in the 1920s, all but neglected before mid-century, has now become a favored field for research. The three presidential elections of the decade have been faithfully measured and weighed, enough to confirm some old notions and to refute others. The legend of the "smoke-filled room" of 1920 has been scotched. The nomination of Harding was not due to a conspiracy by vested oil interests; neither was it due to Senate "bosses" dictating to the convention. A small group of Republican senators did dominate the convention, and they did work for Harding's nomination, but only as a solution to a deadlock and in a more or less open convention. Furthermore, Harding's election did not register a repudiation of the League of Nations.[26]

The intricacies of the 1924 election have begun to be spelled out. Historians have indicated the varied factions in the Democratic party at the time, the significance of the rural-urban split in the party, and the suicidal brawl that the Democrats made of their Madison Square Garden nominating convention.[27] The Teapot Dome affair (traditionally seen chiefly as a morality play) has been viewed from several angles, including an appraisal of its effect in the 1924 campaign. The scandal rose out of the struggle over the conservation of natural resources, but once it had developed as a great party liability in the winter of 1923-1924, it provoked some high political drama and some ingenious maneuverings within and between the two major parties.[28] For the 1928 campaign, the strife over liquor and religion has retained its significance, but recent studies have deepened the analysis, revealed certain ambiguities in the subject, and—perhaps most importantly—examined the election on the state and local level.[29]

These studies of politics have begun to provide, for the first time, depth and complexity for the political history of the 1920s. The structure of the two major parties, the motives that drove certain men into, and others out of, politics, and the relationships of religion to nativism and of prohibition to elections have been appraised. As a result, politics in the 1920s stands revealed as infinitely more varied and subtle than is suggested by the conventional references to "normalcy," the Ohio Gang, and "Keep Cool with Coolidge."[30]

An intriguing but most debatable theme that political historians lately have enlarged upon is that of reform in the 1920s. Studies have begun to reveal survivals of Progressivism and preludes to the New Deal in the decade. Clarke Chambers has found a strong social welfare movement at work in the period, one concerned with child labor, slums,

poor housing, and other problems that Progressives before the 1920s
and New Dealers afterward also sought to alleviate. Preston J. Hubbard
has studied the Muscle Shoals controversy of the 1920s and has demonstrated the essential role that Progressives in the decade played in
laying the basis for the New Deal's TVA system. Donald C. Swain has
shown that much of the conservation program of the New Deal originated in the 1920s. Howard Zinn has shown that Fiorello La Guardia,
as congressman from New York in the 1920s, provided a "vital link
between the Progressive and New Deal eras. La Guardia entered Congress as the Bull Moose uproar was quieting and left with the arrival of
the New Deal; in the intervening years no man in national office waged
the Progressive battle so long." La Guardia in the 1920s was "the herald
of a new kind of progressivism, borne into American politics by the
urban-immigrant sections of the population." Not only his background
and his ideology, but also his specific legislative program, writes Zinn,
were "an astonishingly accurate preview of the New Deal."[31]

Recognition of a surviving Progressivism in the 1920s leading into
the New Deal may be an example of the "consensus and continuity"
themes that John Higham and others have detected and criticized in
recent historiography. On the other hand, historians do continue to
find "conflict" and reaction in the 1920s, as they delineate the decade's
radicalism, nativism, and provincialism. Yet even here, a certain "continuity" is demonstrated by the fact that much of this behavior was
hardly unique with the 1920s. Higham's comprehensive study shows
that "the nativisms that came to the fore in 1920 essentially continued
prewar trends. They consisted largely of hatreds . . . that had gathered strength in the late Progressive era." But the postwar depression,
a fresh wave of immigration, the prohibition experiment, and its ag-
gravation of lawlessness did give a special flavor to the wave of nativism
that arose in the 1920s. In addition, Paul Murphy has shown how the
intolerance traditionally associated with the 1920s was, indeed, virulent,
pervasive, and distinct in form during the decade.[32]

Finally, in diplomatic history one truth has become clearer than ever
before: the "retreat to isolationism," however it be defined, is a dubious
characterization of American foreign policy in the 1920s. Herbert
Hoover, Charles Evans Hughes, Frank B. Kellogg, Henry L. Stimson,
William E. Borah, Dwight W. Morrow, and others who formulated or
criticized policy in the decade were men deeply concerned with the
place of the United States in world affairs. Diplomacy in the decade
may not always have served the best interests of the United States;
nevertheless, policymakers and their critics often showed considerable

energy and ambition in their response to the sweep of change that the Russian Revolution, the rise of anticolonialism in Latin America and the Far East, and the economic and psychological scars of World War I were generating in the world of the 1920s.

Hoover tried to develop American trade and investments abroad in a brand of neo-mercantilism designed to preserve (and profit) a democratic America and to forestall the growth of left-wing unrest in those areas reached by American goods and services. Hughes, for essentially the same reasons, worked to preserve an Open Door not only in the Far East but elsewhere as well. Stimson tried to control a revolutionary element in Nicaragua, but farther north, Morrow, recognizing the Mexican Revolution as a genuine social upheaval, tried with considerable success to come to terms with it while at the same time furthering American interests in Mexico. Kellogg, accepting the legitimacy of the Chinese Revolution, sought to work with the new revolutionary elements in that country. Borah, censurer of many official policies in the decade, called persistently for recognition of the Soviet Union.[33]

It is clear that, as Arthur S. Link has put it, "the period of the 1920s is the exciting new frontier of American historical research."[34] Some areas of the decade's history are still neglected. But others have recently been scrutinized with care, and the findings bear only partial resemblance to numerous portraits offered over the past thirty-five years.[35] The historian of the 1920s is now studying the decade from the sources, pushing aside the veil of memory and oral tradition that obscured the view for so long. The 1920s as a working concept of time and place is durably established, but the revision and amplification of the decade's history presently underway is a signal accomplishment of American historiography for this generation.

NOTES

1. Henry F. May, "Shifting Perspectives on the 1920's," *Mississippi Valley Historical Review*, XLIII (Dec. 1956), 405-27, is a carefully structured survey of "the shifting and changing picture of the decade" held from the mid-1920s to the mid-1950s. Although May analyzes the work of historians, he also appraises views of the period held by businessmen, sociologists, economists, literary critics, and other students.

2. John Spencer Bassett, *Expansion and Reform, 1889-1926* (New York, 1926), v, 293, 303-09. Two of the earliest attempts at a comprehensive view of the 1920s were James C. Malin, *The United States After the World War* (New York, 1930), and Preston William Slosson, *The Great Crusade and After, 1914-1928* (New York, 1930). Few historians of the 1920s have presented so much basic data in one volume as Malin did;

nevertheless, most of his book is limited to economic history and does not include many of the subjects now standard for the period. In contrast, Slosson touched on almost all the things Malin had omitted and severely minimized those Malin had stressed.

3. *Only Yesterday: An Informal History of the Nineteen-Twenties* (New York, 1931).

4. *Only Yesterday*, ix.

5. Examples of the former include Mark Sullivan, *Our Times: The United States 1900-1925* (6 vols., New York, 1926-1935), Vol. VI, *The Twenties*; Samuel Hopkins Adams, *Incredible Era: The Life and Times of Warren Gamaliel Harding* (New York, 1939); and Laurence Greene, *The Era of Wonderful Nonsense* (Indianapolis, 1939). Among more specialized studies, Malcolm Cowley's *Exile's Return: A Narrative of Ideas* (New York, 1956) and Caroline F. Ware's *Greenwich Village, 1920-1930* (Boston, 1935) were notable titles of the 1930s.

6. Significant titles include Adolph A. Berle, Jr. and Gardiner G. Means, *The Modern Corporation and Private Property* (New York, 1932); Harry W. Laidler, *Concentration of Control in American Industry* (New York, 1931).

7. One gauge of political histories during the 1930s was Gaston B. Means' ludicrous tale, *The Strange Death of President Harding* . . . as told to May Dixon Thacker (New York, 1930).

8. May, "Shifting Perspectives," 412.

9. Cowley, *Exile's Return*, 309.

10. Selig Adler, *The Isolationist Impulse: Its Twentieth-century Reaction* (New York, 1961), 219 ff.

11. Frank H. Simonds, *American Foreign Policy in the Post-War Years* (Baltimore, 1935); Denna Frank Fleming's *The United States and World Organization, 1920-33* (New York, 1938). Perhaps the clearest example of an "isolationist" approach to the 1920s was a 1935 article in which Samuel Flagg Bemis declared that America's expansion after 1898 and its entry into World War I in 1917 had been "deplorable blunders." Fortunately, beginning in the 1920s a turn "back to the policies of the Fathers" had been made. "A Clarifying Foreign Policy," *Yale Review*, XXV (Dec. 1935), 221-40.

12. Charles Merz, *The Dry Decade* (Garden City, 1931), was one of the earliest attempts to study the "noble experiment" during its trial decade. . . . Emerson Loucks' *The Ku Klux Klan in Pennsylvania* (Harrisburg, 1936) was not only one of the first historical studies of the Klan but remains one of the few studies yet made for a single state.

13. Karl Schriftgiesser. *This Was Normalcy: An Account of Party Politics During Twelve Republican Years, 1920-1932* (Boston, 1948), is a breezy tale done from a self-proclaimed bias; Henry Morton Robinson's *Fantastic Interim: A Hindsight History of American Manners, Morals, and Mistakes between Versailles and Pearl Harbor* (New York, 1943) is as wordy and free-wheeling as the title suggests.

14. George Soule, *Prosperity Decade: From War to Depression, 1917-1929* (New York, 1947).

15. Kenneth C. Mac Kay's study was published as *The Progressive Movement in 1924* (New York, 1947).

16. John W. Higham's study later appeared as *Strangers in the Land: Patterns of American Nativism, 1860-1925* (New Brunswick, 1955).

17. Samuel Eldersveld, "Influence of Metropolitan Party Pluralities in Presidential Elections since 1920," *American Political Science Review*; XLIII (Dec. 1949), 1189-1206; Samuel Lubell, *The Future of American Politics* (New York, 1952).

18. Frederick J. Hoffman, "Philistine and Puritan in the 1920's," *American Quarterly*, I (Fall 1949), 242-63; Celia Burns Stendler, "New Ideas for Old: How Freudism Was Received in the United States from 1900 to 1925," *Journal of Educational Psychology*, XXXVIII (April 1947), 193-206; R. P. Blackmur, "The American Literary Expatriate," in David F. Bowers, ed., *Foreign Influences in American Life: Essays and Critical Bibliographies* (Princeton, 1944), 126-45; Samuel Putnam, *Paris Was Our Mistress: Memoirs of a Lost & Found Generation* (New York, 1947); G. Louis Joughin and Edmund M. Morgan, *The Legacy of Sacco and Vanzetti* (New York, 1948); Dimitri S. von Mohrenschildt, "The Early American Observers of the Russian Revolution, 1917-1921," *Russian Review*, III (Autumn 1943), 64-74; Mohrenschildt, "The American Intelligentsia and Russia of the N. E. P.," *ibid.*, VI (Spring 1947), 59-66.

19. Charles C. Alexander, *The Ku Klux Klan in the Southwest* (Lexington, 1965); David Chalmers, "The Ku Klux Klan in the Sunshine State: The 1920's," *Florida Historical Quarterly*, XLII (Jan. 1964), 209-15; Robert Moats Miller, "A Note on the Relationship between the Protestant Churches and the Revived Ku Klux Klan," *Journal of Southern History*, XXII (Aug. 1956), 355-68.

20. Kenneth K. Bailey, *Southern White Protestantism in the Twentieth Century* (New York, 1964); Paul A. Carter, *The Decline and Revival of the Social Gospel: Social and Political Liberalism in American Protestant Churches, 1920-1940* (Ithaca, 1956); Norman F. Furniss, *The Fundamentalist Controversy, 1918-1931* (New Haven, 1954); Frederick J. Hoffman, "The Temper of the Twenties," *Minnesota Review*, I (Fall 1960), 36-45; William G. McLoughlin, *Billy Sunday Was His Real Name* (Chicago, 1955); Donald B. Meyer, *The Protestant Search for Political Realism, 1919-1941* (Berkeley, 1960); Robert Moats Miller, *American Protestantism and Social Issues, 1919-1939* (Chapel Hill, 1958).

21. Morrell Heald, "Business Thought in the Twenties: Social Responsibility," *American Quarterly*, XIII (Summer 1961), 126-39; Otis Pease, *The Responsibilities of American Advertising: Private Control and Public Influence, 1920-1940* (New Haven, 1958).

22. James W. Prothro, *Dollar Decade: Business Ideas in the 1920's* (Baton Rouge, 1954); John Philip Gleason, "The Attitude of the Business Community toward Agriculture during the McNary-Haugen Period," *Agricultural History*, XXXII (April 1958), 127-38.

23. Matthew Josephson, *Life Among the Surrealists* . . . (New York, 1962), 6-7.

24. Warren I. Susman, "A Second Country: The Expatriate Image," University of Texas *Studies in Literature and Language*, III (Summer 1961), 171-83; Arthur Mizener, "The 'Lost Generation'," Robert E. Spiller, ed., *A Time of Harvest: American Literature, 1910-1960* (New York, 1962), 73-82.

25. Louise Cowan, *The Fugitive Group: A Literary History* (Baton Rouge, 1959). See also Allen Tate, "Random Thoughts on the 1920's," *Minnesota Review*, I (Fall 1960), 46-56; Frederick J. Hoffman, *The Twenties: American Writing in the Postwar Decade* (Baton Rouge, 1955); Daniel Aaron, *Writers on the Left: Episodes in American Literary Communism* (New York, 1961), is a richly detailed study of the idea of Communism among American writers from about 1912 to about 1940. See esp. 86-190 on the Twenties.

26. Wesley M. Bagby, *The Road to Normalcy* (Baltimore, 1962); and Herbert F. Margulies, "The Election of 1920 in Wisconsin: The Return to 'Normalcy' Reappraised," *Wisconsin Magazine of History*, XXXVIII (Autumn 1957), 15-22.

27. Lee N. Allen, "The Underwood Presidential Movement of 1924," *Alabama Review*, XV (April 1962), 83-99; Allen, "The McAdoo Campaign for the Presidential Nomination in 1924," *Journal of Southern History*, XXIX (May 1963), 211-28; David B. Burner, "The Democratic Party in the Election of 1924," *Mid-America*, XLVI (April 1964), 92-113.

28. J. Leonard Bates, "The Teapot Dome Scandal and the Election of 1924," *American Historical Review*, LX (Jan. 1955), 303-22; Burl Noggle, *Teapot Dome: Oil and Politics in the 1920's* (Baton Rouge, 1962); David H. Stratton, "Behind Teapot Dome: Some Personal Insights," *Business History Review*, XXXI (Winter 1957), 385-402; Robert A. Waller, "Business and the Initiation of the Teapot Dome Investigation," *Business History Review*, XXXVI (Autumn 1962), 334-53.

29. Paul A. Carter, "The Campaign of 1928 Re-Examined: A Study in Political Folklore," *Wisconsin Magazine of History*, XLVI (Summer 1963), 263-72; Gilbert C. Fite, "The Agricultural Issue in the Presidential Campaign of 1928," *Mississippi Valley Historical Review*, XXXVII (March 1951), 653-72; Edmund A. Moore, *A Catholic Runs for President: The Campaign of 1928* (New York, 1956); Ruth C. Silva, *Rum, Religion, and Votes: 1928 Re-examined* (University Park, Pa., 1962).

30. Besides the titles in the above footnote, see Frank Freidel, *Franklin D. Roosevelt: The Ordeal* (Boston, 1954); Freidel, *Franklin D. Roosevelt: The Triumph* (Boston, 1956); J. Joseph Huthmacher, *Massachusetts People and Politics, 1919-1933* (Cambridge, 1959); William T. Hutchinson, *Lowden of Illinois: The Life of Frank O. Lowden* (2 vols., Chicago, 1957); Arthur M. Schlesinger, Jr., *The Crisis of the Old Order, 1919-1933* (Boston, 1957).

31. Clarke A. Chambers, *Seedtime of Reform: American Social Service and Social Action, 1918-1933* (Minneapolis, 1963); Preston J. Hubbard, *Origins of the TVA: The Muscle Shoals Controversy, 1920-1932* (Nashville, 1961); Donald C. Swain, *Federal Conservation Policy, 1921-1933* (Berkeley, 1963); Howard Zinn, *La Guardia in Congress* (Ithaca, 1958). See also Arthur S. Link, "What Happened to the Progressive Movement in the 1920's?" *American Historical Review*, LXIV (July 1959), 833-51; Robert L. Morlan, *Political Prairie Fire: The Nonpartisan League, 1915-1922* (Minneapolis, 1955); George B. Tindall, "Business Progressivism: Southern Politics in the Twenties," *South Atlantic Quarterly*, LXII (Winter 1963), 92-106; James H. Shideler, "The La Follette Progressive Party

Campaign of 1924," *Wisconsin Magazine of History*, XXXIII (June 1950), 444-57.

32. Higham, *Strangers in the Land*; Paul L. Murphy, "Sources and Nature of Intolerance in the 1920s," *Journal of American History*, LI (June 1964), 60-76. See also Stanley Coben, "A Study in Nativism: The American Red Scare of 1919-20," *Political Science Quarterly*, LXXIX (March 1964), 52-75; Theodore Draper, *The Roots of American Communism* (New York, 1957); Paul L. Murphy, "Normalcy, Intolerance, and the American Character," *Virginia Quarterly Review*, XL (Summer 1964), 445-59; Robert K. Murray, *Red Scare: A Study in National Hysteria, 1919-1920* (Minneapolis, 1955); Kenneth B. O'Brien, Jr., "Education, Americanization and the Supreme Court: The 1920's," *American Quarterly*, XIII (Summer 1961), 161-71; William Preston, Jr., *Aliens and Dissenters: Federal Suppression of Radicals, 1903-1933* (Cambridge, Mass., 1963).

33. Joseph Brandes, *Herbert Hoover and Economic Diplomacy, Department of Commerce Policy, 1921-28* (Pittsburgh, 1962); Robert P. Browder, *The Origins of Soviet-American Diplomacy* (Princeton, 1953); L. Ethan Ellis, *Frank B. Kellogg and American Foreign Relations, 1925-29* (New Brunswick, 1961); Herbert Feis, *The Diplomacy of the Dollar: First Era, 1919-1932* (Baltimore, 1950); Robert H. Ferrell, *Peace in Their Time: The Origins of the Kellogg-Briand Pact* (New Haven, 1952); Raymond G. O'Connor, "The 'Yardstick' and Naval Disarmament in the 1920's," *Mississippi Valley Historical Review*, XLV (Dec. 1958), 441-62; Stanley Robert Ross, "Dwight Morrow and the Mexican Revolution," *Hispanic American Historical Review*, XXXVIII (Nov. 1958), 506-28; John Chalmers Vinson, *William E. Borah and the Outlawry of War* (Athens, 1957); Vinson, *The Parchment Peace: The United States Senate and the Washington Conference, 1921-1922* (Athens, 1955); Gerald E. Wheeler, *Prelude to Pearl Harbor: The United States Navy and the Far East, 1921-1931* (Columbia, Mo., 1963); William Appleman Williams, "China and Japan: A Challenge and a Choice of the Nineteen Twenties," *Pacific Historical Review*, XXVI (Aug. 1957), 259-80; Williams, "Latin America: Laboratory of Latin American Foreign Policy in the Nineteen-twenties," *Inter-American Economic Affairs*, XI (Autumn 1957), 3-31; Williams, "The Legend of Isolationism in the 1920's," *Science and Society*, XVIII (Winter 1954), 1-20.

34. Link, "What Happened to the Progressive Movement in the 1920's?" 834.

35. William E. Leuchtenburg's *The Perils of Prosperity, 1914-32* (Chicago, 1958) is a lucid history that incorporates many of the recent findings and interpretations by historians of the Twenties. John D. Hicks, *Republican Ascendancy, 1921-1933* (New York, 1960), presents a more traditional view of the decade.

RECENT STUDIES

Andrew Sinclair, *The Available Man: The Life Behind the Masks of Warren Gamaliel Harding* (New York: Macmillan, 1965).

Paul W. Glad, "Progressives and the Business Culture of the 1920s," *Journal of American History*, LIII (June 1966), 75-89.

Lawrence W. Levine, *Defender of the Faith: William Jennings Bryan: The Last Decade* (New York: Oxford University Press, 1965).

Alpheus Thomas Mason, *William Howard Taft: Chief Justice* (New York: Simon and Schuster, 1965).

Albert U. Romasco, *The Poverty of Abundance: Hoover, the Nation, the Depression* (New York: Oxford University Press, 1965).

XIX

The New Deal, 1929-1941

FRANK FREIDEL

Although the Great Depression and the New Deal are only two or three decades in the past, already they are one of the most written-about phases of American history. The problem facing the teacher is not one of finding materials, but of sorting and sifting from the enormous bulk those writings which will be of use to him in preparing for his classes, and those most readable for various levels of students. There are books that are lively and polemical, others dull and still polemical, and happily a surprising number that are both highly readable and of substantial historic merit. Some of the best historical writing of recent years, firmly anchored on the vast collections of documentary materials already available, has analyzed the depression and the Roosevelt administration.

As a starting-point beyond secondary school textbooks, teachers may wish to examine some of the more recent one-volume and two-volume college level surveys of United States history and especially some of the histories of the United States in the twentieth century. These, although they vary in their individual interpretations, are for the most part full, clear, and factually reliable in their treatment of the years 1929-1941.

From *Interpreting and Teaching American History*, William H. Cartwright and Richard L. Watson, Jr. (eds.), Washington, D.C., National Council for the Social Studies, pp. 264-81. Reprinted with abridged annotation by permission.

They also contain useful selective bibliographies. The most original and extensive of the textbook accounts of the United States during this century is Arthur S. Link, *American Epoch*[1] which contains a full account of the Hoover and Roosevelt administrations. An excellent popular interpretation of American presidents from 1929 is Walter Johnson, *1600 Pennsylvania Avenue*.[2]

THE DEPRESSION AND HOOVER

Several surveys cover the depression through the Hoover and Roosevelt administrations. Broadus Mitchell, *Depression Decade, From New Era through New Deal, 1929-1941*[3] is a rather lengthy economic history of moderate reading difficulty, critical both of Hoover's outmoded, overoptimistic ways of dealing with the depression, and of Roosevelt's nimble shifts among varying economic policies. It deals topically with relief, banking and currency, agriculture, and the like. The author's viewpoint emerges in the final chapter of the analysis "War to the Rescue." Dixon Wecter, *The Age of the Great Depression, 1929-1941* is a vivid, readable social history.[4] Wecter was more favorable toward New Deal economics than Mitchell, but demonstrated no grasp of it. He gathered a wide variety of materials on American life during the depression, occasionally expressing value judgments (as on Hollywood) which were not well considered. The merit of his account is the remarkable way in which he succeeded in conveying to his readers how people felt during the depression, and how they reacted to the New Deal.

The first volume of Arthur M. Schlesinger, Jr., *The Age of Roosevelt*, subtitled *The Crisis of the Old Order, 1919-1933*, covers from the end of the first World War to the inauguration of Roosevelt.[5] In its trenchant, lively analysis of the failures of the economic and political system leading to the depression, and the inability of the Hoover administration to find workable solutions, it takes the view that the "old order" was bankrupt. This volume makes the case against the business leadership, the Republican party, and the Hoover administration during these years. The case for them appears with even greater vehemence, but in a ponderous and uninviting style in the third volume of *The Memoirs of Herbert Hoover*, subtitled *The Great Depression, 1929-1941*.[6] Hoover deplored the stock speculation and weaknesses of the banking system which should have been remedied at home, but viewed the depression as basically an economic hurricane which struck from abroad. His own policies, which in retrospect he affirmed as sound, he believed were bringing a measure of recovery by the summer of 1932 which would have continued except for the accession of Roosevelt and the Democratic party. The last section of his book is a detailed critique of the New Deal along these lines:

> The effort to crossbreed some features of Fascism and Socialism with our American free system speedily developed in the Roosevelt administration. The result was that America failed to keep pace with world recovery. Instead we continued with subnormal levels of lessened productivity, high unemployment, and costly relief measures until our man power and industries were absorbed by the war eight years later, in 1941. [p. vii]

An economist, John K. Galbraith, in *The Great Crash, 1929* explained in a brief, interesting, and easily understandable fashion why the 1929 stock market crash occurred, and why it triggered such an acute depression and deflation.[7] Galbraith saw the causes of the depression as complex and difficult to avoid. Two lively, clear accounts of the twenties, culminating with a summary of the causes of the depression and Hoover's efforts to counter it, are William E. Leuchtenburg, *The Perils of Prosperity, 1914-32* and John D. Hicks, *Republican Ascendancy, 1921-1933*.[8]

The most detailed, relatively dispassionate account of the Hoover administration is Harris G. Warren, *Herbert Hoover and the Great Depression*.[9] Unfortunately, Warren did not have access to the Hoover papers, which are closed to most scholars, and did not use other manuscript collections. Consequently Warren's study contributes little new; his viewpoint is favorable. A forthcoming study of the Hoover administration by Edgar E. Robinson is based on extensive research in manuscript and archival material. Biographies of Hoover published in the forties were popular in content, and in tone have ranged from friendly to adulatory. They add little beyond his own *Memoirs*,[10] although a brilliant critical sketch of Hoover is to be found in Richard Hofstadter, *The American Political Tradition*.[11]

PRESIDENT ROOSEVELT AND THE NEW DEAL: GENERAL TREATMENTS

Among the many books on President Roosevelt and the New Deal, there are a number of distinct merit, based on sound research and written in an effective fashion. These present a variety of challenging viewpoints. The first of these studies was Basil Rauch, *The History of the New Deal, 1933-1938*,[12] written before the manuscript collections were open and based upon *The Public Papers and Addresses of Frank-*

lin D. Roosevelt and the *New York Times*, with a dash of the reminiscences of Raymond Moley and James A. Farley. It set much of the factual pattern for later treatments of the New Deal, and propounds the important thesis that about 1935 there had been a shift from a first rather conservative New Deal emphasizing recovery, to a second, more radical New Deal concentrating upon reform.

A simple, brief survey is Denis W. Brogan, *The Era of Franklin D. Roosevelt*, which has the merit of being written from an English point of view.[13] A more technical English survey of lasting validity is *The New Deal, An Analysis and Appraisal*.[14] A lucid American survey, excellent for high school students, is Dexter Perkins, *The New Age of Franklin Roosevelt, 1932-45*.[15] Perkins, rather deemphasizing the role of Roosevelt, examines broadly the forces creating the New Deal. He feels that the New Deal failed because it fell between two stools:

> It could not restore business confidence; neither could it launch an audacious and far-reaching program of deficit finance. As a consequence, it failed to solve the fundamental problem of unemployment until the conditions of war placed that problem in a new setting. [p. 80]

Out of a careful gathering of evidence, Edgar E. Robinson in *The Roosevelt Leadership, 1933-1945*,[16] came to conservative constitutionalist conclusions. This is the most formidable of the evaluations from the right, far more serious in tone and reasoning than John T. Flynn's bombastic *The Roosevelt Myth*.[17] According to Robinson the effect of the New Deal on American thinking was this:

> Within the nation in these twelve years was developed a distrust of the basic democracy of the republic, as well as a social philosophy that included within its practices, if not in its pronouncements, many of the primary leveling objectives of communism. A whole generation of youth was cut off from the past by an eloquent proponent of revolutionary change. [p. 376]

And the effect upon the role of government in the economy:

> Roosevelt's leadership resulted in fundamental changes in the government itself: in tremendous concentration of power in the Executive; in building up a vast system of bureaucratic control of private business; and by adding direct economic support of the citizen to the careful adjustment of conflicting economic interests in a free enterprise system. [p. 400]

Richard Hofstadter in the concluding chapter of *The Age of Reform*[18] (a book primarily concerned with Populism and Progressivism) also sees in the New Deal a sharp break from earlier traditions, but views with favor what Robinson sees with horror: "If the state was believed neutral in the days of T. R. because its leaders claimed to sanction favors for no one, the state under F.D.R. could be called neutral only in the sense that it offered favors to everyone." In other words, the second Roosevelt moved in a time of depression from a concept of equal rights for all to one of equal privileges for all. Hofstadter points to the large role of organized labor, the interest in regulating rather than smashing big business, and the political alliances with urban bosses, all in contrast to the policies of Progressives.[19]

As its title would imply, Mario Einaudi, *The Roosevelt Revolution* also regarded the New Deal as having wrought vast and permanent changes.[20] Einaudi looked upon these with unreserved enthusiasm, and took issue with Robinson's gloomy views. Students will not find his chapters on Roosevelt and the New Deal as readable as the comparable surveys by Perkins and Brogan, but will find much meat in the introductory "Europe's Image of America," and the concluding commentary, up-dating Tocqueville in the light of the changes first brought about by the New Deal.

Biographical Treatment

Deservedly, the most widely read of the biographies of Roosevelt is the dramatic *Roosevelt: The Lion and the Fox* by James MacGregor Burns, which takes its title from Machiavelli's dictum that the prince must be a fox to recognize traps, and a lion to frighten wolves.[21] Examining Roosevelt and the New Deal from a Keynesian viewpoint, Burns devoted nearly half his book to Roosevelt's second term, which he pronounced a failure. (A brief epilogue covers the war years.) Some of Burns' views are: Congress in 1934-1946 was ready to go further left than the President would move; when he finally went in that direction it was in response to repudiation from the right. His landslide re-election in 1936 created unmanageable Democratic majorities in Congress. These contributed less to his defeat in the abortive effort to increase the number of justices on the Supreme Court than did Roosevelt's tricky tactics. These were made doubly unnecessary, first by the new willingness of the Supreme Court to validate New Deal legislation, second and most important, because Roosevelt could have obtained the objectives the Supreme Court earlier blocked through heavy spending. Burns considered the spending power of the

President the tool with which the depression could have been ended, and Roosevelt's cutbacks in 1937, the cause of the recession. Finally, because Roosevelt did not start early enough to build a liberal party, he suffered new humiliation and defeat when he tried to purge conservative Democrats in the 1938 congressional primaries. In all these and most other things, Burns saw Roosevelt as the fox rather than the lion. Not until the summer of 1940 with England at bay, did Roosevelt conclude the leonine "destroyers-for-bases" deal.

In the second volume of *The Age of Roosevelt*, entitled *The Coming of the New Deal* which covers only 1933 and 1934, Schlesinger presented a favorable interpretation of President Roosevelt and the early New Deal, from a viewpoint of modern economics and liberal politics.[22] Differing from the first volume, which by comparison was a sweeping survey and predominantly intellectual history, *The Coming of the New Deal* topically analyzes in concrete detail the establishment and functioning of the early New Deal policies toward agriculture, industry, finance, relief, natural resources, and labor, and explores Roosevelt's presidential leadership. Behind Schlesinger's smooth-flowing style and vivid anecdotal approach is the exhaustive research in both printed and manuscript materials, and innumerable interviews with participants with which he buttressed his conclusions. Judging recovery agencies like the Agricultural Adjustments Administration and the National Recovery Administration by the economic standards of the end of the fifties rather than the beginning of the thirties, he found much merit in them. He saw in the early New Deal much of the spirit of reform, and much substantial accomplishment. This favorable viewpoint is by no means uncritical. In his analysis of the NRA, Schlesinger pointed out:

> NRA always contained the possibility of becoming a conspiracy of organized business and (in certain industries) of organized labor against the public—a profit-wage conspiracy against the consumer. Under such pressures, NRA tended to promote scarcity and hold back recovery. To this degree, the conventional critique of NRA seems justified. . . . But . . . the economic philosophy of NRA was by no means so mistaken as its conventional critics have assumed. . . . The real cure . . . was to strengthen government labor, and consumer representation in the process of code-making. [p. 172]
>
> . . . .
>
> The more enduring achievements of NRA lay not in the economic but in the social field. Here NRA accomplished a fantastic series of reforms, any one of which would have staggered the na-

tion a few years earlier. It established the principle of maximum hours and minimum wages on a national basis. It abolished child labor. It dealt a fatal blow to sweatshops. It made collective bargaining a national policy and thereby transformed the position of organized labor. It gave new status to the consumer. It stamped out a noxious collection of unfair trade practices. It set new standards of economic decency in American life—standards which could not be rolled back, whatever happened to NRA. In doing these things, it accomplished in a few months what reformers had dreamed about for half a century. [p. 174-75]

As for Roosevelt's leadership, Schlesinger believed that

while he often played at being Machiavelli, he was not really Machiavellian. . . . The rather simplehearted idealism which lay so near the core of Roosevelt's personality could not indefinitely support the experiments in smart-aleckness and trickiness. [p. 557]

An affirmation of the rather simple, humane base of thinking from which Roosevelt embarked into the complicated politics of the New Deal is to be found in Rexford G. Tugwell, *The Democratic Roosevelt.*[23] Tugwell, an ardent, advanced New Dealer, for a while one of Roosevelt's closest advisers, used his own on-the-spot observations and his shrewd afterthoughts. His early chapters analyzing the formation of Roosevelt's character are full of remarkable insights. The section on the first four years of the New Deal, when the President often engaged in complex courses of action, and did not go so far or fast as Tugwell wished, is written in a spirit of affectionate disillusion. The account of events after Tugwell had left Washington at the end of 1936, is less useful.

A projected six-volume biography by Frank Freidel, in the three volumes thus far in print, brings Roosevelt to his election as President in 1932. *The Apprenticeship* covers the period to the end of the first World War; *The Ordeal* to Roosevelt's election as Governor of New York, with emphasis upon his polio attack; and *The Triumph*, the governorship and campaign of 1932.[24]

There is an excellent sketch of Roosevelt, rich in insights, in Hofstadter, *The American Political Tradition*. Recent serious studies of Roosevelt have outdated most of the popular biographies. One exception is John Gunther, *Roosevelt in Retrospect, A Profile in History*, a skillful piece of reporting.[25] Despite minor factual errors, it successfully catches the image of the man and the President. A fine campaign biography, Ernest K. Lindley, *Franklin D. Roosevelt, A Career in Pro-*

gressive Democracy is still worth reading as a portrait of Roosevelt as he appeared before he became President.[26]

There are two scholarly monographs on Roosevelt before he became President, both based on the Roosevelt papers. David R. Fusfeld, *The Economic Thought of Franklin D. Roosevelt and the Origins of the New Deal* gives a detailed account of Roosevelt's training in the political and economic climate of the Progressive era.[27] It takes a view (at variance with that in Freidel, *The Apprenticeship*) that Roosevelt emerged from his economic courses at Groton and Harvard with a fixed and enduring economic philosophy. In a chapter on Roosevelt's views in 1920, Fusfeld relies heavily upon a memorandum probably not the work of Roosevelt or anyone on his staff. Bernard Bellush, *Franklin D. Roosevelt as Governor of New York* is a definitive administrative history, topically arranged.[28]

Memoirs and Diaries

Much of the character of Roosevelt and the flavor of the New Deal emerges in the memoirs and diaries of participants. These, of course, must be used with some caution since, while they can be remarkable for the insights and the freshness of the inside stories they convey, they are also occasionally dangerous in their omissions and distortions. Partly their shortcomings are due to the strong emotions and imperfect memories of the writers, partly to the remarkable way in which President Roosevelt managed to convince any number of people associated with him that they were prime-movers in his enterprises. On the whole these memoirs and diaries are accurate enough, but can present only the facets of the President and his program that were seen by the individual viewer. For some the view was broad, for others, rather narrow.

The most intimate of the memoirs, remarkable for their candor, are Eleanor Roosevelt's two volumes, *This Is My Story* covering up to the White House, and *This I Remember* on the years when her husband was President.[29] From these a moving portrait emerges of Roosevelt as his affectionate, perceptive wife saw him. Unfortunately Mrs. Roosevelt does not always tell as much as a reader would wish about her own major role as a New Deal figure.[30] A pleasant sketch of Roosevelt by one of his sons is James Roosevelt and Sidney Shalett, *Affectionately, F.D.R.*[31]

The finest of the memoirs is Frances Perkins, *The Roosevelt I Knew*, striking in its insight, broad in its view, and friendly but realistic.[32] Miss Perkins, who was Secretary of Labor, also includes much interesting information on the formation of Social Security and the problems of labor. Equally accurate, and full of detail, is Raymond Moley, *After Seven Years*, which is indispensable on the early New Deal.[33] Moley, who had been the key braintruster, left the New Deal as it moved toward the left in 1936. His incisive analysis of Roosevelt's shortcomings, as he saw them, is clearly a description of other aspects of the same man that Miss Perkins writes about. An unreservedly friendly memoir, describing in detail how Roosevelt prepared his speeches and talked with his intimates, is Samuel I. Rosenman, *Working with Roosevelt*.[34]

Among the New Deal diaries, that of Secretary of the Interior Harold L. Ickes created the greatest sensation upon its publication. Ickes, who had entitled his memoir, *The Autobiography of a Curmudgeon*[35] lives up to his self-image in the far-ranging, gossipy, splenetic pages of *The Secret Diary of Harold L. Ickes*, covering 1933-1941.[36] The diary gives Ickes' viewpoint of the inner workings of the Department of the Interior, of feuds with Harry L. Hopkins, Henry Wallace, and other key New Dealers, and of dealings with President Roosevelt, members of Congress, and a host of Washington figures. Much of the information is valuable, most of it is one-sided, and some of it is misleading.

In contrast, readers are not likely to go astray in the carefully organized, clear narrative of John M. Blum, *From the Morgenthau Diaries: Years of Crisis, 1928-1938*.[37] Out of the enormous bulk of the manuscript diaries, Blum wove a detailed account of Secretary of the Treasury Morgenthau's relations with the President and conduct of the business of the Treasury Department. The book contains numerous word-for-word exchanges of conversation between Roosevelt and Morgenthau, from which the reader can picture vividly how Roosevelt worked and relaxed. More than this, it contains invaluable scholarly analyses of the New Deal policies on gold and silver purchases, the debt, taxation, the recession of 1937-1938, and international finance. Although the lucid presentation of these complex matters is the work of Blum, the conclusions are those of Morgenthau. He emerges in these pages as an able administrator, committed to social reforms and humanitarianism, but determined to obtain them within relatively narrow budgetary limits. The theories of Lord Keynes and the New Deal economists never won Morgenthau away from his fruitless aspiration to achieve a balanced budget. An earlier, relatively brief study of one thread of Treasury policy, also based on the Morgenthau diaries, is Allan Seymour Everest, *Morgenthau, the New Deal and Silver*.[38] A contemporary monograph is G. Griffith Johnson, Jr., *The Treasury and Monetary Policy, 1933-1938*.[39]

Marriner Eccles, who as head of the Federal Reserve advocated Keynesian economic policies at variance with those of Secretary Morgenthau, presents his viewpoints and an account of Federal Reserve activities in his memoirs, *Beckoning Frontiers*.[40] Jesse Jones who was proud of the conservative fashion in which he ran the Reconstruction Finance Corporation, quotes extensively from documents in Jesse H. Jones and Edward Angly, *Fifty Billion Dollars, My Thirteen Years with the RFC, 1932-1945*.[41]

Monographs on the New Deal

There is a surprising lack of scholarly monographs on the history of most of the New Deal agencies. The reader often will have to turn to more general works like Schlesinger's *Coming of the New Deal*, or to memoirs and contemporary writings. On the National Recovery Administration, General Hugh S. Johnson's colorful memoir, *The Blue Eagle from Egg to Earth* is still useful although it gives only Johnson's view of the questions over which sharp differences arose.[42] Donald Richberg, with whom he contended, and who succeeded him, presented his contemporary view of the NRA in *The Rainbow* and his afterthoughts in *My Hero*, a facetiously titled autobiography.[43] Leverett S. Lyon et al., *The National Recovery Administration, An Analysis and Appraisal* is a contemporary technical study by Brookings Institution economists.[44]

A compendious survey of agricultural policy during the New Deal is to be found in Murray R. Benedict, *Farm Policies of the United States*.[45] For a readable, anecdotal account, with sketches of some of the policy-makers, see Russell Lord, *The Wallaces of Iowa*, which devotes nearly three hundred pages to the New Deal years.[46] A broad, non-technical contemporary survey is Donald C. Blaisdell, *Government and Agriculture, The Growth of Federal Farm Aid*.[47] More specialized studies are a Brookings Institution monograph, Edwin G. Nourse, Joseph S. Davis, and John D. Black, *Three Years of the Agricultural Adjustment Administration*,[48] and a conservative evaluation, Joseph S. Davis, *On Agricultural Policy, 1926-1938*.[49] Paul K. Conkin, *Tomorrow a New World: The New Deal Community Program* analyzes both the nineteenth century ideological antecedents and the rise and decline during the New Deal of the back-to-land movement and related schools of social and economic planning. These reached their height in the Resettlement Administration and the Farm Security Administration.[50]

The Tennessee Valley Authority, attracting continuing attention within the United States and throughout the world, has been one of the most written-about phases of the New Deal. One of the most thought-provoking of the scholarly monographs is Philip Selznick, *TVA and the Grass Roots, A Study in the Sociology of Formal Organization* which analyzes the decentralization of the TVA, and its consequences.[51] On the vital role of Senator George W. Norris in fostering TVA, see his autobiography, *Fighting Liberal*, and a forthcoming biography by Richard Lowitt.[52]

New Deal labor policy and the growth of unions in the thirties has also been the subject of extensive writing. Milton Derber and Edwin Young, editors, *Labor and the New Deal* is an indispensable collection of essays, relating New Deal developments to the main stream of labor history, contemporary problems, and subsequent policies.[53] The study covers the political relationship between the New Deal and organized labor, the effect of the Wagner Act, the split in the labor movement, and the enactment of protective labor legislation and social security. It also contains a bibliography of several hundred books and articles. One of the most significant monographs is Irving Bernstein, *The New Deal Collective Bargaining Policy*[54] which established that President Roosevelt preferred a paternalistic middle course toward unions, and accepted the Wagner Bill with its strong collective bargaining guarantees only when driven to do so by political necessity. A specialized study on the work of the National Labor Relations Board is Harry A. Millis and Emily C. Brown, *From the Wagner Act to Taft-Hartley*.[55]

Historical studies are yet to appear on the federal relief programs and the establishment of Social Security. However, a forthcoming monograph by C. F. Charles analyzes Harry Hopkins' administration of federal relief; there is a brief account in Robert Sherwood, *Roosevelt and Hopkins*;[56] and Hopkins describes his work in *Spending to Save*.[57] Two valuable monographs on the Works Progress Administration are Arthur W. MacMahon et al., *The Administration of Federal Work Relief*, and John K. Galbraith and G. G. Johnson, Jr., *Economic Effects of Federal Public Works Expenditures, 1933-1938*.[58] The background of Social Security is brilliantly described in Perkins, *The Roosevelt I Knew*. A contemporary analysis is Paul H. Douglas, *Social Security in the United States*,[59] and a later overview, Grace Abbott, *From Relief to Social Security*.[60]

Politics during the New Deal are surveyed in Harold F. Gosnell, *Champion Campaigner: Franklin D. Roosevelt*.[61] The election of 1932 is analyzed in Frank Freidel, *Franklin D. Roosevelt: The Triumph*. A brilliant and readable exposition of the functioning of the Democratic political machinery from the primary campaigns of 1932 through the election of 1936 in James A. Farley, *Behind the Ballots*, which is more useful than his later bitter *Jim Farley's Story*.[62] The positions on the New Deal of three of Roosevelt's presidential opponents can be found in Herbert Hoover, *The Challenge to Liberty*,[63] Alfred M. Landon, *America at the Crossroads*,[64] and the definitive D. B. Johnson, *The Republican Party and Wendell Willkie*.[65] Progressive, Socialistic, and "lunatic fringe" movements culminating in William Lemke's Union party candidacy in 1936 are the subject of Donald R. McCoy, *Angry Voices: Left-Of-Center Politics in the New Deal Era*.[66] The threat from the left was represented most colorfully by Huey Long, the subject of a forthcoming biography by T. Harry Williams, and of several popular studies and novels.[67] An indispensable interpretation of radicalism during the thirties is Murray Kempton, *Part of Our Time*.[68] A perceptive collection of vignettes of political leaders is Raymond Moley, *27 Masters of Politics*.[69] As yet there are only autobiographies or popular biographies of Congressional leaders, as, for example, a biography of the Vice President, Bascom N. Timmons, *Garner of Texas*,[70] and the autobiography of a leading Senator, James F. Byrnes, *All in One Lifetime*.[71] Edgar E. Robinson, *They Voted for Roosevelt* is a compendium and analysis of presidential election statistics from 1932 through 1944.[72]

The controversy over enlarging the Supreme Court has been explored in detail both in contemporary and later books. A distinguished piece of reporting is Joseph Alsop and Turner Catledge, *The 168 Days*.[73] A significant favorable study is Robert H. Jackson, *The Struggle for Judicial Supremacy*;[74] a disapproving account, Merlo J. Pusey, *The Supreme Court Crisis*.[75] There is a clear summary and evaluation in Dexter Perkins, *Charles Evans Hughes and American Democratic Statesmanship*.[76] A thorough analysis of the constitutional changes wrought by the Supreme Court beginning in 1937 is Charles H. Pritchett, *The Roosevelt Court, . . . 1937-1947*.[77] A clever exposition of some facets of New Deal thought is Thurman W. Arnold, *The Folklore of Capitalism*.[78] Arnold discusses the new antitrust policies in *The Bottlenecks of Business*.[79]

CONCLUSION

From the beginning of the New Deal to the end, Roosevelt functioned with a fair degree of consistency. He heartily favored humanitarian welfare legislation and government policing of the economy, so long as these did not dangerously unbalance the budget. He preferred government cooperation with business to warfare with it.

Many of the New Dealers went far beyond Roosevelt in their views, and sometimes saw in his reluctance to support them, betrayal rather than a greater degree of conservatism. They had valid grievances some of the time when Roosevelt stuck to a middle course and seemed to them to be compromising away everything for which they thought he stood, in order to hold his motley political coalitions together. It is a serious moral question whether he compromised more than necessary, and whether at times he compromised his principles. It has been charged that his second four years in the White House represented a failure in political leadership.

In terms of gaining immediate political objectives, like the fiasco of the Court fight, and the abortive "purge" in the 1938 primaries, this is undoubtedly true. In terms of the long-range New Deal program, the reverse is the case. These were years of piece-meal unspectacular consolidation of the earlier spectacular changes. It was many years before historians could say with certainty that these changes were permanent. By 1948 various public opinion samplings indicated that an overwhelming majority of those queried, even though Republican in voting habits, favored such things as social security and the TVA. The election of a Republican president in 1952 did not signify a popular repudiation of these programs. In the years after 1952 they were accepted, and in some instances even expanded, by the Republican administration. The only serious debate over them concerned degree, in which the Republicans were more cautious than the Democrats. The New Deal changes have even come for the most part to be accepted by the business community, although the United States Chamber of Commerce now issues manifestoes against federal aid to education with all the fervor it once directed against Roosevelt's proposals. The fact is that the business community in part bases its plans for the future upon some things that began as New Deal reforms. It takes for granted such factors as the "built-in stabilizers" in the social security system—something, incidentally, that Roosevelt pointed out at the time the legislation went into effect.

In January 1939 Roosevelt, concerned about the threat of world war, called to a halt his domestic reform program. What he said then, concerning the world crisis of 1939, is remarkably applicable to the United States more than two decades later:

We have now passed the period of internal conflict in the launching of our program of social reform. Our full energies may now be released to invigorate the processes of recovery in order to preserve our reforms, and to give every man and woman who wants to work a real job at a living wage.

But time is of paramount importance. The deadline of danger from within and from without is not within our control. The hour-glass may be in the hands of other nations. Our own hour-glass tells us that we are off on a race to make democracy work, so that we may be efficient in peace and therefore secure in national defense.

NOTES

1. New York, 1955.
2. Boston, 1960.
3. New York, 1947.
4. New York, 1948.
5. Boston, 1957.
6. New York, 1952.
7. Boston, 1955.
8. Chicago, 1958 and New York, 1960.
9. New York, 1959.
10. For an interesting account of Hoover's life until he became President, and a disappointingly dull account of the Presidency (other than depression problems), see *Years of Adventure, 1874-1920* and *The Cabinet and the Presidency, 1920-1933*, which are the first and second volumes of Hoover *Memoirs* (3 vols.; New York: Macmillan, 1951-1952).
11. New York, 1948.
12. New York, Creative Age, 1944. General accounts of the social and intellectual history of the thirties are to be found in Dixon Wecter, *The Age of the Great Depression, 1929-1941* (New York, 1948); Frederick Lewis Allen, *Since Yesterday* (New York, 1940); Charles and Mary Beard, *America in Midpassage* (2 vols.; New York, 1939).

   Important documentary collections are: Samuel I. Rosenman, ed., *The Public Papers and Addresses of Franklin D. Roosevelt* (13 vols.; New York, 1938-1950); Elliott Roosevelt, ed., *F. D. R.: His Personal Letters* (New York, 1947-1950).
13. New Haven, 1950.
14. By the Editors of *The Economist*. New York, 1937.
15. Chicago, 1957.
16. Philadelphia, 1955.
17. New York, 1948.
18. New York, 1955.
19. Arthur Link takes the opposite viewpoint that the New Deal was no more than the enactment of an enlarged Progressive program. *American Epoch*, p. 381.
20. New York, 1959.

21. New York, 1956.
22. Boston: Houghton Mifflin, 1959. Since this chapter has been written, Schlesinger's third volume has appeared, surpassing in brilliance even the previous two. This volume consists of four parts: the first part discusses the various radical movements of the early 1930's; the second analyzes the shift from the first to the second New Deal and rather substantially modifies earlier interpretations of this shift; the third considers the crisis of the Constitution and Supreme Court; and the fourth describes the election of 1936. Arthur M. Schlesinger, Jr., *The Age of Roosevelt.* Volume III, *The Politics of Upheaval* (Boston, 1960).
23. Garden City, 1957.
24. Boston, 1952, 1954, and 1956.
25. New York, 1950.
26. Indianapolis, 1931. Among the popular biographies are the dramatic but superficial Alden Hatch, *Franklin D. Roosevelt: An Informal Biography* (New York, 1947); Gerald W. Johnson, *Roosevelt: Dictator or Democrat?* (New York, 1941), an able defense; John T. Flynn, *Country Squire in the White House* (New York, 1940), a clever attack; Emil Ludwig, *Roosevelt: A Study in Fortune and Power* (New York, 1938), a misleading psychological study; and Bernard Fay, *Roosevelt and His America* (Boston, 1933), hasty and laudatory.
27. New York, Columbia University, 1956.
28. New York, Columbia University, 1955.
29. New York, 1937 and 1949.
30. Ruby A. Black, *Eleanor Roosevelt, A Biography* (New York, 1940) and Alfred Steinberg, *Mrs. R.: The Life of Eleanor Roosevelt* (New York, 1958).
31. New York, 1959.
32. New York, 1946.
33. New York, 1939.
34. New York, 1952.
35. New York, 1943.
36. 3 vols.; New York, 1953-1954.
37. Boston, 1959.
38. New York, 1950.
39. Cambridge, 1939.
40. *Beckoning Frontiers: Public and Personal Recollections,* ed., Sidney Hyman (New York, 1951).
41. New York, 1951.
42. Garden City, 1935.
43. Garden City, 1936 and New York, 1954.
44. Washington, 1935.
45. *Farm Policies of the United States, 1790-1950,* . . . (New York, 1953).
46. Boston, 1947.
47. New York, 1940.
48. Washington, 1937.
49. Stanford University, 1939.
50. Ithaca, 1960.
51. Berkeley, 1949.
52. New York, 1945.

53. Madison, 1957.
54. Berkeley, 1950.
55. Chicago, 1950.
56. New York, 1948.
57. New York, 1936.
58. Chicago, 1941; and Washington, 1940.
59. New York, 1936.
60. Chicago, 1941.
61. New York, 1952.
62. New York, 1938; and New York, 1948.
63. New York, 1934.
64. New York, 1936.
65. Urbana, 1960.
66. Lawrence, 1958.
67. See Allan P. Sindler, *Huey Long's Louisiana: State Politics, 1920-1952* (Baltimore, 1956).
68. New York, 1955.
69. New York, Funk & Wagnalls, 1949.
70. New York, 1948.
71. New York, 1958.
72. Stanford, 1947.
73. Garden City, 1938.
74. New York, 1941.
75. New York, 1937.
76. Boston, 1956.
77. New York, 1948.
78. New Haven, 1937.
79. New York, 1940.

RECENT STUDIES

William E. Leuchtenberg, *Franklin D. Roosevelt and the New Deal, 1932-1940* (New York: Harper and Row, 1963).

Bernard Sternsher, *Rexford Tugwell and the New Deal* (New Brunswick: Rutgers University Press, 1964).

Sidney Fine, *The Automobile under the Blue Eagle: Labor, Management, and the Automobile Manufacturing Code* (Ann Arbor: University of Michigan Press, 1963).

Ellis W. Hawley, *The New Deal and the Problem of Monopoly: A Study in Ambivalence* (Princeton: Princeton University Press, 1966).

Otis L. Graham, Jr., *An Encore for Reform: The Old Progressives and the New Deal* (New York: Oxford University Press, 1967).

Lloyd C. Gardner, *Economic Aspects of New Deal Diplomacy* (Madison: University of Wisconsin Press, 1964).

Manfred Jonas, *Isolationism in America, 1935-1941* (Ithaca: Cornell University Press, 1966).

Paul K. Conkin, *The New Deal* (New York: Thomas Y. Crowell, 1967).

William J. Stewart, compiler and annotator, *The Era of Franklin D. Roosevelt; A Selected Bibliography of Periodical and Dissertation Literature, 1945-1966* (Hyde Park, N.Y.: Franklin D. Roosevelt Library, 1967).

XX

American Entry into World War II

WAYNE S. COLE

The aggressive expansion of the Axis powers in Europe and Asia in the 1930's aroused an impassioned debate on American foreign policy. "Isolationists" contended with "interventionists" over the policies adopted by the Roosevelt administration. Though few, if any, of the so-called isolationists wanted literally to isolate the United States from the rest of the world, they joined in opposition to what seemed the major trend in foreign affairs under President Roosevelt. A second phase in the dispute over policy was inaugurated by the attack on Pearl Harbor on December 7, 1941, for with that event the old quarrels became academic. But the policies of the Roosevelt administration continued as the core of dispute between two schools of historians who launched their own war of words over the background of America's entry into war. In the years after 1941 the "internationalist" writers were met by the "revisionists"—the latter term now used almost universally to describe the historians who have written critically of Roosevelt's pre-Pearl Harbor foreign policies and of American entry into World War II. Since the controversy is a continuing one, and because the books and articles on the subject have grown to confusing proportions, some orientation is necessary both for the reader who must work

From *Mississippi Valley Historical Review*, XLIII (March 1957), pp. 595-617. Reprinted with abridged annotation by permission.

his way through the published historical materials and for those attracted to the problem as a field for further research and writing.

Histories of American entry into World War II published during the war defended the pre-Pearl Harbor policies of the Roosevelt administration. Forrest Davis and Ernest K. Lindley had close ties with the administration which enabled them to obtain important data for their volume, *How War Came*.[1] Walter Johnson's book, *The Battle against Isolation*,[2] published in 1944, was a study of the most powerful interventionist pressure groups before Pearl Harbor. Johnson, unlike some later writers, based his study upon previously unused manuscripts—principally the William Allen White papers. In the same year Dexter Perkins provided a concise survey in *America and Two Wars*.[3] The authors of these books shared and endorsed most of the assumptions and convictions of the interventionists and the Roosevelt administration on foreign affairs. The emotional atmosphere of the war years, the necessity for unity in the prosecution of the war, and the inadequacy of available source materials combined to prevent any serious challenge to the pro-Roosevelt interpretation during the war. Pamphlets by John T. Flynn, published in 1944 and 1945, advanced the revisionist point of view, but they received relatively little attention.[4]

During and since World War II growing quantities of raw materials for historical research and interpretation on the subject have been published and made available to scholars. The United States government published special sets of documents related to American entry into the war, beginning with the publication in 1943 of *Peace and War: United States Foreign Policy, 1931-1941*. In addition, the regular *Foreign Relations* series is now being brought close to Pearl Harbor. Military leaders and civilians associated with the Roosevelt administration published personal accounts. Among Americans whose memoirs or letters have been published in full or in part are Raymond Moley, William E. Dodd, Joseph E. Davies, Sumner Welles, Frances Perkins, John G. Winant, Henry Morgenthau, Jr., Henry L. Stimson, Cordell Hull, James A. Farley, Sherman Miles, Eleanor Roosevelt, William D. Leahy, Samuel I. Rosenman, Joseph C. Grew, Ernest J. King, Harold L. Ickes, Husband E. Kimmel, and Jay P. Moffat. Several key figures thus far have not published memoirs—including George C. Marshall, Harold R. Stark, Walter C. Short, Frank Knox, and President Roosevelt. Edited volumes of Roosevelt's speeches, press conferences, and personal letters, however, have been published.[5] Documents, testimony, and reports of the several Pearl Harbor investigations were made available with the publication in 1946 of a total of forty volumes covering the work of the

Joint Congressional Committee on the Investigation of the Pearl Harbor Attack. The war crimes trials in Nuremberg and the Far East added pertinent documents and testimony. Documents on British and German foreign policy before the war have been published. Memoirs of leaders of European states were printed, containing much information of value for an understanding and analysis of American policies. The volumes by Winston Churchill and Count Ciano's diaries are two important examples.[6] And gradually in recent years historians have obtained increased opportunities for research in unpublished manuscripts.

Most of the histories published from 1947 to 1950 on American entry into World War II were based almost exclusively on published sources—particularly on the volumes growing out of the Pearl Harbor investigations and on the memoirs of Hull, Stimson, and others. Most of these early books followed the lead of either the majority (pro-Roosevelt) or the minority (anti-Roosevelt) report of the congressional investigation committee. Among the volumes of this sort defending Roosevelt's foreign policies were *This Is Pearl*, by Walter Millis,[7] and *Roosevelt, from Munich to Pearl Harbor*, by Basil Rauch.[8] Revisionist volumes, based largely on published sources, included *Pearl Harbor*, by George Morgenstern;[9] *President Roosevelt and the Coming of the War, 1941*, by Charles A. Beard;[10] *America's Second Crusade*, by William Henry Chamberlin;[11] *Design for War*, by Frederic R. Sanborn, published in 1951;[12] and *The Final Secret of Pearl Harbor*, by Robert A. Theobald, published in 1954.[13]

Gradually in the late 1940's and early 1950's scholars began to expand into new frontiers by research in unpublished manuscripts. Most of this group wrote from points of view sympathetic with the policies followed by the American government before Pearl Harbor. Robert E. Sherwood used the files of Harry Hopkins as the basis for his Pulitzer-prize-winning *Roosevelt and Hopkins*, published in 1948.[14] *The Battle of the Atlantic* and *The Rising Sun in the Pacific*,[15] by Samuel Eliot Morison, traced the naval side of the background of American entry into the war. *Chief of Staff: Prewar Plans and Preparations*, by Mark S. Watson, analyzed the role of the Army.[16] Herbert Feis's study of American relations with Japan, entitled *The Road to Pearl Harbor*, was based on more extensive research than earlier volumes on that subject.[17] The culmination of the internationalist interpretation came with the publication in 1952 and 1953 of the two-volume work by William L. Langer and S. Everett Gleason under the general title of *The World Crisis and American Foreign Policy*.[18] This massive study, covering the years from 1937 to 1941, was sponsored and financed by the Council on Foreign Relations and the Rockefeller Foundation. These volumes were based not only on published materials but also on extensive research in the records of the Department of State and in the material at the Franklin D. Roosevelt Library at Hyde Park. Since the publication of the Langer-Gleason work, the most recent book written from this same general point of view is *The Passing of American Neutrality, 1937-1941*, by Donald F. Drummond, published in 1955.[19] On the revisionist side, Charles Callan Tansill, after research comparable to that of Langer and Gleason, published his *Back Door to War* in 1952.[20] Harry Elmer Barnes, who had published several pamphlets on the subject earlier, edited a volume called *Perpetual War for Perpetual Peace* that included essays written by most major revisionists.[21] Richard N. Current's critical study, *Secretary Stimson*, was published in 1954.[22] In addition, other books and numerous articles have appeared, particularly since 1950, on specialized aspects of the subject.[23]

The interpretative controversies among historians concerning American entry into World War II are in part a direct extension of the pre-Pearl Harbor debate between interventionists and non-interventionists. Writers of history have not only dealt with the same basic subject and issues, but have also used the same arguments, made the same fundamental assumptions, and advanced similar hypotheses. For most major hypotheses advanced by postwar historians, counterparts could be found in the writings and speeches of prewar interventionists and non-interventionists. Furthermore, the debate among historians aroused some of the same emotional heat, the same ideological dogmatism, the same intolerance of conflicting views, and the same black-and-white portraits —on both sides—as were aroused in the "Great Debate" before Pearl Harbor. There are exceptions, of course, but there were also exceptions before Pearl Harbor.

In many instances the individuals who have written scholarly histories on the subject were involved directly (sometimes prominently) in the pre-Pearl Harbor foreign policy debate—and on the same side that they are now defending in their histories. There is no evidence that any of these writers was persuaded to change his basic point of view as the result of historical research after the war. It is true, of course, that Walter Millis' *Road to War*, published in 1935, was a major revisionist interpretation of American entry into World War I. Millis, however, was on the editorial staff of the interventionist New York *Herald Tribune*, and by 1939 he publicly endorsed the interventionist position. In June, 1940, he signed a petition urging an American declaration of war on Nazi Germany. In 1941 he was a sponsor of the Fight for Freedom Committee—a major pressure group advocating full United States participation in the war against the Axis. Robert E. Sherwood's Pulitzer-prize-winning play, *Idiot's Delight*, with its arraignment of war and war passions, undoubtedly aroused pacifist and non-interventionist emotions. By 1939-1941, however, Sherwood was an interventionist. He actively and prominently supported William Allen White's Committee to Defend America by Aiding the Allies. Harry Hopkins assured himself of the vigor of Sherwood's interventionist views before he added the playwright to President Roosevelt's speech-writing staff in 1940.

Barnes and Tansill refer to the internationalist writers as "Court Historians." One need not endorse the sinister implications of this sobriquet. Many internationalist writers, however, did have sympathetic personal ties and friendships with key figures in the events they described in their histories. Several of them have held important government positions in the administration whose foreign policies they were analyzing and evaluating. Ernest K. Lindley's personal friendship with President Roosevelt and other key administration figures enabled him to obtain special interviews and inside information for the preparation of his sympathetic volume.[24] Robert E. Sherwood assisted President Roosevelt with the writing of his speeches from 1940 until the President's death in 1945. Herbert Feis was an economic adviser in the Department of State from 1931 to 1943 and was special consultant to the Secretary of War from 1944 to 1946. William L. Langer from 1941 to 1946 held various positions in the Office of Coordinator of Information, the Office of Strategic Services, and the Department of State. He served the Central Intelligence Agency in 1950-1951. S. Everett Gleason was with the Office of Strategic Services from 1943 to 1945 and the Department of State in 1945. He has served as deputy executive secretary to the National Security Council since 1950. Samuel Eliot Morison was commissioned in the naval reserve with the sole duty of preparing the history of United States naval operations in World War II. He rose to the rank of rear admiral by the time he retired in 1951. Mark S. Watson's book is a part of the official history of the Army in World War II. None of the major revisionist writers, on the contrary, held important administrative positions under either President Roosevelt or President Truman.

All revisionists for whom specific evidence is available adhered to the non-interventionist position before Pearl Harbor. Charles A. Beard's prewar "Continentalism" as expressed in such books as *The Open Door at Home*[25] and *A Foreign Policy for America*[26] is well known. He publicly endorsed (but did not join) the America First Committee, the leading non-interventionist pressure group before Pearl Harbor.[27] He also testified against Lend-Lease before the Senate Foreign Relations Committee. Harry Elmer Barnes, one of the leading and more uncompromising revisionists regarding the origins of World War I, spoke at meetings of the America First Committee in 1941. Charles C. Tansill in 1938 published the best of the revisionist studies of American entry into World War I.[28] George Morgenstern joined the editorial staff of the non-interventionist Chicago *Tribune* in 1941. For revisionist as well as internationalist it is possible to discern a continuity in viewpoint, extending from the pre- to the post-Pearl Harbor period.

Any brief summaries of the revisionist and internationalist interpretations of American entry into World War II can at best be no more than simplified versions of detailed and complicated accounts. It is necessary in presenting such a summary to pass over countless important details and individual variations in interpretation. There is, nevertheless, a wide area of agreement among writers on each side of the interpretative controversy.

Internationalist writers, looking back to the days before Pearl Harbor, view the Axis powers as extremely serious threats to American security and interests. They point to the strength and speed of the Axis forces which by the middle of 1940 had rolled over Austria, Czechoslovakia, Poland, Denmark, Norway, the Netherlands, Luxemburg, Belgium, and France. Britain alone was successfully resisting Nazi assaults on her home islands. By May, 1941, Hitler was in control of the Balkan Peninsula and was threatening the Middle East. Most authorities at the time expected the Soviet Union to fall quickly after Hitler's *Blitzkrieg* was turned against Russia on June 22, 1941. Axis successes in North Africa raised fears that control of that continent might prove a stepping-stone to the Western Hemisphere. In the meantime Japan took advantage of the European crisis to step up her aggressive campaigns in Asia.

According to the internationalist interpretation, President Roosevelt believed the United States could most effectively increase the possibility of peace in the 1930's by using its power to discourage potential aggressors from provoking war. In this aim, however, he was handicapped by the "isolationist" attitude of the American people and particularly by the powerful opposition in Congress. After war began in Asia and in Europe, according to this interpretation, the President hoped to prevent the United States from becoming involved in the hostilities—providing that could be accomplished without sacrificing American security, vital interests, and principles.

President Roosevelt and his major advisers believed that aggression by Germany and Italy in Europe constituted a more serious threat to American security than did Japanese actions in the Far East. In general, internationalist writers follow the administration view that the defeat of Nazi Germany and Fascist Italy was essential to American peace and security. Like the Roosevelt administration, most of these writers tend to rule out a negotiated peace as a possible acceptable alternative in Europe—particularly after the fall of France. President Roosevelt hoped that his policy of extending aid short of war to the victims of Axis aggression in Europe would prevent the defeat of Great Britain, contribute to the essential defeat of the Axis powers, and thereby enable the United States to maintain both its peace and its security. Among the many steps taken by the Roosevelt administration to aid the victims of aggression in Europe were repeal of the arms embargo, the destroyer deal, Lend-Lease, the Atlantic patrol system, occupation of Iceland, the shoot-on-sight policy, arming of American merchant ships, and permitting the use of those ships to transport goods directly to England.

According to the internationalist interpretation, Roosevelt and Hull wanted to prevent war between the United States and Japan—in part because such a war would interfere with the main task of defeating Hitler. They believed that the best way to preserve American peace and security in the Pacific was to take steps short of war to check Japanese aggression. Among American actions of this sort were the "moral embargo," the termination of the commercial treaty with Japan, various forms of aid to Chiang Kai-shek, keeping the American fleet at Pearl Harbor, and freezing Japanese assets in the United States. The United States was eager to seek a peaceful settlement with Japan—providing such a settlement would not jeopardize American security and principles, and providing it would not require the United States to abandon China, Britain, France, and the Netherlands in the Pacific. As it became increasingly apparent that compromise was impossible on terms acceptable to both countries, the Roosevelt administration tried to delay war to gain time for military preparations.

With regard to the European theater as well as the Pacific, there were distinct variations in the views of administration leaders before Pearl Harbor about implementing American policies and presenting them to the American people. Cordell Hull, hoping to avoid war and fearful of non-interventionist opposition, generally advised caution. He favored limiting action to steps short of war and he explained each step in terms of peace, security, and international morality. Henry L. Stimson, Frank Knox, Henry Morgenthau, Jr., and others were critical of this indirect and step-at-a-time approach. They early came to believe that aid short of war would not be sufficient to insure the defeat of the Axis and they urged the President to take more vigorous action against the aggressors. Stimson believed the American people would support the President in a declaration of war even before Pearl Harbor. Of a different temperament, President Roosevelt, like Hull, was fearful of arousing effective public opposition to his policies and adhered to the step-at-a-time, short-of-war approach.

Internationalist interpretations tend to reflect these variations in attitudes among prewar interventionists. Feis treats Hull with considerable respect. Rauch's interpretation is similar to that advanced by Hull, though the hero in Rauch's book is definitely President Roosevelt. A number of writers, like Davis, Lindley, Millis, and Sherwood, generally feel that in view of conditions then existing President Roosevelt's decisions and methods on foreign policy matters were wise and sound at most crucial points before Pearl Harbor. Dexter Perkins has emphasized that Roosevelt's actions to check the Axis in Europe short of war reflected and expressed the desires of the majority of the American people. Langer and Gleason are sympathetic with the more direct and vigorous approach urged by Stimson—particularly as applied to the European theater. They believe that Roosevelt overestimated the strength of the opposition to his policies among the American people.

Writers of the internationalist school find the fundamental causes for American involvement in the war in developments in other parts of the world—beyond the American power to control by 1941. They do not find the explanation within the United States—except in so far as non-interventionist opposition inhibited administration actions that might have prevented the war from beginning or from reaching such a critical stage. Nearly all internationalist histories are highly critical of the opponents of Roosevelt's foreign policies. Needless to say, they all deny that President Roosevelt wanted to get the United States into war. They are convinced that the Japanese attack on Pearl Harbor was a genuine surprise to the members of the Roosevelt administration. These leaders knew that Japanese armed forces were under way and that war was imminent, but they expected the blows to fall in the south-west Pacific. In that event, administration leaders believed the United States would have to fight—though they were worried about the reaction of the American people to a declaration of war on Japan if American territory was not attacked. In so far as there was any American responsibility for the disaster at Pearl Harbor most internationalist writers blame the military commanders in Hawaii—Admiral Husband E. Kimmel and General Walter C. Short. None of them believe that there were any alternatives

available to President Roosevelt by 1940-1941 which could have prevented American involvement in World War II without sacrificing
American security and principles.

Revisionists have formed an entirely different estimate of Roosevelt's
role and policies. Most of the revisionist interpretation can be summarized under four major headings. First, revisionists believe the Axis
powers did not (or, need not—if the United States had followed wiser
policies) constitute a serious threat to American security and vital interests. Second, they contend that President Roosevelt followed policies that he knew (or should have known) would lead to war in Asia and
Europe and would involve the United States in those wars. Third, while
leading the nation to war, the President deceived the American people
by telling them he was working for peace. And fourth, revisionists maintain that American policies before and during World War II contributed
to the rise of a much more serious threat to peace and security—Communist Russia and her satellites.

In striking contrast to the internationalist interpretation, the revisionists minimize or reject the idea that the Axis powers constituted a threat
to American security. They point out that Hitler had no concrete plans
for attacking the Western Hemisphere. They portray the Japanese attack on Pearl Harbor as an action provoked by American restrictions that
threatened Japanese security and vital interests. In so far as revisionists
concede the reality of an Axis threat to the United States, they believe it
was caused largely by American shortsighted and provocative policies.
Like non-interventionists before Pearl Harbor, the revisionists maintain
that the issue was not primarily security but instead was war or peace.
And revisionists hold that the United States government had the power
to choose for itself whether it would or would not enter the war. Thus,
in contrast to internationalists, the revisionists find the explanation for
American entry into World War II primarily within the United States
rather than in the actions of nations in other parts of the world. In seeking the explanation within the United States, they focus their attention
almost exclusively upon administration and military leaders—and particularly upon President Roosevelt.

Some revisionist historians believe that the Roosevelt foreign policies
helped to provoke and prolong war in Asia and Europe. They interpret
Roosevelt's steps to aid Britain short of war as actually steps to war.
Opinions of revisionists vary on the question of whether Roosevelt deliberately meant these as steps to war. In any event, they contend, these
actions did not provoke Hitler into war against the United States; and

the shooting incidents that occurred in the Atlantic did not arouse American enthusiasm for entering the European war.

Instead, according to most revisionist writers, the Roosevelt administration got the United States into war through the Asiatic "back door" by provoking the Japanese attack on Pearl Harbor. This was accomplished by increasing pressures on Japan while refusing any compromise that the Japanese could accept. The decisive economic pressure in 1941 was exerted through the curtailment of oil shipments, and the key issue on which compromise proved impossible was China. The freezing of Japanese assets in the United States on July 26, 1941, accompanied by parallel action by the British and Dutch, virtually terminated American trade with Japan. This was particularly serious in cutting Japan off from her essential oil supplies. On August 17, 1941, at the suggestion of Churchill, President Roosevelt presented a formal and vigorous warning to the Japanese against further expansion. The President then rejected Premier Konoye's proposal for a personal meeting between the two leaders. Then, Secretary of State Hull, after objections from China and Britain, abandoned the idea of proposing a *modus vivendi*. Instead, on November 26, Hull (though aware that time was running out) submitted a ten-point program to Japan—including the demand that the Japanese withdraw from China and Indo-China. This proposal (which revisionists generally call an "ultimatum") was so extreme that Hull knew in advance that Japan would not accept it. According to most revisionists these and other actions by the Roosevelt administration (out of either design or blunder) provoked war with Japan. The United States confronted Japan with the alternatives of backing down or fighting. With oil reserves falling dangerously low, and believing that their vital interests and security were at stake, the Japanese chose to fight.

Through all of this, according to the revisionists, President Roosevelt deceived the American people concerning his policies and objectives in foreign affairs. Revisionists maintain that Roosevelt publicly committed his administration to a policy of peace while secretly leading the nation to war—a war that these writers consider contrary to national interests and contrary to the desires of 80 per cent of the American people. The most famous expression of this thesis is in Beard's last book and particularly in his final chapter.[29]

Most revisionists maintain that administration and military leaders in Washington gave inadequate, ambiguous, and belated warnings to the commanders in Hawaii and withheld essential information from them. According to their contention, officials in Washington had sufficient information—including that obtained by breaking the Japanese secret diplomatic code—to anticipate an early Japanese attack. Furthermore, most of the revisionists believe that data at the disposal of leaders in Washington were sufficient (if properly analyzed) to have warned of a possible attack on Pearl Harbor. After Pearl Harbor, they say, the administration attempted unjustly to make General Short and Admiral Kimmel, the commanders in Hawaii, scapegoats for the tragedy. Instead of blaming the commanders in Hawaii, the revisionists place the main responsibility upon civilian and military leaders in Washington—including Marshall, Stark, Stimson, Knox, and particularly President Roosevelt. Tansill phrased the idea of Washington responsibility for the war most starkly when he wrote: "It seems quite possible that the Far Eastern Military Tribunal brought to trial the wrong persons. It might have been better if the tribunal had held its sessions in Washington."[30] On this, as on other phases of the subject, some revisionists, including Beard, Current, and William L. Neumann, write in more restrained and qualified terms than either Tansill or Barnes.

Finally, the revisionists insist that the Roosevelt foreign policies failed to serve American national interests. If, as Roosevelt and Hull contended, American aid to the victims of aggression was designed to keep America out of war, these policies obviously failed. If the Roosevelt policies were designed to protect American security, they were, according to revisionists, of questionable success. By helping to crush Germany and Japan the United States removed two major barriers to Soviet expansion and created power vacuums and chaos which contributed to the rise of the Soviet Union to world power and to the resultant explosive Cold War situation. China, which was considered too vital to compromise in 1941, is now in Communist hands—in part, some revisionists say, because of Roosevelt's policies before and during World War II. Revisionists maintain in general that American involvement left the United States less secure, more burdened by debts and taxes, more laden with the necessity of maintaining huge armed forces than ever before in American history. Some revisionists predict that unless the United States returns to a policy of "continentalism" the nation may be headed for the nightmare described by George Orwell in *Nineteen Eighty-Four*, and toward World War III.

It is probable that the reception accorded the revisionist or the internationalist interpretation has been affected as much by the climate of thought and the international developments since Pearl Harbor as by the specific evidence and reasoning relied upon by historians. Emotional, ideological, political, economic, and military conditions from

1942 to 1950 contributed to a widespread acceptance of the internationalist interpretation. The historian who conformed to prevailing modes of thought in the profession did not seriously question the pro-Roosevelt interpretation of American entry into World War II. Revisionist hypotheses were viewed for the most part as biased and unsound. Critical references to the Beard group were in vogue.

With the breakdown of bipartisanship around 1950, the beginning of a new "Great Debate," the development of neo-isolationism of the Hoover-Taft-Knowland variety, and the Republican campaign of 1952, revisionist interpretations found a somewhat more receptive environment. The Cold War tensions and insecurity encouraged the conviction that American entry into World War II had some aftereffects dangerous to American security. These developments were supplemented by a growth of political, economic, and intellectual conservatism that encouraged a more critical attitude toward Roosevelt's prewar domestic policies as well as his actions in foreign affairs. Revisionist volumes and articles were published in increasing numbers. Although most historians continued to express themselves sympathetically toward Roosevelt's foreign policies before Pearl Harbor, there was a more widespread inclination to question specific features of the internationalist interpretation. Internationalist historians, such as Feis, or Langer and Gleason, phrased their accounts in moderate, restrained, and qualified terms. At the same time some revisionist historians became less defensive and more positive in their phrasing. But the neo-isolationism of the early 1950's did not win the dominant position in popular thought or national policies. And revisionist interpretations still failed to gain a really large following among American historians. It well may be that the future attitudes of many historians and of the American people toward American entry into World War II will be shaped as much by the future course of the United States as by the evidence uncovered by historical research.

Historians need not speak disparagingly, however, of the results of their inquiries during a period of only fifteen years on the subject of American entry into World War II. A prodigious amount of research has been accomplished. The diplomatic and military phases have been examined with striking thoroughness within the limits of available sources. Important beginnings have been made in the study of other aspects of the subject. Both revisionist and internationalist writers have advanced provocative and stimulating interpretations and have buttressed them with impressive documentation.

Despite these major accomplishments, there are important deficiencies and much work remains. Individuals will vary widely in their evaluations of what has been done and what remains to be done, but many of the criticisms of existing studies (criticisms which suggest possible directions for future efforts) may be analyzed under two major headings. In the first place, the narrow focus of most publications has left major areas almost untouched by serious historical research. Secondly—though the problem is probably incapable of final solution—there is need for a serious re-examination of the role and limitations of historical interpretation.

When measured by the standards of the "actualities" of pre-Pearl Harbor events, the scope and depth of available publications on American entry into World War II have been quite narrow in terms of time covered, subject matter, and source materials. Only a few books dealing specifically with this subject put it in the time context of the two World Wars. The volumes by Perkins, Chamberlin, Tansill, and Barnes all have this merit. Most studies of American entry into World War II, however, begin with 1940 or 1937. This point of departure is defensible if the scholar remains sensitively aware that he is examining only a tiny segment of the path that led to Pearl Harbor. Many historians, however, write almost as though the years from 1937 through 1941 were separated from and uninfluenced by earlier developments. For example, from a study of most available volumes a reader would not learn that these years were preceded by a devastating world depression with jolting economic, social, ideological, emotional, political, and power consequences that influenced the course of nations to December 7, 1941. Despite many important volumes and articles now available, there is much need for substantial research on foreign affairs in the years from 1921 to 1937. And a more meaningful perspective might be obtained if the subject were put in the broader context of the long-term but changing power relationships, industrialization of the world, the rise of the common man, and the development of secular ideologies designed to explain the mysteries of social, economic, and political changes whose ultimate form can only be dimly and imperfectly perceived.

Most published volumes are concerned largely with diplomatic, military, and some political aspects of the subject. The authors trace in intricate detail the policy planning, the minutiae of diplomatic exchanges, and the reactions of statesmen to the developments abroad. These phases are of major importance. They do not, however, constitute the whole story nor necessarily the most meaningful part. Economic, social, psychological, ethnic, religious, and political conditions that help to give direction and meaning to the diplomacy have been inadequately and imprecisely studied.

Political influences have been given much attention. Even the political analyses, however, often leave much to be desired when the subject is American entry into World War II. A good many historians on both sides have followed the almost standard procedure of charging individuals whose foreign policy views they do not like with partisan political motives. Writers on both sides often seem blind to political influences among those with whom they sympathize. Political analysts also have directed their attention largely to the top administration, military, and diplomatic officials. There has been relatively little serious study of the influence of individual congressmen and of state political organizations on the nation's foreign policies before Pearl Harbor. Furthermore, most references to political figures—even the prominent administration leaders—are of a two-dimensional variety. There is need for thorough biographies of scores of individuals. Frank Freidel's excellent biography of Franklin D. Roosevelt, now being published, suggests the sort of work needed on countless other figures in the story.[31] Some important beginnings have been made, too, in studying sectional variations, but this subject has by no means been exhausted.[32]

One need not be an economic determinist to be disturbed by the neglect of economic influences in existing histories of American entry into World War II. How did foreign policies affect those groups of persons who shared a particular economic interest? How did such effects influence the attitude of those groups toward foreign policy? What influence did those groups exert on policy making? Articles by John W. Masland and Roland N. Stromberg provide important beginnings on this phase of the subject, but much more remains to be done.[33]

Samuel Lubell and John Norman have published studies on the foreign policy attitudes of German-Americans and Italian-Americans.[34] There is need, however, for additional research on the role of numerous ethnic and religious groups in the history of American foreign affairs before Pearl Harbor. Volumes have been published on such pressure groups as the Committee to Defend America by Aiding the Allies, the Fight for Freedom Committee, the America First Committee, and the American Legion.[35] But studies are needed on the attitudes and influence of countless other organized pressure groups of all sorts on American foreign policies before Pearl Harbor. Several books and articles have analyzed the non-interventionists and interventionists—but neither of these groups has by any means been exhausted as a field for constructive historical research.[36]

There has been almost no serious research on the influence of psychological and emotional factors. Both revisionists and internationalists write almost as though the actions of the key figures could all be explained in intellectual and rational terms. It is conceivable that historians could learn as much about American entry into World War II by studying the psychological and emotional make-up of the individuals involved, as by studying the phrasing of the diplomatic dispatches and state papers. Ralph K. White, Harold Lavine, and James Wechsler have published suggestive studies on the role of propaganda in pre-Pearl Harbor developments,[37] but for the most part the role of psychological influences on the attitudes of the American people and of American statesmen has scarcely been touched.

Results of the limited research on these non-diplomatic influences have seldom been integrated into the major works. Thomas A. Bailey's interpretative survey, *The Man in the Street*, contains more data on these phases of the subject than do any of the major volumes on American entry into World War II.[38] But his study is suggestive rather than definitive.

In addition to the narrowness of approach with regard to time span and subject matter, there has been a narrowness in terms of the source materials used. If the focus of the subject matter is to be broadened as suggested in this article, historians will have to demonstrate a high degree of ingenuity in tapping additional source materials—including manuscripts in private hands. This appeal for greater breadth and depth is not meant to disparage the work thus far completed. But much of great importance remains to be done by scholars on the subject of American involvement in the war.

Montaigne's assertion that "nothing is so firmly believed as what we least know" suggests a second deficiency in most major volumes on American entry into World War II. The most heated controversies among historians do not center on those matters for which the facts and truth can be determined with greatest certainty. The interpretative controversies, on the contrary, rage over questions about which the historian is least able to determine truth. Despite the thousands of documents and tons of manuscripts, the written record and the physical remains constitute only a tiny fraction of the reality of America's course toward World War II—and these remains do not necessarily represent the "truth."

With the relatively inexact methods and incomplete data at his command, even the finest historian can often make only semi-informed guesses concerning motives, causes, and wisdom of pre-Pearl Harbor decisions. As Herbert Butterfield phrased it, the historian "can never quite carry his enquiries to that innermost region where the final play of motive and the point of responsibility can be decided. . . . He does not study human nature, therefore, in the way that an omniscient deity might observe it, with an eye that pierces our unspoken intentions, our thick folds of insincerity and the motives that we hardly avow to ourselves."[39] The historian can determine that certain events preceded American entry into World War II and he may find circumstantial evidence suggesting possible causal relationships. But he cannot conduct controlled experiments to measure with any degree of certainty the causal significance of antecedent developments and incidents. Furthermore, these various interpretations of individual historians are based upon different opinions concerning the wisdom of possible pre-Pearl Harbor policies as judged in terms of certain criteria, such as world peace and security, American peace and security, economic order and prosperity, and freedom and democracy. As Sumner Welles phrased it, "The wisdom of any foreign policy can generally be determined only by its results."[40] But in order to measure this wisdom, the results of policies that were actually followed would have to be compared with the results of possible alternative policies that were not followed. It is, of course, impossible to run controlled experiments to determine what would have happened if alternative polices had been followed. Furthermore, the possible alternatives were not necessarily of the simple "either/or" variety. The path to Pearl Harbor was filled with millions of decisions, great and small, each based upon other decisions which preceded it. There were countless forks in the road that led to Pearl Harbor. And no historian can know for certain what lay at the end of the paths that were not followed.

Writers on both sides, of course, are conscious of limitations inherent in historical interpretation. All of them qualify their generalizations with references to the inadequacy of their sources. But they recognize the limitations more clearly when referring to interpretations with which they do not agree. Sanborn, a revisionist, wrote that the internationalists' "first line of defense has always rested and still rests upon a foundation blended of faith, emotion, and hypothesis."[41] Dexter Perkins, on the other side, has written that revisionism is "shot through with passion and prejudice. . . . It also rests upon hypotheses which . . . cannot be demonstrated."[42] To a certain extent both Sanborn and Perkins are correct. But their generalizations apply in varying degree to books on *both* sides in the interpretative controversy.

Probably no one would want the historian to refrain from interpreting the course of events simply because he cannot scientifically prove the truth of his interpretations. The historian could not avoid some degree of interpretation even if he tried. Inadequate though his analyses may be, who is better qualified to perform the function? Both revisionist and internationalist historians have a responsibility to attempt to explain American entry into World War II as they understand it.

Nevertheless, considering the incompleteness and inexactness of their knowledge and understanding, historians do not seem justified in the cavalier, dogmatic tone that they so frequently use. They base their interpretations in part on a personal faith in the wisdom of the policies they support. Like devout believers in less secular faiths, writers on both sides tend to be intolerant of conflicting beliefs. This may not be true of all writers on the subject, but it does apply in varying degree to many on both sides. Historians need to emphasize the limits of their knowledge as well as the expansiveness of it. There is need for more awareness of the tentative nature of human inquiry, for self-criticism and the humility of an Albert Einstein, rather than the positive, dogmatic, self-righteousness of the propagandist. Perhaps in the furious twentieth-century struggle for men's minds there can be no real place for moderation and restraint—even in historical interpretation. Numerous critics, however, both here and abroad, are fearful of the immaturity of American attitudes toward international affairs. If the historian is sensitive to the many-sided complexities of issues and demonstrates intellectual humility and ideological tolerance, perhaps others, influenced by his example, may be less inclined to grasp at simplified, crusading, utopian theories regarding contemporary international affairs.

NOTES

1. *How War Came: An American White Paper, from the Fall of France to Pearl Harbor* (New York, 1942).
2. (Chicago, 1944).
3. (Boston, 1944).
4. *The Truth about Pearl Harbor* (New York, [1944]); *The Final Secret of Pearl Harbor* (New York, [1945]).
5. Samuel I. Rosenman (ed.), *The Public Papers and Addresses of Franklin D. Roosevelt* (13 vols., New York, 1938-1950); Elliott Roosevelt (ed.), *F. D. R.: His Personal Letters* (4 vols., New York, 1947-1950).
6. Winston S. Churchill, *The Second World War* (6 vols., Boston, 1948-1953); Hugh Gibson (ed.), *The Ciano Diaries, 1939-1943: The Complete Unabridged Diaries of Count Galeazzo Ciano, Italian Minister for Foreign Affairs* (Garden City, 1946). See also Togo Shigenori, *The Cause of Japan* (New York, 1956).
7. *This Is Pearl! The United States and Japan—1941* (New York, 1947).

8. *Roosevelt, from Munich to Pearl Harbor: A Study in the Creation of a Foreign Policy* (New York, 1950).

9. *Pearl Harbor: The Story of the Secret War* (New York, 1947).

10. *President Roosevelt and the Coming of the War, 1941: A Study in Appearances and Realities* (New Haven, 1948). See also Charles A. Beard, *American Foreign Policy in the Making, 1932-1940: A Study in Responsibilities* (New Haven, 1946).

11. (Chicago, 1950).

12. *Design for War: A Study of Secret Power Politics, 1937-1941* (New York, 1951).

13. *The Final Secret of Pearl Harbor: The Washington Contribution to the Japanese Attack* (New York, 1954).

14. *Roosevelt and Hopkins: An Intimate History* (New York, 1948).

15. These are Volumes I (1947) and III (1948) of Morison, *History of the United States Naval Operations in World War II* (10 vols. to date, Boston, 1947-   ).

16. (Washington, 1950). This is a volume in the series entitled *United States Army in World War II*, being prepared by the Office of the Chief of Military History, Department of the Army.

17. *The Road to Pearl Harbor: The Coming of the War between the United States and Japan* (Princeton, 1950).

18. *The Challenge to Isolation, 1937-1940* (New York, 1952); and *The Undeclared War, 1940-1941* (New York, 1953).

19. (Ann Arbor, 1955).

20. *Back Door to War: The Roosevelt Foreign Policy, 1933-1941* (Chicago, 1952).

21. *Perpetual War for Perpetual Peace: A Critical Examination of the Foreign Policy of Franklin Delano Roosevelt and Its Aftermath* (Caldwell, Idaho, 1953).

22. *Secretary Stimson: A Study in Statecraft* (New Brunswick, 1954).

23. For example, Hans L. Trefousse, *Germany and American Neutrality, 1939-1941* (New York, 1951); William L. Langer, *Our Vichy Gamble* (New York, 1947); Immanuel C. Y. Hsu, "Kurusu's Mission to the United States and the Abortive *Modus Vivendi*," *Journal of Modern History*, XXIV (September, 1952), 301-307; Norman L. Hill, "Was There an Ultimatum before Pearl Harbor?" *American Journal of International Law*, XLII (April, 1948), 355-67; Richard N. Current, "How Stimson Meant to 'Maneuver' the Japanese," *Mississippi Valley Historical Review*, XL (June, 1953), 67-74; Herbert Feis, "War Came at Pearl Harbor: Suspicions Considered," *Yale Review*, XLV (Spring, 1956), 378-90.

24. Davis and Lindley, *How War Came*, vii-viii; Beard, *President Roosevelt and the Coming of the War*, 243 n.

25. *The Open Door at Home: A Trial Philosophy of National Interest* (New York, 1934).

26. (New York, 1940).

27. Wayne S. Cole, *America First: The Battle against Intervention, 1940-1941* (Madison, 1953), 75.

28. *America Goes to War* (Boston, 1938).

29. Beard, *President Roosevelt and the Coming of the War*, 573-91.

30. Tansill, *Back Door to War*, 629.

31. Frank Freidel, *Franklin D. Roosevelt* (3 vols. to date, Boston, 1952-   ).
32. George L. Grassmuck, *Sectional Biases in Congress on Foreign Policy* (Baltimore, 1951); Ralph H. Smuckler, "The Region of Isolationism," *American Political Science Review* (Menasha, Wis.), XLVII (June, 1953), 386-401; Jeannette P. Nichols, "The Middle West and the Coming of World War II," *Ohio State Archaeological and Historical Quarterly* (Columbus), LXII (April, 1953), 122-45; Wayne S. Cole, "America First and the South, 1940-1941," *Journal of Southern History* (Lexington, Ky.), XXII (February, 1956), 36-47.
33. John W. Masland, "Commercial Influence upon American Far Eastern Policy, 1937-1941," *Pacific Historical Review*, XI (October, 1942), 281-99; Roland N. Stromberg, "American Business and the Approach of War, 1935-1941," *Journal of Economic History* (New York), XIII (Winter, 1953), 58-78.
34. Samuel Lubell, "Who Votes Isolationist and Why," *Harper's Magazine* (New York), CCII (April, 1951), 29-36; John Norman, "Influence of Pro-Fascist Propaganda on American Neutrality, 1935-1936," in Dwight E. Lee and George E. McReynolds (eds.), *Essays in History and International Relations in Honor of George Hubbard Blakeslee* (Worcester, 1949), 193-214.
35. Johnson, *Battle against Isolation*; Cole, *America First*; Roscoe Baker, *The American Legion and American Foreign Policy* (New York, 1954).
36. John C. Donovan, "Congressional Isolationists and the Roosevelt Foreign Policy," *World Politics*, III (April, 1951), 299-316; William Appleman Williams, "The Legend of Isolationism in the 1920's," *Science and Society* (New York, XVIII (Winter, 1954), 1-20.
37. Ralph K. White, "Hitler, Roosevelt, and the Nature of War Propaganda," *Journal of Abnormal and Social Psychology*, XLIV (April, 1949), 157-74; Harold Lavine and James Wechsler, *War Propaganda and the United States* (New Haven, 1940).
38. *The Man in the Street: The Impact of American Public Opinion on Foreign Policy* (New York, 1948).
39. Herbert Butterfield, *History and Human Relations* (New York, 1951), 116-17.
40. Welles, *Time for Decision*, 288.
41. Barnes (ed.), *Perpetual War for Perpetual Peace*, 190.
42. Perkins, "Was Roosevelt Wrong?" *Virginia Quarterly Review*, XXX (Summer, 1954), 372.

RECENT STUDIES

Raymond H. Dawson, *The Decision To Aid Russia, 1941: Foreign Policy and Domestic Politics* (Chapel Hill: University of North Carolina Press, 1959).

Elting E. Morison, *Turmoil and Tradition: A Study of the Life and Times of Henry L. Stimson* (Boston: Houghton Mifflin, 1960).

Raymond A. Esthus, "President Roosevelt's Commitment to Britain To

Intervene in a Pacific War," *Mississippi Valley Historical Review*, L (June 1963), 28-38.

Herbert Feis, *The Road to Pearl Harbor* (Princeton: Princeton University Press, 1962).

Roberta Wohlstetter, *Pearl Harbor: Warning and Decision* (Stanford: Stanford University Press, 1962).

Robert A. Divine, *The Reluctant Belligerent: American Entry into World War II* (New York: John Wiley, 1965).

XXI

A Search for Stability

JOHN HIGHAM

Although World War II caused a widespread lapse of scholarly activity, it did not seem for a time to change the interpretation of American history very much. In fact, as young historians came back to the universities from wartime assignments, progressive historiography entered a kind of Indian summer. Through the late 1940's and into the early 1950's most of the exciting books were written by scholars who had been trained during the Great Depression and who had responded ardently to the influence of Charles A. Beard. Their books in large measure were hearty evaluations of the tradition of democratic reform and protest. Merrill Jensen's *The New Nation* (1950) recorded the advancing struggle of democracy in the 1780's. Arthur M. Schlesinger Jr.'s *The Age of Jackson* (1945) told a similar story about the 1830's. Eric F. Goldman's *Rendezvous with Destiny* (1952) swept bravely forward from 1870 in tracing "the reform movements that culminated in the New Deal and the Fair Deal." C. Vann Woodward's *Origins of the New South, 1877-1913* (1951) focused on the upthrust of democracy under the impact of industrialism. Among somewhat older scholars, Alice Felt Tyler wrote about religious and humanitarian reform in a Turnerian vein; and Henry Steele Commager carried forward Parrington's unfinished story of modern American thought with an optimistic pragmatism the old master had lacked.[1]

A disquieting note sounded in one of the most brilliant of the post-war books. Richard Hofstadter's *The American Political Tradition and the Men Who Made it* (1948) commented mordantly on a current "lack of confidence in the American future" and on "the rudderless and demoralized state of American liberalism." This he attributed partly to the absence of really basic differences between liberal and conservative impulses throughout the national experience. The customary emphasis of American historians on conflict, Hofstadter said, has obscured the underlying agreement that major parties and movements have always shared. Ours has been "a democracy in cupidity," which offers no coherent guidance in a new, more dangerous era.[2] Hofstadter did not press this fateful challenge to progressive historiography. He delivered it as a casual afterthought to a narrative revealing a fascinating variety of political types. He wrote from a position otherwise so sympathetic to Beard and so critical of American business mores that his heresy seemed only a step to the left.

All of these books displayed a keen interest in the role of ideas, particularly as they bore on political action. Many of the authors still held to a primarily economic interpretation of history; but close attention to the impact of ideas on politics inevitably pushed economic causation into the background. From an original concentration on external, material reality, the progressive scholar was turning more and more to a preoccupation with values. And since the values that many of the best books examined were those of the progressive tradition itself, historians were obviously taking stock of their own ideological heritage. While some were assuring themselves of its strength, others probed soft spots. Hofstadter was not alone in showing a new awareness of failures and dilemmas in the liberal record. Goldman worried about the growing relativism it displayed. Other left-of-center historians, newly sensitive to the magnitude of American racial problems, discovered a vein of prejudice in liberal thought; they set about rectifying the insensitivity and disinterest older progressive historians had usually shown on the subject of race.[3]

A more central and thoroughgoing reappraisal of progressive history began in monographs challenging the significance of economic conflicts. No single monograph could make extensive claims or escape the suspicion that its findings were exceptional. By the mid-Fifties, however, the new research was having a cumulative impact on the whole shape of American history. One after another, the great crises, which progressive historians had depicted as turning points in the battle between democracy and privilege, came under fresh examination. In each case the scale of conflict seemed to shrink. Sharp divisions between periods, sections, groups, and ideologies disappeared. Over all, the new digging amounted to a massive grading operation that smoothed and flattened the convulsive dialectic of progressive history. An unsuspected degree of uniformity and agreement appeared in the welter of America's historical experience. Instead of a polarized culture—a culture eternally divided between over- and underprivileged groups, between a party of the past and a party of the future, between noble ideals and ignoble interests— young scholars glimpsed an essentially homogeneous culture full of small, impermanent variations. The continuity that Gabriel had observed in the American "democratic faith" and that Hofstadter criticized in the American political tradition emerged as substantial social reality.

Among the various types of cleavage that progressives dwelled upon, the sectional principle gave way most easily. An attack on sectional differences as fundamental to American history had already developed in the 1930's. It stemmed partly from the revolt against Turner: all anti-Turnerians saw the West as an extension of the East, not its antithesis. The revisionist approach to the Civil War also ran counter to an emphatic sectionalism; for revisionists assumed that North and South were not incompatible civilizations, but basically one. These views simply gained further momentum in the 1940's and 1950's. Now the defensive and aggressive sectional feelings that motivated so much scholarship in the early twentieth century were rapidly dissolving. The standardized urban milieu in which younger historians grew up deprived them of strong regional identities.

Consequently, in postwar scholarship, much that had been described as southern or western either lost significance or merged into national configurations. Following a line of research that Frank Owsley opened in the late 1930's, many southern historians called attention to the democratic features of the Old South. It was, they maintained, primarily a land of middle-class farmers, not of plantation aristocrats.[4] The notion of the antebellum South as a distinctively aristocratic society was a myth; and a northern scholar wrote a book to prove that even the myth had rested on nationwide rather than purely sectional yearnings. *The Southerner as American* (1960) was the title of a collection of essays by a group of young southern historians, and it summed up the general trend of scholarship.[5]

One might equally say of western history that it now dealt with the

westerner as American. Attention shifted increasingly to the post-
frontier West, to cities, economic development, and the impingement
of national politics and institutions on western areas.[6] For many readers
Henry Nash Smith made America's mythology about the West more
interesting than the reality. Smith's powerful book, *Virgin Land*
(1950), capped the assault on Turner by relegating the frontier thesis
—prematurely, it should be said—to the ash heap of dead myths. Simultaneously Walter P. Webb took that thesis out of a sectional context
and put it in an international context. Before World War II Webb
had dwelled on the distinctive features of his own West, the Great
Plains. In 1952 he published *The Great Frontier*, in which America's
frontier experience is linked to European history in a general interpretation of Western civilization.

In view of the reaction against sectionalism, it is little wonder that
academic interest in political conflicts between East, West, and South
fell off markedly. No one could deny, of course, that the Civil War
was a tremendous rupture of whatever unity and continuity America
had exhibited. But few of the younger professional historians coming
along in the wake of Craven and Randall found the causes of the war
an attractive subject for research. While journalists served up great gobs
of Civil War drama to an avid public, the number of significant contributions from professionals declined. A notable exception was the
monumental history of the Civil War era on which Allan Nevins embarked about 1940; but Nevins, writing in the spirit of James Ford
Rhodes, had an old-fashioned appreciation of the triumph of union in
the midst of strife.[7]

If antagonisms between North and South failed to stimulate younger
historians, conflicts between East and West proved still less inspiring.
Events that had been attributed to aggressive western initiative, such
as the War of 1812 and the progressive movement, were reinterpreted
in national terms.[8] Most remarkably, the Turnerian doctrine that the
political democracy of the early nineteenth century came out of the
West received hardly any effective support in post-war research.[9] A
major controversy erupted over the nature of Jacksonian democracy
without any of the leading participants taking seriously the specifically
western elements for which it had been famous.

Not a sectional but a class thesis was at issue in the controversy over
Jacksonian democracy. Not Turner but Beard was the main target of
the newer historians. Turner, having died in 1932, bore the brunt of
the historiographical discontents of the Thirties; Beard's death in 1948
released a similar but fiercer onslaught. While Turner's sectionalism

faded gracefully into the background, Beard's vision of an America divided between the democratic many and a privileged economic class underwent searching criticism. Throughout the late 1940's and 1950's a host of scholars mined and sapped the old economic dualism over most of the span of American history. The first sustained attack developed on Jacksonian terrain simply because a new, highly vulnerable statement of the Beardian approach materialized there.

Arthur M. Schlesinger Jr.'s *The Age of Jackson* was the work of a brilliant, ardent, and very young man charged with the antibusiness spirit of the 1930's. Building on postulates advanced earlier by his father and by Beard, Schlesinger depicted the urban working class as the cutting edge of the Jacksonian movement. That movement involved intellectuals and other "noncapitalist groups, farmers and laboring men." It was a phase of the pragmatic, realistic, "enduring struggle between the business community and the rest of society which is the guarantee of freedom."[10] The line ran straight and true from Jackson to Franklin D. Roosevelt.

Launched in 1945 on a great wave of praise, *The Age of Jackson* soon collided with a backlash of criticism. Many historians, it will be remembered, were turning away from the urgent present-mindedness of the 1930's. The distrusted Schlesinger's heavy emphasis on the features of Jacksonian politics that resembled the New Deal. Further probing into the impressive new evidence he had assembled dissolved the polarity between "the business community and the rest of society." Jacksonian "laboring men" were often merchants and professional people; the "working class" displayed no consistent political allegiance. In fact, acquisitive, business motives entered very largely into the Jacksonian program. Evidently the common man *was* a businessman.[11]

It also began to appear that the ideological cleavage between Jeffersonianism and Hamiltonianism, which progressive historians linked with the distinction between common men and capitalists, was equally misleading. Schlesinger endorsed the usual view that the Jeffersonian spirit triumphed in the 1830's over the monopolistic schemes of the Hamiltonians. But postwar scholarship undercut this dualism too. A modest revival in the study of economic history, beginning in the 1940's, brought out startlingly close relations between government and business in the Jacksonian era.

The revival of economic history owed something to the initiative of Edwin F. Gay, Arthur H. Cole, and the Rockefeller Foundation, and something also to a new climate of opinion. The waning of economic interpretations of history enabled historians to reverse their chain of cause and effect. Attention shifted from economic motives to economic processes, from the economic causes of historical development to the historical causes of economic development. Doubtless the dramatic impact that governmental policies were having on national income and wealth created a special interest in the political sources of economic growth. A Committee on Research in Economic History, appointed by the SSRC in 1941, chose as its first area for investigation the role of government in economic development. The studies it sponsored over the next decade, notably those of Carter Goodrich and his students, revealed a thoroughly mixed economy in antebellum America. An intimate, pragmatic association of state and local governments with "private enterprise" overrode all ideological scruples. One economic historian actually concluded that "it is only meretricious to contrast Hamiltonian with Jeffersonian policy."[12] Others, notably Lee Benson in *The Concept of Jacksonian Democracy* (1961), are redefining party differences with a new grasp of what was constructively liberal in Whig and Federalist programs.

Inevitably, the reaction against an ideologically divided, class-structured history reached back to the Revolutionary era. The basic dialectic of progressive historiography had been established by contrasting the Revolution and the Constitution, the one a democratic social upheaval, the other a capitalistic counterrevolution. Here was the critical test of the progressive approach; and here the sharpest clash of interpretations occurred. In 1943 a modest monograph by Philip Crowl, demonstrating an absence of class conflict in Maryland politics during and after the Revolution, went largely unnoticed.[13] In the 1950's the tide turned. It drastically reduced, though it did not wholly eliminate, the antithesis between a Jeffersonian Revolution and a Hamiltonian Constitution.

Two slashing critics went straight for Beard's *Economic Interpretation of the Constitution*. Forrest McDonald closely re-examined the sources of income of constitutional convention delegates in order to demolish Beard's distinction between personalty and realty interests. Robert E. Brown raked Beard's logic in one book and in another assailed Becker's thesis of an internal social revolution. The widespread participation in government in colonial Massachusetts, Brown claimed, shows that Americans did not gain democracy in 1776 but rather preserved it. Instead of creating a new social order, they defended an old one.[14]

Thus a minimization of class conflict deprived early American history both of a revolutionary and of a counterrevolutionary thrust. Scholars investigating the causes of the Revolution, notably Oliver M. Dickerson, Edmund S. Morgan, and Bernard Knollenberg, discounted the impersonal economic forces and the irrepressible conflicts of Beardian history. Instead, they put forward the old patriotic view that the revolutionists were defending traditional liberties against bungling innovations of British officials. Just as historians in the 1930's rejected Beard's explanation of the Civil War for a theory of inept American leadership, so historians in the 1950's replaced Beard's explanation of the Revolution with an emphasis on inept British leadership.[15] Although the new interpretation of the Revolution was sympathetic whereas the revisionist account of the Civil War was not, the similarity of the two cases suggests again how much a repudiation of determinism contributed to the breakdown of progressive history.

As controversial breezes eddied through the staid ranks of early American historians, a new vigor seemed to enter that field. Never before had professional scholars debated so seriously the issues of the seventeenth and eighteenth centuries. The imperial and progressive schools had worked different sides of the street and had only occasionally encountered one another directly. Now a frontal challenge to the progressive school made early American history, for a time at least, the liveliest area of intellectual ferment. It began to recover from the relative neglect into which it had fallen because of the progressive bias in favor of more recent history. More scholars were willing to focus on the colonial origins of American experience and to understand remote situations in their own terms. Then too, the revulsion against determinism helped to quicken colonial history. A good many postwar historians followed Morison's example of humanizing the colonial scene. Much of the best research appeared in vivid biographies of such people as Jefferson, Ezra Stiles, and Edward Livingston.[16] Fortunately, all these impulses received the timely support of a new research organization, the Institute of Early American History and Culture, which Carl Bridenbaugh started upon a productive career in 1945.

Recent American history may not be faring as well. The study of the twentieth century has shared, of course, in the general reevaluation of the American past. There too the antibusiness spirit of progressive scholarship, with its emphasis on economic conflict, has diminished. There too a revolt against determinism and a more sensitive grasp of the role of political and economic leadership characterize the latest books.[17] But major interpretive revisions, such as we have had for the history of the eighteenth and nineteenth centuries, have been less in evidence, at least for the period since 1917. No established professional historian except Eric Goldman has written seriously about the period since World War II, and some are moving their research back from the twentieth century altogether. There may be some question whether or not the vitality recent historiography had in the 1940's will persist without the explicit present-mindedness of the progressive school.

Enough has been said, perhaps, about particular periods to enable us to ask what over-all meaning the new American past is assuming.

The present generation has not produced a decisive leadership such as Turner and Beard supplied in their day. No one has written a major work shaping our history into a grand design as persuasive as theirs once were. Nevertheless, alternatives to the progressive scheme have been sketched in a number of recent books, all of which depict a relatively homogeneous society with a relatively conservative history.

Historians in an age of unceasing international peril, when national security and the capacity for survival are fundamental concerns, can hardly avoid a somewhat conservative view of their country's history. They can hardly avoid an appreciation of its more cohesive and deeply rooted qualities. Nevertheless, they may trace those qualities to quite diverse sources, and they may disagree widely on the worth and durability of such homogeneity as they perceive. In rejecting a simple cleavage between two Americas, some historians may be most impressed by the wholeness of the national fabric, others by the looseness and multitude of its many strands. Their common concern is with the nature and degree of stability in American experience. Yet their answers are various and often ambivalent.

A key to the present temper of historical opinion lies in the pages of Alexis de Tocqueville's *Democracy in America* (1840), today the most respected of all interpretations of the United States. Tocqueville treated American culture as an organic whole; and his work rested heavily on the concept of national character. During the heyday of progressive scholarship this approach was somewhat suspect, and Tocqueville's influence was at a low ebb. Although progressive intellectuals sometimes indulged in generalizations about national character, they distrusted its heuristic value. Referring as it does to the pervasive, persistent features of a whole culture, "national character" neglects the environmental determination of social conflict. No edition of *Democracy in America* was published in the United States between 1904 and 1945; during most of that time it was out of print. Since World War II, however, at least six hardcover editions have appeared. With them has come a torrent of scholarship and speculation on *the* American experience, character, traits, etc.[18]

In addition to its integral approach, Tocqueville's classic has the special appeal today of rendering a mixed verdict on American democracy. The genial French aristocrat observed a nation at once stable and full of flux. He noticed little class cleavage. But he described a democracy that produced oppressive conformity on the one hand and kaleidoscopic variety on the other. He rejoiced in America's stability while deploring its social fragmentation. These antinomies, which Tocqueville's genius held together, jostle and contend in contemporary historical writing. Today's historians affirm on one side a need for and partial attainment of community in America. They cling on the other to values of dissent and diversity inherited from the progressive tradition. The opposing schools of interpretation that clashed so sharply in the 1930's and 1940's have partially blended, just as general historical theories have done. But the tensions that formerly divided those schools have survived their mingling.

Some of the efforts to sum up American history in recent years primarily emphasize the stability—and therefore the continuity—of American experience over the centuries. Other historians have given more attention to the reverse side of Tocqueville's model, stressing instabilities and thus allowing for a greater degree of change. To the first group belong the Harvard political theorist Louis Hartz and the University of Chicago historian Daniel Boorstin. Both of them have dwelled on the remarkable persistence of basic characteristics throughout American history. Hartz, like Gabriel before him, locates continuity in certain unifying principles or beliefs. Boorstin finds it in the pragmatic, down-to-earth way of life progressive historians often admired. Yet it is Hartz who stands closer to the progressive sympathy for friction and dissent, regretting that America has not had more.

Hartz wrote *The Liberal Tradition in America* (1955) to substitute new categories for the overworked schema of Beard and Parrington. He argued that the absence of a feudal heritage had left America with just one rather than two traditions of thought. A liberal consensus has had so unchallenged a sway, Hartz said, that most American political debate has been shadowboxing. "America must look to its contact with other nations to provide that spark of philosophy, that grain of relative insight that its own history has denied."[19]

Boorstin was equally impressed by the massive stability and unphilosophic harmony of America. He too explained the mediocrity of American political thought as a consequence of the absence of the deep social antagonisms that have existed in Europe. Boorstin, however, had no regrets about this. In *The Genius of American Politics* (1953) and in *The Americans: The Colonial Experience* (1958), he contended that

America from the outset flouished by scrapping European blueprints, dissolving European distinctions, and moving toward a homogeneous society of undifferentiated men. A naïve practicality enabled Americans to unite in a stable way of life, undisturbed by divisive principles.

Significantly, both Hartz and Boorstin got their accent on a stable, continuous national character by looking at the United States as Tocqueville had: from the outside. They too—Hartz especially—adopted an explicitly comparative approach to American history. Hartz came to a comparative approach partly by the accident of having to teach European political theory at Harvard instead of the American theory for which he had been trained. Boorstin came to it through a European education as a Rhodes Scholar (as Lawrence Gipson had many years before) and later as a visiting professor abroad. Certainly both men were responding in a large sense to the heightened awareness of the outside world that the history of the mid-twentieth century thrust upon American historians. The domestic conflicts so apparent in an age of reform had diverted progressive scholars from the international context of American history. The neo-Tocquevilleans of the 1950's partially restored that context and so widened the horizons of scholarship. Unfortunately, their comparative interests were largely confined to contrasts between America and Europe. The insecurities of the postwar era engendered such an urge to define America—to establish its distinctive character—that the parallels and reciprocal involvements of a truly international history remained little attended.

The search for the essential and the permanent in American experience led perhaps more readily in an interdisciplinary direction, for the pursuit of national identity animated literary critics and social scientists as well as historians. One of the most persuasive general historians of the 1950's, David M. Potter, developed an integral and comparative view of American history primarily through contact with anthropology rather than contact with Europe. Like an increasing number of his colleagues, Potter found the theories of contemporary social scientists indispensable to a grasp of American society now that the progressive pattern was dissolving. He stopped writing a conventional sort of political history and made an intensive study of recent findings on culture and personality. More than most postwar historians, Potter wrote in a deterministic vein. His *People of Plenty: Economic Abundance and the American Character* (1954) is an economic interpretation, which transmuted Turner's frontier thesis into the more inclusive and systematic formulas of behavioral theory. For the transitory, sectional abundance of the frontier, Potter substituted a broadly based aptitude for productivity. Whereas the generation of Parrington and Beard had explained basic cleavages on economic grounds, Potter showed our wealth shaping a common, distinctive, and successful way of life.

On a more concrete level of scholarship one of the finest historians who has illuminated persistent features of American history is Edmund S. Morgan of Yale. Hartz, Boorstin, and Potter have explained continuity and stability largely in terms of environment and institutions. Morgan, on the other hand, has looked for and discovered a dogged adherence to fundamental principles. In writing about the Puritan founders of New England, he has emphasized the maintenance of their religious and social standards in the face of many divisive pressures. In writing about the Revolutionary generation, he has shown its undeviating pursuit of consistent principles throughout the tortuous controversy with Britain.[20]

All these historians have been aware of the other side of Tocqueville's America. All of them have noticed the diffuse instability associated in America with rapid mobility; and Boorstin's latest book, *The Image* (1962), reveals a distinct uneasiness over the formless flux he had earlier celebrated. Still, it has remained for another group of scholars, less preoccupied with contrasts between America and Europe, to deal seriously with the dimension of change. It has remained for them to formulate into new patterns the frictions within American life. Although most of the latter historians work on a relatively small scale, close to the stream of events, some of them too have tried to sketch the general course of American history. As a group, they share a common fascination with the tendency of stable structures to break down in a free and fluid culture.

Movement through space and through the ranks of society forms the central theme of our latest students of conflict. Like Potter, they have taken Turner's emphasis on migration out of a sectional context. In effect, they have used the theme of mobility to explode the rigid categories of progressive scholarship while manitaining a sharp interest in conflict and change. In place of classes and sections, they have conceived of a politics of coalition between diverse interests and of a society of shifting status groups. The concept of status has seemed especially relevant because of the very fragility of the honorific and prestigeful considerations that define it. Status is something that is continually pursued and ever on the verge of being lost in a nation of mobile men. As they break free from traditional security in search of better locations, a vast process of disintegration and partial reintegration goes on.

Considering the crucial importance assigned to mobility in this ver-

sion of American history, it is hardly surprising that one of the influential exponents is also the leading authority on immigration. Oscar
Handlin has shaped each of his major books as a story of disintegration
and mobility. Handlin's history begins, characteristically, with a stable,
orderly community—a *Gemeinschaft* in the langauge of German sociology—which makes life meaningful and whole. Then the shock of
migration disrupts the community, breeding strife and freedom; and
uprooted men pursue their separate, clashing purposes. This is the story
of *Boston's Immigrants* (1941), the story of antebellum Massachusetts
in *Commonwealth* (1947), the story of nineteenth century immigration in *The Uprooted* (1951), and the story of us all in *The Americans*
(1963). It is often an anguished story, heavy with a sense of loss and
alienation. It is also highly ambivalent, for the author admires the
growth of freedom while lamenting the decline of order.

A rather similar picture of American development lies behind the
superficially quite different interpretations recently offered by William
A. Williams and Rowland Berthoff, one of them a neo-Marxist, the
other a self-proclaimed conservative. Both Williams and Berthoff look
back to a time of stability and order at the beginning of American history. Both of them observe a breakdown of community in the laissez-
faire world of the nineteenth century as a consequence of excessive
mobility (Berthoff) or expansion (Williams).[21] The three accounts
differ most sharply in their evaluation of the twentieth century. Handlin leaves the outcome confused and uncertain; Berthoff finds America
gradually recovering a healthy balance; Williams sees a capitalist oligarchy restoring but perverting the ideal of community.

Through all these interpretations, through those that stress stability
and those that stress change, runs a question previous generations of
historians in America had never so insistently asked. Most of the major
postwar scholars seem to be asking in one way or another, "What (if
anything) is so deeply rooted in our past that we can rely on its survival?" This has become, perhaps, the great historical question in a time
of considerable moral confusion, when the future looks both precarious
and severely limited in its possibilities. The question is genuinely open-
ended, because neither the partisans of stability nor the connoisseurs of
change assume that history is on their side. Progressive historians, like
the conservative evolutionists who preceded them, relied implicitly on
a faith in progress in charting the relations between past and future.
Assuming an upward gradient, they asked what each period or movement "contributed" or "added" to the march of progress. This faith,
which was shaken in Parrington's day, has since 1940 been so shattered

that historians must soberly ask what is permanent and what is transient in American history. Accordingly, the shedding of a progressive outlook has not left historians accoutered in the conservative evolutionism of the late nineteenth century. Conservative evolutionists were confident that unity would continue to overcome internal strife. They expected that the partnership between union and freedom, which defined their America, would continue to develop and to triumph over obstacles. Today's historians want to know how durable and meaningful are the unities and diversities that already exist. In our postprogressive culture, the relation between freedom and union seems no longer natural but tense and problematical.

Once released from the dream of progress, historians who were alert to conflict and change could face unflinchingly the tragic and ironic elements in the past. In fact, many of our best historians acquired a positive relish for the burdens, the losses, and the intractable dilemmas of history. An early indication of how profoundly this shift in sensibility could affect historical interpretation appeared in the Civil War field. The revisionist school of the Thirties had viewed the "needless" war and the "vindictive" Reconstruction as exceptional interludes in the normal progress of civilization. Like the philosophers of the Enlightenment, the revisionists believed such crimes and follies avoidable if only reason were allowed to work matters out. All of this began to look naïvely optimistic in the 1940's. Relying heavily on Reinhold Niebuhr's powerful critique of the idea of progress, Arthur M. Schlesinger Jr. in 1949 assailed the revisionists for simplifying great moral issues: "Man generally is entangled in insoluble problems; history is consequently a tragedy in which we are all involved, whose keynote is anxiety and frustration, not progress and fulfillment." Before these words were written, the leading revisionist, Avery Craven, was already modifying his position. His writings in the 1950's took more seriously the emotional realities and the moral dilemmas that led to war.[22]

Indeed, much of the best scholarship of the 1950's struck the tragic note. Instead of looking backward from the crest of a historical movement to observe its rise, as progressives usually did, the newer historians often looked forward from the crest to watch its decline. Thus Perry Miller, in resuming the Puritan studies he had commenced in the Thirties, wrote one of the finest books in our historical literature, the second great volume of *The New England Mind* (1953), as an epic of unrelieved defeat. Remorselessly, even gleefully, Miller followed the agonizing, century-long breakup of the intellectual system he had presented in Volume I in its original wholeness. In later work that reflected a growing obsession with the "meaning" of America, Miller shifted to more nationalistic themes. Meanwhile, the stable features of Puritan experience came into view again in Edmund Morgan's writings. But others carried on the analysis of dispersion and loss. Bernard Bailyn, a young historian with a keen understanding of instability in early America, traced through the seventeenth century the fragmentation of social and educational patterns as Miller had traced the fragmentation of beliefs.[23] In writing about the first half of the nineteenth century Stanley Elkins and David Donald discovered similar trends. Where earlier historians had seen a rise of democracy they found a disastrous erosion of all institutional authority.[24]

Into recent history also passed an unprecedented fascination with decline and defeat. Richard Hofstadter's very influential *Age of Reform* (1955) dwelled on the failings of the populists and the progressives. Instead of one evolutionary sequence culminating in the New Deal, he observed the degeneration of each movement into a perverse illiberalism. Henry May's *The End of American Innocence* (1959) examined the cultural ferment on the eve of World War I not as the beginning of a new era but rather as the destruction of a pre-existing scheme of things. C. Vann Woodward, who was perhaps as deeply attached to progressive values as any of our leading historians, nevertheless discovered that experiences of guilt, alienation, and defeat defined the distinctive value and pertinence of southern history.[25]

A crucial book in this mode was Henry Nash Smith's *Virgin Land* (1950), which we have already noticed for its attack on Turner's kind of western history. Although written with deceptive detachment, *Virgin Land* was essentially a study of the death of ideas. It traced three major images of the American West from the late eighteenth century to the end of the nineteenth. In each case Smith's attention fixed on a loss of imaginative richness and social relevance as the image became increasingly debased, exploited, and false to fact. An adequate account of the rise of western myths and symbols remains to be written. *Virgin Land* was the valedictory of a man alienated from the Texas in which he grew up in the 1920's.

Smith's book also announced another theme of great significance in recent historical writing, particularly in the kind that emphasizes instability and change. He handled ideas with a psychoanalytical awareness of their emotional import. *Virgin Land* shares with Hofstadter's *American Political Tradition* (1948) the credit for introducing into professional historical scholarship a large, effective grasp of the nonrational elements in human conduct. Both authors had nourished themselves on modern literary criticism, which became penetrated by psychological interpretations in the late Thirties and Forties. Hofstadter called upon psychology primarily to explain aggression and frustration. Smith, as a professor of English, was less interested in motives than in meanings. A product of the new American Studies movement that was linking literature with history in an integrated study of art and society, he studied the dramatic symbols and pictorial images in which Americans had expressed their deeply rooted hopes and fears. He wrote the history of myths.[26]

Professional historians had been quite slow to make any real use of depth psychology. The first major study of myths in American history, *The Mind of the South* (1941), was written in the 1930's by a tormented literary and social critic, W. J. Cash; but professional historians did not follow up his brilliant insights until the 1950's.[27] Perhaps this was partly because they got little encouragement from the behaviorism that ruled academic psychology. More importantly, a reluctance to accept the nonrational as a legitimate and pervasive dimension of reality was integral to the progressive heritage of American historians. The progressive expectation of steady improvement in human affairs rested on the assumption that men are rational: they ordinarily pursue their individual or collective self-interest, and such interest is either rationally perceived or—at worst—coherently rationalized. Progressive historians treated ideas not as myths, full of extravagant fantasy, but as ideologies that interpret life in terms functional to some interested group. Such, for example, was the method of Charles A. Beard. In the last weeks of his life in 1948 the old man still insisted, "Economics explains the mostest!" Then, after a pause, he added, "But I may have neglected the irrational."[28] The comment was an epitaph to more than one man's career.

In recent years scholarly journals have teemed with articles and university presses with books on historical myths, symbols, images, and the like. A psychological approach may, if it continues to gain momentum, reopen every question in American history. It is seductively congenial to the present climate of opinion; for it enables restless historians who are impressed by the over-all stability of their country to subjectivize the stresses within it. Psychological history turns conflict and change into an interior drama. Divisions, which the previous generation understood as basic opposition between distinct groups, become generalized tensions running through the whole culture. Acts of protest and defiance often acquire defensive, compensatory implications, so that reformers for example are seen acting out their personal and social maladjustments.[29]

Also, the study of myths and images has a special attraction in the postwar period because it focuses on kinds of thinking that unite a people rather than those that divide them. The concept of ideology refers to exclusive and rival creeds. It relates directly to social conflict. The concept of myth, on the other hand, refers to the integrating values that bind men together.[30] All in all, the psychological vogue has given an implicit sanction to harmony or adaptability. It has sustained our sense of the dynamic while expressing our need for social solidarity. It has also raised our appreciation of tragedy in history and depressed our appreciation of rational purpose.

Fortunately, American historians have not yielded wholly to the psychologizing trend. Among those who still respect the force of overt principles, a strain of rationalism persists. It is also reappearing among a small but rising number of historians who are taking a fresh look at organizational patterns. The latter wish to know how groups and agencies—such as political parties, corporations, and communities—have molded behavior and regulated the distribution of power. Deriving partly from studies in entrepreneurial and business history and partly from contemporary American sociology, this kind of history is less concerned with motives than with structure and process. It shows men managing and being managed through rational systems of control and communication. Perhaps we may call this the new institutionalism; for it is bringing back to life a morphological study of organizations, now freed from the formalistic, evolutionary emphasis of nineteenth century scholarship.[31]

Although institutionalists thus far have not gone much beyond the monographic level, the breadth and importance of their contribution seem sure to grow. Yet it is not easy to anticipate that institutional history will in itself alter the main thrust of current scholarship. Institutions are, by their very nature, means of stabilizing the flux of society. If psychological history uncovers in the past the insecurities and pervasive anxieties that trouble many scholars and intellectuals today, institutional history projects the other side of the contemporary spirit: its rage for order. Both the psychological and the institutional approach reflect our fixation on the nature and extent of stability in our past and present. To move beyond that preoccupation historians will need more than a panoply of analytical techniques. They will need a larger and braver vision of the future than most of them now possess.

Meanwhile the profound changes in historical interpretation in the last twenty-five years have left today's scholars with plenty to do. Simply to master the new conceptual resources they have acquired is a herculean task. And the task must be well in hand before one can feel confident that the postwar generation is writing history that will live as a monument of its era, as the history of Henry Adams, of Turner, of Beard, and of Parrington lives as monuments of theirs.

On the concrete, empirical level, many of the newer research objectives remain substantially unfulfilled. The intricate study of social organization demanded by the collapse of the simple categories of progressive scholarship has just begun. The long stultified outward reach of American history into international and comparative dimensions, which suffered first from the environmentalism of progressive scholarship and later perhaps from the inwardness of the American Studies movement, is only now going beyond a few simplified contrasts. The sophisticated moral criticism of the past implicit in our growing psychological awareness has barely revealed its potentialities.

There is work to do also in cultivating a point of view wide enough to integrate these new interests with the unexhausted heritage from which they sprang. Much was sacrificed when the progressive historians largely ignored the constructive insights of the institutionalists. The diverse tendencies in contemporary scholarship suggest that the fault may not be so glaringly repeated. After the stirring historiographical revisions of the Thirties, Forties, and Fifties, it is a good sign that some historians are pondering "the delicate problem of developing an attitude appropriate to the process of absorbing the contributions of predecessors while trying to advance beyond them."[32] Management of this problem would seem to require all the sensitivity historians can muster —sensitivity to progress as well as decline, to the smiling as well as the tragic aspects of life, to the international background as well as the internal narrative, to social patterns as well as psychic tensions, to rational controls as well as irrational impulses, and to the great river of change as well as the bed of continuity.

NOTES

1. Tyler, *Freedom's Ferment: Phases of American Social History from the Colonial Period to the Outbreak of the Civil War* (1944); Commager, *The American Mind: An Interpretation of American Thought and Character Since the 1880's* (1950); Max Savelle, *Seeds of Liberty: The Genesis of the American Mind* (1948); Thomas C. Cochran and William Miller, *The Age of Enterprise* (1942); John C. Miller, *Triumph of Freedom,*

1775-1783 (1948); John Hope Franklin, *From Slavery to Freedom* (1947); Daniel Aaron, *Men of Good Hope: A Story of American Progressives* (1951).

2. Pp. vii-x. This introduction was written, Professor Hofstadter recalls, at the behest of the publisher; he had not written the book with any such clear design.

3. John Higham, "Anti-Semitism in the Gilded Age," *Mississippi Valley Historical Review*, XLIII (1957), 559-78; Kenneth M. Stampp, *The Peculiar Institution* (1956); C. Vann Woodward, *The Strange Career of Jim Crow* (1955).

4. Frank L. Owsley, "The Economic Basis of Society in the Late Ante-Bellum South," *Journal of Southern History*, VII (1940), 24-45, and *Plain Folk of the Old South* (1949); Charles S. Sydnor, *The Development of Southern Sectionalism, 1819-1848* (1948).

5. Edited by Charles G. Sellers Jr.; William R. Taylor, *Cavalier and Yankee: The Old South and American National Character* (1961).

6. Earl Pomeroy, "The Changing West," in *The Reconstruction of American History*, ed. John Higham (London, 1962), pp. 77-80; Louis B. Wright, *Culture on the Moving Frontier* (1955); Douglas F. Dowd, "A Comparative Analysis of Economic Development in the American West and South," *Journal of Economic History*, XVI (1956), 558-74.

7. *Ordeal of the Union* (2 vols., 1947); *The Emergence of Lincoln* (2 vols., 1950); *The War for the Union* (2 vols., 1959).

8. Bradford Perkins, *Prologue to War: England and the United States, 1805-1812* (1961); George E. Mowry, *The Era of Theodore Roosevelt, 1900-1912* (1958).

9. A partial exception was the ingenious reformulation of the Turner thesis in urban terms by two easterners, Stanley Elkins and Eric McKitrick, "A Meaning for Turner's Frontier," *Political Science Quarterly*, LXIX (1954), 321-53, 565-602. Turner's stoutest postwar champion, Ray Allen Billington, gradually modified the claims of the master, muting especially the theme of sectional conflict. See "The Frontier in American Thought and Character," *The New World Looks at Its History*, ed. Archibald R. Lewis and Thomas F. McGann (1963), pp. 77-94.

10. *The Age of Jackson* (1945), p. 307.

11. The most effective critics were Joseph Dorfman and Bray Hammond, whose own books, *The Economic Mind in American Civilization* (5 vols., 1946-59) and *Banks and Politics in America from the Revolution to the Civil War* (1957), were among the major works of the postwar era. For a summary of the controversy see Charles G. Sellers Jr.'s "Andrew Jackson versus the Historians," *Mississippi Valley Historical Review*, XLIV (1958), 615-34.

12. E. A. J. Johnson, "Federalism, Pluralism, and Public Policy," *Journal of Economic History*, XXII (1962), 442. On the origins of this research program see Herbert Heaton's *A Scholar in Action: Edwin F. Gay* (1952), pp. 237-48; on its impressive results, Robert A. Lively's "The American System," *Business History Review*, XXIX (1955), 81-96. Another, more recent approach to economic growth, paying less attention to government and more to markets, is in C. Douglass North's *The Economic Growth of the United States, 1790-1860* (1961).

13. *Maryland During and After the Revolution* (1943).

14. McDonald, *We the People: The Economic Origins of the Constitution* (1958); Brown, *Charles Beard and the Constitution* (1956) and *Middle-Class Democracy and the Revolution in Massachusetts, 1691-1780* (1955). The Beardian approach, modernized and improved, persists in Jackson T. Main, *The Antifederalists: Critics of the Constitution* (1961).

15. Dickerson, *The Navigation Acts and the American Revolution* (1951); Edmund S. and Helen M. Morgan, *The Stamp Act Crisis: Prologue to Revolution* (1953); Knollenberg, *Origin of the American Revolution: 1759-1766* (1960); Esmond Wright, *Fabric of Freedom, 1763-1800* (1961). Other studies are summarized in Jack P. Greene's "The Flight from Determinism: A Review of Recent Literature on the Coming of the American Revolution," *South Atlantic Quarterly*, LXI (1962), 235-59.

16. Dumas Malone, *Jefferson and His Time* (3 vols. to date, 1948-62); Edmund S. Morgan, *The Gentle Puritan: A Life of Ezra Stiles* (1962); George Dangerfield, *Chancellor Robert R. Livingston of New York* (1961).

17. In addition to books by Link and Hofstadter cited elsewhere, see the numerous studies of diplomatic history by Herbert Feis; Arthur M. Schlesinger Jr., *The Age of Roosevelt* (3 vols. to date, 1957-60); William E. Leuchtenburg, *Franklin D. Roosevelt and the New Deal* (1963); Ernest R. May, *The World War and American Isolation 1914-1917* (1959); Alfred D. Chandler Jr., *Strategy and Structure: Chapters in the History of the Industrial Enterprise* (1962).

18. The revival of serious discussion of national character by scholars seems to date from Margaret Mead's *And Keep Your Powder Dry* (1942) and Arthur M. Schlesinger's "What Then Is the American, This New Man?" *AHR*, XLVIII (1943), 225-44.

19. P. 287.

20. Morgan, *The Stamp Act Crisis* (1953); *The Birth of the Republic, 1763-1789* (1956); *The Puritan Dilemma: The Story of John Winthrop* (1958); *Visible Saints: The History of a Puritan Idea* (1963).

21. Rowland Berthoff, "The American Social Order: A Conservative Hypothesis," *AHR*, LXV (1960), 495-514; William A. Williams, *The Contours of American History* (1961).

22. Schlesinger, "The Causes of the Civil War: A Note on Historical Sentimentalism," *Partisan Review*, XVI (1949), 891; Craven, *The Growth of Southern Nationalism, 1848-1861* (1953) and *Civil War in the Making, 1815-1860* (1959).

23. Miller's *The New England Mind from Colony to Province* (1953) is complemented in social and political history by Bailyn's *The New England Merchants in the Seventeenth Century* (1955), *Education in the Forming of American Society* (1960), and "Politics and Social Structure in Virginia," in *Seventeenth-Century America*, ed. James Morton Smith (1959), pp. 90-115.

24. Donald, *Lincoln Reconsidered: Essays on the Civil War Era*, 2nd ed. (1961), pp. 209-235, and the critique by A. E. Campbell, "An Excess of Isolation: Isolation and the American Civil War," *Journal of Southern History*, XXIX (1963), 161-74; Elkins, *Slavery: A Problem in American Institutional and Intellectual Life* (1959).

25. Woodward, *The Burden of Southern History* (1960).
26. Smith took the first Ph.D. in American Civilization at Harvard (1940), an experience that made him a historian; but his essential intellectual experience came earlier as an editor and literary critic in the late 1920's in the Southwest, where his interest in myth was shaped by contact with the New Critics and through the influence of Hans Vaihinger and Henri Bergson. Hofstadter owed more to sociologists like Karl Mannheim and to Sigmund Freud, though his style of historical analysis was also much influenced by the approach of literary critics.
27. E.g., Charles G. Sellers Jr., "The Travail of Slavery," *op. cit.*, pp. 40-71, and Taylor, *op. cit.*
28. Diary of Alfred Vagts. Evidently World War II set Beard—as it set many others—thinking more seriously about irrational motivations.
29. See, for example, Emery Battis, *Saints and Sectaries: Anne Hutchinson and the Antinomian Controversy* (1962), David Donald, *Charles Sumner and the Coming of the Civil War* (1960), Marvin Meyers, *The Jacksonian Persuasion: Politics and Belief* (1957), and Samuel P. Hays, *The Response to Industrialism: 1885-1914* (1957).
30. Ben Halpern, " 'Myth' and 'Ideology' in Modern Usage," *History and Theory*, I (1961), 136-37.
31. William Miller, ed., *Men in Business: Essays on the Historical Role of the Entrepreneur* (1952); Lee Benson, *The Concept of Jacksonian Democracy: New York as a Test Case* (1961); Morton Keller, *The Life Insurance Enterprise, 1885-1910: A Study in the Limits of Corporate Power* (1963); Chandler, *op. cit.* Far from being mutually exclusive, the institutional and psychological approaches are joined in the impressive works, already cited, by Elkins and McKitrick, and in McKitrick's *Andrew Johnson and Reconstruction* (1960).
32. Lee Benson, *Turner and Beard: American Historical Writing Reconsidered* (1960), p. 96.

XXII

The American Past: Is It Still Usable?

J. R. POLE

The past, in the course of its ever-recurring encounters with the demands inflicted on it by the present, enjoys one inestimable advantage: it cannot answer, it is not even listening. "We ask and ask, thou smilest and art still," we might almost say, giving to Arnold's ponderous lines a touch of unintended meaning. In spite of appearances to the contrary, even the American past is in the same position. Even after the lapse (the "revolution," as Gibbon would have said) of more than three and a half centuries of continuous settlement, the historian who has been educated entirely in the tradition and the environment of the United States needs rather more than his European contemporary's normal degree of subtlety if he is to free himself from the peculiarly American version of the space–time continuum.

Those Virginians who still talk about Mr. Jefferson as though he might, at any moment, train his telescope on them from Monticello, the distinguished historian of Reconstruction who, emerging from a southern archive and blinking at the day's newspapers, felt a momentary uncertainty as to which century he was actually in or whether any time had passed, the politicians who invoke the ideals of the Founders as though these gentlemen, if alive, would not in fact be over 200 years old and possibly beyond giving a useful opinion, are all inhabitants of

From *Journal of American Studies*, I (April 1967), pp. 63-78. Reprinted with permission of Cambridge University Press.

this remarkable continuum, this eternal triangle of space, time and political ideology. It is as though any part of the continent, and any period, could be visited simply by virtue of the efficiency of the tourist trade. Although the people who lived in earlier centuries may, by some accident in the providential design, be technically dead, they remain to a peculiar degree the property of their heirs and successors; what one misses is that sense, inescapable in Europe, of the total, crumbled irrecoverability of the past, of its differentness, of the fact that it is dead.

This situation makes room for, and indeed it partly results from, the persistent force of what may well be called the American extension of the Whig interpretation of history.[1] In its cruder recent forms this attitude has been given by some of its critics the inelegant name of "presentism"; by which is meant that the historian plants his own political values, or those which he thinks belong to his own time, in the minds of the people of the past, and approves of their achievements or judges their shortcomings according to these present-day standards. There are, of course, a number of variants, connected in part with varieties of temperament, and in large part with the prevailing political controversies amid which the historian has found himself; but the Whig interpretation, in American hands, has always taken the view that the United States as a nation was responsible for the preservation and advancement of certain ascertained values, and hence to discover, record and celebrate these values was the peculiar duty that the historian owed to his country.

It would be impertinent to suggest that the Whigs have had it all their own way. But patriotic history has almost always been identical with Whig history, and these two strands had an early meeting in the work of George Bancroft.[2] Bancroft, it is true, did not succeed in getting the story of America beyond the Federal Convention of 1787, but he was himself a Jacksonian politician and a dedicated Democrat, and it was he who gave the most effective impetus to the idea that American history should be celebrated as the triumph of democratic principles.

It follows that the works of American politicians and others must be evaluated according to their contributions to the advancement of those principles. Those who obstructed, or who saw their problems in some different light, or who sought a path that went over a precipice—these are mere historical curiosities: what defines them is that by the final test, that of democratic success, they are not truly American. It is the fate of the Loyalists, the Federalists, the Confederacy; if some historians of the New Deal have their way it may even prove the fate of the Republicans; even the Antifederalists have only narrowly escaped it.

Before the end of the nineteenth century, the issues of contemporary politics had begun to suggest the need for some redefinition of the actual objects of American democracy; and it was as a consequence of these conflicts that historians who were themselves dedicated to the Progressive movement began to forge American history into an instrument of political action. The immense, almost oppressive veneration for the Constitution, its use by the courts as itself an instrument of capital against labour, and the bitter strife that had grown up as a result of recent economic development—these things make it seem inevitable that social scientists and even historians should have begun to marshal their own resources on the side of reform. They knew what they were about and soon began to get the feeling of the resources at their disposal; certainly they were not driven blindly into this position by the circumstances of their times. The functional application of historical writing was deliberately proposed in 1912 by James Harvey Robinson in the cause of liberal reform;[3] and was carried forward by a giant stride with the appearance, the next year, of Beard's tract on the economic motives of the framers of the Constitution.[4]

This famous tract performed a service of intellectual liberation that was very badly needed, but it did more than that: by virtue of innuendoes whose implications Beard disclaimed, and by the selection of evidence to support a specific conclusion, it inflicted on more than a generation of historians an excessively narrow view of the issues and an almost unavoidable necessity to take sides in a controversy that even now is not fully worked out. Beard, of course, was striking a powerful blow, not at the Constitution of 1787 but at the Constitution in 1913; and this motive gives the clue to the instrumentalist direction that American historiography was to extract from its Whig foundations. Each stage in the argument was proposed, not by a question (in Collingwood's manner) but by an objective: the significance of the whole procedure being that the objective lay in the historian's own contemporary social and political interests rather than in those properly pertaining to the past.

Instrumental historians gained their sense of direction from social conflict. But in the intellectual development of their views of the nature of historical thought they owed a great deal to European as well as to American philosophy. The leading European influence was that of Benedetto Croce, who as a young man in the 1890s turned against the traditions of positivist realism and whose mature philosophy embraced history as a mode of the historian's own thought—a procedure that tied it down as an expression of "present" experience. American instrumentalists saw in this thesis the justification for their own obvious relativism:

if their historical thought were relative to their own values and interests, so had been those of all their rivals and predecessors! The reception of Freudian psychology, which began early in the century and had great influence in the 1920s, seemed to those who were inclined to read it in that light to go still further towards justifying a psychology and hence a philosophy of subjective and therefore relativist values. On the American side lay the active influence of the specifically "instrumentalist" philosophy of John Dewey.[5]

Beard himself had absorbed much of the feeling of the American Populists and had adopted much of the method learnt from Marx. His instrumentalism, however, is characteristic of that of his more orthodox contemporaries in his method of selecting a simple dichotomy of opposed forces. The broad and rough outline of a division, discernible in the later eighteenth century, between mercantile and agrarian interests, became for Beard a precursor of the class war; the immense weight of landed interest that was thrown behind the Constitution could be bypassed as simply irrelevant to his view of what the struggle was all about. In lining up the two sides Beard assumed that the mercantile and moneyed interests, because "capitalist," were conservative, and by inference opposed to the democratic principles of American progress; which meant that the agricultural interest was also the popular and democratic side in the struggle. The fact that the leadership and probably the bulk of the agrarian interests were in important respects profoundly conservative, while the capitalists were, in an economic sense, dynamically progressive, was overlooked because it was irrelevant to the particular conflict on which his attention was riveted.

It was consistent with this method that when Beard came to the Civil War and to Reconstruction he applied a similar analysis, and that he and his disciples discovered in the capitalist North an aggressive business spirit whose interests explained the Radical Republican programme and their victory in the elections of 1866.[6] The Civil War itself was interpreted as a collision between the capitalist North and the agrarian and basically feudal South—an extension of the dualism that Beard had found earlier in American history. It is perhaps odd that Beard, who wrote with great insight about the clash of interests in politics,[7] and who virtually discovered the 10th Federalist, should have yielded his powerful intellect so easily to the idea of a recurring dichotomy that he virtually overlooked the pluralistic nature of American politics.

These remarks are not made here for the sake of reviving controversies or reviewing the new familiar ground on which Beard and his disciples have grappled with their opponents, but to indicate one of the most persistent styles in American historiography. Running through all the grades of this style, a strand that is once utilitarian and populistic seeks to explain to a sceptical audience that the justification for the study of history is practical; it helps us to understand the present, and can become, in dedicated hands, an instrument of action.

The most extreme statement of this instrumental view of history came, not from the Progressive Movement, but from Conyers Read, in his Presidential address to the American Historical Association in 1949.[8] In a candid and unusual bid to qualify as the Zhdanov of the profession, Read disparaged both the work and the interests of those dedicated historians who take the past seriously for its own sake. "It is the rare bird," he said, "who is interested in the past simply as the past —a world remote, apart, complete, such as Michael Oakeshott has envisaged." Read took the view that the liberal age, "characterized by a plurality of aims and values," was a thing of the past, and that "we must clearly assume a militant attitude if we are to survive." This militant attitude involved the organization of resources and the disciplined interpretation of history towards the propagation of American doctrines. "This sounds," he added, "like the advocacy of one form of social control as against another. In short, it is. But I see no alternative in a divided world." His reassurance that his concept of control meant "no menace to essential freedoms" could hardly have satisfied those whose views and interests might have run the risk of proving inessential.

In a subtler form the instrumentalist version of the Whig tradition reappeared among certain historians whose early political memories were those of the New Deal. Arthur M. Schlesinger, Jr., whose *Age of Jackson*[9] remains after twenty years a work of extraordinary vitality and intelligence, quoted Franklin D. Roosevelt in his preface and argued explicitly that Roosevelt had carried forward a process which Jackson had inaugurated, but which had subsequently been submerged by other issues. It would not be altogether unfair to Professor Schlesinger (at any rate when he wrote *The Age of Jackson* at twenty-eight) to say that in his view the forces on the other side, the Bank of the United States, or the combinations of monopoly capitalism, represent reaction in much the same sense that the Roman Catholic Church represented reaction to earlier historians of Protestantism; and that the Democratic side, which happily emerges as the winning side, is the more American.

Historians of different temperament have always known that there was an alternative to all this. It begins with a fundamental respect for the integrity of the past in which the instrumental view has no place because its aims are irrelevant. It approaches the subject-matter of history without intense presuppositions and with a mind in which convictions (however strongly held) about right and wrong have been subordinated to a profound curiosity as to what was thought about right and wrong in the period under scrutiny. It places a deep absorption in the substance and detail of history on a higher level of priority than the principles which it expects to discover; it starts, of course, with a hypothesis but this hypothesis is almost invariably modified if not abandoned in the course of the research.

The results often tend to be less spectacular and less susceptible of literary grandiosity than those of the progressive, or reactionary, instrumentalists. Yet they are worth noting, because, if they are properly understood, they not only come nearer the truth but they change the message received at this end of the line. Vernon L. Parrington, a literary historian whose work was an outstanding example of the Progressive school, thought that an early example of political progressiveness was to be discovered in Roger Williams, the founder of Rhode Island. Under this impression, Parrington chose to interpret Williams's work as being inspired by political interests and the ideals of democracy. But Professor Alan Simpson, in an article which should be carefully read for its general as well as its immediate reflexions, went back to the texts of Roger Williams's work and showed that his preoccupations were overwhelmingly religious. If he was a "democrat" it was by indirection and as a result of the circumstances he was in.[10]

It would be grossly unjust to suggest that the elders of the present generation have missed the complexities that are more clearly apparent to their successors. The difference has always been one rather of temperament and interest than of age. Professor Carl Bridenbaugh has built up for us a body of information about the early life of American cities in books that will last longer than many a fast-selling work of popularization or propaganda; and the works of those major New England historians, the late Perry Miller and Samuel Eliot Morison, do more to bring the past to life than those which have a point to prove about the present. But there is also, in recent years, an increasing appreciation of the variety of voices that speak from the past to those who are willing to listen, "Each generation," we are often told, "reinterprets history in the light of its own interests." But each generation happily contains many independent minds with a great variety of intelligent interests: so that the arguments for pure historical relativism lead either towards solipsism or, more fortunately, to cancelling each other out.

In each of a variety of fields, the last fifteen or twenty years of American historical scholarship have produced indications of a kind of expertise that tends, not merely to a revision of the last opinion on the subject, but to the suggestion of new categories of question. The trend is perhaps nowhere clearer than in those reviews of twentieth-century foreign policy which have helped to advance our understanding by rejecting the old formalism which dominated American views of the outside world and which culminated, in the actual conduct of foreign relations, in the reign of John Foster Dulles as Secretary of·State. George F. Kennan's trenchant critique of the dominance of moral attitudes in American foreign policy was followed shortly after Professor John M. Blum's unfriendly but cogent analysis of Woodrow Wilson as an agent of moral preconceptions that limited his understanding of political reality.[11] Professor Blum writes from an extraordinary fund of knowledge of recent history and politics, and from a conviction, not perhaps expressed but clearly affecting his method, that the political system he knows so well has enough flexibility to contain and handle the problems that emerge from American society in political form. Meanwhile Professor Ernest R. May[12] has recently opened a searching inquiry into one of the most settled assumptions of American diplomatic historians, the prevailing belief that foreign policy reflects, and, in effect, enacts, public opinion on foreign affairs. It is not necessary for one moment to suppose that such writers have said the last word, or even to agree with their individual conclusions, in order to recognize that their style of approach is refreshing in its coolness, its liberation from the favoured American illusions, and its tone of sceptical pragmatism.

The gains of scholarship resulting from this mood can be traced in such widely different fields as the American Revolution, the character of politics in the age of Jackson, and the motives and achievements of the several interests involved in Reconstruction. American historians of the Revolution are conducting the analysis of politics in a manner that owes, and acknowledges, a great debt to Namier; it is an appreciable irony of eighteenth-century studies that this stance of independence of the Whig tradition should in fact owe more to the example of Namier than to the argument of Butterfield. Students of British politics such as Professor C. R. Ritcheson (and Dr. Bernard Donoughue of the London School of Economics) and students of American politics such as Professor Jack P. Greene,[13] together with specialists in a valuable and increasing number of state or local histories, show a relish for facts, for building up the picture as it looked at the time, which gives us a deeper understanding of the kind of choices that were available at that time.

Revisionism does not invariably mean rethinking. It is often possible and sometimes easy to seem wiser than one's predecessors by virtue of some slight change in outlook which renders a new question more attractive. There is no period of American history under a more intense ferment of revision than that of Southern Reconstruction, and none, certainly, in which it is more important to try to distinguish what is the product of new thinking from what is the product of the altering social opinion. An immense amount of research has been put into Reconstruction during a period that corresponds, very roughly perhaps, with the time since the Supreme Court's decision in *Brown v. Board of Education*—the School Segregation Cases of 1954. Most of the results have appeared in articles, and no synthesis of the period in book form has yet appeared to do justice to the full depth of the work. Professor Kenneth M. Stampp's comparatively brief survey, *The Era of Reconstruction* (1965), presents the principal findings of this revision (including of course Professor Stampp's own research) with the cogent persuasiveness of an authority. When Stampp hands down a verdict he does so in a manner from which there seems little room for appeal. Yet his standpoint is not the only one from which deeper levels of understanding might be attained.

The questions crowd so close upon each other, each entailing the answer to so many others, that any attempt to review the field would require at the least a full-length article to itself. In summary, we risk reducing the subject to a series of paradoxes. When, for example, La-Wanda Cox[14] embarked on a study of the Northern movement to give to the freedmen that fundamentally American form of security, the tenure of freehold land, she clearly expected to find here one of the truly nobler and more redeeming features of the somewhat mixed story of Northern intentions. Her account is scholarly, sound and full of interest: but the interest does not grow any less deep when she arrives, with obvious reluctance, at the discovery that at least some of the congressmen and senators behind this campaign were motivated principally by their anxiety to avert the danger of footloose freed Negroes flooding into the North. Free land would at least keep the Negroes in the South. To take up the problem of interpretation at another level, the historian who regrets the failure of Radical Reconstruction may put his finger on the antipathy between President Andrew Johnson and the Radical majority in the Congress, and may rightly blame the deadlock

on the separation of powers, which emerges as a grave defect in the
Constitution itself. But the historian who does not regret the failure
of Reconstruction will have equal reason to applaud the wisdom of the
Founders, who made it virtually impossible for a temporary majority in
Congress to impose so sweeping a policy.

The rewriting of Reconstruction history has produced notable advances in method which have suggested more complex and more interesting categories. The method which depended on imposing the
concept of class conflict had the defect of introducing broad, inclusive
but basically simple categories. Thus the real force behind the Radical
Republicans was held to be that of the Northern business interests that
were intent on exploiting the resources of the South, laid open for subjection by military defeat. But a significant article by Stanley Coben
began the work of reconsideration by pointing out that no such unit as
that of "Northern business interests" had ever existed, and that in fact
the business interests of the Northeast, which were supposed to be
prominent in the movement, were not only various in content but
divided over Southern policies.[15] Professor Unger's more recent and extensive examination of the social and economic history of the era demonstrates the complexity, the dividedness of the business interests and
renders the old categories obsolete.[16]

> If it is hard to see the consensus in post-bellum America, [Pro-
> fessor Unger observes] it is also difficult to detect a simple Beard-
> ian polarity. On the money question there were not two massive
> contending interests; there were many small ones. If the financial
> history of Reconstruction reveals nothing else of consequence, it
> does disclose a complex, pluralistic society in which issues were
> resolved—when they were not simply brushed aside—by the inter-
> action of many forces.[17]

It can of course be argued that the great revision of Reconstruction
history is itself a form of instrumentalism.[18] There would be an element
of truth in this criticism—an element not to be disregarded because of
one's standpoint on civil rights. Yet much of it has been of such value
in clearing away cartloads of erroneous information and pernicious
mythology—errors about the content of legislation by Southern state
assemblies under Radical rule, errors about the actual composition of
Reconstruction conventions, myths about the scallawags, to name only
a few—that the achievement has been an act of positive liberation.

Yet Southern history, as Vann Woodward has pointed out,[19] has on
the whole been by-passed by the more exhilarating winds of the success

story that Americans love to tell and to hear. The South, unlike the nation, had suffered a shattering military defeat, and the experience of its white population could never be wholly at one with that which was celebrated in the rest of the Union. The best that could be made of it was a great lost cause, to rank in history with those of the Stuarts or the victims of the French Revolution.

One sign of the critical sophistication about the past which seems to have developed since the Second World War has indeed been a moderate revival of interest in lost causes. The Federalists are now being taken more seriously than they used to be by any except political opponents of the Democrats (though it seems odd that a country that can put up a monument to Robert A. Taft cannot find the heart to commemorate Alexander Hamilton); and recent years have shown a new disposition to study and even to redeem the Loyalists of the Revolution. A most important attribute of this approach, not one confined to lost causes but to the rebuilding of historical knowledge in depth, is the attention which historians are giving to local and state history, and to the examination, in great detail, of the composition of communities. Perceptive monographs about New England towns and about state or provincial politics, amplified by articles based on very extensive use of local records, have appreciably added to our picture of the structure of society and the changes brought in it by the War of Independence; that picture seems to change before our eyes, exposing the frailty of surveys made from the continental centre of politics for the very simple reason that there was no centre.

The most influential single product of this detailed social realism has probably been Professor Lee Benson's book *The Concept of Jacksonian Democracy* (Princeton, 1961). Party divisions, and the ideological claims made by rival parties, have always seemed in the past to present an obvious and a legitimate scheme for organizing the political history of the period, and to lead straight from politics to social structure. But Professor Benson rejects these claims, reconstructing the parties from the social ingredients and finding in their rival policies a reflexion of immediate electoral needs rather than serious differences of opinion or principle. Much the same attitude has influenced Professor Richard P. McCormick's important recent work, *The Second American Party System* (Chapel Hill, 1966). It stands out as an interesting conclusion of this study that by the time of the second American party system the capturing of the presidency had become the overriding aim of party organization, and that to this end the second American parties, unlike the first, were willing to subordinate almost all considerations of principle. "Between 1824 and 1840, the 'presidential question,' rather than doctrinal disputes, was the axis around which politics revolved."[20] These investigations will undoubtedly lead to further work on the same lines. They represent a brand of toughness, and a scepticism about the proclaimed ideals of party leaders and theorists, that not only appeals to the mood that has succeeded the Cold War, but is obviously producing tangible results.

Yet it would be a pity if this realism, with its useful appreciation of sociological techniques, were allowed to drive out all respect for the values or principles which Americans said they believed in. The history we have to record is that of the United States under Jackson and Van Buren, not under Clay; yet it is permissible to think that the history of that period would have been significantly different if Clay had been elected in 1832, and that such differences would have been due to genuine differences of purpose. The United States without the Bank had a different economy from the United States with the Bank—to name only one divisive issue—and differences on the question certainly turned on matters of substance.

The inevitable attraction of the great controversies has tended to conceal what is in truth another very significant and at times a very subtle division in American historiography. To put the matter with that simplicity that always does injustice to the nuances, it is the division between those who believe in the primacy of mind and those who believe in the primacy of material fact. The obvious formative and ever-present ingredients of geographical circumstance and economic interest—what may be called the urgency of the economic problem—in American history have not prevented the United States from becoming one of the leading centres of the profession of intellectual history. Even if we discount the influence, which may indeed be very important, of the Puritan founders of New England with their profound sense of mission and their habit of interpreting human affairs as part of a theocentric order, we may be justified at least in tracing the practice of giving a certain primacy to opinions and states of mind back to John Adams. "The Revolution," he declared in a famous phrase, "was effected before the war commenced. The Revolution was in the minds and hearts of the people."[21]

Much of what has been styled the "Whig" method in American historiography has been involved in this process, because of its intense interest in motive. The search for the standard-bearers of progress has meant the search for those who were conscious of their mission; the concept of commitment to preconceived ideals has always been a part of the Whig design for the understanding of the past. It is perfectly legitimate in certain important instances, such as that of the crusaders against slavery; but it becomes misleading to an equal extent when it generalizes and blurs the motives of campaigners who were attacking on some narrow front in the cause of some special interest. And this kind of commitment is more common, and in general more effective. Parrington, largely because of the scale of his achievement, stands out as the leading exponent of this mode of Whig intellectual history, exemplifying both its clarity of design and its defects of interpretation. In contrast is the great example of Perry Miller, a historian who more deeply understood the relation of the minds of earlier generations to their own past and their own age.

Since their day Richard Hofstadter has emerged as the most influential of all the historians with a primary interest in states of mind rather than conditions or series of events. In addition to his own impressive and always slightly disturbing studies, he has helped to inspire studies, such as that of Marvin Meyers on the Jacksonians,[22] which may be said to counteract the progressivism of the more conventional Whig thought. Hofstadter, whose extraordinarily trenchant insight—it is almost an instinct—for historical fallacy, has brought about a reorientation in the views of many more conventional judgments over a variety of fields, has seldom been the victim of any undue propensity for optimism—either about the past or the future. In less incisive hands, the method he has developed of re-creating past states of mind from the records of published opinions, rather than from archival sources, could easily become cloudy and inconclusive. Oddly enough (considering the feeling he generates that something of value is under attack), is was Hofstadter who proposed the view that American political history should be reconsidered in the light of consensus rather than conflict.[23]

In view of the tremendous emphasis on the conflict of mighty opposites which Parrington and Beard had imposed on their generation, the suggestion that American history owed much to an underlying agreement was a very sensible direction to take. On this view, the successes of the American polity were more important and more enduring than its failures, and those successes were due to the absence of any fundamental divisions in ideology. It would be wrong to attribute the main development of the view to Hofstadter, however. Louis Hartz[24] expounded it in much greater detail on the basis of two principles which he discovered in American history. The first of these was Tocqueville's "equality of conditions"—the absence of feudalism and of all the appurtenances and legacies which feudalism left in Europe. The second was an original "liberal principle." It was not the whole of English society, but what Hartz calls its liberal wing, that settled in America, and being settled it grew without the obstruction of any major contrary power or indeed of any contrary ideal.[25] Hofstadter might agree with Hartz that American development can be explained without recourse to fundamental clashes of ideology, though Hofstadter attaches much more importance to conflicts arising from deep social divisions; it seems that for Hartz the trouble with the Federalists or the Whigs was that they were victims of an intellectual error.

The idea of consensus was a useful direction-finder. It is not an explanation. In a sense it may be called a tautology, for the consensus extends only to the principles about which there is agreement, and deep disagreement may be concealed by different readings of the same sacred texts, when opposing sides affirm their allegiance to the source of these texts. Professor Hartz remarked in his Commonwealth Fund lectures that even the Civil War does not represent a real collapse of the American consensus because the Southern states claimed to have adhered to their own view of the Constitution, which they reproduced, with a few modifications, in that of the Confederacy. At this point consensus may be thought to have lost its usefulness. Might one not as well suggest that the French Wars of Religion do not represent a real religious cleavage because both Catholics and Huguenots avowed their faith in the Christian religion?

To reject the concept of basic ideological conflict is not the same thing as rejecting the influence of ideas, preconceptions, states of mind. In contrast to the entire school of intellectual historians there stands a different tradition, whose exponents emphasize the primacy of material forces. The great progenitor of this line was Turner, who seemed to feel that democracy, and all that was genuinely American about American institutions, rose up like a sort of ground mist from the soil of the continent and entered into the bones of the settlers. It was Turner who really implanted this deep strand of geophysical determinism whose influence has affected so much subsequent historical writing but has aroused such deep resentment—partly, perhaps, because its implicit rejection of the formative influence of ideas seems to be a veiled attack on the commitment of the intellectual life of the historian himself.

The great modern exponent of this style of historical thought, though he has arrived there by his own route and his debt to Turner is indirect, is Daniel J. Boorstin. Professor Boorstin has devoted one book to the thesis that the success of American government, the great ability that

Americans have shown in overcoming their practical and political problems, is in fact due to their rejection of preconceived ideological schemes of government. In his major works that have followed, he has extended the same concept to social history in its broadest sense, deliberately extruding ideas or ideals from his terms of reference. As Boorstin shows, in the process of settlement, community came first, government afterwards. Boorstin is not unlike Namier in his hostility to the importation of ideals, ideology, or indeed any form of systematic beliefs—and also, incidentally, in his keen eye for the revealing incident. No contemporary surpasses him in the ability to re-create scenes and situations that bring the past to life; this, we feel, is what it really felt like to be there.[26]

Yet Professor Boorstin's remarkable persuasive powers and the obvious cogency of much of his argument should not conceal two points: First, that it *is* an argument, and as such that it explains the sort of phenomena that primarily interest Professor Boorstin far better than other phenomena that, however, remain significant. The deep and principled convictions that brought about the early political parties, the passions of the antislavery movement, the ratiocinations of Calhoun and other speculative writers, are slighted. And, secondly, that the things that interest the author are presented not merely as one aspect of what he calls "the national experience": they *are* the national experience. The rest is worthy only of rejection because, presumably, it is contrary to the true American genius. The rejects of history that fall into this state of gracelessness, because of that failure, can be rather large, and include the second Bank of the United States, which plays no part in the book which covers its lifetime.

Boorstin is far more subtle and complex in his appreciation of American development than Turner was, and his originality and persuasiveness are sure to exert great influence; much indeed of what he says is more important than what he chooses to leave out. Like Turner before him he sings the virtue of the land, and might for a text have reversed a line of Robert Frost's to read "We were the land's before the land was ours." It is not the less important on this account to appreciate the extent to which his own ideas form a system.

The deep division of interpretation that has been suggested here is concealed by the fact that Boorstin, Hofstadter and Hartz join in some measure of belief, shared by such a solid political historian as McCormick, that ideological conflict has not dominated American life; that agreement to work the machinery has been much more important than conflict over principles. But the fact that rival parties agree to work the same machinery does not mean that they intend to work it for the same objects; and the machinery itself sometimes changes shape under the pressure of strong personalities or principles. The machinery of politics is not neutral; it is not "matter," even though it sometimes seems to be treated as though it were of the order of natural or environmental phenomena rather than of those made by man in America.

This division between mind and matter is less dramatic than those in which the participants are to some extent ideological partisans. It results perhaps from a contrast of temperaments rather than ideals. Yet these alternative views cut deep enough to affect any interpretation of specific events or decisions. It may seem strange that American historians should be moved to take sides over the very question of whether there are any sides to take. But an explanation may lie, to some extent, in the actual nature of the theories that have played so dominant a part in the rewriting of American history during the present century. The Populists, the Progressive instrumentalists and the Marxists asserted the historical primacy of an ideological conflict; and it appears that some historians, anxious to escape this dilemma and convinced of its irrelevance to American development, have in fact been trapped by it. The word "ideology" has itself been given too much work. Ideologies have been thought of as all-embracing, as embodying fundamental views of the state and society, to be wholly accepted or resisted; so that if one rejected "ideological" interpretations one was easily led to deny the relevance, and minimize the intellectual seriousness, of any profound differences of opinion on matters of principle or policy.

But this approach makes too much of the general problem and so, in the end, makes too little of the particular issues. Ideological conflicts may be relatively short-lived, like that between the Federalists and Jeffersonians, and yet intense while they last. Such conflicts, especially when they lead to the adoption of divisive policies, require to be incorporated, not by-passed, in the writing of history. Another of our needs in these matters is to distinguish between the parties who do hold a total view of society and those who are committed to a narrower cause; but it will always be a mistake to trivialize past differences merely because they disappeared with the passage of time.

Time, to come back to the beginning, is the element with which many American historians have had the greatest difficulty in coming to terms; yet they will see into the past, so far as it is given to us to do so, only when they recognize it, in its integrity, as the past. Time is not the enemy of the historian but it is not his friend; it is the prism, the only one, through which we may hope to perceive the dead.

NOTES

1. Herbert Butterfield, *The Whig Interpretation of History* (Cambridge, 1931).
2. George Bancroft: *History of the United States*, 6 vols. (Boston, 1879); *Formation of the Constitution*, 2 vols. (Boston, 1882).
3. James Harvey Robinson, *The New History* (New York, 1912), pp. 15, 24; Chester McArthur Destler, "Some observations on contemporary historical theory," *A.H.R.* 55 (April 1950), 503, n. 3.
4. Charles A. Beard, *An Economic Interpretation of the Constitution of the United States* (New York, 1913).
5. Destler, "Contemporary historical theory," *loc. cit.* pp. 503-6; R. G. Collingwood, *The Idea of History* (Oxford, 1946).
6. Howard K. Beale, *The Critical Year: A study of Andrew Johnson and Reconstruction* (New York, 1930). Charles and Mary Beard, *The Rise of American Civilization*, revised edition, (New York, 1949), chap. xviii.
7. Charles A. Beard, *The Economic Basis of Politics and Related Writings*, compiled William Beard (New York, 1958).
8. Conyers Read, "The social responsibilities of the historian," *A.H.R.* 55, no. 2 (Jan. 1950).
9. Boston, 1946. In the same connexion see Eric F. Goldman, *Rendezvous with Destiny* (New York, 1952).
10. Vernon Louis Parrington, *Main Currents in American Thought*, 3 vols. (New York, 1927-30); Alan Simpson, "How democratic was Roger Williams?" *W.M.Q.* (Jan. 1956).
11. George F. Kennan, *American Diplomacy 1900-1950* (Chicago, 1951); John M. Blum, *Woodrow Wilson and the Politics of Morality* (Boston, 1956).
12. Ernest R. May, "An American tradition in foreign policy: the role of public opinion," in William H. Nelson (ed.), *Theory and Practice in American Politics* (Chicago, 1964).
13. C. R. Ritcheson, *British Politics and the American Revolution, 1763-1783* (Norman, 1954); Bernard Donoughue, *British Politics and the American Revolution* . . . *1773-1775* (London, 1964); Jack P. Greene, *The Quest for Power: The Lower Houses of Assembly in the Southern Royal Colonies, 1689-1776* (Chapel Hill, 1963).
14. LaWanda Cox, "The promise of land for the freedmen," *M.V.H.R.* 45 (1958), 413-40.
15. Stanley Coben, "Northeastern business and Radical Reconstruction: a re-examination," *M.V.H.R.* 46 (1959).
16. Irwin Unger, *The Greenback Era: A Social and Political History of American Finance, 1865-1878* (Princeton 1964).
17. *Ibid.* p. 405.
18. For a specific affirmation of these revisionist views (in this case of the Abolitionists) as serving an instrumentalist purpose, see Howard Zinn, "Abolitionists, Freedom-Riders and the Tactics of Agitation" in Martin Duberman (ed.), *The Antislavery Vanguard: New Essays on the Abolitionists* (Princeton, 1965).

19. "The irony of Southern history," *J.S.H.* 19 (1953), reprinted in *The Burden of Southern History* (New York, 1960).
20. McCormick, *op. cit.*, p. 353.
21. Quoted by Clinton Rossiter, *Seedtime of the Republic* (New York, 1953), p. 4.
22. Marvin Meyers, *The Jacksonian Persuasion: Politics and Belief* (New York, 1957).
23. Richard Hofstadter, *The American Political Tradition and the Men Who Made It* (New York, 1951), Introduction.
24. Louis Hartz, *The Liberal Tradition in America* (New York, 1955).
25. A view developed in Professor Hartz's Commonwealth Fund lectures at University College, London, in 1962 and in *The Founding of New Societies*, ed. Hartz (New York, 1964).
26. Daniel J. Boorstin: *The Genius of American Politics* (Chicago, 1953); *The Americans: The Colonial Experience* (New York, 1958); *The National Experience* (New York, 1965).

XXIII

American Historiography: A Bibliography

COMPILED BY FRANK OTTO GATELL

AND ALLEN WEINSTEIN

GENERAL

Hutchinson, William T. (ed.), *Marcus W. Jernegan Essays in American Historiography* (Chicago: University of Chicago Press, 1937).

Kraus, Michael, *The Writing of American History* (Norman: University of Oklahoma Press, 1953).

Wish, Harvey, *The American Historian* (New York: Oxford University Press, 1960).

Cartwright, William H. and Richard L. Watson, Jr. (eds.), *Interpreting and Teaching American History* (Washington: National Education Association, 1961).

Higham, John (ed.), *The Reconstruction of American History* (New York: Harper and Row, 1962).

Higham, John, Leonard Krieger and Felix Gilbert, *History* (Englewood Cliffs: Prentice-Hall, 1965).

Sheehan, Donald, and Harold C. Syrett (eds.), *Essays in American Historiography* (New York: Columbia University Press, 1960).

Ausubel, Herman, *Historians and Their Craft: A Study of the Presidential Addresses of the American Historical Association, 1884-1945* (New York: Columbia University Press, 1950).

THE NINETEENTH CENTURY

Van Tassel, David Dirck, *Recording America's Past: An Interpretation of the Development of Historical Studies in America 1607-1884* (Chicago: University of Chicago Press, 1960).

Callcott, George Hardy, "Historians in Early Nineteenth Century America," *New England Quarterly*, XXXII (December 1959), 496-520.

Levin, David, *History as Romantic Art; Bancroft, Prescott, Motley and Parkman* (Stanford: Stanford University Press, 1959).

Holt, W. Stull, "The Idea of Scientific History in America," *Journal of the History of Ideas*, I (June 1940), 352-362.

Sorenson, Lloyd Rushford, "Historical Currents in America," *American Quarterly* VII (Fall 1955), 234-246.

Herbst, Jurgen, *The German Historical School in American Scholarship: A Study in the Transfer of Culture* (Ithaca: Cornell University Press, 1964).

Saveth, Edward Norman, "Race and Nationalism in American Historiography: The Late Nineteenth Century," *Political Science Quarterly*, LIV (September 1939), 421-441.

Bassett, John Spencer, *The Middle Group of American Historians* (New York: Macmillan, 1917).

THE TWENTIETH CENTURY

Kraus, Michael, W. Stull Holt, and John Caughey, "American Historical Writing, 1900-1950: A Symposium," *Mississippi Valley Historical Review*, XL (March 1954), 607-628.

Crowe, Charles, "The Emergence of Progressive History," *Journal of the History of Ideas*, XXVII (January 1966), 109-124.

Gold, Milton, "In Search of a Historian," *Centennial Review*, VII (Summer 1963), 282-305.

Cochran, Thomas C. "A Decade of American Historians (1938-1948)," *Pennsylvania Magazine of History and Biography* LXXIII (April 1949), 143-190.

Nichols, Roy Franklin, "Postwar Reorientation of Historical Thinking," *American Historical Review*, LIII (October 1948), 78-89.

Cochran, Thomas C., "A New Era in United States History?" *Revista de Historia Americana*, XXXIII (June 1952), 1-24.

Strout, Cushing, "Historical Thought in America," *Virginia Quarterly Review*, XXVIII (Spring 1952), 242-257.

Bellot, Hugh Hale, *American History and American Historians: A Review of Recent Contributions to the Interpretation of the His-*

tory of the United States (Norman: University of Oklahoma Press, 1952).

Stephenson, Wendell H. "A Quarter Century of American Historiography," *Mississippi Valley Historical Review*, XLV (June 1958), 3-22.

Higham, John "The Cult of 'American Consensus,' Homogenizing Our History," *Commentary*, XXVII (February 1959), 93-100.

Higham, John "Beyond Consensus: The Historian as Moral Critic," *American Historical Review*, LXVII (April 1962), 609-625.

Hollingsworth, J. Rogers, "Consensus and Continuity in Recent American Historical Writing," *South Atlantic Quarterly*, LXI (Winter 1962), 40-50.

Hartz, Louis, "American Historiography and Comparative Analysis: Further Reflections," *Comparative Studies in Society and History*, V (1963), 365-377.

Hoover, Dwight W., "Some Comments on Recent United States Historiography," *American Quarterly*, XVII (Summer 1965), 299-318.

Wish, Harvey, "The American Historian and the New Conservatism," *South Atlantic Quarterly*, LXV (Spring 1966), 178-191.

Wiebe, Robert, "The Confinements of Consensus," *Tri-Quarterly*, No. 6 (1966), 155-158.

Pole, J. R., "The American Past: Is It Still Usable," *Journal of American Studies*, I (April 1967), 63-78.

Unger, Irwin, "The 'New Left' and American History: Some Recent Trends in United States Historiography," *American Historical Review*, LXXII (July 1967), 1237-1263.

POLITICAL HISTORY

Watson, Richard L., Jr., "The Chronicles of America," *South Atlantic Quarterly*, L (January 1951), 109-121.

Dudden, Arthur P., "The New American Nation Series," *Historian*, XVIII (Autumn 1955), 83-104.

Watson, Richard L., Jr., "American Political History, 1900-1920," *South Atlantic Quarterly*, LIV (January 1955), 107-126.

ECONOMIC HISTORY

Hacker, Louis M., "The Anticapitalist Bias of American Historians," in F. A. Hayek (ed.), *Capitalism and the Historians* (Chicago: University of Chicago Press, 1954), pp. 62-90.

LeDuc, Thomas, "Recent Contributions to Economic History: The

United States, 1861-1900," *Journal of Economic History*, XIX (March 1959), 44-63.

Stevens, Harry R., "Recent Writings on Midwestern Economic History," *Ohio Historical Quarterly*, LXIX (January 1960), 1-31.

Woodruff, W., "History and the Businessman," *Business History Review*, XXX (September 1956), 241-259.

Kolko, Gabriel, "The Premises of Business Revisionism," *Business History Review*, XXXIII (Autumn 1959), 330-344.

Cochran, Thomas C., "The History of a Business Society," *Journal of American History*, LIV (June 1967), 5-18.

SOCIAL HISTORY

Fishel, Leslie H., Jr., "The Writing of American Social History," *Midwestern Journal*, IV (Summer 1952), 86-92.

Nevins, Allan, "American Journalism and Its Historical Treatment," *Journalism Quarterly*, XXXVI (Fall 1959), 411-422.

Bornet, Vaughn Davis, "The New Labor History: A Challenge for American Historians," *Historian*, XVIII (Autumn 1955), 1-24.

Berman, Hyman, "A Cursory View of the Jewish Labor Movement: An Historiographical Survey," *American Jewish Historical Quarterly*, LII (December 1962), 79-97.

Saveth, Edward Norman, *American Historians and European Immigrants, 1815-1925* (New York: Columbia University Press, 1948).

Mann, Arthur, "Attitudes and Policies on Immigration: An Opportunity for Revision," *American Jewish Historical Society, Publications*, XLVI (March 1957), 289-305.

Wesley, Charles H., "Creating and Maintaining an Historical Tradition," *Journal of Negro History*, XLIX (January 1964), 13-33.

RELIGION

Clebsch, William A., "A New Historiography of American Religion," *Historical Magazine of the Protestant Episcopal Church*, XXXII (September 1963), 225-257.

May, Henry F., "The Recovery of American Religious History," *American Historical Review*, LXX (October 1964), 79-92.

Cunliffe, Marcus, "American Religious History," *Journal of American Studies*, I (April 1967), 105-113.

Woolverton, John F., "Histories of the Episcopal Church in America; A Survey and Evaluation," *Historical Magazine of the Protestant Episcopal Church*, XXXIV (March 1965), 59-78.

Hill, Marvin S., "The Historiography of Mormonism," *Church History*, XXVIII (December 1959), 418-426.

URBANIZATION

Goldman, Eric F. (ed.), *Historiography and Urbanization: Essays in American History* . . . (Baltimore: Johns Hopkins Press, 1941).

McKelvey, Blake F., "American Urban History Today," *American Historical Review*, LVII (July 1952), 919-929.

Lampard, Eric E., "American Historians and the Study of Urbanization," *American Historical Review*, LXVII (October 1961), 49-61.

Glaab, Charles N., "The Historian and the American Urban Tradition," *Wisconsin Magazine of History*, XLVII (Autumn 1963), 12-25.

INTELLECTUAL HISTORY

Higham, John, "The Rise of American Intellectual History," *American Historical Review*, LVI (April 1951), 453-471.

Higham, John, "Intellectual History and Its Neighbors," *Journal of the History of Ideas*, XV (June 1954), 339-347.

Skotheim, Robert Allen, "The Writing of American Histories of Ideas: Two Traditions of the Twentieth Century," *Journal of the History of Ideas*, XXV (April 1964), 257-278.

Skotheim, Robert, *American Intellectual Histories and Historians* (Princeton: Princeton University Press, 1966).

Curti, Merle, "The Democratic Theme in American Historical Literature," *Mississippi Valley Historical Review*, XXXIX (June 1952), 3-28.

DIPLOMATIC AND MILITARY HISTORY

Van Hoogstrate, Sister Dorothy Jane, *American Foreign Policy, Realists and Idealists: A Catholic Interpretation* (St. Louis: B. Herder Book Co., 1960).

Perkins, Dexter, "American Wars and Critical Historians," *Yale Review*, XL (Summer 1951), 682-695.

Helfers, M. C., "The United States Army's History of World War II," *Military Affairs*, XIX (Spring 1955), 32-36.

Merrill, James M., "Successors of Mahan: A Survey of Writings on American Naval History, 1914-1960," *Mississippi Valley Historical Review*, L (June 1963), 79-99.

CONSTITUTIONAL HISTORY

Haines, Charles Grove, "Histories of the Supreme Court Written from the Federalist Point of View," *Southwestern Political and Social Science Quarterly*, IV (1923).

Bellot, H. Hale, "The Literature of the Last Half-Century on the Constitutional History of the United States," *Transactions of the Royal Historical Society 5th series*, V (1957), 159-182.

SOUTHERN HISTORY

Stephenson, Wendell Holmes, *The South Lives in History: Southern Historians and Their Legacy* (Baton Rouge: Louisiana State University Press, 1955).

Stephenson, Wendell Holmes, *Southern History in the Making; Pioneer Historians of the South* (Baton Rouge: Louisiana State University Press, 1964).

Eaton, Clement, "Recent Trends in the Writing of Southern History," *Louisiana Historical Quarterly*, XXXVIII (April 1955), 26-42.

Noggle, Burl, "Variety and Ambiguity: The Recent Approach to Southern History," *Mississippi Quarterly*, XVII (Winter 1964).

Link, Arthur S., and Rembert W. Patrick (eds.), *Writing Southern History: Essays in Historiography* . . . (Baton Rouge: Louisiana State University Press, 1966).

WESTERN HISTORY

Howard, Joseph Kinsey, "New Concepts of Plains History," *Montana Magazine of History*, II (October 1952), 16-23.

Pomeroy, Earl, "Toward a Reorientation of Western History: Continuity and Environment," *Mississippi Valley Historical Review*, XLI (March 1955), 579-600.

Hamilton, Raphael N., "The Significance of the Frontier to the Historian of Catholic Church in the United States," *Catholic Historical Review*, XXV (July 1939), 160-178.

Hofstadter, Richard, "Turner and the Frontier Myth," *American Scholar*, XVIII (Autumn 1949), 433-443.

Benson, Lee, "The Historical Background of Turner's Frontier Essay," *Agricultural History*, XXV (April 1951), 59-82.

University of Kansas City Review, *The Frontier in American Life: A Symposium on Frederick Jackson Turner and the Significance of His "Approach" Today* (Kansas City: University of Kansas City, 1951).

Stevens, Harry Robert, "Cross Section and Frontier," *South Atlantic Quarterly*, LII (July 1953), 445-463.

Allen, Harry Cranbrook, "F. J. Turner and the Frontier in American History," in H. C. Allen and C. P. Hill (eds.), *British Essays in American History* (London: E. Arnold, 1957), 145-166.

Gressley, Gene M., "The Turner Thesis—A Problem in Historiography," *Agricultural History*, XXXII (October 1958), 227-249.

Rundell, Walter, Jr., "Concepts of the Frontier and the West," *Arizona and the West*, I (Spring 1959), 13-41.

Benson, Lee, *Turner and Beard: American Historical Writing Reconsidered* (Glencoe: Free Press, 1960).

Von Nardroff, Ellen, "The American Frontier as Safety-Valve—The Life, Death, Reincarnation and Justification of a Theory," *Agricultural History*, XXXVI (July 1962), 123-142.

Bolkhovitinov, M. N., "The Role of the 'Frontier' in the History of the U.S.A. (A Critical Analysis of the Views of F. J. Turner)," *Soviet Review*, V (Spring 1964), 22-38.

Noble, David W., *Historians Against History: The Frontier Thesis and the National Covenant in American Historical Writing Since 1830* (Minneapolis: University of Minnesota Press, 1966).

COLONIAL PERIOD

Billington, Ray Allen, (ed.), *The Reinterpretation of Early American History: Essays in Honor of John Edwin Pomfret* (San Marino: Huntington Library, 1966).

Middlekauff, Robert L., "The American Continental Colonies in the Empire," in Robin Winks (ed.), *The Historiography of the British Empire and Commonwealth* (Durham: Duke University Press, 1964), 23-45.

Gay, Peter, *A Loss of Mastery: Puritan Historians in Colonial America* (Berkeley: University of California Press, 1966).

Moore, Leroy, Jr., "Roger Williams and the Historians," *Church History*, XXXII (December 1963), 432-451.

Illick, Joseph E., "Jonathan Edwards and the Historians," *Journal of the Presbyterian Historical Society*, XLIX (December 1961), 230-246.

Morse, Jarvis M., "Colonial Historians of New York," *New York History*, XXIII (October 1942), 395-409.

Persons, Stow, "The Cyclical Theory of History in Eighteenth Century America," *American Quarterly*, VI (Summer 1954), 147-163.

THE REVOLUTION

Smith, William Raymond, *History as Argument: Three Patriot Historians of the American Revolution* (The Hague: Mouton & Co., 1966).

Savelle, Max, "The Imperial School of American Colonial Historians," *Indiana Magazine of History*, XLV (June 1949), 123-134.

Morgan, Edmund S., "The American Revolution: Revisions in Need of Revising," *William and Mary Quarterly*, XIV, 3rd series (January 1957), 3-15.

Greene, Jack P., "The Flight from Determinism: A Review of Recent Literature on the Coming of the American Revolution," *South Atlantic Quarterly*, LXI (Spring 1962), 235-259.

Tolles, Frederick B., "The American Revolution Considered as a Social Movement: A Re-evaluation," *American Historical Review*, LX (October 1954), 1-12.

Higginbotham, Don, "American Historians and the Military History of the American Revolution," *American Historical Review*, LXX (October 1964), 18-34.

Akers, Charles W., " 'New Light' on the American Revolution," *New-York Historical Society Quarterly*, LI (July 1967), 283-291.

Young, Carol Furlong, "A Study of Some Developing Interpretations of the History of Revolutionary Tennessee (1776-1781)," *East Tennessee Historical Society, Publications*, XXV (1953), 24-36.

Butterfield, Herbert, *George III and the Historians*, revised edition (New York: Macmillan Company, 1959).

Smith, Page, "A Case in Point: the American Revolution," chapter 12 of Smith, *The Historian and History* (New York: Knopf, 1964).

Wood, Gordon S., "Rhetoric and Reality in the American Revolution," *William and Mary Quarterly*, XXIII, 3rd series (January 1966), 3-32.

Morris, Richard B., in Morris, *The American Revolution Reconsidered* (New York, 1967).

Green, Jack P., "The Plunge of Lemmings: A Consideration of Recent Writings on British Politics and the American Revolution," *South Atlantic Quarterly*, LXVII (Winter 1968).

CONFEDERATION AND EARLY NATIONAL

Morris, Richard Brandon, "The Confederation Period and the American Historian," *William and Mary Quarterly*, XIII, 3rd series (April 1956), 139-156.

Billington, Ray Allen, "The Historians of the Northwest Ordinance," *Illinois State Historical Society, Journal*, XL (December 1947).

Coleman, Peter J., "Beard, McDonald, and Economic Determinism in American Historiography," *Business History Review*, XXXIV (Spring 1960), 113-121.

Elkins, Stanley, and McKitrick, Eric, "The Founding Fathers, Young Men of the Revolution," *Political Science Quarterly*, LXXVI (June 1961), 181-216.

Nettels, Curtis Putnam, "The Washington Theme in American History," *Massachusetts Historical Society, Proceedings*, LXVIII (1952), 171-198.

Moramarco, Fred, "Hamilton and the Historians: The Economic Program in Retrospect," *Midcontinent American Studies Journal*, VIII (Spring 1967), 34-43.

JEFFERSONIAN

Bellot, Hugh Hale, "Thomas Jefferson in American Historiography," *Transactions of the Royal Historical Society*, IV, 5th series, (1954), 135-154.

Peterson, Merrill D., *The Jefferson Image in the American Mind* (New York: Oxford University Press, 1960).

Pratt, Julius W., "Aaron Burr and the Historians," *New York History*, XXVI (October 1945), 447-470.

Goodman, Warren H., "The Origins of the War of 1812: A Survey of Changing Interpretations," *Mississippi Valley Historical Review*, XXVIII (September 1941), 171-186.

JACKSONIANISM AND MANIFEST DESTINY

Morgan, William G., "John Quincy Adams versus Andrew Jackson: Their Biographers and the 'Corrupt Bargain' Charge," *Tennessee Historical Quarterly*, XXVI (Spring 1967), 43-58.

Friedel, Frank, "Jackson's Political Removals as Seen by Historians," *Historian*, II (Autumn 1939), 41-52.

Martin, Andrew, "The Jacksonian Era: Conflicting Evaluations," *Journal of Social Studies*, VII (Spring 1951), 39-48.

Sellers, Charles Grier, Jr., "Andrew Jackson Versus the Historians," *Mississippi Valley Historical Review*, XLIV (March 1958), 615-634.

Cave, Alfred A., *Jacksonian Democracy and the Historians* (Gainesville: University of Florida Press, 1964).

Wise, Gene, "Political 'Reality' in Recent American Scholarship: Progressives versus Symbolists," *American Quarterly*, XIX (Summer 1967), 303-328.

Schultz, Harold S., "A Century of Calhoun Biographies," *South Atlantic Quarterly*, L (April 1951), 248-254.

Horn, James J., "Trends in Historical Interpretations: James K. Polk," *North Carolina Historical Review,* XLII (October 1965), 454-464.

Zavala, Silvio, "La Historiografía Norteamericana Sobre la Guerra del 47," *Cuadernos Americanos,* VII (March 1948), 190-206.

Barker, Eugene Campbell, "Historiography of American Territorial Expansion," in Barker, *Speeches, Responses and Essays* (Austin: Barker Texas Historical Center, 1954), 205-221.

Esquinazi-Mayo, Roberto, "Historiografía de la Guerre entre México y los Estados Unidos," *Duquesne Hispanic Review,* I (Fall 1962), 33-48; (Winter 1962), 7-35.

Harstad, Peter and Resh, Richard W., "The Causes of the Mexican War: A Note on Changing Interpretations," *Arizona and the West,* VI (Winter 1964), 289-302.

REFORM AND SECTIONALISM

Davis, David Brion, *Ante-Bellum Reform,* Introduction (New York: Harper and Row, 1967), 1-10.

Williams, David Alan, "William Lloyd Garrison, the Historians, and the Abolitionist Movement," *Essex Institute Historical Collections,* XCVIII (April 1962), 84-99.

Ruchames, Louis, "Charles Sumner and American Historiography," *Journal of Negro History,* XXXVIII (April 1953), 139-160.

Nichols, Roy F., "The Kansas-Nebraska Act: A Century of Historiography," *Mississippi Valley Historical Review,* XLIII (September 1956), 187-212.

Alexander, Thomas B., "Historical Treatments of the Dred Scott Case," *South Carolina Historical Association, Proceedings* (1953), 37-59.

Allis, Frederick S., "The Dred Scott Labyrinth," in Stuart Hughes (ed.), *Teachers of History: Essays in Honor of Laurence Bradford Packard* (Ithaca: Cornell University Press, 1954), 341-368.

Whitridge, Arnold, "The John Brown Legend," *History Today,* VII (April 1957), 211-220.

SLAVERY

Mooney, Chase C., "The Literature of Slavery: A Re-evaluation," *Indiana Magazine of History,* XLVII (September 1951), 251-260.

Stampp, Kenneth M., "The Historian and Southern Negro Slavery," *American Historical Review,* LVII (April 1952), 613-624.

Elkins, Stanley M., "Slavery as a Problem in Historiography," in Elkins,

Slavery: A Problem in American Institutional and Intellectual Life (Chicago: University of Chicago Press, 1959), 1-26.

Woodman, Harold D., "The Profitability of Slavery: A Historical Perennial," *Journal of Southern History*, XXIX (August 1963), 303-325.

Genovese, Eugene D., "Recent Contributions to the Economic Historiography of the Slave South," *Science and Society*, XXIV (Winter 1960), 53-66.

Lynd, Staughton, "On Turner, Beard and Slavery," *Journal of Negro History*, XLVIII (October 1963), 235-350.

Sio, Arnold A., "Interpretations of Slavery," *Comparative Studies in Society and History*, VII (April 1965), 289-308.

CIVIL WAR

Beale, Howard K., "What Historians Have Said About the Causes of the Civil War," Chapter III of *Theory and Practice in Historical Study: A Report of the Committee on Historiography; Bulletin 54* (New York: Social Science Research Council, 1946).

Schlesinger, Arthur M., Jr., "The Causes of the Civil War: A Note on Historical Sentimentalism," *Partisan Review*, XVI (October 1949), 469-481.

Geyl, Pieter, "The American Civil War and the Problem of Inevitability," *New England Quarterly*, XXIV (June 1951), 147-168.

Pressly, Thomas J., *Americans Interpret Their Civil War* (Princeton: Princeton University Press, 1954).

Bonner, Thomas N., "Civil War Historians and the 'Needless War' Doctrine," *Journal of the History of Ideas*, XVII (April 1956), 193-216.

Donald, David, "American Historians and the Causes of the Civil War," *South Atlantic Quarterly*, LIX (Summer 1960), 351-355.

Benson, Lee, and Cushing Strout, "Causation and the American Civil War," *History and Theory*, I (1961), 163-185.

Dray, William, "Causal Accounts of the Civil War," *Daedalus*, XCI (Summer 1962), 579-591.

Wooster, Ralph A., "The Secession of the Lower South: An Examination of Changing Interpretations," *Civil War History*, VII (June 1961), 117-127.

Donnelly, William J., "Conspiracy or Popular Movement: The Historiography of the Support for Secession," *North Carolina Historical Review*, XLII (January 1965), 70-84.

Little, Robert D., "Southern Historians and the Downfall of the Confederacy," *Alabama Review*, IV (January 1951), 33-54.

Potter, David Morris, *The Lincoln Theme and American National Historiography* (Oxford: Clarendon Press, 1948).

Curry, Richard O., "The Union as It Was: A Critique of Recent Interpretations of the 'Copperheads'," *Civil War History*, XIII (March 1967), 25-39.

Scheiber, Harry N., "Economic Change in the Civil War Era: An Analysis of Recent Studies," *Civil War History*, XI (December 1965), 396-411.

RECONSTRUCTION

Hays, Willard, "Andrew Johnson's Reputation," *East Tennessee Historical Society, Publications*, XXXI (1959), 1-31.

Castel, Albert, "Andrew Johnson: His Historiographical Rise and Fall," *Mid-America*, XLV (July 1963), 175-184.

Notaro, Carmen Anthony, "History of the Biographic Treatment of Andrew Johnson in the Twentieth Century," *Tennessee Historical Quarterly*, XXIV (Summer 1965), 143-155.

Du Bois, W. E. Burghardt, "The Propaganda of History," Chapter XVII in Du Bois, *Black Reconstruction* (New York: Harcourt, Brace and Company, 1935).

Taylor, Alrutheus A., "Historians of Reconstruction," *Journal of Negro History*, XXIII (January 1938), 16-34.

Simkins, Francis Butler, "New Viewpoints of Southern Reconstruction," *Journal of Southern History*, V (February 1939), 49-61.

Beale, Howard K., "On Rewriting Reconstruction History," *American Historical Review*, XLV (July 1940), 807-827.

Williams, T. Harry, "An Analysis of Some Reconstruction Attitudes," *Journal of Southern History*, XII (November 1946), 469-486.

Franklin, John Hope, "Whither Reconstruction History," *Journal of Negro Education*, XVII (Fall 1948), 446-461.

Weisberger, Bernard A., "The Dark and Bloody Ground of Reconstruction Historiography," *Journal of Southern History*, XXV (November 1959), 427-447.

Green, Fletcher Melvin, "Reconstruction Historiography," Introduction to reprint of William Watson Davis, *The Civil War and Reconstruction in Florida* (Gainesville: University of Florida Press, 1964), xxii-xlv.

Stampp, Kenneth M., "The Tragic Legend of Reconstruction," in *The Era of Reconstruction, 1865-1877* (New York: Alfred A. Knopf, 1965), 3-23.

Cox, LaWanda and John H. Cox, "Negro Suffrage and Republican Politics: the Problem of Motivation in Reconstruction Historiography," *Journal of Southern History*, XXXIII (August 1967), 303-330.

Donald, David, "Historical Synthesis," *Commentary*, XLIV (September 1967), 94-98.

Clark, John G., "Historians and the Joint Committee on Reconstruction," *The Historian*, XXIII (May 1961), 348-361.

Macaulay, Neill W., Jr., "South Carolina Reconstruction Historiography," *South Carolina Historical Magazine*, LXV (January 1964), 20-32.

GILDED AGE

Miller, William, "American Historians and the Business Elite," *Journal of Economic History*, IX (November 1949), 184-208.

Bornet, Vaughn Davis, "Those 'Robber Barons'," *Western Political Quarterly*, VI (June 1953), 342-346.

Bridges, Hal, "The Robber Baron Concept in American History," *Business History Review*, XXXII (Spring 1958), 1-13.

Chalmers, David, "From Robber Barons to Industrial Statesmen: Standard Oil and the Business Historians," *American Journal of Economics and Sociology*, XX (October 1960), 47-58.

Kirkland, Edward C., "The Robber Barons Revisited," *American Historical Review*, LXVI (October 1960), 68-73.

Solganick, Allen, "The Robber Baron Concept and Its Revisionists," *Science and Society*, XXIX (Summer 1965), 257-269.

PROGRESSIVISM AND IMPERIALISM

Saloutos, Theodore, "The Professors and the Populists," *Agricultural History*, XL (October 1966), 235-254.

May, Ernest R., "American Imperialism: Some Answers and Some Questions," *Perspectives in American History*, I (1967), 123-134.

Hitchman, James H., "The Platt Amendment Revisited: A Bibliography Survey," *The Americas*, XXIII (April 1967), 343-370.

Gatell, Frank Otto, "The Canal in Retrospect—Some Panamanian and Colombian Views," *The Americas*, XV (July 1958), 23-36.

Grantham, Dewey W., Jr., "Theodore Roosevelt in American Historical Writing, 1945-1960," *Mid-America*, XLIII (January 1961), 3-35.

Margulies, Herbert F., "Recent Opinion on the Decline of the Progressive Movement," *Mid-America*, XLV (October 1963), 250-268.

Tager, Jack, "Progressives, Conservatives and the Theory of the Status Revolution," *Mid-America*, XLVIII (July 1966), 162-175.

Wilson, R. Jackson, "The Reassessment of Liberalism," *Journal of Contemporary History*, II (January 1967), 93-105.

WORLD WAR I AND THE TWENTIES

Watson, Richard L., Jr., "Woodrow Wilson and his Interpreters, 1947-1957," *Mississippi Valley Historical Review*, XLIV (September 1957), 207-236.

Goodell, Stephen, "Woodrow Wilson in Latin America: Interpretations," *The Historian*, XXVIII (November 1965), 96-127.

Leopold, Richard W., "The Problem of American Intervention, 1917: An Historical Retrospect," *World Politics*, II (April 1951), 405-425.

Smith, Daniel M. "National Interest and American Intervention, 1917: An Historiographical Appraisal," *Journal of American History*, LII (June 1965), 5-24.

Adler, Selig, "The War-Guilt Question and American Disillusionment, 1918-1928," *Journal of Modern History*, XXIII (March 1951), 1-28.

Cohen, Warren I., *The American Revisionists* (Chicago: University of Chicago Press, 1966).

May, Henry F., "Shifting Perspectives on the 1920's," *Mississippi Valley Historical Review*, XLIII (December 1956), 405-427.

Noggle, Burl, "The Twenties: A New Historiographical Frontier," *Journal of American History*, LIII (September 1966), 299-314.

Kirschner, Don S., "Conflicts and Politics in the 1920's: Historiography and Prospects," *Mid-America*, XLVIII (October 1966), 219-233.

NEW DEAL AND WORLD WAR II

Watson, Richard L., Jr., "FDR in Historical Writing 1950-1957," *South Atlantic Quarterly*, LVII (Winter 1958), 104-126.

Chambers, Clarke A., "FDR, Pragmatist-Idealist: An Essay in Historiography," *Pacific Northwest Quarterly*, LII (April 1961), 50-55.

Graham, Otis L., Jr., "Historians and the New Deals: 1944-1960," *Social Studies*, LIV (April 1963), 133-140.

Ferrell, Robert H., "Pearl Harbor and the Revisionists," *Historian*, XVII (Spring 1955), 215-233.

Cole, Wayne S., "American Entry into World War II: A Historiographical Appraisal," *Mississippi Valley Historical Review*, XLIII (March 1957), 595-617.

INDIVIDUALS

ADAMS, BROOKS (1848-1927)

Aaron, Daniel, "The Unusable Man: An Essay on the Mind of Brooks Adams," *New England Quarterly*, XXI (March 1948), 3-33.

Anderson, Thornton, *Brooks Adams, Constructive Conservative* (Ithaca: Cornell University Press, 1951).

Beringause, Arthur P., *Brooks Adams: A Biography* (New York: Alfred A. Knopf, 1955).

Beisner, Robert L., "Brooks Adams and Charles Francis Adams, Jr.: Historians of Massachusetts," *New England Quarterly*, XXXV (March 1962), 48-70.

ADAMS, HENRY (1838-1918)

Ford, Worthington C. (ed.), *Letters of Henry Adams*, 2 vols. (Boston: Houghton Mifflin Company, 1930).

Becker, Carl L., "The Education of Henry Adams," *American Historical Review*, XXIV (April 1919), 422-434.

Samuels, Ernest, *Henry Adams*, 3 vols. (Cambridge: Harvard University Press, 1948-62).

Bayn, Max Isaac, *The French Education of Henry Adams* (New York: Columbia University Press, 1951).

Greenleaf, Richard, "History, Marxism and Henry Adams," *Science and Society*, XV (Summer 1951), 193-208.

Wasser, Henry, "The Thought of Henry Adams," *New England Quarterly*, XXIV (December 1951), 495-509.

Jordy, William H., *Henry Adams, Scientific Historian* (New Haven: Yale University Press, 1952).

Rozwenc, Edwin C., "Henry Adams and the Federalists," in H. Stuart Hughes (ed.), *Teachers of History* . . . (Ithaca: Cornell University Press, 1954), 122-145.

Lindsay, Barbara, "Henry Adams' *History*: A Study in Limitations," *Western Humanities Review*, VIII (Spring 1954), 99-110.

Stevenson, Elizabeth, *Henry Adams, A Biography* (New York: Macmillan, 1955).

Levenson, J. C., *The Mind and Art of Henry Adams* (Boston: Houghton, Mifflin Company, 1957).

Cairns, John, "The Successful Quest of Henry Adams," *South Atlantic Quarterly*, LVII (Spring 1958), 168-193.

Barrett, C. Waller, "The Making of a History: Letters of Henry Adams to Henry Vignaud and Charles Scribner, 1879-1913," *Proceedings, Massachusetts Historical Society*, LXXXI (1959), 204-271.

Donovan, Timothy Paul, *Henry Adams and Brooks Adams: The Edu-*

cation of Two American Historians (Norman: University of Oklahoma Press, 1961).

Peterson, Merrill D., "Henry Adams on Jefferson the President," *Virginia Quarterly Review,* XXXIX (Spring 1963), 187-201.

Vitzhum, Richard C., "Henry Adams' Paraphrase of Sources in the *History of the United States,*" *American Quarterly,* XVII (Spring 1965), 81-91.

Shaw, Peter, "Blood is Thicker than Iron: Henry Adams' *History,*" *New England Quarterly,* XL (June 1967), 163-187.

ADAMS, HERBERT BAXTER (1850-1901)

Holt, W. Stull, *Historical Scholarship in the United States, 1876-1901, as Revealed in the Correspondence of Herbert B. Adams* (Baltimore: Johns Hopkins Press, 1938).

Stephenson, Wendell H., "Herbert B. Adams and Southern Historical Scholarship at the Johns Hopkins University," *Maryland Historical Magazine,* XLII (March 1947), 1-20.

ANDREWS, CHARLES McLEAN (1863-1943)

Eisenstadt, Abraham S., *Charles McLean Andrews* (New York: Columbia University Press, 1957).

BANCROFT, FREDERIC (1860-1945)

Cooke, Jacob E., *Frederic Bancroft, Historian* (Norman: University of Oklahoma Press, 1957).

BANCROFT, GEORGE (1800-1891)

Howe, M. A. DeWolfe, *Life and Letters of George Bancroft,* 2 vols. (New York: Scribners, 1908).

Kraus, Michael, "George Bancroft, 1834-1934," *New England Quarterly* VII (December 1934), 662-686.

Nye, Russel B., *George Bancroft, Brahmin Rebel* (New York: Alfred A. Knopf, 1945).

Hollis, C. Carroll, "Brownson on George Bancroft," *South Atlantic Quarterly,* XLIX (January 1950), 42-52.

Rathburn, J. W., "George Bancroft on Man and History," *Transactions, Wisconsin Academy of Sciences, Arts and Letters,* XLIII (1954), 51-73.

BANCROFT, HUBERT HOWE (1832-1918)

Caughey, John Walton, *Hubert Howe Bancroft: Historian of the West,* (Berkeley: University of California Press, 1946).

Ellsworth, S. George, "Hubert Howe Bancroft and the History of Utah," *Utah Historical Quarterly,* XXII (April 1954), 99-124.

BASSETT, JOHN SPENCER (1867-1928)

Stephenson, Wendell H., "John Spencer Bassett as a Historian of the South," *North Carolina Historical Review*, XXV (July 1948), 289-317.

Stephenson, Wendell H., "The Negro in the Thinking and Writing of John Spencer Bassett," *North Carolina Historical Review*, XXV (October 1948), 427-441.

BEARD, CHARLES AUSTIN (1874-1948)

Blinkoff, Maurice, "The Influence of Charles A. Beard upon American Historiography," *University of Buffalo Studies*, XXII (May 1936), 4-84.

Herring, Hubert, "Charles A. Beard, Free Lance Among the Historians," *Harper's*, CLXXVIII (1939), 641-652.

Morison, Samuel Eliot, "History Through a Beard," in Morison, *By Land and By Sea* (New York: Alfred A. Knopf, 1953).

Borning, Bernard C., "The Political Philosophy of Young Charles A. Beard," *American Political Science Review*, XLIII (December 1949), 1165-1178.

Josephson, Matthew, "Charles A. Beard: A Memoir," *Virginia Quarterly Review*, XXV (Autumn 1949), 585-602.

McMahon, Arthur W., "Charles Austin Beard as a Teacher," *Political Science Quarterly*, LXV (March 1950), 1-19.

Hofstadter, Richard, "Beard and the Constitution: The History of an Idea," *American Quarterly*, II (Fall 1950), 195-213.

Lerner, Max, "The Political Theory of Charles A. Beard," *American Quarterly*, II (Winter 1950), 303-321.

Thomas, Robert E., "A Reappraisal of Charles A. Beard's *An Economic Interpretation of the Constitution of the United States*," *American Historical Review*, LVII (January 1952), 370-375.

Goldman, Eric F., "The Origins of Beard's *Economic Interpretation of the Constitution*," *Journal of the History of Ideas*, XIII (April 1952), 234-249.

Thomas, Robert E., "The Virginia Convention of 1788: A Criticism of Beard's *An Economic Interpretation of the Constitution*," *Journal of Southern History*, XIX (February 1953), 63-72.

Phillips, Harlan Buddington, "Charles Beard: The English Lectures, 1899-1901," *Journal of the History of Ideas*, XIV (June 1953), 451-456.

Marks, Harry J., "Ground Under Our Feet: Beard's Relativism," *Journal of the History of Ideas*, XIV (October 1953), 628-633.

Beale, Howard K., (ed.), *Charles A. Beard: An Appraisal* (Lexington: University of Kentucky Press, 1954).

Deininger, Whitaker T., "The Skepticism and Historical Faith of Charles A. Beard," *Journal of the History of Ideas*, XV (October 1954), 573-588.

Beard, Mary R., *The Making of Charles A. Beard: An Interpretation*, (New York: Exposition Press, 1955).

Sorenson, Lloyd R., "Charles A. Beard and German Historiographical Thought," *Mississippi Valley Historical Review*, XLII (September 1955), 274-287.

Williams, William Appleman, "A Note on Charles Austin Beard's Search for a General Theory of Causation," *American Historical Review*, LXII (October 1956), 59-80.

Nash, Gerald D., "Self-Education in Historiography: The Case of Charles A. Beard," *Pacific Northwest Quarterly*, LII (July 1961), 108-115.

Borning, Bernard C., *The Political and Social Thought of Charles A. Beard* (Seattle: University of Washington Press, 1962).

Kennedy, Thomas C., "Charles A. Beard and the 'Court Historians,'" *Historian*, XXV (August 1963), 439-450.

Kenyon, Cecilia M., "'An Economic Interpretation of the Constitution' After Fifty Years," *Centennial Review*, VII (Summer 1963), 327-352.

BECKER, CARL LOTUS (1873-1945)

Gershoy, Leo, "Carl Becker on Progress and Power," *American Historical Review*, LV (October 1949), 22-35.

Smith, Charlotte Watkins, "Carl Becker: The Historian as Literary Craftsman," *William and Mary Quarterly*, 3rd Series, IX (July 1952), 291-316.

Cairns, John C., "Carl Becker: An American Liberal," *Journal of Politics*, XVI (November 1954), 623-644.

Smith, Charlotte Watkins, *Carl Becker: On History and the Climate of Opinion* (Ithaca: Cornell University Press, 1956).

Zagorin, Perez, and Leo Gershoy, "Carl Becker on History," *American Historical Review*, LXII (October 1956), 1-17.

Gay, Peter, "Carl Becker's Heavenly City," *Political Science Quarterly*, LXXII (June 1957), 182-199.

Noble, David Watson, "Carl Becker: Science, Relativism, and the Dilemma of Diderot," *Ethics*, LXIV (July 1957), 233-248.

Strout, Cushing, *The Pragmatic Revolt in American History: Carl Becker and Charles Beard* (New Haven: Yale University Press, 1958).

Wilkins, Burleigh Taylor, *Carl Becker: A Biographical Study in American Intellectual History* (Cambridge: M.I.T. and Harvard, 1961).

BELKNAP, JEREMY (1744-1798)

Kaplan, Sidney, "The History of New Hampshire: Jeremy Belknap as Literary Craftsman," *William and Mary Quarterly*, 3rd Series, XXI (January 1964), 18-39.

BEVERIDGE, ALBERT JEREMIAH (1826-1927)

Tilden, Richard Arnold, "Albert J. Beveridge: Biographer," *Indiana Magazine of History*, XXVI (June 1930), 77-92.

Donnan, Elizabeth and Leo F. Stock (eds.), "Senator Beveridge, J. Franklin Jameson, and John Marshall," *Mississippi Valley Historical Review*, XXXV (December 1948), 463-492.

Alderson, William T., and Kenneth K. Bailey (eds.), "Correspondence Between Albert J. Beveridge and Jacob M. Dickinson on the Writing of Beveridge's Life of Lincoln," *Journal of Southern History*, XX (May 1954), 210-237.

Levine, Daniel, "The Social Philosophy of Albert J. Beveridge," *Indiana Magazine of History*, LVIII (June 1962), 101-116.

BOLTON, HERBERT EUGENE (1870-1953)

Ives, Ronald Lorenz, "Herbert Eugene Bolton, 1870-1953," *American Catholic Historical Society, Records*, LXV (March 1954), 40-55.

Onís, José de, "The Americas of Herbert E. Bolton," *Americas*, XII (October 1955), 157-168.

BRUCE, PHILIP ALEXANDER (1856-1933)

Powell, William S., "Philip Alexander Bruce: Historian," *Tyler's Quarterly Historical and Genealogical Magazine*, XXX (January 1949), 165-184.

BULEY, ROSCOE CARLYLE (1893-

Mood, Fulmer, "The Theory of the History of an American Section and the Practice of R. Carlyle Buley," *Indiana Magazine of History*, XLVIII (March 1952), 1-22.

BURGESS, JOHN WILLIAM (1844-1931)

Burgess, John W., *Reminiscences of an American Scholar: The Beginnings of Columbia University* (New York: Columbia University Press, 1934).

Loewenberg, Bert James, "John William Burgess, the Scientific Method, and Hegelian Philosophy of History," *Mississippi Valley Historical Review*, XLII (December 1955), 490-509.

CHANNING, EDWARD (1856-1931)

Morison, Samuel Eliot, "Edward Channing, a Memoir," *Massachusetts Historical Society, Proceedings*, LVIV (1930-1932), 250-284.

Fahrney, Ralph Rey, "Edward Channing," *Mississippi Valley Historical Review*, XVIII (June 1931), 53-59.

DeNovo, John A., "Edward Channing's 'Great Work' Twenty Years Later," *Mississippi Valley Historical Review*, XXXIX (September 1952), 257-274.

Weaver, Glenn, "Edward Channing: A Literary Biography," *Social Studies*, LIV (1963), 83-95.

COMMAGER, HENRY STEELE (1902-

Nevins, Allan, "Henry S. Commager as Historian: An Appreciation," in Harold M. Hyman and Leonard W. Levy (eds.). *Freedom and Reform: Essays in Honor of Henry Steele Commager* (New York: Harper & Row, 1967), 6-15.

COMMONS, JOHN ROGERS (1862-1945)

Parsons, Kenneth R., "John R. Commons' Point of View," *Journal of Land and Public Utility Economics*, XVIII (August 1942), 245-266.

Carlin, Edward A., "John R. Commons—Industrial Theorist," *Social Forces*, XXX (May 1952), 379-387.

Blackwood, George D., "Frederick Jackson Turner and John Rogers Commons—Complementary Thinkers," *Mississippi Valley Historical Review* (December 1954), 471-488.

CORWIN, EDWARD S. (1878-

Mason, Alpheus S. and Gerald Garvey, "Edward S. Corwin," Introduction, *American Constitutional History, Essays by Edward S. Corwin* (New York: Harper & Row, 1964), ix-xxiii.

DODD, WILLIAM EDWARD (1869-1940)

Williams, Jack K., "William Edward Dodd: Historian of the Old South," *South Carolina Historical Association, Proceedings*, (1950), 18-29.

Dallek, Robert, *William E. Dodd: Democrat and Diplomat* (New York: Oxford University Press, 1968).

DONALD, DAVID (1920-

Skotheim, Robert Allen, "A Note on Historical Method: David Donald's 'Toward a Reconsideration of Abolitionists,'" *Journal of Southern History*, XXV (August 1959), 356-65.

Ruchames, Louis, "The Pulitzer Prize Treatment of Charles Sumner," *Massachusetts Review*, II (Summer 1961), 749-769.
Goodman, Paul, "David Donald's *Charles Sumner* Reconsidered," *New England Quarterly*, XXVII (September 1964), 373-387.

DRAPER, LYMAN COPELAND (1815-1891)

Harper, Josephine L., "Lyman C. Draper and Early American Archives," *American Archivist*, XV (July 1952), 205-212.
Hesseltine, William B., *Pioneer's Mission: The Story of Lyman Copeland Draper* (Madison: State Historical Society of Wisconsin, 1954).

DuBOIS, WILLIAM EDWARD BURGHARDT (1868-1963)

Broderick, Francis L., *W.E.B. DuBois; Negro Leader in a Time of Crisis* (Stanford: Stanford University Press, 1959).
Wesley, Charles H., "W.E.B. DuBois—the Historian," *Journal of Negro History*, L (July 1965), 147-162.

DUNNING, WILLIAM ARCHIBALD (1858-1922)

Dunning, William A., *Truth in History and Other Essays* (New York: Columbia University Press, 1937).
Harper, Alan D., "William A. Dunning: The Historian as Nemesis," *Civil War History*, X (March 1964), 54-66.

EGGLESTON, EDWARD (1837-1902)

Wolford, Thorp L., "Edward Eggleston: Evolution of a Historian," *Indiana Magazine of History*, LXIII (March 1967), 17-48.

FISHER, SYDNEY GEORGE (1856-1927)

Thompson, D. G. Brinton, "Sydney George Fisher, Son of the Diarist," *Pennsylvania Magazine of History and Biography*, XCI (April 1967), 181-192.

FISKE, JOHN (1842-1901)

Berman, Milton, *John Fiske: The Evolution of a Popularizer* (Cambridge: Harvard University Press, 1961).

FLEMING, WALTER LYNWOOD (1874-1932)

Binkley, William C., "The Contribution of Walter Lynwood Fleming to Southern Scholarship," *Journal of Southern History*, V (May 1939), 143-154.
Stephenson, Wendell H., "Some Pioneer Alabama Historians," *Alabama Review*, I (October 1948), 261-278.

FREEMAN, DOUGLAS SOUTHALL (1886-1953)

Williams, T. Harry, "Freeman, Historian of the Civil War: An Appraisal," *Journal of Southern History*, XXI (February 1955), 91-100.

GIPSON, LAWRENCE HENRY (1880-

Morris, Richard B., "The Spacious Empire of Lawrence Henry Gipson," *William and Mary Quarterly*, 3rd series, XXIV (April 1967), 169-189.

GREENE, EVARTS BOUTELL (1870-1947)

Pease, Theodore Calvin, "Evarts Boutell Greene, 1870-1947," *Illinois State Historical Society, Journal*, XLI (March 1948), 7-15.

HACKER, LOUIS MORTON (1899-

Gerstung, John F., "Louis M. Hacker's Reappraisal of Recent American History," *The Historian*, XII (Spring 1950), 140-166.

HANSEN, MARCUS LEE (1892-1938)

Spear, Alan H., "Marcus Lee Hansen and the Historiography of Immigration," *Wisconsin Magazine of History*, XLIV (Summer 1961), 258-268.

HILDRETH, RICHARD (1807-1865)

Schlesinger, Arthur M., Jr., "The Problem of Richard Hildreth," *New England Quarterly*, XIII (June 1940), 223-245.
Emerson, D. E., *Richard Hildreth* (Baltimore: Johns Hopkins Press, 1946).

JAMESON, JOHN FRANKLIN (1859-1937)

Fisher, Ruth Anna, and William Lloyd Fox (eds.), *J. Franklin Jameson: A Tribute* (Washington: Catholic University Press, 1965).

MAHAN, ALFRED THAYER (1840-1914)

Puleston, Captain W. D., *Mahan: The Life and Work of Captain Alfred Thayer Mahan, U. S. N.* (New Haven: Yale University Press, 1939).
Duncan, Francis, "Mahan—Historian with a Purpose," *United States Naval Institute, Proceedings*, LXXXIII (May 1957), 498-503.
Moll, Kenneth L., "A. T. Mahan, American Historian," *Military Affairs*, XXVII (Fall 1963), 131-140.

MALIN, JAMES CLAUDE (1893-

LeDuc, Thomas H., "An Ecological Interpretation of Grass-Lands History: The Work of James C. Malin as Historian and as Critic of Historians," *Nebraska History*, XXXI (September 1950), 226-233.

Nichols, Roy Franklin, "Kansas Historiography: The Technique of Cultural Analysis," *American Quarterly*, IX (Spring 1957), 85-91.

MARSHALL, JOHN (1755-1835)

Smith, William Raymond, "The Necessity of Circumstances: John Marshall's Historical Method," *The Historian*, XXVI (November 1963), 19-35.

McMASTER, JOHN BACH (1852-1932)

Goldman, Eric F., *John Bach McMaster: American Historian* (Philadelphia: University of Pennsylvania Press, 1943).

Taylor, William R., "Historical Bifocals on the Year 1800," *New England Quarterly*, XXIII (June 1950), 172-186.

MERRIMAN, ROGER BIGELOW (1876-1945)

Mattingly, Garrett, "The Historian of the Spanish Empire," *American Historical Review*, LIII (October 1948), 32-48.

MORISON, SAMUEL ELIOT (1887-

Morison, Samuel Eliot, *By Land and By Sea: Essays and Addresses* (New York: Alfred A. Knopf, 1953).

NEVINS, ALLAN (1890-

Lynn, Kenneth, "Allan Nevins: An Algerian Captive," *Explorations in Entrepreneurial History*, II (July 1950), 245-261.

Walsh, Lyle S., and Michael Lemanna, "A Critical Study of the Biographies of Allan Nevins," *Social Sciences*, XXVIII (January 1953), 34-39.

OBERHOLTZER, ELLIS PAXSON (1868-1936)

Ross, Earle D., "Oberholtzer's History of the United States Since the Civil War," *Mississippi Valley Historical Review*, XXIV (December 1937), 341-350.

O'CALLAGHAN, EDMUND BAILEY (1800-1880)

Guy, Francis Shaw, *Edmund Bailey O'Callaghan, A Study in American Historiography* (Washington: Catholic University Press, 1934).

OSGOOD, HERBERT LEVI (1855-1918)

Fox, Dixon Ryan, *Herbert Levi Osgood* (New York: Columbia University Press, 1924).

PALFREY, JOHN GORHAM (1796-1881)

Gatell, Frank Otto, *John Gorham Palfrey and the New England Conscience* (Cambridge: Harvard University Press, 1963).

PARKMAN, FRANCIS (1823-1893)

Wade, Mason, *Francis Parkman: Heroic Historian* (New York: Viking Press, 1942).

Pease, Otis A., *Parkman's History: The Historian As Literary Artist* (New Haven: Yale University Press, 1953).

Jacobs, Wilbur R., "Some Social Ideas of Francis Parkman," *American Quarterly*, IX (Winter 1957), 387-397.

Jacobs, Wilbur R., *Letters of Francis Parkman*, 2 volumes (Norman: University of Oklahoma Press, 1960).

Doughty, Howard, *Francis Parkman* (New York: Macmillan, 1962).

Vitzhum, Richard C., "The Historian as Editor: Francis Parkman's Reconstruction of Sources in *Montcalm and Wolfe*," *Journal of American History*, LIII (December 1966), 471-486.

PARRINGTON, VERNON LOUIS (1871-1929)

Ekirch, Arthur, "Parrington and the Decline of American Liberalism," *Journal of History of Ideas*, II (October 1951), 391-400.

Filler, Louis, "Parrington and Carlyle: Cross-currents in History and Belles-lettres," *Antioch Review*, XII (January 1952), 203-216.

Friend, Theodore, "The Various Radicalism of Vernon Parrington," *New England Social Studies Bulletin*, XIII (October 1955), 29-39.

Colwell, James L., "The Populist Image of Vernon Louis Parrington," *Mississippi Valley Historical Review*, XLIX (June 1962), 52-66.

Skotheim, Robert A., and Kermit Vanderbilt, "Vernon Louis Parrington: The Mind and Art of a Historian of Ideas," *Pacific Northwest Quarterly*, LIII (July 1962), 100-113.

PARTON, JAMES (1822-1891)

Flower, Milton E., *James Parton: The Father of Modern Biography* (Durham: Duke University Press, 1951).

PAXSON, FREDERIC L. (1877-1948)

Pomeroy, Earl, "Frederic L. Paxson and His Approach to History," *Mississippi Valley Historical Review*, XXXI (March 1953), 673-692.

PEASE, THEODORE CALVIN (1887-1948)

Randall, John G., "Theodore Calvin Pease," *Illinois State Historical Society Journal*, XLI (December 1948), 353-366.

PHILLIPS, ULRICH BONNELL (1877-1934)

Landon, Fred, and Everett E. Edwards, "A Bibliography of the Writings of Professor Ulrich Bonnell Phillips," *Agricultural History*, VIII (October 1934), 196-218.

Landon, Fred, "Ulrich Bonnell Phillips: Historian of the South," *Journal of Southern History*, V (August 1939), 364-371.

Newman, Philip Charles, "Ulrich Bonnell Phillips—the South's Foremost Historian," *Georgia Historical Quarterly*, XXV (September 1941), 244-261.

Hofstadter, Richard, "U. B. Phillips and the Plantation Legend," *Journal of Negro History*, XXIX (April 1944), 109-124.

Stephenson, Wendell H., "Ulrich B. Phillips: The University of Georgia and the Georgia Historical Society," *Georgia Historical Quarterly*, XLI (June 1957), 103-125.

Salem, Sam E., "U. B. Phillips and the Scientific Tradition," *Georgia Historical Quarterly*, XLIV (June 1960), 172-185.

Kugler, Ruben R., "U. B. Phillips' Use of Sources," *Journal of Negro History*, XLVII (July 1962), 153-168.

Genovese, Eugene D., "Ulrich Bonnell Phillips and His Critics," foreword to Phillips, *American Negro Slavery* (Baton Rouge: Louisiana State University Press, 1966).

Genovese, Eugene D., "Race and Class in Southern History: An Appraisal of the Work of Ulrich Bonnell Phillips" [with comments by David M. Potter, Kenneth M. Stampp, and Stanley M. Elkins], *Agricultural History*, XLI (October 1967), 345-371.

PRESCOTT, WILLIAM HICKLING (1796-1859)

Wolcott, Roger (ed.), *The Correspondence of William Hickling Prescott, 1833-1847* (Boston: Houghton, Mifflin Company, 1925).

Ringe, Donald A., "The Artistry of Prescott's *The Conquest of Mexico*," *New England Quarterly*, XXVI (December 1953), 454-476.

Humphreys, Rolphe A., "William Hickling Prescott: The Man and the Historian," *Hispanic American Historical Review*, XXXIX (February 1959), 1-19.

Gardiner, C. Harvey (ed.), *The Papers of William Hickling Prescott* (Urbana: University of Illinois Press, 1964).

RAMSDELL, CHARLES WILLIAM (1877-1942)

Stephenson, Wendell Holmes, "Charles W. Ramsdell: Historian of the Confederacy," *Journal of Southern History*, XXVI (November 1960), 501-525.

RANDALL, JAMES GARFIELD (1881-1953)

Pratt, Harry Edward, "James Garfield Randall, 1881-1953," *Illinois State Historical Society, Journal,* XLVI (Summer 1953), 119-131.

RHODES, JAMES FORD (1848-1918)

Howe, M. A. DeWolfe, *James Ford Rhodes, American Historian* (New York: Appleton and Company, 1929).

Cruden, Robert, *James Ford Rhodes: The Man, the Historian and his Work* (Cleveland: Western Reserve University Press, 1961).

ROBINSON, JAMES HARVEY (1863-1936)

Wish, Harvey, "James Harvey Robinson and the New History," Introduction to Robinson, *The New History* (New York: Free Press, 1965), v-xxix.

ROOSEVELT, THEODORE (1858-1919)

Sellen, Robert W., "Theodore Roosevelt: Historian with a Moral," *Mid-America,* XLI (October 1959), 225-240.

SCHLESINGER, ARTHUR MEIER (Sr.), (1888-1965)

Schlesinger, Arthur M., *In Retrospect: The History of a Historian* (New York: Harcourt, Brace, and World, 1963).

SYDNOR, CHARLES SACKETT (1898-1954)

Bettersworth, John K., "Charles Sackett Sydnor," *Journal of Mississippi History,* XVII (January 1955), 53-55.

THOMAS, BENJAMIN PLATT (1902-1956)

Angle, Paul McClelland, "Benjamin Platt Thomas, 1902-1956," *Illinois State Historical Society, Journal,* L (Spring 1957), 6-23.

TURNER, FREDERICK JACKSON (1861-1932)

Becker, Carl, "Frederick Jackson Turner," in *Masters of Social Sciences* (New York: Holt, 1927). Reprinted in Becker, *Everyman His Own Historian* (New York: Crofts, 1935).

Dale, Edward Everett, "Memories of Frederick Jackson Turner," *Mississippi Valley Historical Review,* XXX (December 1943), 339-358.

Bolton, Herbert Eugene, "Turner, As I Remember Him," *Mid-America,* XXXVI (January 1954), 541-561.

Billington, Ray Allen, "Why Some Historians Rarely Write History: A Case Study of Frederick Jackson Turner," *Mississippi Valley Historical Review,* L (June 1963), 3-27.

Jacobs, Wilbur R., Caughey, and Joe B. Franz, *Turner, Bolton, and Webb; Three Historians of the American Frontier* (Seattle: University of Washington Press, 1965).

Jacobs, Wilbur R., (ed.) *Frederick Jackson Turner's Legacy: Unpublished Writings in American History* (San Marino: Huntington Library, 1965).

Benson, Lee, *Turner and Beard* . . . (Glencoe: Free Press, 1960).

von HOLST, EDUARD HERMANN (1841-1904)

Goldman, Eric F., "Hermann Eduard von Holst: Plumed Knight of American Historiography," *Mississippi Valley Historical Review*, XXIII (March 1937), 511-532.

Goldman, Eric F. (ed.), "Importing a Historian: Von Holst and American Universities," *Mississippi Valley Historical Review*, XXVII (September 1940), 267-274.

WEBB, WALTER PRESCOTT (1888-1963)

Rundell, Walter, Jr., "Walter Prescott Webb: Product of Environment," *Arizona and the West* (Spring 1963), 1-28.

WOODSON, CARTER G. (1875-1950)

DuBois, William E. B., "A Portrait of Carter G. Woodson," *Masses and Mainstream*, III (June 1950), 19-25.

Wesley, Charles Harris, "Carter G. Woodson," *Journal of Negro History*, XXXVI (January 1951), 12-24.